D1124662

Gambetta and the Making of the
Third Republic

Also by J. P. T. Bury

Gambetta and the National Defence: a
Republican Dictatorship in France

GAMBETTA

(Collection Georges Sirot)

Gambetta
and the Making of the
Third Republic

J. P. T. Bury

Longman

WITHDRAWN
UTSA LIBRARIES

Longman Group Limited
London

*Associated companies, branches and representatives
throughout the world*

© Longman Group Limited 1973

All rights reserved. No part of this publication
may be reproduced, stored in a retrieval system
or transmitted in any form or by any means, electronic,
mechanical, photocopying, recording, or otherwise,
without the prior permission of the Copyright owner.

First published 1973

ISBN 0582 50052 4

Printed in Great Britain by
Adlard & Son Ltd, Bartholomew Press, Dorking

LIBRARY
University of Texas
At San Antonio

Contents

Foreword

This book, which has been all too long in the making, is concerned with the part played by Léon Gambetta in securing and moulding the Third French Republic during the first crucial years of its existence. I hope in a further volume to consider his role after the Republican victory in 1877 and to discuss the general significance of his career.

I am indebted to many people on both sides of the English Channel for the help of one sort and another which they have so readily given me during the preparation of this volume. To some I have made acknowledgement in footnotes, but to others I would like to express my gratitude here. On the French side they include M. Jacques Desmarest, who generously lent me the transcripts he possesses of letters from Gambetta to Léonie Léon; M. Baillou, former Director of the Archives of the Foreign Ministry, who allowed me to see Gambetta's papers at the Quai d'Orsay; M. Prioux and other members of the staff of the Library of the Assemblée Nationale, the Directrice of the Archives of the Prefecture of Police, Madame Harburger and her predecessor, Madame Tulard, and Mlle Solente, formerly of the Bibliothèque Nationale, all of whom facilitated my consultation of papers in their care. They also include my friend M. Jacques Millerand who gave me many useful introductions; M. Rupert Nordheim who allowed me to see the papers of Louis Nordheim, Madame Delorme Jules Simon who secured access for me to those of Jules Simon in the Archives Nationales, and M. Georges Wormser who so promptly and patiently answered a number of enquiries.

On the English side they include the late Mr Anthony de Rothschild who permitted me to see the MS news letters of 'C. de B.' in the Rothschild archives in St Swithin's Lane, Mr P. E. Charvet who helped me to unravel knotty problems of translation, and Dr C. M. Andrew, Mr K. Underbrink and Mr Michael Palmer, all of whom kindly helped me in various ways. In addition I must make special mention of my indebtedness to Professor John Roach, who read the whole of the final draft of the typescript and made helpful suggestions for its improvement, and to Mr Andrew Corbett who gave me valuable assistance in all the later stages of preparation. My greatest debt, however, is to my wife who heroically battled with my handwriting and cheerfully typed and retyped almost the whole of what has grown to be a massive volume. To her and to all others who gave me aid or advice I am indeed grateful.

Abbreviations

Acknowledgements

We are grateful to the following for permission to reproduce copyright material:

Editions Calmann-Levy for extracts from *Mémoires du Duc de Broglie, 1871–1875*, Vol. II, by Duc de Broglie; J. M. Dent & Sons Ltd and Translator for extracts from *Letters from Paris, 1870–1875*, by C. de B. translated and edited by Robert Henrey; Editions Bernard Grasset for extracts from *Lettres de Gambetta* by Halevy and Pillias and Librairie Plon for extracts from *Memoires de ma Vie*, Vol. V, by Charles de Rémusat.

'Ce coeur d'homme politique qui semblait toujours prêt à se livrer et qui se dérobait au moment même où l'on croyait le posséder.'

Hector Pessard
(*Mes petits papiers*, 2e série, 1888, pp. 136–7)

'Historiquement, et malgré tant d'écrits, d'éloges et de diatribes, il demeure une énigme.'

Albert Milhaud
(*Histoire du Radicalisme*, 1951, p. 55)

1

Introductory
1838–71

Léon Michel Gambetta was born on 2 April 1838, the son of an Italian grocer living in Cahors, and of Marie Magdeleine Massabie, his wife. It was not until he came of age in 1859 that he acquired French nationality. Some of his political enemies and, later, Right-wing critics after his death, were to take obvious advantage of this alien descent. They would not admit that a man with so much Italian blood in his veins could have the feelings of a true Frenchman. Still less could they endure that a metic should be regarded by vast numbers of Frenchmen as the very model of a French patriot.

In fact he was only half Italian by race and by upbringing hardly at all. Two generations of Gambettas were associated with Cahors before Léon Gambetta was born. His Italian father maintained connection with Celle-Ligure, the fishing village between Savona and Genoa from which his family hailed, and was never naturalised a Frenchman; but he was an Italian living in France; he had settled at Cahors before the birth of his children, and he had taken a Frenchwoman to wife. The mother of Léon Gambetta was of sound Gascon stock, the daughter of a chemist of Molières in Tarn-et-Garonne. Gambetta himself did not visit Italy until he was eighteen and although he marvelled at its beauties and regarded it as a second *patrie* there was never any question but that France came first.[1] France was his home and the centre of all his friendships, interests and ambitions.

It is easy to attribute to the Italian side of Gambetta's ancestry the suppleness, the skill at manoeuvring and the diplomatic talent which were his to a marked degree, and which are popularly supposed to be peculiarly Italian qualities; but those qualities are not necessarily or exclusively Italian, and they were not marked in Gambetta's father. A man of limited

1. For Gambetta's early connections with Italy see my 'Gambetta, *La République Française* e l'Italia', in *Il Risorgimento e l'Europa*, ed. V. Frosini (Catania, 1969).

intelligence, Joseph Gambetta was obstinate, strong-willed and authoritarian. It was these traits, if any, which Léon inherited from his father; he too, was to show an authoritative disposition, strong will and tenacity. In his good nature and vivacity he no less certainly took after his French mother. Beyond this it is difficult to separate the Italian from the Gascon, for earlier generations of Gambettas and Massabies are now little more than names. But if the Italian is elusive, the southerner is evident. Heredity and environment combined to make Léon Gambetta essentially *un homme du Midi*. His manner, his accent, his exuberant conversation betrayed him at once. It was in the south of France that he was born and bred, and spent his life until the great adventure of his setting out for Paris.

As a small boy, he attended the Petits Carmes or infants' school kept by the Fathers of the Sacred Heart of Picpus at Cahors. Then, at the age of nine, he went to board twenty-five miles away at the Petit Séminaire of Montfaucon, where he spent four years. These years were not very happy; terms were long and holidays short and, after an accident to his right eye in the summer of 1849, he had often been in pain.[1] His consequently strange appearance had caused him to be teased or bullied by his classmates, he had fallen behind in his work and it was no doubt a relief when his father took him away from Montfaucon and sent him to the Lycée in his home town of Cahors.[2] But there is no reliable evidence that he had particularly resented his earlier clerical teachers or what they taught. He seems to have been an *anima naturaliter pagana*, and his later anticlericalism would probably have developed had he never set foot in a school that was run by priests, for free thought and anticlericalism were a part of the French Republican tradition.

It was in January 1857 that he made his way to Paris, like so many hopeful or ambitious young Frenchmen, to study law. He quickly succumbed to the fascination of the capital, and found in the Quartier Latin great scope to display his powers. This 'energetic determined-looking young southerner with long black hair' was never so happy as when he had

---

1. The eye was removed in 1867. It used to be and probably still is preserved in a bottle in the Gambetta museum at Cahors.

2. Cf. his letter home of 24 May 1850: 'Je t'anonce que je m'enuis Diablement et qu'il me tarde de voir le sol natal; car, enfin, c'est embêtant: vous êtes là, planté au milieu de 23 élèves, pour la plupart Gaillards que vous ne pouvez pas suivre et vous êtes là comme un lièvre au milieu d'une meute de chiens. Ce qu'il y a de moins amusant pour moi, c'est que je suis le lièvre.' I give the spelling of the original letter in B.N., N.a.fr. 13177, No. 48. It is printed with normalised spelling in P. B. Gheusi, *Gambetta par Gambetta* (1909), pp. 14–15. Gambetta's unhappiness was later made the most of by anticlerical writers, e.g. J. Rouquette (*Célébrités contemporaines* (1872–73)) who related that Gambetta had threatened to cut out his eye if his parents did not take him away from Montfaucon.

an audience to regale with ready talk, vivid recitations from Rabelais, or impassioned declamations from Mirabeau's speeches and Demosthenes' Olynthian orations. The eloquence and memory of the young law student were indeed astonishing; they won him a wide reputation and a large following of admirers, whose affections he retained all the more readily because of his radiant geniality and unaffected good nature. The ease with which he became a leader in the student world of his time confirmed his self-confidence and stimulated his ambition. In despondent moments he admitted the defects of a southern nature, 'a mixture of ferocious energy and of terrible indolence', but the moments of despondency were rare; at twenty-one he believed there was a star awaiting him in 'the firmament of fate', and, strong in this belief, he applied himself resolutely to the task of carving a career.

The first important step was in 1861, when, after taking the oath at the bar, he overcame the strong opposition of his father and remained in Paris to plead. In Paris there were infinite possibilities of advancement for an able and energetic young barrister, and Gambetta entered upon his profession with great enthusiasm: 'I read, I write, I reflect, I listen to good masters, I work in order to become an orator; I give you my word of honour that if energy and desire to succeed, encouragement from my seniors, and the ambition necessary to the beginning of every career can help me to succeed, you can count upon me, I shall reach the goal.'[1] In those days when the cafés of the Left Bank were 'real schools of opposition',[2] each with its own regular orator, his voice was heard in the cafés as well as in the law courts. A Café Procope had echoed with the vigorous loud-voiced speeches of the young lawyer Danton; a Café Procope now resounded with those of the young lawyer Gambetta.

But Gambetta's early life in Paris was not confined to the law courts and the cafés. The bar, then as for long after, was a regular training ground for politicians and he soon forced himself to the notice of men such as Crémieux, Jules Favre, Ernest Picard and Ollivier who were prominent political opponents of the Second Empire as well as noted lawyers.[3] He assiduously attended the sessions of the Legislative Body. He cultivated political acquaintances and he boldly forced the doors of the leading opposition statesman, Thiers, to ask what a budget really was. A Republican

1. Gheusi, *op. cit.*, p. 186.
2. A. Daudet, *Souvenirs d'un homme de lettres* (1889), p. 17.
3. As M. Dogan in *Political Decision-Makers*, ed. Marvick (1961), p. 70, observes: 'Lawyers, more than all the rest go into politics not because they have interests of their own to defend, but because they know how to defend any economic or social interest, sometimes with much sincerity. At the beginning of their political careers they are polyvalent. As a result, they are easily adaptable.'

since the early days when in a letter home from Montfaucon, he had written 'Vive Cavagnac! [*sic*] A bas Bonaparte!' he hitched his wagon to the star of the *Cinq* or five opposition deputies elected in 1857. In doing so, he differentiated himself from the older idealists of the Second Republic. Not for him an attitude of mute protest or an unswerving devotion to rigid principles. He was one of a group of young Republican realists, many of them journalists, who demanded a policy which would produce visible results. In this he went further than many of his associates. For him a liberal reform was a liberal reform, no matter what its source, and he was ready to fight the Empire with the Empire's weapons. The future opportunist statesman of the Third Republic was in effect opportunist from the outset, though not so opportunist as to abandon his Republican creed. Whereas Ollivier, captivated by the charm of Napoleon III, came to believe that all the essentials of democratic liberty could be won without a change of regime, Gambetta always maintained that true democracy and Bonapartist Empire were wholly incompatible.

He took an active part in the 1863 election campaign which gave him valuable experience, but he had to wait another five years before he achieved a national reputation and the prospect of becoming a deputy himself. In 1868 the authorities unwisely prosecuted three newspaper editors who had opened a subscription list for a memorial to an obscure deputy named Baudin, killed on the barricades at the time of Louis Napoleon's *coup d'état* of December 1851. This gave Gambetta his opportunity. At the age of thirty he was engaged to defend Delescluze, one of the editors, and seized the chance to utter a thundering denunciation of the *coup d'état* and the regime it had inaugurated. No such public accusations had been heard in France since the Second Empire began. Gambetta became celebrated overnight. His reputation as an orator of singular power was assured and a political career lay ahead. He was an obvious recruit for the ranks of opposition candidates in the general elections of the following year, 1869. Multiple candidatures were permitted at this time and he was invited to stand both in Marseilles and in what by now had become the most radical working-class district of Paris, namely Belleville—a rapidly growing area in the east of the city.[1] He was successful in both, but although he chose to sit for Marseilles, where he adopted a more moderate tone, the campaign in Belleville was politically more important.

1. 'C'est à *Belleville* désormais, non plus au coeur du vieux *Paris* ouvrier que mûrissent les révolutions, la Commune y trouvera ses plus énergiques défendeurs' (J. Rougerie, 'Belleville', in L. Girard *Les Elections de 1869* (Paris, 1960), p. 3, Bibliothèque de la Révolution de 1848, xxi. This is an invaluable analysis of the Belleville workers and their mentality).

If Gambetta had been no ordinary defence counsel in what was speedily known as the Affaire Baudin, so he had been no ordinary candidate in the Belleville election. His electoral programme was and remains a landmark in the history of French Radicalism. The programme was ostensibly put forward by the electors and in his first electoral address he told them that he would reply to it: 'In this way we shall make a public contract visible to all.' (This notion of a contract between him and his constituents was to be of considerable importance later.) The programme was in fact an elaboration and popular statement of the policy already outlined by a prominent Republican author, Jules Simon, in a book called *La Politique radicale*. How far it represented Gambetta's own views rather than the views he found it convenient to accept at the moment it is difficult to decide. Later he declared that he had never been one of those who denounced standing armies; but the Belleville programme demanded their suppression as 'a cause of ruin to the nation's business and finances and a source of hatred between peoples and of distrust at home'. Election campaigns with mental reservations on the part of the candidate were indeed to be frequent enough under the Third Republic, and the thirst for reform, vigorous reform, but reform tomorrow, not today, would be a feature of 'radical mysticism'. But with some of the Belleville electors' demands, such as those for the disendowment and disestablishment of the Church, for complete freedom of the Press and of meeting and association, and for free elementary education, Gambetta was doubtless in complete sympathy. He had become an anticlerical like so many of his Republican contemporaries. Proudhon's anticlerical *De la justice dans la Révolution et dans l'Eglise* is said to have been one of his bedside books;[1] the Positivist doctrines of Auguste Comte, which he knew mainly through Comte's disciples, the lexicographer Littré and his entourage, influenced him powerfully,[2] and in this year 1869 he had been admitted as a member of 'La Réforme' at Marseilles, a newly founded lodge of the masonic order of the Grand Orient.[3]

1. Deluns-Montaud, 'La philosophie de Gambetta', *Revue politique et parlementaire*, 10 Feb. 1897, p. 255.
2. *Ibid.*, p. 251: 'Il a pu lire le *Cours de philosophie positive*; je ne crois pas qu'il ait jamais lu *La Politique positive*. . . . Je tiens de M. P. Laffitte que Gambetta ne connut pas Auguste Comte personnellement, que c'est sans doute dans l'entourage de Littré ou par des lectures fragmentaires qu'il apprit à connaître la philosophie positive.' This view is not invalidated by J. Reinach's 'Les lectures de Gambetta' in his *La Vie politique de Léon Gambetta* (1918), pp. 200–5.
3. The lodge at this time had forty members, including Maurice Rouvier, who would be a member of Gambetta's cabinet in 1881, Gustave Naquet the Radical journalist, and Gaston Crémieux the future Communard. According to *L'Acacia, Revue mensuelle d'études et d'action maçonniques sociales et philosophiques* (no. 46–47,

To many, the young man who had gaily accepted what seemed to them to be the subversive programme of Belleville was no better than a turbulent demagogue with a facile tongue and an exceptional voice. But in parliament and out of it the new deputy was at pains to correct this impression. He appealed to true Republicans to close their often divided ranks and to form a party 'exclusively composed of citizens who adhere to the same principles',[1] but he did not intend that such a party should be subversive. 'Between the rights and aspirations of Universal Suffrage and the present form of government', he told the Bonapartist Legislative Body, there was complete incompatibility; 'but this does not in any sense mean that, because I am dissatisfied with the present, I shall endeavour to find a remedy by appealing to physical force'.[2] He was an irreconcilable enemy of the Empire, but 'the irreconcilable has recourse neither to violence nor to conspiracy'.[3] He saw the folly of violence and had no sympathy with those revolutionary Republicans who still hankered after insurrection. A Republican government, he said, would be conscious of its duties and know how to make itself respected.[4] Such speeches showed not only that he could be moderate, but also that he was possessed of political sagacity. He soon realised his ambition to be a force in the Legislative Body, and in April 1870, three days after his thirty-second birthday, a speech he delivered opposing the plebiscite and the Emperor's liberal constitution was generally agreed to be a masterpiece. The *Figaro* went so far as to hail in Gambetta a worthy successor of such great orators as Mirabeau, Royer-Collard and Berryer.[5]

Parliamentary Empire, Gambetta had declared in one of his speeches, was merely a bridge between the Republic of 1848 and the Republic that was to come. Were the Republicans but patient, power would fall into their hands like a ripe fruit. Neither Gambetta, however, nor any of his colleagues suspected how soon their hour was to come or in what catastrophic circumstances their capacities for government would be tested.

1. *Discours*, i, 428ff.
2. *Ibid.*
3. For the text of this speech at Belleville, see J. Claretie, *Histoire de la révolution de 1870–1* (1872), pp. 91–2.
4. *Discours*, i, 254.
5. Gheusi, *Gambetta par Gambetta*, pp. 311ff.

Feb.–March 1928) he chose to join *La Réforme* because 'rattachée au Carbonarisme elle se trouvait en fréquentes relations avec des patriotes italiens'. According to *Le Monde Maçonnique* (5 Jan. 1883), he and others had originally intended to found a lodge called Le Réveil maçonnique, but the government had delayed its creation. I owe this information to the kindness of M. Lecottet, formerly of the Bibliothèque Nationale.

In July 1870, like a bolt from the blue, came the Hohenzollern candidature and war with Prussia which led in less than two months to the crushing defeat of one of the main French armies at Sedan and the encirclement of another under Marshal Bazaine at Metz. Thereupon on 4 September there followed in Paris a peaceful revolution and the collapse of the Empire which Gambetta so cordially detested. The Republic was proclaimed and a Government of National Defence, principally composed of all those who had been chosen to represent Paris in the general elections of 1869, was formed to carry on the war. These were the men sometimes alluded to as 'the men of 4 September'. The Bonapartist bridge had been crossed and Gambetta himself had been a principal guide to the new Republican shore. In the scramble for office he had taken possession of a ministry which was of key importance in home administration, especially after a change of regime, the Ministry of the Interior.

He did not remain in Paris for long. The city was about to be besieged, yet the Government ignored suggestions that they should leave for some provincial city, and they sent to Tours only a three-man delegation of some of their oldest members to carry on the conduct of affairs in the provinces. But it was soon evident that the Delegation's policies were in conflict with those of the beleaguered cabinet and that they were not the men to inspire a last dynamic attempt at provincial resistance. Early in October it was agreed that they should be reinforced by the youngest member of the government, and on 7 October Gambetta made his historic escape by balloon from Paris. He happily avoided the German lines and came down in a forest near Amiens. Thence he made his way to Tours and promptly assumed the duties of Minister of War as well as of the Interior. This in itself was a revolutionary step, for the Ministry of War was traditionally in the charge of a general.[1] Only occasionally during the First and Second Republics had a civilian occupied the post.

For the best part of four months Gambetta was virtually dictator in the French provinces not occupied by German troops. With the help of Freycinet, whom he made his chief assistant at the War Ministry, he improvised new armies and sought to relieve Paris and even to continue the war after Paris had capitulated at the end of January 1871.

But the odds were too great. The winter was hard, France was discouraged and war-weary, the German advance forced Gambetta to move the provincial capital from Tours to Bordeaux, and he and his amateur associates inevitably made many mistakes. He had saved France's honour by showing her latent strength even after the humiliation of Sedan, and there was no more effective tribute to his achievement than the wish

1. The Government of National Defence had adhered to the tradition by appointing General Le Flô as Minister; but he was shut up in Paris.

later expressed by one of his German opponents, General von der Goltz, that if Germany ever suffered such a débâcle she would find a man like Gambetta to kindle resistance to the utmost.[1] Yet his efforts ended in fresh defeats and dissension. When Paris capitulated the Government of National Defence had agreed with Bismarck to an armistice of twenty-one days, and to the holding of elections to a National Assembly which was to meet on 12 February. The Delegation at Bordeaux had been ignored and Gambetta's policy of war to the knife even after the fall of Paris was set at nought. All he could do was to try to ensure that the elections suddenly looming so close—and for which the Republicans were seemingly ill-prepared—would not play into the hands of the hated Bonapartists. He therefore issued a decree debarring them from standing for election.[2] This ran counter to the decisions of the government in Paris, and when its representatives, first Jules Simon and then others, reached Bordeaux he was overruled. The Republican party was split again and unless he wished to provoke civil war he had no alternative but to resign. He did so on 6 February, bearing with him, he told one of his prefects, 'as an apanage of our party the grand idea of national resistance'. But he would never again be Minister of War or of the Interior and it would be a decade before he once more held ministerial office.

---

1. C. von der Goltz, *Léon Gambetta und seine Armeen* (1877), p. 231.

2. Ironically, a similar decree had been issued by the Delegation on 1 Oct. 1870, despite the wishes of the Government in Paris, and this had been one of the reasons for sending Gambetta to Tours.

2

Exile
February–June 1871

The Republican Government of National Defence, of which Gambetta had been a member, had rejected his policy of continuing the war against Germany to the bitter end. They had arranged for general elections and they had annulled his decree excluding former servants of the fallen Second Empire from eligibility. The elections held on 8 February 1871, the freest held in France for twenty years, were a further condemnation of his policies and indeed of all that he had stood for. The French people sent as their representatives to the National Assembly which met at Bordeaux some four hundred Monarchists and only some two hundred Republicans. Socially, 'one deputy out of three had blue blood'.[1] The very existence of the regime which Gambetta had helped to proclaim five months earlier appeared to be in doubt. Although he had been elected in as many as ten departments, eight in France and two in Algeria, it was Thiers, the veteran Orleanist statesman more than twice his age, the chosen of twenty-six departments, who was the man of the hour. And Thiers had viewed the prolongation of the war with continued disapproval and had thrown his weight behind those who wished for peace in the final struggle which had led to Gambetta's resignation. When Thiers announced the formation of his cabinet on 19 February it included moderate Republicans who had served in the Government of National Defence, men such as Jules Favre and Jules Simon, but the name of Gambetta was not in his list. His exclusion emphasised the cleavage in the Republican ranks. The 'Dictator' who had so recently governed the provinces and organised the resistance against the invader was now no more than one of six hundred deputies, the majority of whom were strangers to him and detested him. Soon he would not even be a deputy, for he had deliberately chosen to represent the Bas-Rhin, one of the two departments of Alsace, which was doomed to annexation

1. Dogan in Marvick, ed., *Political Decision-Makers*, p. 73. See Map No. 3.

9

by Germany. On 17 February in the Assembly, Keller, one of the representatives for the Haut-Rhin, read out on behalf of the deputies for Alsace and Lorraine a solemn protest against the proposed annexation. It was the work of Gambetta. On 1 March, after the ratification of the preliminaries of peace which confirmed the loss of the two provinces, a further protest of which he was a signatory, was read out by another deputy. Thereupon Gambetta and his twenty-seven colleagues resigned their seats and withdrew at least temporarily into private life. It was a dramatic gesture and a momentous withdrawal, for it perhaps altered the balance of power in the Assembly at a critical moment two years later, so changing the course of the early Third Republic, as Gambetta himself would admit in 1874.[1]

The most prominent of the protesting deputies was one of the youngest members of the Assembly, for he was not yet thirty-three.[2] He had been a forceful figure in French politics in the last years of the Second Empire and he had been carried to power on the crest of a revolutionary wave. But now in the hour of defeat men might well wonder whether he was a spent force, a meteor rapidly extinct, another of those who had enjoyed a brief ascendancy because of a revolution and whom a turn in the wheel of fortune had cast into exile and obscurity.

There were in any case good reasons for Gambetta to retire for a time from the political scene. Although he was a man of great vitality and an exuberant temperament, it is important to remember that he was not strong. He nearly died of peritonitis when he was about eight and, as has been seen, he later lost the sight of his right eye. In his young manhood he had been subject to various ailments and in the summer of 1869 illness had obliged him to spend three months abroad, first taking the waters at Ems and then recuperating on the shores of the Lake of Geneva at Montreux. It was no wonder that the immense strain of the last few months of war, in which he had been unsparing in his efforts to organise resistance, had told heavily upon a constitution which had never been robust.[3] The strain indeed had left visible traces. When he took office in September 1870 he still looked a young man; six months later he appeared middle-aged; his face was lined, his beard and hair were greying, and his old enemy, laryngitis, was threatening him. In letters written in February and March 1871 he confessed that his health had suffered morally as well as physically

1. See below, p. 148. The twenty-seven were the deputies for Alsace (i.e. the Bas-Rhin and Haut-Rhin departments) and all but two of those for the Lorraine department of Meurthe, most of which was annexed by Germany. See Map No. 2.

2. 'Around a third' of the deputies of the Third Republic were under forty when first elected (Dogan, *op. cit.*, p. 61).

3. It told upon others, too: Freycinet, for example, said he felt worn out physically and morally and had to take to his bed for a while (C. de Freycinet, *Souvenirs de 1848–1878*, 6th edn, Paris, 1914, i, 259–60).

and that he felt 'an immense need for solitude and rest'. He was, perhaps, on the verge of a nervous breakdown.

In those dark days when every Frenchman had reason to feel depressed, it would not have been surprising that Gambetta, whose hopes and aspirations had been brutally shattered and who was by nature mercurial in temperament, should feel despondent and embittered. The writer Jules Claretie, who saw him in the little house in Bordeaux which he rented for a month on the morrow of his resignation as Minister, remarked on his freedom from bitterness.[1] But Gambetta's few letters surviving from this time leave no doubt about his gloomy forebodings. He was, he told one correspondent, 'shattered by the infamous happenings' to which France had been subjected. He wrote of 'the horrors of the present time' and, a week later, on 10 March, admitted to being 'more and more gloomy and overwhelmed by the darkest presentiments concerning the domestic future of France'.[2]

He had good reason for his gloom. Another eight days and the Commune broke out in Paris. He learnt the news of this 'convulsion of misery, famine and despair', as he later called it, from a Spanish newspaper on 22 March.[3] Meanwhile, on 11 March, the National Assembly had held its last meeting in the Grand Theatre at Bordeaux. Nine days later it renewed its labours not in Paris, but at Versailles, a move which served only to exacerbate the relations between the capital and the legislature. For more than two months France was torn apart by the horrors of a civil war which was to end in savagery and destruction.

By 18 March, however, Gambetta was no longer in France. A few days after resigning his seat as deputy for the Bas-Rhin he had paid a brief visit to his parents at Cahors and then made his way to San Sebastian on the coast of Northern Spain.

There were political reasons, as well as reasons of health, which pointed to the wisdom of at least temporary withdrawal from France. Had he remained a deputy, it is unlikely that, at the time when his unpopularity was greatest and his prestige at its lowest ebb, he could have influenced the attitude of the Assembly or the policies of the Government. Although he had not been in Paris since he left it by balloon on 9 October 1870, his own experiences before that date had shown him that the city was in a feverish state. Tumultuous events on 31 October and 22 January had threatened the Government and the news subsequently brought from the

---

1. Jules Claretie, *Portraits contemporains* (1873–75), p. 91.
2. *Lettres de Gambetta 1868–1882*, ed. Halévy and Pillias (1938; henceforward cited as *Lettres*), nos. 113 and 114.
3. J. Hansen, *Les Coulisses de la diplomatie. Quinze ans à l'étranger (1864–1879)* (1880), p. 245.

city by deputies of Paris and others who came to Bordeaux, afforded matter enough for gloomy prognostication. Gambetta was unsparing in his criticism of Jules Favre, who had negotiated the armistice, for failing to secure the disarming of the Parisian National Guard: 'After a severe defeat and a prolonged siege', he told his friend Edmond Adam, 'revolution is the first thing that a statesman should dread and guard against'; the acceptance of Bismarck's harsh peace terms would condemn Paris to revolution.[1] But he had assured Thiers that, if the worst came to the worst, he would give the government no trouble;[2] and one writer close to Thiers later averred that Gambetta's voluntary exile was at the pressing request of Thiers, now Chief of the Executive Power.[3] Sun and sea air were indicated as a remedy for his ills, but (if it were made) he declined the offer of the Adams' house on the Riviera near Juan-les-Pins and preferred to go abroad.[4]

The decision was wise, but if Freycinet is to be believed, it was not taken without considerable heart searching. When, shortly before the outbreak of the Commune, Gambetta's friend Ranc had returned from Paris to Bordeaux full of foreboding, Gambetta had at first thought of going to the capital to try to lessen the growing tension. His friends dissuaded him, rightly fearing that he would fail and only compromise himself by attempting to intervene.[5] He gave his views in a letter written as early as 26 March:

> There is only one way to save the situation. It is to declare the definite establishment of the Republic and to introduce the three or four measures which would ensure it free play—the passage of an electoral law, the dissolution of the Assembly, the summons of the new Chamber to meet in Paris, knowing in advance the legislative programme it must follow, and, finally, a bold return to the capital which must be spoken to in a manner fitting for France and for the population of that great city.[6]

Such measures, however, would certainly not have commended themselves to Thiers, who was determined to teach the Parisians a lesson. Later, in the summer, after his return to Paris, Gambetta was said to have told an acquaintance that, had he still been Minister of the Interior, he would

1. Mme Adam, *Mes Angoisses et nos luttes (1871–1873)* (1907), pp. 26–7 (letter from Edmond Adam to his wife).

2. *Ibid.*

3. H. Pessard, *Mes Petits papiers*, 2nd série, 1871–73 (1888), p. 147. According to A. Barthélemy, *Gambetta à Saint Sebastian* (1930), p. 7, the request was conveyed by Gambetta's friend, Antonin Proust.

4. Mme Adam, *op. cit.*, p. 27, As S. Marcos has shown in his notable study *Juliette Adam* (1961), Mme Adam's memoirs are in many ways unreliable.

5. Freycinet, *op. cit.*, pp. 266–7.

6. *Lettres*, no. 118 to Antonin Proust.

have set up his headquarters at the Hôtel de Ville 'with an entourage of good citizens' and then said to the mob:

> 'Here I am. What do you want?' Thus I should have been in a position to mediate between Versailles and Paris and I would probably have settled their differences. Had I written and published my views, people would have said: 'Why doesn't he come himself? Why isn't he here?' But it was already too late. I could not have prevented the disgraceful events that took place. In this sort of business one must act immediately.[1]

In effect, although a letter of 28 March from Antonin Proust indicates that he toyed with the idea, Gambetta had refrained from publishing his views on what should be done.[2] He was as good as his word and abstained from embarrassing Thiers. In Spain he kept silence and did not commit himself. Even to think of politics, one letter suggests, was forbidden him by his friends.[3]

Yet, inevitably, his withdrawal and his silence were criticised. His enemies dismissed him as a charlatan and derided the ex-Dictator, who 'sunned himself amid the orange groves' while Frenchmen were fighting Frenchmen.[4] They declared that he had hurried away to secure the treasures he had amassed during his ministry. They taunted him with fleeing because he feared the consequences of the enquiry which the National Assembly proposed to institute into the acts of the Government of National Defence. In Right-wing circles it was gleefully reported that the authorities were on the look-out for 'this leader of the demagogues' and that the prefects and procurators-general had orders to arrest him whenever he appeared on French soil.[5] Some of those in authority, too, regarded him with suspicion and feared that he was hatching a conspiracy, perhaps secretly in league with the Communards who had connections abroad.[6] It was characteristic of their attitude that, when in June he sought to telegraph from San Sebastian to Paris to prepare his return to politics, he was told that the Bayonne post office would accept no private telegrams to Paris except those relating to the national loan to meet the war indemnity imposed by Germany.[7] Some even of his friends deplored his silence as a shirking of responsibility; they overestimated his influence and, believing

1. Hansen, *op. cit.*, pp. 245–6.
2. B.N., Fond Joseph Reinach, N.a.fr. 13581, f. 107.
3. *Lettres*, no. 116.
4. e.g. P. Lanfrey, *Correspondance* (1885), ii, 239, 16 June 1871. He was still reproached with his retreat to San Sebastian in the Chamber of Deputies in 1876 (*Annales, Chambre*, iii, 213).
5. Freycinet, *op. cit.*, p. 271.
6. *Ibid.*
7. *Lettres*, no. 123.

that any intervention on his part must have been effective, failed to understand why he did not stir.

If he could not have been a successful mediator, neither could he have taken the Commune's side, although he was personally acquainted with many of its prominent figures. He had defended Delescluze and his own compatriot Razoua in court; during the war he had made Rossel commander of the camp at Nevers, and he had employed Georges Cavalier, the notorious 'Pipe-en-Bois', as a kind of factotum and bodyguard at Tours and Bordeaux. But he had also more than once and in all sincerity declared his abhorrence of violent revolution. After the plebiscite of 1870 he had reasserted his conviction that the triumph of the Republican cause under the leadership of extremists such as Flourens, Delescluze and Rochefort would be deplorable. Now, in March 1871, Flourens and Delescluze were prominent among the leaders of the new Parisian revolution. As recently as February, Gambetta had shown his aversion from violence by rejecting the advice of extremists to defy the Government in Paris and to continue the war against Germany. He had thus abjured civil war, and there was no reason for him to condone or support in March or April what he had eschewed in February. One of his most intimate friends, Arthur Ranc, was indeed for a short time a member of the Commune, and one of Ranc's associates was to assert that he had accepted this nomination simply in order to keep Gambetta informed of what was going on.[1] The suggestion is an interesting one and, if true, indicates the importance that Gambetta attached to good intelligence. It could also help to explain his later solicitude for Ranc, whose subsequent career was gravely jeopardised by his brief connection with the Commune; but it is not corroborated elsewhere and Ranc's participation is, by reason of his near-Jacobin views, intelligible without such an explanation. Gambetta might grieve for the people of Paris and understand the reasons which led to the Commune.[2] He could not sympathise with its federalist aims. These, as Proust had written to him on 28 March, could not regenerate the country.[3] Only a short time after the Commune had been overthrown one of its members was to write: 'There is no bond or affinity between the Commune and the present Republican party from M. Target to M. Gambetta. . . . M. Gambetta and the Radical party are further from the Federalist Communal party than they appear to be from Bonapartism!'[4] This view

1. Mme Adam, *op. cit.*, undated letter from Cernuschi, p. 99.

2. Later he was to analyse them briefly in a letter of 29 Aug. 1873 to Castelar (*Lettres*, no. 161 *bis*).

3. B.N., Fond Joseph Reinach, N.a.fr. 13581, f. 107.

4. G. Lefrançais, Charles Rihs, *La Commune de Paris* (1955), p. 201, n. 47. Paul-Louis Target was one of the more conservatively minded Republican deputies. He would help to bring about Thiers's fall in May 1873.

was confirmed about the same time by Gambetta's devoted friend Spuller, when he wrote on 5 June: 'There is no one in France, above all in the Republican party, who does not know that we counted more enemies than co-religionists among those who have just succumbed.'[1]

If Gambetta could not sympathise with the Commune, still less was he disposed to ally himself with a host of his political enemies by giving public support to its repression. In a letter of March, already quoted, he had expressed his fear of a catastrophe: new September days reminiscent of the massacres of 1792 or, before long, a White Terror.[2] He had prophesied only too truly; there was to be a White Terror unexampled in French history and a White Terror was the last thing with which Gambetta could wish to associate himself. By his silence he destroyed no bridges, but he could win credit for restraint as well as abuse for alleged cowardice. The Commune made a new cleavage among Frenchmen and left behind a legacy of great bitterness.[3] As one of the few men in public life who had not taken sides Gambetta would be well fitted one day to play the part of conciliator.[4] Meanwhile he refused to be provoked into condemnation or approval.[5]

The struggle between Paris and Versailles raged for more than two months and culminated in the Bloody Week of 21–28 May. During this time and for a few weeks after, Gambetta virtually passed out of the news. The country round San Sebastian, he had written soon after his arrival, was 'divine' and he quickly abandoned himself to a *farniente* which made the writing of letters a weary burden.[6] Later he told an acquaintance of Danish origin, Jules Hansen, that he had spent more than half his days on

1. *Revue de Paris*, 1 June 1900, p. 466. Later in the year another of Gambetta's collaborators, Challemel-Lacour, explaining to a German friend the aims of the founders of the newspaper called the *République Française*, put things in rather a different light: 'Nous voulons fonder ... la république démocratique, étrangère à la Commune et à ce qu'elle a fait; nous n'en sommes pas moins persuadés qu'en principe elle avait le droit pour elle, que sa résistance et même ses fureurs ont beaucoup moins nui à la République qu'affaibli et découragé les partis monarchiques, qu'en tout cas la politique du gouvernement de Versailles a été insensée, odieuse et lâche' (E. Krakowski, *La Naissance de la IIIᵉ République, Challemel-Lacour le philosophe et l'homme d'état* (1932), letter of 27 Oct. to Herwegh, p. 327).

2. *Lettres*, no. 118.

3. It is of incidental interest to note that one of Gambetta's first teachers, Père Tussier, was shot by the Communards (Gheusi, *Gambetta par Gambetta*, 1909, p. 7).

4. 'Plus tard, ajoutait-il, nous ferons l'amnistie' (Freycinet, *op. cit.*, p. 268).

5. One such vain attempt to get him to disavow the Commune was made in a debate in the Assembly on 9 Jan. 1873 (*Ass. Nat. A.*, xv, 55–7).

6. *Lettres*, nos. 115 and 118. In fact the editors of his correspondence remark on the complete absence of any letters written by Gambetta in April or May. But he himself told A. Proust that he had written ten times to him within a month (*Lettres*, no. 119) and Spuller's letters refer to ones he had received from Gambetta.

the sea among Spanish fisherfolk, that he had read no French newspapers, seen no friends and seriously contemplated abandoning politics for industry.[1] But, like many of Gambetta's accounts of his own doings, this was more impressionistic than exact. Far from being alone in the rooms he had rented in the Fonda Miramar, a house with a view over the bay of La Concha, he was looked after by his devoted aunt, 'La Tata', and attended for a while by his secretary Paul Sandrique.[2] He also probably enjoyed the company of an old flame, Marie Meersmans (alias Estelle or Marie de Moölle, alias the Comtesse de Sainte-M.); she had once been a star in the Parisian demi-monde and mistress of the Provençal poet Mistral, but now she was a lady close upon fifty who, as Gambetta said later, 'looked like my mother by day and like my sister by night'.[3] To San Sebastian, too, came another woman who had first been fascinated by his oratory at the famous Baudin trial in 1868 and who was destined to have a far more profound and enduring influence upon him. But Léonie Léon's hour was not yet; Marie Meersmans was in possession of her 'Loulou', and 'La Tata', vigilant guardian, barred the door against the persistent Creole.[4] Friends there were, too, as well as mistresses, who found Gambetta out in Spain. Thither came Gustave Marqfoy, with his brother Achille, and Freycinet with his draft justification of Gambetta's war ministry, *La Guerre en province*, for his former chief to criticise and approve.[5] Not only did Gambetta see French friends during this period of voluntary exile, but he also made contact with leading Spanish Republicans.[6] The most eloquent Frenchman paid a brief visit to Madrid, visited the Cortes, and renewed his acquaintance with the most eloquent Spaniard, Emilio Castelar. Later in the summer he was to give his young friend Auguste Gérard letters of introduction to Castelar, Figueras and Salmeron.[7]

The delights of San Sebastian could not be enjoyed for ever and those who hoped or prophesied that Gambetta's voluntary exile signified his permanent retirement from politics were soon undeceived. Though with him, as with other charming good-tempered politicians, such as Charles James Fox, ambition might sometimes conflict with the allurements of a life of ease, there is little likelihood that he thought long or seriously about

1. Jules Hansen, *op. cit.*, p. 245.

2. Barthélemy, *op. cit.*, p. 8. A. Tournier (*Gambetta, Souvenirs anecdotiques*, Paris, 1893, pp. 147–8) said that he also had with him his valet, François Roblin.

3. E. Pillias, *Léonie Léon, amie de Gambetta* (1935), pp. 57–8.

4. *Ibid.*, p. 57.

5. Freycinet, *op. cit.*, p. 269; see also below, p. 356.

6. Freycinet, *op. cit.*, p. 270.

7. A. Gérard, *La Vie d'un diplomate sous la troisième République* (1928), p. 12; cf. Gaston E. Broche, *Quelques lettres de Léon Gambetta et de son père à leur cousin Giacomo Galleano, de Celle-Ligure* (Paris/Genoa, 1936), p. 31.

abandoning politics or settling in Spain and going into industry[1] or, as his father advised, returning to the bar. For one who had spent long hours in the Legislative Body, following parliamentary debates when he was still a student, politics were the breath of life. On 18 March he had written to his father of return to Paris after Easter, adding that he did not know when the by-elections, necessitated by the system which allowed a candidate to stand and be elected in more than one constituency, would be held, and that he was not eager for them or to see himself 'forced to return to this ignorant and cowardly Assembly'.[2] But the implication was that he would be forced, that he would return; indeed, before the outbreak of the Commune, he had spoken of disappearing merely for a few months.[3]

By the beginning of June it was expected that the by-elections would take place within three or four weeks.[4] The time was at hand when he must declare himself and decide whether or not to go back to France and stand as a candidate for election. In a letter of 5 June he wrote to ask the advice of Antonin Proust and confessed that he was still very perplexed what to do: 'My present inclination is still not to become a member of an Assembly which I consider is finished and has exhausted its mandate.' But in any case he would propose to send Proust a letter for publication which would explain his position.[5] His continued hesitation was reflected also in a long and revealing letter of the 10th to his old friend Dr Fieuzal and in a further letter to Proust of the 14th.[6] Inactivity was now beginning to pall. To Fieuzal he complained of being without news of many friends, of living 'a sad and embittered existence, alone by the sea', with his heart 'full of anger against the cowards and intriguers who had ruined France and the Republic'. However, his health, he said, was restored to what it had been ten years earlier and he was ready to devote all his energy and intelligence to the defence of 'our sacred cause'. But, he went on,

> to do this effectively, it will be necessary to return and so far I have been unable to do this. I do not know if I have been wrong in yielding to the advice of alarmed friends who have written to urge me to wait yet awhile and have

1. Others, too, under the shadow of France's disasters had temporary inclinations to start a new life elsewhere. Thus on 20 March Clamageran wrote that more than once he had thought of leaving France for good (J.-J. Clamageran, *Correspondance 1849–1902*, Paris, 1905, p. 341).

2. *Lettres*, no. 116. These by-elections had been twice postponed, first because of the peace negotiations and secondly on account of the Commune. They eventually took place on 2 and 9 July 1871.

3. Mme Adam, *op. cit.*, letter from Edmond Adam, p. 27.

4. The decree summoning the electors of forty-seven departments to vote on 2 July was promulgated on 9 June.

5. *Lettres*, no. 119.

6. *Lettres*, nos. 120 and 121.

even declared that a warrant was out for my arrest. I have yielded to this perhaps mistaken advice, but I cannot go on thus; my financial resources are rapidly giving out and I shall soon be obliged to find a means of earning my living.[1]

Again, he expressed his distaste for membership of 'this horrible Assembly': 'Is it really good and politic to return to it? I doubt it and am still debating with myself.'

Meanwhile the attacks of his political opponents in France did not cease. Many cheap jibes about 'the Government of National Expense' and the 'Dictatorship of Incapacity' exercised by 'the Carnot of the Defeat' were to be expected. More serious was the endorsement of the opinion of the majority in the Assembly by Thiers himself, the Chief of the Executive Power. In a speech on 8 June, of which one of the aims was no doubt to widen the rift between moderate and radical Republicans, he pronounced his celebrated condemnation of the men who had sought to prolong the French resistance against Germany: 'They prolonged the defence beyond all reason; the means they employed were the worst conceived in any war at any time. We were all revolted, I—like you—by this policy of raging madmen which placed France in the greatest peril.'[2] Five days later the Assembly set up a Commission of Enquiry into the acts of the Delegation of Tours and Bordeaux, and in doing so reemphasised the wish of the majority to discredit the Republican leaders of the National Defence and, above all, Gambetta. For those of Gambetta's friends and followers who were now eager for his return these onslaughts provided conclusive arguments. 'Had you been there', wrote Eugène Spuller, 'this attack would not have occurred. . . . It is not good . . . for a man who has played a most conspicuous part in contemporary history to allow his actions and intentions to go too long misrepresented. The public will form a false opinion and it will be extraordinarily difficult to revise its mistaken verdicts.'[3] 'Our political enemies', wrote Edmond Adam, 'seek to dishonour you and your collaborators. It is your duty to be with us to defend your friends. Your security calls you, your political future depends on the promptness of your return.'[4]

As so often, it was the advice of Eugène Spuller which seems to have been the decisive influence. Two years his senior, Spuller had been a friend

1. According to Jules Laffitte (*Gambetta Intime*, 1879, p. 23), he had to borrow 20,000 fr. from his father before going to San Sebastian.

2. For the text of Thiers's speech, see *Ass. Nat. A.*, iii, 291–300. After the passage quoted he went on to condemn Gambetta's decree depriving the Bonapartists of eligibility as 'anti-nationale, atroce par ses résultats, arrogante, insolente'.

3. P. Deschanel, *Gambetta* (1919), pp. 133–4.

4. Mme Adam, *op. cit.*, p. 154.

of Gambetta for at least ten years. He was like him in being a bachelor and like him in being the son of a foreigner, for his father was a German from Baden. Moreover, he had attached himself to Gambetta so closely that he was often called his *fidus Achates*. 'It is even said', remarked one newspaper later on, 'that when M. Gambetta has a cold it is M. Spuller who sneezes.'[1] Now in his letter to Fieuzal, Gambetta had complained that he had not heard from that most faithful of friends for a month. But wind of Gambetta's doubts and perplexities had blown through to Sombernon in Burgundy where Spuller was resting and whence he had already written to Gambetta at least five long letters of sage advice. Spuller now came in person to Bordeaux, probably arriving on 15 June. Precisely when Gambetta took the fateful decision to return at once to politics and France we do not know, but on 23 June he accepted invitations to stand as candidate in the three departments of Var, Seine, and Bouches du Rhône.[2] Three days later he reentered the political arena and outlined a whole policy in a striking speech at Bordeaux.

1. *Pouvoir*, 20 Sept. 1876 (A.P.P. BA/1,274).
2. According to the *Bien Public* of 27 June Gambetta replied on 22 June indicating his readiness to stand at Marseilles. An interesting but not very reliable journalist, E. A. Vizetelly (*Republican France 1870–1912*, 1912, p. 208) suggests that Gambetta's decision to return to France was partly due to the arrival in the house in which he was staying of a suspicious-looking individual, who 'came to him begging for assistance on the ground that he had fled from France owing to his participation in the Commune. Gambetta, after questioning the man, did not believe his story, but suspected that he was a police spy sent to watch him.' If true, the incident may have been a factor in his decision.

3

Reentry
June–July 1871

The France to which Gambetta returned on the evening of 25 June 1871 had undergone a considerable evolution since his departure for Spain in March. The Commune had made its bid for power, raged, and been vanquished after the final horror of the Bloody Week, which left many parts of Paris in ruins and was preceded and followed by ruthless repression. The red spectre was laid by a White Terror of wholesale arrest, deportation and execution, but laid it was. The country could once more breathe with comparative freedom. It could turn to the task of repair and reconstruction after a foreign war which had led to the death of nearly 140,000 Frenchmen and the loss of two provinces with a population of one and a half million, and after a civil war which had caused perhaps 20,000 casualties. The members of the National Assembly, so many of them new to the ways of parliaments, were beginning to gain experience, and political groups and parties in all their Latin complexity were attaining a semblance of cohesion. But the future was still obscure: many departments were still occupied by German troops; a large indemnity had to be paid under the terms of the peace treaty of Frankfurt; martial law was still applied in many parts of the country and the great question of the definitive form of French government was still unresolved. Thiers had in February induced the Assembly to defer a decision until after the conclusion of peace and to grant him the title of Chief of the Executive Power of the French Republic. He had pointed out that pacification and reconstruction under the Government of the Republic must come first, and on 10 March he had gone on to declare that he himself would 'observe loyalty to all the parties which divide France and divide the Assembly. What we promise . . . is to deceive no one . . . to prepare no solution of constitutional questions behind your backs.'[1] This promise was to be

1. 'Je dirais que je jure devant l'histoire de ne tromper aucun de vous, de ne préparer sous le rapport des questions constitut ves aucune solution à votre insu.' For the whole speech, see *Ass. Nat. A.* vol. iii, pp. 285–8.

known as the Bordeaux Pact. Thus France, despite the Monarchist inclinations of her National Assembly, was still a Republic in name and fact. From this fact and from the divisions of the Royalists genuine Republicans could derive hope. 'At the moment', Gambetta had written to his father on 19 February, 'I have only one preoccupation: after our fruitless efforts to drive out the foreigner to try to save at least our Republican institutions.'[1] To preserve and strengthen the Republican institutions which had been so hastily improvised after the Revolution of 4 September 1870, here was the obvious goal, the one great urgent object of Republican effort.

Those institutions had been imperilled by the elections of February. It might have been supposed that the Commune must seal their doom, for in the eyes of its enemies the Commune was another exhibition of Republican frenzy, a new identification of Republicanism with violent revolution, a further demonstration of Republican incapacity for government. So, when all attempts to mediate between Versailles and Paris had broken down, there had been moments when Gambetta's friends were filled with gloom about the prospects of the Republic. 'I think the Communalist movement will come to grief,' wrote Spuller on 11 April, 'but ... the Republic ... is running into the greatest dangers. At this moment she has perhaps received her death blow and we shall have to spend our lives bringing up a new generation capable of founding it after having for a moment hoped to found it ourselves.'[2] But Spuller's gloom was to prove unwarranted. The defeat of the Republicans of the Commune by Republican troops strengthened the cause of the Republic. No absolute monarch or military dictator was more determined or relentless in crushing rebellion than 'le petit bourgeois'. Thiers, and the Republic was to be the beneficiary of the energy of this recent and septuagenarian convert to Republicanism. Although France at this moment seemed to be Republican in little more than name and institutions, it was the name and institutions and the attitude of Thiers which were all-important. The name and institutions continued to exist and henceforth could be as well identified with order as with anarchy, while Thiers, the former Orleanist minister on whom Monarchists still placed great hopes, was convinced that the Republic was now the only regime possible.[3] A Monarchy, he believed, must certainly be a prey to Republican insurrection:[4] a Republic

1. *Lettres*, no. 112.
2. E. Spuller, 'Lettres à Gambetta', *Revue de Paris*, 1 June 1900, p. 454.
3. *Lettres de J. Ferry* (1914), p. 116, 15 May.
4. This view was shared by Gambetta's friend Clément Laurier, who, in an interesting unpublished letter of 11 April written to Henry May from Nice, said he was inclined to think that the Republic 'en tant que forme de gouvernement anonyme',

would have far less to fear from Monarchist revolt. Of the dangers of Republican insurrection he had been made well aware. The Commune was not entirely confined to Paris: there had been sympathetic outbreaks in certain other towns. Delegations from the municipalities of some of the most important centres of Republicanism, chief among them Lyons, Marseilles, Grenoble and Toulouse, had come to see him and promised to refrain from alliance with Paris only if he assured them that he was not the tool of a conspiracy hatched by the Assembly to do away with the Republic.[1] Thiers had heeded the warning and reassured his visitors. 'The Republic', he had declared, reiterating a phrase that he himself had uttered twenty years earlier, 'is the regime that divides us least. You may be sure that I will contribute to the foundation of the Republic much better than a veteran Republican.'

Thus the Commune did much to preserve the Republic instead of consummating its ruin and Gambetta is said to have explicitly recognised the fact.[2] The nadir of Republican fortunes had been touched in February. Three months later municipal elections showed that the electoral pendulum was beginning to move towards the Left once more, and, although the Commune was still in being, a conservative like Martial Delpit could deplore the results of these elections as bad,[3] while the Republican Jules Ferry could consider them as satisfactory: 'The Republic is not yet buried. There is life in the "petit bonhomme" yet.'[4] Peace had been concluded with Germany, the reaction against the men of 4 September had diminished in intensity—after all, as Thiers reminded the Assembly on 8 June they had done France the service of getting rid of the Empire—and Republican propaganda, intensified during the war under Gambetta's auspices, was not without effect. But the Assembly still wielded effective power, and, so long as the Assembly continued to exist and to contain a Monarchist majority, Republican institutions must be insecure.

Hitherto the contention of Gambetta and his Republican friends had

1. R. Dreyfus, *M. Thiers contre l'Empire, la guerre, la Commune 1869–1871* (1928), p. 342.
2. Georges Cavalier, *Gambetta* (1875), p. 20.
3. P.-B. des Valades, *Martial Delpit, député à l'Assemblée Nationale* (Paris, 1897), p. 144.
4. *Lettres de J. Ferry*, pp. 110 and 113.

would emerge from the chaos. The South would take fire if the Republican form of government were called in question, and so would almost all the big and middling-sized towns. In other words, the Republic had against her the passive majority, but for her a very numerous and very active minority. 'M. Thiers', he added, 'a trop d'esprit pour ne pas le voir.' I am indebted to Madame Pierre Laroque for a copy of this letter.

been that the Assembly had been elected merely to determine the question of peace or war, and to ratify the peace treaty. But on 11 June, three days after the notable speech in which Thiers had condemned Gambetta's wartime policies, Spuller had written to Gambetta to warn him that it was clear that the Assembly wished to continue in being and that M. Thiers wanted it to do so. 'The Conservative party . . . wishes to prolong what it calls the experiment of the Republic or rather of the unnamed government which has taken the name of Republic.' This, he urged was a great factor. It was, therefore, the duty of the Republicans to enter into action on the ground marked out by Thiers, unsure though that ground was. Moreover, he added, Thiers's attack on Gambetta was perhaps deliberately intended to soften for the Assembly 'the kind of Republican declaration which he wished to make the climax of his speech'. If so, he should be forgiven, 'for in politics much must be endured'.[1] Spuller's diagnosis, which had included a strong appeal to Gambetta himself to return to the fray, was sound. As he said in a further letter, dated the 13th, there was no choice for Gambetta and his friends but between 'complete abstention, which we have never wanted and which today would be more fatal than ever, and vigorous and resolute action on the existing ground'.[2]

On 6 May, just after the municipal elections, a Monarchist deputy, Martial Delpit, noted a rumour that Gambetta, said to be at Lyons, was planning the convocation of a 'Convention which would begin by thrusting the Monarchists out of doors'. Thus, he said, the country would have three sorts of Republic to choose from, the Republic of the Communards, the Republic of M. Thiers and the Republic of Gambetta.[3] Since then the Republic of M. Thiers had annihilated the Republic of the Communards. The questions remained whether the Republics of Thiers and Gambetta were compatible and could be reconciled and whether together or separately they would be strong enough to frustrate the restoration of monarchy.

The young Gambetta of the Second Empire had been regarded by many as an uncouth and violent extremist. Men had forgotten the moderation of his speeches as a deputy in the Legislative Body. They had forgotten how often during the war he and his lieutenants had emphasised that the Republic meant order. What they remembered was that in February he had come to stand for war and the suppression of liberties, two labels that were deadly in France.[4] His policy of war to the knife had been denounced by Thiers, the epitome of bourgeois good sense, and

1. *Revue de Paris*, 1 June 1900, p. 472.
2. *Ibid.*, p. 475.
3. Valades, *op. cit.*, p. 144.
4. J. Gouault, *Comment la France est devenue Républicaine* (1954), p. 57.

it was a policy which had helped to identify him with extreme Left-wing Republicanism. He had been elected at Paris in company with men such as Victor Hugo, Garibaldi and Louis Blanc; he had resigned just before or after men of the extreme Left such as Malon, Pyat, Rochefort and Razoua. His friend Ranc had been, though for a short time only, a member of the Communal Assembly. He was estranged from the Republican ministers in the government and from the majority of his former colleagues in the Government of National Defence. General Trochu, who had been its President, was not the only person to regard him as a 'Red'.[1] But when Gambetta at last returned from his voluntary exile and broke silence on 26 June at Bordeaux, his utterance did not at all accord with this picture of a wild irresponsible radical. Once again the advice of Spuller seems to have been of great importance: 'Upon you now falls the heavy task of reuniting scattered forces, of disciplining men's minds, raising hopes, consoling griefs, calming impatiences and, above all, reconciling the two Frances. . . . The more violent the attacks against you the more easy you will find it to be moderate; and the more moderate you are the more likely you are to succeed.'[2]

The advice was reflected in the speech at Bordeaux of which Spuller corrected the proofs.[3] It was a speech which filled Gambetta's admirers with enthusiasm, a speech which, as Spuller had hoped, impressed Thiers himself by its moderation. Here the Gambetta who had shown himself capable of moderation in prewar days reappeared, took up the thread of old ideas and adapted them to the new circumstances of defeat and the need for 'regeneration'. Given the will and the knowledge, he declared at the outset, the Republican party would succeed in regenerating the country and giving it a free government. So once again he urged that the Republicans must show their fitness to govern, and to this end he preached Republican union: 'I believe that through the union of different shades of Republican opinion we can reveal ourselves to France as a disciplined party, strong in its principles, industrious, watchful and resolved to do everything to convince the French people of its capacity to govern; in short, a party which accepts the formula: power to the wisest and worthiest.' Thiers had said 'The future is to the wisest'. Gambetta took him up—it was a wager to be accepted:

> We accept the formula. We must become the wisest . . . we must maintain and uphold our government, the Republic *de facto* and *de jure*. . . . A government in whose name legislation is passed, peace is concluded, milliards are

1. Valades, *op. cit.*, p. 92.
2. *Revue de Paris*, 1 June 1900, p. 476.
3. For the text see *Discours*, vol. ii, pp. 15–34.

raised, justice is done and insurrections which would have sufficed to over-throw ten monarchies are suppressed, is a lawful and established government whose very acts prove its strength and its rights. This government deserves the respect of all, and anyone who threatens it is a sedition-monger (*un factieux*).

As for the Monarchy, in a shrewd thrust which would appeal to a thrifty peasantry, he said that France was not rich enough to afford it. Moreover, now that the Republic existed in name and that Republican hopes were so far realised, the heroic age of the Republican party was over. Under a government which was Republican in form, opposition must be construc-tive rather than destructive. Once again he declared, as in April 1870, that the task of the great Revolution must be completed: 'But, gentlemen, I mean by this word Revolution the diffusion of the principles of justice and reason by which it was inspired and I entirely reject its identification by our enemies with violent enterprises.'[1]

Just as Italian writers of the sixteenth century had discussed and deplored the failure of their compatriots to meet the challenge of foreign invasion, so Frenchmen now debated the reasons for their defeat of 1870. French degeneracy and its causes had been a frequent subject of argument and speculation since the fall of the Empire and even before. For Renan the cause lay far back in the Revolution and the abolition of Monarchy. For Catholics like Veuillot, impiety, likewise a product of the Revolution, was the root of the evil. Moralists, like Dumas the younger and a whole troop of Republicans, of whom Jules Simon, Marcère and General Faidherbe were among the more reputable, attributed this decline to the slackening of moral discipline in the reign of Napoleon III and phari-saically thundered against 'the orgies of the Empire'. For others, also mostly Liberals and Republicans, the deficiencies of national education were the fundamental reason. The Empire had been a period of infatuation and ignorance and the result was that France had been beaten by the German schoolmaster. In the words of a later writer, impiety was again responsible, but for these men it was impiety towards 'the New Idol of Science'.[2] At Bordeaux Gambetta developed both these arguments at length. The loss of Alsace and Lorraine, he explained, was due to the physical and moral inferiority of France: 'It is the inferiority of our national education which has led us to defeat.' It was the ignorance of the peasantry which had misguided them into voting for Napoleon in the plebiscite of May 1870. The peasant was told 'again and again that it was Napoleon who gave him his land. He confuses Napoleon with the Revolution: he is not far from the belief of Mme de Stael that Napoleon

1. Cf. speech of 19 April 1870 (*Discours*, vol. i, pp. 246–7).
2. A. Bellessort, *Les Intellectuels et l'avènement de la Troisième République (1871–1875)* (Paris, 1931), p. 63.

was "Robespierre on horseback". Well, we must pull him off his horse. We must prove to the peasant that it is to democracy, to the Revolution that he owed not only his land but his rights.'[1] It was essential to remedy this defect so that the adjective 'rural', so lately hurled in contempt at the Assembly, should no longer be a reproach and so that the artificially created antagonism between town and country should disappear. The most urgent task, said Gambetta, echoing a phrase from an article he had contributed to the first number of *La Revue politique et littéraire* in June 1868, was 'to flood the country with education'. This would mark a great step on the way to 'regeneration'.[2] Moreover, the men of the rising generations must be able not merely to read and think for themselves: they must be physically fit, able to be efficient soldiers as well as intelligent citizens. 'Let it be understood that every boy born in France is born a soldier as well as a citizen.' Here too, though he thought of the future, of reconstruction and revenge, Gambetta was echoing the past, not his own words this time but a law of the Convention, which he once described as the greatest assembly France had ever seen: 'Pupils will be taught to read and write; they will learn the records of heroic deeds . . . the boys will be trained in military exercises under the direction of an officer.'[3]

The speech, prudent, but optimistic, radical and yet conservative, sounded the note of what was later to be dubbed opportunism. Inevitably it contained an appeal to revolutionary mysticism; in its references to the plebiscite, its exaltation of the 'exact sciences' and its appraisal of Auguste Comte as 'one of the great thinkers of this century' it was typical of an important section of Republican thought. But in its moderation and its

1. I have borrowed F. H. Brabant's translation in his *The Beginning of the Third Republic in France* (1940), p. 378.

2. The word 'régénération' was constantly on the lips of Gambetta and other Republican speakers after the war of 1870–71, just as it had been one of the stock words in 1789. (Gambetta used it or 'régénérer' four times in this speech at Bordeaux.) In 1871 and after, as in the great Revolution, it often had strong secular and even anticlerical implications, but its overtones were now different. As M. Claude Digeon has indicated in *La Crise allemande de la pensée française (1870–1914)* (1959), pp. 102–3: 'En lui-même, ce mot . . . est intéressant: il promet . . . un avenir purgé du passé plutôt qu'authentiquement nouveau; si l'on compare cette explosion d'espoir au grand mouvement de 1789 et à l'enthousiasme de la fête de la Fédération, on voit que ce désir de renouveau implique un sentiment de culpabilité, la conscience d'avoir fait fausse route. Il signifie: se hausser au niveau allemand, plutôt qu'aller vers un avenir inconnu.'

In no. xxxvii of his forthright *50 Lettres Républicaines* (1875) 'Gervais Martial ouvrier' (Léon Bienvenu) wrote in disillusionment that for more than four years 'nous pataugeons sur place dans le plus affreux des gâchis en nous contentant de répéter sans cesse les mots: régénération, réorganisation'.

3. Law of 27 Brumaire, Year III (17 Nov. 1794).

realism it was also typical of a newer Republicanism which had already been developing in the latter years of the Second Empire and which was very different from that of the Communards. On 8 June Thiers had given a further pledge to the Republicans, for, while reiterating his fidelity to the pact of Bordeaux, he had declared that it implied a loyal working of Republican institutions until the time was ripe for the restoration of Monarchy. After that, as Spuller had urged, it was the easier for Gambetta to ignore Thiers's attack upon himself, to be moderate and extend the olive branch. Thiers was reassured, moderate opinion was reassured and, partly as a result, the by-elections were more than reassuring from the Republican point of view. If Gambetta were to continue in his new course, stressing the Conservatism rather than the Radicalism of his programme, the omens seemed good for eventual cooperation between his followers and the government, for a fusion of the Republic of M. Thiers with the Republic of Gambetta. The most striking comment on Gambetta's reentry into politics came indeed from Thiers's own paper, the *Bien Public*. This had strongly opposed the idea of Gambetta's candidature in Paris, but on 1 July its editor, Henri Vrignault, wrote: 'The speech which made the Empire came from Bordeaux:[1] Bordeaux acclaimed it. Bordeaux has now acclaimed Gambetta. One may hate this man; one may fear and oppose him. One cannot feel indifferent to him. He has been someone who counts and so he will always be.' Already it had said that it would be glad to see Gambetta back in the National Assembly since there ought to be room there for all men of superior merit; moreover, a party leader would be much less dangerous there than plotting revolution on the side.[2]

Gambetta's return to France and his speech at Bordeaux were national events. The place itself was significant as well as the timing. In February Bordeaux had been the scene of Gambetta's discomfiture and he had firmly refused to be a candidate there in the February elections. But now the Bordelais enthusiastically applauded him; the reconciliation was a good omen and henceforward Gambetta, who was always sensitive to opinion, held the Bordelais high in his affections.[3] The speech was reprinted for circulation in Paris and elsewhere. In Paris his supporters adroitly emphasised the idea that he and Thiers were but the two sides of the same coin:

1. The reference is to a celebrated speech by Louis Napoleon in 1852, foreshadowing the proclamation of the Second Empire.

2. 27 June.

3. See P. Sorlin, 'Gambetta et les républicains nantais en 1871' (*Revue d'histoire moderne et contemporaine*, avril–juin 1963, p. 126). Cf. H. Taine, letter of 5 Aug. 1872 to Mme Taine: 'Bordeaux is running after Gambetta. He is just the man for the Southerners' (*Life and Letters of H. Taine 1870–1892*, London, 1908, p. 92).

they distributed a leaflet which declared that a vote for Gambetta was a vote for the Republic and for a balance of power which would give the Republic two leaders, Thiers and Gambetta, one Tory, the other Whig, and thereby finally close the door to Monarchist conspirators.[1] Gambetta also stood in two other departments as well as the Seine, namely the Bouches du Rhône, where he had first been elected in 1869, and the Var, one of the ten departments which had voted for him in February.[2] When the results were known he proved to be one of the only three candidates who were elected in as many as three departments. The other two had also been notable figures in the war: they were Colonel Denfert-Rochereau, the defender of Belfort, and General Faidherbe, former commander of the army of the North. Gambetta expressed his satisfaction: the elections had shown that the Republic was more firmly based than people thought: 'We will now found a moderate and rational Republic which will save France.'[3] Moreover, it was particularly encouraging in a state in which two-thirds of the population were country dwellers, that many country districts had voted Republican: 'Mark this', he exclaimed to an acquaintance, 'the Republic has planted her feet in the peasants' sabots and she will not cast them off.'[4]

Yet it was noteworthy that this wild man who had spoken so moderately now chose to sit for the Seine or, in other words, Paris, rather than for his old constituency at Marseilles in the Bouches-du-Rhône. Of the twenty-one deputies elected for the twenty-one Parisian arrondissements he came seventh in popularity. But for him, of course, given the position he had taken up and the programme he had adopted in 1869, Paris must inevitably mean the 20th arrondissement which included Belleville. And Belleville, already regarded as a red suburb in 1869, seemed more than ever red in 1871, for in May its hills on the eastern edge of the city had been the last

1. French printers and journalists have never been good at mastering the complexities of English names. In the copy of the leaflet preserved in the Bibliothèque Nationale the word 'Whig' appears as 'Wigh'.

2. The Var, like the Bouches-du-Rhône, had a reputation for Radicalism. On 10 April 1873 *The Times* correspondent wrote that it was at Luc between Hyères and Cannes that 'the most Radical Committee in France holds its meetings, a Committee with which no candidate will find favour unless he is prepared to regard the heads of citizens as so many poppyheads, and to strike them off when it may be convenient or agreeable to do so'.

3. Hansen, *Les Coulisses de la diplomatie*, p. 246; *L'Eclipse* of 30 July published a caricature by Alfred le Petit showing Gambetta winning an electoral sackrace and carrying off the 'Cocarde des Vainqueurs', the Bordeaux speech sticking out of the mouth of his sack.

4. G. Jollivet, *Souvenirs d'un Parisien* (1928), p. 156. In 1872 11,234,899 people in France's total population of 36,102,921, lived in communes of more than 2,000 inhabitants (F. Carrière and P. Pinchemel, *Le Fait urbain en France*, 1963, p. 86).

fierce bastion of the Communards' resistance.[1] Belleville was 'Belleville of ill fame', as the Royalist *Gazette de France* was wont to call it and many moderate men might still ask themselves whether the moderation of Gambetta was no more than skin deep and whether 'the dictator of Bordeaux' was not after all a wolf in sheep's clothing.

Gambetta's personal triumph was overshadowed by that of Thiers and the essentially moderate and rational Republicanism for which Thiers now stood. Of the 114 seats to be filled on 2 and 9 July Republicans of one shade or another gained as many as ninety-nine. As early as 6 June a Monarchist observer, who signed himself 'C. de B.', had reported that there was no doubt that the Assembly was losing ground in the country, which put its trust in Thiers. Thiers, he believed, would therefore take the opportunity in the forthcoming elections to ally with the Left and to bring about the entry into the Assembly of sixty or eighty more or less moderate Republicans who would displace the majority and make him complete master of the situation until he was overthrown by his new allies.[2]

The first part of his prognostication was more than fulfilled. The Monarchists were still more divided than the Republicans and they had no outstanding leader with a popular following. The Republican electoral organisations had been bolder and more efficient[3] and the Republicans had not hesitated to avow their allegiance, whereas the Monarchists had seldom declared themselves as such. This was one cause of the latter's weakness. But more important was the fact that, since the Republic was the existing regime, they now appeared revolutionary because they wished to overthrow it. They also appeared to be the party of war because they wished to restore the temporal power of the Papacy which had been swept away when the Italians entered Rome in the autumn of 1870. But the country wanted no more of revolution or of war. It was noteworthy that candidates who had been in any way associated with the Commune such as Victor Hugo, Clemenceau, Ranc and Floquet were not elected. Indeed Gambetta had thought Ranc's candidature untimely and refused to support it.[4] As C. de B. had divined, the majority of French people trusted in the good sense of Thiers and wanted him to carry on as

1. See J. Rougerie, *Paris libre* (1971), pp. 253–5.
2. Unpublished letter by C. de B. (Rothschild pp.).
3. In its leader of 14 Nov. 1871 Gambetta's paper, *La République Française*, was to refer to 'the societies formed during the war to organise local defence and subsequently maintained for the elections of April, July and October'.
4. Ranc's widow asserted of her husband's candidature: 'Il fut porté à son insu—il ne voyait absolument personne' (Ranc, *Souvenirs—Correspondance 1831–1908*, 1913, p. 198).

he had begun. France, a French correspondent in New York wrote shrewdly to an under-director of a well-known bank, the Crédit Lyonnais, 'is Thierist, as yesterday she was for Napoleon III: what she wants is to be left in peace to get on with her business. She begins to understand that times [*sic*] is money, so if we have the Republic let us keep her.'[1] The elections of 2 July were indeed above all a sweeping vote of confidence in the little old man whom Jules Favre and Jules Ferry called their 'little king', the man who had made peace and vanquished the Commune. This was the same man who, only a few days before the electors went to the polls, had launched a brilliantly successful loan to pay off the war indemnity imposed by Germany and had taken the salute at an imposing military review on the racecourse at Longchamp. Both testified to the revival of French national pride and self-respect.

The Monarchists were confounded and dismayed, the more so because in less than a week their hopes suffered another blow. The elections of 2 July were disastrous, yet they had been eager for them and had believed that they would profit from the change which in April they had introduced into the electoral law, whereby voting took place in the commune instead of in the chief place in the district or canton.[2] But four days after the polls there was published by the Monarchist Pretender 'Henri V', the Comte de Chambord, a manifesto which to many appeared tantamount to abdication. In recent months the Monarchists had made strenuous attempts to heal the schism between Legitimists and Orleanists which dated back to 1830. They had secured a declaration from the Orleanist Duc d'Aumâle acknowledging that there was but one royal family and one monarchy and adding that his eldest brother, the Comte de Paris (the Orleanist Pretender), would be at the disposition of the Comte de Chambord. The 'fusion' or reunion of Orleanists and Legitimists, so often sought but hitherto never achieved, had seemed to be in sight and on 8 June the abrogation by the Assembly of the laws condemning members of former ruling houses to exile had been widely interpreted as the prelude to a speedy restoration of the Bourbon monarchy. But in the famous manifesto of 6 July, which Chambord persisted in publishing despite the earnest pleading of some of his most devoted supporters, the Pretender declared himself unable to abandon the white flag of the Bourbons for the tricolour of the Revolution and the Empire: 'Henry V cannot give up the flag of Henry IV.' This meant that he would not consent to become King of France except on his own terms, which were hardly acceptable

1. Letter of 22 July 1871, quoted in J. Bouvier, 'Des banquiers devant l'actualité politique en 1870–1871', *Revue d'histoire moderne et contemporaine*, avril–juin 1958, p. 151.
2. For the text, see Gouault, *op. cit.*, p. 108.

to the France of 1871. Moreover, he had issued this declaration before any formal reconciliation with his Orleanist relatives. The Comte de Paris consequently adjourned the visit he had contemplated making to the senior Pretender and the relations between the two royal houses and their followers remained in suspense. In one of his letters to Gambetta from Sombernon Spuller had expressed the hope that the proposed monarchy might at the last moment collapse of itself.[1] That hope now seemed likely to be fulfilled and Republicans rubbed their hands with delight. Thiers wittily called the Comte de Chambord the founder of the Republic, the French Washington.

But the Legitimists, though gravely perplexed and embarrassed by the action of their 'King', refused to despair. They declared that their belief in the desirability of a hereditary monarchy for France, but with the tricolour flag, was unimpaired. Moreover, Monarchists generally could hope that 'fusion' might yet somehow be accomplished. The Comte de Chambord, who was fifty-one and childless, might die and thus leave the way open to the Orleanists who had stood for the tricolour from the first. Meanwhile, the supporters of Monarchy, still a majority in the Assembly, might yet put many an obstacle in the way of the definite establishment of a Republican constitution. But the results of the elections of July 1871 were a grave warning that time might not be on their side, and time, since the return of Gambetta and the action of the Comte de Chambord, was likely to be more than ever an important factor in determining the future government of France. No wonder that when Thiers ironically congratulated the Orleanist Duc de Broglie on Chambord's virtual abdication, which seemed to clear the path to power for the Orleanists, the Duke replied: 'The suicide of the Comte de Chambord does not console me for the resurrection of Gambetta.'[2]

1. *Revue de Paris,* 1 June 1900, p. 467.
2. Brabant, *op. cit.,* p. 350.

4

Back in the Assembly: the first ten weeks July–September 1871

Despite Gambetta's denunciation of it as ignorant, cowardly and illegal, the National Assembly of some 650 to 750 deputies to which he was elected and reelected in 1871 has a strong claim to be considered as one of the great parliaments of French history. Few were more rich and varied in their composition, few had weightier business to determine, few were more dignified, more industrious or more productive of important legislation. It presided over the reconstruction and recovery of a defeated country; reorganised its army and administration; and endowed it with a constitution which was to endure longer than that of any other regime since 1789. Looking back on it many years later, a contemporary declared that it might well be said that the man who had not attended its deliberations did not know what a parliament should be, what heights eloquence could attain, or what resources the strategy of the lobbies offered to the clever and ambitious.[1] Even Gambetta himself in 1881 recalled it with enthusiasm as full of intelligent and cultivated men—a Chamber which it was a pleasure to address.[2]

Although the Commune had been vanquished and the capital was once again fully controlled by the forces of order, the National Assembly continued to sit at Versailles. This preference gave an unwonted animation to a historic town which had fallen into decline. At the same time it made the old, cramped Gare St Lazare at the lower end of the rue d'Amsterdam at Paris a constant rendezvous for the politically curious, since it was from this station that there ran the 'parliamentary trains' which conveyed deputies to and from Versailles. Such commuting was indeed a novelty and, in the opinion of one memorialist, the constant to-ing and fro-ing and catching of trains at fixed times induced in the members of the Assembly a nervous tension which helped to explain the

1. Paul Bosq, *Souvenirs de l'Assemblée Nationale 1871–75* (1908), p. 133.
2. Brabant, *op. cit.*, p. 414, n. 3.

incoherences and violence that sometimes marked their political conduct.[1] On the days of important debates station and trains were crowded; top-hatted deputies, journalists and spectators were jumbled together, and at Versailles there was keen competition to secure a box in the red and gold Assembly hall. This had once been the Opera House built by Gabriel for Louis XV: it 'is the fatality of this Assembly', wrote a contemporary journalist, 'that it has always sat in theatres and voted on the stage'. Invariably dressed in white, the Russian Princess Lise Troubetz-koï seldom missed an important speech of Thiers, who frequently honoured her salon, and after the elections of July 1871 Madame Adam was usually to be seen when Gambetta was expected to take part in a debate.[2] She was there to watch him make his first speech after those elections; she saw him drag himself, 'big, heavy and badly dressed' to the tribune and, when he sat down again in his corner seat on the second bench on the the left, she contrasted his fine head with the weasel-like face of his old friend Clément Laurier and the pale inconspicuous visage of Dréo beside him.[3] Meanwhile deputies on the Right and their sympathisers, who had not set eyes on Gambetta before and who regarded him as a 'Red', used to point him out 'as though he were a strangely fierce beast or a particularly curious animal in a menagerie'.[4]

In that first speech, on 22 July, he seized the opportunity to follow up his oration at Bordeaux and once again to demonstrate his support for Thiers. Right-wing agitation concerning the temporal power had continued and, after a pro-Papal declaration by the Comte de Chambord, a number of French bishops had petitioned the Assembly in favour of the restoration of papal sovereignty. In conversation Gambetta had described the petition as monstrous[5] and, when they heard that he intended to intervene in the debate it occasioned, friends and foes alike expected an early diatribe, an anticlerical explosion. But Thiers, through Edmond Adam, had soon after the elections privately appealed to Gambetta and his friends to show 'a difficult prudence' if they did not want the Republic to elude them.[6] Gambetta again responded. He waited until Thiers had astutely answered those who demanded French intervention in Italy and then surprised his hearers by a brief speech of studied moderation in which the most remarkable point was the speaker's warm approval of the attitude

1. Pessard, *Mes Petits papiers*, p. 118.
2. Bosq, *op. cit.*, p. 82.
3. Mme Adam, *Mes Angoisses*, p. 183; cf. Pessard, *op. cit.*, p. 134.
4. Pessard, *op. cit.*, p. 82.
5. *Ibid.*, p. 182.
6. *Ibid.*, p. 178.

adopted by Thiers. 'You will see,' he had said to Freycinet, 'I shall be M. Thiers's last defender.'[1] He could not have caused a greater sensation, wrote one historian, 'if he had proposed that the Vatican should be burned down'.[2] The widespread belief that there was a secret alliance between Gambetta and Thiers seemed to be confirmed and the Right were all the more outraged.

'Gambetta', C. de B. had written at the end of June, 'will shortly be elected, but his appearance in the Assembly will lead to violent storms.'[3] He was a true prophet. As the historian Hanotaux put it, Gambetta's appearance at the tribune 'secured silence, his words unchained the storm'.[4] No sooner had he declared his acceptance of the agenda or order of the day, proposed by a member of the Left Centre, Marcel Barthe, and approved by Thiers, than Keller, speaking for a section of the Right, said that the significance of the order of the day was changed by Gambetta's acceptance of it and that he and his friends could no longer support it. Thiers at once sharply denounced such a display of personal animosity and, with reference to Gambetta's support, declared that he had not sought agreement with anyone but that he did not flee from it when it came to him. Meanwhile Gambetta, understandably roused by the attitude of the Right, had gone to the tribune again and denounced his enemies' 'mad desire to compromise the future of the country and the peace of Europe'.[5] But his further attempts to speak were said to have been continually interrupted by cries such as—'There are no dictators here!' 'No! No! This is not the place for dictatorship.' 'We are not at Bordeaux!'[6] Such was the temper of the Right that the prudence and support of Gambetta were an embarrassment rather than a help to Thiers. By a large majority the Assembly approved the report of the Commission which had considered the bishops' petition and recommended it to the attention of the Minister for Foreign Affairs. The Minister was still Jules Favre and the decision of the Assembly made the situation of this former Republican member of the Government of National Defence, already difficult for other reasons, still more difficult. He resigned and was

1. Freycinet, *Souvenirs 1848–78*, p. 276.
2. Brabant, *op. cit.*, p. 418.
3. Rothschild pp.: letter of 28 June.
4. Quoted in H. Stannard, *Gambetta* (1921), p. 125. Bosq (*op. cit.*, p. 87 n.) noted that, as in previous parliaments, speakers in the Assembly 'reliaient leurs discours et faisaient un bout de toilette à leurs improvisations'. Gambetta, he said, usually entrusted this chore to his friends Challemel-Lacour and Spuller.
5. For the text of Gambetta's interventions, see *Ass. Nat. A.*, vol. iv, pp. 257–62, and *Discours*, vol. ii, p. 43.
6. *Ibid.*, p. 53. These interruptions are omitted from the *Annales* of the Assemblée Nationale.

succeeded by one of Thiers's personal friends, Comte Charles de Rémusat, who was not a member of the Assembly.

The Monarchists, however, had also been embarrassed by the debate and by the apparent alliance between Gambetta and Thiers. Of this Thiers was aware: since the Monarchists were now virtually without a king he himself appeared to be all the more indispensable. He was consequently tempted to strengthen his position by inducing the Assembly to agree to a proposal of his old friend Rivet, a former prefect of the July monarchy, that his powers should be clearly defined. Rivet was now a firm Republican, who at Bordeaux had added the words French Republic to Thiers's title and claimed thereby to have put a nail in the Monarchists' shoe.[1] His new proposal was intended to be a 'fishbone in their throats'. The moment was well chosen, for the Monarchists were unprepared; they could indeed be rid of Thiers, under whose rod of iron they were often restive, but they dreaded any Republican substitute and, although many names such as those of General Changarnier and of Louis Philippe's son, the Duc d'Aumâle, were again canvassed, they had as yet no agreed candidate of their own to put in his place. Since the Comte de Chambord had failed them their plans were in confusion and their divisions tended to reopen. By using the threat to resign, a device he had already employed, Thiers might hope to extract from them as much as he wished. Accordingly on 12 August Rivet brought forward the motion that Thiers should be given the title of President of the French Republic and that he should exercise for three years the powers which had been delegated to him by decree on 17 February. Such a proposal, however, meant that, since he would be both chief minister and President and could not be dismissed, ministerial responsibility, the basic principle of parliamentary government, would cease to exist. This was more than the Assembly was prepared to swallow, and the Commission, whose spokesman, M. Vitet, reported on the proposal sixteen days later, made some important modifications. The motives prefixed to the Bill in its amended form explicitly stated that the Assembly had constituent powers, and the text accorded Thiers his powers not for three years but for the duration of the Assembly and under its authority. He must remain responsible to it.

In this form the Bill placed Gambetta and his friends in a delicate situation: they did not wish to embarrass or offend Thiers by their opposition, but they were still more reluctant to admit the constituent powers of a Monarchist Assembly. In a speech which was again constantly interrupted and which at one moment became a defence of the revolution of 4 September Gambetta opened a public campaign in favour of the dissolution of the Assembly and the election of a new constituent body. He had

1. R. Dreyfus, *La République de Monsieur Thiers (1871–1873)* (1930), p. 108.

no wish for a Republic, he said, which was the creation of an Assembly not legally competent to create it.[1] The National Assembly had been elected merely in order to settle accounts with the foreigner.

> When you are founding a regime, whether it be a monarchy or a republic, the preoccupation of the founders should be to create a fortress that can be defended against the factions who attack it, not a tent or hangar which is open to all the winds and which can be overturned by any passer-by. This is what you would be doing if you were to deliberate about a constitution with your present lack of powers. I say this from the Monarchist as well as the Republican point of view.

And then he added a prediction which was to be conspicuously falsified:

> Should a Republican constitution emerge from this place I declare in all conscience that I should not think myself sufficiently well armed to strike at those who might dare to attack it.

The effect of this speech was not perhaps what Gambetta intended it to be, but it satisfied Thiers, for the opposition of Gambetta and his Radical followers brought all the rest of the deputies save the extreme Right and a handful of Bonapartists to his side: the Bill was passed on 31 August by a large majority (491–94). Thiers had thus gained much, though not all that he wanted, while the majority had secured formal recognition of their constituent powers and done as much as possible to prolong their own life.

The whole transaction, as a future President of the Republic, who became Gambetta's biographer, later pointed out,[2] contained a singular element of paradox. The Left, who denied the constituent powers of the Assembly, were not yet ready to urge that the Rivet Law which gave Thiers the title of President of the French Republic should have the force of a constitutional law, whereas the Right, who so loudly claimed constituent powers, insisted that the law was an ordinary measure which could easily be revoked. Not for the last time the Extreme Right and the radicals on the Left had momentarily joined forces in opposition. But the significance of what had been done was not lost on a shrewd deputy of the Right Centre, Léonce de Lavergne: 'You win,' he told a Republican colleague. 'The Republic has been made despite Gambetta and despite Vitet! It has been made and by royalists!'[3]

1. Professor Guy Chapman has argued that Gambetta's claim that the Assembly had no mandate to be a constituent body was technically unsound; see Appendix IV in his *The Third Republic of France, the first phase 1872–1894* (1962). For the text of Gambetta's speech, see *Ass. Nat. A.*, vol. v, pp. 246–50.

2. Deschanel, *Gambetta*, p. 138.

3. Dreyfus, *op. cit.*, p. 128.

During this month of August the Monarchists were still highly nervous and indulged in the gloomiest prognostications. If new elections were held now, declared Martial Delpit on 12 August, the result would be the return of a Red Assembly in which Gambetta would be on the Right, the Socialist Tolain in the Centre and the Internationalists and Communards on the Left. The hostility of the Left to the Assembly and any prolongation of its powers was reported to be such that 'a veritable Jacquerie' was being prepared in the south;[1] and when on 20 August General Faidherbe resigned as deputy for the Nord because, he said, he did not consider that his constituents had given him a mandate to make a constitution, it was alleged that this was only the first act of a plot to force the Assembly to dissolve—other resignations of Republican deputies would speedily follow.[2]

Dissolution was one dread of the Monarchists. Paradoxically, the death of Thiers was another. The demise of the Comte de Chambord might solve some of their difficulties, but the death of Thiers would complicate them still further. There were reports, too, of increasing Bonapartist propaganda in the provinces: 'Anything may happen', wrote C. de B. on 11 September. 'We are living under a Provisional Government run by an old gentleman of seventy-four! He could disappear any day and then you would see the crisis—the crisis for which the Bonapartists want to be ready.'[3] The supposed pact between Gambetta and Thiers had, moreover, led to the belief that Gambetta was the successor intended by Thiers himself, 'the Dauphin', as Madame Adam heard him dubbed by a Right-wing deputy.[4] She and her friends had at once playfully adopted this name for him and he himself replied humorously one day to someone who suggested that the moment had come to make an attack on Thiers: 'Oh, no! He is an uncle one may succeed. He must be treated with consideration.'[5] This was amusing enough in informal conversation, but when a somewhat unscrupulous journalist, Edouard Portalis, published an article on 1 October entitled 'Democracy's Pretender'[6], Gambetta rapped him over the knuckles:

> Although this expression can be seen simply as an antithesis I believe that it upholds the monarchical idea and I think that in future we ought all to avoid such drawbacks. As for me, however flattering in some respects the name of the Democracy's Pretender may be, I cannot accept it, for in my view in a

1. C. de B. (Rothschild pp.) 24 Aug.
2. *Ibid.*, letter of 29 Aug.
3. *Letters from Paris*, ed. R. Henrey, 1942, p. 171.
4. *Mes Angoisses*, p. 185.
5. Valades, *Martial Delpit*, p. 218.
6. In *La Constitution*.

Democracy there can and ought to be only citizens called upon to render services and never pretenders.[1]

But five days later the Acting British Chargé d'Affaires (who had no doubt read Portalis's article and Gambetta's reply) was reporting to Lord Granville that, if a crisis occurred, it was 'more than probable that Mons. Gambetta would succeed to power'.[2]

Such a prediction truly indicated the remarkable change in French politics and the striking revival of Gambetta's influence which had taken place since February. But that influence was probably much greater in the country than in the Assembly. The parliamentary group consisting of Gambetta and his radical followers which towards the end of the year met in new premises in the Rue de la Sourdière was presently to be known as the Republican Union, but the name denoted aspiration rather than actuality.

All parties in opposition tend to be divided and this had always been true of France's Republicans. During the last years of the Second Empire the division had roughly been threefold, first between the moderates in parliament who were ready to ally with liberal Monarchists in opposing the regime and those like Gambetta who believed that such alliances were compromising and that the Republicans must close their ranks, and secondly between both these parliamentary groups and the various brands of extreme radicals who would have no truck with an imperial parliament and were ready to work for violent revolution. The collapse of the Empire on 4 September 1870 had temporarily rallied all Republicans to the new *de facto* regime, but this harmony had been shortlived. The Government of National Defence had comprised both groups of parliamentarians, but it had soon been hard pressed by the revolutionary forces which had gained fresh strength during the war and finally exploded in Paris and elsewhere in the Communal movement of March 1871. Meanwhile, as has been seen, there had been a further cleavage in February between the majority of the Government of National Defence, who had concluded the armistice, and Gambetta and his supporters who had wished to continue war to the knife. At the same time the advent of the supposedly Orleanist Thiers to power as the *de facto* chief of the Republic meant that there was a new group of Thierist Republicans in the making. In these circumstances Gambetta, because of his past and his belligerence, inevitably found himself allied to the extreme Left in the Assembly after the July by-elections; while the old revolutionary Left were for the most part in prison or in exile after the suppression of the Commune. Thus he

1. *Lettres*, no. 129.
2. P.R.O., F.O. 146, 1543.

was temporarily on the extreme Left in French political life as a whole. It was an exposed position and he now in a sense shifted his ground. Whereas before the war he had opposed the 'open Left' advocated by moderate Republicans, in the summer of 1871 he became its chief advocate.

On the eve of his first speech in the Assembly since his reelection Gambetta had described the situation as 'very obscure: much talk and little action. However, it will be necessary to shake up the Left.'[1] He sought, it appears, to shake up the Left, already dividing loosely into groups, by proposing that the Republican deputies should unite to form but a single parliamentary group or party. Such a union would mark a great step on the way to realising his dream of a two-party system. But this was not to be. At a meeting at the Jeu de Paume on 3 August he had vainly tried to convince his fellow-Republicans of the expediency of uniting the forces of the Left.[2] The breach between Gambetta and his more moderate colleagues at the end of the war was not easily to be healed. The leaders of the main body of the Left, 'the four Jules', Jules Grévy, now President of the Assembly, Jules Simon, Jules Favre and Jules Ferry, were lukewarm or hostile and that body had no desire to be wagged by a radical tail.[3] They were Thierist, rather than Gambettist Republicans, and Thiers, though reassured by Gambetta's moderation, was still far from sympathetic. It was essential to Thiers to maintain as much influence as possible over the more moderate groups and so he wished to keep the Left Centre and the Republican Left for himself: 'What can I say to the Right Centre', he argued, 'if they say my friends are shaking hands with such an extremist as Louis Blanc?' Gambetta might be a possible heir, but Thiers had no intention of sharing his command with him. So it was decided that the Left should remain divided into three groups of the Left which would remain 'open but quite separate'.[4] The moderate Republican party, Thiers informed the British Ambassador, Lord Lyons, with satisfaction on 10 August, 'now numbered two hundred votes in the

1. *Lettres*, no. 125.
2. *Le Siècle* (5 Aug.) said that a further general meeting was to be held on the 8th, but on the 10th it recorded no such meeting but the constitution on the 8th of the Republican Union.
3. A. Scheurer-Kestner, *Souvenirs de Jeunesse* (1905), p. 266. 'Jamais Guelfe n'eut plus d'horreur pour un Gibelin qu'un ami de Gambetta pour un de ceux qui s'étaient rangés à Bordeaux autour de M. Jules Simon' (Pessard, *op. cit.*, p. 257).
4. Scheurer-Kestner, *op. cit.*, p. 266. Deputies could, however, and did sometimes enrol in more than one group. René Goblet, for instance, was a member of both the Republican Left and of the Republican Union (R. Goblet, 'Souvenirs de ma vie politique', *Revue politique et parlementaire*, 10 Sept. 1928, p. 368). This practice of 'double appartenance' continued until 1910 when it ceased for a while.

Assembly, and it was a very significant circumstance that Gambetta had sought and had been refused admission to their ranks. Gambetta was thus left with about thirty supporters instead of two hundred and thirty which an imprudent policy on the part of the government might have given him.'[1] Little did Thiers think that the existence of a united Left might in the long run have been to his advantage, making it less easy for the Right to effect his own overthrow less than two years later.

So Gambetta had for the time being to be content with the leadership of a small group in the Assembly, but with this, too, he had his difficulties. Many of the younger men such as Scheurer-Kestner, Laurent-Pichat, Lepère and René Goblet readily followed him, but the surviving 'vieux' of 1848 were often awkward colleagues. Their Republican notions were very different from his, they could not easily be disciplined and they objected to the very name of Republican Union which he insisted on substituting for Radical Left. Peyrat, Victor Schoelcher and Victor Hugo he gradually won over, but all his charms could not endear him to the 'grey-haired cherub' and historian Edgar Quinet or to the diminutive author of l'*Organisation du Travail*, Louis Blanc.[2] As in the latter years of the Second Empire, there was a conflict of generations, a conflict between the old men of 'the heroic age', which Gambetta now declared to be past, and the younger men, utilitarian and practical in outlook, some of whom would eventually be dubbed opportunists. But the men who were spoken of as ghosts (*revenants*) or backwoodsmen before the Empire fell were more than ever ghosts in the parliaments of the postwar decade. When Madame Adam wrote of the parts played in the National Assembly by Louis Blanc, Ledru-Rollin, Quinet, Schoelcher, Littré and Hugo, she said that they were more and more like 'great Elysian shades astounded by terrestrial compromises', astounded and no doubt shocked.[3]

Thus Gambetta's position in the Assembly ten weeks after his reelection

1. P.R.O., F.O. 146, 1540, Lyons to Granville, 11 Aug.
2. Gambetta's papers in the Quai d'Orsay (M.A.E., vol. 49) contain an amusing example of his or his entourage's contempt for Louis Blanc. It is the copy of an announcement of a new paper, *Le Jour*. This announcement contained a pompous paragraph stating that Louis Blanc was to direct the paper. The paragraph was marked in ink by Gambetta or one of his associates who wrote beside it:

> 'Boum ! Deux sous à qui
> Boum ! ! lira ça sans souffler !
> Boum ! ! !'

For further evidence of Gambetta's dislike of Louis Blanc, see Edouard Millaud, *Le Journal d'un parlementaire (de l'Empire à la République, mai 1864–février 1875)* (1914), p. 141.
3. *Mes Angoisses*, p. 267.

lacked a broad basis and he was still much on the defensive. He had not yet succeeded in dominating a hostile audience as he had often dominated the Legislative Body of the Second Empire, and some of his friends were dismayed that he had not at once reestablished a parliamentary ascendancy. When a Monarchist, the Vicomte de Meaux, expressed to Gambetta's friend Laurier his disappointment with Gambetta's oratory, Laurier shrewdly replied that there was a degree of ill-will which no orator could overcome: 'And then when one has been a god for six months it is not easy to change.'[1] A rare glimpse of him at the end of the session was, however, charmingly recorded on 12 September by an acute observer, Ludovic Halévy, once secretary to the Duc de Morny. While 'no matter who was saying no matter what on I know not what subject', he noted,

> I looked at Gambetta. I had not seen him since the month of November, at Tours, during the war. He was sitting at the end of a bench on the left. He had that good-natured innocent look he used to have, the look he had when he was nobody. . . . But I am wrong. Gambetta has always been somebody. In 1862 or 1863 when he was not yet twenty-five he was already treated with great deference by the Five.[2]

There was, moreover, another frequent observer in the Assembly who admired him, a man whose reputation in a different sphere was to equal if not surpass his own. Among those who were assiduous in attending the debates was an artist who filled his notebook with sketches of Gambetta and eventually sought to persuade him to give him some sittings. But Gambetta, for whatever reason, would not comply with Edouard Manet's request. Furious that Gambetta seemed to scorn his talent, Manet is said to have exclaimed in disgust: 'He's yet another of those who are wedded to Bonnet!' (Bonnet was a very conventional but fashionable artist) and to have added, 'These Republicans are all of a piece. Talk to them of art and you are faced by the worst reactionaries.'[3]

A few days later the members of the Assembly adjourned for a long and well-deserved vacation of two and a half months: they were not due to reassemble until 4 December. Gambetta now had other opportunities to extend and reassert his influence outside the Chamber. Here he had

1. Vicomte de Meaux, *Souvenirs politiques 1871–1877* (1905), p. 243.

2. L. Halévy, *Notes et Souvenirs 1871–1872* (1899), pp. 223–4. The Five were the five Republican deputies elected to the Legislative Body in 1857; see above, p. 4.

3. E. Moreau-Nelaton, *Manet raconté par lui-même* (1926), i, 131. It would appear from this account that Manet finally gave up his efforts to obtain sittings only some time after the foundation of Gambetta's newspaper, the *République Française*, in November 1871.

already met with considerable success. During the last four months of 1871 he was able to apply ideas which he had long been harbouring and so to develop methods and means of propaganda which would immensely strengthen his hand.

5

Outside Parliament
June–September 1871

On his return from exile Gambetta had gone back to his old abode in Paris, namely a flat on the first floor of No. 12 in the rue Montaigne. It was, according to a police report, 'a decent enough house in every respect'.[1] His maiden aunt, as usual, was there to supervise his household and was reputed to keep a watchful eye over her nephew. Thus the woman to whom Gambetta was to become attached for life, Léonie Léon, went there only rarely for dinner, although she sought to win 'La Tata' by gifts. As for other visitors, 'La Tata' was said to inspect them carefully before allowing them in.

> If [wrote C. de B.] she was entirely satisfied with the caller's credentials [she] would magnanimously accord him an audience after dinner to drink a cup of coffee, adding in her inimitable accent of the Midi: 'Té, my good friend, as you're a "bon", come for coffee. One cup more or less is no great matter.' One was thus admitted into Gambetta's intimate coterie, but though Mme Massabié [sic] did not grudge the coffee she kept an eagle eye on her nephew's cigars and the fact that he insisted on having a box of 'Londrès' on the table filled her with fear lest he should offer one to a friend.[2]

The functions of valet and general servant were fulfilled by François Roblin, a former member of the Garde Mobile who had been with him at Bordeaux. The furnishings of the three main rooms, Gambetta's study and bedroom and the dining room were, according to one of his visitors in July, as simple as those of any young barrister.[3] Only in the study were there ornaments of unusual interest: in the centre of the mantelpiece a large bronze given to Gambetta by admirers in Alsace and, flanking it,

1. A.P.P., BA/917.
2. *Letters from Paris*, pp. 217–18, 16 March 1876. C. de B. was, of course, a Royalist.
3. Hansen, *Les Coulisses de la diplomatie*, p. 244.

two statuettes—one of Liberty bequeathed to him by Colonel Charras, the military historian, the other of Mirabeau, whom he once called the greatest political genius France had had 'since the incomparable Cardinal Richelieu'.[1] On the walls there hung pictures which also bore witness to their owner's political sympathies, portraits of Danton and of Marie, one of the men of 1848, and another tribute from Alsace—Henner's 'La jeune Alsacienne'—recently presented to him.[2]

Like many Frenchmen, he is said to have been an early riser, normally getting up at 6 a.m. He generally spent the morning before midday receiving callers and went out in the afternoon, but if he stayed at home he would see more visitors after lunch. His callers appeared to the watchful police to be 'very mixed'. So too was his correspondence. Fortunately some of the letters which he received between the end of June and the beginning of October 1871 have survived.[3] They are presumably but a small and seemingly random remnant of the voluminous correspondence which is the lot of any prominent politician and which must have absorbed part of Gambetta's time[4] and still more of that of Spuller (in whose hand are several of the drafts or copies of Gambetta's replies) and of Gambetta's young secretary, Paul Sandrique; but they help to fill in the picture of his activities during a period in which, it has been said, he wrote and spoke very little.[5] They show him granting appointments to all sorts of people who wished to see him, giving instructions that signed photographs should be sent to three Republican lady admirers, and encouraging fervent Republicans, however unlettered, who had written to him about the state of affairs in their departments, to write again and keep him informed. 'I am watching: please keep me *au courant*' was his note on a letter from a Marseilles workman denouncing the 'unheard of propaganda of the Monarchists'. Many simple folk all over the country must thus have been encouraged to believe that Gambetta had their

1. Emile Labarthe, *Gambetta et ses amis* (1938), p. 99. Charras was one of Cavaignac's henchmen in 1848 and went into exile in consequence of the *coup d'état* of 1851.

2. Vizetelly, *Republican France*, p. 207. For other descriptions of Gambetta's flat, see *L'Evénement*, 24 Aug. 1872, and H. Thurat, *Gambetta, sa vie, son oeuvre* (1883), pp. 306–7.

3. M.A.E., Fond Gambetta, vols. 49 and 59–61. After October the correspondence preserved is much more fragmentary.

4. ' "My work in the Assembly", Gambetta was reported as saying early in January 1873, "is a very small matter compared with my natural and ordinary duties" and as he spoke he pointed with a half-pitying, half-despairing smile to a huge pile of letters which a secretary or man servant . . . had brought in' (*New York Herald*, 27 Jan. 1873).

5. Pierre Sorlin 'Gambetta et les Républicains nantais en 1871', *Revue d'histoire moderne et contemporaine*, avril–juin 1963, p. 126.

interests at heart. He is consulted by students eager to engage in Republican propaganda,[1] by journalists, by provincial politicians and by men who want his backing for some new project, whether it be the founding of a newspaper or the creation of some local Republican club. But his funds were limited and when on 1 August Jules Magnan of Limoges wrote to ask for 4,000 francs to enable him to found a paper to be called *La Fusion Républicaine* devoted exclusively to Gambetta's interests, he had to reply that, while such a publication could not fail to succeed if it had the support of 'the patriots of Limoges', the state of his personal fortune did not allow him to send the sum asked for. When at the end of the month Magnan returned to the charge and further asked him to write for the proposed paper Gambetta's answer was sharper in tone: much as he would like to, it was absolutely out of the question for him to give financial aid; and as for a weekly unsigned article, how, he asked, did Magnan suppose that he had time to write an article every week in the midst of his daily tasks and of all the business concerning the general interests of the Republican party? 'First of all, it is not my profession and, secondly, I have neither the leisure nor the ability.' So, too, he declined an invitation to contribute a few lines to a new paper 'in the manner of *Charivari*' to be called the *Chat Botté*; he was too busy: 'besides, I am not much accustomed to expressing my thoughts in writing'. A request from Gustave Naquet, formerly director of the Marseilles paper *Le Peuple*, asking him to approve and write a preface for a brochure entitled *L'Europe délivrée*, which contemplated a Republican federation of the 'United States of Europe' in twenty years' time called forth a more specific statement of Gambetta's views. He asked to be excused from contributing a preface, not only

> because, as you know, writing is hardly my business, but also because I do not agree with you on the fundamental basis of your book . . . I have never been a subscriber to this vague and deceptive theory of a Republican United States of Europe . . . after the hard and severe lessons given us by recent events I absolutely reject this theory as fatal for the regeneration of France, false as a matter of general history, and dangerous for democracy and the freedom of the world.[2]

Unlike many Republicans, Gambetta had been a realist in foreign policy before the war. Indeed on one occasion in the Legislative Body in April 1870 he had confessed that he was 'pretty chauvinist'.[3] Now, as a result

1. e.g. the youthful Committee of the Fédération des Ecoles founded in Montpellier on 29 May 1871.
2. Naquet's brochure was published none the less before the end of the year: its full title was *L'Europe délivrée, histoire prophétique de 1871 à 1892*.
3. 5 April 1870. *Annales du Sénat et du Corps Législatif*, vol. iii, p. 304.

of the experience of the war, his naturally realistic, and indeed nationalist, outlook was reinforced. Almost at the same time he wrote to the organiser of the Fifth Congress of the League of Peace and Liberty, shortly to be held at Lausanne, that he had never been a warm partisan of cosmopolitan ideas and principles. Their effect was to lessen the love of one's country and, in France's present situation, it was more than ever important for people to cling to the principle of loyalty to the nation and 'to rediscover their strength in the idea of France'.[1]

Rejecting Utopianism, Gambetta also refused to be identified as a feminist. In a draft letter, marked 'keep but do not send', which may, however, be presumed to have represented his views, he replied to an invitation to become a member of a recently created 'Association pour les droits des femmes' saying that he did not see of what use could be the adherence of a man like himself who had little familiarity with such complex problems as those which it was proposed to raise! Moreover, his own view was that the question of women's rights would be near to being resolved, once the rights of the citizen were established and legally recognised: 'We shall reach this goal, Sir, by firmly maintaining the Republican constitution and by extending education in floods (*à flots*) to the new generations. That is why I have consented to become a member of the Ligue de l'Enseignement which, in the present state of our habits (*moeurs*) seems to me to reply as effectively as possible to the questions you put forward.'[2]

While Gambetta in some of his letters defined his role and his attitude to certain questions of general importance and, incidentally, made it clear that he had renounced any idea of returning to the bar—having taken the 'irrevocable decision to devote all the time at my disposal to the duties of my mandate as a deputy and to the general interests of the Republican party'[3]—his correspondence also illuminates his views or reemphasises opinions he had already expressed on various more immediate problems.

1. This letter was published. See *Lettres*, no. 127.
2. This draft is undated, but answers a letter of 26 Sept. The Ligue de l'Enseigne-ment had been founded in 1866 by the Republican freemason Jean Macé and was one of the most important agents of Republican propaganda. A note in Gambetta's papers indicates that in October he sent 50 francs in response to an appeal from the Committee of the Cercle Parisien de la Ligue de l'Enseignement asking for support for a 'Mouvement national du sou contre l'ignorance. Pétition en faveur de l'instruc-tion obligatoire et gratuite.' This petition was backed by 1,267,267 signatories and was regarded as a great success for the Ligue. Nearly 400,000 of the signatories also wanted secular education (G. Compayré, *Jean Macé et l'instruction obligatoire en France*, 2nd edn., Paris, 1902, p. 85).
3. Letter of September 1871 to a M. Amiel who had written on 31 Aug to ask Gambetta to defend him in a lawsuit.

It was important to encourage good Republican candidates and organisations, but it was also essential to stress that they should be moderate and act strictly within the limits of the law. It was also necessary for him to define more clearly his attitude to the assumption of constituent powers by the National Assembly.

So far as candidates were concerned, the most striking example of Gambetta's concern to use or continue to use good men was his letter of 27 September to General Faidherbe, who had resigned from the Assembly on 20 August, precisely because he did not believe himself empowered by his electors to grant it constituent powers. Gambetta's long letter was an eloquent plea to the General to return to parliament no matter how repugnant this might be to him.[1] But Faidherbe was not to be moved and devoted himself mainly to philosophy and archaeology until he became a senator in 1879. Gambetta's unpublished correspondence also shows him advising Freycinet, his former delegate at the War Ministry in Tours and Bordeaux, whose election in Paris he had failed to secure on 2 July,[2] and reveals his concern for less prominent Republicans. Thus in August he looked forward to seeing a former proscript of December 1851, Théodore Karcher of the *Courrier de l'Europe*, and talking about his candidature in the next elections in the Ardennes, and in October he wrote very cordially to the Comte de Marquessac who was standing as a candidate for the General Council in Gambetta's own native department, the Lot. Marquessac was a convert to the Republican cause and Gambetta had once spent some time on board the frigate of which he was captain: now Gambetta told him that he was particularly glad to know that through his example the Republic was making daily progress in the countryside: 'Support such as yours is precious.' Three days later, when a local elector had written to enquire whether Marquessac should be supported, Gambetta's friend Alphonse Péphau, who also sometimes acted as secretary for him, wired back: 'Let all sincere Republicans place his name in the urn and take all necessary steps on his behalf.'

Gambetta had significantly played no part in the debates about the organisation of the departmental General Councils for which these elections were held in October. They concerned the greatest opportunity to decentralise French government which had occurred for decades, yet in the final vote on 10 August on the law as a whole he had abstained. Thus he had not disclosed whether he shared the opinion of the majority in the Assembly that these bodies should be allowed to express political wishes or whether he thought with Thiers, that conservative and authori-

1. *Lettres*, no. 128.
2. Fond Joseph Reinach, B.N., N.a.fr. 13581, ff.14–15 (Freycinet to Gambetta 15 Sept.) and ff.16–18 (Gambetta to Freycinet 19 Oct.).

tarian believer in centralisation, that their activities should be narrowly restricted. But in October, after the law had been voted, he was ready to declare himself. An enquiry from Cornil, the newly elected Republican president of the General Council for the Allier, who had 'rolled to victory under the banner: "the republican principle is the conservative principle par excellence" ',[1] gave him an admirable opportunity once again to show both his own moderation and the extent to which he could on occasion agree with Thiers. After claiming, as he would subsequently in speech after speech, that the election results were democratic and registered a further Republican advance,[2] he asserted that they showed that light was penetrating to 'the lowest strata' of society and that the influence of local notables was diminishing. A new world was coming into being: 'the people, petits bourgeois, workers and peasants have every day a clearer perception of the connection between their affairs and politics. They wish to have their own representatives and soon they will provide them. This constitutes a revolution.'[3] Here was an anticipation of the famous phrase about 'a new social stratum' (*une couche sociale nouvelle*) of which Thiers was to disapprove and which was to raise such a storm a year later.

On the national level Gambetta's diagnosis was exact—more clearly than most he divined the real tendencies of this postwar age, but so far as the General Councils were concerned, there is no certainty that the clearer political perceptions of 'the people' meant a lowering in the social level of the representatives chosen in the 'seventies. The General Councils might become more professional and their political allegiance might gradually become more markedly Republican, but for a long while to come they were still predominantly filled by local 'notables'.[4] Yet, if the

1. Sanford H. Elwitt, 'Politics and social classes in the Loire: triumph of Republican order, 1869–1873', *French Historical Studies*, vol. vi (1969), no. 1, p. 111.

2. e.g. on 14 Dec. 1872: 'Le pays nomma en grande majorité des républicains.' But, according to Lord Lyons, 'apathy, timidity and weariness kept the majority of the Electors away from the Poll ... the votes given were so few, as to afford no sufficient test of the comparative strength of these Parties' (to Lord Granville, 29 Dec. 1871, P.R.O., F.O. 146, 1545). Ludovic Halévy, too, commented on abstentions amounting to sixty per cent and asked whether the electorate was going on strike. He cited an amusing conversation he had had with a farmer in Seine-et-Marne who had been one of the abstainers: 'Moi ... Oh! non, par example, je n'ai pas voté.—Et pourquoi cela?—Pourquoi ça? ... Plus souvent que j'irais me déranger pour voter, maintenant qu'on est libre.—Comment libre?—Mais oui, on est libre. Sous l'Empire il fallait marcher. ... mais à présent c'est fini ... Tenez, dimanche, j'ai vendu une vache, j'aime mieux ça que d'avoir voté' (*Notes et Souvenirs 1871–1872*, pp. 246–7).

3. For the text of Gambetta's letter to Cornil, see *Discours*, vol. ii, pp. 473–83.

4. In this connection, see the interesting analysis in pp. 177–80 of *Les Conseillers Généraux en 1870* by L. Girard, A. Prost and R. Gossez (1967).

political sense of the people was becoming more acute, Gambetta now made it clear that he did not think that the departmental Councils should be turned into political assemblies. More than ever, he urged, administration should be kept free of politics; the departmental Council ought not to become a sort of petty legislature.[1] If he were a Councillor he would not indulge in any sort of political resolution: 'I would not demand the dissolution of the Versailles Assembly, the proclamation of the Republic, or any other general political measure . . . I should regard myself as the business agent of my constituents.' It should be the task of the councillors to make methodical studies of the social conditions of the department; to make themselves fully acquainted with the state of education, public health and poor relief, with the condition of industry, agriculture, communications and finance. Thus they would become a nursery for the education of the administrators and politicians of the future.

Moderation was the keynote, too, of much of the advice contained in Gambetta's unpublished correspondence during the late summer and early autumn. When Paul Motté of La Ferté Bernard wrote to say that he and his friends would like to celebrate the anniversary of 4 September, the date of the overthrow of the Second Empire and the proclamation of the Republic, Gambetta replied that the idea of a commemorative banquet had never seemed to him to be a good one 'in these times of such trouble and difficulty. Not that I reject this date: but the time has not come to celebrate it. This moment will not come until the territory has been completely freed.' Any festivity, he pointed out, would be a gift to the enemies of the Republic. 'Let us avoid all such traps and celebrate 4 September in a fitting way by serious reflection instead of by meeting at banquets.'[2] His reply to the President and Secretary of a newly formed Central Committee of Republican Propaganda in Loir-et-Cher, who had about the same time sent him the statutes of their committee for his approval, was particularly interesting and illuminating. While he agreed with them, he said, when they declared that the problem was to protect the Republic from *coups d'état* and that the solution lay in the creation of committees such as theirs, there was one point which he could not sufficiently emphasise, namely that they should never go beyond the bounds of legality: 'You know how strictly limited the right of association is in

---

1. There were, no doubt, two good political reasons for this advice. One was that it was the Legitimists who in 1851 had vainly introduced Bills to enhance the powers of the General Councils in order to give them an important political role and who ever since had sought to maintain their own local influence through these bodies. The other was Thiers' opposition to any widening of the powers of the Councils.

2. This letter, merely dated September, appears to be either a draft or a copy of the one presumably sent (M.A.E., Fond Gambetta, vol. 49).

France today as it has been in the past. Do not transgress those limits, if you wish to do useful and lasting work. Devote yourselves to such works of established utility as the founding of newspapers, the creation of libraries and lectures for adults and finally to securing the success of Republican candidates in the elections.' Here spoke the advocate of education *à flots* and member of the Ligue de l'Enseignement, the shrewd politician who knew that, whatever might happen in the Assembly, those were the means with which to consolidate the hold of the Republic on the country at large.[1] In this connection a letter of considerable interest is preserved in the Scheurer-Kestner papers.[2] It was from Alcide Dusolier and dated 19 July 1871. The writer stated that he and Jules Barni (who would at the third attempt, in June 1872, be elected Radical deputy for the Somme) were forming a provisional Central Committee of the Société d'instruction républicaine, whose work had been interrupted by the war:[3] 'Some departments', he said, 'are not yet converted and the others need to be confirmed in their democratic faith.' He wanted a definitive Central Committee to be formed and it would be good to have on it some members of the Republican Left: 'Speak about it to Gambetta and get the help of some of the most active and influential democratic papers. . . . We are in course of establishing ourselves in the Dordogne, this poor Dordogne which has just sent M. Magne [a former Bonapartist minister] to the Assembly and which is in great need of being told about the advantages of a Republican regime.' Whatever the form of propaganda, however, legality was at this time always a prime consideration. Thus, when a M. Beaudemont of St Quentin and some of his friends wrote to say that they were founding a Central Electoral Committee of the Aisne department and enquired about their legal position, Gambetta encouraged them to go ahead: 'The creation of a centre of action is simply the exercise of one of those necessary freedoms which the President of the Republic once so eloquently demanded.'[4] But he insisted that their committee must preserve its exclusively electoral character and that,

1. This letter, too, is a draft or copy, dated September. Jean Macé, the founder of the Ligue de l'Enseignement, also did notable work in helping to establish public libraries and reading rooms. The Ligue had close associations with freemasonry.

2. B.N., N.a.fr. 22409.

3. This society published a weekly paper called *Le Patriote;* it organised lectures, founded libraries and issued brochures; see D. Halévy, *La Fin des Notables*, Appendix III (p. 292), which also contains notes on other collections of Republican propagandist brochures. The *R.F.* of 29 April 1872 announced the forthcoming appearance of ten more 'popular publications', price fifteen centimes each, published by the Society. It included three on the peasantry and three on the French Revolution, one written by one of Gambetta's former collaborators in the National Defence, Jules Cazot.

4. An allusion to a celebrated speech of Thiers in 1864.

whilst always being prepared, they should make use of it only during the electoral periods, that is to say at the times when it would be called upon to produce its maximum effect.[1]

The importance of these Republican committees in the provinces and their organisation can hardly be overestimated. It was soon to be recognised in early numbers of Gambetta's paper, *La République Française*, and the historian Daniel Halévy later drew attention to it in his *La Fin des Notables*.[2] From Gambetta's correspondence and other evidence it is clear that he was in frequent touch with many of these bodies and that they constantly turned to him for advice or to report progress. One such progress report, contained in a letter of 12 October from the President of the Republican Society of the Drôme, gives an interesting insight into the kind of network which was being developed. The writer claimed that the Republican successes in the elections to the General Council were due to the organisation of his society which covered almost all the department:

> The Communes are divided into sections which correspond with the cantonal sections which in their turn correspond with the central section in the chief town. But all sections can correspond directly with the Central Committee. . . . This organisation has enabled us by means of monthly subscriptions to meet the numerous expenses entailed by the elections and to form a compact group obeying the decisions taken by the Society's delegates whether they concern the choice of a candidate or any other measure of general interest.

These methods had aroused the interest of Republicans in other departments, including the Allier and the Basses-Alpes, 'whom we are organising by correspondence. The Ardèche is poorly organised and we shall have completed our work there within a month. Although the courts have ordered the dissolution of the societies of the Isère they are still actively functioning.' But, he added, money was always a problem.[3] This was no

1. Cf. the draft or copy of a reply of September to a correspondent who had sent Gambetta the programme of the Ligue Républicaine d'Epinal. In this Gambetta expressed particular approval of the fifth paragraph 'concerning the essentially peaceful and legal character that you intend your institution to have. This is an extremely important point for we must admit that we shall not succeed in conquering the liberties which we lack except by the patient and wise use of those which we have.' He added that he would always be glad to have news of the progress of the society and particularly of the extension of its influence on the electoral terrain.

2. pp. 121–2; see in particular the R.F.'s leader of 14 Nov. 1871. Some of these Republican organisations, such as the Alliance Républicaine, had emerged during the war. For Radical activities in the Hérault in 1871–72, see D. Stafford, *From Anarchism to Reformism* (1971), pp. 6–7.

3. Unfortunately, this letter bears no comment by Gambetta or his entourage and Gambetta's reply, if any, is unknown. For a suggestion of a similar sort of Radical organisation, see the following satirical passage in the Bonapartist publication *Bleus,*

doubt also true elsewhere, and such an elaborate organisation as that in the Drôme was probably rare. In the Loire, for instance, a recent historian has written, the Republicans did not constitute a political party so much as 'a nexus of social and personal relationships'.[1]

The other main question illuminated by Gambetta's private correspondence during these months is that which had caused such a furore in August, namely the constituent power of the Assembly. A contributor to the three-year-old *Progrès de la Côte d'Or et Dijon* had sent him an article on the attitude to be adopted by the Left. In his reply Gambetta said that, when in the debate on this question he had declared that the majority would not exercise this power, this was not a challenge but a reasoned conviction:

> In effect when the Assembly meets again after being prorogued for two months during which its members will have individually been able to size up the real state of opinion in the provinces, I do not think it will raise the constitutional question again nor above all do I think that it will have the necessary prestige and strength to solve it in a monarchical sense. So I think that it is above all necessary to let this question of constituent power slumber and confine ourselves to the idea that the existing assembly which has no mandate for it is incapable of exercising it in spite of all its pretensions.

He agreed that it would be better for Republican deputies to abstain from voting on constitutional measures than to resign from the Assembly *en masse*, but added that 'what we must do is to follow the movement of public opinion, so far as concerns dissolution'.

The movement of public opinion—this now meant in particular the mustering of petitions for the dissolution of the Assembly organised by various groups of Republicans. Here, too, Gambetta was asked for his advice. On 8 September M. Buisserand of Epineuil-près-Tonnerre in the

---

1. Elwitt, *art. cit.*, p. 104. But on 9 July 1875, C. de B. reporting on the extent to which Buffet had been impressed by Radical organisation in the South, declared that the Radicals had maintained 'cette Ligue du Midi établie précisément pendant la guerre pour constituer le radicalisme communal dans tout le sud de la France'.

Blancs, Rouges, Lettres Réactionnaires adressées au Directeur du Paris-Journal par un provincial (Paris, 1873), p. 23 (letter of 5 Sept. 1872): 'Oui, monsieur, Sainte Anne, commune de 1,153 habitants, possède un comité radical, qui correspond avec le comité du chef-lieu d'arrondissement, lequel correspond avec le comité du chef-lieu de département. Les quatres polissons qui forment le comité de Sainte Anne se sont réunis au Café National.' On the other hand the historian of the Allier comments on the lack of organisations on a departmental scale in 1871 (J. F. Viple, *Sociologie politique de l'Allier. La vie politique et les élections sous la Troisième République*, 1967, p. 87).

Yonne wrote to ask whether or not he should urge people in his commune and the neighbourhood to sign. The answer was 'Yes', and when on 14 September he was sent a cutting from the *Echo de l'Aisne* containing a reply by E. Evrard to a letter from Waddington, the future President of the Council, expressing surprise that a petition for the dissolution of the Assembly should be organised at Château Thierry, Gambetta noted on it: 'M. Evrard's reply has my entire approval. To go on with the petitions is the way to be rid of the conspirators.'

So the campaign for the dissolution of the Assembly was given encouragement by its chief protagonist. He himself was soon to carry it a stage further in a series of public speeches and in his own newspaper. Thereby he was to follow Spuller's advice to him while he was still at San Sebastian and to set out 'to conquer France'.[1]

1. Letter of 11 June (*Revue de Paris*, 1 June 1900).

6

The République Française
March–December 1871

At the end of September and the beginning of October 1871 Gambetta
was confined to his flat with an attack of phlebitis in the left leg.[1] This
prevented him from spending part of his vacation with his friends the
Edmond Adams in their villa on the Riviera, but it does not seem to have
seriously retarded his plans for extending his influence both inside and
outside the Assembly. One of his main preoccupations at this time was the
completion of preparations for launching a new daily paper.

'The Press is everything', that veteran Republican Adolphe Crémieux
had once exclaimed, 'if the Press is ours we shall have the rest.'[2] In a party
which contained a high proportion of journalists the importance of the
Press was unlikely to be underestimated and opposition papers had played
a considerable part in the last phase of the Republican struggle against the
Second Empire. But though many of these, such as Delescluze's Réveil,
had been categorically Republican, none had exactly corresponded to the
conceptions of the new school of young Republicans. So it was that
Gambetta had long harboured the ambition of running a paper to voice
his own views and those of his associates. As early as 1865 he and his
friends Allain-Targé, Brisson and Jules Ferry had considered taking over
a paper called the Liberté which was about to be started by a Legitimist.
But the negotiations came to nothing.[3] Again in 1866, after consulting
Allain-Targé, whose assistance had also been sought, he had refused an
invitation from Ollivier to work with him on the Presse. As Allain-Targé
wrote to his father: 'Together we might have made the Presse a power:
but in whose service and to what end?'[4] The paths of Emile Ollivier,

1. See Lettres no. 130: but in the draft of his letter of 19 Oct. to Freycinet he
referred to the right leg!
2. C. S. Phillips, The Church in France 1848–1907 (1936), p. 189.
3. H. Allain-Targé, La République sous l'Empire (1939), p. 33.
4. Ibid., p. 58.

future minister of Napoleon III, and of Gambetta and his contemporaries were indeed clearly more and more divergent. Eventually, in 1868, with Brisson, Challemel-Lacour, Allain-Targé and Laurier, Gambetta had helped to found and had even written an occasional article for the *Revue politique et littéraire*; but this had been a weekly review of limited circulation, and it had lasted only seven months. What Gambetta wanted was a serious paper, a daily vehicle of Republican opinion, comparable in importance to but different in spirit from the moderate Republican *Siècle*.[1] He had persevered with the idea, and in 1869 he and another friend, André Lavertujon, were planning the publication of a paper to be called the *Suffrage Universel*—a significant title in days when universal suffrage was still insecure. They hoped it would have the financial backing of M. Dubochet, a prominent industrialist and former Saint-Simonian, in whose château in Switzerland, Les Crêtes, near Clarens in the canton of Vaud, Gambetta was a welcome visitor.[2] But this project, too, had come to nothing. Then the war had brought weightier preoccupations; it had also led to a cooling in the relationship between Gambetta and two of those who had been closely associated with some of his early journalistic plans, namely Laurier and Lavertujon.[3]

The first of his surviving letters from San Sebastian had, however, shown that Gambetta had not abandoned his long-cherished ambition: 'When we return to Paris', he had written on 18 March 1871, to Antonin Proust, 'we must think of founding a big newspaper and we ought already to be thinking about its composition and the plan of campaign.'[4] Three months later he was asking Proust anxiously: 'And the paper? What's the position? With whom? How? I have a great many observations to make!'[5] After his return to France eleven days later the opportunity and the need for such a paper appeared to be all the greater. This was pointed out in a

1. A. Lavertujon, *Gambetta inconnu* (1905), pp. 126–8. The *Siècle* had had a circulation of about 50,000 in the early 1860s. It still had one of the largest circulations in 1872 (I. Collins, *The Government and the Newspaper Press in France 1814–1881*, 1959, pp. 140 and 168). Its now somewhat old-fashioned character was reflected in the Gothic lettering of its name on the front page.

2. See *Lettres*, nos. 50, 54, 59, 60, 62, 66.

3. Laurier, however, gave generous financial help to the *République Française*, taking up twenty-three of the initial shares of 1,000 fr. (see 'La République Française journal de Gambetta' in *Etudes de Presse*, vol. xii, nos. 22–23, p. 13, n. 1). According to Halévy and Pillias (*Lettres*, no. 388, n. (a)), Laurier became an Orleanist and from about 1872 ceased to be one of Gambetta's political friends, although the two men remained on cordial terms. Laurier died suddenly in 1878 and an article upon him in the *Figaro* of 2 October that year entitled 'Le Morny de M. Gambetta' asserted that, despite their apparent rupture, Laurier had continued to be one of Gambetta's righthand men.

4. *Lettres*, no. 115.

5. *Lettres*, no. 121.

letter of 5 July from one of Gambetta's friends, Armand Ruiz; he referred to an indecisive meeting at Versailles two months earlier at which the idea of founding a paper had been discussed and said that he might now be able to raise the necessary funds.[1] His friends Challemel-Lacour and Edmond Adam were among those who agreed that the enterprise must be a new one, not merely the revivification of an existing paper.[2] What part Ruiz played in obtaining funds and where they came from is not clear,[3] but it was not long before Gambetta had succeeded 'without too many difficulties' in procuring enough money at least to start the paper. More would have been forthcoming had the founders been willing to accept the help of certain financiers and businessmen, such as the chocolate manufacturer, Menier, but they had refused such offers in order to preserve their freedom of action.[4] Gambetta's ambition, however, was realised at last and the new paper made its first appearance on Tuesday, 7 November 1871. Various names suggested for it such as *La Revanche* or *Le Patriote* had been rejected in favour of the more comprehensive *La République Française*, for which Freycinet claimed the credit. It still remained to raise additional capital and here Gambetta hoped to obtain a considerable proportion—in a letter to Albert Boell of Wissembourg, he spoke of 60,000 francs—from Alsace and Lorraine.[5] But although Gambetta urged that patriotism would be the ruling principle of the paper and that the affairs of Alsace and Lorraine would have a privileged place in its columns, the agent he selected to operate in the lost provinces, Puthod, who had been prefect of the Ain during the war, appears to have been ill-chosen and did not succeed in obtaining more than 55,000 francs.[6] The sum eventually raised among political sympathisers with the help of Scheurer-Kestner and others was substantially larger. It enabled the constitution in October 1872 of a limited company, the Société de la République Française. This had a limited capital of 125,000 francs divided into 1,000 franc shares bought by thirty-two shareholders, the largest of whom were Clément Laurier

1. Letter to Gambetta Fond Joseph Reinach (B.N., N.a.fr.. 1351, ff. 116–7).
2. Mme Adam, *Mes Angoisses*, p. 168.
3. E. de Marcère in *L'Assemblée Nationale de 1871* (1904, pp. 128 and 251) asserted that the paper had been launched with aid from the wealthy family of Arnaud de l'Ariège. One of Dubochet's nieces, Suzanne Guichard, married Frédéric Arnaud de l'Ariège and later became one of Gambetta's intimate friends.
4. Letter of 27 Oct. from Challemel-Lacour to his German friend, the poet Herwegh (quoted in G. Wormser, *Gambetta dans les tempêtes, 1870–1877*, 1964, p. 125). The refusal of help from Menier is mentioned in a police report of 22 Aug. 1872 (A.P.P. BA/917).
5. Letter of 12 Nov. 1871, in H. Galli, *Gambetta et l'Alsace-Lorraine* (Paris, 1911), pp. 45–7.
6. 'La République Française journal de Gambetta: Extraits du journal inédit de Scheurer-Kestner', *Etudes de Presse*, vol. xii, (1960), nos. 22–23, p. 14.

(twenty-three shares), Charles Bloch of Sainte-Marie aux Mines (twenty shares), Edouard Le Pelletier and Joachim Bruel of Paris (twelve and ten shares respectively) and two members of the Péphau family, Alphonse and Antoine, who took eight shares each. In addition, Gambetta as founder of the paper, received 125 so-called 'industrial' shares of 1,000 francs each in addition to his salary of 12,000 francs as director.[1] The *République Française* was therefore of crucial importance to him financially. He had no private means, and since he had ceased to practise at the bar and to draw a ministerial salary, he had little other income apart from his annual stipend as a deputy, namely 9,000 francs, the equivalent of £360 in English money at the time. The creation of the *République Française* and its success would eventually ensure him a steady income, relative affluence and a more assured financial situation than he had ever known before.

The new venture from the outset played a major part in Gambetta's existence. He visited its offices at 16 rue du Croissant almost every evening when he was in Paris, and later, in 1876, when these were moved to a more spacious building in the Chaussée d'Antin, he left his flat in the rue Montaigne and took up his abode on the premises. True to his belief that he had no gift for writing, he seldom, if ever, contributed an article in written form. His usual practice was to gather his collaborators around him and let them talk; without seeking to influence them he would intervene and sum up the discussion. Thus he inspired and directed the policy of the paper through the spoken word, generally leaving it to his entourage to translate his views into article form, but sometimes there and then himself dictating the leader of the morrow.[2]

From the outset, too, the *République Française* was a rallying point for several of his closest adherents. He told them to regard themselves not as journalists, but as future ministers.[3] And so indeed many of them were. As one later commentator remarked with pardonable exaggeration: 'All the Third Republic was gathered there.' Gambetta's intimate friend and constant companion, the friendly and ever-willing Eugène Spuller ('le Badois', as he was familiarly known from his Germanic origin) occupied the post of editor-in-chief, originally destined for Lavertujon.[4] Home

---

1. *Ibid.* p. 13, n. 1. and communication of M. P. Albert at the Colloque Gambetta held at Nanterre on 13 May 1972.

2. See Freycinet, *Souvenirs 1848–1878*, p. 296.

3. In a circular letter of appeal to his compatriots of Alsace and Lorraine he wrote that 'this paper is divided into ministries' (Galli, *op. cit.*, p. 48).

4. Scheurer-Kestner in his unpublished journal (of which an extract relating to the *République Française* was printed in *Etudes de Presse*, vol. xii, 1960, nos. 22–23, wrote that Spuller had irritated Gambetta in 1876 by signing his election posters 'Rédacteur en chef de la *République Française*' and that this was false: 'A cette époque, il n'y avait pas de rédacteur en chef par la raison que Gambetta n'en avait pas voulu.' (*contd.*)

affairs were treated mainly by Ranc and Challemel-Lacour. Freycinet, a future President of the Council, and now the director of an iron works in the Landes, was until 1876 the specialist on military affairs and public works. Antonin Proust, 'the artist and aesthete of the young Republic, slightly faded like the pictures by Detaille and Meissonnier of whom he was the champion', took charge of foreign affairs;[1] Allain-Targé, later Gambetta's Minister of Finance, and Rouvier, another future premier, handled economic and financial topics, while the physiologist Paul Bert, who would become Gambetta's Minister of Education and of Public Worship, wrote especially on scientific and educational subjects, and Gustave Isambert, formerly one of Gambetta's 'personal guard' at Bordeaux, directed the editorial secretariat, the *secrétariat de rédaction*.[2] Others enlisted were Dionys Ordinaire, Charles Floquet, Emmanuel Arène, Berthelot and Louis Combes; later there would be several young recruits who would play a conspicuous part in the political life of the Third Republic, for Gambetta had a remarkable flair for spotting and encouraging young men of ability. Among these were Gaston Thomson, future Minister of Marine, who was to have the distinction of representing the Algerian constituency of Constantine for fifty-five years; Camille Barrère, future ambassador in Rome; Gabriel Hanotaux, historian and future Minister for Foreign Affairs, who wrote 'Variétés historiques' every month and Marcellin Pellet, a later deputy and diplomat. Perhaps only the *Journal des Débats* could rival the *République Française* in the brilliance of its

1. G. Hanotaux, *Mon Temps*, vol. i, *De l'Empire à la République* (1933), p. 146. Wormser, *op. cit.*, p. 124, asserts that Spuller had charge of foreign affairs. Mme Adam (*Nos amitiés politiques avant l'abandon de la revanche* (1908, p. 72) mentions Ranc's father as writing on sport. This was confined to giving accounts of race meetings. The art critic was Burty.

2. For portraits of Isambert and other leading members of the R.F.'s staff, see Henri Avenel, *Histoire de la presse française depuis 1789 jusqu'à nos jours* (1900), facing p. 650. In a letter of 6 July 1871 Henri Sainte-Claire Deville said that since the outbreak of the Franco–Prussian war Gambetta was the only person who had publicly referred to French science (B.N. Fond Joseph Reinach, N.a.fr.13581, ff. 118–9). The scientific chronicles were an important feature of Gambetta's paper.

The R.F. incidentally expressed its desire to give science 'une part propre à la place qu'elle mérite d'occuper dans une conception vraiment démocratique de notre organisation sociale'. The author of its first Revue Scientifique on 4 Dec. 1871 said that it must be admitted that 'le bataillon scientifique de la France est peu nombreux et fort mal armé. . . . La nécessité d'une réformation dans l'organisation et dans l'outillage est criante'. The conditions for developing disinterested theoretical research must be improved: 'Il faut que l'on se déshabitue de l'impatiente question: à quoi sert-il?'

However, a police report of 14 March 1872 and the paper itself on 1 Oct. 1873 had called Spuller chief editor and most authorities agree that he was, at least till 1876.

team of contributors. After Gambetta, Challemel-Lacour was the oracle of the establishment. Both were brilliant talkers and both were severe critics; yet there was a complete contrast of manner between 'the Master' and this right-hand man. Gambetta was generally genial, expansive and *bon enfant*; Challemel-Lacour, the pessimistic disciple of Schopenhauer, prematurely white-haired and menaced by tuberculosis, was dry and dictatorial; he hated familiarity, was irritated by contradiction and, according to a recruit of 1876, Joseph Reinach, treated his collaborators like a class of schoolchildren.

The day of the cheap Press based on advertisement was dawning, but Gambetta did not at first succumb to the temptations offered by modern techniques and popular appeal. Like the *Journal des Débats* and the *Siècle*, the *République Française* appeared in the morning, its leaders being dated the preceding day, whereas most Parisian dailies were published in the afternoon or evening. With its four large pages it was typical of the more serious papers of the time and any advertisements were normally confined to the last page. It was intended to be a missionary enterprise, the 'breviary of Republicans', as Challemel-Lacour's wartime associate at Lyon, Le Royer, was said to have put it.[1] Indeed in December 1872 in a notice of Marcellin Pellet's book on *Elysée Loustallot et les Révolutions de Paris*, Gambetta's anonymous reviewer (later revealed as Georges Avenel) exalted Loustallot as the ideal journalist, the journalist who above all

ought to be a knowledgeable and conscientious man, a man of good sense, of dignity, quick to spot injustice but a man whose indignation as a citizen must never resemble hysterical anger. In short the journalist should (though men may laugh at this today) believe himself to be entrusted with a priestly mission; it is his duty not only to keep a watch on the mandatories of the sovereign but to diffuse amongst the members of the sovereign the habits of a free people.[2]

As part of this missionary enterprise the *République Française* reinterpreted the French Revolution as well as enunciating the doctrines of modern Republicanism.[3] It was sold in Paris for the same price as the *Presse* and the *Figaro*, namely fifteen centimes a copy, five centimes less than the *Journal des Débats* but five more than such papers as the *Radical*, which had

1. Mme Adam, *Mes Angoisses*, pp. 219–20. This was recognised also by Republicans abroad. Thus the Spaniard Castelar wrote to Gambetta on 9 Nov. 1871 that the paper would be 'a focus for our ideas'; he would do his best to make it widely known (Reinach pp., B.N., N.a.fr. 13580, ff. 107–8).
2. *R.F.* 31 Dec. 1872, pp. 3–4. Loustallot (1762–90, sometimes spelt with one 'l') was a champion of freedom of the Press in the early days of the French Revolution. For fourteen months he was the main contributor to *Les Révolutions de Paris*.
3. See Paul Farmer, *France Reviews its Revolutionary Origins* (1944), p. 38.

made its first appearance only three weeks earlier,[1] and that favourite of the Parisian working class, the *Rappel*. Its articles were, unlike those in most papers, unsigned, since Gambetta appears to have been convinced that anonymity spelt both authority and integrity;[2] it aimed, in Challemel-Lacour's words, at being 'prudent and moderate in form, at least to begin with',[3] while in tone it sought, as he also said, to dethrone the *Figaro*. It was, therefore, eminently serious and often dogmatic.[4] The 'Red' ex-dictator would in journalism as in politics show that he was no wild man of the woods, and if his own gay spontaneity was in print submerged by the seriousness of Spuller and the austere self-righteousness of Challemel-Lacour, so much the better. Moreover, the paper aimed at a high standard in its new service,[5] and it contained much besides politics to interest serious readers. In consequence, since everyone knew that it was Gambetta's organ and that it reflected his views, it rapidly gained an established position among the chief journals of the day. Hitherto, as one of its early numbers declared, democratic opinion had lost much of its force because the channels by which it found expression had been too many and too small. Now the *République Française* provided a useful focus for much of

1. The first political daily to be published for 5 centimes was the Orleanist *Soleil* founded in 1873 (Avenel, *op. cit.*, p. 682). The *Radical*, the first daily of that name, was to exist 'sans gloire et sans éclat' until 28 June 1872 when it was suppressed (see J. Kayser, *Les Grandes batailles du Radicalisme des origines aux portes du pouvoir 1820–1901*, 1952, pp. 56–7).

2. Freycinet, *op. cit.*, p. 282. Cf. R.F. leader of 14 Nov. which declared that signed articles had made for corruption: 'Rien n'a plus contribué à faire si souvent de la presse un théâtre où des artistes, avec ou sans talent venaient à tout prix se faire une provision de renommée.'

3. Letter of 3 Nov. to Herwegh, quoted in Krakowski, *Challemel-Lacour*, p. 329.

4. *Ibid.* Daniel Halévy (*La Fin des Notables*, pp. 128–9) wittily argued that the tone of the new paper marked a conscious reaction against the Second Empire: 'La France était souriante sous l'Empire, et *La République Française* condamne tout ce qui était en faveur sous le règne coupable. On avait de l'esprit sous le Second Empire, *La République Française* n'en aura donc pas. On était sceptique sous le Second Empire, *La République Française* sera donc dogmatique. . . . L'enthousiasme est fort surveillé; les romantiques en avaient abusé, on répudie leurs errements. Ils avaient fait un large emploi du point d'exclamation! on le proscrit.' In a speech in 1875 Spuller described the paper as 'L'instrument de la méthode nouvelle, méthodique, positive, pratique, qui n'avance pas trop pour ne pas avoir à reculer, mais qui ne se jette jamais en arrière, par peur des idées nouvelles, ni de côté pour faire des trouées dans l'inconnu' (*R.F.*, 2 Nov. 1875).

5. In a letter of 27 Oct. urging his German friend Herwegh to contribute a weekly news item, Challemel-Lacour said: 'Nous ne vous demandons que deux choses: informations rigoureusement exactes (vos correspondances n'auront d'autorité qu'à ce prix), et que tous les sujets soient traités, présentés au point de vue française'. A week later (3 Nov.) he repeated: 'exactitude d'informations, sûreté irréprochable dans le détail des faits' (Krakowski, *op. cit.*, pp. 328–9).

this opinion, even though a hostile critic like Marcère could later write that it was the organ of a man rather than of a party and that the party effaced itself too much before the man, like courtiers before a man of destiny.[1]

The *République Française*, however, although it was to give a lead to Republican papers throughout the country, was above all a Parisian journal. Although its price was the same in the departments as in Paris it could not take the place of the provincial Press nor was it within the means of all potential Republican readers. But, just as Gambetta had long wished to have his own paper, so, before the war, he had recognised the importance of the local newspaper as a vital instrument of propaganda. Nowhere was this more clearly expressed than in a letter to the editor of the *Réveil du Dauphiné* which he had written before the war and which had been printed in *Paris Journal* on 26 June 1870. There was a great need, he said, for incessant Republican propaganda amongst the people in the country districts. The two Frances should be brought close to one another by making the political education of the country people as good as that of the towns. Therefore, he urged his correspondent, he should, day by day and line by line, set out to prove that the material interests of property, well-being and wealth (*aisance*), as well as the superior rights of man and the citizen could be developed only within a democracy freely and regularly established as a Republic:

> This demonstration ought to derive from a thousand details of the life of the people studied in the individual, the commune, the department, the state. Each line in the budget ought to provide you with a text with which to argue successfully to the profit of democracy against the bureaucracy. If we triumph of set purpose over the bureaucracy we shall form a free democracy.

In 1871 after the fall of the Second Empire Gambetta no longer campaigned against 'bureaucracy' as such although he often attacked particular groups of officials. But the work of converting the country people to the Republic still had to go on. The by-elections of 2 July had been remarkably encouraging. Thus, for example, in the Loir-et-Cher the Republicans had formed a bloc against the Monarchists and Bonapartists in support of the mayor of Blois, Dr Dufay, who had polled more than double the number of votes obtained by the Republican candidate in February and easily won the seat. What was particularly encouraging was the support he had won in such a rural area as the Sologne, in which the conservative influence of the big landowners had previously been very marked. Perhaps Dufay's succinct election address promising peaceful progress,

1. Marcère, *op. cit.*, p. 251.

liberty of conscience and, last but not least, cheap government was well designed to appeal to the peasantry, as were the tactics of the newspaper *l'Indépendant* which supported him and which depicted the opposition candidates as fanatical clericals who would oblige everyone to go to mass.[1]

'Devote yourselves to such works of established utility as founding newspapers', Gambetta had written later, in September.[2] Two months later still the contribution made to Republican electoral success by the provincial Press was recognised in an early number of the *République Française*:

> It is to the Press in the departments that we owe a large part of the work which has been done. The Republican papers in the departments have taken in hand and by themselves firmly held the floating reins of public opinion. . . . Behind each of these papers we perceive the men who support them. Our thoughts accompany and would wish to encourage these devoted groups, this unknown France, the hope and strength of democracy. . . . We make no mystery about it, it is with this part of the Press that we are above all anxious to enter into and to maintain an intimate relationship.[3]

These sentiments suggest an attempt on the part of Gambetta and his friends to construct a network of connections with the Press in the departments and thereby both to gather provincial news for the *République Française* itself and to intensify the effort to republicanise the rural populations. Indeed in the Loire one of Gambetta's former prefects, César Bertholon, founded a paper specially for them entitled *La République des paysans*. It is, however, far from clear whether such a network was established systematically. Many provincial papers of all parties borrowed articles from their Parisian confrères: thus in the Doubs in this period the local *République* and *Démocratie-Franccomtoise* gave hospitality to the *République Française* as well as to the *Siècle* and the *Rappel*. Some parties made use, too, of a regular correspondence service for the dissemination of their news and views, one of the best-known examples being the 'Correspondance Saint-Chéron' utilised by the Legitimists. As a French historian of the Press has written: 'The propaganda effort of Gambetta

---

1. G. Dupeux, *Aspects de l'histoire sociale et politique du Loir-et-Cher 1848–1914* (1962), pp. 460–4.
2. See above, p. 50.
3. *R.F.*, 14 Nov. 1871. The passage is quoted in D. Halévy (*Fin des Notables*, p. 125) who erroneously implies that the *République Française* first appeared in October 1871. In his letter to A. Boell (see p. 56 above) Gambetta claimed that the paper 'à peine à ses débuts a déjà pour lui les sympathies de la presse provinciale'. It is perhaps worth noting that the price in the provinces was the same as in Paris, namely fifteen centimes. Many papers added five centimes to the price of copies on sale in the provinces.

and his political friends was considerable and was supported by many papers in the departments. But it is impossible to say exactly whether all these papers were really connected with one another by a systematic network of information or if there was merely a very supple organisation which was above all based upon personal ties and friendships.'[1] The statement in a police report of 12 November 1872, to the effect that Gambetta's party proposed to make use of private letters rather than of a correspondence service suggests that, at any rate at that time, personal relationships were still the key to the extension of its influence by means of the Press.

How great this extension was is also something that in the nature of things it will hardly be possible to estimate with precision, even should the day come when the whole provincial Press has been studied in detail. On the basis, however, of two contemporary documents which analysed the provincial Press in 1873 and 1874 respectively, a French historian has estimated that forty Radical dailies were founded in the provinces during the postwar period as well as thirty-nine papers which she labels as Thierist Republican in sympathy, whereas the number of new Monarchist or Bonapartist creations was only thirty-one.[2] Even supposing that a number of the Radical papers were ephemeral and that not all of them were directly influenced by Gambetta, the figures suggest that his conscious efforts to work through the provincial Press were far from fruitless. Already in February 1872 Taine, in a letter to the editor of the *Temps*, had written: 'A few months ago' in 'a small town in Central France, I entered a café and asked for a newspaper. A Radical paper was brought to me, and when I asked for a different one, a still more revolutionary sheet was produced. "Have you nothing but these Radical papers?" I inquired. I was informed that such papers were supplied free of charge and that this saved a subscription to other papers.' Possibly, commented Taine, 'the free supply has come to an end; nevertheless this incident, and similar ones ... is most instructive, for it shows the strength of the Radical propaganda.'[3] In the diffusion of this propaganda, it is to be noted, the

1. M. Pierre Albert in a personal letter to me dated 30 Sept. 1964. Prof. Sanford H. Elwitt, however, writes of 'a network' in the Loire where Gambetta's friend and former colleague in the Government of National Defence, Pierre Dorian, together with César Bertholon founded two papers, the *République de la Loire*, 'a general interest paper for businessmen and professionals' and the *République des Paysans* mentioned above. In addition there were two local papers, one, *L'Eclaireur*, covering Saint-Etienne while the other the *Courrier de Roanne* covered the Roanne district (Elwitt, *art. cit.*, *French Historical Studies*, vol. vi, 1969, no. 1, pp. 100–1).

2. Jeanne Gaillard, 'La Presse de province et la question du régime au début de la IIIe République', *Revue d'histoire moderne et contemporaine* (Oct.–Dec. 1959), p. 307.

3. Taine, *Life and Letters of H. Taine 1870–1892* (1908), vol. iii, pp. 80–1.

café played an important part. Thus a historian of the Allier has written that in each commune of that department of Central France there was a 'red' café and a 'white' café; 'The former was more plebeian and had a larger clientèle. People read the papers there at a time when subscriptions were dear and when it was risky for one's job to be known as a subscriber to a Left-wing paper, even a weekly.'[1] This influence of the Republican Press was not, moreover, confined to Central France. In the late summer of 1872 a Bonapartist testified to the strength of 'Radical' propaganda in the west—'the workers buy only Radical papers, the most detestable pamphlets find their way into the smallest towns'[2]—while in May 1873 an agent of the same party reported to Rouher that the only papers to be found in the hotels, railway stations and cafés of Eastern France and particularly Franche-Comté were Radical papers which had come from Paris or which were published in the chief towns of the departments and arrondissements.[3] No doubt one of the papers which had come from Paris was the *République Française*.

1. Viple, *Sociologie politique de l'Allier*, p. 84; cf. p. 261.
2. *Journal de Fidus*, vol. iii, *L'Essai loyal* (Paris, 1890), p. 106.
3. See Roger Marlin, in 'La Presse du Doubs et l'établissement définitif du régime républicain', in J. Kayser, *La Presse de province sous la Troisième République* (1958), pp. 120-1, where a long passage from this interesting report by F. Perron is quoted.

7

A French O'Connell: Saint-Quentin and anticlericalism November 1871

Eloquence had been the foundation of Gambetta's career. His voice with its power of moving masses was one of his greatest assets. His sage counsellor, Spuller, knew its value and, while Gambetta was still at San Sebastian, urged the part it should take in ensuring victory. Until the Republic was definitely proclaimed and securely established, he wrote, Gambetta should take a leaf out of Irish politics and be 'a Republican O'Connell, touring the countryside, travelling from town to town, constantly orating, making the public aware of him, aware of a Republican programme and of a Republican party as an active progressive force, rallying the scattered troops of Republicanism throughout France'.[1]

These seeds of counsel fell on good ground. By the autumn of 1871 Gambetta had already done much to raise Republican hopes; he had shown his willingness to forget and forgive where this was politically expedient; he had made some preliminary sketch of the shape he wished the Republic to take; and he was about to launch a new vehicle for the propagation of his views, the *République Française*. But the *République Française* was an instrument which might be slow, even if sure in effect. As Gambetta himself was to say at Angers, 'Frenchmen do not travel enough and what we know least is our own geography'.[2] His own knowledge had been vastly extended by his wartime journeyings and by experience of governing the provinces from Tours and Bordeaux. Now, once he had recovered from his phlebitis, he was ready to act on Spuller's advice, extend his knowledge still further, and tour the country as a Republican O'Connell or, to use the contemptuous term of an adversary, which he later adopted with pride, as the 'commercial traveller of the democracy'.[3] The question was, however, whether he would be allowed

1. Letter of 9 May 1871 from Spuller at Sombernon (*Revue de Paris*, 1 June 1900, p. 460).
2. *Discours*, vol. ii, p. 229.
3. In his speech of 18 April 1872 at Le Havre (*Discours*, vol. ii, pp. 260–1).

to do so when parts of the country were still subject to martial law or in German occupation and when the authorities gave no encouragement to public meetings of a political character. A word from Thiers might effectively have prevented Gambetta's voice from being heard at all in the way that Spuller intended. But no presidential veto was pronounced. Gambetta and his friends renounced any attempts to organise open meetings in favour of private banquets, to which admission naturally had to be by ticket. Thiers, for his part, although he had in the end been worried by the famous electoral reform banquets of 1847–48 and declined to attend them, was for the time being ready enough to allow Gambetta to use this means of propaganda, provided that public order was not disturbed. He no doubt reckoned that Gambetta could not afford to be extreme in his utterances and that the note of moderation sounded at Bordeaux would be reechoed at Saint-Quentin. Thus, though the Republic of Gambetta might not be the same as the Republic of Thiers, Gambetta in his own way might do yeoman service in consolidating the Republic *tout court*. But in this new banquet campaign of the early 1870s, when, in the words of one English observer, Gambetta was '(as the Americans term it) stumping . . . part of France',[1] his voice would not be heard in Paris or Lyon—'no doubt Thiers wished him to avoid stirring up the two capital cities'.[2]

Few political speeches bear reading in their entirety even by contemporaries and those of Gambetta are no exception. His eloquence was often turgid and formless—'it's not French', said Jules Grévy on one occasion, 'it's horse language', but his audiences did not gather to hear some impeccable stylist of the French Academy;[3] what mattered was that

1. Col. Connolly to Lord Lyons (P.R.O., F.O. 146, 1591).
2. D. Halévy, *La Fin des Notables*, p. 129.
3. Political opponents were naturally critical. Thus to F. Giraudeau, the Bonapartist author of *Bleus, Blancs, Rouges* (1873, pp. 56–8), Gambetta's reputation as an orator was 'singulièrement surfaite. Il a adapté à la politique une langue à la fois pédante et romantique, mélange confus de mots savants et de métaphores *voyantes*, qui éblouissent la foule, mais sous lesquels le chercheur ne trouve rien. Citez-moi, dans son oeuvre, un beau mouvement oratoire, une phrase saisissante, une idée neuve, cinq lignes enfin, que l'histoire puisse conserver et transmettre à nos neveux? Supprimez l'accent coloré du Midi, le geste violent, impérieux, l'attitude léonine, la crinière renversée par un brusque coup de tête, toute cette mise en scène de la passion révolutionnaire; prenez le discours en lui-même, épluchez-le, analysez-le. Que trouverez-vous? Une pensée banale, une forme inégale, çà et là des phrases si creuses . . . que le plus hardi plongeur n'en saurait découvrir le fond.'

On the other hand, it is interesting to note a subsequent tribute by Jaurès in an undated letter from the Marquise Arconati-Visconti to Joseph Reinach (B.N., N.a.fr. 24889, f. 179): 'Beppo carissimo . . . je viens vous dire ce que Jaurès m'écrit ce matin: "Je viens de trouver dans ma bibliothèque rustique un volume dépareillé des

unrecorded richness of voice, the warmth and exuberance, the enthusiasm and overpowering vitality which can never be recaptured and which were all the more exhilarating in the communicative warmth of the banquets at which these speeches were delivered. He was, said an otherwise critical witness, 'one of the few orators of our time, perhaps the only one, who could make an audience experience that divine shudder which tightens the throat and makes one's hair stand on end'.[1] And a later writer, Albert Thibaudet, declared that he was one of three men who knew how to speak to Frenchmen, the other two being Mirabeau and Lamartine.[2] Moreover, his subjects were subjects that mattered; in these utterances he touched on many of the great questions which were to agitate the Third Republic during the first thirty years of its existence. The series of speeches which Gambetta delivered at intervals during the ten months between mid-November 1871 and the end of September 1872 was to be notable for the way in which he enlarged upon the theme of regeneration already enunciated at Bordeaux and on other great problems, not least those of clericalism and education.

The first of the series was delivered at Saint-Quentin on 16 November, less than ten days after the launching of the *République Française* and three weeks before the return of the National Assembly after its long vacation.[3] The occasion and the topics chosen by Gambetta for this opening move in his new campaign were naturally of particular significance. The occasion was a patriotic one, a commemorative banquet attended by some seven hundred Republicans in honour of Saint-Quentin's resistance to the Germans just over a year earlier. It was time for the man whom the lost provinces regarded as their foremost champion, the incarnation of the idea of revenge, to declare himself. Wiser than the belligerent champions of the temporal power, Gambetta was as discreet as a man with his record could be less than a year after the conclusion of the armistice. The war, he said, had been the result of a long premeditated act, scientifically prepared. French resistance had failed because of the debilitating effect

---

1. J. Delafosse, *Figures contemporaines* (1899), p. 191. For another notable appraisal, see Ch. Chesnelong, *Les derniers jours de l'empire* ... (1932), pp. 11–12. Chesnelong was a Monarchist.

2. Quoted in D. Halévy, 'Gambetta connu par ses lettres' (*Revue des Deux Mondes*, 1 March 1938, p. 133).

3. For the text, see *Discours*, vol. ii, pp. 170–89.

---

discours de Gambetta (de la période de 1871 et 1872). Je les ai relus avec passion et admiration. Contrairement à un préjugé très répandu même chez nos amis, je trouve qu'il n'y a pas seulement de la puissance, du mouvement et de l'habileté, mais une sûreté et une beauté de forme qui en font une oeuvre immortelle, l'abondance jaillissante et classique tout à la fois de Notre XVI Siècle ... ".'

of the Empire. Fortunately, France, 'with her admirable resources of every kind, still counted in the world and needed only a little order and quiet and suitable organisation to repair her grievous losses with prodigious speed'. And then came the exhortation, later to be simplified into the famous phrase 'N'en parlons jamais, pensons-y toujours': 'Let us never speak of the foreigner, but let it be understood that we are constantly thinking of him. Then you will be on the real path of revenge because you will have learnt to govern and control yourselves.'

This said, and memorably said, Gambetta passed rapidly to the domestic problems which occupied the greater part of his speech, the successes of the Republicans in the recent elections to the General Councils, the need for more propaganda, the need for reform and, above all, for the provision of a good system of free, compulsory, and 'absolutely lay' education. Now the cat was out of the bag. These two words 'absolutely lay' were the prelude to a full-scale attack on the clergy and the Papacy. 'With all my heart', he declared, 'I want not only the separation of the Churches from the State, but also of the schools from the Church.' He entirely rejected the charge of being hostile to religion and of wishing to manufacture atheists or install antireligious teaching in the schools,[1] but, he asserted, because of their educational pretensions, the clergy had ceased to be a great religious body and had become a political faction. They had been the instruments of secular power under the most corrupt and usurping regimes; they were also 'the passive agents of a foreign and occult power', men who had become accustomed no longer to think of themselves as French citizens, but who took pride in 'being the servitors of the theocratic power which sends them its dogmas and its commands'. This onslaught not unnaturally caused 'a profound sensation', as did his later assertion, after a reference to the papal condemnation of the rights of modern society,[2] that, if his hearers were to entrust to such men the education of future generations, they would find, when the moment came to speak of sacrifices and the duties of the citizen, that they were confronted by 'a soft and debilitated kind of being, resigned to the acceptance

---

1. This point is important: 'Est-ce à dire que la religion sera sacrifiée?', he asked and answered 'No': 'chacun restera dans son rôle, . . . la morale sera enseignée laïquement, et la religion sera enseignée dans les endroits consacrés à la religion, et chaque père de famille choisira pour son enfant le culte qui lui conviendra, chrétien, juif ou protestant' (*Discours*, vol. ii, p. 176). He elaborated on this theme in his speech at Albertville ten months later (*ibid.*, vol. iii, p. 80) and Emile Pillias in his *Léonie Léon, amie de Gambetta* (p. 65) suggested that this tolerance was perhaps due to the influence of Léonie Léon. But since his liaison with her began only in April 1872 this thesis is unnecessary. For all the intermittent violence of his language Gambetta was by nature a generous and basically tolerant man.

2. In the *Syllabus of Modern Errors*, 1864.

of every kind of misfortune as the decree of Providence'. For eighty years, he said, ever since 1789, two systems had confronted one another and waged a bitter warfare, which explained why France had continually alternated between revolt and repression, anarchy and dictatorship. It was time to end this conflict, to let religious education be a matter of free choice and 'to separate these two worlds'.

At this point Gambetta came back to the still bigger question of the separation of Church and State, but only to say that he did not think it opportune to discuss the various phases through which it had passed. It was significant that the man who had accepted separation as a main plank in his Belleville programme two years earlier now trod more cautiously. The reasons for this prudence are not disclosed, but perhaps one was the fact that the most recent 'phase' of the question was that provided by the Commune which had promulgated separation in a decree of 2 April. Separation was for Gambetta still, no doubt, an ultimate aim, but what had prior claim was clearly lay education. At this point, too, the tone of his speech changed. He had in his onslaught on religious education attacked both 'a dominant party in the Church' and Rome itself, but the violence of his language might well lead his hearers to believe that all the clergy equally were condemned. Whether because he feared he had overreached himself or because from the outset he had intended to soften his blows and to try to sow divisions among the clergy themselves, he now became more explicit and sharply differentiated between the upper and the lower clergy. Since the disappearance of the old Church of the *Ancien Régime*, he asserted, the upper clergy had gradually, and eventually exclusively, been recruited from among the representatives of the pure Roman doctrine to such an extent that there really were no French clergy, at least in the higher ranks. But there remained a section reminiscent of the old France—the *bas clergé*, 'often so haughtily treated by their superiors': he was not, he said, cold to such men, to men like the humble curé, both a peasant and a priest, who lived in the midst of the rural populations, seeing their hard struggle for existence, helping and consoling them. Amid the dangers of invasion, he himself had seen how such men had shown themselves

> devoted and ardent patriots; they belong to the democracy, they value it and, if they could confide in us, more than one of them would admit to being a democrat and a Republican. . . . You see that, far from being the enemies of the clergy, we only ask to see them return to the democratic traditions of their forbears of the great Constituent Assembly [of 1789–91] and to associate themselves like other Frenchmen with the life of a Republican nation.

Gambetta's tribute was probably sincere, but his words found little response: it would be long before the Republic won many priestly converts, even among the simple parish clergy.

'Clericalism, there is the enemy!' This was no new cry in France. Peyrat of the *Avenir National*, now a member of the Republican Union, was said to have uttered it in 1864.[1] Gambetta was to repeat it in different words in a famous speech in 1877. But, in effect, this was what he was already proclaiming at Saint-Quentin in 1871, and this was at once recognised by one of the most vigorous and influential members of the French episcopate, Mgr Dupanloup, Bishop of Orléans and a deputy for the Loiret. Dupanloup replied in an open letter to Gambetta challenging him to give account for the war he had declared on the Church and religion. It contained a slashing attack on Gambetta's conduct since 4 September and ended with the words: 'The former Dictator makes me wary of the candidate who aspires to establish liberty. No, rather to kill religion and to seize power. You are not an apostle but a pretender. La République c'est moi! That is your programme and the whole object of your speech....'[2] Gambetta, it has been said, never forgave the Bishop for this onslaught.[3]

Anticlericalism had been given a new impetus during the Second Republic (while Gambetta was a schoolboy at the Petit Séminaire at Montfaucon) by the lively attacks made on the Church by such Republican free thinkers as the Positivist Littré and Edgar Quinet. It was then that Quinet had published his book *L'Enseignement du Peuple* (1850), outlining a whole programme of secular education for a State which should be strong and independent of the Church; it was then that the Republican village schoolmaster began to emerge as a rival mentor to the curé. The argument had continued under the Second Empire and had grown in intensity as a reaction to the apparent revival of the alliance of Throne and Altar in the 'fifties. In 1858 Proudhon had entered the fray with his influential *De la justice dans la Révolution et dans l'Eglise* which had categorically asserted 'Christian or Republican—there is the dilemma!' In the 'sixties the revival of freemasonry and its infiltration by Republicans, because it was one of the few kinds of group which could meet without fear of disruption by the police, had added a new and formidable element to forces of secularism, which were already being strengthened by the growing cults of Positivism and Science and by the Pope's ill-judged denunciation of Liberalism in the *Syllabus of Modern Errors* of 1864.

1. But see Chapman, *The Third Republic of France*, p. 171 n: 'Gambetta's friend Peyrat had in fact written nothing of the kind.' Chapman implies that Gambetta had misremembered a phrase in a letter by Peyrat of 9 April 1863 to the *Temps* opposing a possible electoral alliance of the Republicans with the Legitimists and Ultramontanes and saying that 'les cléricaux' were still their enemy.

2. *Lettre de M. l'évêque d'Orléans à M. Gambetta* (n.d.).

3. L. Capéran, *Histoire contemporaine de la laïcité française*, vol. i (1957), p. 33.

Thus, as has been seen, when Gambetta was a law student in Paris in the early 1860s, anticlericalism and free thinking had pervaded the atmosphere breathed by young men of Republican sympathies on the left bank of the Seine. Anticlericalism had been a major Republican tenet and Gambetta had already publicly adhered to it at Belleville in 1869 when he had agreed to campaign for 'the suppression of the budget of public worship and the separation of the Church and the State' as well as for lay, free and compulsory education. He had been, as he now declared at Saint-Quentin, 'won to free thought' and put nothing higher than the study of man (*la science humaine*). So it was with most of his friends and political associates before and after the war: Scheurer-Kestner had been a materialist since the age of twenty-two and later became a Positivist of the school of Littré; Ranc, Challemel-Lacour, Jules Ferry and Brisson, were all freemasons, most of them much more ardently so than Gambetta who never rose above the rank of apprentice and whose name disappeared from the Réforme's list in 1872. In Madame Adam's circle, which Gambetta frequented for several years after the war, most of the Republicans, old or young, were without religious beliefs and strong anticlericals. Her friend, Dr Maure, was an old Voltairean, the Socialist Tolain thought the Christian acceptance of suffering monstrous, Spuller and Adam himself were the only deists, while Arnaud de l'Ariège, the only Christian among them, had separated from his wife because she would not consent to the baptism of their son. 'With us', wrote the hostess, 'a religious ceremony of marriage, baptism or burial was enough for you to be accused of clericalism. . . . Clericalism! After the Prussians this was the great enemy! The hold of the priest upon thought!'[1]

The quarrels of Church and State and disputes about education had, however, for the most part been forgotten during the war. Why then did Gambetta seek to revive them at the end of 1871 by emphasising them so conspicuously in his harangue? This action and the campaign which he thus renewed and continued and intensified during the following decade could to some historians of a later generation, preoccupied with social problems, appear to be a blunder of the first magnitude, perpetuating outmoded divisions and diverting the attention of French politicians from matters of greater importance for the welfare of France. In the long run when the fires of sectarian strife were rekindled from decade to decade this criticism could indeed appear to have some validity.[2] But to apply it to the Republicans of the 'seventies, fanatical in their

---

1. Mme Adam, *Mes Angoisses*, pp. 209, 249, 270–1.
2. The embers have still glowed from time to time in the second half of the twentieth century; cf. the account in *Le Monde* of 7 July 1959 of speeches delivered at the annual congress of the Syndicat National des Instituteurs.

anticlericalism though many of them were, is to ignore genuine fears and preoccupations which the regime of Moral Order that was to be in the ascendant from 1873 to 1877 seemed amply to justify. The Monarchist majority in the National Assembly *was* predominantly Catholic and clerical in sympathy. The clergy *were* predominantly Ultramontane and did look to a Pope who had recently condemned the proposition that the Roman Pontiff could and ought to be reconciled to and come to terms with progress, liberalism and modern civilisation.[1] The question how Frenchmen had best be educated *was* a real problem, which the Prussian victory had rendered more urgent.[2] Against such a background Republicans could not but be aware that the wealth and power of the Church in France had increased in many ways during the last quarter of a century. The value of the property of the authorised religious orders, estimated at only forty-three million francs in 1850 would have nearly decupled by the end of the 'seventies. The numbers of unauthorised teaching orders had more than doubled in the twenty years 1850 to 1870 and, since the passage of the Loi Falloux in 1850, the 'free' or predominantly Catholic schools had greatly multiplied.

The influence of the clergy had thus grown considerably both in public and private education. Moreover, the Ligue de l'Enseignement had its counterpart in the Société générale d'éducation et d'enseignement founded by an important group of Catholics in 1868 and its work on behalf of Catholic schools was reinforced by that of the recently founded Catholic Committees.[3] Yet, despite this activity, the quality of the education purveyed by the clergy left much to be desired. The priests, undoubtedly poor and generally virtuous though most of them were, were men who had received an antiquated training imparted by old-fashioned methods. The teaching they provided was correspondingly out of date. Their textbooks were in Latin, their studies of philosophy stopped short of Kant, and their knowledge of French history came to a halt with the outbreak of what they deemed the great Evil, the French Revolution; of advanced mathematics and natural sciences they knew little or nothing. Half a century or more behind the times, they were, as has been said,[4]

1. Articles 45–48 of the *Syllabus of Errors* had condemned the system of secular schools controlled by the State.
2. See, for example, Emile Blanchard's pessimistic article on the state of French education in the *Revue des Deux Mondes* of 15 Oct. 1871.
3. A copy of a circular issued by the Comité Catholique with an enclosed form of petition addressed to MM. les Deputés opposing free compulsory and secular education is preserved in M.A.E. Fond Gambetta, vol. 58, with a note written in ink: 'pétition occulte préconisée par les ultramontains de la Chambre'.
4. By Adrien Dansette in his *Histoire religieuse de la France contemporaine: sous la IIIème République* (1951), p. 23.

ready to cope with Voltaire but not with Renan, and, ill-equipped to refute contemporary critics, they too often fell back on abuse as a substitute for argument. Yet influential clergy such as Mgr de Ségur, whose recently published *Vive le Roi!*[1] had met with particular approval from the Comte de Chambord himself, urged the abolition of the State-controlled University and the freeing of children from the perverting influence of the schoolmaster (*instituteur*). Whereas for Gambetta and his colleagues free, compulsory, *lay* education was essential to France's regeneration, for French Catholics France's defeat was due to her de-Christianisation and the confessional school was therefore all the more necessary. No wonder then that Gambetta was concerned both about the attitude of the clergy and about the fitness of the Frenchmen they educated to play an adequate part in the modern world. No wonder that, for all his love of the classics and conscious debt to the classical education he had himself received, he was on the side of the scientists in the battle between the Classics and the Sciences; no wonder that in his speech at Le Havre in April 1872 he would declare that children in secondary schools must not be allowed to spend all their time 'in the sterile study of a little-known antiquity from which after some years . . . they emerge with buzzing ears and empty minds'.[2] No wonder, finally, that he and his friends demanded 'a truly modern education' and emphasised as he did at Saint-Quentin that the world 'for which we are made . . . is the modern world . . . the world which thirsts for science, truth, free will and equality'.[3]

These were general reasons enough to explain this main theme of Gambetta's second great speech in the provinces after his return from exile. But there were also specific reasons which gave the question of education actuality. In particular, the Minister of Public Instruction, Jules Simon, was preparing a Bill to make education free and compulsory (but not secular) and Dupanloup had written a letter on the subject to *L'Impartial du Loiret* opposing the abolition of fees on the grounds that it would lead to absenteeism and be the undoing of the Catholic schools which would not be able to compete with the free communal schools supported by the State. This provided the *République Française* with the theme for a leader on 8 November, the second day of its appearance. After castigating both Dupanloup and, for different reasons, Jules Simon, Gambetta's antagonist at Bordeaux ten months earlier,[4] the paper somewhat

1. This book had been published at Poitiers earlier in 1871. It had a considerable success in Legitimist circles.
2. *Discours*, vol. ii, p. 255.
3. *Ibid.*, p. 178.
4. Later, on 27 Dec., the *R.F.* denounced Simon's Bill as 'un projet étroit et contradictoire, une illusion, un mensonge, un trompe l'oeil'. Gambetta, of course, had no love for Simon, his antagonist in the events leading to his resignation in February 1871.

portentously declared that no question was more lofty, more ripe, or more urgent than that of public instruction; 'We still have to fight for principles accepted by all enlightened and intelligent men for more than a century. . . . For the thousandth time we shall demonstrate that the spirit of modern societies is a secular spirit.' There was much more on the same theme. Gambetta, the director of the *République Française*, had already pointed the way for Gambetta the French O'Connell at Saint-Quentin.

The speech at Saint-Quentin, enthusiastically received by its hearers, was widely printed and commented upon.[1] It was, said the *Figaro*, reproduced and discussed by the whole of the Press—Thiers was the only other person to whom 'this evidently exaggerated honour' was paid.[2] Yet, curiously enough, the passages attacking the clergy were not those which caused most comment, except in Catholic papers. Madame Adam in her memoirs said that Gambetta had surpassed himself, but what she professed to remember was his patriotism, not his anticlericalism.[3] The *Siècle*,[4] while expressing its wholehearted approval of what he had said about the need for lay education and separation of Church and State,[5] reproduced not these paragraphs but the last part of the speech in which he had reiterated his demand for a new assembly, anathematised the plebiscite of 1870, and urged not only those who had then been deluded into voting 'Yes' but also the men of the past ('whose pretensions were known but whose party was now dismembered') to recognise that the Republic was the most liberal of regimes and to take their place within it. 'In the democratic system', he had said, taking up the theme of the leaflet about Whigs and Tories distributed in Paris at the time of the July election campaign,[6] 'there must be two parties . . . a reforming party and . . . a second party no less necessary which acts as a brake. . . . It is on the equilibrium of these two political sectors . . . that in my view the functioning of republican government and good order depends.'[7] These were words of which Thiers's paper the *Bien Public* could approve.[8] The word *ralliement* was to be famous twenty years later: but already in 1871 in his notable peroration to this speech at Saint-Quentin, Gambetta, although he used

1. It moved one Corbeau père, son of Georges Corbeau 'fusilié [*sic*] par les Chouans le 24 Juin 1797' to compose and offer to Gambetta a waltz which he called *The San Sebastian* (M.A.E. Fond Gambetta, vol. xlix).
2. *Le Figaro*, 20 Nov.
3. *Mes Angoisses*, p. 223.
4. *Le Siècle*, 19 Nov.
5. Two questions 'qui doivent figurer dans le programme de tout Français véritable et de tout bon républicain'.
6. See above, p. 28.
7. *Discours*, vol. ii, p. 188.
8. 21 Nov. 1871.

the word only once, had issued a categorical invitation to its enemies and to those who wavered to 'rally' to the Republic.[1]

What did all this really mean? This was what some papers enquired. Gambetta, said the *Figaro*, represented a party, but what does this party want? 'Apart from compulsory education and the separation of Church and State we do not know', and it added more unkindly, 'we see only that M. Gambetta is nothing and that he aspires to be something.' The same question troubled the much more friendly *Radical*.[2] Beneath the majestic phrases of the speech, it said, people are looking for the precise principles of the programme that he will carry out when he is in power. 'He has principles, but principles that he subordinates to their opportuneness. . . He says one must only give one's opinion when it is a means of increasing the general prosperity.' The *Radical* understood Gambetta's reasons for prudence, but added that some innovations could not be introduced too soon. Yet, in general, it approved his attitude and graciously said that it would not reproach him for his 'Lamartinian elegy on the good country priest'.

The interest roused by the speech at Saint-Quentin was, however, soon forgotten in the excitement caused by the reassembling of the National Assembly after its long vacation. Perhaps the new session would impel Gambetta to elaborate his programme with greater precision.

1. He used the word in the final paragraph, which began as follows: 'Ainsi donc, nous pouvons nous séparer en affirmant que la France s'est définitivement ralliée à la République, et qu'avant peu il faudra bien que tous les partis se renouvellent.'

2. Of 20 Nov. Cf. the Catholic *Correspondant* of 25 Nov.: 'Take away from him the hatred of priests and the taste for impious declamations, take away from him the Jacobin excitations and the vindication of '93, and there remains nothing for him to say, nothing to promise that one cannot say and promise, with more sincerity, in the name of Liberal monarchy' (quoted in M. C. A. Gimpl, *The Correspondant and the Founding of the French Third Republic*, 1959, p. 70).

8

A Winter of Discontent and the Radical Programme December 1871–April 1872

The advent of winter had cooled the ardour of many deputies for debating the affairs of the nation amid the chilly splendours of Versailles. Snow was on the ground in early December when they were due to reassemble. The Republicans objected in principle to the dethronement of Paris as capital, and Thiers, despite the burning of his house by the Communards and his earlier experiences in 1848, would have preferred to govern from Paris and to reside at the Elysée rather than at the Préfecture of Versailles, which some dubbed the Palais de la Pénitance. But in the eyes of the Monarchists the cold and discomfort of the winter journeyings to and from Versailles were small evils compared with the dangers of return to the Red and revolutionary capital, whose mobs had invaded the Chamber in 1848 and 1870 and established the Commune only nine months earlier. So the responsible officers, the Questors, had set to work to improve the parliamentary amenities. They had devised all sorts of expedients to improve the seating accommodation in a hall not originally intended to hold more than four hundred; gas lighting was installed, and what Hector Pessard wittily called 'the reactionary stove' was heated to the maximum.

The new session began quietly, perhaps because of menaces just uttered by Bismarck as a result of Franco-German friction; but there were soon to be debates as tumultuous as any in the first months of the Assembly's existence. Once again the position of Thiers and his attitude to the parties, and theirs to him were all important. Once again the life of parliament was punctuated by by-elections which appeared to strengthen the flow of the electoral tide towards Republicanism and to make a Monarchical restoration still more hazardous. But the opponents of the Republic, certainly of the Republic of Gambetta, still had a handsome majority; for him the atmosphere of the Chamber was still unfriendly and during the first four months of the new session he again spoke but rarely. These are indeed months in which the biographer of Gambetta can see him only through a glass darkly. Not only did he speak little, but he also wrote little—at least very few letters are known to survive—and his friends are strangely silent about his doings. His views are, of course, reflected in the *République Française*, but he himself is glimpsed only fitfully. All this and much else suggest that for him these were not easy months. Nor were they for France, and their history cannot be ignored because Gambetta himself appears to be largely withdrawn into the shadows. Moreover, the speeches he did make together with various leaders and articles in the *République Française* at least throw some further light on his policies and on the picture of the Republic as he would have it.

The first important event of the new session was the presidential message delivered by Thiers in person on 7 December. The politicians were eager to hear it, looking for light and leadership and hoping for clear signs that Thiers was steering the ship of state towards their own particular haven. But they listened instead to a lengthy discourse, likened by one journalist to an American President's review of the state of the nation, in the course of which Thiers castigated the parties, asserted that he was a mere administrator and told the Assembly that it was sovereign. Of the Republic there was no mention. This omission and the recognition of the sovereignty of an Assembly he wished to be rid of naturally angered Gambetta and his friends on the Left. The *République Française* was sharp in its criticisms. The session, it declared, had been a humiliating one. For more than two hours, the President of the Republic had lowered his authority and dignity before men who were the enemies of the Republic. Furthermore, the views he had expressed on the finances, the army and the administration were those he had always held: 'He rebels against the most necessary innovations and refuses even to try and understand them. To subscribe to his programme would be to give up any hope of better things and to see the rebirth of an ensemble of bourgeois institutions with all the risks of catastrophe which they would bring with them.' The Left, hitherto divided in its attitude towards Thiers, should now unite to make him understand the country's will, to replace or supplement his declining powers, and to undertake the reforms which he was unable to conceive or to propose.[1]

There was some substance in these strictures, but they did not push Thiers further into the arms of the majority, who had, on the day after the message, rejected a motion in favour of returning to Paris sponsored by his supporters in the Left Centre. He had in any case to perform a difficult balancing act, but the vehemence of the reaction of the *République*

1. *R.F.*, 9 Dec. 1871. It is interesting to note the pejorative use of the word 'bourgeois' by a paper such as the *R.F.* which could hardly be termed Socialist!

Française was perhaps a factor which induced him to give reassurances to the Left sooner than he had intended. The first was conveyed privately to Gambetta through Freycinet, whom Thiers had expressed the wish to see again and who, with Gambetta's approval and encouragement, now called upon him.[1] Thiers received Freycinet cordially and, having indulged in his habitual denunciation of the folly of continuing the war after Sedan, said that what was done was done and that all that he himself wanted was to see the German troops of occupation out of France. He hoped that the Assembly would give him time to be rid of them; but the Monarchists were in a hurry and already wanting to restore the Monarchy: 'None the less your friends may rest tranquil. As long as I am here, I will not allow the form of government to be touched. After me they can make their own arrangements. If your friends behave themselves prudently they will be the masters. France is on their side and does not want any upheaval.'

In happier circumstances these contacts between Thiers and Freycinet might have led to a direct rapprochement and a closer understanding between Thiers and Gambetta. But it was to be some time before such an understanding came about and then fate decreed that it should be too late to be as fruitful as Gambetta hoped. In 1872 three obstacles stood in the way. First of all, the memories of the National Defence were still too vivid. 'I could see clearly', wrote Freycinet, 'that M. Gambetta, though he did not wish it to be seen, was still wounded by the injurious epithets M. Thiers had applied to him. ... For his part, M. Thiers could not bear that his advice and entreaties at Tours had been ignored. He believed that he had preached wisdom and his pride was hurt because this had not been recognised.'[2] Secondly, there was the difficulty of Franco-German relations. In Bismarck's eyes Gambetta represented the war party in France. Any close association with Gambetta at this time could jeopardise Thiers's freedom of negotiation with Germany. Thirdly, Thiers had still to face a Right-wing majority in the Assembly and if he were to ally too openly with the Left his own position might be imperilled. So he may well have told the Adams that their friends should be careful, otherwise the Republic they wanted so much would escape them.[3]

The warning was heeded. In consequence of these obstacles Gambetta was not to be seen at the soirées which, before long, to the delight of

---

1. Freycinet, *Souvenirs 1848–1878*, pp. 290–1. Freycinet does not give the date of the interview, but merely says: 'Je me présentai chez M. Thiers peu de jours après son message présidentiel.'

2. *Ibid.*, p. 293. For two obscure references by Gambetta to his meetings with Thiers at Tours in 1870, see *Lettres* nos. 159 and 205.

3. Mme Adam, *Mes Angoisses*, p. 178.

politicians and Parisians alike, Thiers began to give at the Elysée. There were many rumours of secret contacts between the two men, but an all too allusive letter to Gambetta suggests that, apart from a conversation at Versailles sometime in the summer of 1872, they had no serious private talk between Gambetta's return to political life in June 1871 and Thiers's fall from power in May 1873.[1] In consequence of these obstacles, too, the Radicals were constantly critical of Thiers's policies in detail, both in the Assembly and the Press, though they often supported him with their votes. Thiers, however, soon and unexpectedly followed up his private assurance to Freycinet that he would not abandon the Republic, with a public assurance in the Assembly. Suddenly, on 26 December, in the course of a speech expressing his utter opposition to an income tax, he went out of his way to tell his hearers that they rightly wished to give the Republic a sincere trial (*un essai loyal*) and that the trial must be sincere— they all wanted it to be so. He asked 'those who have a real concern for the Republic, who sincerely wish to establish it, and I am of their number' to reject the tax.[2] If the Left had been irritated by the message of 7 December, how much more was the Right disturbed and angered by this unpalatable medicine administered to them on the 26th! Thiers, the former servant of the House of Orléans, had only a week earlier shown his irritation at the decision of the two Orléans princes, Aumâle and Joinville, to occupy the deputies' seats to which they had been elected in February. Now it was clearer than ever that neither Orleanists nor Legitimists could count on his support for a restoration. 'The Bordeaux Pact' by which Thiers in February 1871 had promised not to work in favour of any particular regime, was, as the *République Française* remarked a little later, as good as dead.[3]

The Monarchists, in consequence, once again sought to heal their differences and bring about a 'fusion'. They also thought of putting forward the Duc d'Aumâle as successor to Thiers should Thiers be overthrown. Aumâle might thus keep the place of head of the state warm for 'the king'. But, once again, the efforts of the moderates came to

---

1. This letter from Léonie Léon was dated 19 Sept. 1872. It contained the following sentence: 'Il faudra que vous voyiez au retour le grand maître de nos destinées sur lequel votre conversation de Versailles a eu tant d'influence' (Ass. Nat., p. 27). Scheurer-Kestner, who was in a good position to know, states emphatically (*Souvenirs de jeunesse*, p. 287) that Gambetta did not have any talk with Thiers until early in the year; this was not a *tête-à-tête*, but an interview at which he was accompanied by Generals Chanzy and Faidherbe and requested considerate treatment for officers who had served under the Government of National Defence when they came under review by the Commission appointed to review wartime ranks.

2. *R.F.*, 27 Dec. 1871, p. 3.

3. *ibid.*, 17 Jan. 1872.

nothing because of the intransigence of the extreme Legitimists[1] and of the Comte de Chambord himself. When General Ducrot went to see Chambord at Antwerp and suggested the Aumâle solution, the Pretender, perhaps consciously echoing his ancestor Louis XIV, declared that no Prince of the Blood should absent himself from the entourage of his King;[2] and when the Comte de Paris again prepared to go and meet his cousin, Chambord, on 25 January, issued a new uncompromising manifesto which prevented such a reconciliation: 'I will not allow any impairing of the monarchical principle which is the patrimony of France and the last hope of its grandeur and freedom. . . . Nothing will shake my resolution or tire my patience and nobody, on any pretext, will induce me to consent to become the legitimate king of Revolution.'

It was no wonder that in these circumstances the Monarchists made little progress in the by-elections of January and February. They won a seat indeed in Savoie in January, thanks to the efforts of the local clergy, but in February they lost one in the Côtes-du-Nord and their candidate came bottom of the poll in the Eure. For the Radicals, however, and—this was the novelty—for the Bonapartists, these elections were relatively encouraging and important.

The by-elections in January 1872 were for fifteen seats in thirteen departments, including one seat in Paris and two in constituencies which had elected Gambetta himself in July, namely the Var and Bouches-du-Rhône. For Gambetta they provided an opportunity to reemphasise some of the main points of his programme, to renew old contacts and to make new ones.

The points singled out by the *République Française* for the electors to consider were three: an amnesty for the political prisoners taken in the repression of the Commune—there were still some 20,000, many of them confined in appalling conditions in improvised prisons; an end to martial law, which still applied to forty departments and to cities such as Lyons and Marseilles; and the dissolution of the Assembly.[3] Above all, it urged, candidates should be chosen who would demand dissolution. In the Bouches-du-Rhône the imperative mandate imposed on the Radical candidates included three further points, namely the return of the Govern-

---

1. The extreme Right had shown their displeasure with the Orleanists by putting forward a motion of their own in the debate on the validity of the Orleanist princes taking their seats. The Left were delighted: 'Gambetta nous dit: "Vous êtes incapables d'un concert monarchique, il ne vous reste qu'à vous dissoudre" ' (*Journal politique de Charles de Lacombe*, ed. A. Hélot, 1907, vol. i, p. 89).

2. Louis XIV said 'les fils de France ne doivent jamais avoir d'autre retraite que la Cour' (P. Goubert, *Louis XIV et vingt millions de Francais*, 1966, p. 47).

3. *R.F.*, 28 Dec. 1871.

ment to Paris, compulsory free and secular education, and separation of Church and State. The demand for return to Paris was nothing new and the other two points were part of the Radical stock-in-trade, but it was significant, as a French historian of the elections of this period has pointed out, that 'many Republicans no longer hesitated to confront the electorate with a precise programme which borrowed nothing even superficially (*en apparence*) from the political conceptions of the Conservatives. This boldness did not prevent the electorate from voting more and more for the Left-wing or extreme Left-wing Republican candidates.'[1] The precision which had seemed to critics to be lacking at the time of Gambetta's Saint-Quentin speech was now beginning to emerge and the parliamentary debates of the winter session were to give his programme still further definition.

In the south-east Gambetta himself took a hand in the campaign. He was reported to have wanted to secure the adoption of Freycinet as a candidate in the Var,[2] and he was equally interested in the election in the Bouches-du-Rhône where one of the candidates for the two vacant seats was none other than Challemel-Lacour. But this foray into Provence does not seem to have been the sort of triumphal tour that before long he would be used to. Freycinet was not adopted in the Var or Isère. Gambetta was prevented from speaking at a meeting at Marseilles,[3] and his only reported utterances, at an election meeting and a dinner given in his honour at Toulon, were relatively insignificant.[4] They merely repeated his demand for dissolution of the Assembly and reaffirmed his belief in democracy, attacked the Empire and adjured his hearers to choose their deputies with foresight, intelligence and prudence, and they are curiously omitted from Joseph Reinach's comprehensive edition of

1. Gouault, *Comment la France est devenue Républicaine*, p. 140.

2. *The Times*, 1 and 3 Jan. 1872. Freycinet in his *Souvenirs* makes no mention of this attempted candidature, but in a letter of 15 Sept. 1871 to Gambetta he said that he proposed to stand in Isère and would like also to stand in the Var if Gambetta would support him. A draft reply by Gambetta, dated 19 Sept., approved Freycinet's trying his luck in Isère, but said that he could not help him in the Var, since there was only one seat vacant and the electors would not wish to give the election 'un caractère moins avancé que celle du 2 juillet'. Had two seats been vacant, he might well have been accepted along with a more 'advanced' candidate (B.N., Joseph Reinach pp. N.a.fr. 13581, ff. 16–18).

3. Ironically, the prefect who threatened to ban the meeting was Kératry, who had raised Breton forces for the war in the provinces, but quarrelled with Gambetta and resigned. Marseilles had had its own shortlived Commune from 23 March to 4 April 1871.

4. See *The Times*, 5 and 8 Jan., pp. 8 and 9 respectively and, in addition, see the hostile comments of Paul Cambon, the new Secretary-General of the prefecture at Marseilles (P. Cambon, *Correspondance*, vol. i, 1940, p. 36, letter of 8 Jan.).

Gambetta's speeches and pleadings. To the correspondent of *The Times*, writing on 2 January, it seemed that Gambetta's star was beginning to pale and that he was too moderate for the hot-headed Radicals of south-eastern France:

> The young Dictator sees before him the fate of Beales, Odger, and moderate demagogues of that kind. He will be left behind. Already the ugly word 'réactionnaire' has been applied to him. His Democracy is far too mild in its character to suit the extreme tendencies of the day. . . . Since he has been in the Chamber he has done absolutely nothing towards organising a party [here, surely, the correspondent was ill-informed]. He is not even regarded as a leader; his advice is never followed, and as he never speaks he has done nothing to acquire an influence in the House'.[1]

Gambetta, however, was biding his time and no doubt continuing to give much of his attention to the *République Française*, still relatively in its infancy. In the south-east it did not need a major speech from him to secure the election of Challemel-Lacour and Bouchet at Marseilles or to gain a handsome majority for the former prefect Cotte in the Var, while in Isère Denfert-Rochereau's Radical successor Brillier was elected unopposed.[2] In the Doubs, however, where Denfert-Rochereau had again to be replaced, the Radical only just scraped home, thanks to the divisions among the Conservatives, and in the Somme Jules Barni, the Radical candidate and former editor of the *Bulletin de la République Française* which had been distributed in the provinces during the war, was defeated by a very moderate Republican. Moreover, in Paris another moderate Thierist Republican, Vautrain, President of the Municipal Council of Paris, was victorious, despite all the efforts of the *République Française* to secure the election of the poet Victor Hugo as the man of the future and its denunciations of the 'senile obstinacy' of the *Siècle* for supporting Vautrain, the man of the past.[3] So, in its leader of the 11th appraising the results, the *République Française* wisely did no more than claim that they had in general been favourable to the strengthening of Republican

---

1. *The Times*, 5 Jan., p. 8. In Gambetta's draft letter to Freycinet, quoted in n. 2, p. 81 above, apropos of Freycinet's wish to stand as a parliamentary candidate there was a significant phrase indicating his dependence on the extreme Radicals. The electors might, he said, accept the candidate he recommended, but just because he was wholly responsible he could not 'me déterminer à faire revenir le département du Var en arrière sur sa dernière manifestation'.

2. Cotte and Brillier had both gone into exile after the coup d'état of 2 Dec. 1851. Brillier indeed had been with Baudin, the Republican deputy killed on the barricades.

3. *R.F.*, leader of 7 Jan. 1872.

government. But for Gambetta probably not the least valuable consequence was the addition of six new recruits to the Republican Union.

No less significant was the relative success of the Bonapartists. Their
increasing propaganda had continued and its momentum had already
been reflected in such views as were reported, for instance, by C. de B. on
5 December:

> The peasants and workmen are sorry that the Second Empire has disappeared
> because under that regime they were so prosperous that they did not have to
> envy the rich. . . . It is no good talking to them about the military disasters of
> Napoleon III because they answer that the emperor was betrayed by the wealthy
> classes. They excuse his capitulation at Sedan by saying that he did this to prevent
> shedding the blood of his soldiers uselessly. . . . A deputy heard a woman shout-
> ing to a couple of peasants in the fields one day last week: 'Ah! If only we could
> have our good Napoleon III back again, what splendid times we should have.'[1]

One of the chief centres of this Bonapartist feeling was the Pas-de-Calais
where the Bonapartist candidate was returned by a handsome majority
on 7 January. Another was Corsica, where in February the sitting
Bonapartist deputy stood down to make way for Rouher, the former
Minister of State of the Second Empire. Needless to say, Rouher's candidature was bitterly attacked by the *République Française*,[2] but he was
elected by an overwhelming majority. The Bonapartists in consequence
now had in the Assembly a man of national reputation who promptly
formed their handful of deputies into a group known as L'Appel au
Peuple. But their influence was not measurable simply in terms of their
parliamentary strength. To *The Times* correspondent writing on
30 December it seemed that, in view of their experience and

> with all branches of the public services crammed with adherents, with no
> character as a party to lose, with unrivalled capacity for conspiracy and hordes of
> active emissaries and perfectly trained instruments working gratuitously, the
> chances of the overthrown Dynasty were not to be despised: looked at from a
> purely Newmarket point of view . . . it has always seemed to me that the odds
> were slightly in their favour . . . not because they have got a better horse, but
> because they have been on the turf all their lives.[3]

His opinion was shared by the British Ambassador. Lord Lyons believed
that if a free vote were taken a majority would probably be obtained for
the restoration of Napoleon III,[4] and on 10 January the *République*

---

1. *Letters from Paris*, p. 178.
2. *R.F.*, leaders of 24 and 25 Jan.
3. *The Times*, 1 Jan. 1872, p. 10.
4. Lord Newton, *Lord Lyons: A Record of British Diplomacy* (London, s.d., Nelson
Library of Notable Books), p. 292.

Française thought it necessary to print a leader rebutting the Imperialists' pretensions to be the only serious rivals of the Radicals.[1] But it took them seriously. A month later, on 16 February, it began a serial story by J. G. Prat called 'La Tour du Jaï' exposing the 'exploits' of Bonapartists in the Var at the time of the coup d'état of 1851. In April this was followed by 'Sous L'Empire' of which the author was no less a person than Gambetta's friend on the Paris Municipal Council, Arthur Ranc. In September it recommended a little brochure, just put on sale for fifteen centimes, entitled *Histoire de Napoléon III* and based largely upon the *Petite Histoire du Second Empire* 'written by M. E. Spuller on the eve of the fatal plebiscite of 8 May 1870'. The 'M. E. Spuller' was Gambetta's *alter ego*, Eugène Spuller and the tone of these writings can easily be imagined.

The relative success of Bonapartism and the exaggerated fears it aroused were, of course, due in part to the continued confusion and uncertainty prevailing among the other parties and to the continued stuggle to decide the nature of the regime which must ultimately emerge. At the end of December and in January this confusion was enhanced by differences on financial and economic questions which ranged free-traders against protectionists and divided parties still further.

In *La Fin des Notables* Daniel Halévy remarked on the admirable simplicity of the Radical programme: 'on fiscal reforms, nothing; on working-class reforms, nothing ... on the Communards led to the prison-ships and being shot, not a word. There remains the struggle against the Church. The whole ardour of the party is directed to this.'[2] Broadly true, this judgement is, however, too simple. A Radical motion, calling for an amnesty for all condemned or prosecuted for political crimes or lesser offences at Paris and in the provinces during the past year, had been introduced in the Assembly as early as 18 September 1871 and Gambetta had been one of its signatories.[3] As has been seen, an amnesty was still one of the foremost demands of the *République Française* and of Radical electoral programmes at the turn of the year. At the same time Edmond Adam and others were busy raising money for the relief of the families of prisoners and Gambetta was one of those who contributed to their fund.[4] Moreover, important questions of reform came up for discussion during this session on which Gambetta and his friends were bound

1. In his diary on 6 Jan. the Bonapartist writer 'Fidus' wrote: 'De son côté, M. Gambetta dit audacieusement: "Il n'y a que l'Empire et moi!"' (*Journal de Fidus*, vol. iii, *L'Essai loyal*(1890), p. 43).

2. p. 127.

3. See Jean T. Joughin, *The Paris Commune in French Politics* (1955), p. 68. Consideration of the motion was deferred to the following session.

4. *R.F.*, 26 Dec. p. 1, 1 Jan. 1872, p. 3; see also a pressing appeal for further funds in *R.F.* of 27 March (p. 1).

to adopt a policy. These were, in particular, the reform of the Conseil d'Etat and of the magistrature, of education, of the army and, most immediately pressing, of the finances.[1] This last was connected with the problems presented by the budget and by the need to meet an anticipated deficit of some 250 million francs because of the extra financial burdens which had to be carried by a defeated and partly ravaged country.

There were various means of raising the additional funds. Some proposed a general increase on all existing taxes, some, the introduction of an income tax, and others a return to protection and an increase in customs duties, particularly on raw materials. The old Radical panacea for taxation was the single land tax, advocated, for instance, by Jules Simon in the 'sixties in his *La Politique Radicale*.[2] But now it was the income tax proposal, sponsored by distinguished economists such as Henri Germain and Wolowski and by an important section of the business community, which won the support of Gambetta and of the *République Française*, the paper's key argument being that the country's great and growing share capital (*richesse mobilière*) made a quite inadequate contribution to the exchequer.[3] Gambetta encouraged one of his most useful new lieutenants, the Alsatian Scheurer-Kestner, to return to the charge on 16 January and make his maiden speech largely in support of an income tax (which did not necessarily mean a progressive tax although this was what many of his colleagues wanted). Thiers, however, was both an ardent protectionist and bitterly opposed to any such proposal, which on one occasion, he referred to as 'socialism by means of taxation'. The debates on this question came to a conclusion at the end of December and, when a vote was taken, many of the Left, no doubt partly in recognition of Thiers's pledge to make 'a sincere trial' of the Republic, refrained from opposing him. The proposal was therefore dropped, but such a tax became one of Gambetta's abiding objectives: in August the *République Française* urged that it should be the subject of one of two resolutions it would like all General Councils to put forward in their summer session.[4]

1. See above, p. 68. For Gambetta's attitude to the problems of the Conseil d'Etat and the army, see p. 231, n. 1, and Chapter 22 below.
2. 2nd edn (1868), p. 36.
3. R.F., 25 Dec. 1871, p. 1.
4. R.F., 19 Aug. The other 'voeu' was to be for 'une éducation obligatoire et laique pour le peuple'. An income tax also found a place in many Radical election programmes, e.g. in that of Paul Bert in the Yonne in June 1872 and in the 'contractual mandate' accepted by Victor Hugo in the election campaign of January 1872; this demanded 'a truly proportional tax upon incomes'. To *The Times* of 25 Jan. it seemed that Gambetta's party had 'one fixed idea, which is that, if they can get an Income-tax established in principle, they will convert it into a progressive tax, which would be the first step towards levelling incomes'.

The prospective deficit had still to be met and a fresh series of passionate debates took place between 10 and 19 January. The protectionist policy advocated by Thiers was all the more serious in that it entailed the renegotiation or abrogration of France's commercial treaties, particularly those with England (which had expired a year earlier) and Belgium. Gambetta in a subsequent intervention on 1 February said that if he defended free trade it was not because he was a doctrinaire, but because he believed it was the key to France's prosperity. The free-trade treaties had indeed been 'a cause of difficulties and even of ruin for some' but

> in a very great part of the country there were industries which had courageously faced the struggle and ... had succeeded in dominating the situation and now remained unrivalled in the world.... Consequently, alongside the interests which protest and say: 'We ask for the revision of treaties' ... there is the vast majority of the population of France, the consumers, who say: 'We have bene-fited from these treaties, we have gained from them.'[1]

In the interest also of good relations with England, he urged adjournment of a decision so that negotiations might continue. But by then the die was virtually cast and France soon returned to her old path of sterile protectionism. Gambetta's plea was unavailing and shortly afterwards the French Government denounced the Anglo-French treaty of 1860.[2] Nevertheless he continued to be regarded as a champion of free trade and it was no doubt for this reason that in May 1875 he was made a member of the London Cobden Club.

The dénouement of the free trade issue had not been reached without a major struggle, which reached its climax in a governmental crisis. Having dropped their campaign for an income tax, the free traders and their sympathisers substituted a proposal for a tax on turnover. To Thiers this seemed no less inquisitorial than an income tax and, despite the protests of industrialists and Chambers of Commerce throughout the country, he fought tenaciously to carry his cherished tax on raw materials. To *The Times* correspondent it seemed 'hardly comprehensible' that Gambetta should throw away 'the magnificent opportunity' of leading the opposition which the 'feeble policy' of the Government afforded him.[3] But Gambetta took no part in the debates of this momentous week, presum-ably because he had no wish for a direct collision with Thiers. While they were still in progress, however, he wrote to the wife of his old friend

---

1. *Ass. Nat. A.*, vol. vii, pp. 343–5. According to *The Times*, 3 Feb., p. 5, his speech was 'delivered with great energy and warmly applauded by the Left'.
2. A new treaty was, however, negotiated and signed in November 1872.
3. *The Times*, 20 Jan., p. 6.

Clément Laurier what is perhaps one of the only two of his letters to have survived from this period. In language that was characteristically and tantalisingly imprecise he expressed his anxiety:

> We have been very close to the abyss over which the Republic is leaning. M. Thiers's obstinacy and narrow-mindedness, his absurd *amour propre* and also a weakness for the Monarchist parties had put us within an inch of this calamity. Thanks to our desperate efforts we have been able to plaster over the cracks and for some days we have been breathing more freely. But the situation is still very grave and I foresee that it will only get worse until all is shattered.[1]

The climax came on 19 January in what *The Times* of the following day described as 'the most riotous and exciting' sitting of the Assembly since the opening of the winter session. The motion in favour of a tax on raw materials supported by Thiers was rejected by forty-two votes and an alternative one was adopted by a majority of seventy. This time Gambetta and his friends voted with the majority.[2] The free-trade issue had split the parties to the undoing of Thiers, and Gambetta, as a champion of the consumers, was prominent in supporting the alternative motion, one of whose chief sponsors was the Legitimist advocate of the silk interests of Lyons. This desertion by the Republicans particularly irritated Thiers who had, he said, devoted himself on their behalf for a year: 'They have no political sense. They will never be a party fit to rule.'[3]

On the following morning Thiers carried out the threat so frequently made and resigned. Consternation followed in the Assembly when the decision was announced and eventually all but eight deputies, seven Legitimists and one Bonapartist, voted in favour of a motion appealing to 'the patriotism of the President of the Republic' to resume office and refusing to accept his resignation. According to *The Times* correspondent, Gambetta had miscalculated in urging the Left to vote as they did, for he had not believed that Thiers would go to the point of resignation. As a result, the Left 'became indignant with Gambetta and frantically alarmed

1. *Lettres*, no. 131 of 17 Jan. The other letter of the period 1 Dec. 1871 to 31 March 1872 printed by Halévy and Pillias is no. 132 of 17 March to his father.
2. According to Lacombe, a Monarchist deputy, Gambetta 'près de la tribune, à l'extrême gauche, pousse les orateurs contre le projet du gouvernement, donne le signal des applaudissements et paraît mener toute l'affaire' (Hélot, *op. cit.*, vol. i, p. 93).
3. For the debate, see *Ass. Nat. A.*, vol. vii, pp. 96–109. The motion adopted read as follows: 'L'Assemblée Nationale, réservant le principe d'un impôt sur les matières premières, décide qu'une commission de quinze membres examinera les tarifs proposés et les questions soulevées par cet impôt, auquel elle n'aura recours qu'en cas d'impossibilité d'aligner autrement le budget.' In other words, the principle of a raw material tax was reserved instead of being accepted by the Assembly as Thiers had demanded.

at the consequences of their own action. Thus on Friday Gambetta did all he could to push his party to vote against the Government; on Saturday he was tearing wildly about with an *ordre du jour* which never saw the light, by which the Government should be kept in office.'[1] However, his failure did not affect the issue. The officers of the Bureau of the Assembly headed by the father of the house, M. Benoist d'Azy, set out on foot to take the Assembly's appeal to Thiers at his residence, the Prefecture of Versailles. Some members of the Left are said to have dashed from the debating chamber and hurled themselves into such cabs as were available in order to be the first to tell Thiers of the Assembly's vote,[2] but Gambetta is unlikely to have demeaned himself in this way. Perhaps he was among 'the immense majority of the Assembly' who, according to the editor of his speeches, followed the Bureau in their pilgrimage to the Prefecture.[3]

Thiers was, of course, delighted to have the Assembly at his feet and graciously withdrew his resignation. The *République Française*, looking back on the crisis, deplored it as unnecessary. It might have been avoided had Thiers been less rigid. It was to the honour of the Left that they had not given way to him: indeed they had shown themselves to be the true protectors of the industrial interests and the nation's wealth. M. Thiers, however, had diminished in stature and the Assembly had also discredited itself. Once again, the moral was that dissolution was more than ever necessary. It was a measure of public safety.[4]

Thiers had indeed triumphed. He had momentarily demonstrated his indispensability, but he could not be sure that the Assembly would always allow itself to be browbeaten in such a way with impunity. On some other occasion it might be less willing to play a suppliant role and beseech its vain and aged ruler to resume office. Meanwhile, the crisis had unsettled French politics still further and created an unfavourable impression abroad. Thiers himself had described France as 'a country which may be called a universal contradiction, where everybody is divided on everything'.[5] His own obstinacy had added to the divisions. 'I have never known the French so depressed and so out of heart about their internal affairs', wrote Lord Lyons. 'They don't believe Thiers can go on much longer and they see

1. *The Times*, 25 Jan., p. 10.
2. C. de B. (Rothschild pp.), 22 Jan.
3. *Discours*, vol. ii, p. 192.
4. R.F., leaders of 21, 22, 23 Jan. To *The Times* (leader of 22 Jan.) the conduct of the Assembly was reminiscent of Don Quixote and his helmet: 'Bent on testing the temper of his head-piece, the knight shattered it by a single blow; but he immediately picked up the pieces, put them together as he best could and wisely determined to submit it to no further experiment.'
5. 13 Jan. *Ass. Nat. A.*, vol. vi, p. 580.

nothing but confusion if he is turned out. . . . It all tends to raise the Bonapartists.'[1]

'All' was not 'shattered' by the crisis as Gambetta had foretold it would be, but his letter of 17 January containing the prophecy suggests that he must certainly have shared in the depression referred to by Lyons. The message of Chambord and the continued confusion in the Monarchist ranks no doubt soon gave him fresh heart, but at much the same time he encountered a vexation of a different kind; he became the victim of two of the best-known and wittiest playwrights of the day.

In a brief work, dated 21 January and entitled *Nouvelles lettres sur les choses du jour*, Alexandre Dumas *fils*, moralist and author of *La Dame aux Camélias*, made one of his relatively rare descents into the political arena. From time to time, he said in language which at moments resembled that of a Hebrew prophet, nations gave themselves to and were guided by Chosen Leaders. 'But a man'—he mentioned no name—'who united in himself much error and good faith and believed himself to be such a Chosen Leader (*l'Elu promis*)' bore none of the marks by which a Leader could be recognised:

> he is branded with those marks by which one recognises the eternal rebel and, in consequence, the eternally defeated . . . this man, half seer or half-blind,[2] is doomed to final impotence like all those who confine themselves to the earth. . . . He has shut himself up in the little black box of atheism . . . he wearies and exhausts himself in running about and speechifying . . . it is not with words that a nation can be saved or a fatherland reconstituted.

Dumas's brochure, however, made less stir than Sardou's play.

In the first week of February all Paris was competing for seats at the Vaudeville Theatre to see Victorien Sardou's new five-act comedy, *Rabagas*. Any new play by Sardou was an event, but the interest and excitement over *Rabagas* was all the greater because of its political satire. The theme was the threat to the government of Monaco by a set of revolutionary radicals and the masterly way in which it was foiled by the Prince, counselled by his American *dame du palais*, Mistress Eva Blounth. The Radicals' headquarters were a tavern called Le Crapaud Volant, which overlooked the palace gardens, and their leader was a demagogic

1. Newton, *op. cit.*, p. 295.
2. No doubt a reference to Gambetta's loss of an eye. Dumas *fils*'s damning views on Gambetta are also reflected in a letter (date not given) from Mme de Pierreclos to Juliette Adam (see Mme Adam, *Mes Angoisses*, pp. 368–9). Gambetta had his revenge when Dumas was received into the French Academy in February 1875. The *R.F.* (13 Feb.) wrote a scornful account of Dumas's speech which it described as 'lourd, pâteux et embarrassé'.

lawyer named Rabagas. The play was a highly amusing satire on Republican demagoguery, some said on the men of 4 September. In particular, Rabagas, described by his sovereign as 'a jovial good fellow, a great consumer of beer,[1] who knows everything and has a little speech for everything', a man who, when he was made prime minister, assured the Prince that, as a lawyer, by virtue of his profession he could do everything and would therefore 'make strategy for you when you want it. Such as has never been made before!' was widely interpreted as a caricature of Gambetta. The actor Grenier, who played the part of Rabagas, was said to have been made up to resemble him and to have imitated his gestures.[2] Moreover, the second act depicting Rabagas as the oracle of the Republican newspaper, *La Carmagnole*, could be taken as an uproarious skit on the *République Française* and its clientèle.

What Gambetta's own reactions were we do not know. But the story was told that an acquaintance pointed, as they were passing by, to the theatre in which *Rabagas* was being played and said: 'If you want to see an Aristophanes of the boulevards, you should go in there.' 'No', replied Gambetta laughing, 'I prefer to read the real Aristophanes.'[3] Of the irritation of his supporters, however, there is no doubt. The *République Française* showed its vexation in an article attacking Sardou,[4] and Madame Adam no doubt truly recorded that she and her friends were revolted and scandalised.[5] Indeed she claimed that 'all the Republicans', even the moderates of the Left Centre, had urged M. Thiers to forbid the play and that he had agreed and wired to the Governor of Paris, General Ladmirault, to do so. But Ladmirault, she alleged, an Imperialist general who detested Gambetta, guessed what was in the telegram and so did not open it until after the first performance had ended amidst 'a storm of contending cheers and hisses'.[6] Thus the play went on and the printed version ran through

---

1. For long the favourite drink of Gambetta and his friends: 'le bock symbolisera pour eux le souvenir de leur chère jeunesse, ardente, expansive, assoiffée' (R. Dreyfus, 'Les Premières armes de Gambetta (1869–1873)' (I), *La Revue de France*, 15 Dec. 1932, p. 676, n (1).

2. Mme Adam, *Mes Angoisses*, p. 254.

3. Claretie, *Portraits contemporains*, p. 60.

4. *R.F.*, 4 Feb., p. 2: 'Cet amuseur veut être un satirique . . . cette diatribe sans goût, sans esprit, sans observation.'

5. *Mes Angoisses*, pp. 253–4: *The Times*, 6 Feb., p. 4. *The Times* correspondent saw little resemblance between Rabagas and Gambetta and thought that 'in their anxiety to convict M. Sardou of indecorum, the Radicals wantonly sacrifice their unlucky leader and discover a resemblance which does not really exist' (7 Feb., p. 4).

6. *The Times*, *ibid*. 'Even during the performance the interruptions and counter-interruptions were loud and frequent. Republicans like Jules Claretie jumped up from their seats and shouted that the "play was insupportable", that the only fitting

many editions before the year was out. It did not deflect the course of French politics, but there must henceforth have been many Parisians and others who could not think of Gambetta without thinking of Rabagas, and *Rabagas* furnished a precedent for some of the libels later levelled at Gambetta, the leader of the Opportunists and maker and unmaker of governments. Meanwhile, however, the Left found some consolation in the renewed prestige of Victor Hugo, their great man of letters. His celebrated play *Ruy Blas*[1] was revived in the same month of February and in the spring the publication of his dramatic poem, *L'Année Terrible*, dealt the Bonapartists a resounding literary blow[2]—the great poet, long since a sworn enemy of 'Napoléon le Petit', now pilloried him as 'L'homme tragique', who 'Vint s'échouer, rêveur, dans l'opprobre insondable', and Sedan as 'le nom funèbre, où tout vient s'éclipser/'Crache-le, pour ne plus jamais le prononcer.'

Apart from his interventions on the free-trade treaty and later on the Conseil d'État, Gambetta spoke but little in general debate during the remainder of the winter session. He figured in a couple of the tumultuous incidents, so frequent in this Assembly, in which Right and Left engaged in bitter taunts, but this was all. He was not, however, the only conspicuous personality who in this way disappointed an expectant public. Looking back on the session soon after its ending, *The Times* correspondent commented that M. Rouher had 'rivalled in silence the Orléans Princes or Gambetta'.[3] Towards the end of February, however, Gambetta was reported to have spoken in his bureau in favour of a Bill sponsored by the new Minister of the Interior, Victor Lefranc, which empowered the government to prosecute for seditious libel any newspaper which attacked the rights and authority of the Government or Assembly. As this was a sweeping and draconian measure, the report caused a certain stir and provoked a somewhat embarrassed explanation in the *République Française* of 26 February.[4] It was necessary it said, to distinguish between the two clauses of the Bill. The first could be voted for, since it gave the government the support it needed, but the second (which forbade the

1. It was warmly reviewed in the *R.F.*, 20 Feb., p. 3.
2. The poem was the subject of an enthusiastic article in the *R.F.* of 7 May, pp. 1–2.
3. *The Times*, 11 April 1872.
4. The *R.F.* had printed leaders critical of the Bill on 22 and 23 Feb. 1872. For the text of the Bill, see *Ass. Nat. A.*, vol. vii, p. 686.

conclusion to it could be the cry of "Vive l'Empereur!"—a challenge which the pugnacious Paul Cassaignac [*sic*] instantly met by crying "A bas les Communards!" ' When the play was performed at Bordeaux at the end of June and at Marseilles in July there were demonstrations and several people were arrested (*ibid.*, 28 June, p. 12, and 22 July).

reappearance elsewhere in France of a paper suppressed or suspended in a place subject to martial law) was inadmissible since it decreed new restrictions on the liberty of the Press. Gambetta had spoken neither for nor against the Bill: he had contented himself with speaking 'on the actual position'. The Bill was eventually withdrawn because the Monarchists introduced amendments unpalatable to the government, but the qualified support at first given to it by some of the Left was a measure of the shock administered to them by Thiers's resignation. Fearful of the activities of the Bonapartists in particular, they had been ready to support a measure which would strengthen the authority of Thiers even at the expense of the freedom of the Press, the more so because by implication it might involve a recognition of the Republic as the definitive form of government.

At much the same time a curious glimpse of Gambetta at a well-attended meeting of the Cercle Républicain is given in a letter of 26 February from the Calvinist Radical J.-J. Clamageran to his brother-in-law Ferdinand Hérold. Numerous orators addressed the meeting including Gambetta and Louis Blanc. To Clamageran the best speech seemed to be that of Louis Blanc, who was not at all sectarian, whereas 'Gambetta declaimed against the bourgeoisie in a deplorable way. Both were much applauded. Gambetta's declamations I found trying. I thought that events had done little to mature him. He is always the same: very eager and sometimes very stirring but with his head fuller of images than of ideas, plenty of warmth and little light.'[1] This reference to Gambetta's declaiming against the bourgeoisie is curious and tantalising, since he had so lately allied with industrialists and textile manufacturers over the free-trade question. Moreover, it was apparently about this time that, according to Madame Adam, her Gambettist friends were being helped by the support and approval of big traders and Parisian industrialists who, during the war and the siege, had abhorred the phrase-making of the Jules Favres and the Trochus but had respected Gambetta as a man of action.[2] The clue no doubt lies in an article of the *République Française* quoted above.[3] Gambetta was not turning Socialist but merely declaiming against the kind of diehard bourgeois conservatism represented by Thiers and his friends and against the reluctance of many middle-class people to renounce

1. Clamageran, *Correspondance 1849–1902* (1906), p. 367. There does not appear to be any reference to this meeting in the *République Française*. A very hostile observer, who saw Gambetta in the Assembly at the end of February, described him as rolling about on his bench 'gros, gras, rouge, factieux, paresseux, luxurieux' (*Journal de Fidus*, vol. iii, p. 56, 1 March).

2. *Mes Angoisses*, p. 268.

3. p. 77, cf. Gambetta's later condemnation of 'une notable partie de la bourgeoisie française' in his celebrated speech at Grenoble on 26 Sept. 1872 (*Discours*, vol. iii, pp. 100–1).

their Monarchist sympathies. It would not be the last occasion on which he did so.

With the coming of spring and the prospect of a vacation, for the Assembly was to be prorogued for three weeks from 29 March, Gambetta was more cheerful. Nine Radical papers in the provinces, charged with criticising the Commission of Pardons set up by the Assembly, had been acquitted by juries.[1] The Monarchists had failed to effect a fusion, there had been no Bonapartist *coup*, and it was now hoped that M. Thiers would consent to remain in office as long as the Assembly remained in being.[2] 'Everything', Gambetta told his father when he wrote him a birthday letter on 17 March, 'leads us to believe that our efforts, long unrecognised, are more and more appreciated from day to day and that they will not have been fruitless either for the honour of France or for the future of the Republic.'[3] Within the next few months his returning optimism seemed to be amply justified.

---

1. See *R.F.*, leader of 8 March.
2. See *R.F.*, leader of 21 March.
3. *Lettres*, no. 132. In a letter of 24 March Clamageran (*op. cit:*, p. 368) reported that rightly or wrongly people were pretty optimistic at the Cercle Républicain.

9

'I am a traveller and salesman of democracy' April–October 1872

The spring recess gave Gambetta the chance to resume the propaganda campaign of which the speech at Saint-Quentin had been a mere fore-taste. Full of ardour, he escaped from the 'whirlpool'[1] of a life divided between Versailles and Paris and, on 4 April, boldly set out on a tour of the conservative West carrying the war into the enemy's country. His first main port of call was Angers, the chief town of a department whose eleven deputies, with one exception, were all Monarchists, the home of a considerable Legitimist monarchist paper, *L'Union de L'Ouest*, and a city in which two of the most influential figures were the well-known Monarchist Comte de Falloux and the energetic Bishop of Angers, Mgr Freppel. There he stayed with his friend Allain-Targé, and there, on the 7th, he told Marie Meersmans, he was to go to a huge banquet.[2] It was at this banquet, attended by some four hundred people, including the Mayor of Angers, that he delivered the first of the new series of speeches.[3] He was in splendid form, full of verve and humour which at once captivated his audience. He had felt a need, he said, to visit a part of France which was misjudged and belittled, and of which people alleged that it was made up of steppes and heaths inhabited by ill-formed and peevish folk. But he knew well that it was not such a sterile region. The welcome he had received had shown him what a unity of outlook there was between different parts of the country, that the Republic was the same everywhere and wanted equally by different populations. Only these populations acted differently according to their temperaments, some demanding the Republic, some making ready for it, some awaiting it. In union lay strength and, if they put aside the differences of origin and theory which must always exist in a great party like theirs and

1. *Lettres*, no. 133, 3 April 1872.
2. *Ibid.*, no. 134.
3. For the text, see *Discours*, vol. ii, pp. 226–47.

displayed this unity when it came to the vote, they would gain a lasting victory. The first-fruits of victory had already been seen in the region and the progress of Republicanism there had thrown the ranks of the adversary into confusion. And then Gambetta, after as usual dismissing the Empire with the utmost scorn—'this accursed empire whose name should be uttered only with a kind of physical nausea'—enjoyed himself holding the Monarchists up to ridicule; they were 'paladins whom it was impossible to convert', who took no account of all that had happened since the Restoration, and to whom it was impossible to talk of reason because they knew only of faith. They believed that they were the servants of tradition; they presented themselves to France and France did not recognise them. They themselves were now aware of this, and that was why they wanted to hang on to their seats.

So Gambetta came to his central theme, the theme so often reiterated, and now to be voiced more insistently than ever by the Radical campaigners—'dissolution!' Each time universal suffrage had been consulted, he declared, whether in the municipal elections or in the elections to the General Councils—and on these he laid particular stress[1]—it had uniformly replied 'Restore my sovereignty!' Then, however, the Legitimist and Orleanist parties had entered on the scene—the Bonapartists were not a political party, but a rabble—and 'en pleine République' they had gone abroad to seek a king to bring back and install in place of the existing government: 'And this is not called conspiring, this is not called a danger to public peace and well-being or indulging in culpable manoeuvres! What a thing, to act in this way under the eyes of the enemy encamped on our soil! No, you are wrong, it is the party of respectable people which is acting in this way and what it is doing is called seeking to guarantee order!' (Repeated applause.) Then, having ridiculed the 'excessive number of pretenders', Gambetta had no difficulty in arguing that it was in fact the Republican party which had shown to all that it was 'the true party of order' and that those who spoke so much of 'order' were no more than common and impotent agitators.

This main theme with various subordinate developments was accompanied by a commentary on the French Revolution more complete than any yet given by Gambetta. What he said was not original, but there were still men living who had been children during the Revolution, and, because of the cleavages it had created in French society, its place in French history could still be and was once again more than ever a matter of passionate debate. Thus, only four months earlier, in December, Renan

1. 'On ne se lasse pas d'envisager les conséquences fructueuses, les conséquences, permettez-moi de le dire, incalculables pour nos idées, de ces élections aux Conseils généraux.'

had published his *La Réforme intellectuelle et morale de la France* which
contained a searing indictment of the later stages of the Revolution and
of the 'ignorant and limited men who took the destinies of France in
hand at the end of the last century'.[1] A man might be gauged by his
attitude to the Revolution, and so Gambetta's interpretation of it was
much more than a mere historical exercise. First and foremost was his
claim, commonly made by the Left, that it was still in progress. Gambetta
did not, as would Clemenceau later, declare that it was a 'bloc', something
to be accepted in its entirety, but he did assert that it was incomplete
because its progress had been crossed by 'dynasties, kings, pretenders and
adventurers'.

Secondly, he asserted that it had brought order. The Republicans, the
party of the French Revolution, were accused of threatening property, the
family and freedom of conscience. In fact, it was they who had introduced
property 'into the French World', who had taken over two-thirds of the
nation's wealth on which no taxes were paid, and handed it over to men
who worked, it was they who contrived that individual property should
take the place of royal domains and entailed estates, they who had given
land to the peasant, rescued him from slavery and made of him 'a proprie-
tor, a citizen and man!'[2] As for the family, was there any dogma more
inviolable than the dogma of the family established by the French Revolution? It had 'freed man by civil marriage' and delivered all those 'pariahs
of the old society', Jews and Protestants. It had destroyed privilege even
in matters of inheritance by declaring the equal rights of children to a
share in the partition of real property. To say that the Republicans were
enemies of freedom of conscience was also a calumny—but here
Gambetta's language was less precise; he wisely avoided direct reference
to the French Revolution but asked rhetorically whether it was the
Republican party which had ever persecuted freedom of conscience in
whatever form it might be manifested, prayer, worship or meeting?

The dispassionate twentieth-century historian may shudder at the
violence done to historical truth by some of Gambetta's oratorical asser-
tions,[3] but these passages on the French Revolution were among those

---

1. pp. 11–13 of the edn by P. E. Charvet (1950). The review of the book in the
R.F. of 13 April was naturally unfavourable: 'Nous l'avons lu avec fatigue et nous
l'avons fermé avec dégoût.'

2. This claim he repeated at Albertville on 25 Sept. 1872: 'c'est de la Révolution
française . . . que date la création de cette immense quantité de petits propriétaires . . .
qui représentent la force et la sève de la France' (*Discours*, vol. iii, pp. 85–6); cf. speech
of 14 July at La Ferté-sous-Jouarre: 'il n'y eut qu'un cinquième de terres libres et
réservées aux citoyens les cultivant de leurs propres mains' (*ibid.*, vol. ii, pp. 380–1).

3. e.g. one later, at Chambéry on 22 Sept., when he said that the Republic of 1848 had
arrived 'in the midst of absolute peace and general prosperity' (*Discours*, vol. iii, p. 28).

which drew the greatest applause from his audience. Moreover, his conclusion, linked to the French Revolution, was remarkably adroit. The Revolution, he declared, was now daily threatened. 'But ask the peasant, the worker, the bourgeois, all those who have a feeling for truth, if they want to let everything be compromised by an impotent and incorrigible band.'[1] What reinforced his faith in the future was that 'the man who is at the head of the government cannot forget his origins or his studies or the lessons of experience; he knows, he ought to know, that there is something finer than having written the annals of the French Revolution and that is to complete it and crown his work by the loyalty and sincerity of his government'.[2]

Gambetta had indeed proved himself a 'fine player'[3] of the political game. Thiers had perhaps muzzled him at Marseilles in January but there had been no ban on his speaking at Angers and the maintenance of Thiers in office was now more than ever a main concern of the Left. In reasserting the claims of his party to be a party of order and in publicly paying tribute to Thiers in the peroration of this first speech of the new provincial campaign of 1872, Gambetta might well hope to continue his tours with Thiers's sanction, if not his positive blessing.

Gambetta sat down amidst prolonged applause and repeated cries of 'Vive la République! Vive Gambetta!' He was understandably delighted and wrote to Marie Meersmans that he had been 'extremely well received and been able to ascertain that our affairs are going splendidly'.[4] From Angers he went on to Le Mans and Nantes and thence to Brest, which he reached on the night of 9–10 April. A week later he was at Le Havre where on the 18th, at a still bigger banquet for some six hundred people, he delivered his second campaign speech of the Easter recess.[5]

This was a less humourous discourse and in the main repeated the themes already elaborated: the demands for dissolution and for the

1. Here he echoed a phrase in a speech of 30 March at the close of the recent parliamentary session, in which Thiers had spoken of 'the incorrigibility and impotence of the parties'. It is worth noting that the *R.F.* went out of its way to review books relating to the French Revolution. Thus on 22 and 29 April 1872, it printed a very lengthy notice of Ernest Hamel's *Histoire de la Révolution Française: sous le Directoire et sous le Consulat* and a month later, on 20 May, a substantial review of Michelet's *Histoire du XIXe Siècle: Directoire–Origines des Bonaparte*. Of the latter, the anonymous reviewer, probably Georges Avenel, wrote enthusiastically, ending with an apostrophe to the author: 'O maître, achevez vite, et que vite aussi un abrégé de cette Vie nouvelle soit mis en petit livre, en brochure et coure les campagnes ... il faut que le Michelet soit l'antidote du Béranger.'

2. Thiers was the author of a history of the Revolution in ten volumes (1824–27).

3. Daniel Halévy's phrase, 'ce beau joueur' (*La Fin des Notables*, p. 133).

4. *Lettres*, no. 135, n.d.

5. For the text see *Discours*, vol. ii, pp. 249–65.

election of a Republican Assembly as a matter of urgency ('if we linger in this provisional state which enervates us ... we run the greatest dangers'), for an armed and educated nation, for educational reform at all levels;[1] it reiterated the arguments that the Republican party was 'not a party of revolution but of conservatism; that it was not 'a closed party', but that those who had 'failed by error' would be welcome in it, provided their conscience was pure; and that it alone could assure order, 'not the order of silence and fear ... but order based on legality, on legitimacy established by the general will'. Apart from a spirited defence of one of his most criticised wartime collaborators, Jules Le Cesne, and apart from his assumption of the title of 'commercial traveller of the Democracy', the main novelty in the speech was one of Gambetta's rare allusions to the social question.[2]

At Angers, a town of some 50,000 inhabitants, but the only one of any size in the rural department of Maine-et-Loire, there had been no need to refer to the social question. But Le Havre was a different matter. It boasted three shipyards and important docks and its port handled a quarter of French trade. Its population was 70,000, that of Rouen in the same department of Seine-Inférieure was 100,000. Here and in nearby regions of Normandy there were a proletariat on the one hand and great business interests on the other, and so, almost in parenthesis, Gambetta grasped the nettle. The development of the intellectual and military reorganisation of the country along with respect for secular principles in the State, for 'philosophic liberty', for orderliness in the finances, for economic freedom and for freedom of worship—these, he asserted, were 'a sufficient task for the generation to which we belong'.

> But this is not to say that I in any way deny the existence of misery and suffering and legitimate grievances in part of our democracy. I am not the man to belittle the power there is in this world of labour. . . . Here is a whole new world which we know too little and which has suffered and groaned too long. . . . But we must all beware of the Utopias of those who, dupes of their imagination or ignorantly behind the times, believe in a panacea. . . . Believe me there is no social remedy because there is not a social question. There is a series of problems to be resolved, of difficulties to be overcome, which vary according to localities,

1. According to Juliette Adam, Scheurer-Kestner, who heard Gambetta deliver the speech recommended the Adams to read above all 'le magnifique passage sur l'instruction primaire, "qui doit apprendre au paysan quelle est sa dignité, dans quelle société il vit, quelle est sa place et son lieu de solidarité avec ceux qui l'entourent. L'instruction primaire doit lui montrer quel est son rang dans la commune, dans le département . . . Ah ! la grande éducatrice que l'instruction primaire, nationale!"' (Mme Adam, *Mes Angoisses*, p. 278).

2. *Discours*, vol. ii, pp. 262–3.

climates, customs and sanitary conditions, economic problems which change within the interior of a single country; well, these problems must be resolved one by one and not by a single formula. . . . There is, I repeat, no social panacea; there is progress to be made daily, but there is no immediate definitive and complete solution.

This declaration was heard without either interruption or applause by Gambetta's audience, but elsewhere it was immediately recognised as a significant pronouncement. It caused widespread comment in the Press and involved the *République Française* in a brief controversy with Louis Blanc.[1] It was, however, quite consistent with the terms in which Gambetta had in 1869 accepted the Belleville mandate. This had, in laboured phraseology, demanded 'economic reforms related to the social problem, the solution of which, though subordinated to political change, ought to be a matter for constant study and research in the name of the principle of justice and social equality'. In his acceptance, Gambetta had carefully avoided referring to 'the social problem' or 'question' as a single entity and had declared:

Like you, I think that a loyal and orderly democracy is par excellence the political system which most readily and certainly gives effect to the moral and material emancipation of the greatest number and which best assures social equality in its laws, acts and customs. But, like you too, I hold that the progressive series of these reforms absolutely depends on the political regime and on political reforms.[2]

His attitude could be regarded as another proof of his realism, but his vagueness concerning specific social reforms, both in 1869 and now in 1872, could also be held to show a lack of any genuine interest in social questions.[3] Had he been directly taken to task on this in 1872, his answer would almost certainly have been that the political issue, the question of the regime, was all important and that to add to his programme a number of specific social reforms of a controversial nature would merely have

1. See *R.F.*, leader of 24 April and article on 26th (p. 2). Alluding to it in a letter to a friend later on in the year Emile Ollivier cynically commented that the phrase 'Il n'y a pas de question sociale' meant 'Bourgeois, n'ayez pas peur; je massacrerai comme vous les socialistes' (*Lettres de l'exil 1871–1874*, 1921, p. 128).

2. For the French text, see e.g. J. P. T. Bury, *Gambetta and the National Defence* (1936), pp. 286–7.

3. The *R.F.* in its leader of 24 April replying to the criticisms of Louis Blanc was no more specific: 'Ce qu'on demande aujourd'hui, à la place d'un socialisme nourri de chimères et d'illusions, c'est un régime de liberté et de progrés où les problèmes sociaux seront successivement résolus par la science et conformément à la justice, dans l'intérêt de ceux qui souffrent.'

confused the main issue and have risked scaring the peasantry and dividing the ranks of the Republicans at a time when greater unity was essential.[1]

Two months later, in the conclusion of a moving and patriotic speech at a banquet given on 24 June at Versailles to commemorate the birth of one of the military heroes of the French Revolution, General Hoche, he returned, though much less categorically, to the theme that there was no short-cut to Utopia: 'I recall another formula that he [Hoche] had made his own . . . : "Ago quod ago", I do what I do. Yes, let us do what we do, do not let us seek to settle everything, do not let us think that there is a way to make general happiness uniform.'[2] Three weeks later still at La Ferté-sous-Jouarre he was a shade more precise on one social question, the question of property:

> What we demand is that property should be accessible to all, and especially to those who can make it fructify. It is through a more equitable distribution of wages and taxes, a difficult problem to resolve, but one which must be tackled . . . that we may hope to reach a solution; it is by making possible the accumulation of savings and in consequence the acquisition of capital in the form of land that capital in the form of money is increased and that property is made accessible to the greatest number.[3]

Such vague utterances might well lead *The Times* correspondent to think that political economy was not the strong point of Gambetta and his friends, but further than this sort of generalisation he would not go. Thus in September at Firminy in the Loire department he spoke at a banquet at which many workers were present and later in the same evening to a gathering exclusively of workers; these would have been admirable opportunities for him to enlarge upon social questions, but Gambetta

1. An intelligent follower of Gambetta in the Loire, César Bertholon, had early in the year founded a paper expressly aimed at winning peasant support, *La République des paysans*. In the number of 16 May he put his own gloss on Gambetta's views: 'I want to see the Republic securely established, so that we can get on with the business of reform in a practical and sensible manner and face without danger social questions. It is no longer a question of overthrowing the existing order, but of modifying it as we feel the need' (Elwitt, *art. cit.*, *French Historical Studies*, vol. vi, 1969, no. 1, pp. 102–3).

2. *Discours*, vol. ii, p. 364.

3. *Ibid.*, vol. ii, p. 392. Cf. speech of 1 June 1874, at Auxerre: 'à chaque propriété qui se crée, c'est un citoyen qui se forme; car la propriété . . . est, à nos yeux, le signe supérieur et préparateur de l'émancipation morale et matérielle de l'individu. Ce n'est pas de la propriété que nous sommes les ennemis . . . mais plutôt de sa raréfaction. . . . Ce que nous demandons, ce qui se fait, ce qui est une loi sociale de démocratie, c'est que la propriété se divise, c'est qu'elle aille à celui qui l'exploite et qui la féconde de tous ses efforts pour lui faire produire chaque jour davantage, à son avantage personnel, mais aussi au plus grand avantage social' (*Discours*, vol. iv, pp. 155–6).

carefully avoided any reference to them and stuck to his well-worn themes.[1] Three years later, a leader in the *République Française* showed that he had not budged from the position he had adopted at Le Havre; the view that there was *a* social question was a chimera, but all questions had a social aspect of which public men should be aware.[2]

The parties of the Right were naturally angered by Gambetta's speeches at Angers and Le Havre and by the mounting campaign which he was directing for the dissolution of the Assembly,[3] and a Bonapartist deputy, Raoul Duval, a doughty hammerer of Radicals, who had previously made two onslaughts against Ranc, questioned the government about the banquets when the Assembly reconvened and elicited from the Minister of the Interior an official condemnation of the conduct of the Mayors of Angers and Le Havre for attending such political manifestations. But that was an outcome which did no harm to Gambetta and his cause. The speeches were indeed splendid propaganda. Not only were they printed *in extenso* by the *République Française* but they were reproduced separately by Ernest Leroux of the rue Bonaparte and sold for ten centimes each. Large numbers were said to have been run off for distribution by Radical clubs and committees in the provinces.[4] Later in the summer the well-known photographer Etienne Carjat was advertising portraits of Gambetta, Victor Hugo and various generals of the National Defence. Meanwhile *The Times* correspondent had pertinently asked: 'Why don't Gambetta's opponents follow suit? Their answer', he went on to report, 'invariably is "Ce n'est pas dans nos habitudes"', and he added that the 'notion of a party propaganda here is to send little coloured pictures about, for instance there is a whole sheet of military achievements of the Orléans Princes'.[5] In fact, the *République Française* had already, in commenting on the anger of the Orleanist *Journal de Paris* at Gambetta's Angers speech, remarked that 'it was doubtful whether MM. the Royalist deputies

1. For the text of these speeches, see *ibid.*, vol. iii, pp. 1–9.
2. *R.F.*, 29 Sept. 1875. In a letter of 23 June 1874, commenting on an article on Babeuf by Ranc, Gambetta did, however, remark that the war of 1870 had been accompanied by a social revolution 'qui sera de longue haleine', and that if 'le machinisme' developed as Babeuf had foreseen, 'c'est la classe ouvrière qui deviendra prépondérante à moins que la classe bourgeoise ne conserve sa supériorité en technique et en savoir comme en attitude d'autorité morale' (quoted in G. Wormser, *Gambetta dans les tempêtes*, 1969, p. 148).
3. There were two more leaders on the subject in the *R.F.* on 28 April and 19 May 1872.
4. In a letter of 12 June the secretary of a workers' union in Lot-et-Garonne told Gambetta that he had heard that the *R.F.* was placing at the disposal of the democrats of the departments 100,000 copies of his speeches 'pour les faire lire dans les campagnes'.
5. *The Times*, 25 April 1872, p. 12.

would dare to face as many as a hundred electors at a time'. It would be delighted to see them adopt this practice of a free country, but if many did so, 'if it became the fashion for the deputies to go and visit the electors in order to render account to them or come to an understanding with them, it would soon be necessary to enlarge and ease the right of meeting'.[1]

To the leaders of the other parties, however, 'stumping the country' was no doubt something foreign which savoured of demagogy, the demagogy of a man who, it seemed to the *Correspondant*, set out to flatter, excite, blind and delude the people.[2] They still, as the *République Française* remarked, preferred 'to conduct polling behind closed doors between "gens comme il faut" ' and to indulge not in the eloquence of the banquet or balcony but in that of the sofa.[3] Perhaps, too, they knew that they could not hope to compete with Gambetta in oratorical power. So when he continued his banquet campaign in the summer, after a two months' break imposed by the demands of parliament, he was still without competitors.

Meanwhile, before the banquets resumed, four more by-elections had taken place. Another Bonapartist was returned in Corsica, but on the mainland the victors in the three departments concerned, the Nord, the Somme and the Yonne, were all Republicans and two of them Radicals. In the Nord the moderate Republican Deregnaucourt, whose election by a few hundred votes as recently as January had been invalidated by the Assembly, was reelected by an immensely increased majority. In the Somme Jules Barni, who had been beaten in January, won by a comfortable margin over the Bonapartist runner-up.[4] In the Yonne a well-known Radical, already a general councillor in the department, the scientist, atheist, and expert on education, Paul Bert, replaced the former conserva-

1. *R.F.*, leader of 12 April 1872.
2. See Gimpl, *The Correspondant and the Founding of the French Third Republic*, p. 105.
3. *Ibid.* The remark about 'eloquence of the sofa' is no doubt a reference to the Doctrinaire Monarchists of the 1820s, so small a group that they were sometimes known as the Sofa party, since they were all supposed to be able to sit on a single settee.
4. Among his helpers was one of the department's deputies in the previous year, General Faidherbe, who sent round a circular on white paper expressing his support for Barni and also, according to *The Times* of 19 June (p. 12) 'had carried through the country villages and towns the sword of honour presented to him by the inhabitants of Lille. Beneath the hilt figured the words "Massive gold" and above it the words "Vote for Burni [*sic*]".' Barni's victory was also in part a reflection of the rivalry between the influential moderate Republican, Dauphin, mayor of Amiens and friend of Thiers, and Frédéric Petit, an able local Radical manipulator (G. Lenormand, 'Le mouvement républicain dans la Somme au début de la IIIe République (1870–1877)', *Revue Historique*, vol. cxcvi, Jan.–March 1946, p. 20).

tive Republican, L. Javal; he easily defeated both Javal's son and the Monarchist Duc de Clermont-Tonnerre. Here was another important recruit for the Republican Union and Gambetta, delighted, sent him an enthusiastic letter of congratulation: 'There you are, a past master at the first attempt!'[1]

Gambetta and his supporters had indeed every reason to be exultant. 'Gambetta taught us', Scheurer-Kestner once noted in his diary, 'that the best manifestoes are Republican votes.'[2] In the Nord it looked as though all the new voters who had abstained in January now supported the Republicans.[3] In the Somme and the Yonne the electoral tide was swinging away from the Republic of Thiers to that of Gambetta. 'The peasants were following the workers and the North the South.'[4] On 12 June the *Journal des Débats* went so far as to declare that 'this triple success of the Radical party' was 'the most significant electoral development in France since the elections of February 1871. . . . It is not only the Monarchy that has been beaten, but also and above all the moderate Republic . . . the Republic of M. Léon Gambetta has triumphed over the Republic of M. Thiers.' The alarm in Conservative circles was such that forty Monarchist deputies, including the Duc de Broglie, deputy for the Eure, who had resigned the London Embassy in order to devote himself more fully to politics, suggested to the Left Centre group a common *démarche* to urge the President of the Republic to govern in a conservative manner. But their negotiations came to nothing: each side was Monarchist or Republican before it was Conservative, and the new president of the Left Centre, General Chanzy, declared that his group could join in the *démarche* only if this was in effect a declaration that the Republic was the definitive form of government; to such a condition the Monarchists were unable to subscribe. The Radicals were, of course, delighted and the *République Française* commented: 'Perhaps it will never have been more truly said: France is Left Centre.'[5] Disappointed though they were, however, the Monarchists ill-advisedly decided to go ahead and to send a delegation of nine to make representations on their own. Ill-advisedly, for as Broglie later wrote: 'From the moment that we were no longer simple conservatives asking M. Thiers to undertake the defence of social principles, we were royalists

---

1. Cit. Léon Dubreuil, *Paul Bert* (Paris, 1935, p. 49). This letter of 10 June is not printed in *Lettres*, and Halévy and Pillias in their introduction say that the letters received by Paul Bert were destroyed when there was a fire at his house at Auxerre in 1904. Bert wrote many of the weekly articles on science in the *R.F.* (Dubreuil, p. 36).
2. *Journal inédit*, vol. iii, p. 351, B.N. N.a.fr. 12. 706.
3. Gouault, *Comment la France est devenue Républicaine*, pp. 148–9.
4. D. Halévy, *La Fin des Notables*, p. 135.
5. Leader of 21 June.

reproaching him for not establishing the Monarchy quickly enough.'[1] An interview of two hours on 20 June got them nowhere. Indeed Thiers declared that he had accepted the Republic at Bordeaux: 'It is not enough to refrain from opposing it; you must help to consolidate it.' His concluding remark was poor consolation for his discomfited visitors: 'What will you? The Republic is one of those things that the Empire has bequeathed to us along with so much else.' The Radicals were now no less delighted with Thiers, and, if Juliette Adam is to be believed, Edmond Adam privately congratulated him on Gambetta's behalf.[2] The *République Française* exulted: Thiers's words were those of a head of state who intended to be respected. They were 'a decisive, terrible blow, struck at all the Monarchist parties'.[3]

Gambetta's personal prestige, moreover, was soaring. On the day before the unhappy *démarche* of the Fur-Caps (*Bonnets à poil*), as Broglie and his friends were quickly dubbed,[4] a friend wrote to Ernest Picard, a moderate Republican who had been a member of the Government of National Defence:

> M. Gambetta, whose paper is well made... grows daily in importance. His name is gradually becoming synonymous with that of the Republic for the vast majority of Frenchmen. You have read M. d'Haussonville: 'Gambetta's reign is beginning.'[5] M. Gambetta is as it were *a latere* to Thiers, in the position of a successor who is listened to all the more because he is thought to be strong enough to be able, if need be, not to wait for the succession.[6]

1. *Mémoires du Duc de Broglie*, vol. ii, *1870–1875* (Paris, 1941), p. 113.
2. Mme Adam, *Mes Angoisses*, p. 311.
3. Leader of 23 June. Six weeks later, on 5 Aug. the *R.F.* printed a profile of Broglie. It was in the characteristically harsh tone in which the paper treated all its political enemies, witness this sentence: 'Déjà éclate l'esprit jaloux, et tout l'odieux d'un caractère égoiste et vindicatif, autoritaire et tyrannique, — petit, — petit !'
4. 'Sous Louis Philippe, certaines compagnies d'élite de la garde citoyenne portaient avec orgueil le majestueux bonnet à poil des grenadiers de l'Empire, et, le 15 Mars 1848, indignes de sa suppression comme du pire scandale révolutionnaire ces privilégiés tentèrent un mouvement de la rue contre le Gouvernement provisoire, mais furent étrillés par une foule gouailleuse' (Dreyfus, *La République de M. Thiers*, p. 205).
5. D'Haussonville had written a very long letter, published in the *Journal des Débats* of 17 June complaining that France was suffering from lack of direction—'Nous ne nous sentons pas gouvernés'—and appealing to Thiers to take a stronger line. In it there occurred the following passage: 'Nous sommes de moins en moins gouvernés. Le règne de M. Thiers s'achève; celui de M. Gambetta s'annonce. On croyait au triomphe de la république modérée, et l'on trouve devant soi le radicalisme victorieux.'
6. Ernest Seligmann to Ernest Picard, 18 June 1872 (B.N. Fond Ernest Picard. N.a.fr. 24370). Cf. the Orleanist deputy, Eugène Chaper, to his wife 21 June: 'Pour moi, je n'ai plus aucune confiance dans sa politique et je regarde le succès légal des

Was it perhaps at this time that in the Assembly he sat down 'in a very sprightly mood' beside that inventive memorialist the Marquis de Castellane and took out a teetotum from his pocket? 'On two sides was written, in big black letters, the word "Republic", on the two others, "Monarchy". And he began to set it spinning. How did he manage it? This much is certain', wrote Castellane, 'that the teetotum stopped ten times running at the word "Republic". And the great man walked away in delight, splitting his sides with laughter.'[1]

Thiers, however, was not worried. When some three weeks later some deputies commented indignantly on Gambetta's speech at La-Ferté-sous-Jouarre he was reported to have listened calmly and to have remarked: 'But Gambetta is more politic than you think'; and when they expostulated that Gambetta's policy meant the destruction of any social order incompatible with Radicalism, he replied tranquilly: 'Radicalism! but one can live with Radicalism; look at Switzerland, where there is a radical government, it is calm and happy.'[2] So Thiers would not muzzle the most eloquent of all the Radicals of the day, and Gambetta would for the time being be free to continue his role as 'commercial traveller' of the Republic, provided that he was prudent and that his utterances did not foment public disorder.

'Whenever . . . we encounter an anniversary, an occasion to be commemorated, a great souvenir to be recalled, a great example to be studied, we must not fail.'[3] These words of Gambetta in a speech later in the year at Chambéry are a vivid reminder of the way in which historical celebrations were part of the political warfare of the time. The Bonapartists had their anniversaries, which they were once again beginning to mark by demonstrative manifestations, the anniversaries of the great Napoleon's birth (15 August) and death (5 May), the birthday of the Empress Eugénie (15 November) and others.[4] But their historical arsenal was not so rich as that of the Republicans and perhaps there was something in Gambetta's claim that the Republican party's persistence in wishing to teach and comment upon its history 'must be a source of mortal anxiety to the rival

1. Antoine, Marquis de Castellane, *Men and Things of my Time* (1911), p. 125.
2. C. de B. (Rothschild pp.), 19 July.
3. *Discours*, vol. iii, p. 55.
4. As early as 15 Aug. 1871, at mass at the church of Saint-Augustin in Paris, young men had appeared wearing the Bonapartist flowers, violets, in their buttonholes (*Journal de Fidus*, vol. iii, p. 10).

candidats radicaux comme assuré, grâce à lui [Thiers]. C'est à dire que d'ici à peu de temps, nous aurons une Chambre radicale et Gambetta président légal de la République' (P. Barral, *Les Périer dans l'Isère au XIXe siècle*, Paris, 1964, p. 180).

parties'.[1] His party's 'preoccupation' with its history was not only, of course, a facet of its concern to set the French Revolution in a favourable light: it reflected the continual need of Gambetta and his friends to defend it from the charge of being the party of disorder and incompetence.[2] So it was that on 24 February and 15 July the *République Française* had devoted many columns to the history of the proclamation of the Second Republic in 1848 and to that of the fall of the Bastille in 1789. So it was that, of the three notable speeches which Gambetta delivered outside parliament during the summer session, two were at commemorative banquets, namely the one at Versailles, in memory of Hoche, and the one at La Ferté-sous-Jouarre which took place on 14 July.[3] And in the great autumn campaign one of the main series of addresses he delivered was at Chambéry on 22 September, the anniversary of the founding in 1792 of the First Republic.

There is no need to examine in detail the historical accuracy of Gambetta's eloquent portrait of Hoche as 'a great citizen, a captain of the élite, a statesman, a warrior, a politician, an administrator, a man of conscience, and a great hero'. But the speech also contained shrewd hits at Napoleon, the man who 'among other generals' went to the Vendée, but 'feared to get involved in a bad business, saw the country, returned, and it was never possible to send him back there again' and 'the ambitious egoist who caused the Republican armies to be denatured and to deteriorate so that they ended by bringing the country to ruin'. And there were adroit allusions to contemporary politics: 'He [Hoche] at once brought out of the ranks those whose merits he recognised; new men were needed, he improvised them. Was he not himself a new man, an improvised leader who had broken with the old representatives, with the laggard supporters of the old monarchies?' How many of Gambetta's audience did not at once think of Gambetta himself, also an improvised leader, a new man in new times? And then there was the veiled allusion, greeted by a 'triple salvo of prolonged applause', to the vexed question of an

1. *Discours*, vol. iii, p. 55.
2. At La Ferté-sous-Jouarre he spoke of 'ce parti républicain, outragé, calomnié, décimé, transporté sans trêve ni repos depuis soixante-dix ans'. *Ibid.*, vol. ii, p. 380. The *R.F.*'s concern with the French Revolution was illustrated *inter alia* by its printing of a series of reviews by Georges Avenel of books on the Revolution, later published under the title *Lundis révolutionnaires 1871–1874* (1875). In his introduction the author wrote that after the war and the Commune 'l'affolement des esprits était à craindre. Je crus ... qu'il importait surtout de leur rappeler la grande époque où s'était constituée la France nouvelle et de leur faire la glorification raisonnée du régime républicain qui avait sauvé cette France à son berceau.'
3. Gambetta had also been invited to speak at Bordeaux on 14 July. For his letter declining this invitation, see *Discours*, vol. ii, pp. 393–4.

amnesty for the Communards: 'After having proclaimed martial law, on the morrow of the day on which he [Hoche] was the victor, he proclaimed an amnesty.' The whole speech was warmly applauded, as indeed it deserved to be, for it was a moving performance, but, according to a police report, in certain parts of the hall there were repeated cries of 'Rabagas'.[1]

This Versailles audience had been one of deputies, members of the Republican Union, and other notables. At the little town of La-Ferté-sous-Jouarre in Seine-et-Marne, where several tents had been arranged to form a vast hall holding eighteen hundred people Gambetta addressed a very different crowd, most of them country folk, many of whom had travelled long distances despite rain so torrential that it twice obliged him to interrupt his speech.[2] Here again he extolled the French Revolution and, in particular, 14 July, 'the day on which our New Testament was given us'. But the speech was more directly topical and political and perhaps its most significant passages, apart from the now customary demands for dissolution and lay education, were those stressing the need to multiply such gatherings, particularly in country districts, the need for incessant propaganda, and the need for a new unity, a breaking-down of the barriers between town and country, a rapprochement of bourgeois, worker and peasant, a federation of interests as in 1789. Here, at La Ferté-sous-Jouarre, Gambetta had a still warmer reception; his speech was constantly interrupted by applause, the applause of an audience which was unlikely to have seen or read *Rabagas*.

The Assembly concluded its summer session on 3 August and was prorogued until November. Before the session ended Thiers had slightly modified his attitude towards the Right. In particular, he disavowed any connection with the Left's demands for dissolution: 'I owe everything to the Assembly', he said in substance; 'if I were to treat with its enemies I should think I was conspiring against the sovereign.' What were his real intentions? Léonie Léon wrote to Gambetta and asked whether he would not see 'the master' during the recess: 'I should be infinitely glad if he more or less explained his plan to you so that you could support him with full knowledge if it is favourable to you or oppose it if you dislike it.'[3] But there is no record that such a meeting took place[4] and what was probably Gambetta's reply of 21 July shows with what cool calculation

1. Report of 25 June. A.P.P., BA/917.
2. For the text, see *Discours*, vol. ii, pp. 367–93, and for a later tribute of a Bonapartist writer to 'Ce genre d'éloquence dans lequel il ne sera jamais dépassé', see J. Richard, *Le Bonapartisme sous la République* (2nd edn, Paris, 1883), p. 290.
3. Letter dated 'Jeudi' from Bourg-la-Reine (Ass. Nat., p. 17).
4. Unless it was the conversation at Versailles referred to above, p. 79.

he regarded the President:

> You must not be too quickly alarmed by the changes and half-treacheries of the greedy old man who governs us. I have always said that we must try and attach him to us, to compromise him, to be of use to him so far as is right and useful, but without alienating or abandoning anything and without being duped or blinded.
>
> He will still struggle often enough in the net which envelops him; he can still cause us many seeming setbacks, but at bottom he is powerless to disentangle himself and ruin us. . . . And if he were to betray us we've thought of this too; we have never presented him to our friends as anything but a needful auxiliary, a man condemned to help us out (*un convict*). We should change our position without difficulty and he would soon know what we were like in opposition. The wounds he has inflicted upon our democracy are still bleeding and we would have only to remove the dressing with which we have concealed them in order to rouse the sick man and make him utter cries of vengeance.[1]

A month after the deputies had dispersed another Republican anniversary fell due, 4 September, the second anniversary of the proclamation of the Republic and of the Government of National Defence. Unsympathetic to Radicalism and afraid of disturbances, Lefranc, the Minister of the Interior, sent a circular to the prefects instructing them to prohibit all banquets and public meetings on 4 September, as well as those which, 'affecting to be private, might none the less assume a public character or risk provoking . . . troubles outside'.[2] Although some Radicals wished to celebrate the anniversary, Gambetta, as he had indicated in the previous year,[3] was not among them. The *République Française*, while professing to be shocked that the Minister should give his prefects such arbitrary powers, declared that 4 September was not a day that the Republic would wish to count in the number of its festivals,[4] and to Republicans at Château Renard who had invited him to address them at a commemorative banquet, Gambetta wrote that he would rather meet them at some other time, 'not that I in any way whatsoever repudiate what took place on that memorable day, but because it was preceded and followed by events that every good Frenchman would wish to erase from our history'.[5]

Gambetta did, however, wish to celebrate the anniversary of the founding of the First Republic on 22 September. In October more

1. L.G. 'The wounds . . . ' was, of course, a reference to Thiers's suppression of the Commune.
2. The text was printed in the *R.F.* of 30 Aug.
3. See above, p. 49.
4. *R.F.*, 30 Aug., p. 1, leader.
5. *Le Soir*, 6 Sept., p. 2. Gambetta's correspondence in M.A.E., vol. 49, contains a number of letters written in August inviting him to banquets planned by Republican enthusiasts in different parts of the country.

by-elections were to be held and, with these in mind, he had shrewdly planned another 'commercial traveller's' tour, which included speaking at a commemorative banquet to be held that day at Chambéry. Did Lefranc's circular imply that he would have to cancel his tour? When he raised the question with the authorities it was referred to Thiers himself, and Thiers, who told his minister that he did not at this juncture want to have a head-on collision with Gambetta and his friends, wisely said that there should be no more circulars and indicated a compromise solution. Banquets might take place, but they must not assume the form of public meetings and the speakers should steer clear of certain subjects. In Thiers's own words, 'that these gentlemen should speak of the Republic of 1792 and other things to their taste, well and good, but what we must preserve from all attack are the Chamber and Peace. So nothing should be said about dissolution or revenge; for the rest—liberty.' He added an interesting and characteristic comment: 'We must always point out to the advanced Republicans that if we ask them to abstain more than other people it is in their interest, for their health needs it. They should remember that the Republic suffers from all their blunders and by contrast benefits from [such manifestations as the pilgrimages to] La Salette and Antwerp.'[1]

Thus Gambetta was free to embark on what was to be one of the most celebrated of his political campaigns. On the day after the compromise was reached he left Paris for a visit to the Lyonnais, Dauphiné and Savoy which lasted for nearly three weeks. He had been to the south-west in June 1871, to the north-east at Saint-Quentin in November, to Provence in January and to the west in the spring. Six departments in the east were still in German occupation and therefore forbidden ground.[2] The regions to the south-east and south-west of Lyon were important areas which he had not yet penetrated. One of the deputies of the Seine was Frédéric Dorian, a Republican colleague of Gambetta's in the Assembly and formerly Minister of Public Works in the Government of National

---

1. G. Bouniols, *Thiers au pouvoir* (1921), pp. 239–40. (Telegram of 11 Sept. from Thiers at Trouville to Lefranc at Versailles.) La Salette had become a great place of pilgrimage for French Catholics and Monarchists. Antwerp was where the Comte de Chambord had received deputations of his supporters earlier in the year. On the same day Gambetta wrote to Edouard Millaud, a Radical deputy, who was to attend a banquet at Arbresle on 22 September, telling him of the arrangement which had been reached and emphasising that one point above all must be avoided, 'c'est tout développement relatif à ce que l'on appelle "*la revanche*"'. But, it is interesting to note, the letter, as printed by Millaud in his *Le Journal d'un parlementaire*, vol. i (*de l'Empire à la République Mai 1864–Février 1875*) (1914), p. 161, makes no reference to the subject of dissolution. This letter is not in Halévy and Pillias's *Lettres*.

2. Marne and Haute-Marne (evacuated in November 1872), Ardennes, Vosges, Meuse and Meurthe (evacuated along with the canton of Belfort by 1 Aug. 1873).

Defence, who had been largely responsible for the production of arma-
ments during the war. Dorian was himself an ironmaster in the Loire
department, and this gave Gambetta a favourable opportunity to visit
many of the factories in that area. His continuance of his journey farther
east was, like the visit to Angers and the west, a deliberate reconnaissance
into enemy country, for Savoy was a region in which clerical influence
was still strong and which in January had returned a Monarchist deputy.[1]
But it was also more than this, for apart from the Revolutionary and
Napoleonic period, it had been French for only twelve years. In consequence, when the defeats of 1870 had been followed by the débâcle of
January 1871 and when the ensuing elections had opened up the prospect
of the restoration of Monarchy, some Savoyard Republicans had begun
to talk of separatism and union with Republican Switzerland. Although
nothing had come of this movement, such separatist sentiments still
existed in 1872. The idea of inviting Gambetta to Savoy at this juncture
probably emanated from one of his neighbours in no. 12 rue Montaigne,
Nicholas Parent, a prominent Chambéry lawyer, anxious to see unity
restored among Savoyard Republicans whom separatism had tended to
divide.[2]

The tour of the Loire with Dorian took five days and finished with the
banquet on 19 September at Firminy already mentioned above.[3] Thence
Gambetta went by way of St Etienne and Lyon to Chambéry in Savoy
where a local journal had rashly invited the public to come and hear
him. The result was that on the 21st, the day before it was to be held, the
Prefect of Savoie formally banned the banquet which had been arranged
as well as the meeting. Gambetta and the Republicans of Chambéry,
however, were not to be outwitted. On the one hand he insisted that the
terms of the prohibition should be strictly complied with, thus demon-
strating his wish to preserve law and order. On the other, while the
banquet had to be foregone, it was decided that as many as possible of
those who were to have taken part should be received and addressed by
Gambetta in his own suite at the Hôtel de la Poste. This was what
happened, and on the following day Gambetta made no less than five
speeches and shook the hands of five successive deputations. Moreover,
instead of a banquet on the 22nd, he was given a private dinner by local
notables on the 24th, at which he also made a speech. The prefectoral
ban had been a mistake. It helped to spread the fame of his visit and when
he went on to Albertville the next day village deputations intercepted

1. At Thonon, complained a local correspondent of the *R.F.* (4 Oct.), they had not
even got a democratic club; he had tried to form one, so far without success.
2. J. Lovie, *La Savoie dans la vie française de 1860 à 1875* (1963), p. 540.
3. See above, p. 100.

him on the way. It was no wonder that he was tired when at Albertville he had to attend a banquet and make another speech, so tired that he had to beg his audience to applaud less since their 'marks of approbation' risked interrupting his train of thought. No wonder that at Pontcharra in Isère on the 27th (after having at Grenoble on the 26th delivered at another dinner the most famous of all the speeches of this autumn campaign) he began his address with the words 'In spite of my state of fatigue as a result of my journey' or that at Thonon three days later he began with 'However tired I am . . .' and 'In spite of my state of fatigue and exhaustion, it is impossible for me not to reply. . . .' Four (brief) speeches at Thonon, two at Bonneville, one at La Roche, four at Annecy and on 2 October one at Saint-Julien, such was the final tally of the flow of oratory which had begun at Firminy and which, with explanatory matter, takes up 193 pages in the collected edition of Gambetta's speeches.[1] It was by far his greatest oratorical effort and also the most wearing. In a letter to his aunt he wrote of 'the terrible fifteen days I have just passed crossing all the valleys and mountains of Savoy'.[2] But Spuller was with him and, at the end of the tour, Gambetta's wealthy and 'excellent friend', Dubochet, came to the rescue and gave him a few days' well-earned rest in his château across the border in the Swiss canton of Vaud.

This greatest oratorical tour was also the one which made the greatest impression. It was a triumphal progress which an adorer at a distance compared to the entry of Alexander the Great into Babylon![3] At the station of Grenoble he was welcomed by a crowd of more than six thousand, at Pontcharra by two thousand. At Thonon five steamerloads of people from both shores of Lake Geneva came to see and hear him. Choirs sang and brass bands played at various points on his route. His audiences applauded him with enthusiasm and emotion, and cries of 'Vive Gambetta!' resounded along with those of 'Vive la République!' But, as on various occasions, he adjured his audiences to applaud not a man but the Republic. At Thonon and Bonneville, moreover, he effectively grasped the separatist nettle and emphasised the 'scandal' which would result from any 'further mutilation of the country'.[4]

The triumphal reception accorded to Gambetta and the scorn he incessantly heaped on the Monarchist parties, whom he declared to be

1. Vol. iii, pp. 1–193.

2. *Lettres*, no. 138.

3. Léonie Léon, undated letter to Gambetta from Bourg-la-Reine, beginning in English 'My dear love' (Ass. Nat., p. 19).

4. See especially *Discours*, vol. iii, pp. 132–8 (in which Gambetta astutely made immense emotional play with France's misfortunes—e.g. 'la France que, dans sa défaite, on calomnie, que l'on outrage; oh ! cette France-là, je l'aime comme on aime une mère') and 146–52.

finished and no longer of any account—henceforward there would be only two real parties, the Republican democrats and the great enemy, the clerical party[1]—both preoccupied and infuriated the members of the Right. Moreover, despite his reiterated efforts to present his own party as the true party of order and to divest Radicalism of any alarming implications,[2] many moderate men such as General Chanzy and Jules Grévy were concerned by this autumn progress.[3] Above all, it was a speech at Grenoble which gave alarm: it worried conservatively minded men in France, including Thiers himself, and it confirmed the prejudices of those in Germany and elsewhere who believed that the advent of Gambetta to power would endanger both social order and peace.

1. See especially the speeches at Bonneville and St-Julien, *ibid.*, pp. 142, 145 and 191. At Bonneville he declared that the touchstone for genuine Republicanism was acceptance of free, compulsory, secular education (*ibid.*, p. 144).

2. e.g. at Chambéry, *ibid.*, p. 63.

3. In a letter to H. Pessard, Chanzy declared that Gambetta's tour was harmful to the cause he claimed to serve. All had been going well and now Gambetta was making the Republicans into a sect which put the triumph of its own political opinions before the interests of the country (Pessard, *Mes petits papiers*, vol. ii, pp. 284–5).

10

The Grenoble speech and its aftermath
October–December 1872

'An incident which at many moments in these sixty years would have seemed ordinary enough had very different consequences. It was a speech by Gambetta, the importance of which did not exceed that of a newspaper article.' Thus wrote Rémusat in his memoirs[1] later on, while Hector Pessard, another close associate of Thiers, looking back, remarked: 'Today the Grenoble harangue would be a blancmange, a white cream sauce for our cloyed palates, but in 1872, this speech, sprinkled with Cayenne pepper, stuck in the throats of the men of Versailles.'[2]

The deputies of the Right were indeed furious and their Press was loud in denunciation.[3] The *Gaulois* demanded Gambetta's prosecution, the *Univers* declared that he stood for drunkenness and corrupt bargains and that he was the incarnation of false reports and cynical histrionics. Even the sober *Journal des Débats* commented: 'Scratch the demagogue and you will find a slave and a tyrant.' The abuse hurled against him in Paris and Versailles was echoed in the provinces. For the *Journal du Maine-et-Loire* 'the briefless barrister of the Empire had never succeeded in anything except the demonstration of his incapacity and folly'; for the *Echo de la Dordogne* the speech was 'essentially revolutionary, tyrannical and Jacobin'; for the *Union du Sud-Ouest* the speech 'of this third-rate café orator' was dangerous; 'any ambitious grocer could now dream that his son might exercise sovereign power'; while for the *Journal de Bordeaux* 'the dictator' was preparing civil war; he was 'a disturber of the peace who ought to be locked up'.

What had Gambetta said to merit such obloquy? In fact, the speech contained little that was new. It was the manner in which he had enlarged on certain themes, the vigour or humorous scorn with which he

1. Charles de Rémusat, *Mémoires de ma vie*, vol. v (Paris n.d.), p. 422.
2. Pessard, *Mes petits papiers, deuxième série 1871–1873*, p. 284.
3. For these quotations, see Kayser, *Les Grandes batailles du radicalisme*, pp. 60–1.

had amplified them, that made the sensation. In the autumnal calm of the parliamentary vacation his words resounded like a thunderclap and heralded fresh storms.[1]

Once again he had refuted the charge that his party was the party of disorder. Once again he had ridiculed the restrictions on freedom of speech and meeting—'What is democracy if men are cooped-up and subjected to a prison-like regime?' If fifteen hundred people were not allowed to meet because their gathering together constituted a public meeting, while three hundred could, the effect was the same. What was said in the meeting of three hundred was bound to be repeated and published abroad. The authorities might put their hands over the light, but light filtered through their fingers. In a republic such proceedings, which could only engender moral disorder, must be abandoned. Yet there were still people unwilling to recognise the consequences of the French Revolution and that Monarchy was in all its forms condemned and finished. But Gambetta did not leave his reference to such people at that. He drove home his point in a way that infuriated many of his readers: 'It is in the lack of courage and resolution of a notable part of the French bourgeoisie that I find the origin and explanation of all our misfortunes and weaknesses and of all that is still uncertain, hesitant and unhealthy in present-day politics.' How, he asked, could such people be so obstinate, how could they shut their eyes to the emergence since the fall of the Empire of a new and eager generation which had begun to take part in local affairs? This attack on the bourgeoisie was the prelude to the development of one of those points in his speech which were to create such a furore, the point already made unobtrusively in his letter of October 1871 on General Councils.[2] It was here that he delivered himself of the famous passage and the famous phrase subsequently quoted in innumerable speeches and books:

> Had they [the bourgeoisie] failed to see a new personnel, a new political electorate appear all over the country ... ? Had they not seen the workers of town and country, the working world[3] to whom the future belongs make its entry into politics? Did not their entry give notice that, after having tried many forms of

1. For the text see *Discours*, vol. iii, pp. 88–120. The *R.F.* printed it in full on 2 Oct. in place of its usual leader.

2. See above, p. 48.

3. As M. Pierre Barral has pointed out this phrase of Gambetta—'ce monde du travail' is ambiguous, but 'dans l'acceptation positiviste', it was not limited to working men but extended 'aux patrons, aux artisans, aux commerçants, à tous ceux qui exercent une activité professionnelle' (*Les Fondateurs de la Troisième République*, 1968, p. 230, n. 1). In July 1873 he again used the words in this sense, referring to the new social strata as ... 'ce monde qui est heureusement arrivé non seulement au travail, à la propriété, mais à la capacité politique'.

government, the country was turning to another social stratum in order to experiment with the Republican form? (Yes! Yes!—prolonged sensation.) Yes, I foresee, I feel, I announce the coming and the presence in politics of a new social stratum which has been taking its part in politics for some eighteen months and which, to be sure, is far from being inferior to its predecessors.[1]

'A new social stratum'—this in particular was the phrase which caused so much controversy and which soon became part of the political vocabulary. Instead of judging this new personnel at work, Gambetta continued, the Monarchist parties cried out at the triumph of radicalism and sought to alarm the country and exploit its fears, 'for fear, Gentlemen', he exclaimed, as would many French writers ninety-six years later, 'is the chronic disease of France—political fear'. Since this exploitation of fear was their enemies' resource, the Republican party must cure France of this disease: once again the remedy must be prudence (*la sagesse*) and refusal to be provoked. For the moment there was only one thing to be done, it was to behave peacefully and legally, invoking universal suffrage, whose will to transform the embryo Republic into one that was definitive, genuine and progressive could not long be delayed. So Gambetta came to two of the other points which so infuriated the Right. The reactionaries, he first of all declared, had loudly proclaimed the need for an immediate restoration of the Monarchy with 'fusion'; they had abandoned this, first for a moderate Monarchy without 'fusion', then for a loyal trial of the Republic, but of a Republic without Republicans, then for a conservative Republic and now they were talking of a constitutional Republic. What did this mean? That dissolution was at hand: 'For if they were not convinced that dissolution was there, like the grave-digger ready to throw a last spadeful of earth on the corpse of the Assembly of Versailles ... you may be sure that they would not talk of this marriage *in extremis* with the Republic.' Secondly, while he recognised that compromises and adjustments were necessary in politics, for no healthy society could result from a clean sweep, Republicans must beware of those who climbed on the bandwagon at the last moment, men who might do what had been done twenty-two years earlier and 'take the Republic, set it upon a chariot, adorn it with flowers and lead it to fall beneath some aristocratic butcher's knife'. (Profound sensation—prolonged applause.) So in the next elections he would like it to be understood that only those who offered sufficient guarantees should be admitted to the Republican lists: 'You see, Gentlemen, my idea is to separate the leaders from their so-called army; the army can enter the ranks of the

1. *Discours*, vol. iii, p. 101.

democratic party but, as was the way with the early Christians, the leaders must be left for a while to do penance at the door of the Church.' (Approving laughter—Applause.)

Dissolution—he had often demanded it before—but to proclaim its imminence in this way, to assert that the Assembly was a corpse, to appeal to a new social stratum to replace it and to veto the admission of distinguished men of the Right into the Republican ranks, this was too much! This was, as Broglie later wrote, 'a veritable provocation to rebellion against our authority and our laws'.[1] And Broglie was all the more irritated because Gambetta had so trenchantly denounced his own stratagem. Crestfallen at their discomfiture when they had waited on Thiers in June, Monarchists like Broglie had decided to retaliate by offering to recognise the Republican form of government 'at least for the moment', provided that Thiers agreed to make an outspoken break with Radical principles. 'At least for the moment', wrote Broglie later, for it was important 'to find a means of giving the Republic only a temporary existence, that is to say of opening the door legally and easily for the restoration of Monarchy should circumstances become more favourable'.[2] But Gambetta had seen through these machinations of which the *République Française* had had wind as early as mid-September. 'Today', he had declared, 'people seek to employ the same means as the Liberal Empire . . . We have been told that . . . the Monarchist party has asserted that it wanted the Republic. . . . Ah, Gentlemen, for the sake of our honour and our safety, for the honour and greatness of our country, beware of being taken in by such an ignoble comedy.'[3]

Such was the speech which created such a furore. It was viewed with disfavour by many moderate Republicans including the President of the Assembly himself, Jules Grévy, who was reported to have remarked that it confirmed his opinion that Gambetta was 'a below-average politician who floated on the surface only because he was empty'.[4] In these circumstances the Right were given a fresh opportunity to try to drive a wedge between Thiers and Gambetta, whom they still suspected of being in

1. *Mémoires*, ii, p. 123. The alarm was such that, according to a police report of 30 Sept., Isambert of the *R.F.* was instructed to write to moderate Republican groups in the departments to assure them that 'M. Gambetta n'a pas cessé d'être un homme de gouvernement et pour les mettre en garde contre les interprétations intéressées des monarchistes' (A.P.P., BA/917).

2. *Mémoires*, pp. 119, 121.

3. *Discours*, vol. ii, p. 117.

4. Pessard, *op. cit.*, p. 285. Cf. Cambon (*Correspondance*, vol. i, p. 37), letter of 5 Oct. to Casimir-Périer, in which he said about Gambetta that the Grenoble speech had proved 'ce que savaient déjà tous ceux qui le connaissent, à savoir qu'il n'aura l'étoffe d'un homme d'état'. Cambon was at this time Prefect of the Aube.

collusion.[1] Their first move was to rouse the Permanent Commission of the Assembly which met fortnightly at Versailles and held a kind of watching brief during parliamentary vacations. Thiers, to his irritation, had to interrupt his holiday at Trouville in order to answer the Commission's questions concerning Gambetta's tour. On 18 October in the privacy of the Commission's meeting place he could afford to express his disapproval and to appease the Right. The speech, he declared, 'was a bad one, very bad'. It was regrettable 'from the point of view of those who think that the existing form of government is the only one possible and it has been more of a setback for the Republic than any that could be effected by the handiwork of its enemies'.[2] In particular, he attacked Gambetta's phrase about the new social stratum:

> I do not admit of class distinctions. . . . To make distinctions within the nation is to provoke class war. There are only Frenchmen, citizens who are to be distinguished from one another only by their merit and their wisdom. The man who distinguishes between classes in such a way as to rely on one alone becomes a factious and dangerous person. Had Parliament been sitting I should have attacked the Grenoble speech with all my power.[3]

The disdain with which Thiers voiced his disapproval delighted the Duc de Broglie, whom it reminded 'of the best days of Thiers's fight against demagogic passions in 1849'.[4]

This and similar attacks by Right-wing papers and speakers necessitated a defence and the *République Française* hastened to explain that by the term 'new social stratum' 'the leader of the Left had merely wished to state a well-known fact, namely the capacity shown since their advent into politics by the men who had been excluded from it before 1848 and who had subsequently refused to play a part in the shameful tragi-comedy of the government of December'.[5] Nine months later Gambetta personally defended his expression in the Assembly after a Right-wing deputy had referred to a party, which had 'excited certain social strata against the so-called ruling classes. The new social strata'—he now employed the plural—had, he explained, been 'created by the French Revolution' and had gradually become more aware of their identity with the help of

1. For the *Guienne* of Bordeaux 'Gambetta et sa secte ne sont que le produit logique du sophisme révolutionnaire que personnifie M. Thiers' (*cit.* Kayser, *op. cit.*, p. 62).
2. This was virtually the phrase already used by the *Bien Public*, Thiers's paper, on 2 Oct.
3. Quoted in Dreyfus, *La République de M. Thiers*, p. 262.
4. *Mémoires*, vol. ii, p. 123.
5. 16 Oct.

universal suffrage. Each electoral system corresponded to a social system.[1]
Later still, at Auxerre in 1874, he would give a much fuller explanation
of this view of France's social development.[2]

Meanwhile Thiers's remarks to the Permanent Commission in October
1872 did not mean that Thiers was surrendering to the Right. As the
République Française pointed out, what was important was the reply
Thiers was reported to have given to the Duc de Rochefoucauld-Bisaccia:
'Since you have just uttered the words "Conservative Republic", I take
the opportunity to say "Yes, henceforward the Republic is a necessity
for this country. People are free to be Monarchists but serious men cannot
conceive of any form of government other than the Republic." '[3]

In his recent speeches it was noteworthy that Gambetta had carefully
abstained from any reference to Thiers until at Annecy on 1 October the
organiser of the meeting had given the toast of 'two great citizens of the
French Republic: Thiers and Gambetta'. Then Gambetta had had no
choice but to associate himself with the toast to Thiers, saying that he was
happy to drink first to the Republic and then to its President, whom he
described as 'this experienced, witty, resourceful old man who is so
familiar with the difficulties of politics, so amazingly active and full of
ardour for the public good, so quick in comprehending the trend of
public opinion, so wise in the measures by which he suggests resolving the
difficulties which present themselves'. What Thiers thought of this
encomium we do not know, but a few days later in a letter to an important and very recent recruit to Republicanism, Casimir-Périer, he condemned the Radicals and passed a memorable judgement on Gambetta,
by whose conduct he professed to be relatively unconcerned:

> M. Gambetta is as you depict him. At one moment he wants to make his advent
> to power possible and he adopts the language and the wariness of a man capable
> of governing, then he fears losing his followers and he makes the Grenoble
> speech twice over (*a deux éditions*), but he will never have the decided views of a
> real statesman. His evolutions are not yet finished. We shall see him again in the
> guise of a man of government, but he will always fall back into the role of a
> tribune imposed upon him by his party, a role that he plays more naturally than
> the other. He has done the country a little harm during these recent days, but it is
> only a passing harm while he has done himself much more. Credit has suffered a
> little and Europe has been alarmed, but all that will pass.[4]

Thiers's confidence could appear justified, despite such temporary
vexations. He, like the well-known writer Daniel Stern (the Comtesse

1. 12 July 1873 (*Ass. Nat. A.*, vol. xix, pp. 141–4).
2. See below, pp. 198–9.
3. *R.F.*, 11 Oct.
4. Bouniols, *Thiers au pouvoir*, p. 257 (letter of 7 Oct.).

d'Agoult), might still have good reason for satisfaction. An English visitor to Paris could still remark on 'the ghastly gutted look' of the ruins left by the Commune as seen by gaslight,[1] but in a letter to Emile Ollivier the Comtesse wrote of the 'daily improvements' in the state of the country.

> Our debts are paid, the harvests are splendid, people are setting to work again with a will and moderate opinions manifestly prevail—all this is a counterweight to the Lourdes pilgrimages, the Grenoble banquets, the intrigues of the discontented. . . . After this disastrous war I was prepared for plague, famine, bankruptcy and the rest. We are flourishing; we are eating again; we pay our taxes; there is order in the streets if not in men's minds.[2]

The results of the further by-elections of 20 October, which had been one of the reasons for Gambetta's recent tour, were also satisfactory from the Republicans' point of view. Once again, except in the strongly conservative Morbihan, the Monarchists were discomfited and five out of the six vacant seats were won by Republicans, Thierist or Radical. Attempts at electoral cooperation by the Right Centre with the Left Centre had come to nothing and the *République Française* could declare that if, 'as is possible, the Grenoble speech has prevented what has been called "the conjunction of the Centres", if it has nipped this formidable intrigue in the bud, then the Grenoble speech was a masterly stroke'. There would now, it said, be 'no more monarchy, whether Caesarian, traditional or parliamentary in the manner of 1830'; what had emerged was 'the definitive Republic without ambiguity or reservations . . . the elections . . . will, we are sure, encourage the first magistrate of the Republic [i.e. Thiers] to act . . . he must now choose: will he opt for the Assembly, will he opt for France?'[3]

Thiers's answer would be given in his presidential message of 13 November at the opening of the new session. Meanwhile the Pretender at Frohsdorff had, in the words of *The Times*, again come before the French nation 'with the same imperturbable insistence with which the ancient Sibyl . . . stood in the presence of the Roman Monarch'.[4] He had dealt a blow to Broglie's policy by issuing a new directive absolutely forbidding his followers to associate themselves with the proclamation of a Republic: 'To cling to the illusion of a moderate and sincere Republic would be to forget the warnings of Providence and the lessons of the

---

1. A. Mackie, *Italy and France. An editor's holiday* (1874), pp. 320 and 365.
2. Jacques Vier, *La Comtesse d'Agoult et son temps*, vol. vi (1963), pp. 44–5 (letter of 15 Oct.).
3. *R.F.*, leader of 23 Oct.
4. *The Times*, 23 Oct., p. 9.

June days of 1848.' A moderate conservative Republic was, however, what Thiers himself was now more than ever determined on, for it was what he was convinced the country wanted. But it must be definitive and without *arrière-pensées*. So in his message he made his choice:

> The Republic exists; it is the legal government of the country; to want something else would constitute a new Revolution of the kind most of all to be feared. Do not let us waste our time in proclaiming the Republic, but let us employ our time in giving it the characteristics which are necessary and desirable. ... The Republic will be conservative or it will not exist.

The Left loudly applauded this unequivocal reaffirmation of Thiers's Republican convictions. The *République Française* declared that he had cut the cable and had never been better inspired: 'Happy the men, who on certain days of their lives, can thus interpret the wishes of a whole people.'[1] Conversely the Right, for all Thiers's emphasis on Conservatism, were furious at what appeared to be the final breach of the Pact of Bordeaux. Thiers had betrayed them. For Broglie, his words were so many 'drops of burning oil upon an open wound'.[2] Henceforward the Right would be on the offensive and, unless Thiers could be brought to reason, would force his overthrow. It remained only to determine the opportune moment and to be sure of a successor on whom they could rely.

Thus the message of 13 November was a crucial utterance and inaugurated a new period of crisis, a period in which stormy debates within the Assembly were appropriately matched by winter storms and floods without. The immediate tactics of the Right were first of all to exploit the Radical bogey to the utmost and secondly to curtail Thiers's influence by restricting his freedom to intervene in the Assembly's debates.

So far as Radicalism was concerned, they seized again on Gambetta's now famous Grenoble speech and made it one of the chief weapons in their arsenal. One prong of their attack was thrust home on the 18th, when the vain and octogenarian Orleanist General Changarnier[3] demanded that the government should wholly dissociate itself from a 'factious' man—a colleague who was disposed to overthrow everything in order to resume 'a disastrous dictatorship, the return of which would ruin France for ever'. He was later followed by Broglie who venomously asserted that it was on 18 March 1871 that the new social stratum had appeared, 'and the wretches who represented it were so mediocre and

---

1. *R.F.* leader of 15 Nov.
2. *Mémoires*, vol. ii, p. 126.
3. 'Mon pauvre ami Changarnier', wrote Rémusat, 'n'était plus qu'un vieillard prétentieux et dénudé' (*op. cit.* vol. v, p. 427).

vile that they have not succeeded in engraving their names in our memories even though they wrote them with fire and blood on our walls'. The Grenoble speech was, he declared, 'a great, an immense scandal. A man has set himself up before you and said to this Assembly, the sole legal power in the country: "you no longer exist".' Thiers had vigorously condemned such scandalous doctrine in the Permanent Commission. He should now repeat the condemnation in the Assembly so that the whole of France might know of it and applaud. Such a summons, however, profoundly irritated Thiers. In an impassioned reply he refused to repeat the condemnation and demanded a vote of confidence. The demand was granted, but the motion eventually supported by the Government none the less contained an explicit disapproval 'of the doctrines professed at Grenoble'. In consequence, the extreme Left and part of the Left as well as some other deputies abstained from supporting it. The government's majority of 263 votes to 116 with 277 abstentions was regarded as a setback for Thiers. As the *République Française* had already remarked, he could no longer be sure of not being put in a minority,[1] but, it had added, 'he can be sure of the majority of the country; there only remains one thing to be done, to liberate the country and to consult the wishes of France by means of general elections'.

This new political crisis caused widespread anxiety and swelled the crowds at Versailles and the Gare St Lazare. On the evening following the debate in which he had been so vigorously attacked, a throng of Gambetta's supporters gathered in the Salle des Pas Perdus to show him their sympathy on his return from Versailles. Estimated at several hundred, when he arrived at the end of the hall they 'formed into two lines, respectfully uncovering before him—a manifestation which the young Dictator duly acknowledged by walking hat in hand between them'. This little scene, reported by *The Times*[2], was early and moving testimony to Radical discipline.

Meanwhile the Assembly had also begun to launch its attack on the powers of the President of the Republic. It had appointed a commission containing a majority of members from the Right and Right Centre to consider what reply if any should be made to the presidential message of 13 November.[3] The report produced by its *rapporteur*, Batbie, was also a renewed and ferocious attack on Radicalism. In the words of Daniel Halévy, it was 'above all perhaps a reply to the speech of Grenoble.

1. R.F., leader of 15 Nov.
2. 23 Nov.
3. Rémusat pointed out that the motion to appoint such a commission would have been rejected had not Thiers misjudged the situation and said he accepted it: 'Cette faute de tactique eut les plus grandes conséquences' (*op. cit.*, pp. 426–7).

Gambetta had outlawed the ruling classes and, speaking in their name, Batbie demanded the outlawing of radicalism.'[1] 'Far from being a party in our eyes', he declared, 'radicalism [*sic*] is the enemy of all respectable parties. How could this faction, whose audacious formula [i.e. Gambetta's 'nouvelle couche sociale' and his refusal to accept recruits 'de la dernière heure'] outlaws all who are an obstacle in its path, return within the bounds of political impartiality?' He demanded a fighting government (*gouvernement de combat*) to resist its progress.[2] The majority of the Commission, moreover, considered that the cause of the existing political malaise lay in the personal participation of the President in the Assembly's debates and they therefore proposed the appointment of a commission of fifteen to prepare a Bill on ministerial responsibility. There were many who expected that Thiers would resign rather than take such unpalatable medicine. But instead of doing so, Thiers, through his Minister of Justice, the experienced septuagenarian Dufaure, put forward a counterproposal. In return for the limitation of the President's powers the Assembly should set to work and tackle the constitutional problem as well as that of ministerial responsibility. After a heated debate, in which Gambetta preserved a masterly silence while Thiers again threw himself into the mêlée with passionate zeal, Dufaure's proposal won the day by 372 votes to 335. This narrow victory for the government would not have been possible without the support of the Left. Gambetta had, in a sense, come to the rescue of Thiers, in spite of the harsh things said about the doctrines of Grenoble by Thiers and his government; this, noted a Monarchist observer, was 'the grave factor in the situation'.[3] 'Everyone in France', wrote Broglie, in his *Mémoires*, 'thought that all was over and that the Republic had been made by Thiers's alliance with the Radicals.'[4] The vote of 29 November was indeed a crucial one, for Thiers had forced the Monarchists against their will to face the task of constitution-making which they claimed as their right, but which was a right whose exercise they still wished to evade. Yet Gambetta was as ever opposed to any admission of the Assembly's constituent power. 'So you want to make a constitution', he exclaimed one day to a deputy of the Left Centre, Marcère, 'you are making a great mistake. You will get the government into a defile it won't be able to get out of.' 'Bah!' answer Marcère, 'we will widen the defile.' When Marcère recounted this exchange to Thiers, the latter's comment was that Gambetta feared for his own position.[5]

1. *La Fin des Notables*, pp. 204–5.
2. For Batbie's speech, see *Ass. Nat. A.*, vol. xiv, pp. 254–8.
3. C. de B., (Rothschild pp.) letter of 30 Nov. 1872.
4. p. 133.
5. Marcère, *L'Assemblée Nationale de 1871*, p. 275.

In the meantime, the *République Française* had on 25 November announced the imminent publication of a collection of the speeches Gambetta had delivered in Savoy. The volume, which was to cost two francs, contained a prefatory 'Note by the Publishers' which the *République Française* thought fit to reproduce *in extenso*. The interest of the speeches, the note pointed out, transcended the immediate circumstances in which they had been delivered.

It can be said that the collection . . . is a sort of summary of the questions which will in an undoubted future inevitably be called upon to appear in the election manifestoes (*professions de foi*) and programmes of candidates who seek the support of the Republican voters, and nothing can be of greater use to the electors than to prepare them in this way for the electoral battle which an early dissolution of the Assembly will necessitate. M. Gambetta's speeches aim not only at warning the democratic party of the traps to be avoided but they also show how the party should act in order to enter into peaceful and regular possession of this legal authority which will enable the Republic to be established for all time. . . . The Republican orator has provided the models for the speeches and addresses that all good citizens devoted to the cause of the Republic can and should deliver in the clubs they attend and the meetings they can organise. . . . In this respect . . . the collection is of unmistakable interest and it is not excessive to claim that it is a veritable manual of Republican propaganda.[1]

Thus, as ever, Gambetta and his friends were mindful of propagating their aims with an eye to elections and the verdict of universal suffrage. The Bonapartist 'Fidus' noted in his journal in the fourth week of November that the Radicals were far from having lost courage:

The petitioning for dissolution continues more actively than ever and in a few weeks, in accordance with M. Gambetta's threats, six or seven million signatures will be presented and the Assembly will be summoned to retire. M. Thiers is secretly backing this movement and is preparing to profit by it: in the new elections he is believed to intend to be a candidate in all eighty-six departments at once.[2]

Fidus was wrong in his estimate of the number of signatures that would be obtained—Gambetta himself did not claim that there were more than

1. The correspondent who reported to the *République Française* on Gambetta's tour in Savoy wrote that he had heard the wish expressed that Gambetta's speeches there should be published as a brochure (*R.F.*, 6 Oct., p. 2). C. de B. asserted in his letter of 19 Nov. that the Radical party was about to print and put on sale a cheap edition of a million copies of Gambetta's speeches to be sold at ten centimes.

2. *Journal de Fidus*, vol. iii, p. 135.

just over a million[1]—but he was almost certainly right in believing that the petition campaign was secretly backed by Thiers, for the *Siècle*, whose political director, Leblond, was in frequent contact with Thiers, now took the initiative in organising it. Naturally Radical papers such as the *République Française* and the *Rappel* were zealous in support. Then, early in December, certain parliamentary groups began to take a hand; on the 10th the Republican Union, now under the presidency of Louis Blanc, met and issued a manifesto calling for dissolution and new elections, the only remedy, it claimed, for a political crisis which was having serious economic repercussions. This manifesto was printed in place of its customary leader by the *République Française* on the 12th, together with a request that provincial papers should copy it, and it was reprinted again on the 14th.[2] On the same day, at the instance of a deputy of the Right Centre, the Assembly debated the petitions.

Thus far in the new session the greatest orator in France, the man whose speeches and principles had given rise to such political ferment, had kept silence. But now, as was fitting for one who had been a foremost advocate of dissolution for more than a year, he opened the debate in a speech which lasted more than two hours, held the attention of the house, despite many interruptions, and was notable for the moderation of its language. Even Rémusat conceded that his argument was 'really shrewd' (*politique*), even a Monarchist opponent admitted that it was 'closely knit, logical and adroit; the style was often bad; there were faulty passages, incoherences and impossible phrases, but all this was secondary and this speech was powerfully constructed and devoid of empty rhetoric'.[3] The main burden of Gambetta's argument was twofold—the Assembly had no mandate to act as a constituent body and it had reached such a pitch of ineffectiveness that it was powerless to create a stable majority, no matter what the parliamentary stratagems to which it might resort. It could only prolong the state of crisis due to uncertainty of the morrow. He had no doubt that it might muster many votes against dissolution, but this could not prove that it was agreed on government organisation or on reforms, but only that it was agreed not to die. The country, he declared, reacted to the proposed 'gouvernement de combat' in a spirit of conservatism, 'conservation' was a word which was not the monopoly of any one party. As for the Radicals—and this was the part of his speech which, according to a

1. C. de B. alleged that no more than 300,000 people had signed and that these included minors, criminals and illiterates (Rothschild pp., letter of 27 Dec. 1972).

2. The *R.F.*, also printed an appeal to all Republicans to sign the petitions; this appeared every day from 16–22 Dec. inclusive.

3. *Op. cit.*, p. 433; Charles Chesnelong, letter of 15 Dec. to Joseph Chesnelong, in Chesnelong, *Les Derniers jours de l'Empire et le gouvernement de M. Thiers*, pp. 229–30.

British Embassy observer, attracted the most attention[1]—the Radicals who had been so much decried were 'simply Republicans who think that the Republic is the only form of government compatible with universal suffrage; who are ready to defer to the will of the country so long as it is not with them, but who believe that if the country is consulted the victory of the Republic will emerge'. Outside the Assembly people said that the one real issue at stake was the policy outlined in Thiers's message and, as the Assembly was not truly in harmony with this policy, the country would continue to demand dissolution. 'I know well that you will resist, Gentlemen, but the resistance of besieged towns and Assemblies has a limit.' The need for a new Assembly rested on three basic considerations; material interests—the interests of business, the interests of France's foreign policy—patriotic interests, and the need to put an end to rumours such as those of an imminent *coup d'état*. The day was not far off

> when you will decide to sacrifice yourselves because the people who have sent you here will themselves warn you and tell you that your vote today and your subsequent votes on the new petitions they will send you will be votes preparatory to future elections. On that day universal suffrage will know how to recognise its own and how to choose between those who have delayed and those who have helped to prepare the definitive triumph of the Republic.[2]

Gambetta sat down amidst repeated applause from the Left and such uproar on the Right that the session had to be briefly suspended. This was only the beginning of a debate which extended to a night session and in which another formidable and eloquent onslaught on radicalism was launched, this time by the Duc d'Audiffret Pasquier, who spoke, he said, as a Liberal. The Radicals, said Pasquier, were a party who undermined the essential bases of society; they believed in the most dangerous and revolutionary theory in the world, that of the sovereignty of numbers 'regardless of the inherent rights' of human personality. This was a theory which led to the brutal despotism of the multitude and they were a party who attacked religion, family, property and *Patrie*. He rejected them not because he was a Monarchist but because he was a Liberal.[3]

Gambetta was right in prophesying that his enemies would muster a large number of votes against the petitions. They were rejected by the very substantial majority of 483 to 196, a majority which many at the

1. P.R.O., F.O. 146, 1609, report of 15 Dec. by Mr Lee Hamilton.
2. For the text, see *Ass. Nat. A.*, vol. xiv, pp. 561–73, and *Discours*, vol. iii, pp. 225–267. On the 17th the R.F. issued a special supplement which reprinted Gambetta's speech from the *Journal Officiel*.
3. For the text of the Duke's speech see *Ass. Nat. A.*, vol. xiv, pp. 573–9.

offices of the *République Française* found disconcerting, for they had hoped that the Left Centre would support the petitions. But Gambetta, 'always', as Freycinet said, 'confident or wishing to appear so', told his followers that the number of votes mattered little. 'The bell has sounded', he said, 'they will come to it.'[1] What was indicative, however, of a new twist in the political labyrinth was the fact that the government of Thiers, the man who had secretly encouraged the petitions, now condemned them. Dufaure, once again its spokesman, and a master of sarcasm, alluded derisively to Gambetta in a reference to 'travelling personages' and declared that dissolution was synonymous with agitation.[2] In Broglie's view, he had 'really floored' Gambetta who remained glued to his place while the Assembly applauded Dufaure.[3] No wonder that at a meeting of the Republican Union on the 17th Dufaure's speech was fiercely criticised. But the Assembly had marked its approval by voting that it should be posted up in every commune.[4]

The fact was that in the precarious situation in which he had been placed both by the Grenoble speech and by his own message, Thiers was more than ever obliged to perform a balancing act. In order to facilitate the final negotiations with Germany for the liberation of the territory he had to emphasise the conservatism of his policy; in order to play for time and to maintain his position as long as he could he had to placate the Right. At the end of November the Right, in forcing the resignation of Lefranc, the Minister of the Interior, had brought about a fresh crisis and Thiers himself more than once thought of resigning.[5] Alarmed by this prospect, however, the Left had rallied round him and on Sunday, 1 December a deputation of sixty of its members had waited upon him to express their sympathy and support. At half past twelve that night, according to *The Times* correspondent,

> M. Gambetta might have been seen pacing anxiously up and down the 'salon [*sic*] des pas perdus' [i.e. at the Gare St Lazare] . . . waiting for the arrival of his

1. Freycinet, *Souvenirs 1848–1878*, pp. 295–6.
2. According to C. de B. (Rothschild pp., letter of 13 Dec.) Thiers was ready to support an 'ordre du jour' condemning dissolution, provided that the Commission of Thirty agreed to discuss constitutional proposals before it discussed ministerial responsibility.
3. *Mémoires*, p. 134.
4. *R.F.*, 18 Nov. 1872. Not to be outdone and, as ever, mindful of the value of propaganda, Gambetta and Louis Blanc, the other main defender of radicalism during the debate, had their speeches reprinted in pamphlet form, Gambetta's being published by Ernest Leroux at fifteen centimes.
5. According to Rémusat (*op. cit.*, p. 432), Thiers went so far as to show him a draft message of resignation which he had written, but 'le lendemain, il semblait n'y plus penser (6 décembre)'.

friends to hear from them the result of their audience, for the Radicals are in fear lest the President may break the last link that binds him to them. . . . Gambetta waiting for the report of his friends, appears in the position of some brigand chief, whose prisoner is allowed to live at home on a payment of blackmail.[1]

Thiers, however, did not pay blackmail. What he said to the deputation is not recorded, but instead of rewarding the Left for their support on 29 November he veered to the Right and modified his cabinet in such a way as to give it something of the guise of a government of combat. In particular, he transferred a member of the Right Centre, Goulard, to the key post of Minister of the Interior and removed from the office of Under Secretary in that department a man named Calmon who was suspected of Radical sympathies.[2] This government would before long go into action and, by administrative and legislative measures particularly distasteful to the Radicals, force Gambetta to reconsider his attitude to the Conservative Republic and the 'old stadtholder'[3] who presided over it. But immediately Gambetta expressed satisfaction. The new ministry, he said, was a 'little chef d'oeuvre of the maître Scapin who governs us'. Thiers had played his game admirably. There was no need to worry. ' "Le Pouvoir" will be our hidden ally as in the past.'[4] This notion was curiously reflected in a letter written four days earlier by one great literary figure to another. 'If the bourgeoisie were to be consulted now', Gustave Flaubert told George Sand, 'it would make Father Thiers King of France. Were Thiers to be removed it would throw itself into the arms of Gambetta.'[5] As for Thiers, in one of his witty moments he had simply said of himself and his 'reformed cabinet': 'I oscillate, my ministers see-saw.'[6]

---

1. *The Times*, 4 Dec., p. 10.
2. P.R.O., F.O. 146, 160, Lyons to Granville, 10 Dec. 1872.
3. 'The Stadtholder', 'the Pensionary', or the 'Grand Pensionary' were names frequently given by Gambetta to Thiers in the autumn and the winter of 1872–73: see e.g. *Lettres*, no. 141.
4. Letter of 8 Dec. to Léonie Léon (L.G.).
5. Gustave Flaubert, *Correspondance*, vol. vi (1930), p. 457.
6. *The Times*, 23 Dec., p. 7.

11

The Constitution and the
Radical tide
December 1872–May 1873

Apart from his speech of 14 December 1872 demanding the dissolution of the Assembly and a little-known interview given to a correspondent of the *New York Herald* early in January, the four months following Gambetta's tour of Savoy and Dauphiné were months in which he was still more silent than in the previous winter; silent everywhere, as Daniel Halévy remarked, silent both within the Assembly and without.[1] In these months he delivered only that one political speech and wrote only one letter that has been preserved. He was, as he explained in it, condemned by 'the cruel goddess of Politics' who commanded his life, to remain in Paris, keeping an hourly watch on Thiers, on the 'Thirty Tyrants' as he called the newly elected constitutional Commission, and watch, too, on his dissolutionist friends. So he could not escape to Nice and visit his father during the Christmas recess.[2] Politics and the *République Française*, as always, absorbed him. But other sources provide a few scattered glimpses of other activities, of his going early in November with Freycinet to visit the chocolate manufacturer Menier on his estate in Seine-et-Marne,[3] of his talking about the general situation one day a little later to the English Radical Charles Bradlaugh,[4] and of his speaking on 5 January 1873 at a dinner in honour of Littré's completion of his celebrated *Dictionary of the French Language*.[5] They show him busy learning German, probably still from the former Danish agent, Jules Hansen,[6] confined to

1. *La Fin des Notables*, p. 213.
2. *Lettres*, no. 139.
3. A.P.P., Carton BA/917, 71800, report of 12 Nov. 1872.
4. *Ibid.*, report of 19 Nov. Perhaps this was the occasion, reported by Bradlaugh's daughter in her biography of her father, when the two men had an argument about anticlericalism 'which went far into the night' (H. B. Bonner, *Charles Bradlaugh*, 2nd edn, 1895, vol. i, p. 331).
5. For the text, see *R.F.*, 8 Jan. 1873, p. 3.
6. *New York Herald*, 27 Jan. 1873; Hansen, *Les Coulisses de la diplomatie*, p. 247.

bed for a while in January by an attack of bronchitis, and one day taking time to listen to a young philosopher of later fame, Fouillée, being examined on his thesis at the Sorbonne.[1] He found time, too, for other young men of ability such as the future ambassador, August Gérard, who was just beginning a three-year spell at the Ecole Normale. Gérard used to see him regularly on Thursdays or Sundays and sometimes accompanied him to Versailles. On Sundays he often lunched with Gambetta at his flat in the rue Montaigne, lunches at which the other guests were usually some of his host's most intimate associates, such as Spuller and Challemel-Lacour, old friends from Cahors, or Freycinet and other former collaborators in the National Defence. After lunch, when the guests had dispersed and other visitors had been received, Gambetta would take Gérard for a drive in the Champs Elysées or in the Bois de Boulogne where they would get out and stroll, Gambetta 'thinking aloud as he walked'.[2]

Undoubtedly, however, his most precious moments of leisure were spent quite otherwise, in the company of a woman who had replaced Marie Meersmans in his affections, to whom he would write some three thousand letters[3] and on whom he was increasingly to depend. On 27 April 1872 he had for the first time visited Léonie Léon in her flat in no. 7, rue Bonaparte,[4] and he thereafter cherished the anniversary of this day which had seen the beginning of their enduring romance. This self-possessed woman of mystery had, as she herself admitted, intermittently 'pursued' him since she was both carried away by his eloquence in the Baudin trial of November 1868 and in it divined a meteoric future. To this meteor she was determined to become attached. Her father, part Jewish, part Creole, was a colonel in the army who had gone mad and died in 1860; her elder sister, to whom she was devoted, was to have a similar end in 1875. In 1864 she had become for a while the mistress of the widowed Louis Alphonse Hyrvoix, a handsome and charming man who was then Inspecteur-Général de Police des Résidences Impériales and who became in 1865 the father of her only child, Léon Alphonse.

---

1. D. Halévy, *La Fin des Notables*, p. 213. Halévy (p. 220) also recounts an exchange with Thiers: 'Tel soir de janvier . . . Thiers etait au Luxembourg où Calmon, son ami républicain, recevait les républicains. Gambetta y était aussi, fort sage et écoutant les propos du Président qui dissertait, très en verve, sur les arts. "Monsieur le Président," lui dit-il, "votre république est vraiment une république athénienne . . . " — "Non pas, répliqua Thiers, florentine !" '

2. *Mémoires d'Auguste Gérard*, pp. 13, 16 and 22.

3. 'Tous les soirs en réglant le journal pour le lendemain, Je glisse dans le paquet de la poste la lettre qui t'est destinée' (letter of 2 June 1872, L.G.).

4. 'Voilà un nom de rue qu'il faudra changer' (Gambetta to Léonie Léon 13 Oct. 1872: *ibid.*).

She was devoted to this delicate but clever boy, to whom, in her letters to Gambetta, she mysteriously referred as 'la Chine' and she constantly reported his doings. Yet, such was her discretion, that her son was brought up to call her 'aunt' and perhaps never to the day of his death at the age of twenty-six knew their real relationship. Léonie indeed had what someone called 'a genius for self-effacement'. Her liaison with Gambetta lasted until his death, but, although most of his friends came to know of her existence, few of them ever met her and those who did were struck, even repelled, by her extreme reserve. Until in 1877 he bought 'Les Jardies', a modest house at Sèvres Ville d'Avray, as a rural retreat, she continued to live either in her own apartment or with her mother, her son, and, until her death, her sister at Bourg-la-Reine near Sceaux, a few miles south-south-west of Paris. It was only when they went on holiday that she and Gambetta lived together. This discretion, as her biographer has remarked, served him in good stead. Wholly wrapped up in him, she not only gave him relaxation and as complete and secluded a domestic tranquillity as he could hope for outside matrimony, but she protected him from adventures, which, given his nature, might well have been damaging, if not fatal to his career.[1] This did not mean, as she knew to her sorrow, that he was always faithful. She indeed, the woman who had pursued him, had also hoped that he would marry her. But he refused, for reasons that have never been disclosed: it was only towards the end of his life that he changed his mind and then she in turn was unwilling.

Léonie Léon, only seven months younger than Léon Gambetta, was not beautiful, but she had a certain distinction, she dressed well, she was well read and she was shrewd. Ambitious as well as self-effacing, she above all had 'as much as and perhaps more than intelligence, a feeling for and passionate interest in politics'.[2] She, too, helped, as had Madame Adam, to civilise Gambetta and make him presentable in society; she, still more, became his constant political confidante and adviser, and his

1. Cf. these words in a letter of 14 May 1873 when Gambetta was at St Nazaire: 'J'y devine de gracieuses et élégantes admiratrices qui solliciteront des regards que vous n'accorderez pas toujours; car c'est une grande force pour un homme, un homme d'Etat surtout, que de renfermer dans son coeur un sentiment assez sérieux pour le préserver de toutes les séductions passagères qui pourraient distraire son attention du but qu'il poursuit' (Ass. Nat. p. 53). See also Pillias, *Léonie Léon, amie de Gambetta* (1935), p. 61. This perceptive and excellently documented study, whose author was killed in the Second World War, is indispensable. I have leant heavily upon it.

2. *Ibid.*, p. 68. Cf. an undated letter from Léonie Léon to Gambetta written probably in 1872 from Bourg-la-Reine: 'Pourquoi ne me dites vous pas un mot de politique, sachant l'immense attraction qu'a pour mon esprit cette fascinante préoccupation, cet élément dans lequel j'aurais voulu vivre exclusivement. N'est-ce pas cette noble passion qui a attaché ma pensée a votre personnalité ... ?' (Ass. Nat., p. 9).

comforter when things went wrong. At first a devout Catholic, she eventually under his influence for a while lost her faith; meanwhile, however, her Catholicism perhaps strengthened his natural disposition to tolerance.[1]

Such was the woman whom the young lawyers in the house opposite sometimes spied lifting her curtains to gauge the weather and quickly letting them fall when she saw she was being watched. One of them remembered often seeing a stout man descend from a cab and enter number 7, holding a handkerchief to his face to disguise his identity. He did not guess that this man was Gambetta.

In a letter of 29 December 1872 to his father, Gambetta had written that he was 'relatively satisfied and reassured' about the political situation. The intrigues of the Monarchists would fail. M. Thiers would end by forcing them to capitulate or by dissolving the Assembly. Meanwhile he was paying the Prussians and hastening on the liberation of the territory. This in itself meant hastening the day of dissolution. The country was daily inclining more and more to the Republic and 'everything leads me to suppose that in May or June France will make her voice heard and put everyone back in their right place'.[2] This satisfaction was expressed more emphatically in the interview Gambetta accorded to a correspondent of the *New York Herald* early in the new year: the Republican cause, he said, had never looked better. From all parts of France he had the most positive information concerning the spread of Republican ideas. Dissolution would probably come in May: 'M. Thiers has only to say "I cannot govern France with the aid of the Assembly" and the work is done.' Meanwhile the petitioning campaign had been a success and petitions had been signed more widely in the country than in the towns, such was the change that had come over the peasantry.[3] Only a few days later satisfaction was also expressed by a very different personage, the Comte de Paris. In a letter of 12 January he wrote that calm had returned since Dufaure's speech against the Radical campaign for dissolution; the unity achieved between the government and the majority of the Assembly was a guarantee of the period of repose which France needed in order to recover before deciding her future destinies. The Commission of Thirty was pursuing its labours conscientiously and patriotically and would

1. See above, p. 68n.
2. *Lettres*, no. 139.
3. *New York Herald*, 27 Jan. 1873. The dispatch containing the report of this remarkable interview, which extended to four and a half columns of small print, was dated 9 Jan., but the correspondent did not say when it had taken place. Since it referred to Napoleon III's illness and operation it must have occurred between 2 and 9 January. The interview was partly reproduced in *The Times* of 26 Feb., p. 12. It was also the subject of a leader in the *New York Herald* of 27 Jan.

certainly succeed.[1] This letter and Gambetta's earlier one help to illustrate the equivocal nature of French politics at this time. The political outlook was fraught with ambiguities and when certain important events occurred their significance was differently interpreted.

One such event was the death at Chislehurst on 9 January of the ex-Emperor Napoleon III. It put an end to elaborate schemes for a new 'return from Elba' which had been planned to take place in March and which, among other things, involved dealing with the Assembly by the picturesque stratagem of boxing up the parliamentary train in the tunnel of St Cloud between Versailles and Paris. When the news came, Gambetta, who was 'for nearly two hours walking up and down the tombstone gallery [the Galerie des Tombeaux] with a couple of old friends, with his hat on his head and a cigar in his mouth', was said to have treated it with relative indifference: 'There is no longer a Bonapartist party! We see now its last convulsions. The so-called great conservative party will now be a mask for general desertion from the Imperialist camp! Show me a single Imperialist that can afford to wait for five or six years till the child [i.e. the Prince Imperial] becomes something like a man!' Such were the comments he was alleged to have made to those who enquired his views.[2] But to the Emperor, even on his deathbed, Gambetta showed no compassion. A few days earlier, he had remarked: 'We should have known better where he would lead us to—the *misérable*!' 'It is difficult', commented the *New York Herald*'s reporter, 'to give an idea of the intense and bitter energy, the sarcasm—which may have been anger, but most likely hatred—which darkened the speaker's face as he threw out the . . . word *misérable*.'[3] The *République Française* faithfully echoed Gambetta's views: all was over, it said, and the Bonapartist party was about to break up now that the ex-Emperor, 'this maniac . . . this somnambulist', was in his grave.[4] But not all observers adopted this interpretation. Moreover, despite the apparent indifference with which the news of Napoleon's death was received by ordinary Frenchmen, time would soon show that Bonapartism was not a spent force.

Another event which suggested that Republicanism was really on the march was the abdication of Spain's Italian monarch and the proclamation

1. Letter of 12 Jan. 1873, written from Chantilly to an unknown correspondent (in the author's possession).
2. *New York Herald*, 8 Feb. 1873 (p. 4, despatch of 11 Jan.).
3. *Ibid.*, 27 Jan. 1873.
4. Leader of 11 Jan. 1873; cf. also leader of 12 Jan. The Comte de Paris took a similar view: 'Sa mort met fin aux espérances du parti césarien qui entretenait toujours grâce à la juste crainte qu'inspirent les radicaux l'espérance malsaine d'une révolution violente en faveur de l'Empire' (letter of 12 Jan. 1873 quoted above).

there of a Republic on 11 February.[1] But how stable would this Republic be and would its advent, making the forces of conservatism more alarmed, drive them to compromise or render them more aggressive?[2] This was a moot question. The effect of a third event was less uncertain. In a letter of 8 February the Comte de Chambord, again like 'an ancient Sybil' in the words of *The Times*, once more gave haughty utterance against fusion and any compromise on the national flag. When Dupanloup, the Bishop of Orléans, to whom the letter was addressed, digested its contents he is said to have exclaimed in despair: 'Well! here is something which will further the business of the Republic! Poor France! All is lost!'[3]

As early as 8 August 1872 the Monarchist Lacombe had told his friend the Comte de Falloux that the next session of parliament would be decisive and that proposals would be put forward for organic laws and a second chamber.[4] Since the meeting of the Assembly many schemes for endowing the Republican regime with greater stability had been canvassed. Some suggested that Thiers should become President for life, others that he should be supported by an elected Vice-President; many favoured an upper house and some proposed a partial renewal of the Assembly or even a restriction of universal suffrage.[5] Gambetta, too, had views which he volunteered in the surprising interview already alluded to and given, probably in his flat, to the Paris correspondent of the *New York Herald*.[6] He was vehemently opposed to partial renewal of the Assembly [canvassed among others by Grévy] and preferred a President elected not by universal suffrage, but by the Assembly for a term of four or five years. As for the Assembly, it should be elected for two years and be reduced to some four hundred deputies, since the existing body was probably the largest in the world, and, he feared, enjoyed the distinction of being the most turbulent.[7] These views were unremarkable, but it

1. For the *R.F.*'s reactions, see leaders of 16, 17 Feb. defending Spanish Republicans against French Right-wing attacks.
2. Cf. a letter of Léonie Léon to Gambetta dated 'Dimanche' in which she claimed that the Spanish movement was leading the Monarchists to make concessions and 'tromper le pays en instituant une République qui sera selon les désirs de M. Thiers, complice de leur fourberie, une monarchie constitutionnelle sous le nom de République' (Ass. Nat., p. 38).
3. G. Hanotaux, *Le Gouvernement de M. Thiers 1870–1873*, vol. ii (1925), p. 221.
4. Lacombe, *Journal politique*, vol. i, p. 106.
5. This idea had naturally been attacked by the Radicals, see e.g. Gambetta's speech at Chambéry, *Discours*, vol. iii, p. 22; *R.F.*, leaders of 6 and 26 Oct. 1872.
6. See above p. 131. For the text of the part of the interview relating to constitutional arrangements, see Appendix.
7. In 1868, annotating a copy of Prévost-Paradol's *La France Nouvelle*, Gambetta

was remarkable that he should advocate the creation of a Grand Council of State of eighty members to be 'a great conservative strengthening force, a balance-wheel as it were, acting as a check upon an Executive with despotic aspirations and a sedative upon an angry and unreasonable Assembly'. It was also remarkable that he should reject ministerial responsibility. When *The Times* correspondent in Paris reported the interview at the end of February, his comment was that the American interviewer had contrived to damage Gambetta's influence with his party more effectually than the combined efforts of all his political enemies put together.[1] As for the *New York Herald*, in a leader devoted to the interview it concluded that France was unlikely 'to throw herself into the hands of Gambetta. It is evident that the underthought of this able and daring young man is that there can be no republicanism without a strong executive and that no executive would be as strong as Gambetta.'[2]

Were these Gambetta's real long-pondered views which he could not resist divulging but which, because they were so at variance with orthodox Radical doctrine at certain points, he preferred to divulge only to the correspondent of a transatlantic paper unlikely to be read by Frenchmen? For lack of corroborative evidence this question is very difficult to answer. Had the interview not been genuine it would surely have been promptly repudiated by the *République Française*, but that paper ignored it and, strangely enough, *The Times* correspondent, who wrote so fully on French politics, often treating the same theme time and time again, never reverted to it or its alleged effect upon Gambetta's standing with his party.[3]

Meanwhile Gambetta's 'Thirty Tyrants', the Commission instituted after the vote of 29 November 1872, had been busy. But as they contained a majority of deputies belonging to the Right or Right Centre they had little zeal for constitution making. They preferred to concentrate on the *chinoiseries*, as Thiers called them, of devising a procedure to restrict the freedom of the President of the Republic to address the Assembly. For

1. *The Times*, 26 Feb. p. 12. The correspondent presumably made this allegation because of Gambetta's wish to reduce the numbers of the Assembly and to make the Grand Council of State into a kind of second chamber. For Gambetta's views on the Conseil d'Etat as expressed in debate in 1872, see p. 221, n. 1, below.

2. 27 Jan.

3. It is of interest to note that *The Times* correspondent's own interview with Gambetta in Dec. 1874 was ignored by all except two Legitimist papers (see below, p. 221, n. 1). This fact supports the view that it was the insularity of the French Press which caused the *New York Herald* interview to be ignored.

had written against a passage where Paradol suggested six hundred deputies as the right number: 'C'est beaucoup trop! A mon sens 400' (Reinach, *La Vie politique de Gambetta*, p. 215).

several weeks President and Commission were at loggerheads, until Thiers adroitly suggested a compromise. He would accept the *chinoiseries* provided the Thirty in their turn accepted an additional article relating to constitutional arrangements. The proposal was at first rejected, but then certain Orleanists, shaken and angered by Chambord's reply to Dupanloup, deserted their Legitimist allies and agreed to the transaction. The additional article provided that the National Assembly would not break up until it had decided on the organisation of the executive and legislative powers, on the creation and organisation of a second Chamber, and on an electoral law. As Broglie later pointed out, the word 'Republic' was not mentioned, but everyone knew that the article meant that, 'if nothing new occurred', the Assembly would bequeath France a Republican constitution. 'Only', Broglie went on, 'this constitution ought to be effected by simple laws which would be revocable in accordance with ordinary legal procedure. This would make it possible to get out of the Republic when Monarchy became possible without running the risk of a revolution.'[1] But there was no time limit set for this and when Broglie presented his report on behalf of the Commission on 21 February the main questions of constitutional principle were reserved. His proposals were, as one deputy wittily remarked, confined to the regulation of the ceremonial entries and exits of M. Thiers to and from the Assembly. In other words they were concerned with the *chinoiseries*. But by limiting Thiers's opportunities to exercise his remarkable power of directly influencing the Assembly in debate they were of constitutional significance, and were to undermine his position and make his fall more easy.[2]

The warfare between Thiers and the Thirty and then their compromise, Thiers's balancing acts, the ambiguities in Broglie's report, the shifting majorities in the Chamber all made this a baffling period in French politics. And so it was, even for Gambetta. What attitude should he maintain towards Thiers; how far should he continue to keep silence and, if he spoke, was it to be in honeyed words of moderation or should he give way to pressure on his Left and launch new Radical thunderbolts? In a letter to Léonie Léon of 25 February he admitted that he was 'very anxious, very preoccupied, very divided even', in his views: 'I find that my head is full of the most contradictory courses which are struggling one against the other; at one and the same time I have the liveliest fears

---

1. *Mémoires*, vol. ii, p. 130.
2. See D. Thomson, *Democracy in France* (3rd edn, 1958), p. 85; for a different view, see Deslandres, *Histoire constitutionnelle de la France*, p. 200. The Bill was officially described as a 'projet de loi tendant à régler les attributions des pouvoirs publics et les conditions de la responsabilité ministérielle'.

and the most enthusiastic hopes.'[1] One important reason for maintaining silence was the need, allegedly impressed on him at Thiers's instance by Edmond Adam, not to prejudice the negotiations with Germany for the evacuation of the remaining German troops from French soil.[2] He decided, however, to intervene in the long series of debates on the Bill resulting from Broglie's report and, 'with perspicuity, moderation and logic', did so on 28 February.[3] Naturally he condemned the Bill as puerile (an adjective also used by *The Times*), and as dangerous because it was obscure and equivocal, whereas the country wanted to see its way clearly and to know whether it was being led towards Monarchy or Republic. Naturally he reiterated his party's denial of the Assembly's constituent power and referred to the dissolutionist petitions which were still flowing in. These were but old arguments adapted to the particular situation. What was of real general interest was the opportunity given him by the equivocal character of the Bill to restate his ideal of a democratic and liberal Republic. Every regime, he said, must have its conservatives, but the Republic could not be made with conservatives alone, and certainly not with 'those of a certain category'. He and his friends could not understand the organisation of a Republic whose only programme was 'to repel democracy', which could conceive only of monarchical institutions and could not make concessions without which such a Republic was purely and simply an embodiment of the abuses of the past. 'And so', he declared, alluding to D'Audiffret Pasquier's attack in December,

> we want no Republic which is not based upon that sovereignty of universal suffrage which you have so disdainfully called the sovereignty and brutality of numbers and treated almost as though it were an abject tyranny. We are hurt and wounded by these threats and big words of the *grand seigneur*, and tell you: 'If that is the conservative Republic, it will not be the Republic.' We want the Republic with its basic rights and freedoms, freedom of the Press, of meeting and of association.[4]

What was of real particular interest, both in the light of future developments and of Gambetta's recent advocacy of 'a Grand Council of State', was his categorical rejection of the idea of a second chamber by which Thiers among others set such store. Such a 'Chamber of Resistance', he

1. *Lettres*, no. 140. In no. 141, dated by the editors 'Février–Mars 1873', he wrote of 'les fastidieuses besognes que me prodigue la triste situation que nous traversons'.
2. Mme Adam, *Mes Angoisses*, p. 383.
3. *The Times*, 3 March, p. 10. For the text of his speech, see *Discours*, vol. iii, pp. 272–301 and *Ass. Nat. A.*, vol. xvi, pp. 224–33.
4. *Discours*, vol. iii, p. 295.

declared, would be a perpetual cause of conflict. It was a chimera. The history of second chambers in France, 'except perhaps for a few years in the first restoration'[1] had been lamentable. A second chamber meant the mutilation of universal suffrage: to invite Republicans to take part in such a creation would lead not to political or social peace but to catastrophe.

This doctrine of a single chamber had not been included in the Belleville programme, but it was, of course, part of an old Jacobin and radical tradition that Gambetta had already uncompromisingly reasserted in the Legislative Body in April 1870[2] and it is noteworthy that, although his speech was sometimes interrupted, no one flung in his teeth the proposals attributed to him by the *New York Herald*. Gambetta was seemingly tempted to return to the topic of a second chamber some days later but thought better of it. Thiers had recently had a brief but alarming attack of faintness. Gambetta did not choose to attack one of his pet schemes again at such a time: 'after all', he wrote, 'he is the best sort of constitution we have at the moment and I would not for the world wish to impair it. So I will hold my peace for the time being.'[3]

The Bill was voted upon on 13 March and passed by a handsome majority—407 to 225. But the majority was an artificial one[4] and hopes that it would ensure and inaugurate a period of appeasement and governmental stability were disappointed, despite the almost simultaneous success of Thiers's final negotiations with Germany. On 15 March a treaty was signed providing for the evacuation by a date in August of the last German troops from all remaining occupied territory except Verdun. The day on which Thiers communicated the treaty to the Assembly was a great parliamentary occasion. A motion was passed which included a declaration that Thiers had deserved well of his country and one hundred and fifty members of the Left accompanied the delegation deputed to convey the news to Thiers at the Préfecture. Gambetta may not have been one of them, but he did not hesitate to reiterate his appreciation of what 'the old Stadtholder' had done.[5]

1. The context suggested that Gambetta meant the Bourbon restoration generally as opposed to that of the Empire under Napoleon III.
2. *Discours*, vol. i, pp. 224 and 226–9.
3. 'J'ai à peu près renoncé à parler sur la seconde Chambre; j'ajourne un projet' (*Lettres*, no. 142 to Léonie Léon, 9 March 1873). What sort of 'projet' this was there was no indication. It is tempting to speculate that he half thought of airing his Grand Council scheme. Even the former Liberal Imperialist, Emile Ollivier, admitted at this time that Gambetta was showing much good sense (Ollivier, *Lettres de l'exil 1871–74*, p. 173).
4. 'Entente des conservateurs du centre droit et des républicains *thiéristes* du centre gauche, fragilement unis pour la dernière fois contre les purs royalistes et les radicaux de Gambetta' (Dreyfus, *La République de M. Thiers* p. 307).
5. Mme Adam, *Mes Angoisses*, p. 382.

But this rapprochement between Thiers, 'the Protector', as Léonie Léon preferred to call him, and the Radicals was not to last.[1] His 'government of combat' was still busy combating Radicalism, and Thiers himself in the Assembly on 4 March pointed to the Left and said, 'There you have the kind of Republic which happily does not suit a large number of Republicans!' A law of 18 February had modified the electoral provisions in the interests of the Conservatives. Radical papers such as the *Rappel*, the *Radical* and the *Républicain de l'Est* as well as others were prosecuted and Gambetta was impelled to demand the ending of martial law.[2] Above all, the alleged misdeeds, past and present, of Lyon, the second city of France, provided grounds for assault.

Lyon had a long history as one of the most turbulent towns of nineteenth-century France. It had had its own revolution on 4 September 1870, set up a Committee of Public Safety, flown the red flag on the Hôtel de Ville and claimed to treat with the Government of National Defence as an equal. During this difficult period the Prefect of the Rhône had been Gambetta's future collaborator on the *République Française*, Challemel-Lacour. He had proceeded circumspectly and on the whole preserved order, but, of course, he was a Radical who could be accused of being too indulgent to such a subversive society as the International and too careless in his conclusion of war contracts. These were the charges levelled against him by the Right, acting through the Commission set up to investigate war contracts. It was expected that the accused would be easy prey, but when the debate took place on snowy days at the end of January Challemel-Lacour proved himself a first-rate speaker and more than a match for his opponents. Gambetta, through the *République Française*, expressed his delight and the Republican Union at its meeting on 8 February voted that the speeches of Challemel-Lacour and of his colleague Ferrouillat should be printed and distributed.[3]

The attack on Challemel-Lacour thus turned out to be a damp squib. As *The Times* sarcastically commented: 'Three days have just been spent in discussing whether Lyons or the State ought to pay 30 millions of war expenditure incurred by the southern city, and the result finally arrived at is that it is a very wrong thing to hoist a red flag.'[4] Nothing daunted,

1. Men like Spuller were often restive at their dependence on Thiers. According to a police report of 29 Jan., Spuller had told a friend: 'M. Thiers est une vieille canaille, mais en ce moment, nous ne pouvons que le suivre.... C'est un vieux bateau troué, auquel nous sommes contraints de nous raccrocher sous peine de couler à fond' (A.P.P., BA/1.274).
2. *Ass. Nat. A*, vol. xv, p. 491, 15 March 1873.
3. *R.F.*, 9 Feb. For the *R.F.*'s reactions to the debates, see leaders of 2, 3 and 4 Feb.
4. *The Times*, 7 Feb. 1873, p. 7. Cf. Hanotaux, *op. cit.*, pp. 254–5: 'La plus violente

however, the Right proceeded to turn their attention to the Lyon municipality which had pursued an anticlerical policy bitterly contested by
Catholics. For a man like Broglie this body was 'composed of the most
extreme Radicals, those who during the war and revolution of 1870 had
committed every excess except that of courage'. It was 'a miniature
Commune', which had dispossessed innocent teaching congregations and
replaced them by secular schools 'given over to veritable orgies of
impiety'.[1] Thiers, who had done nothing to curb the secularist policies of
the municipality, would have been content to suppress the central mayor-
alty and leave the administration of the city in the hands of district authorities, but this did not satisfy the Right, and in spite of Thiers's opposition,
the Minister of the Interior, Goulard, was persuaded to promote a bill not
only to abolish the central administration, but to transfer its duties to the
prefect of the Rhône. The measure, put forward at the end of March,
drew violent Radical protests and occasioned stormy debates in the
Assembly, but it became law on 4 April and had a considerable effect on
certain forthcoming by-elections. Meanwhile, as the result of a trivial
incident in the debates, Jules Grévy had resigned his office as President of
the Chamber, refused to withdraw his resignation, and been succeeded by
Buffet, a member of the Right. Buffet's victory, although by a very narrow
majority over Thiers's friend Martel, who was supported by the Left, was
the presage for Thiers of worse defeats to follow. The first of these would
also be a direct result of the suppression of the Lyon municipality.

By the end of March a 'little general election' was pending, since there
were vacant seats in twelve constituencies, including, as ill-luck would
have it for the Government, the Seine and the Rhône. The Government
decided to hold eight of these elections, including the one in Paris (the
Seine) on 27 April and did not convoke the electors in the other four
departments, including the Rhône, of which Lyon was the chief city,
until 13 April for a vote on 11 May. This appeared to the Radicals to be a
deliberate attempt to prevent the two chief French cities from going to the
polls on the same day and simultaneously exhibiting their hostility to an
Assembly of 'rustics' (ruraux). Yet the election in Paris might not have
caused such a furore but for Thiers's insistence on putting forward the

---

1. Mémoires, vol. ii, p. 145; cf. Rémusat, Mémoires de ma vie, vol. v, p. 453: 'On sait
que la ville de Lyon est de toutes la plus profondément dévorée par le socialisme et la
démagogie. Le conseil municipal misérablement composé, le maire et les adjoints,
gens du dernier ordre, après avoir un temps essayé de l'administrer au mépris des lois,
se contentait de l'administrer au mépris du bon sens.' But he admitted: 'Cependant
depuis huit mois tout était tranquille.'

---

attaque dirigée contre le gouvernement de la Défense nationale ... avait abouti à un
vote unanime contre le drapeau rouge.'

candidature of his old friend and colleague Rémusat, who, as Minister for Foreign Affairs since August 1871, had been his righthand man in the negotiations with Germany so recently and successfully concluded. Rémusat was the only member of the Government who was not a deputy. In urging him to stand, despite Jules Simon's warning that he would be accused of reviving the obnoxious practice of 'official candidature', Thiers hoped to strengthen his own hand by winning fresh acclamation for his foreign policy. But he miscalculated. Rémusat, an aristocrat and former Orleanist, was not the man to win the favour of Radicals increasingly critical and suspicious of Thiers. Was he indeed a genuine convert to Republicanism? Louis Blanc publicly doubted it and so, as Daniel Halévy remarked, Rémusat, Thiers's chosen candidate, came under the ban pronounced by Gambetta at Grenoble.[1] His candidature indeed placed Gambetta in a dilemma. When after initial hesitation Gambetta decided to oppose it, he, too, made what in the long run seemed to many a grave miscalculation. The joint misjudgements of Thiers and Gambetta led to one of the most exciting by-elections in the history of the Third Republic, one which had grave consequences for both.

It was not long since Thiers had written of Gambetta: 'We shall see him again in the guise of a man of government, but he will always revert to the role of tribune imposed upon him by his party.'[2] Such a moment of reversion was now at hand. At first, according to Hector Pessard, Gambetta had deemed it stupid to think of opposing Rémusat and laughed when it was suggested that his Radical 'tail' (*queue*) might have other views; 'My tail!', he exclaimed, 'I'll give it a white tie and we'll go into society together!' But when a few hours later, at dinner with Emile de Girardin, Pessard repeated Gambetta's views, he observed that a tall young man 'with rather slit, cold, lack-lustre eyes' was listening to him. 'When I had finished my story, the young man raised his head and quietly asserted that Gambetta would change his mind. He held to this opinion despite our protests . . . and told us that the man whom Paris would elect would be M. Barodet. The prophet was M. Edouard Portalis . . . at that time director of the *Corsaire*.'[3]

What caused Gambetta to change his mind and to support not Victor

---

1. *La Fin des Notables*, p. 243.

2. See above, p. 118.

3. Pessard, *Mes petits papiers*, pp. 312–13. Unfortunately he does not give the date of these conversations. (The *Corsaire* was a Radical paper.) Cf. Mme Adam, *Mes Angoisses*, p. 390. Earlier in her book (p. 336), and also without giving a date, Mme Adam recorded a supposed conversation in which Gambetta's friend Laurier reproached him with being too faithful to the Belleville programme: 'tu n'auras jamais le courage de couper ta queue. Je ne la couperai pas, répondit Gambetta, mais je la dévisserai si doucement qu'on ne s'en apercevra pas.'

Hugo or Ledru-Rollin, both of whom were mentioned as possible candidates, but the relatively obscure Désiré Barodet, whose only claim to fame was that he happened to be mayor of the doomed municipality of Lyon? Evidently pressure from that 'tail' which he had affected to disdain, pressure from obscure clubs and committees, groups that Portalis and others were said to have been organising for months,[1] pressure from free-masons and pressure from all those among whom 'the old leaven of the Commune' was said to be working. These were the forces which may be assumed to have contrived that Barodet's candidature should appear to emerge 'spontaneously' as the result of a great upsurge of popular opinion, which gained the ear of the more Left-wing members of Gambetta's own entourage, men such as Ranc and Challemel-Lacour with their particular associations with Paris and Lyon, and which, through them and Spuller, won Gambetta himself.[2] In doing so they convinced him that here was both a chance to 'teach Thiers a lesson'[3] and to demonstrate beyond doubt that, for all his parliamentary trimming, Gambetta was still a Radical at heart. In the words of the *Figaro*, 'the ravening wolves of the Radical Republic were eager to devour the frightened sheep of the conservative Republic'.[4] Perhaps, too, Gambetta was attracted precisely by the fact that, instead of being a celebrity such as Ledru-Rollin or Hugo, Barodet was no national figure, but yet an admirable representative of the new social stratum whose advent to power he had hailed at Grenoble.[5] Already, moreover, the Grenoble speech had seemed to some to show Gambetta's thirst for the backing of the 'demagogic elements in the big towns', especially Paris. Hector Pessard later drew particular attention to the moving peroration in which the orator had spoken of Paris—'this Paris which is deprived of the national parliament, this Paris that men have sought to strike down and insult after not knowing how to defend her;

1. See e.g. A. Lefèvre, *Histoire de la ligue d'union républicaine des droits de Paris* (1881), p. 361.
2. Electioneering in the Radical 3e arrondissement in Paris in 1876, Spuller claimed: 'Le premier . . . qui songea que le devoir de Paris était de venger la seconde ville de France . . . c'est moi' (*R.F.*, 8 Feb. 1876).
3. The phrase reported by Jules Hansen (*Les coulisses de la diplomatie*, p. 264); but the *R.F.* of 12 April (p. 2) specifically disclaimed this intention: 'Nous ne voulons pas non plus faire une protestation stérile, ni donner une leçon au gouvernement.'
4. Kayser, *Les Grandes batailles du radicalisme*, p. 67.
5. He may also have been influenced by a different sort of consideration put forward by Léonie Léon in a letter dated 'Mercredi': 'Ne serait-il prudent d'opposer au ministre un personnage tout à fait insignifiant? afin que s'il succombe dans la lutte, vous puissiez vous donner aux yeux du gouvernement le mérite de lui avoir abandonné le terrain tout en sauvant les apparences à l'égard de votre parti. Si au contraire votre candidat est vainqueur votre triomphe devient d'autant plus écrasant pour le gouvernement que vous ne lui avez opposé qu'un homme à peu près nul' (Ass. Nat. p. 50).

this Paris which has never lost the confidence of France, for whenever her name is uttered in the provinces, even in the humblest village, it is hailed as the head and heart of the *patrie*'.[1] This, commented Pessard, was Gambetta's indirect way of making his peace with the Commune.[2]

Now he had an opportunity to make it directly. But would it have been possible if the Radical committees and his Belleville constituents had known what he was alleged to have said in that strange interview with the *New York Herald*?: 'You know, of course, that I am detested by the Commune. I am well aware of it. Were they in power they would shoot me. I was in Spain during the Commune and I am sure, had I returned, I should have been shot more eagerly ... than the Archbishop of Paris.' However, the view that the 'old leaven of the Commune' was stirred by the high-handed suppression of the municipality of Lyon has much to commend it. When polling day came 'all the ordinary people, the workers of the suburbs, the elements more or less involved in the Commune'[3] who had been afraid to vote in January 1872, answered Gambetta's appeal and turned out to vote against the candidate of Thiers, the man they had not forgiven, the Commune's bloody suppressor.

Gambetta's opposition to Rémusat's candidature did not take long to develop. The candidature was first mooted on 22 March and already on the 27th the *République Française* printed a leader declaring that, if it were persisted in, it would be necessary to oppose it with the utmost energy. If it were persisted in—the first move was to try to induce Rémusat to desist. But a delegation of Radical deputies who had been to see Rémusat on the 25th had not succeeded in persuading him to stand down.[4] Reluctant candidate though he genuinely was, he believed he must stand since Thiers wished it. Gambetta's own later attempt, through Freycinet, to induce Thiers to withdraw the candidature was likewise unsuccessful,[5] while Rémusat, for his part, was equally unable through the good offices of Jules Hansen, to persuade Gambetta to renounce his opposition.[6] Rémusat, the *République Française* pointed out, was member of a cabinet which was going to put forward a new electoral law adverse to universal suffrage and propose a second Chamber, member of a cabinet which still

1. *Discours*, vol. iii, p. 188.
2. *Mes petits papiers, deuxième, série 1871–1873*, p. 284. A police report of 1 Oct. 1872 noted that the Grenoble speech had much enhanced Gambetta's stock in the 11th, 18th, 19th and 20th arrondissements of Paris (A.P.P., BA/917).
3. Gouault, *Comment la France est devenue Républicaine*, p. 155.
4. *The Times*, 26 March, p. 5.
5. Freycinet, *Souvenirs 1848–1878*, pp. 298–9. Freycinet recorded Thiers's irritation: 'Vos amis sont fous. Ne voient-ils pas qu'ils font le jeu des royalistes ... ? Ils seront responsables de ma chute.'
6. Hansen, *Les Coulisses de la diplomatie*, pp. 263–4.

maintained martial law in Paris and in forty-three departments. His election would be a victory for the Right Centre; he was being used to set a dangerous trap for the Republican party and the city of Paris.[1]

The election programme that Barodet put forward contained only three articles but they succinctly reflected the grievance of those Parisians who still felt they were humiliated by the existing regime. They were: (1) the immediate dissolution of the Assembly of Versailles; (2) the absolute and genuine integrity of universal suffrage, i.e. no tampering with it by reactionary electoral laws; (3) the early summoning of a single Assembly (i.e. no second Chamber), 'which alone can vote for an amnesty and for ending the state of siege'. An amnesty would indeed be a generous and conciliatory act, for as *The Times* correspondent pointed out, there were many cases of injustice, where people fortuitously caught up in the Commune were still in prison, while the ending of martial law would remove a cause of humiliation to a great city. This programme was imposed upon Barodet not by Gambetta but by the delegates of the Radical committees met together in a Federal Committee of Electoral Action. But Gambetta, once he had been convinced that Barodet was the man who must be supported, even at the cost of splitting the Republican ranks, put all his abundant energy into directing Barodet's campaign. And it was no ordinary campaign. Barodet was a symbol of opposition and of injured municipal liberties rather than a personality in his own right and he did not appear once in Paris during the official campaigning period.[2] Gambetta directed the *République Française*'s vigorous polemics on his behalf.[3] It was Gambetta who drafted for him his election manifesto and counselled him at every stage.[4] It was Gambetta whose eloquence and versatility of argument won for him the support of the Republican Union,[5] in spite of Adam's warning that the Assembly would be more

1. Leader of 30 March. Thus Rémusat, in his own words written on polling day, had to his astonishment become 'l'homme dont tout le monde parle, sur lequel la France et l'Europe même ont les yeux . . . me voilà devenu la carte sur laquelle se joue la situation du gouvernement, sa durée, peut-être l'avenir du pays; me voilà, chose plus étrange, devenue la garantie nécessaire de la République !' (*Mémoires de ma vie*, vol. v, p. 459).
2. For his anxiety not to have to meet his constituents, see my article 'The Seine and the Rhône. Two French by-elections in 1873', *The Historical Journal*, vol. x, (1967), no. 4, pp. 391–9.
3. See *Lettres*, no. 145.
4. *Ibid.*, nos 144, 146–52 and 154–6.
5. Scheurer-Kestner's diary, p. 122 (B.N., N.a.fr. 12, 707). But Crémieux, Scheurer-Kestner and Edmond Adam were not persuaded and still preferred Rémusat. Gambetta's main arguments, summarised by Scheurer-Kestner who acted as secretary and wrote the minutes of the meeting, were that Rémusat's candidature was undemocratic; that the provinces were sick of the Republic without Republicanism; that

tenacious of life if Barodet were elected and that Thiers's prestige would be greatly weakened, and it was Gambetta whose resounding election speech at Belleville on 22 April made the greatest sensation.[1] Yet in that speech the name of Barodet was not once pronounced. The issue, he declared, was not a struggle between two men; it was the question whether democracy would be given its rightful share in the affairs of the country.

The name of Barodet was not pronounced by Gambetta at Belleville, but it was plastered all over Paris as was that of Rémusat. And some of the most effective posters, describing Barodet as 'belonging to this working world which for the last eighteen months has made its entry into public affairs. . . . He belongs to this new social stratum',[2] were undoubtedly inspired by Gambetta. The war of posters was indeed unprecedented in volume—it was estimated that more than 1,200,000 were stuck up in a fortnight—and it added to the intense excitement. When polling day came, namely 27 April, the electors turned out in larger numbers than at any time since the plebiscite of May 1870 and they did so in spite of pouring rain. The men who had previously abstained turned the scale. Barodet was elected by 180,045 votes to Rémusat's 135,028, while 26,644 went to the Bonapartist Colonel Stoffel who was supported by the Legitimists but not by everyone in his own party. This last candidature had thus further advertised the Monarchists' inability to unite and Barodet had had an overall majority over both his rivals.[3] The result was a triumph for superior organisation, an overwhelming victory for Radicalism and a stinging defeat for Thiers, the suppressor of the Commune. The Radicals triumphed, too, in three of the seven other departments which voted that day, namely the Nièvre, Gironde and Bouches-du-Rhône; in each a Monarchist was replaced. In the provinces it was once again the Monarchists who were the losers. A fortnight later polling took place in the other four departments where there were vacant seats. Three Radicals and one Bonapartist were elected: 'the repudiation of the Monarchist Assembly and even of Thiers's conservative Republican government was still more

1. For the text, see *Discours*, vol. iii, pp. 333–66.
2. *Cit.* Kayser, *Les Grandes batailles du radicalisme*, p. 69.
3. *The Times*, 3 May, p. 9, in a leader commented caustically: 'The Monarchists who are now shrieking that society is in danger, actually thought fit . . . to set up a candidate of their own. . . . The absurdity of the Stoffel nomination. . . . ' 'Many Parisian Bonapartists, discontented by the alliance with the Legitimists, voted for Barodet' (J. Rothney, *Bonapartism after Sedan*, 1969, p. 114).

now was the time to find a man whose conduct demonstrated that the Republicans were fit to administer—Barodet was such a man, for he had wisely looked after a city of 800,000 inhabitants; that Rémusat wanted the Assembly's powers to be prolonged; that Thiers sought to govern with the support of the two Centres, men of no real party, and that if he triumphed there would be no prospects for real Republicans.

striking than in April'.[1] And of the elections of 11 May not the least
significant was that at Lyon of a Paris municipal councillor, none other
than Gambetta's enigmatic and influential friend Ranc, who had known
the Paris Commune from the inside. A Barodet for a Ranc! Perhaps this
was, as Juliette Adam suggested,[2] part of the secret of Gambetta's readiness to support Barodet, for Gambetta liked to look after his own;
conscious that he had been unwilling to back Ranc's candidature in Paris
in July 1871 he may have been all the more ready to help him in 1873. In
any case Ranc's election by a large majority emphasised anew the solidarity
of Radicalism in the two largest cities in France.

Delighted though he was with the triumph of Barodet, Gambetta at
once realised that it was necessary to be prudent in exploiting it. Significantly he told Barodet not to celebrate his victory with the customary
banquet; 'it would be a great mistake and give the police and reactionaries
a pretext for agitation. We must not play into the hands of the coalition of
the Right.' He struck the same note on 16 May in a notable speech at
Nantes in which he drew the moral from the by-elections as a whole.[3]
Successive elections had demonstrated the splendid movement of the most
numerous and basic strata (*couches*) towards the Republic, demonstrated it,
he claimed, to such a point that after these last elections it was reckoned
that, even if the urban electors who voted Republican were subtracted
from the lists, the Republicans would still triumph. If the triumph had
been incomplete, it was because of clerical influence in the neighbouring
department of Morbihan—hence, once again, the need for Republican
propaganda in the country districts—and because of administrative pressure by the adherents of the successful candidate, Boffinton, a former
Bonapartist prefect. Boffinton's former subordinates were still in place and
had worked on his behalf: such were the fruits of a Republic without
Republicans.[4] The result of the elections proved beyond doubt that the
country wanted two things—the Republic with universal suffrage unimpaired and the Republic with democratic institutions. But the reactionaries, those who had sworn mortal enmity to the Republic, had been
busy organising a campaign of panic and were capable of resorting to
desperate and violent courses. He therefore appealed to Thiers not to
falter:

1. Gouault, *op. cit.*, p. 157.
2. *Mes Angoisses*, p. 390; cf. her *Nos amitiés politiques avant l'abandon de la revanche*,
p. 5.
3. For the text, see *Discours*, vol. iii, pp. 267–90.
4. 'Cette élection', commented Léonie Léon in her daily letter to Gambetta, 'est un
fait isolé et sans importance. Le bonapartisme n'est pas l'ennemi du présent; il deviendra
peut-être celui de l'avenir' (Ass. Nat., p. 52).

Do you not see the abyss into which France may be hurled? We Republicans are with you, be with us: let us pass wise measures with a . . . loyal administration and not a corrupt one that contains too many representatives of previous regimes which France has definitely repudiated. . . . What has universal suffrage, whose imposing and repeated decisions appear to alarm you, meant to say, what has it recalled? It has recalled and demands the policy of the message of 13 November, this message which is your greatest claim to fame.

This was indeed a moving appeal, but Gambetta could not let things rest there. What if Thiers did falter or slide into the enemy camp?

We must not despair, for however eminent the man . . . a people does not perish if a man fails it. . . . Citizens, the session which is about to open will be grave and full of perils. Our adversary is in the position of the sailor who feels his ship sinking and prefers to blow himself up rather than surrender.

He therefore urged his hearers as never before not to let themselves be provoked, but to be disciplined and united and to redouble their prudence and good behaviour (*sagesse*).

This appeal to Thiers, these solemn words, were eloquent testimony to the way in which the situation had deteriorated since the by-elections. The Radical victories had alarmed the Right as never before. They appeared to them to mark the triumph of mediocrity and vulgar passions; they seemed, as C. de B. wrote, to signalise the burial of the Conservative Republic and to show that the only kind of Republic now possible was a Radical one.[1] The reign of Gambetta, with all the terrors that was supposed to imply, now seemed to be at hand. Already in the Assembly on 14 December d'Audiffret-Pasquier had denounced the Radicals as 'the party of destruction' out to attack family, property, *Patrie* and religion. Now, recorded the Bonapartist 'Fidus',

The Radicals are openly announcing their plans: 'We will seize power', they say, 'after having overthrown M. Thiers, in the next elections; we will change all the government personnel. If there is a violent movement of opposition we will stop it as ruthlessly as Republics can. The bourgeoisie will be frightened; no one will budge. Then all will return to normal and the Republic will be founded.' This is the sort of language being held in the offices of the *République Française*: 'You ought to see these people', a man who knows them said to me, 'they have the gravity and calm of future ministers; they are real Jacobins, real Saint-Justs.'[2]

And this Jacobin note was still more vividly echoed by Lord Lytton; he reported having met a man who said that Ranc had declared that 'a fall of

1. See Gimpl, *The Correspondant and the Founding of the French Third Republic*, p. 104; Rothschild pp., letter of 28 April.
2. *Journal de Fidus*, vol. iii, pp. 201–2.

nearly thirty thousand heads' was, 'according to his most careful calculation, still required by the Revolution before this country can be "set to rights".'[1] Behind Gambetta the Right saw the spectre of the Commune. The Right, both through genuine fear and of set purpose, were indeed busy sowing panic. Moreover, the fact that Gambetta, in his speech at Belleville, had gone out of his way to pay tribute to Thiers,[2] while opposing Thiers's protégé, Rémusat, had only confirmed their deep suspicions that Thiers was in league with the Left.[3] His speech at Nantes angered them still further: Changarnier, according to Madame Adam, loudly demanded that the Permanent Commission should 'twist the neck of this commercial traveller in eloquence'.[4]

The Right were not alone in their alarm. The Barodet election had also scared certain sections of the financial and business world connected with the Left Centre. Thus, for instance, on 5 May the head of the Paris branch of the Crédit Lyonnais bank wrote gloomily that, were elections to be held, Gambetta would become President of the Republic: 'Then there would be a general mess the outcome of which it is impossible to foresee.'[5] Before long the defection of such men and their political associates would be crucial. In fact, the Right, as the *République Française* pointed out in a leader of 6 May, had already decided that Thiers must be brought low as speedily as possible. In March, after the Assembly had voted its approval of the treaty with Germany, Jules Simon had laughingly said to Thiers: 'Now your work is done; you must say your *nunc dimittis*.' Thiers had looked at him thoughtfully and replied: 'But they have nobody.' 'They have Marshal MacMahon,' said Simon. 'Oh! As for that,' Thiers had quickly retorted, 'I'll answer for it, he'll never accept.'[6] But Thiers was wrong. At the opening of the new session the Republican Union submitted a draft Bill, signed by Gambetta and fifty-nine others, requiring the Assembly within fifteen days to fix the date of its dissolution. This was but a belligerent gesture. The Right went into battle against Thiers and the Radical menace, brushed the Government's constitutional proposals aside and with the decisive aid of fourteen deserters from the Left Centre won

1. P.R.O., F.O. 146, 1669, Lord Lytton to Lord Granville, 1 May.
2. *Discours*, vol. iii, p. 337.
3. In an article on the Paris election *The Times* correspondent reported Ranc as having said: 'Nous allons couvrir M. Thiers de fleurs comme il convient à une victime'; the correspondent commented that the *République Française* had 'been busy all the week distributing the garlands' (5 May, p. 12).
4. *Mes Angoisses*, p. 396.
5. J. Bouvier, *Le Crédit Lyonnais de 1868 à 1882* (1967), vol. i, p. 423, n. 1. Cf. his interesting article 'Aux origines de la Troisième République. Les Réflexes sociaux des milieux d'affaires' (*Revue Historique*, vol. ccx, Oct.–Dec. 1953), pp. 282–6.
6. Hanotaux, *op. cit.*, p. 250.

the day for a motion critical of the President. This was a moment when Gambetta must have regretted the resignation of the twenty-seven other deputies of Alsace and Lorraine in March 1871.[1] Thiers, despite his indignant and eloquent repudiation of any association with a Communard radicalism which he hoped had been crushed for a long time to come, was defeated by fourteen votes and promptly resigned. His successor was one of those who had been most strongly opposed to his ideas on army reform in the Conseil Supérieur de la Guerre. Responding in soldierly fashion to the call of duty, Marshal MacMahon accepted the presidency.

1. In the course of a debate on 4 June 1874 when someone challenged him to resign, Gambetta replied: 'Il n'est jamais bon de donner sa démission dans une Assemblée, à quelque parti qu'on appartienne. Ce qui le prouve, c'est que . . . si les démissionnaires étaient présents, nous aurions fait la République, et vous en seriez peut-être aujourd'hui les serviteurs !' (*Ass. Nat. A.*, vol. xxxi, p. 304).

12

The battle against 'moral order' and restoration May–October 1873

Gambetta, often an optimist, was given to optimistic predictions. On 24 April 1873 *The Times* reported that he had 'laid a wager that M. Barodet will have a majority of 40,000 votes at the first scrutiny'. Four months earlier he had predicted, as has been seen, that there would be a dissolution in May or June. He had been as good a prophet on the Barodet election as he was a bad one on dissolution; and where dissolution was concerned he himself had seemingly played a major part in making its early achievement impossible. The Barodet and other by-elections had determined the Right to seize power precisely in order to prevent dissolution and to stem the Radical tide. Had Gambetta, by supporting Barodet as he did, made a crucial misjudgement, losing, as it turned out almost for good, the opportunity once again to govern France? Had he at the same time committed an act of political cowardice?[1]

It is probable that he had misjudged the consequence of his action. Thirty years later Juliette Adam wrote that her husband had been unhappy —the more he thought about the Barodet candidature, 'patronised by Portalis', the more he came to the conclusion that it was a manoeuvre of Gambetta's worst enemies both within and outside the party. She also alleged that, after the event, Gambetta himself was anxious and admitted to regretting an election which had awakened the appetite of the Communards and served as an argument to those who dreamed of *coups de force* against what they called the Revolution.[2] Two factors were all-important in the situation which had resulted: time and the conduct of Thiers. Earlier in the year many prophets besides Gambetta had foretold a general election in 1873, most probably after the liberation of the territory,

1. As suggested, for example, by E. Durier in a letter of 16 April 1873 to Ernest Picard (B.N., Papiers Ernest Picard, N.a.fr., 24370).
2. *Mes Angoisses*, p. 394; cf. her *Nos amitiés politiques avant l'abandon de la revanche*, p. 5.

namely in the late summer or early autumn, when Thiers, they thought, would resign and go to the country. But it was also widely prophesied that a general election would bring a Radical victory, and the Right, scared further by the by-elections, had no intention of granting time. They brought about Thiers's resignation before the liberation of the territory. Given their resolute anti-Radical attitude, already proclaimed in 1872, and given the results of the by-elections in the provinces in the spring of 1873, the Right might well have forced a crisis in May or June quite apart from the Paris election result.[1] But they might not so soon or easily have been victorious had Rémusat been unopposed or Barodet been defeated. To this extent Gambetta's part in securing Barodet's overwhelming victory had indeed played into their hands and made it easier for them to procure Thiers's defeat and forestall the general election. In doing so, however, they had gambled on Thiers's resignation. Yet he need not have resigned. As the historian Seignobos once pointed out:

> One who had been a Republican from the start would have hesitated to place the Republic in the power of its enemies: the President had the right to remain until the end of the Assembly.... But Thiers the former Orleanist was too accustomed to parliamentary usages to stay on after a hostile vote. Perhaps...he thought the Assembly would soon be obliged to recall him to power. He behaved like a Prime Minister rather than a President of the Republic.[2]

Gambetta and his colleagues likewise bowed to parliamentary usages. When at Nantes Gambetta made his moving appeal to Thiers to stand firm and not to make concessions to the Right, it was not an appeal to him to stand firm and remain in office whatever the upshot of debate. Later, in December 1874, Gambetta told *The Times* correspondent that Thiers's resignation had been a great mistake: he 'should have retained office, taken a Cabinet from the Right, and waited till that Cabinet...had fallen amid the applause of the country, and thus restored him his freedom of action'.[3] But at the time the Left did not appear to have made any attempt on 24 May, as they had on an earlier occasion, to induce Thiers to go back on his decision.[4] They, or rather Gambetta and the Radicals

1. One factor which is impossible to assess with precision is the effect first of Barodet's candidature and then of his election on the elections in the provinces. Would the results have been substantially different had he not stood?

2. C. Seignobos, *Le Déclin de l'Empire et l'établissement de la 3e République* (1921), p. 359.

3. *The Times*, 22 Dec., p. 5.

4. See p. 88. Perhaps the only person to do so was MacMahon, who went to see Thiers and urged him to remain and change his ministers: if so, he (MacMahon) would decline the Presidency (J. Silvestre de Sacy, *Le Maréchal de MacMahon Duc de Magenta (1808–1893)* (1960), p. 269.

among them, had sought both to teach Thiers a lesson and to maintain him. In so doing they had, in Thiers's view, naturally made fools of themselves, and pursued ends which were incompatible.

Gambetta's miscalculation seems evident, but it is not possible to plumb the depths of the human heart and to know how far miscalculation was prompted by fear. Once he had failed to secure Rémusat's withdrawal he was on the horns of an inescapable dilemma; he must either support Rémusat and alienate his 'tail' or support Barodet and still further alienate moderate Republicans like Grévy. It would, however, have required the greater courage to support Rémusat, for had he done so, he would have risked at least temporarily being a leader separated from his troops. As it was, he kept his troops and regained or reinforced his hold on the more belligerent and on his old constituents at Belleville where he had first been elected in 1869. His speech at Belleville on 22 April was indeed a masterly performance, delivered with tremendous verve and humour. He made but a passing reference to the stagnation of business, yet, although Belleville, one of three areas in the city with the greatest concentration of industry, was also one of those most hit by unemployment and consequent distress, he was loudly applauded by his authentically Parisian audience.[1] Apart from its exposé of the general political situation, the speech was remarkable for Gambetta's review and defence of his own conduct. He was, he said, the same man whom his constituents had elected in 1869. But the need to substitute a legal parliamentary opposition for the heroic militancy of earlier Republicans had necessitated in the Assembly, 'the natural ground for political compromises', all kinds of 'precautions and wariness and in short the resort to an infinity of middle courses'. Hence on five or six occasions he and his colleagues had given the government support without which it would have fallen. But if he had been ready to compromise in parliament this could not be so when it came to elections. After referring to the electoral situation and the failure of the Assembly to give the country the educational, army and tax reforms it wanted, he went on to point out the dangers that beset a man in the forefront of politics. All sorts of flatterers and men from other parties were liable to approach him and say that they could do business with him and that he might thus become the instrument of the best reforms. 'They said: "Why don't you get rid of those worthless people? One isn't a statesman if one doesn't know how to cut off one's tail."' But that, said Gambetta, was to betray one's party. The real place of a statesman was in the ranks, 'in the

1. The *arrondissement* of Ménilmontant in which Belleville was situated was one of those in which the proportion of immigrants from the provinces was lowest (see L. Chevalier, *La Formation de la population parisienne au XIXe siècle*, 1950, charts on pp. 82–3).

midst of those who have upheld you and sustained you, to enlighten them, instruct them, moderate them when they are angered, stimulate them when they lose courage, in short to govern them'. The real question was whether democracy should be given its fair share in the affairs of the country. The new social strata of which he had spoken represented the working world which wished to enter the world of politics because it was its right and it was capable of doing so. Such things were right and useful to say 'here in Belleville of ill-repute (General laughter)'.

Thus did Gambetta reassert control and 'govern' his 'tail'. But in his speech he astutely inserted the remark that the policy of parliamentary compromise and support of the government when expedient should be continued after the liberation of the territory.[1] It was a pointer to Gambetta's innate opportunism or sense of political realities.

Prudence, *sagesse*, this note, as has been seen, he had sounded much more urgently at Nantes and, although on the fatal day of 24 May he was reported to have been striding through the corridors of the Assembly like an enraged bull,[2] he soon recovered his self-control and took a lead in reiterating the Republican appeal for calm. Calm was, of course, essential in order to give the lie to the thesis of the Right that the Radicals stood for violence, revolution and destruction. Gambetta had, ever since his speech at Bordeaux at the end of June 1871, preached moderation and ever since then the Republicans had begun, in Daniel Halévy's phrase, to play a new game for them, the game of legality.[3] Now in the summer of 1873 came the first great tests of Radical nerves, the tests presented by the 'parliamentary *coup d'état*' of 24 May, the inauguration of the reign of 'Moral order' and the biggest effort of the Right to effect a monarchical restoration.

'Moral order'—ironically enough these words which were now to attain such celebrity had been used by Gambetta in his speech at Grenoble. Denouncing the inadequacies of the government's legislation he had declared that its only effect was to engender moral if not material disorder when it was moral order with which statesmen ought above all to concern themselves.[4] Now 'moral order' of a very different sort from that envisaged by Gambetta was, in the words of an inaugural letter from MacMahon,

---

1. It is interesting to note that the R.F. of 16/17 July 1873 (p. 2) would praise the Spaniard Castelar's definition of politics as 'une série de transactions entre l'idéal et la réalité, et une autre série de transactions entre les divers partis qui se disputent le gouvernement'.

2. A. Laugel, 'Le Maréchal de MacMahon et le 16 mai', *Revue de Paris* (1 Aug. 1966), p. 502.

3. *La République des ducs* (1937), p. 8.

4. *Discours*, vol. iii, p. 100.

to be reestablished, and reestablished by a veritable 'gouvernement de combat'.

Gambetta, if the *New York Herald* correspondent is to be believed, had shared Thiers's view that McMahon would refuse the presidency. 'He has,' he said, 'no fancy for politics; no skill in public affairs. He is a pure simple soldier, no more no less, with all the skill of a sergeant-major.'[1] Here again he had proved a bad prophet, although he was correct in his diagnosis that MacMahon, despite a certain shrewdness, had no fancy for politics or skill in public affairs. But wisely he and the *République Française* refrained from attacking the Marshal, although, in his inaugural message, the Marshal had referred to the Assembly as a bulwark of society which was threatened by 'a faction which menaces the repose of all peoples and seeks your dissolution only because it sees in you the principal obstacle to its plans'. They gently reminded him that he was only the first servant of France and should be above parties[2] and they reserved their fire for the new cabinet which was now truly the real government of France.[3] Its leader, the Vice-President of the Council of Ministers, was Broglie, who had played such a prominent part in the debates of the last two sessions, but who was a novice of fifty-three and had never before held ministerial office. He had conducted his campaign with great ability, but he was at the disadvantage of having troops who were divided in allegiance. The very composition of the government, as he wrote in his *Mémoires*, dictated its policy. There were three 'pure Monarchists', three constitutional Monarchists or Orleanists, namely himself and two others, one Bonapartist—the only man with previous experience as a Minister—and one Conservative Republican. Hence, in his words:

> The reform of the administration which contained too many revolutionary elements left over from 4 September, the restraint of abuses by the Press, in short, a struggle against those passions inimical to all social order, and incompatible with any government, these were the only objectives which a cabinet composed of such elements could set itself. Had it sought to give the country a constitution it would at once have been divided. We had a tacit agreement to defer any

---

1. 27 Jan. 1873. Later, however, at dinner in 1881 with the Marquis du Lau, according to Ludovic Halévy, Gambetta professed to have 'prévu l'avènement de MacMahon. Changarnier se tenait prêt. J'étais, dit Gambetta, au mieux avec Changarnier; je lui disais: "Vous savez, ce ne sera pas vous, ce sera MacMahon." Il me répondait: "Ce n'est pas possible, c'est l'homme le plus bête de l'armée. — Ce sera lui, ce sera lui." Et ce fut lui' (L. Halévy, *Trois dîners avec Gambetta*, 1929, p. 44).

2. *R.F.*, 29 May.

3. MacMahon in a message of 26 May had specifically stated that the magistrate entrusted with the executive power was merely the delegate of the Assembly in which the real authority lay.

question of this kind for some time and to maintain the unity of the Conservative party.[1]

Unity—this, too, was Gambetta's foremost preoccupation. Already at Nantes on 16 May he had urged that the Republican party should present a unified front in the face of the enemy.[2] Back from Nantes two days later, he had attended a meeting of the Republican Union at which he had spoken urging his hearers 'to forget their late disagreements and become united again against the Monarchists'.[3] It was notable that it was the Republican Union which now for a while took the lead among the groups of the Left. On 25 May, the morrow of 'the sad and lamentable day' of Thiers's overthrow,[4] the Radical papers printed an appeal for calm over a hundred and fifteen signatures. The men who headed the list were leaders of the Union, Peyrat, Gambetta, Lockroy and Louis Blanc. Their manifesto urged Frenchmen to avoid anything which would add to public excitement: 'never was the calm that comes from strength more necessary. . . . The safety of France and the Republic depend on this.' On the same day a full meeting of the Union had agreed that 'with calm, coolness and vigilance, there was no danger that could not be met', and at another full meeting on 5 June deputies back from the provinces were reported to be full of confidence in the 'good disposition' of the people in their departments.[5] If the Radicals were, despite all, confident compared with the more moderate Thierist Republicans, there is little doubt that this was partly due to the resilience and indomitable cheerfulness of Gambetta. 'The situation is excellent', he soon reassured his friends; 'this man, M. Thiers, tumbles into our arms along with the Republic; we shall profit from his popularity.'[6] 'After all', he told Freycinet, 'we now have a more clear-cut situation. . . . The people can see who are their friends. There are now only two parties: those who want to destroy the Republic

1. *Mémoires*, vol. ii, p. 195.
2. *Discours*, vol. iii, p. 389. The *R.F.* of 26 May (p. 4) announced that Gambetta's speech at Nantes was on sale for ten centimes.
3. *The Times*, 19 May 1873. *The Times* report spoke of the meeting as one of 'the Extreme Left', at which several deputies who had supported Rémusat were present.
4. *R.F.*, 26 May.
5. *R.F.*, 6 June.
6. Goblet, *art. cit.*, *Revue politique et parlementaire* (10 Sept. 1928), p. 363. But to judge by what Lord Newton asserts that Gambetta told Lord Lyons's private secretary, George Sheffield, there was still no love lost between Gambetta and Thiers: 'He expressed great delight at the fall of Thiers . . . and said that under him no real self-acting Republic could ever have been formed, that it would have fallen to pieces at his death, and indeed that the best thing Thiers could do for the Republic would be to die' (Newton, *Lord Lyons*, pp. 350-1).

and those who wish to preserve it. The hybrid party of the Republic without Republicans has fortunately disappeared.'[1]

The appeals for unity were effective, at any rate for the time being. Jules Ferry, whose acceptance of the post of Minister at Athens, offered him by Thiers in May 1872, had been damned with faint praise by the *République Française*,[2] resigned and rejoined his Republican colleagues; prominent journalists such as Adrien Hébrard of the *Temps*, which had engaged in sharp controversy with the *République Française* during the Barodet election, and Edmond About, editor of the *XIXe Siècle*, whose conversion to Republicanism Gambetta's paper a year earlier had treated with scorn,[3] forgot their differences. Even Jules Grévy temporarily concealed his antagonism to Gambetta in the interests of a common cause. The ability of the Republicans to close their ranks was indeed impressive. So was their *sagesse* and their restraint in refraining from vain agitation. The new regime might pose as the restorer of moral order and seek to silence its adversaries; but it could not dispel an economic recession nor could it claim to be the saviour of a society in the throes of revolutionary violence.

The two prime objectives of the new Cabinet and the parties it represented, namely purging the administration and restraining the Press, were indeed aimed at silencing the enemy on the Left. Thiers had been overthrown, but the Radical leader Gambetta was still to be reckoned with. Everything that administration could do to discredit him and muffle the sound of that too persuasive voice would surely be done. An administrative purge was no new thing in France; it was 'the normal and often the most definite outcome of every revolutionary crisis',[4] and Gambetta and his colleagues had promptly embarked on one after the Revolution of

1. Freycinet, *Souvenirs 1848–1875*, p. 302.

2. *R.F.*, 16 May 1872: 'bien que le député de Paris ait depuis longtemps perdu de vue la théorie "des destructions nécessaires" [a phrase Ferry had used in the election campaign of 1869], bien que le gouvernant du 4 Septembre ait singulièrement méconnu la pensée qui l'avait porté au pouvoir, nous voyons toujours avec satisfaction M. le président de la République s'adresser de préférence à qui a conservé encore la nuance républicaine, si décolorée que soit cette nuance. . . . Ecrivain prudent et mesuré, M. Ferry n'est pas toujours maître de sa parole, et il est à craindre qu'il ne devienne un agent compromettant apres avoir été un homme politique compromis.' Pessard, commenting on this passage (*Mes petits papiers*, 2me série, p. 258) remarked: 'les douceurs, sans cesse répétées, ne facilitaient pas la concentration des forces républicaines dans l'Assemblée et n'étaient point faites pour amener les hésitants à la République. Les mouches, même celles du coche, n'ont aucun goût pour le vinaigre.'

3. *R.F.*, 12 May 1872. He had been attacked by the *R.F.* again as recently as 30 March 1873, as a man who had long 'fourragé sur les ailes de tous les partis'. Cf. Marcère, *L'Assemblée Nationale de 1871*, vol. i, p. 252.

4. Marcère, *op. cit.*, p. 9.

4 September 1870. Although the crisis of 24 May was less revolutionary he purge undertaken by Broglie and his colleagues was remarkably thorough, and the series of changes in prefects and subprefects which took place at the end of May and at intervals during the summer ensured that most of the key posts in the departments were soon in the hands of supporters of 'moral order', many of whom had had administrative experience under the Empire. Such men could be relied on to apply pressure at election time and enforce restrictive Press laws with zeal. The *République Française* had often had cause to criticise Thiers for his maintenance or nomination of officials whom it regarded as reactionary.[1] But if the prefects of Thiers had chastised with whips those of 'moral order' would chastise with scorpions.

The Radical Press was understandably one of the first targets of the new administration. In the eight months before Thiers's fall the campaign for compulsory secular education had continued with the publication of pamphlets such as Jean Macé's series called *Les Idées de Jean-François*, and new Radical papers had been founded and welcomed by the *République Française*.[2] In mid-May, greeting the début of the biweekly *Républicain du Lot*, it had reiterated the importance of propaganda, especially through the Press: since the Press was 'the most effective and certain agent', it was the development of the Press which should be the prime object of the Republican party's care.[3] The Radical Press had already suffered when Goulard was Minister of the Interior, particularly in March when various papers had been prosecuted, suspended or suppressed. In spite of powerful criticism in the Assembly by Gambetta's friend and colleague Rouvier and others, the Minister had taken no active steps to curb the activities of military governors and prefects. Forty-three departments were still under martial law and in these areas military governors had the right to regulate the Press in accordance with the needs of public safety; but their powers were ill-defined and they were under no obligation to account in public for the way in which they exercised them. Moreover, by a law of July 1849 which was still on the statute book, prefects could virtually force out of existence any papers of which they or the government disapproved by refusing licences to hawk such papers.[4]

Thus when the Broglie government came to power it inherited effective

1. e.g. R.F., 30, 31 Oct., 1, 3 Nov. 1872.
2. e.g. 22 Oct. 1872 (*Le Républicain* of the Nièvre); 23 Nov. (*La Résurrection*); 8 Jan. 1873 (*La Tribune Républicaine* of Marseilles). On 3 June it hailed the arrival of *L'Impartial de l'Aisne*.
3. R.F., 12 May 1873.
4. Early in July Gambetta and his colleagues tabled a Bill for the repeal of the offending clause in the 1849 law.

weapons with which to 'restrain' the Press, and it soon showed that it intended to make full use of them.[1] The editors of the *République Française* and its Radical fellows had to walk very warily during the coming months.[2] But occasionally the administration overreached itself and then the Radicals could get their revenge. Indeed, as early as 10 June a debate in the Assembly on the suppression of the *Corsaire*, Portalis's paper which was not for the first time in trouble, gave Gambetta a splendid opportunity to discomfit Broglie and his colleagues. Unknown to Beulé, the Minister of the Interior, a zealous Under-Secretary in his Ministry named Pascal had issued a confidential circular requesting prefects to send in a full report on the state of the Press in their departments and to find out, among other things, the financial circumstances of conservative papers 'or those which might be tempted to become so' as well as 'the value they might attach to the sympathetic aid of the administration'. A copy of the circular came into Gambetta's hands[3] and, although such governmental efforts to influence the Press were no new thing in nineteenth-century France, their revelation at the outset of a new ministry of 'moral order' could not but make a bad impression. Gambetta exploited the situation with prodigious enjoyment and skill. He read the circular aloud, gleefully and dramatically commenting on each sentence.[4] 'Such a circular, if it is authentic', he declared, 'enables us to judge the kind of moral order which is being introduced into the administration.' The unhappy government still kept its majority, but it accepted Pascal's resignation and some weeks later appointed him prefect of the Gironde. For Broglie and his colleagues the affair was a parliamentary setback from which, one Left-wing journalist claimed, they never recovered.

If the Radical Press in general was one of the government's first targets, an individual Radical journalist, none other than Ranc, Gambetta's close friend and collaborator on the *République Française*, was one of their early

1. On 27 Aug. the R.F. (p. 2) stated that since 24 May five papers had been suppressed and sixteen been stopped from being sold in the streets. In September sixteen provincial papers were suppressed, fifteen of them in the South of France.

2. On 24 Aug. the R.F. reported that its street sale had been forbidden in Savoy.

3. The *Bien Public* of 15 June denied the report (accepted by Seignobos, *op. cit.*, p. 363) that the copy of the circular had been given by a prefect to Thiers who had passed it on to Gambetta. Thiers indeed affected to ridicule the whole affair: 'Se plaindre qu'on achète les journaux', he said, 'c'est se plaindre que l'on corrompe une fille publique' (quoted in R. Dreyfus, 'La déception monarchique de 1873', *Revue de France*, 15 June 1933, p. 661).

4. For the text of his intervention, see *Ass. Nat. A.*, vol. xviii, pp. 264–6, and *Discours*, vol. iv, pp. 6–11, and for a brilliant and lively sketch of the scene, C. Pelletan, *Le Théâtre de Versailles. L'Assemblée au jour le jour du 24 mai au 25 février* (1875), p. 47.

and particular victims. In attacking Ranc, Gambetta truly, if egotistically, observed they were aiming at him.[1] Ranc had been an object of suspicion to the Right ever since his shortlived association with the Commune.[2] Their papers had frequently assailed him and they had been infuriated by his recent triumphant election to the Assembly by the people of Lyon. Broglie had already marked him down as a prey when in his speech of 23 May he had referred to a colleague who, 'but for an as yet inexplicable tardiness in the execution of justice, would have had to give an account of his conduct'.[3] A few days later General Ladmirault, the Military Governor of Paris, demanded the account and on 14 June the bureaux of the Assembly met to appoint a Commission to examine whether there was a case for prosecution.[4] In the fourth bureau Gambetta did his best to defend his friend. He pointed out that the charges brought had already been examined and that Ranc had appeared before tribunals and not been incriminated. His case had been discussed in the Assembly as the result of an interpellation on 20 December 1871, the Minister of Justice had declared that nothing could be done, and the Assembly had passed the 'order of the day pure and simple' and gone on to the next business.[5] Gambetta also drew attention to the fact that it was only since his election as a deputy that Ranc was now the intended object of a new prosecution; public opinion would regard General Ladmirault's action as a deplorable act of reprisal.[6] But, despite Gambetta's intervention and the leaders on the subject printed by the *République Française* on seven successive days,[7] the case went forward. On 20 June the Assembly voted in favour of prosecution by the substantial majority of 467 to 140. Meanwhile Ranc, in *The Times*'s phrase, had deemed 'it prudent to seek a change of air'. No doubt Gambetta was among those who urged him to slip across the frontier into Belgium, and so it was in his absence that he was on 13 October condemned to death by the third Court Martial of Versailles. It was unlikely that the death sentence would have been carried out, but in prison or transported, like Henri Rochefort a few weeks later, to New Caledonia, Ranc would have been of little use to

---

1. *Lettres*, no. 157.
2. See above, p. 14.
3. *Ass. Nat. A.*, vol. xviii, p. 31.
4. In accordance with its règlements or house rules the Assembly divided itself monthly into a number of bureaux, the members being chosen by lot. These bureaux gave preliminary consideration to proposed legislative measures, etc., and then each chose 'one of its number to serve as a member of the special committee which was to study the proposal and to report on it to a public session of the Assembly (R. K. Gooch, *The French Parliamentary Committee System*, 1935, p. 33).
5. For the debate of 20 Dec. 1871, see *Ass. Nat. A.*, vol. vi, pp. 197–208.
6. See *The Times*, 16 June.
7. 14–21 June inclusive.

the Radical cause. In Belgium he was accessible;[1] he settled down in Brussels, played dominoes regularly, and could still render yeoman service as a contributor to the *République Française*. Yet Gambetta's paper which had defended him persistently in June kept silent when condemnation came in October. The silence was prudent and calculated, if not courageous, and there were good reasons for it. The threat of a restoration of Monarchy still loomed large and at such a juncture Gambetta could not bear to risk the suppression of the *République Française* by the ever-vigilant guardians of moral order. So Spuller had to write to Ranc: 'As you can imagine we have only been able to record this absurd and sinister trial without commenting upon it. It is more than ever necessary for us to be prudent; they are looking for any opportunity to find fault with us and on the first that arises we shall be seized. There is no need to tell you more: you would have been the first to recommend us to keep silent.'[2]

Silence, in this summer of 1873, was also to be the order of the day for politicians outside the Assembly, while the discussion of constitutional questions within it was to be deferred until after the summer vacation. These issues, however, gave Gambetta an opportunity to intervene in the none the less noisy debates which marked the end of the session. In the Assembly on 2 July Dufaure, who had introduced the previous government's constitutional proposals just before Thiers's fall, demanded that a commission should be appointed to examine them. In doing so he remarked that the only people who could logically object to his request were those members of the Republican Left who had consistently denied the Assembly's constituent power. Thereupon Gambetta seized the chance to leap to the tribune—according to *The Times* he used to ascend it 'as if he were about to vault over it', he 'throws back his hair, puts his hands into his pockets while he waits for silence and . . . throughout his speech looks

---

1. At 3 p.m. on 7 July Ranc fought a sword duel at Bettembourg in the Grand-Duchy of Luxembourg with Paul de Cassagnac, editor of the Bonapartist paper *Le Pays*. In an article in January Cassagnac had written: 'Vous êtes Ranc le communard, Ranc l'ami des incendiaires et des égorgeurs, Ranc l'exécuteur des basses oeuvres du parti radical, le bras droit de Gambetta.' Gambetta who was much attached to Ranc took a great interest in the duel and in the choice of Ranc's seconds. He and Edmond Adam left secretly for Belgium in order to be at hand when the duel was fought (Mme Adam, *Nos amitiés politiques avant l'abandon de la revanche*, p. 17). They then went on to Brussels. Ranc was wounded in the arm. Duelling, it has been said (Christopher Andrew, *Théophile Delcassé and the Making of the Entente Cordiale*, 1968, pp. 6–7), 'was in a real sense an occupational hazard of French journalism at a time when many writers felt it a point of honour to have at least one encounter to their credit'. A month later Hervé, editor of the *Journal de Paris*, fought a duel with About, the editor of the *XIXe Siècle*.

2. Letter of 14 Oct. (Ranc, *Souvenirs-Correspondance 1831–1908*, pp. 214–15). The trial was recorded in the *R.F.* of 15 Oct., pp. 2–3.

round as if expecting interruptions'.[1] Interruptions there were in plenty as Gambetta reiterated his familiar plea for dissolution, but now that Thiers had fallen and despite the fact that there were by now several seats vacant, it was a plea which had less effect. Broglie tersely replied that the Assembly had not waited for Gambetta's permission to be born and that it did not need it to live and to rule France. The Assembly agreed, moreover, with Broglie that the appointment of a constitutional commission before the vacation was inopportune and had best be deferred until a month after the winter session began. Thus Broglie successfully played for time.

Meanwhile the government made clear that it would forbid the celebration of inconvenient anniversaries such as 14 July,[2] 21 August (the proclamation of the First Republic) or 4 September, which might be the occasion of unwelcome Republican demonstrations and oratory. So far as oratory was concerned, it was evident that they had Gambetta particularly in mind. There should be no more 'speeches of Grenoble'. Already at Versailles at the end of June, when Gambetta had again been invited to speak at the annual commemoration of General Hoche, the prefect had forbidden a public banquet in a hotel and Gambetta had had to content himself with delivering his defence of freedom of speech and his vigorous assault on the new administration to a comparatively small gathering in a private house.[3] Now towards the end of July the government promoted a Bill giving the Permanent Commission the right during the vacation to authorise proceedings against persons committing offences against the Assembly 'by way of publication'. Gambetta twice intervened in the turbulent debates preceding the passage of the Bill.[4] He demanded 'fair play' and the right of meeting and freedom of propaganda as basic liberties and he protested against a measure directed *ad hominem*, in other words to preventing Gambetta himself from exercising what one speaker scornfully called 'the freedom of the balcony'. But he protested in vain, and when it became law the Bill was to a considerable extent effective in muzzling him, although he could not be wholly silenced. During the

1. 9 July. For the text of Gambetta's intervention, see *Ass. Nat. A.*, vol. xix, pp. 12–14.

2. The *R.F.* of 15 July (in which the leading article was dated '14 juillet') announced that, 'à l'occasion de l'anniversaire du 14 juillet', it would not appear 'demain'. This, as D. Halévy remarked, was 'une autre manière de le fêter. Gambetta (qui l'eût attendu de lui?) apprit ainsi au duc qu'il y avait une éloquence de silence' (*La République des ducs*, p. 38). But it was not so silent as not to publish a series of commemorative articles in its number of 15 July.

3. But the speech was soon printed by E. Leroux and put on sale for ten centimes. For the text, see *Discours*, vol. iv, pp. 15–27.

4. For the text, see *ibid.*, vol. iv, pp. 53–67, and *Ass. Nat. A.*, vol. xix, pp. 154–6 and 364–9.

vacation he made only a few comparatively brief speeches and, such was the repressive atmosphere of 'moral order', the *République Française*, which normally published its patron's utterances in full, contented itself with printing brief summaries culled from a local paper. As for the two main speeches, those delivered at Périgueux and Châtellerault, it did not print a line of them, and the sale of the *Siècle*, which did, was promptly forbidden in the streets of the Seine department.[1] Thus there was war to the knife between Gambetta and the 'gouvernement de combat'; but it was a war which transcended personal vendettas. It was, the *République Française* claimed in a leading article on the significance of 14 July,[2] a duel without quarter between the French Revolution and the past, while the government's tortuous policy was now revealed as above all a policy of clericalism.[3] This indeed could seem a warranted charge, for the climate of 'moral order' was such that French Catholics and Legitimists had taken great heart and were loud in clamour and activity. The Prefect of the Rhône forbad civil burials after 6 a.m. in summer and 7 a.m. in winter. The Assembly itself voted the building of a great expiatory church that would dominate Paris from the heights of Montmartre and, while Radical voices were hushed, many parts of France resounded to the tramp and chanting of pilgrims who invoked the Sacred Heart and prayed for the restoration of Pope and King.

With the advent of the parliamentary vacation—on 29 July the Assembly was prorogued until 5 November—the duel between the government and the Republicans entered a new phase.[4] On the first day of the vacation the Republican Union met and issued a statement which was given wide publicity in Republican papers. It claimed that the parliamentary revolution of 24 May had strengthened the discipline and unity of the Republican party. Its members must continue to struggle with all legal means against the promoters of restoration and to enlighten democracy as to its true interests. It was with 'genuine confidence in the loyalty of the declarations made by the first magistrate of the Republic' that the representatives of the Republican Union were going to visit their constituents, 'not without having promised to devote this too long vacation to the

1. R. Dreyfus, 'Gambetta et la naissance de l'opportunisme' (*Revue de France*, p. 415), suggested that Gambetta's editorial colleagues might well have feared 'de propager des paroles dont le modérantisme risquait d'effaroucher prématurément les purs du parti'. But the two speeches were soon printed as usual by Ernest Leroux and sold together as a brochure for fifteen centimes.

2. *R.F.*, 15 July.

3. *Ibid.*, 30 June.

4. A police agent's report of 4 August alleged that Sandrique, Spuller and others 'l'avaient (i.e. Gambetta) champagnisé à force ce matin ... aux environs de Paris' (A.P.P. BA/918). No doubt this was a celebration of the beginning of the holidays.

defence and propagation of their ideas. They think that they owe it to their electors to visit and talk to them and above all to convince them of the political necessity of the dissolution of the National Assembly.'[1]

This statement contained two references of particular significance: one to 'the promoters of restoration', the other to 'the loyalty . . . of the first magistrate', in other words, MacMahon. If the Republican Union did not intend to be idle during the vacation, nor did the Right. 'Given the situation we now occupy in the Assembly and the country', Broglie had written to a confidant of the Comte de Paris 'it would be unpardonable for us not to attempt to restore the monarchy.'[2] Thiers, in fact, had been right in his fighting speech before his fall to point out that the burning issue was still not that of Conservatism or Radicalism, but of Republic or Monarchy. The attempt at restoration was to be the great enterprise of the Monarchists during the vacation. But in any such enterprise the attitude of the actual holder of executive power must at some moments be crucial. In one of his declarations immediately after his election as President MacMahon had affirmed that there would be no interference with existing laws and institutions. Gambetta in his speech at Versailles on 24 June had seized on this and uttered a solemn appeal and warning to the Marshal. MacMahon's declarations, he said, constituted 'a solemn pact with the whole country, a sacred contract which could only be broken by a *coup de force* from below or an attack from above'. In either case resort to violence would be unpardonable and 'the world and history would pass the severest judgement on the man who deserted legality to enter upon crime'.[3]

MacMahon's character, however, was such that he needed no warning from Gambetta. Indeed he may well have resented such apostrophes from a man of whom he fundamentally disapproved although he had admired his wartime role.[4] He would be no party to a *coup d'état* but, elected by the Assembly, he intended to abide by its law. Thus if only the barest majority ('even that of a single vote') 'were to decide to bring back the King, the Marshal would without hesitation carry out the sovereign decree; he would ensure the support of the army'.[5] But early in October he thought it his duty to make it clear that the army was wedded to the tricolour and that to offend it where the flag was concerned would risk provoking most

1. For the text, see *Discours*, vol. iv, pp. 67–9. The statement was printed by the R.F. of 31 July instead of a leader. The R.F. of 13 Aug. printed several letters to their constituents written by deputies of the Republican Union.

2. Cit. Seignobos, *op. cit.*, p. 365; cf. Broglie, *Mémoires*, vol. ii, p. 196.

3. *Discours*, vol. iv, p. 25. Cf. R.F. leader of 13 Aug. reemphasising MacMahon's undertaking to maintain existing laws and institutions.

4. See Deschanel, *Gambetta* (Paris, 1919), p. 161.

5. R. Dreyfus, 'La déception monarchique de 1873' in *La Revue de France*, 15 June 1933, p. 663.

serious trouble;[1] and a month later he refused to receive the Comte de Chambord, when, as a last gamble, the Pretender came privily to Versailles hoping to win over the Marshal and, by a sudden appearance with him in the Assembly, take that body by storm and be acclaimed as King. Both MacMahon's actions were crucial and wholly in character. The latter gave the *coup de grâce* to Chambord's hopes of restoration and made certain that, unless he renounced his rights or the internal situation dramatically changed, there would be no restoration during his lifetime.

But for the best part of three months Monarchist hopes had been soaring. The Comte de Paris had at last visited his cousin, meeting him in Vienna early in August and this reconciliation between the two Pretenders was widely believed to imply 'fusion'. There were many subsequent comings and goings in the Monarchist camp and eventually things seemed to have proceeded far enough for the preparation of a constitutional bill whereby, it was hoped, the Assembly would effect the restoration of Henry V along with the maintenance of the tricolour flag. The royal carriages were ordered and shopkeepers in Paris were getting ready to sell white flags and cockades against the entry of the King. But now, as all along, there was a basic misunderstanding. The Orleanists would not abandon the tricolour and, despite the pressure put upon him, Chambord remained intransigently loyal to his 'principle', of which for him the white flag was the embodiment. After many misunderstandings and equivocations Chambord on 27 October wrote a letter to the Catholic deputy Chesnelong, who had been the chief intermediary between the Pretender and the Monarchists in France. It cut the ground away from the feet of all those who had been working for his restoration. He would not sacrifice his honour or abandon 'the standard of Arques and Ivry'. The letter was for the Monarchists a shattering and irreparable blow.

How seriously were the prospects of restoration taken by Gambetta and his colleagues and what measures, if any, did they adopt to reduce them, apart from the summer communion with constituents advocated by the Republican Union? That they were worried there can be little doubt. Madame Adam related how Gambetta, sometime after 24 May,[2] had talked one evening of a plan for forming 'central electoral committees' rather on the pattern of the Charbonnerie of the 1820s.

> Those enrolled will undertake to risk their lives in defence of the Republic. They must be resolved not to dispute any order; only one member of each

---

1. MacMahon's latest biographer denies that he uttered the famous phrase 'à la vue du drapeau blanc, les chassepots partiraient tout seuls' (Silvestre de Sacy, *Le Maréchal de MacMahon*, p. 281).
2. As all too often she is exasperatingly imprecise in her chronology.

committee will know what are the directives from above and he will know the name of only one of the members of the directing committee. The head of a central regional committee will be like a military commander. He will be able to summon the members under his orders to act without any discussion. Since the Monarchists have declared that the Monarchy could be established by a majority of a single vote, we must at all costs prevent this from being possible. The only programme would be that of defending national sovereignty against the coalition of the Right-wing groups; the only watchword: the Republic must not capitulate at Versailles in the way that France capitulated to the Prussians. Each military leader of the central regional committees would command a group of two or three hundred experienced and reliable citizens each of whom would have under their orders ten or twenty men who would know only them.

'It would be impossible', added Madame Adam, for the government to lay hands on such an organisation.'[1] It seems equally impossible for the historian to do so. Did such an organisation ever come into existence or was it simply an invention of Juliette Adam's or a bright but hardly original idea of Gambetta's? In default of further evidence it must be supposed that it remained in the realm of ideas. The plans put forward later were probably less dramatically conspiratorial.

While the *République Française* for the most part adopted a confident, belligerent and disdainful tone throughout the crisis, Gambetta himself, as might be expected, was pessimistic or optimistic according to his mood and his latest intelligence. There was pessimism first of all, recorded by Hébrard of the *Temps* who dined with him soon after he had had the news of the meeting of the two Pretenders in Austria. Unlike Thiers, whom Hébrard had recently seen and who thought that Monarchy had no chance, Gambetta was 'very anxious'. He believed that the country was weary and that the mass of the people would resign themselves to a restoration. Indeed the best thing would be to let the restoration take place: the restored Monarchy would prove ridiculous and collapse without the firing of a shot. But he feared that everyone would not show restraint: there might be excesses in the small towns and a peasant *jacquerie* with the destruction of churches and the burning of châteaux. This would compromise the Republican cause.[2] Gambetta's pessimism was in contrast with the relative optimism of Spuller at about the same time. 'All the news, written or oral, which comes to us from the provinces', he told Ranc, 'agrees in saying that Republican views are making astonishing progress in the country districts. The peasant wants the Republic . . . because he sees

1. *Mes angoisses*, pp. 404–5.
2. 'Les Carnets de Ludovic Halévy, II', *Revue des Deux Mondes* (1 Feb. 1937), p. 544, entry of 13 Aug. 1873. D. Halévy summarised and dramatised this conversation in *La République des ducs*, p. 40.

that the priest and the nobles and people of that ilk do not want it.'[1] Later in the month, however, Gambetta, too, wrote to Ranc and expressed a prescient and guarded optimism: 'It is certain . . . that there is a hitch in the fusion . . . it seems virtually certain that the Comte de Chambord does not mean to give way on the white flag and reserves the right to grant a Charter . . . we must be ever on the watch. But . . . it seems to be definite that serious disagreements have arisen in the fusionist camp.'[2]

Conviction that these disagreements were seriously impeding the Monarchists' plans no doubt encouraged him to enjoy a brief holiday abroad, his first since his San Sebastian exile. Enjoy it he did, as an enthusiastic letter revealed,[3] all the more so since he took it in the company of his new inamorata, Léonie Léon, 'la petite reine', whom a police agent wrongly supposed he must have married a fortnight earlier.[4] They travelled incognito, using the surname of his colleague of the *République Française*, Péphau, and went, probably by way of Brussels, to The Hague and Amsterdam, returning via Spa. He had never, he wrote, had such a delicious journey, never felt so continuously happy or glad to be alive. It was a buoyant and vigorous Gambetta who summoned the real Péphau to meet him on his return to Paris at 11 p.m. on the evening of Sunday, 14 September.

Meanwhile the deputies of the Republican Union, or such of them as were able to be in Paris, had begun to hold fortnightly meetings which were to be continued throughout the vacation. The second of these took place on 16 August. Once again the statement issued was confident. As in the autumn of 1872, so in the autumn of 1873 more by-elections were pending and the Radicals as ever had a keen eye on the electorate. 'Information specially received', said the statement,

from the eleven departments which will have to fill up vacancies . . . concurs in proving that there exists to the north as well as the south of the Loire a perfect harmony between all shades of the Republican democracy, and it appears . . . from town and rural districts alike that the triumph of the Republican candidates, if delayed by the temporising of the Administration of May 24, will be none the less remarkable.[5]

The meeting broke up with the firm conviction that the session of the General Councils about to open would prove 'the accuracy of the reports . . . as to the moral and political position of the country'. General Councils as well as by-elections—from the first Gambetta and the *République*

1. Ranc, *op. cit.*, p. 236, letter of 7 Aug.
2. *Lettres*, no. 161, 22 Aug. (Cf. the confident leader of 25 Aug. in R.F.)
3. *Ibid.*, no. 162, 4 Sept.
4. Police report from Brussels, 2 Sept. (A.P.P., BA/918).
5. *The Times*, 18 Aug.

Française had nursed the General Councils, in which he professed to see the 'new social strata already at work', and now the fruits were beginning to ripen; on 17 August Republicans were returned in elections in five departments and in many Councils the presidents made declarations of loyalty to the Republic which were given wide publicity. As for the by-elections, there might be eleven vacancies, but the 'temporising of the Assembly' or rather of the government would mean that only four would take place during the summer recess.[1] But the results of these by-elections of 12 October in the Nièvre, Puy-de-Dôme, Loire, and Haute-Garonne would justify the optimism of the Republican Union, 'surpass all expectations' according to the *République Française* on the 15th, and mark a further setback for the Monarchists;[2] in two of the constituencies Monarchists were replaced, one by a moderate and the other by a conservative Republican, the latter being none other than Rémusat. What was particularly striking was the increase of the Republican vote in rural areas. To a large extent this was due to the way in which the Republicans, and not least the Radicals, had exploited the peasants' fears, fears of war, war with Italy for the restoration of the Pope, and fears of social changes to their detriment. The Right had earlier raised the spectre of the Commune; the Left had now conjured up that of the *ancien régime*, of the return of feudalism and the rule of priest and noble. It had disseminated popular *images d'Epinal* depicting the unhappy lot of the peasantry under the *ancien régime* and in places there was almost a pale reflection of the *grande peur* of 1789: in one village in the Loire the peasants were said to have penned their livestock in the belief that Henri V would demand a levy of beasts to mark his accession.[3]

By the time of the by-elections the restoration crisis had entered its final phases. There was less than a month to go before the Assembly returned to work and it was widely expected that, if they were able to proceed with their plans, the Monarchists would lose no time in putting the restoration to the vote. In view of this threat to 'established institutions' the Republican forces began to mobilise as never before, but now it was not Gambetta, but Thiers who was the real head of the combined forces of opposition. The ex-President had no intention of retiring from politics. It was seldom anything but enforced leisure which confined him wholly to his 'chères

1. A seat could be left vacant for six months. According to C. de B. (Rothschild pp., 13 Sept.) the government was deferring the elections as long as possible because the prefects' reports still indicated that the Radicals were 'maîtres du terrain'.

2. Léonie Léon wrote to Gambetta on the 13th: 'Il n'y a rien de tel que des élections comme celles-là pour guérir le rhume, aussi après un pareil triomphe je ne demande plus de vos nouvelles' (Ass. Nat., p. 92).

3. See Hanotaux, *Histoire de la fondation de la troisième république*, vol. iii (1926), p. 162.

études' and a few days after his fall he had reappeared in the Assembly in his capacity as a deputy of the Seine and taken his seat on the Left. The occasion had been seized by all the groups of the Left, including the Republican Union, to give him a great ovation. Now he had returned from a holiday in Switzerland, having been enthusiastically acclaimed on his way there by the newly liberated people of Belfort and Nancy. As the man responsible for the liberation of the territory, just completed on 16 September, he was riding the crest of a new wave of popularity and he made no secret of his attitude to 'the threatening danger of a Monarchist restoration'. Resentment at the way he had been overthrown and dislike of the policies of his successors now made him a natural ally of the Left which had assiduously courted him since his fall. As Lord Lytton put it on 7 October, 'M. Gambetta and the chiefs of the advanced Republican camp, having sagaciously agreed to range themselves . . . behind M. Thiers, the ex-President is at this moment the virtual leader of all the anti-Conservative forces in France'.[1] But though he was said to have shaken Gambetta by the hand in the Assembly early in July,[2] there is no evidence that Thiers met Gambetta face to face to concert policies. Their collaboration was probably still effected through intermediaries.[3]

The mobilisation of opposition had two main purposes: the mustering of the groups in parliament for unified action and for pressure on the waverers in the Centre who might swing the Assembly's vote for or against restoration, and the rallying of opinion outside parliament in such volume as to frighten the Monarchists and deter them from their enterprise. Essentially it was a war of nerves. So far as the first objective was concerned, *The Times* of 4 October reported that the members of the Extreme Left, by which it meant Gambetta's party, had already agreed to follow the lead of the Left and Left Centre, in other words of the two groups with whom Thiers was most in sympathy, and it was proposed to put pressure on vacillating deputies by getting up petitions in their departments urging them to vote for the Republic. The three groups had also, it said, agreed with the Republican newspapers in the provinces to present a united front when general elections were held to support candidates who would vote for the Republic irrespective of their antecedents. Three days later the Republican Union agreed to appoint a liaison committee to

1. P.R.O., F.O. 146, 1678. Lytton to Granville. Cf. letter of 30 Sept. from Republicans at Figeac to MM. Thiers, Louis Blanc et Gambetta and Louis Blanc's reply (L. Blanc, *Questions d'aujourd'hui et de demain*, 2e série, 1874, pp. 477–86).

2. *Journal de Fidus*, vol. iii, p. 226.

3. D. Halévy in *Le Courrier de M. Thiers d'après les documents conservés au département des manuscrits de la Bibliothèque Nationale* (1921) remarks (p. 497): 'Rien ne nous éclaire sur les négociations qui sans doute eurent lieu entre Thiers et Gambetta.' Freycinet, an earlier intermediary (see above, p. 78), is silent on the matter.

concert action with similar committees nominated by the other groups, and on the 27th Adam, Brillier, Lepère, Peyrat and Scheurer-Kestner were selected for this task. Thus the Republicans were learning to 'concentrate' their forces and 'concentration', a new word in the French political vocabulary, as the *République Française* pointed out, was the order of the day.[1]

Meanwhile the mobilisation of opinion outside parliament had been going on apace and here such glimpses as we have of him show Gambetta playing a characteristically vigorous part, first in the south-west and then in Paris.

Gambetta's autumn sortie took him to the Périgord on 22 September and kept him until early in October in a part of the south-west he had not yet visited since his return to France after the war. *The Times* rightly surmised that his tour, 'which the Royalist journalists have turned into ridicule, representing the Democratic leader as faring sumptuously in castles and holding formal receptions as if he were a Sovereign or a President, was not merely to visit friends and to make speeches which could not be reported'.[2] Once again Gambetta was carrying the war against his political enemies into fresh territory: once again the time was well chosen, within three weeks of the forthcoming by-elections, when the restoration question was becoming critical, and also within a week or so of the final liberation of the territory. At Périgueux, therefore, in his first main speech, at a banquet commemorating General Daumesnil, the defender of Vincennes in 1814, it was natural for him to strike an emotionally patriotic note, but he also denounced the iniquities of the existing administration which had recently removed his host from the office of mayor.[3] Later at the Château de la Borde near Châtellerault it was equally appropriate for him to speak to his hearers of their common anxiety:

> In spite of these festive airs ... we feel ourselves at grips with a terrible enemy ... whom we must overcome at all costs ... if we return voluntarily beneath the yoke of the monarchy, new punishments and new misfortunes await us (Hear! Hear! Applause). ... The rights of those who are members of a nation cannot be transmitted like toys from cradle to cradle (General approval—Bravos). ... What do we see today? People want to take us back to the *ancien régime*. And who are they who plan this enterprise? Men who are the unworthy descendants of the great liberal and national bourgeoisie of 1789!

1. R. Dreyfus, 'La déception monarchique de 1873', *Revue de France*, 15 June 1933, p. 681.

2. 6 Oct., p. 10. According to a police report Gambetta and Spuller returned to Paris on 6 Oct.

3. The deputy-mayor was subsequently suspended for two months for having allowed Gambetta to speak at this banquet without making any protest. For the text of the speech, see *Discours*, vol. iv, pp. 72–9.

But, happily, he said, there were some who did not desert their traditions, and so he came to the most remarkable part of his speech, a strong appeal to the bourgeoisie to rally to the defence of the Republic and to the union of all Republicans in face of the enemy. On previous occasions, he had appealed to the peasants and heralded the new social strata; now he struck a new note, recognising that, just as in the Assembly the attitude of the Centre groups would be vital, so in France as a whole the attitude of that central block in society, the bourgeoisie with their great influence, could be all important.[1] This might indeed be so. The Monarchists were full of confidence and their confidence could be infectious. On 26 September one of them, Decazes, wrote to a friend that the Left was demoralised and that Léon Say, one of the well-to-do and influential members of the Left Centre had said to him the day before: 'The Monarchy is made. You will have 400 votes.'[2]

But the two speeches at Périgueux and Châtellerault were only a part of Gambetta's activities during his stay in the south-west. He and Spuller spent a week at the Château de Sept-Fonds near Périgueux and received a stream of visitors, mostly, but not only, Republicans from Périgueux. On Saturday, 27 September, some three hundred and fifty to four hundred people, many of them mayors and General Councillors, were reported to have made their way to 'the vast country house'. Gambetta received them in groups of fifty to sixty at a time, exchanged views with each group and then summed up and gave his hearers advice 'which was appreciated as much for its firmness as for its prudence'. One group was particularly important; it consisted of visitors from the six neighbouring departments, Charente, Creuse, Lot, Lot-et-Garonne, Haute-Vienne and Vienne.[3] The pattern of these receptions resembled that at Chambéry a year earlier, yet the net was much more widely spread and the official standing of many of the visitors more significant. But did they come only to talk and then to hear a 'pep-talk' from their leader? Were there in Gambetta's speeches directives which the *République Française* thought it wiser not to mention? Several French papers, according to *The Times*, had spoken of 'a plan for organising popular manifestations intended to alarm the Monarchists and the Government. Nothing of the kind has yet occurred.'[4] C. de B. went further and on 28 October wrote that the Radicals were organising centres of resistance to the Monarchy throughout France in agreement with the General Councils and municipalities in which they had a majority. The first act, he added rather surprisingly, would be to

1. For the text see *ibid.*, pp. 80–7.
2. M.A.E., Fond Chaudordy, vol. i, *Correspondance avec le Duc Decazes.*
3. See the detailed account printed in the *R.F.* of 1 Oct.
4. 6 Oct.

kidnap the Marshal's niece, the Marquise de MacMahon, who lived in Saône-et-Loire.[1]

Such reports of plans for resistance were borne out by Juliette Adam when, in her memoirs published thirty years later, she wrote: 'We the conspirators all knew that a large number of guns had been diverted when the National Guard was disarmed, that munitions had come in across the Swiss frontier and been stored near Lyon. The resistance to a restoration had been very cleverly organised, Gambetta devising the plan together with Bardoux.'[2] Perhaps such a contingency plan for resistance had been drawn up, but the evidence concerning it is understandably very slender and it seems very doubtful whether Gambetta would have been eager to implement it. On the contrary, when Francisque Ordinaire went to see him as the emissary of a 'Central Committee' in Lyon to discuss armed resistance he is said to have tapped meditatively on the window in his flat and then exclaimed 'No! No insurrection. You must understand, my dear friend, that in this country nothing durable has ever been founded on force.'[3] So, too, Alphonse Gent, a deputy for the Vaucluse and one of Gambetta's wartime prefects, was said to have met with a similar refusal to countenance the use of force when he offered to raise the South.[4] Thus, while there is no doubt that the Radicals deliberately tried to frighten the Monarchists by talk of economic stagnation, disorder, and civil war, it is most unlikely that any of 'the manifestations' recommended by Gambetta at the Château de Sept-Fonds were of a violent kind.[5] Rather it is to be

1. C. de B., *Letters from Paris*, p. 144: the text has been badly paraphrased by the editor. Chapman (*The Third Republic*, p. 178), writing of the later crisis in 1877, says that the Republicans had committees in each canton 'drawn from Jean Macé's Ligue de l'Enseignement and the masonic lodges'. He does not give his evidence for this statement.

2. *Nos amitiés politiques*, p. 42. It is not clear from what Mme Adam wrote whether the plan was a development of the one for 'central electoral committees' mentioned above, p. 163.

3. 'La déception monarchique de 1873', *Revue de France*, 15 June 1933, p. 683.

4. F. Pisani-Ferry, *Le Coup d'état manqué du 16 mai 1877* (1965), p. 72.

5. For the rumours of imminent violence and civil war, see e.g. letter of 25 Aug. by C. de B. (Rothschild pp.) reporting that a Republican leader had said to him: 'Si vous essayez de renverser la république, attendez-vous à des massacres dans les campagnes'; cf. Gustave Flaubert (*Correspondance*, vol. vi, Paris, 1930, p. 81), letter of 4 Nov. in which he expressed his relief at the failure of the restoration, because 'je ne veux pas qu'on brûle les églises et qu'on tue les curés, ce que l'on s'apprêtait à faire en Bourgogne, au dire du maire de Reims à moi-même, et dans le Midi, comme me l'a assuré Mme Espinasse. L'Est se serait soulevé pour le père Thiers, la Provence pour Gambetta . . . '; cf. also the letter of 17 Oct. to Paris municipal councillors signed by Gambetta and other deputies of the Seine (*Discours*, vol. iv, pp. 88–9). It spoke of 'une tentative dont le succès aurait pour suite prochaine le désordre ou la guerre civile'. But men like the highly intelligent journalist J. J. Weiss, who later became a supporter

supposed that they were to form a part of the immense enterprise of mobilising public opinion, of inducing every possible individual and group of individuals to write to the papers and form deputations to wait upon prefects and ministers and others in authority and express their alarm at and opposition to the contemplated Monarchy. This process came to a climax in the last ten days of October.[1] On the 20th Gambetta wrote to an unknown correspondent informing him that the Republican Union had decided that all over the country 'delegations of one, two or several active and influential men should be formed who would immediately take the train, make their way to Paris and ask to see the President of the Republic to tell him the state of opinion among their fellow-citizens and demand of him the maintenance of the existing institutions.' One of two things would happen, said Gambetta; MacMahon would either receive them or show them the door. In the second case they should see Thiers and members of the various Republican groups and set forth their views. The story of their *démarches* would be published in the papers, they would return home and render account, their compatriots would subscribe to their declarations and the whole process would snowball and win over the waverers.[2] The plan was at any rate partly put into action. On 28 October *The Times* reported that delegations from Dordogne, Vaucluse, Côte d'Or and Loir-et-Cher had arrived to protest against restoration and that Mac-Mahon had refused to see them, but that they had been received by Thiers and Léon Say.

Meanwhile Gambetta, who had been to the countryside, appealed to the

---

1. The *R.F.*, for its part, published daily from 16 Oct. until November a series of letters and addresses from Republicans either directed to MacMahon and protesting against any Monarchist restoration or congratulating the Left or Left Centre on their firm stand in defence of Republican institutions.

2. *Lettres*, no. 164.

---

of Gambetta, did not think much of this sound and fury. In an article written in 1878 he declared that in 1873 France was ready to accept the Monarchy: 'Ceux qui s'en défiaient ou la haïssaient, les paysans dans les campagnes, les ouvriers dans les centres populeux ne possédaient aucun moyen de résistance. Le Midi, à la vérité, était couvert d'affiliations bruyantes où l'on agitait vaguement des projets de sédition. . . . C'étaient des affiliations sur le papier, disséminées, trop nombreuses pour ne pas renfermer beaucoup d'éléments incertains et mobiles. Des colonnes volantes . . . en auraient eu facilement raison. Le gros de la bourgeoisie attendait la restauration sans défaveur et l'espérait' (de Meaux, *Souvenirs politiques 1871–1877*, p. 162 n. (1)). Rémusat (*Mémoires*, vol. v, entry of 15 Oct., p. 485) also discounted the danger of civil war, while Ludovic Halévy recorded ('Les Carnets de Ludovic Halévy', ii, *Revue des Deux Mondes*, 1 Feb. 1937) on 3 Nov. (pp. 555–6): 'Jamais la tranquillité intérieure et matérielle n'a paru plus complète. . . . La monarchie du comte de Chambord était évidemment impopulaire, on l'aurait acceptée cependant.'

bourgeoisie and mobilised mayors and General Councillors. At the same time he appears not to have neglected the workers. According to a police report of 22 October, he had for some days been receiving in his flat workers' representatives to find out what they would do in the event of a Monarchist *coup d'état*.[1]

All these moves were the peaceful civic gestures of a man who had constantly preached the need to keep within the law. He and others might talk of disorder and civil war, but neither side sought them—the memories of and exhaustion following from the German war and the Commune were all too recent. Yet when passions were aroused incidents might all too easily occur. There was therefore much truth in the remark of 'an old French politician' to *The Times* correspondent: 'It all depends upon the army.'[2] The army was not neglected by the Republicans in their war of nerves. After the Royalist Commission of Nine had on 19 October published its note suggesting that all obstacles to restoration had been overcome, Thiers and Gambetta were said to have 'betrayed the liveliest concern and put it about in the papers that some generals and officers were ready to oppose the restoration'.[3] But the Minister of War with the backing of the Marshal had taken steps to preserve order. He did not hesitate to remove from his command the disgruntled General Carrey de Bellemare for having written to him that he would refuse to serve under the white flag. Carrey de Bellemare was a man whom Gambetta had championed[4] and police reports indicated that Gambetta was in touch with other generals[5]—but there were no others who followed Bellemare's example. 'There was no reason to fear sedition', wrote MacMahon's biographer. 'The Marshal knew that by remaining within the limits of the law he would command the army's absolute obedience. He was legally the mandatory of the Assembly and he himself saw many of the corps commanders' and 'reminded them that they must accept the decisions of the majority of the Assembly even though it was a majority of only one.'[6]

But there would be no disturbances. On 30 October, when excitement and tension were at their height, Chambord's letter to Chesnelong was published in the Legitimist *Union*. It was, said a Right-wing deputy, 'like a blow from an oar on a drowning man who thought he was in reach of

1. A.P.P., BA/418.
2. *The Times*, 6 Oct.
3. Silvestre de Sacy, *Le Maréchal de MacMahon*, p. 283.
4. When he appealed against his treatment by the Commission for reviewing war-time ranks. Léonie Léon (letter of 1 Nov. to Gambetta, Ass. Nat., p. 101) suggested that Mme de Bellemare might not be 'étrangère à cette détermination qui la ramène à Paris'. Carrey de Bellemare was stationed at Périgueux.
5. For Gambetta's relations with army officers, see Chapter 22 below.
6. Silvestre de Sacy, *op. cit.*, p. 283.

the lifeboat'.[1] The Monarchist campaign came to an abrupt and inglorious end. 'We had', wrote the Duc d'Audiffret-Pasquier in disgust, 'sought to reconcile France and Royalty: we were thrown back into complete demagogy.'[2]

1. See C. de B., *Letters from Paris*, pp. 194–5.
2. Duc d'Audiffret-Pasquier, *La Maison de France et L'Assemblée Nationale: Souvenirs 1871–1873* (1938), pp. 257–8.

13

Towards opportunism
November 1873–June 1874

The Right had intended to force restoration through the Assembly when it reassembled in November 1873 but the Comte de Chambord had torpedoed their plans and left them deeply embarrassed. Léonie Léon, in her retreat, speculated whether Broglie would fall and, if so, whether Mac-Mahon would not feel impelled to resign, for 'without de Broglie he is a body without a spirit and the ex-majority [*sic*] without its sword is a body without a weapon'.[1] But a sword, in the person of the Marshal, was precisely what Broglie intended to fall back upon. The idea of prolonging MacMahon's powers had been ventilated earlier and Broglie himself had indicated that, unless a restoration could be effected quickly, he would support 'the maintenance of the party truce together with the prolongation of Marshal MacMahon's powers for a considerable time'.[2] The proposal at least kept the peace for a while between the parties who made up his own majority, and he secured their support for the extension of the Marshal's term for ten years irrespective of the life of the Assembly. But this was too long a period for many—the Left proposed five years instead of ten, hoping perhaps to force the Marshal's resignation, and, were this to happen, Léonie Léon had visions of her 'dear Divinity' becoming 'the master of events'.[3] This, however, was not to be. Eventually at the end of a long and stormy debate Broglie carried the compromise solution of seven years. MacMahon, a staunch Conservative, would thus continue to hold the fort. Much might happen within seven years—Chambord's health was none too good although he was only fifty-three; he might die and he was still childless. Moreover, France might be given institutions sufficiently conservative to make the transition to some eventual restoration comparatively smooth. As Broglie wrote in his *Mémoires*, 'time gained in this

1. Letter of 7 Nov. to Gambetta (Ass. Nat., p. 104).
2. *Mémoires*, p. 211.
3. Letter of 16 Nov. to Gambetta (Ass. Nat., p. 107).

world is always something and sometimes indeed it is everything in a mortal lifetime!'[1] Monarchist hopes were deferred but not wholly abandoned. Léonie Léon's prophecy as early as September 1872, when there had been talk of Thiers's adopting MacMahon as Vice-President, seemed to have been fulfilled: it was that 'MacMahonism would be the *refugium peccatusum* [*sic*] of all the disappointed parties'.[2]

While Broglie and 'the doctrinaires', as the *République Française* was wont to call his particular associates, continued in power there would hardly be the relapse into complete demagogy feared by his fellow duke, D'Audiffret-Pasquier. But from the first the Septennate laboured under the disadvantage of being equivocal. It was 'a waiting room, the antechamber to the definitive'.[3] It continued a provisional state of affairs and men argued as to whether it was personal or impersonal, a perpetuation of power personal to MacMahon in order to keep the place open for Monarchy, or impersonal and therefore in fact a consolidation of the Republican regime already in being. Broglie, embarrassed, was harried on this point of interpretation by both Right and Left. But his major task, once the Septennate had come into being, was to tackle the constitution-making deferred at the end of the summer session of 1873. A new Commission of Thirty, again containing a majority of members of the Right, was laboriously chosen and slowly set to work, as though, wrote the *République Française*, it was marching to Calvary.[4] It began to elaborate an electoral law while Broglie planned the *pièce de résistance* which was to be his undoing in May, a truly conservative second Chamber. Meanwhile he had remodelled his ministry, himself assuming charge of the Ministry of the Interior, and his government continued to act as a government of combat. It smote the Press and now not only the Radical papers. It also tightened administrative controls still further, notably by a law of 20 January 1874, which removed the choice of mayors from municipalities and entrusted it to the Government and its agents, the prefects.

Such was the background to another period of comparative self-effacement in Gambetta's career. He and his party had naturally voted against the Septennate in which he professed to see the looming shadow of dictatorship. But he took no part in the debates. The leading role for the time being fell to the Left and Left Centre groups and the chief speakers against the prolongation of MacMahon's powers were men such as Jules Simon, Jules Grévy and Dufaure. So it was for some time to come. Thus in the New Year Gambetta tabled an important interpellation on the

1. p. 185.
2. Letter of 21 Sept. 1872 to Gambetta (Ass. Nat., p. 28).
3. *R.F.*, leader of 23 March 1874.
4. 19 Feb. 1874.

implications of the Septennate arising from a government circular relating to the law on the mayors, but when it came to be debated in March he did not speak himself but entrusted the task to Challemel-Lacour because, said Madame Adam, Challemel had a more cruel irony than he![1] When he did speak in the Assembly it was on relatively technical matters. The reasons for this self-effacement can only be guessed. Perhaps it was part of an understanding with Thiers; perhaps it was due to a feeling of frustration with 'this Babel-like Convention called Septennate'[2] and to genuine uncertainty about the means of escape from the impasse of a Republic now governed by men whom Léonie Léon scornfully called 'Lilliputians'[3] and who certainly were no Republicans. He was content to watch and wait his opportunity, never neglecting the *République Française* (though this, too, might be a burdensome labour when politics seemed tedious and unreal) and keeping an ever-vigilant eye on universal suffrage.

No doubt, too, he was happy during the winter to have a little more time to relax. Thus he was as jolly as a sandboy in escaping from Paris on 30 December to spend ten days in the Midi, although he could not take Léoni Léon with him and had to be content with writing to his 'chère petite femme adorée' from the Adams' sumptuous villa, Les Bruyères.[4] On the journey he read d'Alembert's 'magnificent preface to the dictionary of the Encyclopédie'. At Marseilles he and his companions 'lunched gloriously'. At Cannes he was met by his family. At Les Bruyères 'an incomparable night fête with ball and supper' awaited him and the company was entertained by a comic opera of his hostess's own composition. One day he picnicked with the Adams in the dry bed of a mountain torrent behind Nice, but the news of his presence had got abroad and on their return he found a crowd awaiting him in the main square at Vallauris expecting a speech; so he preached to his Republican flock his 'usual sermon on the wisdom, hopes, activities and virtues of democracy'. To escape further such attentions, he went to Nice to visit his father and then on to Italy to San Remo to see 'one of our unhappy friends in exile', presumably a Communard, who had 'been condemned to death under M. Thiers'. He even continued as far as Savona where, in the garden once enjoyed by Pius VII, he picked 'a little red flower for the hair of his *mignonne*: "A Pope blesses our love".' But political duties would not be kept at bay. He could not, he said, resist the need to reorganise the party in

---

1. *Nos amitiés*, p. 105. Challemel's notable speech was put on sale for twenty centimes by Ernest Leroux and duly advertised in the *R.F.* For an arresting description of Challemel's oratory, see C. Pelletan, *Le Théâtre de Versailles*, pp. 131–3.
2. Letter of 1 Feb. 1874 to Léonie Léon (L.G.).
3. Letter of 16 Dec. 1873 to Gambetta (Ass. Nat., p. 119).
4. Letters of 2, 3 and 7 January 1874 (L.G.).

the Alpes-Maritimes where the problem was difficult because French and Italians were at loggerheads on every kind of issue (*dans presque tous les cartons*). He thought he had done some good at Antibes and Grasse and he hoped to meet party members from Nice and Cannes.[1]

He returned to Paris in the best of health, but, his hostess alleged, inadvertently leaving behind on his bedroom table a telegram destined for 'Mlle. L.L.... the person who is to be seen at the Assembly's sessions whenever Gambetta speaks'.[2] Back in Paris, he resumed his artistic and sociable habits of the Second Empire: 'He was to be seen at the theatre and at the Sorbonne and in the evening he appeared at the beautiful Juliette Adam's',[3] for she, too, had returned to the capital where she and her husband reopened their salon in no. 23 Boulevard Poissonnière. But he did not find time for what Léonie Léon had regarded as an act of great political importance. A year earlier she had expressed her regret that no busts or paintings of her hero had been submitted to the selection committee for the annual exhibition: 'The more you efface yourself the less people will seek to see you.... If you were to have two busts and three portraits in the Salon this would be proof of a strong and sure popularity which would influence many of the hesitant; quite apart from the effect which your handsome, attractive and regular features (*votre si régulière et si séduisante beauté*) could not fail to produce!'[4] Léonie Léon had to content herself with what was said to be a striking likeness of Gambetta in the form of a medallion wrought in iron by Alfred Gauvin and exhibited on the landing of the main staircase.[5]

In fact Gambetta's quiescence during the winter and spring of 1873–74 was to some extent a reflection of the general state of French politics. When Marcère, a prominent member of the Left Centre, looked back on 1874 he wrote that it was a year in which the National Assembly itself 'seemed to slumber'.[6] Parliamentary life was still full of incident and during the year Gambetta's own policies were to take a momentous new turn, yet each side was playing a game of patience. On the one hand the Right and the government were angling for time while maintaining administrative controls, so that the din of political strife continued partly to be muffled; on the other the Left were waiting for the majority to

1. Letter of 7 Jan. (*ibid.*).
2. *Nos amitiés*, pp. 70–84.
3. Halévy, *La République des ducs*, pp. 142–3. A cryptic letter of 26 Dec. from Léonie Léon to Gambetta suggests that some charming Englishwoman had 'l'anglomanisé' in a single evening (Ass. Nat., p. 124).
4. Letter to Gambetta dated 'Mercredi' (Ass. Nat., p. 46).
5. *R.F.*, 2 May, p. 3, and 13 May, p. 3.
6. *L'Assemblée Nationale de 1871*, vol. ii, p. 112.

disintegrate. 'This', wrote C. de B. as early as 29 November 1873, 'is the *mot d'ordre* for the whole Left: to keep quiet, to allow divisions to break out in the majority and to prepare people for the day of the election; it is better, say the leaders of the Left, to wait for another two years than to compromise success by being in too much of a hurry.'[1] 'Genius', declared the *République Française*, 'lies in patience.'[2] The game looked promising. The defenders of 'moral disorder', as the paper preferred to call it, had rallied to Broglie for the moment, but they were not happy. In particular, the Legitimists of the extreme Right were restive and distrustful. The basic cleavage between two different conceptions of Monarchy and society remained as deep as ever despite the reconciliation of the Princes in the summer of 1873.[3] Now the Legitimists, baulked of their restoration, regarded the Septennate as an Orleanist device and were tempted to make Broglie the scapegoat for their own miscalculations.

At the same time the Right Centre was uneasy and divided, many of its members again yearning for that co-operation with the Left Centre, that 'conjunction of the Centres' which the *République Française* had formerly denounced as dangerous. All this was not lost upon Gambetta and his friends in the rue du Croissant. The essential thing, recalled Freycinet, was to keep alive the mutual distrust of Orleanists and Legitimists; so it was decided 'to embark on a guerrilla warfare against the majority . . . and to exploit each incident in such a way as to leave poison in the wound'.[4] As for the 'conjonction des Centres', which would mean the establishment of a conservative Republic to the exclusion of the Radicals, Gambetta and his colleagues kept a vigilant and discouraging eye on any overtures from the Right Centre to the Left and on any tendency to rapprochement between the two groups. In Robert Dreyfus's picturesque image 'the Radical wolf does not commit the blunder of disguising himself as a good Conservative shepherd, but watches the coveted flock from the corner of his eye and prevents it from straying into the adjoining meadow'.[5] It would need not just a traffic in consciences and portfolios, but an approximation of ideas and principles to bring the two Centres together, the *République Française*

1. Rothschild pp.
2. Leader of 15 Dec.
3. Cf. R. Rémond, *La Droite en France de 1815 à nos jours* (Paris, 1954), pp. 138–9: 'En dépit de certains points communs, légitimistes et orléanistes . . . continuent bien de représenter, parfois à leur insu, deux systèmes, deux religions, deux histoires, deux sociétés.'
4. Freycinet, *Souvenirs 1848–1878*, pp. 307–8. For articles designed to exploit the mutual suspicions of the two Monarchist parties, see *R.F.*, 6, 28 Nov., 25 Dec. 1873, 20 Jan. 1874.
5. 'Gambetta et l'opportunisme' (1873–1874) (1), *Revue de France*, 1 Dec. 1934, p. 426.

had asserted, and that did not really exist.[1] To be sure, it declared, the Left Centre and the undecided members of the Right Centre distrusted radicalism, but they equally mistrusted 'clerical intolerance, aristocratic pretensions and doctrinaire impertinence'. And when the possibility of such a conjunction was ventilated again in mid-March, the paper devoted two leaders to warning the Left Centre that such an arrangement would be a 'marché des dupes': no true alliance was possible, one Centre would be bound to swallow the other.[2] The *République Française* was right. If Broglie hoped to offset the possible defection of the Legitimists by such an alliance, he was doomed to disappointment. He was likewise disappointed in the repercussions of his law of 20 January concerning the mayors.

The mayors' law, which enhanced the powers of the prefects of the 'government of combat', was at once denounced by the *République Française* as a prelude to the revival of the official candidatures of the Second Empire.[3] It might indeed have been effective had it not been implemented with excessive zeal and tactlessness, with the result that many moderate as well as Radical mayors were removed from office and as often as not replaced by men who had served the Empire. In consequence, the measure created much unnecessary resentment. The Left, who had urged Republican mayors not to resign in protest against the law, were particularly angered and more than ever vigilant. Thus it is noteworthy that on their behalf Jules Simon kept watch on the movement of civil administrators just as Gambetta later would keep watch on the personnel of the army. There is extant a letter of Simon to an unknown correspondent requesting information about the changes of mayors in his department and explaining: 'I want the Left to be informed of the character of the whole movement. . . . I am even seeking information concerning the changes in the nominations of justices of the peace, various inspectors, etc.'[4] But in making such changes Broglie and his henchmen grossly overplayed their hand. In April Gambetta could go so far as to claim that the law had 'set the seal on the popularity of our party's men and ideas'.[5]

Meanwhile universal male suffrage as well as municipal liberty had become a target of the Right. It had, apart from a brief period in the 1850s, operated in France since 1848, and in 1869 Gambetta had declared its 'liberation from every sort of tutelage, obstacle, pressure and corruption' to be the most urgent of all reforms. But its introduction in 1848 was regarded by many men of the Right as the great aberration and they still

1. *R.F.*, 8 Nov.
2. *R.F.*, 11 and 13 March 1874. See also leader of 8 April.
3. e.g. leader of 15 Jan. 1874.
4. Letter of 7 Feb. 1874 in the author's possession.
5. *Lettres*, no. 185, 25 April 1874.

nourished a profound suspicion of 'le nombre'. This suspicion had been eloquently voiced in D'Audiffret-Pasquier's denunciation of Gambetta's Radicalism on 14 December 1872: 'You are a Radical because when you spoke for the first time in the Legislative Body in the session of 5 April 1870, you put forward the famous theory of the sovereignty of numbers ... the most dangerous and revolutionary theory in the world, the doctrine of 1793.' So, too, in a significant passage in a letter of 18 August 1872, the Comte de Falloux had told his friend Lacombe, that order would be less well guaranteed under even the most monarchical of monarchies with unrestricted suffrage than under a Republic in which universal suffrage was 'contained and directed by the normal influences operating in any civilised country'. A second Chamber was, in his view, useless as a bulwark of order without 'a good electoral law'.[1] It was clearly impossible in the 1870s to revert to the kind of property qualification which had served to define the electorate of the July Monarchy. But the Commission of Thirty were ingenious in their proposals to 'contain' universal suffrage. Among other things they envisaged raising the voting age from twenty-one to twenty-five, thus disqualifying, according to Gambetta, between two and a half and three million young electors.[2] They also provided for a three years' residence qualification for voters living away from their birthplace, as though, wrote the *République Française*, they had forgotten that France was a mobile society no longer living in the Middle Ages.[3]

These proposals, made public in advance, were naturally obnoxious to the Left. In this context Gambetta's constant concern both for universal suffrage and election results was vividly reflected in his paper's exhortations to its readers at the end of January when the register of electors was due for revision. They must, it urged, check that their names were on the register, and it was all the more important to do so because this year would see municipal elections, a partial renewal of the General Councils, and 'finally, perhaps general elections for the National Assembly'. 'The electors know their duties and their rights: we must hope that in the grave circumstances in which the country is placed they will not slumber in a culpable and fatal neglect.'[4] A little later the paper recorded having received letters from people who thought that they might be disqualified under the proposed new electoral law and asked what point there was in their enrolling. 'Our reply', it said,

---

1. Hélot, *Journal politique de Charles Lacombe*, vol. i, p. 118.
2. *Discours*, vol. iv, p. 179.
3. 2 May, p. 2. Cf. Gimpl, *The Correspondent and the Founding of the French Third Republic*, pp. 96 ff for Liberal Catholic criticisms of universal suffrage.
4. *R.F.*, 22 Jan. 1874, p. 2, and 25 Jan.

will be absolutely clear. Citizens who are thus threatened by a more or less certain disqualification should be all the more zealous in seeing that they are inscribed. . . . At the last moment the majority may draw back before taking such grave responsibilities. It may also be transformed by elections between now and the day when the electoral law will be debated.[1]

And when, soon after this, by-elections were held, the *République Française* claimed that because of these threats to the franchise the electors of the Pas-de-Calais and the Haute-Saône, were fighting 'on behalf of the electoral rights of several million Frenchmen'.[2]

These elections in the Haute-Saône and Pas-de-Calais were part of a new series. But, although the government spaced out by-elections and introduced legislation such as the mayors' law, its measures did not avail to reverse the Republican tide. Already on 16 November in the Seine-Inférieure a moderate Republican general had been returned in place of a deceased Orleanist, while a Republican had succeeded a Republican in the Aube. These were victories which led Léonie Léon to tell Gambetta that France was already his at heart if not in fact.[3] On 14 December when there was polling for four vacant seats, four Republicans, including two Radicals, were elected, the sensation being the defeat of the Legitimist candidate in Finistère by a moderate Republican with the Hibernian name of Swiney. On 8 February 1874, in the Haute-Saône a Radical prevailed over the son of the former Orleanist member, the Duc de Marmier, and on 1 March Republicans were elected in the traditionally conservative Vienne and in Vaucluse, where the victor was none other than Ledru-Rollin, the veteran Radical of 1848–49.[4] Finally, on the 29th of the same month a Conservative Republican replaced an Orleanist in Haute-Marne and a Radical succeeded a more moderate Republican in the Gironde, gaining a majority over his Monarchist and Bonapartist rivals combined. The *République Française* was exultant: 'whether they act as a coalition or whether they are divided', it observed, 'all the adversaries of the Republic are henceforth condemned to defeat. These are the most frankly and clearly Republican elections that have yet taken place.'[5] The Monarchist adversaries might well be dejected; although a Bonapartist had been elected on 8 February in the Pas-de-Calais, not a single Legitimist or Orleanist had won a seat. This lack of success did not make them happier

1. 27 Jan.
2. 8 Feb.
3. Letter of 17 Nov. (Ass. Nat., p. 108).
4. Thiers played an influential part in securing the Republican victory in Vienne and, after it had been announced, Spuller wrote to Mme Adam: 'Thiers *for ever* oui, mais République encore plus *for ever*!' (*Nos amitiés*, p. 98).
5. R.F., leader of 1 April.

bedfellows. Already on 15 December the Legitimist C. de B. had noted that Thiers and his friends were jubilant and saying to the government: 'You accused us of being responsible for the progress of radicalism; now under your regime you see that it is making still more headway.'[1] One reason for this progress was, no doubt, the Radicals' studied moderation, a moderation which did not, however, according to *The Times*, exclude 'appealing to the passion for equality, denouncing existing burdens upon land and promising to replace them by taxes on the rich'.[2] Peasants, moreover, were sent pamphlets in a series known as the Collection Républicaine which included a poem entitled *Les Radicaux de l'An I* that contained the following comforting verse:

> Cherchons donc le bonheur sur terre
> Aimons le bien, fuyons le mal,
> Dans chaque homme, voyons un frère,
> Voilà l'ordre du Radical ... [3]

Some months earlier *The Times* had remarked that the Assembly might 'become a Long Parliament, but individual members die and as they are replaced by men the large majority of whom are charged to demand an immediate dissolution the end must come and at no very distant day'.[4] That day now seemed nearer and Broglie was therefore all the more anxious to proceed with his constitutional proposals, in particular with his conservative second chamber, which was to be the great buttress for the Septennate. Meanwhile Gambetta and his friends continued to demand the dissolution of a 'Chambre plus "introuvable"' than any previously recorded in history. 'Where', asked the *République Française* at the end of January 1874, 'is the Gladstone who will advise our Assembly to dissolve? ... Dissolution and the formation of a new Assembly are no longer party questions, they are national.'[5] On 23 March Gambetta and more than eighty members of the Left tabled a motion demanding the maintenance of the existing electoral law and calling upon the Assembly to dissolve on 28 June. It was reminiscent of the Bill sponsored by Gambetta and his colleagues in May 1873[6] and it was, of course, equally fruitless.[7] The general

1. Rothschild pp.
2. 19 Jan., p. 8.
3. Kayser, *Les Grandes batailles du radicalisme*, p. 87 n. (*a*).
4. Leader of 26 May 1873, p. 10.
5. *R.F.*, 28 April 1874. Gladstone had at the end of January 1874 declared his intention to dissolve parliament. A general election followed in February.
6. See above, p. 147.
7. The Republican Union at its last meeting before the Easter vacation also issued a resolution reiterating the demand for dissolution and 'l'intégrité du suffrage universel' (see *R.F.*, 1 April, p. 1).

election they had hoped for in 1873 would, despite Broglie's imminent fall, not take place in 1874 or even in 1875. But soon the oft-reiterated demand for dissolution would be heard less frequently and then rather as a ritual cry. Gambetta, who had led it, was to perform a *volte-face*, concede to the Assembly the constituent powers he had so long denied it and extract from it the Third Republic. This was the classic manoeuvre which was to win the name of Opportunism. Acute observers might have seen it fore-shadowed in Gambetta's appeal to that bourgeoisie, whom he had earlier denounced, in his autumn speeches near Châtellerault[1] and in a significant article in the *République Française* in November.

At the Château de la Borde in the autumn he had asked who it was who had given to the world the great idea of justice set forth in the Declaration of Rights:

> Who promulgated the declaration of rights? Who founded the indestructible union of the French nation? Was it demagogues or obscure people who had escaped from their workshops or from cultivating the soil? No, it was the bourgeoisie to whom is due the honour of emancipating the whole people. A solemn hour is about to sound for the bourgeoisie. It can regain a great ascendancy over the French people. It will depend upon its representatives in the Assembly to act politically in such a way as to rid us for ever of anarchy and dictatorship. Yes, if these bourgeois, small or big . . . understand the gravity of the moment, they can by rallying firmly around the flag of the Republic . . . save it with their own hands, that is to say that they can ensure for themselves and for their descendants many long and beneficent years of influence on the direction of public affairs, . . . and establish the recovery and even the greatness of France upon a pact of indissoluble alliance between the proletariat and the bourgeoisie . . . . Why should we be forbidden to hope that these men will understand the extent and the nobility of their mission? . . . Rights and interests alike are united in indicating a similar line of conduct both to those who are the heirs of the French Revolution, the descendants of that bourgeoisie which used to be called the Third Estate, and to those who belong to the new social strata . . . who wish to exercise their rights.[2]

Confronted by the Restoration threat, Gambetta had naturally enough preached the union of all classes; but it was the appeal to the bourgeoisie and the linking of the new social strata with the bourgeoisie which was the novelty. A novelty, but not a surprising one in a man who was basically moderate, who was himself a petit bourgeois and in many ways admired the virtues and enjoyed the good things of an affluent bourgeois society. Madame Adam had already laboured to make him acceptable in such

1. For these speeches, see above, pp. 168–9.
2. See *Discours*, vol. iv, pp. 84–6.

society; Léonie Léon was continuing the task and the Alsatian industrialist, Scheurer-Kestner, had lately also begun to play his part.[1] He had sensed, he wrote, that Gambetta valued him as a representative of the well-to-do bourgeoisie. He believed that he could help Gambetta to win the political sympathies of people of their class and he realised that Gambetta was 'passionately anxious' to get into touch with a social group which was then one of the strongest elements in the Republican 'concentration'. In consequence, without consulting Gambetta, Scheurer-Kestner arranged a fortnightly dinner in his flat in the rue des Mathurins. The guests were usually colleagues of the Republican Union, 'the demons of demagogy' as Gambetta humourously wrote to Scheurer-Kestner's wife,[2] that is to say, apart from Gambetta and Ranc (before his exile), men such as Challemel-Lacour, Peyrat, Spuller, Lepère and three whom he called the three musketeers, namely Clemenceau, Lockroy and Georges Perin. The dinner was followed by a soirée to which other politicians, among them prosperous members of the bourgeoisie, were invited.[3] The invitations naturally enough did not extend to members of the Right Centre but they attracted men of the Left Centre such as Marcère, Bardoux and Duvergier de Hauranne (whom Gambetta charmed on his very first visit). It was the well-to-do members of the Left Centre or at the edge of it who might turn the scale, men of what Robert Dreyfus called 'that shifting region of the parliamentary arena in which some hesitant liberals hardly knew themselves whether at the moment of a decisive vote circumstances would lead them to vote along with the extreme Right or with the extreme Left'.[4] These were men who wanted political stability as a guarantee of economic prosperity and who would be ready enough to accept a Republic if it protected their financial interests. It was their fellows, industrialists who had exhibited in the Vienna Exhibition of 1873, that Gambetta was ready in 1874 to support as nominees for gold medals and the Legion of Honour.[5]

At the same time the salons doubtless subtly contributed to Gambetta's evolution. One evening in the spring of 1874, so Juliette Adam claimed, her husband was to be heard urging the need for Republicans to penetrate into Conservative circles. It was time, he said, to destroy the idea that they

1. *Journal inédit*, vol. iv, B.N. N.a.fr. 12, 707.
2. *Lettres*, no. 172 of 9 Feb.
3. Scheurer-Kestner, *Journal inédit*, vol. iv, pp. 106ff (B.N., N.a.fr. 12, 707). There were, of course, other dinners of this sort, e.g. the Tuesday dinners at the Café Riche of 'the Council of Ten', a self-constituted committee which included representatives of the three Left-wing groups. According to Juliette Adam the Republican Union's representatives were Lepère, Fourcand, Scheurer-Kestner and Adam (*Nos amitiés*, p. 14).
4. 'Gambetta et l'opportunisme' (*Revue de France*, 1 Dec. 1934, p. 496).
5. 23 June 1874, *Ass. Nat. A.*, vol. xxxii, pp. 360–5.

were Hottentots. Gambetta must not laugh at the idea, he said: 'be sure of it, you don't go far in Paris if you are not one of "the people whom one can see". You can belong to the opposition in cafés, but you can only belong to the government by being in society (*le monde*); it is in the salons that governments are made.'[1] Already for some months an *habitué chez* Madame Adam, where, as Daniel Halévy put it, 'people hardly knew whether it was he or she who was receiving',[2] Gambetta together with other notables of the Republican Union and *République Française* also frequented the salon of that other 'précieuse radicale', the cultivated and statuesque Madame Arnaud de l'Ariège.[3] It was about this time, too, namely in 1873 or 1874, that he began to visit the witty and charming Princess Lise Troubetzkoï, a friend both of Thiers and of the Russian Chancellor, Prince Gortschakoff. But although she presided over a celebrated and cosmopolitan salon she preferred to receive him, and he perhaps to go to her, privately.[4]

Along with the other papers of the Left the *République Française* had vigorously denounced the proposals to prolong the Marshal's powers, but on 21 November 1873, the very morrow of the passage of the Septennial law, it had shifted its ground in a remarkable manner. On 16 August 1871, with Gambetta's approval, Ferdinand Boyer had declared: 'We shall enter the Republic by the main door and not by the side one of riots, surprise or expedients.'[5] But now the leading article in Gambetta's newspaper contained the following significant passage:

> They have given power for seven years to an elected and revocable magistrate who bears the title of President of the Republic. During all this time . . . what will be the political status of the French nation? Will it be Monarchy? No: no one will venture to maintain this. If it is not the Monarchy, then it will be the Republic and if the power granted for seven years lasts for seven years, if during

1. *Nos amitiés*, p. 117. Marcère, *L'Assemblée Nationale de 1871*, vol. ii, p. 96: 'A l'époque . . . où nous sommes, la politique exerçait une influence prépondérante dans les relations même mondaines. Les divers partis avaient trouvé asile dans des salons présidés par des femmes distinguées.'

2. *La République des Ducs*, pp. 142–3. Sometimes, however, he played bezique or dominoes with his host, Spuller, and Peyrat, or the celebrated actor Coquelin. (Mme Adam, *Nos amitiés*, p. 185; Marcos, *Juliette Adam*, p. 397, n. 155.) For a description of Mme Adam as hostess, see E. A. Vizetelly, *Republican France 1870–1912* (1912), pp. 188–9.

3. Marcère, *op. cit.*, p. 96. The only references to Mme Arnaud in Gambetta's *Lettres* date from 1882. She was a niece of Gambetta's wealthy supporter, the industrialist Dubochet, a director of the Paris Gas Company.

4. The first letter from Gambetta to the Princess in his *Lettres* is no. 196 of 24 July 1874. But a police report of 26 March 1872 asserted that she had recently received him in her flat in the Place Vendôme (A.P.P., BA/918). For a lively (perhaps too lively?) description of her see Mme Adam *Après l'abandon de la revanche* (Paris, 1910), pp. 9–12.

5. *Ass. Nat. A.*, vol. iv, p. 653.

this period it is organised and strengthened, what will be founded if not the Republic? Is this the intention of those who the day before yesterday voted for prorogation? Undoubtedly no ... but the force of circumstances is more potent than men. Who knows? The day before yesterday people thought that they were escaping the Republic; but perhaps this time we have entered upon it definitively and for good and all. Ah! we know, it is the side door ... we are far from that admirable ideal of the poet who speaks somewhere of the new generations of the French democracy entering the Republic and passing

> Sous la haute porte azurée
> De l'éblouissant avenir

But perhaps this is the mysterious fate of the Republicans of our day.

And another leader two days later declared that the Bonapartist Rouher had been right in exclaiming immediately after the vote in favour of the Septennate 'the outcome will be the Republic! (la République sera)'.

The social taming of Gambetta no doubt contributed to his political evolution, but the moment when he would help to complete the building to which the side door gave entrance depended on political circumstances, on 'la force des choses', a force which, ironically enough, his old enemy Napoleon III used so often to invoke. Four factors, Broglie's hauteur and lack of the bonhomie and charm which were among Gambetta's chief political assets, the failure of the Legitimists and Bonapartists to support him, his consequent fall, and the activities of the Bonapartists, combined to create that force.

The queen with which Broglie hoped to checkmate the Radical king, opposing, as he put it, 'the representation of intelligence and interests to the representation of crude numbers'[1] was his proposed Second Chamber or Grand Council. This body was to be composed of several *ex officio* members, such as cardinals, marshals and admirals, of a number of life members nominated by the President of the Republic from among men distinguished in various walks of life, and of members elected in each department for seven years by an electoral college of local notables, including members of the General Councils. Someone remarked that it resembled nothing so much as an Assembly of Notables of the *ancien régime*. Gambetta's shrewd comment has often been quoted: 'If the Right has the good sense to accept this plan, democracy in France will be set back for fifty years.'[2]

But the Right had neither the unity nor the good sense to secure the acceptance of Broglie's Bill which was first presented to the Assembly on 15 May. Its reactionary character stunned most of the Left; the Bona-

1. *Mémoires*, vol. ii, p. 278.
2. D. Halévy, *La République des ducs*, p. 136.

partists had become increasingly disillusioned with its author, and the Extreme Right were *frondeur* as ever. In consequence, when on the following day Broglie demanded priority for the electoral law elaborated by the Commission of Thirty over one relating to municipalities, and when he made the vote virtually a vote of confidence, he was defeated by a combination of the Left, the Bonapartists and the Extreme Right. He resigned at once although his pet Grand Council scheme had not yet been debated and this time his resignation was not refused. French politics had seldom been more confused. But on the Left there was joy unbounded at the fall of the man who himself had caused the fall of Thiers a year before. After a week of crisis the Marshal formed a relatively colourless Right-wing ministry presided over by a general; many people regarded it as little better than a caretaker government.[1] Gambetta, attentive to Broglie's difficulties with his majority, had already prophesied his imminent fall[2] (the Duke had indeed nearly been defeated at the end of March) and when the fall occurred he wrote optimistically to Ranc that he had never since 2 July 1871 known a moment more favourable to Republican interests. The Easter holidays had brought a large number of visitors to Paris from all parts of France and they were all confident and reassuring about the state of public opinion.[3] As for the recent crisis, it had demonstrated that, throughout, the Assembly's one concern had been to prolong its own existence. The new cabinet had, in his view, been formed simply with the idea of reassuring it about the improbability of an early dissolution. It was a MacMahonian cabinet: 'These people live from day to day. They have no plans, views or projects. The Marshal wants to continue in power and anyone else in his place would do as much.' Some people talked of the likelihood of a *coup d'état* but this was absurd; there had never been and could not be any question of such a thing.[4]

The letter of 26 May to Ranc which contained these judgements had begun with a discussion of another by-election which created a great stir. The Bonapartist catalyst was beginning to work.

Gambetta loved flowers and Léonie Léon sent him the first periwinkle to open, but she refrained from sending a bunch of violets when she

1. As did its members themselves. C. de B. (Rothschild pp., 27 May) reported that he had talked with one of the new ministers: 'Ils sont toujours décidés à ne prendre aucune initiative, à la laisser à l'Assemblée souveraine sur toutes les questions importantes et à jouer le rôle de simples exécuteurs.'

2. *Lettres*, no. 187.

3. *Lettres*, no. 191, 20 May.

4. *Lettres*, no. 193, 26 May. C. de B. wrote on 19 May that there were people about the Marshal who urged him to suspend the Assembly, govern without it and arrange elections when he was master of the situation. But, he said, 'le maréchal est loin de ces idées' (Rothschild pp., 19 May).

remembered that the violet was a Bonapartist emblem.[1] She was wise, for the Bonapartists, whom he held responsible for the defeat of 1870, he always regarded as his chief enemies, the men for whom he reserved his direst scorn and invective. He had optimistically dismissed the death of Napoleon III in January 1873 as the end of Bonapartism,[2] but if this was a serious judgement it soon proved erroneous. The movement still had plenty of vigour and it could survive both the loss of the fallen Emperor and the trial and condemnation to death of Marshal Bazaine towards the end of the same year. The Bonapartist policy outlined by Rouher in February 1874 accepted the Septennate but looked forward to a plebiscite, 'l'appel au peuple', when the Marshal's term expired. Then, it was hoped, the Third Empire would displace the Third Republic. It was a policy which seemed shrewd enough. As the author of *L'Année politique* was to write: 'The Bonapartists' attitude was perfectly legal and then, by contrast with the petty restrictions imposed upon the electorate by the Monarchists, the plebiscite began to take on an air of incontestable grandeur.'[3] Moreover, this policy would give Napoleon III's son, the Prince Imperial, time to mature. Meanwhile, for many, such as the peasants encountered in the Sarthe by the elder Caillaux, the Marshal was well enough until 'the little one' grew up.[4]

Napoleon III and Bazaine had been borne down by the millstone of defeat. But Napoleon's only child, the Prince Imperial, was young and personable, a romantic exile, and he had reached the age of eighteen, the age of political majority according to the Imperial constitution, on 16 March 1874. The event had been a pretext for great celebrations and seven thousand people from all over France had made their way across the Channel to Chislehurst for the occasion. The *République Française* might write scornfully about 'this new child of the miracle', 'this dud' (*fruit sec*),[5] but the extent of the loyalty shown to him was a rude shock to Republicans and Monarchists alike. The shock was all the greater when the Bonapartists won a by-election in the Nièvre at the end of May. The Nièvre, a constituency which in 1873 had twice returned a Radical, now sent the Bonapartist Baron de Bourgoing to the Assembly. Already in April Lord Lyons had reported that, while the great majority of the people were Republican, the next most numerous party was the Imperialist. Now on 29 May he wrote: 'The Adherents to monarchical principles and indeed strong conservatives of all shades of opinion have gone over to the

---

1. Letters dated 'Lundi' and 'Bourg-la-Reine Jeudi' (Ass. Nat., pp. 136 and 139).
2. See above, p. 132.
3. A. Daniel, *L'Année politique 1874* (1875), p. 143.
4. J. Caillaux, *Mes Mémoires*, vol. i, p. 36.
5. 2 March.

Imperialist cause in very great numbers, and the eventual restoration of the Empire has become less and less improbable in the eyes of those most opposed to it.'[1] Lord Lyons's earlier judgement has been borne out by a recent French historian who has shown that, whilst the votes polled by the Republican candidate were not greatly less than in 1873, the result was above all another blow to the Monarchists and demonstrated that the Republicans were likely to find the Bonapartists the more serious adversaries.[2] The *République Française* had declared that the electors of the Nièvre would be arbiters of the political crisis resulting from Broglie's defeat and resignation: 'They can ... exercise a decisive influence and hasten the end of a provisional state of affairs so enervating for all interests.'[3] It was therefore all the more embarrassing that the electors had made the wrong choice. But Gambetta took a level-headed view. He deplored the fact that some of his friends were panicking and crying that all was lost:

> Ah! it's a hard job for a poor man like me who has constantly to reinstil courage into a public so lacking in energy! The Nièvre affair is indeed a serious matter, but there are many reasons which account for it. First of all M. de Bourgoing was an exceptionally well-chosen candidate; then there is the influence of the Bonapartist mayors who have all been reinstalled in the Nièvre; finally there is the weariness, impatience and uncertainty of the future which has affected so many people as a consequence of 'moral order'. But we must remember that we cannot without vainglory expect to win every encounter in our war against the monarchist coalition. We have won sixteen out of eighteen elections and now because one is unfavourable people cry that all is lost. This is quite absurd.

He added that the Empire had always been the Republicans' chief foe and 'today this is evident'. The Legitimists had been defeated in November; the Orleanists had lost on 16 May when the Broglie ministry was overthrown; now the Bonapartists remained. 'As for me,' he said, forgetting his optimism on the death of Napoleon III, 'I have always thought that they would give us a lot of trouble. ... What seems to attract the people is this phrase "appel au peuple" ... an effective phrase which seems to say

1. P.R.O., F.O. 146, 1745 to Lord Derby, 3 April and F.O. 146, 1747, 29 May. Cf. Rémusat, on 30 March (*Mémoires de ma vie*, vol. v, p. 491): 'Le temps semble venir où il n'y aura plus de candidats que ceux de l'Empire et ceux de la République'.

2. Gouault, *Comment la France est devenue républicaine*, pp. 180–2. Cf. Rouher's letter to a newspaper editor of Puy-de-Dôme, 11 Feb.: 'le jour venu, il n'y aura en présence que deux formes de gouvernement: la République, l'Empire' (Daniel, *L'Année politique 1874*, p. 110).

3. 22 May, p. 1. Cf. leader 24 May; 'M. Gudin [the Republican candidate] a posé ... la question de la dissolution. Ce voeu ... est le voeu de toute la France ... les électeurs de la Nièvre ont la parole; qu'ils en usent au nom du pays tout entier.'

something and which is but a fresh lie. So we must fight Bonapartism to the utmost.'[1]

The fight was on indeed, although, as has been seen, it was one that the Radicals had never ceased, and Gambetta threw himself into it with a will. On 1 June in 'the centre of France' at Auxerre, where Napoleon III had delivered a celebrated discourse eight years earlier, he uttered one of his most powerful denunciations of the 'clientèle which was now returning and prowling around *la patrie*'. Above all he denounced their double dealing. They were men who counterfeited democracy with their plebiscitary 'appel au peuple'. To the country people they presented themselves as the foremost of democrats:

> They know just what to say to the agricultural worker and the small proprietor: they will give him security, credit, peace and a definite share and influence in the commune and the canton. Nothing of the sort, gentlemen, and you know it. . . . As soon as they meet a man of the Church . . . what do they tell him? That they are at his service. . . . Was it not they who sent expeditions to Rome, China and Mentana? Didn't they maintain the Pope's temporal power for twenty years . . . ? But when they met someone belonging to a more educated people they instinctively knew that they were facing adversaries. They changed tone: they offer him their protection; unable to flatter or corrupt him they try to intimidate him because they excel in exploiting fear (Sensation—Bravos). Fear . . . that is their great political weapon . . . and when they have frightened a certain class of citizen, they come forward as their saviours (Prolonged bravos).

But, he declared, they had already tried this game and all those who had been duped by such charlatanism had already called down curses upon 'this band of adventurers who exploited France for twenty years'. The country by itself had proved strong enough to annihilate the intrigues of the Monarchists: 'There now remains only the empire in this final duel against the Republic.'[2]

Nine days later the duel was renewed in a stormy debate in the Assembly concerning the alleged nefarious activities of the Bonapartist Comité Central de l'appel au peuple in the Nièvre election. Gambetta became involved in a violent altercation with Rouher in the course of which he cried that there were some who had no title to demand that the Revolution of 4 September should render account, namely 'the wretched men who had brought France to her ruin' (les misérables qui ont perdu la France). 'Never', wrote *The Times* correspondent, 'was he more vehement

1. *Lettres*, no. 193, of 26 May to Ranc.
2. For the text of his speech, see *Discours*, vol. iv, pp. 135–64. In an obituary notice written when Gambetta lay dying, the Bonapartist Jules Richard singled out as a 'phrase restée célèbre: "La conscience française proteste contre cette fraude immonde qu'on cache aujourd'hui sous le nom de plébiscite"' (*Le Bonapartisme sous la république*, p. 292).

and violent. Scorn flashed from his eye and burst from his lips as he stood gesticulating in the Tribune and hurling his denunciations . . . at the cowed Bonapartists.'[1] Uproar ensued. Gambetta was twice called to order and the President of the Assembly threatened to suspend the sitting.[2]

The battle in the Assembly was soon transferred elsewhere. Already at the end of January Gambetta had nearly been involved in a duel with a Bonapartist deputy named Haentjens.[3] Now he was to suffer a different sort of physical encounter. There were tumultuous scenes at the Gare St Lazare when he appeared there on his way to Versailles on 10 June. He was greeted by angry Bonapartists with cries of 'Down with Gambetta!' and, according to *The Times*, one of them tried to attack him but, 'M. Gambetta raising his stick drove the fellow off as he was preparing to rush at him'.[4] The climax came on the 11th after the publication in the Bonapartist *Le Pays* of a violent article which called Gambetta a drunkard and attacked 'the cowards of the National Defence who let besieged Paris die of hunger'. Crowds again assembled at the station and Gambetta on his return from Versailles was struck in the face by a former officer of the zouaves of the Imperial Guard named Henri de Sainte-Croix. There were further scenes on the following day, but this time the Republicans gathered in force to support their leader and cries of 'Vive Gambetta! Vive Gambetta!' were said to have 'made the gallery ring'.[5] Eventually the

1. *The Times*, 11 June, p. 5. The correspondent went on to observe 'in justice to M. Gambetta, that he has always shown respect to the Committee of Inquiry and that he has accepted on various occasions many hard things from the majority, and especially from the Duc d'Audiffret-Pasquier, without attempting angry and violent retorts. But to be taken to task by a Bonapartist, was more than he could endure.' It was, in fact, Gambetta who had uttered the first provocative words by alluding to the Bonapartists as 'une faction détestée'. For the text, see *Ass. Nat. A.*, vol. xxxii, pp. 78–9.

2. On the second occasion Gambetta was called to order 'avec inscription verbale'. This meant losing half his deputy's stipend for fifteen days, i.e. losing 187 fr. 50 c. or £7 10s. according to the contemporary sterling equivalent (see *The Times*, 18 June).

3. This was due to a misunderstanding. Haentjens had said in the course of a speech: 'M. Gambetta a fait aussi à la tribune de la propagande involontaire pour l'indiscipline'. Gambetta did not hear the word 'involontaire' and called Haentjens a liar. When the matter was settled amicably the Bonapartist paper *Le Pays* accused Gambetta of cowardice: 'on sait que la prudence de ce Génois dépasse de beaucoup son hâblerie' (see Mme Adam, *Nos amitiés*, pp. 87–9).

4. 11 June, p. 5.

5. *The Times* of 12 June gave a long and vivid account: 'Several thousand persons belonging to all ranks of society were walking about in the immense hall. Most of them seemed to have received orders to go there and observed complete silence. Suddenly, towards 1.15, cries of "There he is" were heard from one end of the gallery to the other . . . M. Gambetta was coming. . . . When the riot was at its height, a number of policemen charged the crowd, dealing out fisticuffs right and left with great impunity. . . . The police drove away the crowds and made a passage for M.

government sent troops to maintain order and the unseemly manifestations came to an end.

They naturally caused a great sensation, but *The Times* correspondent's fear that they would interfere with the greatest racing event of the year, the Grand Prix de Paris, was happily groundless. Meanwhile Gambetta's friends were anxious and he received many messages of sympathy, including one from the workers in the Dorian factories at Firminy whom he had addressed in 1872.[1] His assailant was sent to prison for six months and fined two hundred francs, but to his fury the jury at the assize court of the Seine on 2 July acquitted the powerful and virulent Bonapartist journalist Paul de Cassagnac of exciting to hatred and contempt by his scurriless articles in *Le Pays*.[2] Nevertheless the Bonapartists had made themselves too conspicuous. Resort to violence did them no good, particularly in the Assembly where Monarchists as well as Republicans had already taken alarm at the resurgence of Bonapartist activity. Indeed the shadow of the Empire provided the Assembly with an unexpected excuse for resisting dissolution. What if the Imperialist triumph in the Nièvre were to set a pattern for the general election? There was only one way to avert such a menace: the constituent Assembly must complete its task. Hitherto it had laboured reluctantly and often like Penelope undone its own work. Now there might be a greater sense of urgency and better prospects, for Gambetta, though he still talked of dissolution, was ready to take a hand.

1. See above, p. 100; cf. *Lettres*, no. 195 of 16 June to Mme Dorian. Gambetta asked her to thank them on his behalf and to get a works foreman to distribute to the signatories of the address 'une série de cartes'. 'Quantum mutatus ab illo!' exclaimed one of his recent biographers, M. Georges Wormser (*Gambetta dans les tempêtes*, p. 150): 'L'ancien Gambetta eût été les remercier d'un violent discours.'

2. Gambetta's anger at this 'scandalous' acquittal was voiced in a letter of 2 July to Léonie Léon (L.G.).

Gambetta. The crowd followed and accompanied him with their acclamations. M. Gambetta, after bowing two or three times, went on his way, saying.... "Keep calm; don't give them any pretext." The shouts continuing, the police arrested several persons, whom the crowd tried to set at liberty, crying "Vive la République!" A few shouts of "Down with Gambetta!... Down with Rabagas!" were heard.' 'Le pauvre diable! Quelle destinée!' wrote the admiring Spuller to Ranc: 'C'est lui qui fait tout, dans ce parti. Il prononce les grands discours, il rédige les ordres du jour, dit les paroles les plus vibrantes, reçoit les coups de poing, et personne ne l'aide.... Hier soir, il était un peu amer, et à bon droit' (letter of 13 June in Ranc, *Souvenirs—Correspondance*, p. 300). This bitterness was reflected in a letter of the previous day to Léonie Léon in which he referred to 'cette assemblée, la plus vile, la plus lâche, la plus sotte qui se soit jamais rencontrée' and said that 'les grands hommes de gauche ont été plus bêtes que la Providence ne devrait le permettre. C'est à rougir d'être leur allié et leur voisin. Il y a des moments où j'ai dégoût de la vie Publique' (L.G.).

14

A Constituent Assembly after all!
March–November 1874

Gambetta may have taken things more easily in the winter of 1873–74, but the early months of 1874 had for him their moments of weariness, frustration and anxiety. There were weary moments for the director of the *République Française* when he had to deal day after day with what in the jargon of the 1970s would be called 'non-events'.[1] There were anxious and frustrating moments for the Republican leader concerned to maintain a united Republican front and concerned also for his own position. On 12 March *The Times* correspondent had gone so far as to assert that Gambetta had lately sustained two moral reverses which it was urgent for him to retrieve. On the one hand, he was 'in danger of dwindling into a mere subaltern' because of 'the high position' of Thiers, whose public support had (as the *République Française* had readily acknowledged) largely contributed to the success of the Republican candidate in the recent by-election in the Vienne.[2] It was all very well for the Republicans to present a united front when no elections were pending, but by-elections could subject the front to considerable strain. The point here was one that Gambetta himself touched upon in a letter later on in the year. At each such election it was part of the tactics of 'le Vieux de la Montagne', as he called Thiers, to demand the selection of a candidate of his own choosing: but, he wrote, 'we will yield to him as seldom as possible'.[3] He had, however, yielded in the Vienne and, if *The Times* was right in hinting that he had hoped to find consolation by securing a seat for his old friend and

---

1. *Lettres*, no. 183 of April to Ranc: 'Vous n'imaginez pas quel supplice c'est de parler tous les jours sur ce qui n'existe pas. A ce jeu on s'use vite.' Cf. earlier no. 176 of 15 March to his father, with its reference to 'Les innombrables et écoeurantes besognes qui dévorent tout mon temps'.
2. See above, p. 181, n. 4.
3. *Lettres*, no. 205 of 4 Sept. to Mme Adam. Cf. no. 213 in which he wrote of 'l'avidité de M. Thiers et ses amis'.

collaborator Freycinet in the Gironde, he had not succeeded.[1] The candidate adopted was a much more obscure and Radical figure named Roudier.

On the other hand, said *The Times*, Gambetta was 'menaced by the old Radical renown of Ledru-Rollin'. The reemergence of Ledru-Rollin was in fact but one element in the problem of the Radical doctrinaires. Every Left-wing party periodically has trouble with its extremists and for Gambetta in 1874 the maintenance of Republican unity was more difficult on the Left than on the Right. From the first he had had a delicate task in keeping on good terms with the 'revenants' of 1848, men who had been in politics when he was still a child. In the spring of 1873, at the time of the Rémusat-Barodet contest in Paris, he had conspicuously been faced with the problem of humouring his 'tail'. Always the clever parliamentary tactician had to reckon with the disapproval of the intransigent men of principle. These divergences were manifest in various ways from the late autumn of 1873 to the voting of the constitutional laws in 1875. They were reflected in the Republican Union, in parliament and in electoral tensions.

So far as the Republican Union is concerned there is during the six months or so following the failure of the Monarchist restoration a curious phenomenon. The group which had been so prominent in organising opposition to the 'government of combat' appears to go to ground. The *République Française* which continues to report meetings held by the Left and Left Centre is silent about the Union. Was this because of excessive prudence or because the Union did not meet? Or did the paper keep silent because the members of the Union met only to disagree? The last is a possible hypothesis, if not the only one. Certainly there were divergences in the Radical camp concerning the by-election campaign in the Vaucluse in February 1874 when Ledru-Rollin, also an illustrious 'revenant' of 1848, was adopted as the Republican candidate. Gambetta had opposed the suggested replacement of Barodet by Ledru in the famous Paris election of April 1873 and now in 1874 Ledru's candidature in the Vaucluse had been supported if not engineered by 'the arch-radical and demagogue' Alfred

---

1. *The Times*, 12 March. For previous reference to these elections of February and March 1874, see above, p. 181. Gambetta had paid a brief, sudden, and 'strictly incognito' visit to Bordeaux at the opening of the Gironde election campaign (see *Lettres*, no. 175). Freycinet makes no mention of any such possible candidature in his *Souvenirs*, but a letter of 20 Oct. 1873 to Gambetta from Gustave Marqfoy indicates Freycinet's desire to stand as soon as opportunity occurred. In a letter of 5 March to Léonie Léon Gambetta recalled his days at Bordeaux during the war: 'J'ai failli verser des larmes . . . quand je me suis vu installé à l'hôtel qui fait face à la Préfecture, et que de ma fenêtre j'ai pu apercevoir par les fenêtres entr'ouvertes le cabinet où j'ai tant travaillé, tant souffert et si inutilement pour mon grand et malheureux pays. . . . J'ai fait ici mon temps d'enfer' (L.G.).

Naquet and the extreme section of the party.[1] These, along with Louis Blanc and others, were men who did not discourage oral propaganda to the effect that Gambetta was 'colourless and pusillanimous'.[2] Indeed Spuller told Ranc that the attacks made on him by Louis Blanc at Marseille had caused Gambetta to make a hasty journey south toward the end of February.[3] No wonder that the *République Française* was distinctly cool on the subject of Ledru: 'We waited to speak of his candidature until it had been approved by the delegates of Vaucluse.' 'We have not to defend M. Ledru-Rollin. We do not know what he will do or say.'[4] Although it eventually admitted that his candidature was a striking manifestation on behalf of that universal suffrage which Ledru had introduced in 1848, it is clear that Gambetta was not enthusiastic about this veteran recruit to the ranks of the Radical deputies.[5] It is also clear that he was nettled by the allegations of his own pusillanimity or inaction: there would always be a little group of dissidents, he told Ranc, 'discontented, cantankerous, jealous, bewildered and timid people who, when met together, will want to do *something*. One must do something: excellent; but what? Issue manifestoes? They hardly ever mention them any more. Make speeches? But they have no effect. What then? Impossible to get anything out of them except this irritating phrase: "something must be done".'[6] Fortunately for Gambetta their attempt to 'do something' by founding their own daily paper came to nothing, since Ledru, on whom they counted for funds, was not easily parted from his money. Gambetta, of course, affected in any case to make light of such a possible rival: 'It is not simply a question of bringing it out. You have to fill it and fill it well. . . . There are people who think that it is perfectly easy to create a paper. No one knows better than I what efforts, what tension, what integrity, patience and self-sacrifice are involved. I mean, of course a paper which means to do useful work.'[7] Fortunately, too, for Gambetta, Ledru's first great speech to a crowded house on 3 June disappointed his audience. He did indeed seem a wellnigh extinct volcano.

1. *The Times*. Spuller told Ranc that Naquet appeared to have been supported by Lockroy, Georges Perin, Tony Révillon, Ordinaire, Ballue and Saint-Quentin (Ranc, *op. cit.*, p. 289). In a letter to Scheurer-Kestner dated 2 Oct. 1875 Naquet wrote: 'J'espérais trouver en Ledru-Rollin un homme avec lequel on pourrait battre en brèche la politique de Gambetta' (B.N., N.a.fr. 22409, p. 122).

2. Mme Adam, *Nos amitiés politiques*, p. 220.

3. Letter of 22 Feb. 1874 (Ranc, *Souvenirs-Correspondance*, p. 290).

4. *R.F.*, 20 and 22 Feb. 1874.

5. Ledru-Rollin was elected on 1 March with a majority of 3,500 over his Legitimist opponent.

6. *Lettres*, no. 187, undated letter of April or May. Cf. Spuller to Ranc 22 and 23 Feb. (Ranc, *op. cit.*, pp. 288–97).

7. *Lettres*, no. 184, 19 April.

It was more serious when the differences in the Radical ranks were publicly reflected, as at the end of March, in an important vote in the Assembly. Then a Legitimist named Dahirel had demanded urgent consideration for a motion whereby the Assembly should definitely decide in favour of a Republic or a Monarchy by 1 June at latest.[1] The motion was highly inconvenient for Broglie who himself went to the tribune to oppose it. Allied to Dahirel and his followers the Left could have overthrown the ministry. What a chance! But forty-nine Republicans refused to let their consciences capitulate to expediency and to take part in such an unholy alliance. The *République Française* was very angry: ·

> Instead of the imposing unity which could have given us victory at so slight a cost we had in the ranks of our own party the sad and deplorable spectacle of the most unhappy misunderstandings and most regrettable divisions.... We were present at the session: we have never seen anything like it. What was asked for? A simple vote on the question of urgency and nothing more. Let no one talk of questions of principle.... A grave blunder has been committed.[2]

It was necessary to paper over the cracks as soon as possible and this was effected at a meeting of the Republican Union on 29 March at which a grave sort of manifesto suitable for publication was unanimously agreed upon. It referred to renewed Monarchist intrigues and threats to universal suffrage and declared that in the eyes of the Union dissolution was still the sole remedy for the crisis. 'At this present moment, a strict discipline is necessary for all Republicans; for the issue is the decadence or recovery of France.'[3] In the next few weeks the *République Française* took pains to devote more than one article to the admirable cohesion and discipline now to be found in the Republican ranks![4] In private Gambetta told Ranc that most of those who had saved the Broglie ministry had repented of having done so and had disclaimed any intention of seeking to break the Republican Union. He thought the intransigent would be more politic in future. As for himself he recognised that such disagreements were inevitable and he regarded them with sang froid. He would do his best to avoid giving pretexts for them, make timely concessions in order to avoid them, and if

1. See *Ass. Nat. A.*, vol. xxx, p. 658.
2. Leader of 29 March. Those who voted against urgency included Louis Blanc, Ledru-Rollin, Edgar Quinet, Barodet, Crémieux, Delpit, Deseilligny, Esquiros, Millaud, Naquet and Ordinaire. Gambetta's bitterness was reflected as late as 12 May when he wrote in a letter to Léonie Léon that he and his friends were 'résolus à rester impénétrables jusqu'au moment décisif au mépris de ce que les Pontifes appellent les Principes, s'il faut sacrifier les Principes à la Fortune. Ce n'est pas nous qui laisserons périr la République pour des chimères et des syllogismes' (L.G.).
3. For the text of this 'procès-verbal', see *R.F.*, 1 April.
4. See, e.g., articles of 5, 7 and 21 May.

things did come to a head, after having maintained his own views, he would do his best to repair the momentary damage.[1] This was a sound assessment and a sensible attitude to adopt. For the time being, moreover, it worked. When there were further contentious votes during the Assembly's summer session the now vaunted unity was better maintained.

Meanwhile with the coming of spring Gambetta's natural optimism had returned. The influence of the *République Française*, he told Ranc, had never been greater: indeed it was read more by the Right than by the Left. There had never since 2 July 1871 been a time more favourable to Republican interests. The *gouvernement de combat* had surpassed his hopes and by its actions converted the masses to Republicanism.[2]

The fall of Broglie and the Bonapartist challenge had a still greater effect. It was as though in the warmth of early summer Gambetta had escaped from the toils of a spider's web and taken wing like a noble peacock butterfly finding honey in gardens both new and old. Once again he spoke outside the Assembly, while within it he reasserted himself, violent and conciliatory by turns, but more than ever a master of tactics and once more a dominating personality. With Broglie out of the way and the Right once more in disarray the Assembly might yet become an instrument of Republican construction. But for this to happen, as Gambetta had already recognised, the most moderate group on the Left, the Left Centre, must continue to play the leading role.[3]

Outside the Assembly Gambetta spoke three times in a month and on each occasion he took the opportunity to enlarge upon the sort of theme on which he had already touched in the autumn of 1873. At Grenoble he had created a furore by appearing to hold out the image of an exclusive and intolerant regime monopolised by the 'new social strata'. He himself had often since sought to correct this image and Challemel-Lacour, in his notable speech in the Assembly in March, had eloquently described a Republic which, while 'resolved to defend itself against all agitators, anarchists or monarchists, nevertheless remains open to all, because she knows neither class nor caste and takes account only of services rendered and avowed good will'.[4] Now in his first public utterance after Broglie's fall, a funeral oration by the grave of a Republican aristocrat, Comte d'Alton-Shée, Gambetta was at pains again to substitute for the picture of an exclusive Republic that of one which would be tolerant and also

1. *Lettres*, nos. 185 and 187 of 21 April and April–May, to Ranc.
2. *Lettres*, nos 184 and 185 of 19 and 21 April. Cf. Spuller to Ranc 23 Feb. expressing similar optimism (Ranc, *op. cit.*, p. 292).
3. Letter of 12 May to Léonie Léon (L.G.).
4. This speech and this passage in it were singled out for praise in a leader in the R.F. of 25 March.

'Athenian' in its elegance and distinction.[1] He had already made overtures to the bourgeoisie at the Château de la Borde eight months earlier:[2] now it was the turn of the aristocracy. 'In a great society like ours . . . there is room for everyone, above all for those who more than others seem to represent the past and its traditions of elegance, wit and dignity. The old aristocracy from which d'Alton-Shée was descended, belongs to France. It can still serve her.'[3]

But, in spite of the presence of so many deputies of noble birth in the Assembly, the bourgeoisie were now a much weightier force than the aristocracy. Gambetta's second speech outside the Assembly at this time, the speech at Auxerre on 1 June was, as has been seen,[4] dominated by his onslaught on the Bonapartists, but it also contained significant passages of another kind. At one point he slipped in a remark which was greeted with laughter and general approval, but which with hindsight the historian can see as a deft indication of the direction in which his mind was working: 'I have too often been represented as the systematic enemy of the Assembly; I have nothing more to say about it and I prefer to keep silence on this subject, because we have much more important things to consider together.'[5] These important things included a fresh wooing of the bourgeoisie and an encomium of the 'new social strata' in which he skilfully laid all his emphasis on their economic and most solidly bourgeois virtues. After expressing his disappointment that many of the liberal opponents of the corrupt government of the Empire had not, when it fell, become 'liberal democrats', he went on to say that nothing was ever lost with the French bourgeoisie. 'Moreover, it is impossible to say where this bourgeoisie, to which the nation owes so much, begins and ends . . . it is impossible to deny its qualities which it could so nobly employ for the greater good of the country.' Conversions, he pointed out, had already taken place and he paid particular tribute to the Left Centre which had played such a decisive and patriotic part at the time of 'the Restoration conspiracy'.

Then there followed his most noteworthy exposition of the development of the 'new social strata'. It was, he declared, thanks to the economic development of 'that loathed and corrupting regime, the Empire' that a kind of new France had been formed, that new *travailleurs* had been

---

1. In a letter to Ranc of 26 May (*Lettres*, no. 193) he referred to his speech and said: 'Le soir, dans les bons cercles et cafés d'amis, on se piquait un peu sur la république athénienne. En 1848, on disait la République démocratique et sociale. C'est vrai, mais que voulez-vous? Tout le monde n'est pas athénien et n'a pas le désir de le devenir.'
2. See above, p. 183.
3. For the text of the oration, see *Discours*, vol. iv, pp. 125–9.
4. See above, p. 190.
5. *Discours*, vol. iv, pp. 144–5. For the text of the whole speech see pp. 135–64.

created, and that property and shareholders had multiplied. It was due to this economic movement that a world of small proprietors, industrialists and shopkeepers had emerged, the world of the new social strata—'I said new strata, not classes'—which through its prosperity and ability increased the country's wealth and intelligence. These strata formed the democracy in which men had the right to choose the government most suited to their interests and in which, when eight out of ten million electors were liable to pay taxes on land, they must surely choose the Republic. But what Republican democracy demanded was not 'a closed, exclusive Republic; it is a national Republic; the Republic of all, the Republic of ten million electors'. Apart from the attack on the Bonapartists, the speech was a brilliant exercise in conciliation. Moreover, the definition of the 'new social strata' emphasised a highly important point, namely the extension of the habit of buying shares. As a twentieth-century historian has put it: 'the mass of investors in government ten per cent stock strengthened the new regime. Capitalism and the Republic both gained thereby.'[1]

It was to the bourgeoisie, too, that he alluded once more in the last of his three speeches outside the Assembly, a speech once again delivered at the annual commemoration of the birth of General Hoche. As in 1873, the Minister of the Interior forbade a public banquet and, as then, the ceremony took place in a private house. But the man whom Gambetta extolled was not so much Hoche as Thiers, to whom a toast had been proposed, Thiers the supreme convert, 'this illustrious statesman who has given the phalanx of experienced parlementarians, great landowners, important industrialists, great merchants, considerable citizens of all kinds' an example in sacrificing his old opinions to the higher interest of France, recognising that the Republic was the only means of restoring her to her rank. From this rapprochment between Thiers, 'the most typical [*exact*] representative of the French bourgeoisie', and the party of Republican democracy there had sprung 'this great national party which wants the Republic and which has become the shield of order and liberty'. In consequence, Republicans understood 'the need to abjure the old spirit of exclusiveness and hostility' towards all those who sincerely wished to enter into this alliance. They would have no greater satisfaction than in seeing the establishment of the Republic assisted by the very men who hitherto had been unwitting obstacles in its path.[2]

1. J. Bouvier, *Les Rothschild* (Paris, 1967), p. 221.
2. For the text of this speech, see *Discours*, vol. iv, pp. 16–21. Already in a leader on 22 April the *R.F.* had claimed that while the Republican party could not at first have 'le calme, la pondération, l'esprit politique, la connaissance des affaires', the accession of the 'classes libérales les lui ont apportées. De cette union féconde est résulté un parti national vraiment complet. C'est ce parti qui remplit aujourd'hui les avenues du pouvoir.'

These conciliatory gestures made by Gambetta outside the Assembly were paralleled by some of his utterances within it. While Broglie's fall automatically entailed the burial of his scheme for a Grand Council, though by no means that of all plans for a second chamber, the reactionary electoral reform Bill drafted by the Commission of Thirty had yet to be debated. The *rapporteur* of the Bill was one of Gambetta's former law professors, Batbie, and in opposing a second reading on 4 June Gambetta adopted a tone of good-humoured banter which delighted the house:[1] 'There is great virtue in moderation', wrote *The Times* sententiously,

> and yesterday M. Gambetta was moderate; he was also witty and amusing, which . . . is a great treat in a Chamber where, as in most Chambers, so much dreary twaddle is talked. . . . M. Gambetta may boast with truth that he yesterday not only won the applause of the Left . . . but that he also commanded, in great measure, the silence of the Right, a feat much more difficult to achieve. . . . His moderation of tone was remarkable, and gives hope that he may yet shine as a member of that Conservative Republican Government which, we are taught to believe, is one day to establish complete liberty, order and prosperity in France.[2]

This was high praise from *The Times*. Yet it omitted to observe that in humourously remarking that he did not wish to place himself on constitutional ground, for 'you know with what hesitation I venture upon this difficult soil', and in referring to dissolution, but not making it a main plank in his speech, Gambetta had as good as accepted the Assembly's constituent power and assumed that it would be exercised. Apart from this, although the Assembly voted in favour of a second reading the criticisms levelled by Gambetta, Louis Blanc, Ledru-Rollin and others virtually killed the Bill.[3] The Commission of Thirty withdrew it and brought forward a revised version on 24 July, but this was too near the summer vacation for it to be debated, and later on it was decided that the completion

---

1. For the text, see *Ass. Nat. A.*, vol. xxxi, pp. 302–6 and *Discours*, vol. iv, pp. 168–85. The *R.F.* of 6 June described Gambetta's intervention as 'une improvisation étincelante de verve ironique, admirable de vigueur. . . . Quand M. Gambetta est descendu de la tribune d'éclatants applaudissements ont retenti.' For another tribute, see Pelletan, *Le Théâtre de Versailles*, pp. 158–9: 'Jamais il ne fut plus prestigieux. . . . Comment analyser cet admirable discours, qui est de l'action autant que de la parole, et dont le souffle changeant, comme par bouffées de rafale, passant de la brise à la bourrasque, sort tout entier de la situation du moment, du milieu.' The speech was soon after put on the market as a brochure by E. Leroux along with Gambetta's speech at Auxerre. The former cost ten centimes, the latter twenty, but the two together might be had for twenty-five.

2. 6 June 1874, p. 5.

3. Pelletan, *op. cit.*, pp. 155–9, singled out Louis Blanc's as the other great speech of the day.

of the electoral law should be deferred until after the framing of the constitution. Thus Gambetta played his part in preserving that 'integrity of universal suffrage' which he held so dear. The *République Française* could even claim that the session of 4 June would remain 'famous in parliamentary history and in the annals of French eloquence. It can be said that it will remain a unique example of an oratorical battle in which one of the parties to the fight was so superior that the adversary himself had the grace to recognise . . . that the joy and enthusiasm of the victors was justified by the greatness of their triumph!'

At one time and another Gambetta and the *République Française* had paid tribute to the Left Centre. But the Right Centre had understandably distrusted it, fearing that it must one day pay for the support of the Radicals and that the conservative Republic would be merely a halfway house to the 'Red' Republic of the Radicals. Now, however, when the Right Centre was in disarray after Broglie's fall and alarmed by the Bonapartist revival, the Radicals could regard it in a rather different light. On 29 May an eavesdropping police agent, asserting that he had no doubt of what he heard, reported the sense of a conversation between Gambetta and three companions as they left the Gare St Lazare on their way back from Versailles.

> It is certain [they agreed] that M. de Bourgoing's election must bring the Right Centre closer than ever to the Republicans. Yet the danger for the Republic will not be any the less, on the contrary. But if an alliance could be brought about momentarily, thus providing a significant majority in the Assembly, dissolution could soon follow and we would then see, according to the real strength of the Republicans, who would form the new assembly, how we can bring the Orleanists to a reckoning and fight them. If things happen this way elections will take place in November . . . if they do not there will be a delay of at least a year. But we can wait.[1]

This, if accurately recorded, was a revealing conversation. The Right Centre, the group consisting largely of Orleanists, were thus the men to be alternatively frightened and courted, but for purely tactical reasons. The *République Française* had in fact already set to work. The 'doctrinaires', as it loved to call them, were, it said on 28 May, playing into the hands of the Legitimists in the Assembly and of the Bonapartists in the country, and three days later it printed a leader urging them to abandon their chimeras and to throw in their lot with the Republicans. By 3 June, however, it had decided that, while the group was condemned to break up, there were in it only a certain number of intelligent men who might be persuaded to

1. A.P.P., BA/918.

abandon a suicidal policy and 'join the liberal-conservative standard now upheld by the Left Centre'.[1]

Under these and other pressures part of the Right Centre did indeed begin to waver, while the Left Centre, no doubt largely directed by Thiers, took the lead in going over to the offensive. On 15 June a prominent member of the group, a notable convert from Orleanism, Thiers's friend Casimir-Périer,[2] son of Louis Philippe's celebrated minister, moved a highly important motion. It was that, in view of the Bonapartist menace, the Assembly's Constitutional Commission should proceed to organise the Republic on the basis both of Dufaure's Bill of 19 May 1873, which had declared that 'the Government of the French Republic is composed of two Chambers and of a president, the head of the executive power', and of the law of November 1873 entrusting the presidency of the Republic to Marshal MacMahon for seven years. In the words of a French constitutional historian, this motion sought to 'consecrate' the Republic, 'for it extended the name no longer only to the President but also to the government itself, Chamber and President'. At the same time it gave guarantees to the Conservatives: two Chambers, the continuance of the Septennate until 20 November 1880, and the possibility even of a complete constitutional revision which could permit the institution of a Monarchy.[3]

Casimir-Périer demanded urgent consideration of his motion. To have any chance of passing, it required support not only from the Right and Left Centres but also from the other two Left-wing groups, and this implied their readiness sooner or later both to recognise the Assembly's constituent power and also to swallow a second chamber. Although the *République Française* throws no light on the matter, no doubt the influence and eloquence of Gambetta were decisive in swinging the majority of the Republican Union into line on 13 June. 'The thirty years that followed', wrote Hanotaux, 'were daughters of that day.'[4] But this, as a French biographer of Gambetta has remarked, was to attach too great significance to a tactical gesture: 'A vote on the urgency of a proposal did not *ipso facto* imply the adoption of a constitutional system or a definite political choice.'[5] This, indeed, had been demonstrated by Gambetta's attitude in March to

1. For further articles on this issue, see, e.g., *R.F.* of 8 and 9 June.
2. The *R.F.* of 27 June called him 'le grand ministre de la bourgeoisie'.
3. M. Deslandres, *Histoire constitutionnelle de la France*, pp. 292–3.
4. *Cit.* Deschanel, *Gambetta*, p. 169. E. Renard (*La Vie et l'oeuvre de Louis Blanc*, 1922, p. 150) says that in the discussion in the Republican Union before the debate, Louis Blanc was one of those who opposed supporting the demand for urgency. In the vote on the 13th he abstained, as did two other members of the Republican Union, namely Peyrat and Edgar Quinet. Their reasons are set out in Blanc's *Histoire de la Constitution de 1875* (1882), pp. 32–9.
5. Wormser, *Gambetta dans les têmpetes*, p. 157.

the Dahirel motion.[1] Nevertheless, Gambetta had patently shifted his ground. He was ready, if need be, as he had admitted in a letter of 12 May to Léonie Léon, to 'sacrifice Principles to Fortune' and Louis Blanc warned him that he had taken the first step on a slippery slope.[2]

It is interesting to observe how the *République Française* prepared the way for this evolution and at the same time contrived to clothe itself in the unsullied mantle of consistency. Already on 3 June it had remarked that people could express the most varied opinions concerning the Assembly's constituent power, but there was one point on which everyone was agreed, namely that the Assembly could not any longer defer the fulfilment of its undertaking: 'Make a constitution or dissolve yourselves', such was now the dilemma, a dilemma which the nation would not permit its mandatories to elude. On the 15th, the day on which the urgency of Casimir-Périer's motion was to be put to the vote, the paper's leading article explained that the great ill which France was suffering from was uncertainty. No proposal or parliamentary act whose object was to put an end to this uncertainty could meet with the paper's hostility or indifference. Casimir-Périer's motion posed the dilemma: Republic or dissolution.

This paper's policy is known. It has never varied ... the dissolution of the Assembly ... seems to us more than ever the only possible and complete solution of the difficulties of all kinds which at present beset us. We will abstain from prejudging the results of the vote which is to take place today. It is possible that the motion will be adopted: the fundamental questions will still be reserved; but the true situation will nevertheless be delineated; it is, to repeat it again, the alternative already indicated: Republic or dissolution.

The motion in favour of urgent consideration was in fact adopted by the narrow margin of four votes (345 to 341). Thirty-four members of the Right Centre had supported it. The *République Française* exulted. This was 'an immense event' and the Republicans were now near their goal.[3] One observer, Flaubert, told his niece that the Republic had been recognised by a majority of four and that this was the direct consequence of the fear of the Bonapartists resulting from Sainte-Croix's assault on Gambetta: 'There is an example of the way in which trivial causes have great effects.'[4] It was, indeed, as Gambetta's later disciple, Joseph Reinach, was to write,

1. See above, p. 196.
2. L.G.; Blanc, *op. cit.*, p. 18.
3. 17 June. On the following day the historian Taine, away with his family at Menthon-Saint-Bernard, wrote to his friend Emile Boutmy, 'it seems to me that within a year's time (unless Prussia upsets things generally) either this Chamber or the next will bring in the Republic' (*Life and Letters of H. Taine*, Part iii, p. 135).
4. Flaubert, *Correspondance*, vol. vii, p. 150.

the first step towards the definitive constitution of the Republic made by those who had so often declared it to be fatal and impossible.[1] But it was only a first step and the Republic eventually constituted would be very different from that envisaged by the more radical members of the Republican Union.

The motion had still to be referred to the conservatively-minded Commission of Thirty. After a fortnight the Commission rejected it and elected a subcommittee of three to put up different proposals. A confused situation at the beginning of July was rendered still more confused by a fresh manifesto unexpectedly issued by Chambord and by the rejection of a government motion endorsing the Septennate. The cabinet therefore resigned, but was kept in being by MacMahon: shortly afterwards, however, it lost its two Bonapartist members and this was widely interpreted as a blow to Bonapartist influence. As the menace of Bonapartism appeared to recede people no longer thought that the Casimir-Périer motion represented the only bulwark against a return of the Empire.[2] So when it and other constitutional proposals were the subject of a general debate on 23 July it in turn was rejected by 374 votes to 333.[3] The Duc de Broglie had reentered the fray and in one of his best speeches ridiculed the inconsistencies of Republican doctrine, the government had thrown their weight against the motion and the Right Centre had rallied to their support. Gambetta in a letter to Princess Troubetskoï affected to regard the defeat as a slender one.[4] The *République Française* had reiterated that the choice was between the Republic or dissolution; the Republic had been turned down, dissolution remained. The Left Centre, Gambetta told the Princess, were so angered by the failure of the Casimir-Périer motion that they were eager to press for dissolution. There were only fifteen votes to be won and the decisive blow might be struck within a week. But Gambetta was an optimist and his arithmetic was faulty. It was indeed a notable event for the Left Centre to take the initiative in proposing a motion for dissolution. But when this motion, proposed by Léon de Maleville of the Left Centre, in favour of general elections on 5 September followed by an immediate dissolution was debated on 29 July it was defeated by 369 votes to 340. In ordinary times, as Rémusat remarked, an Assembly of which 330 to 340 members demanded dissolution would have been as good as dissolved.[5] But these were extraordinary times, as indeed Gambetta's own intervention ironically served to emphasise: the erstwhile denier of the

1. *Discours*, vol. iv, p. 214.
2. See *The Times*, 21, 23 July.
3. Quinet and Louis Blanc again abstained, as did Jules Grévy.
4. *Lettres*, no. 196, 24 July.
5. *Mémoires de ma vie*, vol. v, p. 507.

Assembly's constituent authority now made a powerful plea that it should exercise its sovereignty 'and make a last effort to give this country a definitive government!'[1] But the Assembly was deaf to the plea. There had been a prolonged heatwave and 'the great party of the weary' (*le grand parti des Fatigués*) prevailed. Already General Changarnier (who, it is true, was an octogenarian) had remembered his Horace and expressed his desire:

> Nunc veterum libris, nunc somno et inertibus horis
> Ducere sollicitae jucunda oblivia vitae.[2]

So far from striking 'a decisive blow', the Assembly made haste to take an even longer vacation than usual. It acted, wrote Gambetta, 'like the desperately ill, who take opium in order not to feel the final agonies'.[3] It adjourned from 6 August to 30 November. The *République Française* scornfully remarked that people at Versailles 'no doubt rejoiced at the thought of gaining five or six months and of still for a whole season counting as deputies on hotel registers and visiting cards'.[4]

---

1. For the text, see *Discours*, vol. iv, pp. 241–56, *Ass. Nat. A.*, vol. xxxiv, pp. 97–101.
2. Ibid., vol. xxxiii, p. 338, 24 July.
3. *Lettres*, no. 197, 26 July. He repeated the simile in no. 200 of 2 Aug. to Mme Scheurer-Kestner. To Léonie Léon he wrote: 'nous sommes vaincus pour six mois' (letter of 29 July, L.G.).
4. 28 July. C. de B., however, claimed that public opinion was delighted to see the Assembly go on holiday—the longer the better (Rothschild pp., 25 July).

15

'The too long vacation' July–November 1874

On the eve of the long summer recess which the National Assembly, now sometimes derisively called 'the National Agitation',[1] had voted itself, the Republican Left held a meeting and issued a statement. This reminded its adherents that among the adversaries of the Republic some were members of the government armed with the discretionary powers of martial law, others had since 24 May 1873 been in occupation of most of the administrative posts and yet others were reiterating their right to use the recess for yet another attempt at monarchical restoration. Moreover, 'the organisation even of a personal power opposed by every party' was at the moment more possible than the creation of a definite government. In face of these adversaries and dangers the Republicans, the statement declared, should remain absolutely calm and disciplined. During the recess, it continued, they would have several opportunities of manifesting their firm desire to found a Republican government.[2]

The Republican Union and the *République Française* which reproduced the statement would no doubt fully have endorsed it. Moreover, there were, as it said, to be several opportunities for the Republicans to show their strength because elections were again in the offing at various levels: by-elections, cantonal elections for the partial renewal of General Councils, and municipal elections. Gambetta's long vacation would be far from idle, as his letters to Juliette Adam were to show. When she departed to spend the latter part of the summer at Les Bruyères he promised, as her 'resident minister' in her 'good town of Paris', to write to her frequently.[3] As a result she became the recipient of some of the longest letters he ever

---

1. *The Times*, 21 Aug., p. 5.
2. For the text, see *R.F.*, 7 Aug.
3. According to Mme Adam, when she asked him to write, he replied: 'J'écris si peu! Hum! Hum! fait Spuller. Nous sourions tous, sachant que de très nombreux billets prennent le chemin de la rue Bonaparte' (*Nos amitiés*, p. 142).

wrote—one spread over several days extended to fourteen pages when it was later printed. They are fascinating letters in which he frankly admitted his mercurial temperament and in which he wrote freely about his political preoccupations. These were foreign affairs and electoral problems at home.

The Bonapartists' influence might have been removed from the cabinet but their power and propaganda were still feared as an electoral force in the provinces. The Republicans had the reputation of being better organised than any other party,[1] but local organisations might become lax and they varied in strength from locality to locality. All parties, no doubt, had to contend with the 'profound indifference towards any sort of politics' observed recently among the country-dwellers in Eastern France by Taine. 'I take it', he wrote, 'that if voiced the general feeling is: "Don't worry us. Give us any government you like, as long as it provides police and roads, but for heaven's sake let there be no quarrelling!"'[2] So people, Gambetta said, were more ready to criticise than to act:

> The Press gets little support, money is contributed too sparingly, committees are formed only with great difficulty: laziness is the great ill. Our best friends take things too easily. They content themselves with writing three or four pages on the last session, send their prose to a local paper and think that they have done their duty by their electors. . . . This isn't so in the least; universal suffrage supports those who cultivate it untiringly; the voters need to be visited, enlightened and informed and I do all I can to urge our colleagues to this missionary work.[3]

Gambetta indeed did not spare himself. An old propaganda weapon was incidentally refurbished at the beginning of August when Leroux announced that his collection of Gambetta's speeches was now out of print

1. See *The Times*, 3 July, p. 10: 'It is said that in every Commune of France there is a Republican Committee of 30 persons, and that the President of each committee reports to a chief. A head-centre is appointed in every Department. It is probable that the efforts of the Bonapartists are more desultory and less combined.' Cf. police report of 16 June: 'On s'occupe très sérieusement de . . . propagande républicaine Gambettiste dans les campagnes capables de combattre la propagande bonapartiste. . . . Tous les membres actifs du parti républicain de Paris donneront les renseignements sur leurs provinces et se mettront en relations avec les maires et conseillers municipaux révoqués' (A.P.P., BA/918).
2. Taine, *Life and Letters*, Part iii, p. 134. This apathy was the subject of the fourth of the *50 Lettres Républicaines de Gervais Martial ouvrier, recueillies par Touchatout* (1875), a letter 'où l'on voit Gervais Martial savonner fortement son copain d'atelier Roger, dit Pisse-froid, au sujet de sa coupable indifférence en matière politique'. Martial (a pseudonym of Léon Bienvenu) was a doughty Republican.
3. *Lettres*, no. 203, 25 Aug. to Laurent-Pichat.

and that he was reissuing them in more durable form. This, he claimed, would be very useful on the eve of the inevitable general elections.[1]

This might be so, but Gambetta's more immediate concern was with by-elections which the government continued to defer and to space out as far as possible, with the result that hardly a month passed without an election somewhere in France. The first of these to take place in the long vacation was that of 16 August in Calvados and the result, a handsome victory for the Bonapartist candidate over his Legitimist and moderate Republican rivals, seemed to confirm the fears of all those who believed in the danger of a restoration not of Monarchy, but of Empire. But Gambetta had been prepared for defeat. As early as mid-June he had told a police agent that the Bonapartist candidate was bound to be elected, since his Republican opponent, Lecesne, had, undeservedly, a bad reputation. Indeed, he added that he rather hoped for such a result, for then the Bonapartists would be bound to overreach themselves and the effect would be to rally the Monarchists to the Republic.[2] To others he explained that the Bonapartist candidate, Leprovost de Launay, had been one of the best of the prefects of the Second Empire.[3] After the event the *République Française* expressed dismay but refused to be alarmed.[4] It did, however, admit defects in the local organisation: above all, the Republican candidate eventually selected instead of Lecesne had been chosen too late. Whereas Leprovost de Launay's candidature had been mooted three months before the election, the Republicans had decided on their man, a lawyer named Aubert, a bare twelve days before it took place and this had been quite insufficient time in which to build up an adequate electoral machine.[5]

1. *R.F.*, 31 Aug. The volume was advertised for 3.50 fr. in-18° or 6 fr. in-8° in the *R.F.* of 4 Dec. and intermittently thereafter.

2. A.P.P., BA/918, report of 18 June from an agent who from now on was in frequent touch with Gambetta. The idea of Lecesne's candidature seems to have been dropped, probably soon after this conversation.

3. *Lettres*, no. 200 of 2 Aug. to Mme Scheurer-Kestner.

4. 19 Aug. In its attempts to rally the electors of Calvados against the Bonapartist candidate the *R.F.* had made the most of 'the traitor' Bazaine's escape from the fortress in which he was confined. It had also reprinted a 'remarquable brochure: La vérité sur Sedan par un officier supérieur', lately published by the Bibliothèque de l'instruction républicaine. At the end of the year (27 Dec., p. 3) it mentioned a further series of pamphlets 'que des écrivains et des libraires patriotes opposent courageusement aux millions de pamphlets et de feuilles volantes' of the Bonapartists; in particular it commended *L'Appel au peuple* by Jules Barni, *Les Décembriseurs* by Schoelcher, *Ce qu'ont fait les bonapartistes* by an Alsatian, *Invasion IV* by P. Lefranc, and *République et prospérité* by Gazeau de Vautibault.

5. 20 Aug.: 'il ne paraît pas qu'il y ait eu autre chose pour appuyer M. Aubert qu'un comité unique à Caen et quelques activités individuelles dans des centres comme Lisieux, Vire et Honfleur. Non-seulement il n'existait pas de comités cantonaux, mais, dans un grand nombre de cantons, le comité de Caen n'avait même

Accordingly, as other by-elections were likely to be held before long, the Republicans must not in future be taken by surprise. No doubt the law must be scrupulously observed and 'the time appointed by law must be awaited before committees can enter into direct contact with the electorate and hold public meetings etc.' But they could greatly further their task by preparatory private meetings and correspondence, and the *République Française* praised its 'friends' in the Nord for already going to work to choose a candidate for an election to be held in November.[1]

The next by-election was in fact one to which Gambetta attached particular importance. It was to be held a month later in Maine-et-Loire, a department in which Monarchist and clerical influences had been powerful, which had not voted since 8 February 1871, and which incidentally was the home of Gambetta's friend and collaborator Henri Allain-Targé. It was an election in which the Bonapartists were once again presenting a candidate and it was to be the first occasion on which the Savary Law of 18 February 1873, became operative. This law, passed at the instigation of Monarchists, who thought it would work to their advantage, had reinstated the practice of a second ballot a fortnight after the first if the leading candidate did not succeed in obtaining an absolute majority of the votes cast. Gambetta had set to work at once to prepare the ground. On the very day of the death of the former minister Beulé, which created the parliamentary vacancy, he wrote to Allain-Targé to tell him to start visiting his friends. It was clear that he hoped to secure his adoption as the Republican candidate.[2] In the end, however, the man put forward was Maillé, a moderate Republican and a former Mayor of Angers who had been dismissed by Broglie's first ministry. But Allain-Targé, guided from Paris by Gambetta, took an active part in organising the electoral campaign. Gambetta at the end of August was writing to urge him to attack the election manifesto of the Bonapartist candidate, to organise meetings in country districts, and to distribute anti-Bonapartist propaganda.[3] Optimistic on 5 September that Maillé would lead and force his Bonapartist and Legitimist opponents to a second ballot,[4] he confessed on the 12th, the eve of the poll, that he had never awaited election results with greater anxiety: 'It is', he wrote to Madame Adam, 'a dangerous game (*une grave*

1. *R.F.*, 1 Sept., cf. 18 Sept.
2. *Lettres*, nos 178 and 181 of 4 and 11 April.
3. *Ibid.*, no. 204 of 27 Aug. In particular he thought that the brochure called *La Vérité sur Sedan* (see p. 208, n. 4 above) would have an excellent effect.
4. *Ibid.*, no. 205 to Mme Adam.

pas un correspondant régulièrement accrédité sur qui il pût compter. Le zèle et l'activité des membres du comité caennais ne pourraient se répandre en quelques jours sur six arrondissements et sur une population d'un demi-million d'habitants.'

partie); if we fail after our reverses in the Nièvre and Calvados I fear that the plebiscitary gangrene will spread; if on the contrary fortune returns to us, our victory will also be contagious and from now on until the return of the Assembly we shall have a series of triumphs. Our Lady of Les Bruyères pray for us!'[1]

Whether or not Madame Adam prayed, fortune returned. In the first round Maillé polled 45,517 votes compared with 26,374 gained by the Legitimist Bruas and 25,524 by the Bonapartist Berger. A second ballot was necessary, Berger withdrew and Maillé won. Meanwhile in the next instalment of this same long letter Gambetta was bubbling over with delight. The results of the first round exceeded the Republicans' hopes, he wrote, and victory was certain a fortnight later. The fury of the reactionaries was 'beyond description'. The Bonapartists had owed their previous success to the complicity of officialdom, all the government's attempts to exert official pressure had failed. It was a débâcle: 'the Septennate pure and simple has for the first time appeared before universal suffrage;[2] it has been tried and executed. It will meet with the same fate at the hands of the Assembly when it reassembles.' The death on the 12th of Guizot, 'this portentous genius'—Gambetta in private was never the man to heed the maxim 'De mortuis nil nisi bonum'—was just another example of the reactionaries' ill-luck. The significance of this by-election was indeed such that *The Times* had devoted a leader to it. The result showed, it said, that French Conservatives were being converted to the Republic. The honour of this conversion was due to Thiers, but, it added, 'to the leaders of the Left and especially to M. Gambetta must not be denied the credit of having rendered it possible by an exercise of moderation and reticence too rare in the political history of France.'[3]

If the result in Maine-et-Loire was to set a pattern, it was indeed important, for there were to be no fewer than seven more parliamentary elections before the end of the vacation. In general the results were satisfactory for Gambetta. In February 1871, as the *République Française* wrote a little later, on 21 November 1874, the Republicans in the Assembly had numbered only 120: now they were 340: 'Twenty more victories and they will be in

1. *Ibid.*, no. 206. According to a report on the same day by a police agent who said he had had twenty-five minutes' talk with Gambetta, Allain Targé wrote to Gambetta every morning about the situation in Maine-et-Loire (A.P.P., BA/918).

2. M. Bruas had stood as a supporter of MacMahon. He was derided by the *R.F.* 25 Aug.) as 'une ombre de candidat', as (1 Sept.) like 'Hippolyte étendu sans forme et sans couleur', and (4 Sept.) as 'le candidat qui n'aura d'opinion que dans sept ans'. The government's dismay was noted by C. de B. (Rothschild pp., 14 and 28 Sept.).

3. 15 Sept. It is interesting to note that it was at this time that *l'Eclipse* of 13, 20 Sept. and 4 Oct. published three celebrated caricatures by Gill: 'L'homme qui rit', Thiers; L'Homme qui parle', Gambetta; and 'L'homme qui pense', Victor Hugo.

the majority.' Of the twenty-eight deputies elected since 24 May 1873, twenty-three were Republicans. The Monarchists were again the party which lost most ground. They failed to retain two seats, one of them in the Nord being won by a Republican convert, Edouard Parsy, Mayor of Cambrai, about whom Gambetta had written with revealing enthusiasm: 'He is perfect', he told Madame Adam, 'very rich, a Republican "de la veille", still young, well enough educated and with a real facility for speaking.'[1] But it was a disappointment that a candidate whom Gambetta himself visited on 1 October,[2] could not prevent a Bonapartist victory in Pas-de-Calais after a second ballot, for the *République Française* had hoped that a Republican triumph there would 'complete the ruin of the Bonapartists'.[3] It was, moreover, 'deplorable' that in the Oise on 8 November divisions in the Republican ranks and the consequent appearance of two Republican candidates had led to the election of another Bonapartist, the Duc de Mouchy; indeed the *République Française* was all the sadder when it reflected that a department which had suffered so much in the German invasion had acclaimed 'a young grand Seigneur who was more concerned with pleasure than the public interest' and whose only recommendations, so it said, were his personal fortune and his connections with the abhorred Imperial family. Once again the Republicans had failed because of defective organisation.[4] It was dismaying, too, that there had been a high proportion of separatist votes in Nice (the Alpes Maritimes) in spite of Gambetta's attempts to exert his personal influence there in the previous winter.[5] And in the Drôme, which had gone to the polls on 8 November, a small but uncomfortable cloud had appeared. The successful Republican candidate, Madier de Montjau, a veteran of 1848 whose candidature the *République Française* had cordially supported, was in fact one of those intransigent Radicals à la Louis Blanc, who in his campaign had not hesitated to declare his disagreement on various points with Gambetta.[6] He would continue to do so.

Meanwhile there had been another set of elections early in October, elections to the importance of which the Republican Left, in their

---

1. *Lettres*, no. 206, 7 Sept. Cf. *R.F.* 1 Sept. Parsy's election was hailed by the *R.F.* (11 Nov.) as a great political event and Gambetta congratulated his friend Testelin, already one of the deputies for the Nord, enthusiastically upon it on 10 Nov. (*Lettres*, no. 220 *bis*).

2. *Lettres*, no. 213 of 1 Oct. His visit was primarily to induce François Brasme, whose wife did not want him to stand, to agree to be the Republican candidate.

3. 9 Oct.

4. See the severe leaders of 10 and 11 Nov.

5. For Gambetta's annoyance at this, see *Lettres*, nos 210 and 221. For his visit to the Alpes Maritimes, see above, pp. 176–7.

6. Gouault, *Comment la France est devenue républicaine*, p. 179.

statement of 5 August, had drawn particular attention, namely those for the partial renewal for six years of the membership of the General Councils.[1] Normally under a definitive form of government, the statement had pointed out, local interests were chiefly at issue and the electors could make their own choice on administrative grounds. But this was not so in present circumstances—every election was now a political one. This was particularly true, it asserted, of the elections to the General Councils, not only because the Tréveneuc Law of 1871 had assigned the Councils a special role 'in the event of attacks on the national sovereignty', but also because it was now proposed to find in them electors and candidates for an Upper Chamber.[2] Gambetta shared this view of the importance of these elections. He wrote to friends like Dr Testelin in the Nord urging them to prepare the ground for his party's success[3] and, resuming, as he jokingly told Allain-Targé, his old functions as Minister of the Interior, he followed up the Republican Left's statement with a 'circular' of his own. This took the form of a second 'Letter to a General Councillor', reminiscent of the one he had written in 1871.[4] It went over familiar ground, reviewing the course of Republican electoral victories since April 1871, and claimed that the excellence of the candidates chosen in the municipal and cantonal elections of that year had been proved in the restoration crisis of 1873: 'France owed it to the calm, loyal and resolute intervention of the local assemblies that she escaped a new upheaval which would have been "the most frightful of them all".' Once again he referred to the new social strata (which he defined as 'this democracy, petite bourgeoisie, workers and peasants') and praised the attention that, as members of General Councils, they had given to the practical problems of roads, prisons, public health, pauperism, and above all, railways. Once again he stressed the diversity of social problems, each requiring a particular solution so that in the long run each was a problem of a political order. Now in 1874 he urged that in view of the manifest impotence of the Assembly to fulfil its constitutional mandate, France must speak out: in consequence the elections to the Councils must everywhere have a political, Republican character. They would be a veritable preparation for a general election;

1. They were renewable by half every three years, those cantons in which this procedure was to be followed first, i.e. in 1874, having been selected by lot in 1871. The *R.F.* printed lists of the sitting members in these cantons in its issues of 17–28 Sept. inclusive. Lists of Republican candidates were also printed thereafter.

2. See *The Times*, 7 Aug., p. 5.

3. *Lettres*, no. 204 *bis*, 1 Sept.: 'Je vous prie de bien recommander à nos amis ... de faire lever les listes électorales par arrondissement, de faire préparer cinq ou six bandes pour chaque électeur, afin de pouvoir leur envoyer à domicile les bulletins et les journaux, et les professions de foi.'

4. See above, pp. 48–9.

no 'servant of the democracy' must decline to stand, if called upon to do so, and Republican successes in them should remove the last hesitations of those deputies who, 'without any marked aversion to the Republican regime had not yet dared to accept it'.[1]

Although the *République Française* claimed that these elections were an immense success despite all sorts of obstacles,[2] it is uncertain whether Gambetta's hopes were really fulfilled. It was by no means easy, as *The Times* remarked, to assess the political outlook of fourteen hundred local notables, and the more candid Parisian papers confessed their inability to do so.[3] In a report to Lord Derby, Lord Lytton estimated that the anti-Republican votes taken together showed 'a collective majority of about ten per cent, as compared with the united Republican Party. This last . . . has not lost much ground, but it undoubtedly has lost *some* ground.' But in view of official pressure, he thought that the Republican party had stood up to 'an ordeal specially devised by its oponents [*sic*] in the hopes of its discomfiture' remarkably well. The losses had been chiefly 'in the south where republicanism is ultra-radical, their gains chiefly in the north where republicanism is moderate.'[4] The official figures showed the return of 606 Republicans compared with 604 Monarchists and 156 Bonapartists. In forty-three out of eighty-six mainland departments Republicans had the satisfaction of seeing their men elected Presidents of their General Councils.[5]

The Maine-et-Loire by-election had been so crucial in Gambetta's opinion that he dared not take a holiday until it was over. Then, on 1 October, accompanied not, to her vexation, by Léonie Léon but by Spuller, his *fidus Achates*, as he himself called him, he set off for a twelve days' break.[6] A growing stoutness was beginning to vex him—'the harder

1. For the text see *Discours*, vol. iv, pp. 462–74, or *R.F.* 28 Sept. in which it was printed as a leader. It was subsequently sold as a brochure for ten centimes.

2. 6 Oct. Cf. leader of 7 Oct. On 26 Sept. the paper had complained: 'dans bien des cantons, nous manquons encore de candidats, et l'on nous écrit trop de lettres où l'on nous dit que personne, parmi nos amis, ne se sent la force d'entamer la lutte.'

3. *The Times*, 7 Oct., p. 5.

4. P.R.O., F.O. 146, 1753, Lytton to Derby, 12 Oct.

5. Deslandres, *Histoire constitutionnelle*, p. 304.

6. According to Mme Adam (*Nos amitiés*, p. 189), relations between Gambetta and Spuller had recently been strained. Gambetta had not said anything to Spuller about his plan to go to Holland and Spuller had been much upset at this. It was, she claimed, she who had persuaded Gambetta to take Spuller with him, perhaps because Spuller had been quite ill towards the end of August (Gambetta, letter to Léonie Léon, 21 Aug., L. G.). But there is no hint of this persuasion in Gambetta's letter to her of 7 Oct. (*Lettres*, no. 217). He reported quite simply: 'j'ai jugé que le moment était venu de donner à mon bon et fidèle Achate quelques jours de repos et de plaisir.' Léonie Léon's vexation is suggested by the tone of Gambetta's letters to her of 10 and 14 Oct. (L.G.).

I work the stouter I become', he told his mother.[1] This *embonpoint* was not reduced by copious meals such as the 'Pantagruelic' lunch he gave to his Spanish friend Castelar soon after the holiday was over.[2] It was indeed a development which, according to police reports of the following spring, was beginning to cause his friends anxiety: he was taking on the appearance of 'a barrel of tallow'. They feared he might have apoplexy; besides, 'a fat Radical was not the sort of Radical for the people . . . Barbès and Blanqui are thin'.[3] Gambetta himself admitted that he ought to go and walk in the mountains to reduce his weight; but he did not. Instead he and 'the philosopher'—another of his names for Spuller—went for their holiday to the flattest of countries, Holland, picking up Ranc, 'the colonel', in Brussels on the way.

The three bachelors—Edmond Adam had not long before remarked that wives and widows would be lacking in the Republic that was to come, since Gambetta, Spuller, Ranc and Challemel-Lacour were all unmarried[4]—admired pictures in Brussels, explored Rotterdam, spent a sunny day on the beach at Scheveningen, gazed in ecstasy at Paul Potter's 'Bull' in the museum at The Hague and ended up with three days in Amsterdam and one in Antwerp. Gambetta had a genuine love of art and wrote at length both to Léonie Léon and to Juliette Adam about what he had seen. A letter to Léonie Léon contained a glowing description of Millet's *Angelus* and a fine appreciation of Constable, 'a man without whom perhaps the great school of French landscape artists would still be copying . . . the basic work of Eustache Lesueur, Poussin, the earlier Vernet, Girodet and other lovers of Greek temples lost in the midst of zinc and carbon trees'. But the three good companions admired Reynolds still more; as in Millet's *Angelus*, so in Reynolds's *Widow* everything seemed to be brought together—'nature and humanity, and what nature!—the fresh shade of a vast English park, and what humanity! grace embodied in mother love, a sad and delicious moment chosen by the artist for carrying out his idea'. The scene reminded Gambetta of the splendid verse of Homer in which Hector's young wife, bidding goodbye to the hero about to die for his country, smiled through her tears as she showed him the young Astyanax calmly playing with the plume of the warrior's helmet.[5]

1. *Lettres*, no. 208, 27 Sept. As early as 8 Jan. 1872 Paul Cambon had referred to Gambetta's 'gros corps essoufflé' (Cambon, *Correspondance*, vol. i, p. 36).

2. *Lettres*, no. 219, 22 Oct. to Mme Adam.

3. A.P.P., BA/918, report of 1 May 1875; cf. also one of 9 March. Prince Hohenlohe, who saw Gambetta at Versailles in June 1874, described him as 'a fat undersized person with long black hair' (*Memoirs of Prince Chlodwig of Hohenlohe-Schillingsfuerst*, ed. F. Curtius, vol. ii, 1906, p. 116).

4. Cf. *Nos amitiés*, pp. 310–11.

5. *Lettres*, no. 214, between 2 and 5 Oct and 217. 7 Oct.

But the holiday was all too soon over and Gambetta returned to piles of accumulated work amid which fine bunches of flowers from Madame Adam were one of his consolations. Among his preoccupations there remained the preparations for the third category of electoral contests during the long recess, namely the municipal elections which were to be held in the country as a whole on 22 November and in Paris on the 29th. In these, a leader in the *République Française* of 7 November explained, it was important to bring on new and young men. The municipal elections were not political elections in the sense that they were concerned with recruiting the men who would conduct the general business of the Republican party, but Republican democracy must 'appear to be the elite of the country from the triple point of view of work, competence and initiative'. That was why Republican candidates must be put forward. The men of the 'new social strata' must face the duties imposed on them by their emancipation as citizens. This was an immense task, he told Madame Adam, and he was extremely proud of having had lists made out of every municipal council in France; 'When you come back', he wrote, 'I will show you these splendid lists which cover the whole Republican party from the smallest commune to Paris. You will be able to see at a glance the whole of the Republican party with the names and professions of all its members. I am quite proud of my invention, for I do not think that any government so far has effected or applied it.' It would, he thought, be of great interest for future elections and therefore he was keeping quiet about it so that no one else should steal his device.[1] So far as the country as a whole and, in particular, the big towns apart from Paris were concerned, Gambetta was confident. His task was rendered the easier because the Monarchists, for lack of agreement and inability to put forward common candidates, largely advocated abstention. This enabled the Radicals at last to show their independence of Thiers's Conservative Republicans. 'In almost all the chief places', according to *The Times*, the moderate Republicans 'prepared lists which they endeavoured to induce their more Radical friends to accept. . . . In some . . . a "transaction" was effected, but in most it has been found impossible to induce the Radicals to give way.' The elections were mainly an inter-Republican battle and the results were a striking victory for Radicalism, especially in the big towns such as Lyons, Marseilles, Bordeaux and Nantes. The Bonapartists and Legitimists, it asserted, like all factions which wished 'to convulse the state', had voted for extremists, hoping that the triumph of Radicals would cause panic and provoke a reaction in their own favour.[2] But, if this was so, it was, as so

1. *Ibid.*, no. 219 of 22 Oct.
2. Leader of 24 Nov., p. 9. The *R.F.* (30 Nov.) took issue with this article: *The Times*'s suggestion that the conservatives had abstained in order to let the extreme

often, a gamble which did not come off. One of their papers might assert that the red flag was now hoisted on every church steeple, but Radicalism no longer had such terrors; indeed the Legitimist C. de B. noted the curious fact that the more victories the Radicals won the more the financial world gained confidence.[1]

The pattern was similar in Paris, though for Gambetta the preparation of electoral lists had been a much more complicated matter.[2] Paris, he told Juliette Adam, was a 'tower of Babel' in which the candidates were 'as numerous and more intolerable than flies in spring'.

> I do not know whom to listen to, I do not want to be too moderate or too advanced. What we want in the present crisis is a Republican municipal council, composed of men who are resolute but sensible and able, one that includes names liked and respected by public opinion and who can in a word earn the respect of our enemies and the esteem of our party. We must prevent a situation in which people could cry Commune and seek to create a municipal commission as under the Empire. But we must also avoid falling into the hands of intriguers who want to be revenged for Barodet's election and to puff themselves up as men of influence on future occasions. You see the elements of the problem. It is difficult and complicated but . . . I think we have nearly resolved it and I dare to think that as a Parisian, an artist and a Republican (and a bit of an aristocrat whatever you may say) you will be pleased with our selection and the final outcome of our colossal undertaking. In a few days' time the paper [i.e. the *République Française*] will give you the complete list of our aediles.[3]

1. Rothschild pp., 24 Nov. The *R.F.*, of course, hailed the results as an immense success, not for Radicalism, but for the Republic (leader of 25 Nov.).

2. The *R.F.* of 17 Aug. and following days had published a notice urging Parisian electors to check the lists which were being revised between 10 and 29 Aug. and gave a list of persons in each *arrondissement* who could if necessary advise them about procedure. On the 20th and following days the notice was modified. Many electors, it said, had written to say that they had been omitted from the lists although they were fully qualified. In consequence, it insisted, in large letters, that 'Tous les électeurs, sans exception aucune' must check their lists.

3. *Lettres*, no. 221. The list was printed in the numbers of 28–30 Nov. Cf. C. de B. (Rothschild pp., 19 Nov.) saying that the Radical campaign was directed from the offices of the *R.F.*: 'c'est de là que part la consigne pour les comités et les journaux des départements.' In a leader of 28 Nov., however, the paper declared: 'la *République Française* ne prend l'initiative d'aucune candidature . . . nous avons toujours porté

Radicals triumph, it dismissed as puerile: 'Un parti ne s'abstient jamais quand il croit avoir quelque chance de l'emporter. Si donc les "conservateurs" et les "bona-partistes" se sont abstenus, comme le prétend le *Times*, c'est parce qu'ils avaient la certitude . . . d'être honteusement battus.' In a separate article on the same page it naturally took the line that it was the moderate Republicans who had rejected Radical overtures.

The list was indeed a veritable array, the Radicals putting up candidates in every ward but three.[1] Once again there was no united Right-wing list; once again the Conservatives lost a large number of seats and many moderate Republicans were displaced by Radicals. The new municipal council comprised eleven members of the Right, twenty-seven moderate Republicans and as many as forty-two Radicals. Sixty-six out of the seventy-seven candidates supported by the *République Française* had been returned. The paper might well be triumphant and applaud Paris as 'great and admirable'.[2] So indeed, in its view, was the whole country. It had already quoted with particular approval an article in the *XIXe Siècle* which declared that from one end of France to the other universal suffrage had pronounced the word 'Republic' and added that the arrival of the new social strata was now an accomplished fact: 'the "classes dirigeantes" are no more'.[3] But was this so in the Assembly and would the word 'Republic' make any impression on its majority? There Gambetta divined only 'irresoluteness, fear and hatred; the three furies who stir our politicians of today'.[4] There the *République Française* still discerned the obstructive power of a narrow oligarchy personified in the so-called 'ruling classes'.[5]

1. The *R.F.* was very proud of having induced the celebrated architect, Viollet-le-Duc, to stand in the 9th *arrondissement* (Faubourg Montmartre section) and devoted its leader of 19 Nov. to his candidature.

2. 'Grand et admirable Paris!... toujours grand, ferme, généreux, républicain, semblable à lui-même' (leader of 1 Dec.). Cf. Gambetta to Léonie Léon 29 Nov.: 'Les Elections de Paris sont triomphales. C'est la plus éclatante défaite que nous ayons jamais infligé aux troupes réactionnaires.... Mais tout ce triomphe ne serait qu'une vaine pompe si ton âme ne m'appartenait plus tout entière... je te confonds à ce point avec l'image de la Patrie que c'est d'un même amour que je vous embrasse toutes les deux' (L.G.).

3. *R.F.*, leader of 27 Nov. The Radical victories in the towns were in general gained by the help of primary school teachers, doctors and lawyers (Kayser, *Les Grandes batailles du radicalisme*, p. 86).

4. *Lettres*, no. 220 *bis*, 10 Nov. to A. Testelin.

5. 1 Dec., cf. 9 Dec. For earlier articles making scornful reference to these 'classes dirigeantes', see *R.F.* 2, 15, 16, 18 and 20 Dec. 1873 and 2 Jan. 1874.

en tête de nos colonnes les candidats choisis par les comités républicains...', but 'entre plusieurs candidatures il serait impossible que nous n'eussions pas nos préférences... nous considérons comme un devoir de les rendre publiques'.

16

A Republican Constitution at last
December 1874–February 1875

The beginning of a new session after a long summer recess was always a time of excited anticipation. The Assembly might be dying 'of anaemia'— 'the terrible moment'[1] might be approaching fast, but death, too, has its fascination. Towards midday on 30 November 1874, crowds again gathered at the Gare St Lazare to see the deputies make their way to the Versailles train. By now a new class of middlemen had come into being, the men who had attended regularly at the station, rendered small services to deputies and came to know most of them by sight. These men were important personages in the eyes of the more ignorant onlookers, for they could point out who was who and even exchange a word with individual legislators. They had in fact become showmen, the deputies being the show. On this 30 November there were two chief exhibits whom the spectators wished to see. The first was Thiers, of whom Gambetta's aunt Jenny approvingly remarked a few weeks later: 'You've only to see the way he walks to realise how cunning he is.'[2] The second was Gambetta of whom a well-known writer, Jules Claretie, had just written a glowing eulogy in a popular series of *Portraits contemporains*.[3] The onlookers did well to stare at Gambetta. He was to play a vital role in the next few months.

In his recent correspondence with Juliette Adam Gambetta had taken a gloomy view of the forthcoming session. In spite of the good harvest and returning prosperity,[4] which he did not mention, and in spite of the

1. *R.F.*, 4 Dec. 1874.

2. *The Times*, 1 Dec., p. 5; police report 11 Jan. 1875 (A.P.P. BA/918).

3. These 'portraits' were a weekly series beginning on 16 Oct. 1874. For Gambetta's letter of thanks to Claretie, see *Lettres*, no. 224.

4. *The Times* 7 Nov., leader p. 9: 'The country is settling. . . . Money is coming back in a continuous stream through the demand for French productions, . . . and . . . the stagnation of industry and the distress of the workmen . . . are falling away. A fine harvest and a splendid vintage have blessed the cultivator of the soil.'

Republicans' electoral successes, which he did, the situation, he said, was far from being clearer or calmer: the parties were 'at a climax of mutual exasperation' and people were more concerned to seize power in order to strike at their foes than to found 'a legal government which would set things to rights'. The clash in the Assembly would be sharp and the Septennate, he thought, would in any case reach its moment of crisis and be unable to survive the parliamentary debates of 1875.[1] The situation was, in fact, still much as *The Times* had described it on 25 July: 'Nothing remained but the old distracted Assembly vainly endeavouring to give birth to something which an indulgent world might call a Constitution. The Marshal, his Army, a chaos of factions at Versailles, and a legion of agitators throughout the country—these were the political powers of France.' It was no wonder that towards the end of the year Lord Derby wrote that he could not make 'head or tail of French internal politics', and that he presumed most Frenchmen were in the same condition![2]

The clash on constitutional issues was in fact deferred until the New Year since it was agreed to give priority to debates on the army and education during the brief period before Christmas. Meanwhile the Marshal, in a presidential message to the Assembly on 3 December, had reiterated his desire for the support of 'all men of good will'. It appeared that he was ready to accept the idea of a Republican constitution and that he was appealing to both Centres to organise one. At the same time he had extolled the Septennate and at one moment Gambetta and Challemel-Lacour suspected that some even of the Left Centre had committed themselves 'to organise the Septennate' rather than the unambiguous Republic that was Gambetta's goal. These suspicions were probably communicated by the Adams to Thiers when he visited Nice on his way back from Italy, but they were seemingly unjustified.[3]

The attitude of the two Centres and their possible 'conjunction' was indeed once again a crucial issue. On the very day on which the Assembly met again, on 30 November, it had been the common topic of conversation in the lobbies.[4] Eight months earlier the *République Française* had declared that any such alliance must be a fools' bargain and that the Left Centre would be swallowed by the Right.[5] In May, however, Gambetta and his friends had been heard to discuss the expediency of a momentary alliance.[6] In June thirty-four members of the Right Centre had been

1. *Lettres*, nos 219 and 221 of 22 Oct. and 15 Nov. Cf. *R.F.*, leader of 3 Dec.
2. Newton, *Lord Lyons*, p. 326.
3. *Lettres* no. 221; Mme Adam, *Nos amitiés*, pp. 202–3.
4. *The Times*, 1 Dec., p. 5.
5. See above, p. 179.
6. See above, p. 201.

found to vote for urgent consideration of the Casimir-Périer proposal and the *République Française* had rejoiced. Now in November Gambetta told a friend that he would not be the man to reject the least chance of constituting the Republic even though it might be with the aid of unworthy collaborators. The important thing was to round the cape of the provisional; 'once we have crossed the bar of the personal Septennate and recognised the Republic . . . we can proceed to a new policy of action. Until then you will always find me ready to beat about and tack along the coast.'[1] More than ever the question was whether thirty or so men of the Right Centre could again be found to vote for a motion like that put forward by Casimir-Périer and so to secure a majority for a definitively Republican constitution. It was the question forcefully put by Gambetta in conversation on 21 December with *The Times* correspondent and an unnamed deputy of the Right Centre as they made their way to the Assembly from Versailles station. Gambetta declared that he asked for nothing better than to vote for the organisation of the Marshal's powers: 'Only let the Constitution be headed the Government of the Republic, the legal Government of France, and I will vote for all the Constitutions you like, and, probably, even for more stringent a Constitution than you would like.' To the objection of the Right Centre deputy that Gambetta could obtain the Republic by organising the Marshal's powers and passing other laws afterwards he replied that he wished to get rid of ambiguity:

> I do not wish you to have the appearance of voting a Republican Constitution which may serve to create a Monarchy. I want the legal existence of this Republic to be inscribed at the head of the Constitution, so that once it is voted, people can neither cry nor write 'Vive le Roi', 'Vive l'Empereur'. On this condition we will recognise the constituent right of the Assembly, and help you in framing laws and measures which you may think requisite to prevent that Republic from deviating from the principles of order and social protection which you demand. You ask me to assist you in creating an ephemeral, defenceless power resting on understandings and which disarms itself beforehand against all the attacks by which it will be assailed. You wish to create a nominal Republic which will merely serve to discredit that form of Government. . . . I want you to decide on creating a Government which finds in its organisation the strength necessary to defend itself against all attacks, no matter from what side. . . . I . . . do not force you to organise the Republic; I only ask you to organise it sincerely. . . . On this condition, I repeat, I recognise the Marshal's power for seven years.

Indeed he claimed that Thiers was now more Radical than he was, and when his companions began to laugh, he said: 'It is quite correct; for M.

1. *Lettres*, no. 220 *bis*, 10 Nov., to A. Testelin.

Thiers rejects the Marshal, while I accept him for seven years, and people may even make him eligible for reelection if they like.' In any case, he pointed out, the Conservatives now had before them the examples of Thiers and Casimir-Périer and all who had rallied to the Republic: 'Nobody thinks of thwarting them; we all think of supporting them . . . we are ready to discuss with them a programme of Government . . . and to agree on such a programme, taking account of their sympathies, leanings and natures. . . . Only', he added, as he and his two companions reached the doors of the Assembly, 'it is necessary for thirty Monarchists in the Chamber to join us. Without that, we have not a majority, and as long as we have not a majority we adhere to our refusal to take part in a comedy.' 'You will have the thirty,' remarked the Right Centre Deputy; 'I know some of our Party who will be with you.'[1]

The Right Centre Deputy was right, but it took time for the thirty votes to be mustered. In particular there were two difficulties to be overcome: the first was the question of priorities—which should be voted first, a law organising a Second Chamber or one organising the Marshal's powers—a law on the transmission of powers as it was called—and the second was the character and composition of the Second Chamber. For the Right the word 'Republic' itself in any law on the transmission of powers could still be a stumbling-block; for the Left a Second Chamber was still something to be approached with extreme circumspection.

Meanwhile, since the resolution of these difficulties was postponed until the New Year and since the Assembly adjourned for a fortnight on Christmas Eve, Gambetta and Spuller were able once again to make a winter escape from Paris and pay the Adams a brief visit on the Riviera.[2] Gambetta arrived in poor health, but was soon restored by relaxation in brilliant weather. He went over to Nice for a day to see his parents. He played dominoes and spillikins, and again one evening watched a play written, produced and partly performed by his versatile hostess. Yet politics could not be wholly excluded. Gambetta's local admirers, once they knew where he was, would once again not be denied a speech and so one day he addressed them from the balcony of 'Les Bruyères', telling them of the regeneration of France, declaring that the Assembly had

1. *The Times*, 22 Dec., p. 5. *The Times* correspondent, presumably Blowitz, naturally thought he had pulled off something of a coup in securing this interview with Gambetta and he was dismayed that only two Legitimist papers, the *Gazette de France* (24 Dec.) and the *Union* reprinted it, the former inviting the R.F. to rectify it if need be. It was indeed remarkable that it was, he said, not even mentioned by any other papers (*ibid.*, 27 Dec.). The R.F. itself ignored it.

2. Mme Adam says that Gambetta arrived on 20 Dec. (*Nos amitiés*, p. 208). *Lettres* no. 229 to Léonie Léon makes clear that he did not leave Paris until the morning of the 24th.

already voted in favour of the principle of liberty of education, and prophesying that 1875 would see the voting of constitutional laws and then, at last, dissolution. This holiday in the south perhaps encouraged him to adopt a playful mood with some of his new English acquaintances, one of whom was Sir Charles Dilke. When in January they discussed the constitutional problem, Gambetta suggested that the National Assembly should continue to govern 'without filling up death vacancies, and with the provision that when at last it became reduced to one member, he should take any title or give to any person that he pleased any title, or adopt any form of government that he should think fit!'[1] The holiday also spared him what might have been the somewhat embarrassing necessity, had he been in Paris, of attending the funeral of Ledru-Rollin who died on 31 December.[2] 'Who is Ledru-Rollin?' asked Lord Randolph Churchill three months later. Astonished and then vastly amused at meeting someone who had never heard of Ledru, Gambetta burst out laughing and explained that he had been a Republican in the days when there were no Republicans: 'That is why we insisted on giving him a first-class funeral.' The explanation, if brief, was true. Ledru had remained a man of 1848 and was in the 1870s no more than a historic survival.[3]

The question of constitutional priorities was posed in a new message from the Marshal-President on 6 January 1875. The time had come, he said, for the serious discussion of the constitutional laws, since the country would not understand any further delay. In particular, he recommended the Assembly to give consideration to a law concerning a second chamber which he regarded as 'a necessary complement' to his government and as a guarantee of the 'conservative interests' which he had been charged to defend.[4] The debate which ensued was once again a debate on the Septennate itself, for, when asked for what sort of regime the Senate was to be

1. S. Gwynn and G. M. Tuckwell, *The Life of the Rt. Hon. Sir Charles Dilke*, vol. i (1917), p. 185.
2. See police report of 4 Jan. 1875 (A.P.P., BA/918). But the R.F.'s leader of 2 Jan. 1875 was generous in its praise of 'one of France's "plus nobles citoyens", one of the national democracy's "chefs les plus vénérés" '. It could afford to be. *The Times* in its obituary notice (1 Jan. 1875, p. 10) spoke of Ledru's 'second appearance on the political stage' as 'a pitiable failure' and went on to pay a tribute to Gambetta: 'The fact that M. Gambetta's fame and his political influence have steadily grown while M. Ledru-Rollin's crumbled away at the first touch of reality is most instructive and encouraging. M. Gambetta's success is due to the power of moderation and tact, to a talent for the arts of conciliation that is most rare among Frenchmen of extreme opinions, and to the perception of the truth that all politics are matters of compromise.'
3. Gwynn and Tuckwell, *Life of Sir Charles Dilke*, vol. i, p. 188.
4. 'Commencer par le Sénat!', exclaimed the R.F. scornfully, '... avant d'avoir dit à la France qu'elle sera une République ou une monarchie! n'est-ce pas le comble du ridicule et de l'insanité?' (leader of 7 Jan.).

created, the government spokesman, Chabaud-Latour, declared that it was
for the Septennate and that the Assembly had already decided, a few
months earlier, that the Republic should not be proclaimed as the government of France. In other words the question of the regime was to be
deferred until 20 November 1880, or at least until the Marshal's death,
should this occur earlier. Such a suggestion was, of course, intolerable to the
Republicans and when it came to a vote on giving priority to the creation
of a Second Chamber rather than to the other constitutional laws they
were supported by the Legitimists. The government was defeated. As
Gambetta had prophesied, the Septennate, in the character of a special
regime not to be touched for six years, did not survive even the first
important debate of 1875. The defeat was, moreover, a defeat for the
Marshal as well as the ministry. In consequence, in Gambetta's view, a first-
class crisis had arisen and the situation was the most puzzling he had yet
known. The Marshal, he said, was more seriously wounded than he had
been at Sedan.[1] He had a hundred times repeated that he would stay in
office until the end of his seven years, and Gambetta now feared that, finding
his position intolerable, he might on the specious pretext of protecting
conservative interests, declare himself against a hostile majority in the
Chamber and resort to a *coup d'état*. Moreover, if, as people expected,
Broglie were to form a new government and preside over a dissolution,
what sort of elections would result? Perhaps Bonapartist ones which
would lead to the recall of Napoleon IV, whereupon Broglie and the
Marshal himself would soon be driven from the scene.[2] Gambetta's acute
fear of the Bonapartists was no doubt increased when they won yet
another by-election, one in the Hautes-Pyréneés on 17 January.[3]

The Marshal did indeed send for Broglie, but Broglie refused to accept
office in such difficult circumstances, preferring, as he wrote later, to
reserve himself for the last great struggle, the general election which now
looked inevitable before long and in which he still hoped to rebuild a
united Right-wing front to bar a Republican victory.[4] Deprived of the

1. *Lettres*, no. 231 of 7 Jan. to Mme Adam and no. 232 of 12 Jan. to Ranc.
2. *Lettres, ibid.* Cf. the long letter from Spuller to Mme Adam printed in Mme
Adam, *Nos amitiés*, especially pp. 218–19.
3. The Bonapartist candidate won on the second round. In the first round on
3 Jan. there had been two Republican candidates, one Thierist and one Gambettist
who subsequently stood down. Gambetta had been taxed with this in his conversation
with *The Times* correspondent on 21 Dec.: ' "In that Department", said the Right
Centre Deputy . . . "your candidate will not do, but rather a Thiers candidate." "I
do not ask for anything better", replied M. Gambetta, and it is only through rigorous
obedience to a principle that I do not support such a candidate." "So", said I, "when
people talk of a Thiers candidate, it does not mean an anti-Gambetta candidate?"
"Certainly not", replied M. Gambetta' (*The Times*, 22 Dec.).
4. Broglie, *Mémoires*, vol. ii (1941), p. 337.

support of the most astute of his noble henchmen, the Marshal saw no alternative but to ask the twice-defeated ministry to carry on. It was not a happy state of affairs. There was in effect no government, wrote the *République Française* sarcastically; 'the executive power no longer has any instruments with any authority'.[1] One consequence, as has been remarked, was that when the constitutional debates resumed, the Government had no one of sufficient prestige to defend the executive: 'The Constitution would be the work of the Assembly alone, which was naturally disposed to favour parliament, exaggerate its prerogatives and make it the first if not the only power in the state.'[2]

Although the *République Française* violently attacked the idea of a new Broglie government,[3] Gambetta, anxious, watchful and astute, despite a heavy cold, appears to have exerted all his influence during the ministerial crisis to prevent his friends from provoking the Right in such a way as to goad them into reforming their disunited ranks.[4] And when the discussion of the constitutional laws was resumed on 21 January (the anniversary, as many people remarked, of the execution of Louis XVI) it was not he or Thiers who spoke for the Republicans but men such as Jules Favre, Jules Simon and Laboulaye of the Left Centre.[5]

Priority for discussion of the second chamber having been refused, the proposals of the Committee of Thirty were once more to the fore. During the last ten days of the month the most important debates were about the organisation or transmission of the public powers or, in other words, the crucial question of the form of government. They were often bitter and often confused and when they were about to begin the *République Française* wrote gloomily that there was no agreement on anything and that the Assembly was infinitely divided. On the 28th, however, the Casimir-Périer motion of July was reintroduced in the form of an amendment to the first article of the Commission's draft Bill. Its promoter, Laboulaye, had a great success and it looked as though at long last a sufficient number of deputies of the Right Centre would be won over for the amendment to

1. Leader of 14 Jan. 1875. In debate on 12 Feb. Gambetta would dub the cabinet 'Un ministère six fois battu et toujours présent !' (*Ass. Nat. A.*, vol. xxxvi, p. 499).

2. Deslandres, *Histoire constitutionnelle* (1937), p. 311.

3. e.g. leader of 10 Jan.

4. See the editors' footnote to *Lettres*, no. 232: 'Il semblait qu'on fût au seuil d'une double crise, présidentielle autant que ministérielle. Les très habiles instances conciliatrices de Gambetta furent alors très fécondes. Cissey resta aux affaires, et l'on entreprit le vote des premières lois constitutionnelles.'

5. In his letter of 11 Jan. to Ranc (no. 232) he spoke of the danger that a speech by Thiers would excite the Assembly 'au plus haut point', but we do not know whether Thiers intended to intervene and was dissuaded by Gambetta. For a glowing account of the speeches of Favre and Simon, see Pelletan, *Le Théâtre de Versailles*, pp. 236–43.

succeed. But the vote did not take place at once and the impression made by Laboulaye's eloquence ebbed away amid the shifting and tedious sands of subsequent speeches. In particular, Louis Blanc, once again refusing to toe the Gambettist line, made a brief and much interrupted intervention in which he criticised the way in which the motion was presented and said that his conscience would not allow him to vote for two Chambers or for a Republic with a President. The vote was in fact deferred until the following day, the 29th. It was regarded as so vital that ailing deputies staggered to the Chamber or had themselves transported there, but the amendment was lost by twenty-three votes (359 to 336 with twenty abstentions) compared with forty-four in July.[1] The Right-wing majority was diminishing but Gambetta was furious with Louis Blanc, and others—even Rochefort, before long a bitter critic of Gambetta—were furious, too, on Gambetta's account. 'M. Louis Blanc', declared the *République Française* in its most sourly portentous manner, 'has thought fit to take a different line from his party. We leave this grave responsibility entirely to him. We hope that it will not weigh too heavily on such a scrupulous conscience once the gusts (*bouffées*) of his well-known vanity have been wholly dispersed.'[2] And when one of his wartime collaborators, Gustave Masure, director of *Le Progrès du Nord*, printed reports critical of the majority of the Left Gambetta himself took him severely to task: 'Be assured we are not constitution-making, we are engaged in battle against the Monarchists of every hue. . . . In short it's a question of victory first, we can philosophise afterwards. . . . I beg you to follow us and I count on your doing so.'[3]

On the very day on which the *République Française* printed its onslaught on Louis Blanc a new amendment introduced by a quiet and scholarly Catholic named Wallon was carried by a single vote (353 to 352). On the one hand the opposition of the intransigent quintet, Louis Blanc, Quinet,

---

1. In the later part of the debate, after the rejection of Laboulaye's amendment, the Assembly resumed discussion of the scheme of the Commission of Thirty. When the Legitimist Boyer began to speak against it 'the Ministers, Deputies, spectators and servants', according to *The Times* correspondent (30 Jan., p. 5), 'began one of the most animated and noisy conversations yet heard in the Assembly. It reminded me of the "Aria dei Sorbetti" formerly recited in Italian theatres when a singer of either sex was sacrificed beforehand and made to sing on the stage while the public took refreshments. The Left was much excited. Messrs Gambetta and Arago called and gesticulated in the midst of the Radical Deputies. The entire Left must be made to vote for the inoffensive project of the Committee in order that the famous Wallon amendment may be reached. The latter is the indirect substitution of a Septennial Republic for a Republic without any adjective.'

2. Leader of 30 Jan.

3. *Lettres*, no. 235, 3 Feb.; cf. e.g. *Le Progrès du Nord*, 1 Feb., criticism of those who wanted 'à tout prix et ont récemment tenté encore de faire constituer la République par une Assemblée qui contient en majorité des ennemis de la République'.

Madier, de Montjau and Peyrat had been overcome by Gambetta and his friends; on the other a sufficient number of deputies of the Right Centre had joined the Left-wing groups in support of Wallon's proposal.[1] And so the third Republic was born. The Laboulaye amendment had begun with the phrase 'The Government of the Republic is composed of two Chambers and a President'. The word 'Republic' which the Right still found so difficult to swallow was in the first line. But Wallon's amendment began, 'The legislative power is exercised by two assemblies, the Chamber and the Senate' and it was not until the second line that 'the Republic' was inconspicuously mentioned: 'the President of the Republic is elected by a majority of votes by the Senate and Chamber of Deputies met together as a national assembly'. 'The President of the Republic' was a familiar title which held no terrors for it had been in use since 1871. But Wallon's amendment subtly changed the situation. It 'separated the title from its holder, made it impersonal, created an office and, above all . . . made permanent a transitory form of government by substituting a septennial President for a septennial Republic'.[2]

Thus the Republic did indeed slip in by the side door and not 'sous la haute porte azurée'.[3] 'You can imagine', wrote Broglie later, 'the mingled exclamations and laughter with which this result was greeted in the Chamber and the galleries. A government, and what a government! . . . proclaimed by a majority of one! After four years of struggle, after the expenditure of so much eloquence, after so much din on both sides, to come to such a burlesque ending! At first it was impossible to take what had happened seriously.'[4] In writing thus Broglie conveniently forgot that in 1873 his friends had been equally ready to restore the Monarchy even if it secured no more than a majority of one.

Had the Monarchy been restored by even one vote only there would no doubt have been a paean of rejoicing in the Monarchist Press. It was not so with the Republican papers. They would have chanted triumphantly if the Laboulaye amendment had carried the day, but the Wallon amendment was a different matter, an obscure second best adopted by a weary Cham-

---

1. They included Savary, the Comte de Ségur, de Saint-Pierre, the Vicomte d'Haussonville. Deslandres' list, *op. cit.*, p. 333, is in part erroneous.

2. Stannard, *Gambetta*, p. 161. But *The Times* correspondent wrote (31 Jan., p. 5) that the Wallon amendment only had a majority because 'it creates nothing immediate and postpones the difficulty until 1880, when it provides for a fresh Septennial term. . . . The members of the Right Centre who voted for it thought that, if in seven years the Comte de Paris could not arrive at power, he had an uncle, the Duc d'Aumâle, who had no heir, and whom nothing would prevent from accepting the post of President of the Republic.'

3. See above, p. 186.

4. *Mémoires*, vol. ii, p. 348.

ber. Gambetta, indeed, was reported by one observer to have been 'beside himself with joy' on the day when the amendment was carried[1] and Freycinet related that the offices of the *République Française* were illuminated that night. But he added that Gambetta urged his colleagues to calm themselves: 'We shall reach our goal but there are still plenty of difficulties to overcome.'[2] Indeed Republican papers such as the *Temps* and the *République Française* were remarkably cautious, seemingly having to convince themselves that the vote really did consecrate the Republican form of government. Thus the *République Française* wrote in very laboured fashion. It

> could not but recognise and state that a constitutional provision which ... determines the mode of transmitting the power of a high authority which it confirms and which declares that this authority is essentially elective in character, is a provision which breaks down and destroys the very principle of monarchy, namely hereditary transmission in a family; and, that in consequence it is not only possible but reasonable to regard a law of this kind as essentially Republican.

The majority, it admitted, was so slight that it could be said not to exist. Yet the Assembly was leaning to the side of France.[3] A subsequent vote giving priority to a second Wallon amendment, which conferred the right of dissolution not, as the Commission of Thirty proposed, on MacMahon alone, but on the President of the Republic, subject to the agreement of the Senate and the holding of an election within three months, was carried by a majority of no less than 182 on 2 February. These two votes had, the *République Française* declared, consolidated the Republic, 'not, to be sure, the Republic such as we understand it and such as the country demands', but it was necessary to be content with modest beginnings. In the absence of Monarchy the nation had gradually become Republican just as a sturdy seed in fertile soil could without human aid grow into a majestic plant not easily uprooted. Throughout the country, it claimed, there was a feeling of satisfaction, relief and hope.[4] Before long it was writing of 'the victory of 30 January'.[5]

Nevertheless the *République Française* prudently warned its readers on 5 February that it would be 'a grave error to think that all is finished. ...

1. See Deschanel, *Gambetta* (1919), p. 173.
2. *Souvenirs 1848–1878*, p. 317.
3. Leader of 1 Feb.
4. Leader of 5 Feb. The view that there was a general feeling of relief was shared by *The Times* (leader of the same day).
5. Leader of 7 Feb. Cf. letter of 2 Feb. from Gambetta to Léonie Léon: 'Vive la République! Elle est faite' (*cit.* J. Chastenet, *Gambetta*, 1968, p. 238).

There are serious and delicate negotiations to be pursued.' The warning was necessary and Gambetta was to play an important though ill-documented part in the negotiations. On 3 February in its further deliberations on the law on public powers the Assembly had given the Chambers the right to revise the constitution (although in a form of which Gambetta disapproved)[1] and the Commission's spokesman had categorically stated that this included the right to change the form of government. Moreover, the old Conservative bloc had formed again to prevent by five votes the transfer of the seat of government from Versailles to Paris. This was a sign that it might still rally and have power to obstruct. The law on public powers had been passed on its second reading on 3 February by a large majority, but the second round of debates on the vexed question of the Senate had yet to come. Meanwhile three by-elections had been held since the beginning of the year. In the first, as has been seen, the Bonapartist candidate in the Hautes-Pyrénées had on the second round easily defeated his Republican rival. Once again the shadow of the Empire was cast upon the political landscape: 'The Pyreneean election', says one French historian, 'perhaps played an important part in the vote on the Wallon amendment some days later by an Assembly which feared the Bonapartist peril above all others.'[2] In the other two elections, however, on 7 February, the peril seemed to have been conjured. In the Seine-et-Oise the Bonapartist candidate was defeated by the Republican Valentin, a protégé of Thiers, and in the traditionally Monarchist Côtes-du-Nord a Legitimist won for the first time for two years. These results, wrote Lord Lyons, might give the Right 'an impulse in the direction contrary to the Republic, which may deter them from voting any measures which tend to the establishment of that form of government, even though it be only by implication'.[3]

And so it was, but not before another vote in the Assembly had given the Right an unexpected shock. The debate on the Senate was resumed on

1. The conditions under which constitutional revision might be effected had often been of vital importance in earlier French history. Gambetta urged that revision should be carried out not by the two Chambers sitting together, but by a specially summoned constituent assembly. He reserved the right to introduce an amendment to this effect on the third reading, but refrained from doing so when the time came (*Ass. Nat. A.*, vol. xxxvi, pp. 421–2).

2. Gouault, *Comment la France est devenue républicaine*, p. 187. The evidence of Bonapartist conspiracy given by the strongly anti-Bonapartist Prefect of Police, Léon Renault, before the commission of enquiry into the Nièvre election may also have been a factor (see Chapman, *The Third Republic of France*, pp. 60–1).

3. Lyons to Derby, P.R.O., F.O. 146, 1808, 9 Feb. 1875. For the composition of the Assembly after these elections, see Gouault, *op. cit.*, Annexe iv. The Bonapartists still had only thirty-two Deputies.

11 February after the traditional break for the Lenten carnival. To the general astonishment, the Assembly by 322 to 310 voted an amendment by the Radical Pascal Duprat proposing that the Senate should be chosen by the same electors as the Chamber, in other words by universal suffrage. Most of the Bonapartists, protagonists of universal suffrage, had voted for it and many Legitimists had abstained. It was, wrote Gambetta, 'an admirable and decisive day contrary to my earlier expectations'.[1] When they realised what had happened most Conservatives from the Marshal downwards were profoundly dismayed. As Broglie wrote later, it was already asking a lot for the Marshal to accept the Republic, but to let it be organised by Pascal Duprat was indeed to pass beneath the Caudine Forks. Such a second chamber would be but an offshoot of the first, a younger child soon disowned and disinherited.[2] He and his friends naturally wanted a Senate which would be independent, a brake on the Chamber and a stronghold of Conservatism. The Right Centre intimated that it would not vote for the third reading of the Bill on the Senate and on the 12th the Marshal let it be known that ministers could not take part in debates which led to consequences so detrimental to Conservative interests.[3] Accordingly, by 368 to 345, the Assembly refused to proceed to a third reading. Naturally enough it also rejected a proposal for urgent consideration of dissolution, once again put forward by the Left. An impasse and something like chaos resulted. The struggling infant of the Republic, deprived of one of its vital organs, appeared, in Broglie's words, to be smitten by death in its cradle.[4]

But it was in such a situation that Gambetta was at his best. In the confusion of the continuing debate he had intervened with what Broglie, whom he so often and so bitterly attacked in the *République Française*, described as one of the happiest improvisations he had ever heard from any orator.[5] After castigating the Assembly for replacing a true majority by an artificial one and the ministers for sheltering behind the Marshal's sword, Gambetta made great play with the concessions already given by the Left:

> We are taking it upon us to surrender into your hands if you are willing to create a moderate and conservative government. (Further bravos and applause on the Left. Exclamations on the Right.) We have agreed to a division of power, to the creation of two Chambers; we have agreed to give you the

1. To Léonie Léon, 11 Feb. (L.G.).
2. *Mémoires*, vol. ii, pp. 350–1.
3. Camille Pelletan commented that the Marshal's veto was a 'formule singulière, qui porte sur une autorisation tout platonique, car les ministres jusqu'ici n'ont apporté que leur silence dans le débat' (*op. cit.*, p. 26).
4. *Mémoires*, p. 352.
5. *Ibid.*, p. 353.

strongest executive power ever set up in a country with democratic elections; we have given you the right of dissolution . . . we have given you the right of revision; we have given you everything.

And yet this had not been enough: after all this the majority still wanted their own Senate, a Senate that would be exclusively theirs. The speech was a powerful indictment of the Orleanists, but in the hand of Gambetta, the warrior of the Republican Union, there was an olive branch as well as a spear: 'I know that there are still some of you who are pushing the spirit of political wisdom and compromise (*transaction*) to the point of heroism and who think they may yet find . . . auxiliaries for this impossible task.' Later, however, he told the Assembly, it would be said that they had perhaps missed the only opportunity to establish 'a really strong legal and moderate Republic'.[1]

Confusion was the order of the day, but Gambetta with his sense of political realism and love of political accommodation had pointed to the way out—the path of 'transaction' or bargaining. Fortunately MacMahon was wisely counselled against adopting the desperate courses advocated by some members of the Right—the formation of a new ministry of combat which would withdraw the constitutional Bills and arrange for the Assembly to be renewable by thirds. The way was thus open for the negotiations which, the *République Française* insisted, 'must continue to the last day and the last vote'.[2] The men of the two Centres came together again, groups and splinter groups were buzzing with activity and from a welter of ingenious projects there emerged a new proposal for the constitution of the Senate. It, too, was sponsored by Wallon, and it was a 'transaction' after Gambetta's own heart.

The new plan was for a Senate of 300 members, 225 elected by the departments and colonies and seventy-five by the National Assembly. The seventy-five were to hold office for life (to be *inamovibles* in the French term), but to be replaced, as and when vacancies occurred, by men elected by the Assembly and the election was to be by *scrutin de liste*. The 225 were similarly to be chosen by *scrutin de liste* by a departmental electoral college comprising four categories of elector, the deputies of the department, the general councillors, the *conseillers d'arrondissement* and one delegate from each commune, regardless of its size, chosen by the municipal councillors of that commune. In this new Chamber there were to be no *ex officio*

1. For the text, see *Discours* vol. iv, p. 276, and *Ass. Nat. A.*, vol. xxxvi, pp. 500–2. The speech was promptly printed and sold by Leroux as a separate sheet for five centimes and *en brochure* for ten centimes. For an eloquent and enthusiastic eulogy of it and Gambetta's oratory, see Pelletan, *op. cit.*, pp. 265–7.

2. Leader of 22 Feb.; cf. leader of 21 Feb. For a detailed and critical account of the negotiations which ensued, see Blanc, *Histoire de la constitution*, pp. 132–209.

representatives of intermediary and elite bodies and no nominated members, for the Marshal, to the intense dismay of his entourage, had been induced to surrender his proposed right to nominate Senators in return for that of nominating Councillors of State, a right which this same Assembly had in 1872 denied to Thiers.[1] At the same time electoral influence was heavily weighted in favour of the rural communes so that the Conservatives could believe that their interests were safeguarded. The principle that Senators should be elected and not nominated was what the Republicans had fought for and Gambetta undoubtedly was one of those who saw that this could be all-important in the long run. There is little evidence, however, to determine what part if any he took in shaping the Wallon–Ricard proposal, as it came to be known, but the particular interest he had shown in elections to municipal and general councils and in the work of the latter suggests that he may well have backed the idea that municipal and general councillors should compose part of the electoral college on whom the responsibility for choosing the Senators was to devolve.[2]

Such was the plan presented to a meeting of the deputies of the Left Centre on the 19th: but the Left were still a trinity of three in one and one in three and the meeting was largely attended by representatives of the other two Left-wing groups. The chief critic was the austere Jules Grévy, who thriftily added to his carefully calculated reputation for independence,

1. For an interesting account of this *volte face* and glimpses of Gambetta's attitude to the Conseil d'État, see R. Dreyfus, 'Le choix des Conseillers d'état (1872–1875)' in his *De Monsieur Thiers à Marcel Proust* (Paris, 1939). Dreyfus's interpretation was contested by Daniel Halévy (e.g. *La République des Ducs*, p. 181, n.). On 15 Sept. 1870 the Government of National Defence had suspended the Conseil d'État of the Second Empire and replaced it by a Provisional Commission. In the debates of 1872 Gambetta defended the Conseil d'État as one of the best creations of the Monarchy, criticised the proposal that the councillors should be selected by the Assembly— such a Conseil would, in his view, be 'une sorte de Chambre haute avant la lettre'— and argued that decisions of this kind were premature before there had been a decision on the form of government. Thus he appears to have had a kind of premonition of the way in which the problems of choosing the members of the second chamber and of the Conseil d'État might become interdependent.

2. It is impossible to know how much weight to attach to the first part of the following comment by Juliette Adam: 'Certains de nos amis disent que Gambetta n'a pris la défense du Sénat que parce qu'il a vu dans sa récréation un affaiblissement du pouvoir exécutif et surtout la possibilité d'annihiler ce même Sénat à l'aide de la manipulation plus aisée du suffrage restreint.

'Le fait est que Gambetta est passé maître dans l'art du groupement des influences républicaines dans les provinces, dans les communes. Comme il me l'a écrit lui-même, il connaît en détail les forces dont il dispose' (*Nos amitiés*, p. 232). According to Blanc, *Histoire de la constitution*, p. 132, the idea of General Councillors and *conseillers d'arrondissement* forming part of the electoral college originated in a proposal by the future prime minister Waddington, who also wished to include the Assembly itself and the Institut.

arguing that only a dissolution would satisfactorily resolve the crisis. Thiers was alleged to share this opinion.[1] But, said *The Times*, 'the Left have now found an adviser who is certainly able to assume the demeanour of states-manship. M. Gambetta has been the moderating spirit of his Party ... he combated the views of M. Grévy, the gist of his argument being simply that they must take the Republic on the conditions proposed, or give up the hope of obtaining it at all.'[2] Two days later the Republican Union held a meeting which was also attended by members of the other two groups. Three Radicals, Marcou, Barodet and Madier de Montjau in turn attacked what was now known as the Wallon–Ricard plan for the Senate, but Gambetta bore down their opposition.

> He urged that the features of the scheme, although not quite conformable to Republican principles, were of minor importance in comparison with the necessity of organising the Republic. He gave a vivid sketch of the political situation at home and abroad, showing the perils to which not only the Republic but France itself would be exposed by the absence of a regular Constitution.

He also

> produced a great effect when he reminded his hearers how the belief that the Monarchy was impossible followed close on the letter of the Comte de Chambord, which destroyed the plans of the Fusion. If the present attempt to constitute the Republic should fail, would it not be said that the Republic also was impossible? What then would remain possible in the eyes of the people he left his hearers to consider for themselves.[3]

Once again Napoleon IV was a splendid card to play![4] 'The interests of the country being at stake, how, he asked, could patriotic Republicans hesitate? For his own part, he could not do so, being anxious, above all things, to save France.'[5] His appeal was so moving that it was said to have drawn tears from some of those present.[6]

Largely as a result of Gambetta's intervention the meeting decided with

---

1. *The Times*, 20 Feb., p. 5. He abstained when the final vote was taken on the law on the Senate. But C. de B. reported: 'M. Thiers s'est concerté hier soir, avec les chefs des deux Gauches [sic] et les a pressés vivement d'adhérer sans hésitation, pour sauver la République, au projet Wallon. M. Gambetta est de cet avis et ne met pas en doute le vote favorable de la majorité des Gauches' (19 Feb., Rothschild pp.).

2. Leader of 24 Feb., p. 9.

3. *The Times*, 22 Feb., p. 5.

4. Incidentally 'Napoleon IV', the Prince Imperial, had just passed seventh out of a numerous class at Woolwich (see *The Times* 17 Feb., leader, p. 9).

5. *The Times*, leader of 24 Feb., p. 9.

6. Mme Adam, *Nos amitiés*, p. 227.

only two dissentients to vote for the Wallon–Ricard plan and against any amendment which, on the pretext of improving it, might be devised to break up the newly formed majority: 'If the Bonapartists propose any Universal Suffrage Amendment the President of the Union will explain the grounds on which the Republicans will oppose it.' The discipline of the Left was, not for the first time, impressive. Later historians such as Daniel Halévy (and others after him) argued that it could not be explained simply by 'Gambetta's genius at manoeuvring' or by the promptings of Positivist writers like Littré and Renouvier. They divined another source for it in the 'powerful association with which in a few months' time Littré and Ferry would become conspicuously associated', namely freemasonry.[1] During the Restoration that fascinating secret association the Chevaliers de la Foi had an important influence on the discipline maintained among the Ultras in the Chamber by Villèle. Did Masonry play a similar role among the members of the three Left-wing groups in 1874–75? It is an interesting surmise, but not more. If Gambetta alone was not the magician of solidarity, there were others whose political influence was considerable and who could have a reason for maintaining the unity of the Left in face of Bonapartism and to the detriment of the Septennate. Not least among them was Thiers who tends to be forgotten because his role in the winter of 1874–75 is so ill-documented. As Rémusat pointed out a little later, what eventuated was an involuntary return to the policy of Thiers: 'He had always said that the Monarchy was impossible and that it was therefore necessary to cling to the Republic; that moderate men should agree to organise it upon a conservative basis and that they should not reject but might even win the support of the pure Republicans.'[2]

The debates on the Senate were resumed on the 22nd and the third reading of the Bill relating to the organisation of the public powers followed on the 24th and 25th. 'Never had the Assembly been so full or excited', reported *The Times*. 'Every bench was occupied and the galleries were crowded to suffocation.' These 'new days of February' would long be remembered.[3] The *République Française* was no less impressed by the momentousness of these days, these 'truly extraordinary sittings'.

Those most knowledgeable on the History of Political Assemblies never remember having been present at more remarkable and moving scenes than

1. Halévy, *La République des Ducs*, p. 170. For Littré's and Ferry's admission to the ranks of freemasonry, see below Ch. 17, p. 249.
2. *Mémoires*, vol. v, p. 520. The idea that Thiers was now more revolutionary than Gambetta was one which it may have amused both men to encourage, but it is not clear that it had any real substance; for a story to this effect printed in *Le Français* of 12 March, see Halévy, *Le Courrier de M. Thiers*, pp. 499–500.
3. 23 Feb., p. 5, and leader of 24 Feb., p. 9.

these. The struggle is intense. . . . The past puts up an unbelievable resistance—there is a rain of amendments. The ground is disputed foot by foot. Nothing gets through without first being held up. But everything yields, gives way, and disappears before the mounting wave of the new mood (*l'esprit nouveau*). The old world is submerged. Yesterday we heard the Marquis de la Rochejacquelein pronounce a kind of funeral oration for the Monarchy. . . . Thus has Monarchy with fourteen centuries behind it come to its end.[1]

The discipline of the Left which Gambetta had done so much to secure operated once again, although there was now a larger number of abstentions: the Left 'had made up its mind to vote and not to talk'. In consequence the whole Bill on the Senate as proposed by Wallon and Ricard was eventually carried by 435 votes to 234 and that on the public powers by 425 to 254.[2] The Republic had been secured. Perhaps the most remarkable tribute paid, in retrospect, to Republican discipline and Gambetta's perspicacity during these weeks was that later penned in his memoirs by one of his most resolute adversaries, the Duc de Broglie. The passage merits quotation almost in full:

> Since the arrangement was the result of mutual concessions . . . it would have been a consolation to see at least some of the violent members of the extreme Left reproach their moderate colleagues for the steps they had taken to meet us. M. Grévy . . . and M. Gambetta might then have found themselves in an embarrassment more or less similar to mine . . . and the public would have understood that what it was seeing was a bargain and not a capitulation. But the Left showed political sense: it understood that . . . the sole fact that the Republic for the first time assumed the form of a regular government and entered into law by the door of a peaceful and legal majority vote and not as in 1792 and 1848 by the breach of insurrection was a success which they should recognise and then fully exploit. . . . It resolved to appear satisfied at all costs, and, in fact, it was, for it had the true satisfaction valued by all parties: it saw its enemies furious and in despair.
>
> I have reason to believe that this astuteness, which contrasted with the ruinous disorder which reigned in the ranks of the Right was almost exclusively due to the political judgement and most happily directed activities of M. Gambetta. Since then I have heard many people boast of the skill of this Italian tribune

1. R.F. leader of 26 Feb.
2. On the 24th there was nearly a last minute hitch over Article 9, an article belatedly inserted as the result of a Right-wing amendment, which named Versailles as the seat of the executive and legislature. Gambetta was furious over it, insisting on a return to Paris: 'Nous avions été', wrote Paul Cambon, 'à deux doigts de voir tout cet édifice laborieux s'écrouler.' But the discipline of the Left told once more; Gambetta gave way and the Left remained silent at the crucial moment. 'Et quelles chandelles, quels cierges on doit à cette Gauche qui s'est tue!' added Cambon in concluding his account of this incident (Cambon, *Correspondance*, vol. i, pp. 58–60).

whom they would make into a rival of Machiavelli. . . . I do not wholly share this admiration and I venture to think that his subtleties which are generally more or less (*assez*) apparent do less honour to his inventiveness than discredit to the mentality of those whom they ensnare. But on the present occasion he really showed his practical cleverness. He at once saw the advantage to be gained from the word *Republic*, especially when it was commented on by the furious lamentations of the Extreme Right and he determined to sacrifice everything to ensure that this word was at least inscribed at the top of a regular constitution.[1]

Yet it was still by the side door that the Republic had entered, a fact which the *République Française* emphasised by reprinting part of its leader of 20 November 1873. 'We have discovered the politic method, the method of patience and solicitude. . . . It will bring us other successes. But we must not exult too loudly over what we have just obtained. . . . The difficulties are not smoothed away, they are beginning.'[2] If the mood of the *République Française* was thus one of quiet and realistic satisfaction, it was very different with the men of the Right Centre whose attitude had been so crucial. Lord Lyons met some of their leaders at the Elysée on the very evening of 25 February and made an interesting report:

> They all, and particularly Decazes, looked to me very unhappy, and indeed they did not affect to be at all satisfied with the occurrences in the Assembly. Like the horse in the fable who invited the man to get on his back, the Right Centre have let the Left get on their backs to attack Bonapartism, and don't know how to shake them off again.[3]

To Broglie and many others looking back later the pattern seemed simple. It was not so simple at the time. In fact neither side were then wholly sure of having gained what they wanted and if they found consolation it was in the clause which provided for constitutional revision. Gambetta, too, would shortly declare that he would not have voted for the laws had there been no allowance for revision. God was not invoked, commented Halévy: this constitution was a pact between men and one which did not even pretend to be lasting.[4] Because it lacked such pretensions it endured the longer.

1. *Mémoires*, vol. ii, pp. 370–1.
2. Leader of 27 Feb.
3. Newton, *Lord Lyons*, p. 328. For an interesting but embarrassed attempt by a deputy of the Right Centre to justify his party's conduct, see *The Times*, 2 March, p. 5.
4. *La République des ducs*, p. 173. Cf. L. Halévy in 'Nouveaux Carnets' on 28 Feb. 1875 (*Revue des Deux Mondes*, 28 Feb. 1937): 'Nous voilà donc en République ! En République définitive. Les journaux républicains impriment cela sincèrement. Une chose définitive en France !'

17

Opportunism and the last months of the National Assembly February–December 1875

'The difficulties have not been smoothed away; they are beginning.' For Gambetta they were of two kinds, one personal and one institutional. It was one thing to win the votes of a coalition in the Assembly for policies which he had previously denounced: it was another to convince the electorate at large, and in particular his own constituents, that those policies were the right ones. The old Gambetta had denied the constituent power of the Assembly, the new Gambetta had supported it and been one of the midwives of a Republic which would include two Chambers and looked suspiciously Conservative.[1] The Radical had become an Opportunist although the name was not yet in use as a party label. How could the Opportunist sell this Conservative Republic to his Radical electors? Once again Gambetta was confronted by the difficulty presented by his 'tail'.

The second problem was institutional, for the laws just voted in the days of February 1875 had established no more than the framework of a seemingly Conservative Republic. As a severe French constitutional historian noted: 'After men had waited for them for four years' the two fundamental laws of the new regime 'had been put forward and voted in little more than a month'.[2] The lacunae remained to be filled by a third constitutional law and by legislation to regulate the elections to the Chamber and Senate. Finally, the Assembly would have to complete its work by electing seventy-five of its own members to the Senate. Thus there was scope enough for possible difficulties and scope, too, for the manoeuvring in which Gambetta excelled. There would also be found business enough, barring generously long vacations, to occupy the Assembly for another ten months, secure against dissolution and still free to determine the date of its own demise.

1. Deschanel, *Gambetta*, p. 182, says that 'some friends, Freycinet in particular, had contributed to convert Gambetta to the acceptance of a second chamber'.
2. M. Deslandres, *Histoire constitutionnelle de la France*, p. 371.

The difficulties that Gambetta had encountered from the extreme Radicals in the spring of 1874 had been smoothed over, but they had not been resolved. At the end of July one of Gambetta's supporters in the Republican Union had written optimistically that in the end Peyrat, Edgar Quinet and even Louis Blanc himself would be won: 'Gambetta will get the better of Peyrat, I shall try to convince my intransigent friend Edgar Quinet and, as for Louis Blanc, he is too large-hearted for us to despair of his patriotism!'[1] But when it came to the debates of January and February 1875 the compromise Republic championed by Gambetta was too bitter a pill for these three musketeers of 1848 to swallow whole. The desperate struggles of the Right, the funeral orations of expiring Monarchy were indeed moving; but so, too, were the pangs of conscience of these Republicans of an earlier era. The *République Française* might scoff in anger at Louis Blanc's speech of 28 January,[2] but when he and his colleagues did in the end vote for the Laboulaye amendment they did so, Blanc recalled, 'to the sound of immense applause which was like arrows in our hearts'. They had made 'the most painful sacrifice for the sake of friendship and of the unity of the Republican party'. It was a sacrifice that they could not continue to make. Broglie in his memoirs[3] no doubt forgot that when the final vote was taken on the vexed question of the Senate the three were joined in abstention by thirteen other Republicans. For Louis Blanc and his friends the compromise solution advocated by Gambetta meant 'the stifling of the big towns by the small, of the small by the villages, of the villages by the hamlets. It was the defeat of day by night.'[4] So, too, when the vote on the third reading of the law on the organisation of public powers was taken on 25 February, eleven Republicans abstained. The numbers were insignificant but the split between the 'pure' Radicals and the rest was something that Gambetta had been unable to prevent even though he exerted the strongest personal pressure.[5] This cleavage was part of the birth travail of the Third Republic. It would endure and cause him further trouble.

Among the abstainers, apart from Louis Blanc, was Quinet, who at one point was moved to tears: another was Barodet. Quinet and Barodet—a

1. Millaud, *Le Journal d'un parlementaire*, vol. i, p. 196.
2. Blanc, *Histoire de la constitution*, p. 101.
3. i.e. the passage cited on p. 234 above.
4. Blanc, *op. cit.*, p. 152.
5. Witness the undated letter from Barodet cited by Blanc (*op. cit.*, p. 171): 'Au moment où la Constitution allait être votée, MM. Gambetta et Challemel-Lacour vinrent me trouver à mon banc et m'adjurèrent, sur le ton de l'amitié, de voter avec eux. Pour me dérober à leurs instances, je m'échappai par les couloirs. Ils m'y poursuivirent, me cernèrent en quelque sorte, et insistèrent avec une grande véhémence sur toutes les considérations qu'ils croyaient de nature à me décider.'

veteran and a relative newcomer to national politics. Quinet had been the first president of the Republican Union, but, like Ledru-Rollin, he was one of those who were honoured but no longer drew the multitudes. He had, moreover, long been a sick man, but Gambetta on 25 February could have had no notion that his next important speech would be by Quinet's grave. He died suddenly on 27 March. Gambetta had not intended to speak, but his friends urged him that it was time his voice was heard again.[1] So he followed the other orators, Victor Hugo, Brisson the new president of the Republican Union, and Laboulaye, and addressed the great throng of mourners who had crowded to the cemetery of Montparnasse and who were estimated to number 100,000. There was no religious service and many of those present wore 'the yellow and red everlastings peculiarly affected by freethinkers'.[2] Inevitably Gambetta had to refer to the differences which had separated him from some of his elders, to 'certain differences which our enemies exaggerate in order to exploit them'. But, he claimed, there had never been disagreement over fundamentals:

> We shall always agree to pursue the same aims ... the victory of a wise and hardworking democracy, stubborn and patient ... the great and generous democracy which has inscribed on its banner the slogan which will give us victory: Alliance of the bourgeoisie and the proletariat. ... I repeat we are following the traditions of our predecessors. Their principles are ours: it is only the methods to protect and defend them that have changed. When one is in the majority one must govern. ... So it is necessary for us to force ourselves to work, discipline, patience and [he adroitly slipped in the words] to a spirit of compromise and understanding.[3]

Thus Quinet's funeral gave Gambetta the chance to make a public defence of his new tactics. His rhetoric was as vague but as warm as ever and his new reference to the alliance between the bourgeoisie and the proletariat which he had first mentioned at the Château de la Borde in 1873[4] was greeted with prolonged applause. It was a first gesture of propitiation to his 'tail'. But not all the proletariat were to be easily won. In one of a series of open letters Léon Bienvenu, a workman who wrote with effective pungency under the pseudonym of Gervais Martial, took Gambetta to task for uttering such a hollow phrase and 'putting a heap of

1. Police report, 30 March (A.P.P., BA/918).
2. *The Times*, 30 March, p. 5.
3. For the text, see *Discours*, vol. iv, pp. 289–98; cf. Mme Adam, *Nos amitiés*, p. 238, for the plan of the speech, which Gambetta showed her and of which she made a copy.
4. See above, p. 183.

large sugar lumps into principles made to be drunk pure'. The two words bourgeoisie and proletariat were, he pointed out, vague denominations which did not correspond to any precise classification. If Gambetta meant, as he supposed, the poor and the rich, then the only excuse for such a fantasy was his ardent wish to be conciliatory which led him and many others 'to sweeten the pills for fastidious stomachs':

> You speak of an alliance between the bourgeoisie and the proletariat. Against whom ... and against what? ... Where is the common enemy? ... The bourgeoisie is hard, egoist, full of pride ... and will never of its own accord do anything for the proletariat. On the other hand the proletariat cares little for an alliance with the bourgeoisie which could only take the form of protection. ... The proletariat has no alliances to conclude. It has rights to assert.

Such an alliance would be as impossible to bring about 'as to obtain the signature of a millionaire for a petition asking for a progressive income tax'.[1] Gambetta must have taken heed. Not until 1877 would he again proclaim this 'alliance between the bourgeoisie and the proletariat' as a slogan of victory.

'My tail. I'll give it a white tie and we'll go into society together.' So Gambetta was alleged to have remarked in April 1873.[2] His 'tail' meant first and foremost his working-class constituents, the proletariat, in Belleville. The last time he had delivered a major speech in his constituency was on 27 April 1873, in support of Barodet. But he had paid a well-timed visit there on 21 June 1874, soon after the Bonapartist attacks on him at the Gare St Lazare, and returned well satisfied.[3] Nevertheless the situation was awkward. Barodet's electoral programme in 1873 had contained three demands: the immediate dissolution of the National Assembly; the absolute integrity of universal suffrage; and a single chamber 'which alone can vote for an amnesty and an end to martial law'. Now, two years later, the National Assembly was still in being; universal suffrage was to be diluted when it came to the choice of a Senate, and the Republican constitution was to comprise two chambers instead of one. Moreover, Barodet had been one of those who had abstained from voting for the constitutional law on 25 February. Such were the circumstances in which Gambetta had to face his electors and justify his conduct. It would be a difficult

---

1. *Les 50 Lettres Républicaines de Gervais Martial ouvrier, recueillies par Touchatout* (1875), no. xi.
2. See above, p. 140.
3. 'Je rentre de Belleville un peu fourbu, mais fort satisfait de l'esprit, de la fermeté, de la sagesse de tous les braves gens. ... Ce sont de bonnes et salutaires fréquentations. Je regrette vivement de ne pouvoir les multiplier' (letter of 21 June 1874 to L. Léon (L.G.)).

enterprise. On 12 April when he went with the Adams to see Bornier's *La fille de Roland*, in which Sarah Bernhardt was playing, he was said to have encountered one of his extremer colleagues in the Assembly, Georges Perin, who told him that the men of Belleville would not swallow the Senate: 'You know that the Belleville programme is my group's programme. We owe its formulae to you. . . . You can go back on them in part or in whole, but we will cling to them. Take care; if you go too far in cutting loose from them we shall use your own weapons to fight you.' But Gambetta professed confidence. He said that he had taken care to see his leading Belleville supporters on the morrow of the vote establishing the Senate. He would win the day and added that in any case Belleville was not France.[1] But the previous parliamentary session had exhausted him and at the beginning of April he was still tired and in the doctors' hands;[2] now, as the time drew near for the ordeal he was understandably anxious. 'My heart is beating fast', he confessed to Léonie Léon on the eve of the Belleville encounter.

> I have to weather a big storm and I shan't get over my nervousness until I'm on the spot; till then I fiddle and fiddle again with a thousand things without concentrating on any. My brain feels as though it were filled with a floating and sticky mist, something like the atmosphere which must have preceded the emergence from chaos. . . . Happily love is my cordial and it is it that I invoke, with it and for it that I am going to do battle. Léonie *ora pro nobis*.[3]

He fought his battle in the dance hall of 27 rue Ménilmontant on the evening of 23 April 1875. Police agents were busy and their estimates of the numbers in the audience varied from 1,300 to 3,000, but all were agreed that Gambetta's speech had an immense effect.[4] Happily, his leading supporters had done their duty. His task was facilitated by the opening words of Blanchet, the chairman, who pointed out that the Republic was now the legal government of France and that, 'rudimentary and incomplete' though it might be,

> we, citizens of the 20th *arrondissement* of Paris, prefer to consider the act of 25 February as a point of departure, a first step towards the . . . realisation of the ideas of political and social justice which constitute the ideal of the Republican party. On this score we shall not grudge our support . . . and we express our gratitude to citizen Gambetta for the part he has played in the transformation of our institutions.[5]

1. Mme Adam, *Nos amitiés*, pp. 242–3.
2. *Lettres*, nos. 238–9.
3. *Ibid.*, no. 242. Cf. Mme Adam, *op. cit.*, p. 244.
4. A.P.P., various reports in BA/918.
5. *Discours*, vol. iv, p. 300. For Gambetta's speech, see *ibid.*, pp. 300–40.

Gambetta could sense that his constituents were still proud of being represented by one of the foremost Republican leaders and by the greatest popular orator in France. He started boldly with a reminder and a question: 'We began with a contract. Does it still stand?' 'Yes! Yes!' replied the audience amid 'Bravos' and prolonged applause. All was well. He could proceed to increase their good humour by a clever exploitation of the charges made by his enemies:

> People may say we are incendiaries (laughter), at one time that we are hypocrites, at another Italians brought up in the school of Machiavelli, at one Caesarians, at another Orleanists (fresh laughter). Two years ago I uttered a word which people still throw in my teeth—they accuse me of being from Belleville . . . of not having wished to cut off my tail (fresh hilarity). I haven't done so, I am not ready to do so and the proof is that I am here among you.

Such was the prelude to a tremendous rhetorical effort which fills thirty-nine pages of print in the fourth volume of Gambetta's collected speeches, the prelude to a review of the two years since he had last addressed his constituents and then to a still longer exposition and defence of the new Republican constitution. Gambetta was well aware of the point often severely commented on both by contemporaries and by later constitutional historians;[1] a constitution had been made, but he admitted that 'it was not subject to a great deal of discussion. Public powers have been organised, they have not been very minutely or very analytically scrutinised and coordinated.' 'And yet', he went on, 'do you know what has happened? The work is probably better than the circumstances which produced it . . . it may well be that this Constitution . . . offers Republican democracy the best instrument of enfranchisement and liberation that has yet been put into our hands.' It was not surprising that this assertion caused a 'profound sensation'. He then went on to examine the component parts of the instrument. The President would not be 'superior or anterior to the representatives of the country . . . elected for a specified term, obliged to register the will of the Assemblies and to promulgate the laws they make, responsible to them . . . he is neither a potential monarch nor a prince who is preparing to don the Caesarian purple. Modest though his situation is it is great enough for the authority in his hands to be worthy of France.' As for the Senate, it was true that those who first thought of it did so with the idea of resisting Republican democracy, but 'if we look at it . . . we shall find that instead they have organised a power which is essentially democratic in its origins, its tendencies and its future'. His audience might well have been astonished when he proceeded to declare not merely that this second Chamber was now the law of the country to be respected as

1. e.g. Deslandres, *op. cit.*, p. 371.

such but also that 'we must regard it as the sheet-anchor upon which the ship of state must rest'. But he pressed on to explain the way in which the Senators would be chosen. He had hesitated, he said, to believe that the Assembly would agree to give the Senate the most democratic thing in France, 'the spirit of the commune, that is the thirty-six thousand communes of France'. But this was what had happened. Political activity would circulate; from hamlet to town the communes would deliberate . . . and to do what? 'To dictate their wishes, that is to say to rule (Salvo of applause).' After such deliberations what would result? 'A Senate? No, citizens, the result will be the Grand Council of the French Communes.' Thus did he sell the rural communes to the townsmen, guessing, as one historian has remarked, that 'the prodigious inequality instituted by the law between the Parisian electors and those of Saint-Cuenta would not be noticed. Provided the elector has a vote and does not see anyone with two, he is hardly aware of it, if according to the play of coefficients, his vote has a thousand times less weight than someone else's.'[1] 'The Grand Council of the French Communes'—here was the happy formula with which, to loud applause, Gambetta made a now enthusiastic audience swallow the potion that had at one time been so unpalatable.[2] Having done so, he pointed to the importance of the senatorial elections and of getting the right men chosen for the electoral college, and then, returning to the constitution in general, he added that he would not have voted for it if it had been impossible to revise it. As for the future, he said he would not sketch out any programme, for nothing was more sterile than a programme 'en l'air', but—a highly significant but—'the State must be secular (*laïque*) . . . let France be a secular nation par excellence—and the public powers must be free from the encroachments of the priesthood just as much as from those of the empire'. Gambetta's vision of the secular state and nation was greeted by a chorus of 'Hear! Hear!' and a 'double salvo of applause'. He could sense that anticlericalism might of itself be a programme sufficient to secure him the continuing allegiance of his tail.

Gambetta's speech was a *tour de force*, a masterpiece of political oratory, for he made a bargaining concession appear a notable victory. He won over

1. Marquis de Roux, *Origines et fondation de la troisième République* (1933), pp. 266–7. Gambetta himself was, of course, aware of the inequality. Later, in a letter of 14 Nov. to Ranc (*Lettres*, no. 256), he wrote: 'Depuis quelques mois, on proteste contre le manque de proportionnalité dans le nombre des délégués sénatoriaux. Certes, en cela, il est illogique, antidémocratique et dangereux qu'une ville de cent mille habitants n'ait qu'un électeur sénatorial tout comme une bourgade de cinq cents âmes. . . . Sur ce point la réforme s'impose et sûrement s'inscrira dans la rédaction des futurs cahiers électoraux.

2. The cynical Rochefort did not think that the Belleville electors would swallow such doses for long (*Nos amitiés*, p. 248).

his working-class audience. They would not desert en masse to Louis Blanc. He gave them white ties by preparing them to shake hands with Senators of their own choosing.[1] He told the peasants that through the communes and the Senate they held their destinies in their own hands and were the arbiters of the nation. At the same time anticlericals could rejoice. That acute observer G. de Saint-Valry remarked that no doubt the speech would be denounced by the papers of the Extreme Right as an ultra-revolutionary manifesto; but, he added, 'in dealing with such a skilful *toreador* you should not hurl yourself blindly upon the red flag like a beast in the circus; you must watch the Genoese sword in the other hand'. Gambetta's objective, he thought, was fundamentally the same as that dreamt of by Ollivier (a comparison Gambetta would scarcely have relished); for both it was a question of organising and disciplining democracy.[2] Others also realised this and the Press generally hailed the speech as significant and statesmanlike.[3] Even the Radical *Rappel* approved Gambetta's policy of compromise and went so far as to declare that 'politics was generally nothing but an uninterrupted series of more or less felicitous bargains (*transactions*)'. Thus for the time being, though only for the time being, Gambetta had brilliantly resolved one of the difficulties confronting him at the end of February 1875.

This was something that could be achieved by the heroic effort of a single night. The institutional problems were of a different order. The passage of the constitutional laws was but 'a truce, an armistice between two virtually equal parties'.[4] The battle was quickly resumed and it would be prolonged over several months.

Once the law on the Senate and the constitutional law of 25 February had been passed it was impossible for MacMahon any longer to retain his

1. Even the critical Gervais Martial wrote an open letter to congratulate him for refusing to 'cut off his tail' (no. xxvii of *Les 50 Lettres Républicaines*). Martial pointed out the stupidity of the constant references by reactionaries to the tail of the Republican party: 'Où commence-t-elle pour eux la queue du parti républicain? Si on leur donnait un grand couteau avec la faculté de couper cette queue eux-mêmes, ils ne seraient même pas capables de s'entendre entre eux sur l'endroit où ils désiraient couper cette queue.' Gambetta's speech was at once printed in pamphlet form and sold for fifteen centimes by E. Leroux, 28 rue Bonaparte. According to a police report of 2 May, it was distributed in large numbers all over the south of France (A.P.P., BA/918).

2. G. de Saint-Valry, *Souvenirs et réflexions politiques* (1886), vol. i, pp. 116–19.

3. In a leader on 27 April, *The Times*, which had been critical of Gambetta's speech at Quinet's funeral, described the Belleville speech as 'a great oration, a real manifesto of the leader of the Left . . . in no part is it dull or insignificant . . . its phrases are chosen to make an impression and to pass from mouth to mouth'.

4. J.-J. Chevallier, *Histoire des institutions politiques de la France de 1789 jusqu'à nos jours* (Paris, 1952), p. 314.

discredited and oft-defeated ministers. As Gambetta saw, the formation of a new ministry at this juncture was a matter of particular importance. Not only would it be the first of the now legally established Republican regime, but in all probability it would be the cabinet under whose auspices the general elections would be held. The new majority in the Assembly implied a more liberal cabinet, but MacMahon, with his conviction that he stood for the defence of Conservative interests, was the last person to move far in a Liberal direction. The man he selected to form a ministry was Buffet, a Conservative, who had grown in stature in the role of President of the Chamber which he had occupied ever since Jules Grévy's resignation in 1873. But Buffet ran into difficulties, and it was a poor omen for the cabinet-making of the Third Republic that its first ministry was nearly a fortnight in the making. A general difficulty was the Marshal's wish to see in it as many men of the Right as possible, while the Left asserted their claims since the regime was now formally Republican. A specific difficulty was the key post of the Ministry of the Interior. The Left would have been happy to see this in the hands of the Duc d'Audiffret-Pasquier, a prominent member of the Right Centre whom they regarded as relatively liberal and with whom Gambetta was said to be on good terms, in spite of the Duke's earlier denunciation of Radicalism.[1] But Buffet feared that his appointment would give unnecessary provocation to the Bonapartists and in the end he took the post himself.

That Gambetta played an active part in these negotiations is certain. He told Léonie Léon on 4 March that he was wholly absorbed by the 'thousand ministerial combinations' which were being exchanged and that he was overcome by fatigue.[3] But his precise role is not wholly clear. No doubt, as Lord Lyons commented on 2 March, the Left had begun by supporting Buffet in the hope of placing him under an obligation.[4]

In his persuasive intervention in the Republican Union on 21 February Gambetta was said to have used as one of his arguments in favour of the constitutional laws the prospect of a liberal cabinet 'which would exceed all our hopes'; and when a voice queried: 'A D'Audiffret-Pasquier ministry?' he replied, 'Better than that.'[5] The upshot was clearly not better, but worse. D'Audiffret-Pasquier was not even in the cabinet and all their

1. See, e.g., C. de B., Rothschild pp., 17 March.
2. 'Le duc d'Audiffret-Pasquier, dont le talent d'orateur aurait été un sérieux appoint pour le Ministère, avait été pressenti pour l'Intérieur, mais Buffet garda pour lui ce département ministériel pour ne pas rester sans portefeuille et dans la crainte de susciter les préventions des bonapartistes hostiles au duc' (Silvestre de Sacy, *Le Maréchal de MacMahon*, p. 314).
3. L.G.
4. Lyons to Derby, P.R.O., F.O. 146, 1808.
5. L. Blanc, *op. cit.*, p. 166.

efforts did not secure the Left more than two posts which went to Dufaure and the economist Léon Say, both of the Left Centre.[1] But, according to Thiers's friend, Rémusat, who was in touch with many of the principals in the negotiations, Gambetta, in particular, was determined to be conciliatory:

> He was happy to appear so accommodating, thinking that this was clever. And to be sure he had his reasons. He imagined by this unexpected change in attitude he would accelerate the dissolution of the Assembly. He was above all anxious that the elections should be held under a government which was neither Bonapartist nor repressive. Lastly, although he did not tell everyone this . . . he saw that the Republic was losing ground and that the election results were not as certain as they had been. It was therefore necessary to press on, not to push things to extremes and to avoid the last extremities of reaction.

And, Rémusat added, this was indeed the attitude of many of his friends: 'Let us accept this cabinet and allow it to live until the elections.'[2] But Thiers himself in a moment of asperity was said to have commented that Gambetta was far too ministerial and not sufficiently Republican.[3] It was a strange comment from such a quarter!

Rémusat, in his subtle analysis of the events of February and March, had described the new majority in the Assembly as 'precarious'. No doubt this was another factor that Gambetta had in mind when he spoke of the difficulties that were beginning. The constitution had been voted by 435 to 254, but, Rémusat pointed out, 'in the 435 there are many who, by eagerly falling in with the views of authority, will seek to contain it within the narrow circle of the Conservative system'.[4] To such men the new ministers appeared to listen all too readily. Their initial declaration affirmed that their

---

1. According to *The Times* (11 March, p. 5) the Left had demanded an additional portfolio for a member of the Left Centre if D'Audiffret-Pasquier did not take the Ministry of the Interior, but an attempt to reach an agreement on this basis broke down. The final composition was submitted by Bocher, President of the Right Centre, to Gambetta, Ricard, Bethmont and Casimir-Périer in one of the committee rooms and by the end of a discussion which lasted 1¾ hours 'the Left capitulated once more'. Rémusat (*Mémoires*, vol. v, p. 524) gives a different version, saying that Bocher went up to Gambetta during the Assembly's sitting and asked him to go with him to a committee room: 'Là, en tete à tête, il lui a rendu compte de l'arrangement projeté, lui demandant s'il l'approuvait. Gambetta a répondu *Placet* et le ministère a été fait.'

2. *Mémoires*, vol. v, p. 525. Cf. Gambetta to Léonie Léon, 4 March: 'Je ne crois pas que le Premier Cabinet qui sortira de tous ces manèges soit bien fameux, mais . . . nous le pousserons vers la solution: Des Elections générales, avec un Programme net, un personnel plus dévoué et plus libéral, et une constitution à défendre' (L.G.).

3. C. de B., Rothschild pp., 11 April.

4. *Mémoires*, vol. v, p. 519.

policy would be 'very distinctly Conservative' and it did not even mention the word 'Republic'. Martial law was to be continued, the mayors' law to remain in being, although it was hoped that mayors might be selected from municipal councillors 'so far as possible', and a new Press law was to be prepared. It was no wonder that the *République Française* in disillusionment criticised the ministry for letting it be believed that nothing was changed in France[1] and that Gambetta a fortnight later declared that 'the time of ambushes was not yet ended'. It was a relatively small consolation that d'Audiffret-Pasquier, a candidate warmly supported by Gambetta and accepted by the Left, had been elected to succeed Buffet as President of the Assembly.

Always ready for a vacation, the Assembly had dispersed from 20 March to 11 May. Two by-elections were due to be held on 30 May, one in the Lot and the other in the Cher, and Gambetta took the opportunity to make a journey to the south on election business and also to visit Pau.[2] But by-election business was soon suspended, for, although there were now fifteen seats vacant, the Assembly after its return to its labours agreed that no more by-elections should be held since general elections were not far away.[3] Meanwhile the government had been preparing the further constitutional legislation and proposed to refer it to the famous Commission of Thirty. At once Thiers and others protested against reference to a body so out of tune with the new majority. When a vote was taken they carried the day and the Commission, now known as Penelope because of its long and often abortive labours, resigned. The *République Française* was jubilant: 'The cable has been cut.... A new Commission is to be nominated. So the time of dissolution is drawing near.'[4] When it came to electing a new one the Left groups could not agree with the Right Centre upon the allocation of places and decided to put forward their own list. One of the Right Centre groups headed by Léonce de Lavergne joined them and, although Gambetta who was a candidate was not elected, the new alliance swept the board. The Right gained only four seats and were indeed downcast. 'I fear', wrote C. de B., 'that the Right Centre will no longer be able to form a Conservative majority.'[5] This was only too probable now that the

1. Leader of 14 March.
2. Reports of Gambetta's movements were contradictory.
3. According to Lacombe (*Journal*, ed. Hélot, vol. i, pp. 187–8) Gambetta particularly feared a Bonapartist success in the Lot and had therefore been eager to put a stop to this and other by-elections. The R.F., however (e.g. leader of 26 March), had urged holding all the pending elections on the same day.
4. 20 May. Only one member of the Republican Union, Cazot, was elected to the new Commission.
5. Rothschild pp., 28 May.

Lavergne group had swung to the Left and soon adopted the name of Constitutional Centre. But Gambetta, for his part, was afraid that the victory would go to his friends' heads and cause them to commit some folly: 'What people about the President are looking for', he told Léonie Léon, 'is an explosion and a rupture with the Left.'[1] This was the last thing he wanted and, once again, he set out to preach prudence and moderation. This did not, however, mean that he was not exasperated by the slowness of the Assembly's progress in completing its constitutional tasks and by the unconciliatory conservatism of Buffet and his cabinet. With the first he expressed his disapproval firmly but moderately on 24 June at the annual dinner in memory of Hoche and with the second more passionately in a further debate in July on the Nièvre election of 1874.

When the evening for the Hoche commemoration drew near the government once again forbade a public gathering and the company had to meet in the house of one of the municipal councillors of Versailles. Gambetta seized the opportunity to make an eloquent encomium of the 'necessary Republic' and at the same time to be frank and acknowledge that it was not yet perfect. Thus an important measure now being put forward relating to Catholic higher education was, in his view, characteristic of the last efforts of the reactionaries 'against the very genius of our country'. There was much truth, too, in the criticisms of those who said that the constitution of 25 February was 'confused and obscure, full of ambushes and traps' and that it was stamped too much by some of the principles of constitutional Monarchy, by certain parliamentary practices which represented a compromise between the theories and wishes of the old parliamentarians and those of the Republican party. But the remedy lay in dissolution and the verdict of the great mass of eleven million electors who wanted the Republic, 'not a disguised monarchy' but 'a Republic of justice and progress. (Yes! Yes! Hear, Hear!).' Finally he seized the chance to make an incidental and oblique defence of his opportunism, virtually declaring that consistency was not a reasonable rule of life:

> People assert that some of us have changed our tune. Of what use would the passage of time and lengthening life be if they did not teach us experience? But those of whom this is said . . . are immovable and inflexible in their attachment to the French Revolution and its legitimate and essential consequences. (Lively approval.) The pact between the old and new servants of the Republic

---

1. Letter of 29 May (L.G.). Cf. *R.F.*, leader of 27 May: 'Ne triomphons pas trop et surtout ne triomphons sans nos alliés nécessaires. . . . Il faut maintenir la majorité du 25 février.'

is not a contract between strangers, it is rather a kind of mutual recognition on which we should congratulate ourselves all the more on account of its necessity.[1]

He had spoken cheerfully and prudently and his speech was commended by *The Times*, but by the end of the month the continued procrastinations and intrigues at Versailles led him to write one of the most despondent of his wellnigh daily letters to Léonie Léon: earlier in the summer the more optimistic prophets had spoken of the Assembly's completing its constitutional and other work by the end of the summer session and of a general election being held in October, but now that vision began to recede. 'Precious time', Gambetta said,

> is being lost and I am beginning to despair of dissolution. The number of the timid, the low and the envious, the . . .[2] is becoming truly frightening and I am very anxious about the future. Were it not for my feeling of duty towards our mutilated country . . . I should quit politics . . . and seek calm and studious leisure in my profession. For the first time in my life discouragement is nigh upon me.

When he wrote this the Assembly had become absorbed by what seemed an interminable debate on a railway question. 'We shall never get them out of Railways', he was reported to have remarked in more jocular mood, 'except by telling them that the art of steering balloons has been discovered.'[3] Two days later the three Left-wing groups for the first time held a general meeting, presided over by Laboulaye, at which they went so far as to agree upon a joint resolution, strongly supported by Gambetta, to confine discussion to the narrowest limits and to forgo multiplying amendments and speeches. But even this self-denying ordinance, damming the natural springs of Left-wing eloquence, would not in the end achieve their aim.

Meanwhile the battle between Catholics and anticlericals was intensified as the summer wore on.[4] On the one hand Gambetta took part in a ceremony which consolidated a new alliance of anticlerical forces; on the other he was bitterly dismayed by the Catholic victory on the higher

1. For the text, see *Discours*, vol. iv, pp. 341–54. According to a police report of 26 June, it angered 'les purs'.
2. There is an omission here in the transcript of this letter of 29 June (L.G.).
3. *The Times*, 1 July, p. 7.
4. Catholic newspapers such as the *Correspondant* had been increasingly critical of Republican policies and asked, for instance, whether Gambetta was not committing 'a singular error in making atheism one of the necessary marks of the Republic' (Gimpl, *The Correspondant and the founding of the French Third Republic*, p. 177).

education Bill, which he had denounced in his speech at the Hoche banquet.

On 8 July, in 'the vast halls' of the masonic order of the Grand Orient, Jules Ferry, a notable Republican politician, and Emile Littré, a notable Republican thinker, were admitted members of the Clémente-Amitié lodge. The occasion, wrote the *République Française*, recalled one of the most splendid days in the annals of French Masonry, that on which Voltaire had been received in Les Neufs Soeurs.[1] It was honoured, claimed About's *Dix-Neuvième Siècle*, by the presence 'of the Republican élite, the flower of French liberalism, the greatest orators in the Assembly and the most brilliant writers in the Press'.[2] And it was *the* greatest orator in the Assembly, Gambetta, who made the final speech, thereby giving the ceremony his blessing and, in the words of the *République Française* placing it 'under the patronage of science'. He urged his hearers to imitate in the field of action the strenuous labours of Littré in the field of thought and 'to fight the great fight of science against obscurantism, of liberty against oppression, and of tolerance against fanaticism'.[3] This event symbolised the clash of two worlds, the Catholic world of Mgr Dupanloup and the Positivist anticlerical world of Gambetta, and it revealed the coalition of Positivism and Masonry. To Dupanloup it was an event of horrible significance and, taken with its consequences, it seemed later to the historian Daniel Halévy, to be as considerable perhaps even more considerable for the history of the French soul than 1789.[4] It was indeed significant. A year later, on the anniversary of his initiation, Ferry virtually claimed that Positivism had taken over freemasonry: a year later still the Grand Orient demonstrated its Positivist trend by voting to eliminate from its constitution the paragraph affirming belief in God and the immortality of the soul. Later still Juliette Adam was to relate that, soon after the ceremony of 8 July 1875, Gambetta and Challemel-Lacour had admitted to her that it was with the help of freemasons such as Ferry and Littré that they intended 'to fight the great fight against clericalism'.[5]

That ceremony and the alliance with freemasonry may have heartened Gambetta, but his discouragement with the Assembly (certainly not the first in his life!) was not alleviated by the course of the debates on the higher education bill. The defence of Catholic interests was by now one of the few issues which could rally the Right. The Bill aimed at allowing

1. Leader of 10 July.
2. Quoted in Capéran, *Histoire contemporaine de la laïcité française*, vol. i, p. 8.
3. *Ibid.* The R.F. curiously refrained from printing Gambetta's speech; it only printed Littré's.
4. *La République des Ducs*, p. 233.
5. *Nos amitiés*, p. 262.

any Frenchman to found institutions for higher education. These *facultés libres* were to be given the right to confer degrees. The proposals were strenuously opposed by anticlericals as well as by representatives of the University, who argued that it was the duty of the state to ensure proper standards and that it alone should confer degrees. But all the oratory of Gambetta's friends and colleagues, such as Jules Ferry, Challemel-Lacour and Paul Bert, was powerless to prevent the Bill going forward. Eventually a compromise was reached and the Assembly agreed that candidates for degrees awarded by *facultés libres* must present themselves before juries composed equally of professors in state and free universities chosen by the Minister for Education. Yet the fact that the *facultés libres*—which in practice meant Roman Catholic faculties—were authorised was a notable triumph for Catholicism. Although Gambetta had foreseen this outcome a month before,[1] when the law passed on 12 July he could not help writing in disgust to Léonie Léon: 'Yet another detestable day, we have been furiously defeated by this clerical majority. France is monk-ridden for a long time to come. The Recluse of Varzin [Bismarck] must be laughing at the trump cards "freely" put in his hands. It's enough to make one mad with anger. My only hope now is in dissolution, but it's coming very slowly.'[2] A solemn leader written on 14 July in the *République Française* bade its readers remember that they were 'the sons of Voltaire and of the French Revolution',[3] and five weeks later the paper began a campaign to demonstrate from the Belgian example to what decadence France was being led by *liberté d'enseignement*.[4]

It was thus against a background of irritation—an irritation enhanced perhaps by miserable weather and a challenge to a duel from a sixty-eight year old Bonapartist (which he loftily declined)[5]—that Gambetta on 15 July again and more dramatically vented his spleen against Buffet. The interminable affair of the Nièvre election of 1874 had come up anew with a debate on the second report of the parliamentary commission of enquiry. In the course of it Buffet took the opportunity to steer a middle course and to remind his hearers that the political dangers were not on

1. Police report of 9 June (A.P.P., BA/918).
2. 12 July (L.G.).
3. *R.F.*, 15 July.
4. Gambetta asked Ranc to document him and send books used in Belgian Catholic universities (*Lettres*, nos. 248–9).
5. A. Granier de Cassagnac complained that the *R.F.* had accused him of venality. A statement in the *R.F.* of 7 July explained that the reporters of the paper were individually responsible for their articles. M. Granier de Cassagnac must know that 'Monsieur Gambetta n'est pas et ne saurait être à la disposition du premier ou du dernier venu de ses adversaires ou de ses ennemis politiques. Il a d'autres charges et d'autres devoirs envers son parti, envers la France et la République.'

one side only: 'If the Bonapartist party goes to take its orders in Camden Place, the home at Chislehurst of the Empress Eugénie and the Prince Imperial, the revolutionary party goes for its orders to Geneva, London, Brussels and, I might add, nearer still. . . . The government will be vigilant!' This was too much for Gambetta who rashly jumped up and appeared to identify himself with 'the revolutionary party'. In a speech which was constantly interrupted, he declared that the men responsible for the Bonapartists' nefarious activities were 'those who have sought to govern the Republic with the aid and the personnel of the ill-omened (*néfastes*) men who had brought France to her ruin . . . there is only one set of men responsible, M. de Broglie and his successors'.[1] But Gambetta had momentarily met his match. Buffet stoutly defended his officials and challenged the Left to move a vote of no confidence. Gambetta, quite unprepared for a ministerial crisis, evaded the issue. The cabinet in consequence gained an overwhelming vote of confidence (392 to 264). Buffet had for the time being strengthened his hand and the debate had, as a result of Gambetta's intervention, been deflected from the Bonapartists who thus escaped condemnation. If the Radicals rejoiced in the attack on Buffet, Gambetta's friends of the Republican Left and Left Centre were none too pleased and the *République Française* found it necessary twice to embark on a laboured defence of its patron's conduct.[2] Whether this had been another calculated gesture to the extreme Left or merely, as *The Times* thought, 'a burst of foolish passion',[3] there is no doubt that Gambetta was increasingly irked by those whom he called 'the incompetent men who are governing us' and their 'ill-will'.[4]

'After seventy-two years of the most extraordinary reign in history', the *République Française* had written in May, 'Louis XIV on his deathbed had the supreme good sense as well as the courage to say to his mourning servants: "Why do you weep? Have you believed me to be immortal?" The Assembly of Versailles would have done well to remember these words of the great King whose palace it inhabits.'[5] But the Assembly was still loth to end its days. Although the members of the Left had, for the most part, attempted to honour their self-denying ordinance to limit unnecessary speeches and amendments and although the remaining constitutional legislation was hastily discussed and easily passed, a majority of the deputies voted for another session rather than prolong their labours

---

1. *Discours*, vol. iv, p. 380. For the whole of Gambetta's intervention, see pp. 368–389 and *Ass. Nat. A.*, vol. xl, pp. 94–100.
2. *R.F.*, 18 and 19 July.
3. Leader of 17 July, p. 11.
4. *Lettres*, no. 247 of 17 Aug. to Léonie Léon.
5. 16 May.

into the middle of August.[1] So the summer vacation of 1875 began on 3 August and Gambetta celebrated its advent soon after by an outing to Fontainebleau with the Adams.[2] Meanwhile, as a final 'end-of-term' gesture, he was reported to have proposed at a meeting of the Republican Left that the three groups of the Left should instigate a debate on the date of the general elections, the suspension of by-elections and the municipal law. 'The meeting, however, decided that the Left ought to be satisfied' with the success it had achieved during the session and that these questions should be deferred until November. It was 'desirable to avoid any debate which might impair the alliance with the Liberal-Conservatives'.[3] Gambetta had readily accepted this decision and his proposal was perhaps but another gesture to the extreme Left. No one knew better than he the importance of humouring the men of the Centre.

Once the vacation began there were many rumours that he intended to embark on a great oratorical tour, but he was not so rash. When asked in September by a reporter in Vienna whether he would engage on an autumn campaign to prepare the people for the elections, he replied that he could not tell: France was 'like a woman who must be left quiet when she desires it'.[4] His exhortations in fact would be by letter and he would leave it to others, including the reemerging Thiers, to do the speaking.[5] Relieved, too, of the necessity of mustering his troops for by-elections, aware that the general elections could now hardly be held before 1876, he felt free to travel further and longer than usual abroad. One of his main objects was to take soundings on the international situation, by which he like many other Frenchmen, had been increasingly preoccupied because the menacing attitude of Bismarck earlier in the year had appeared to threaten France with a preventive war.[6]

Meanwhile the politicians and the Press had already long been speculating and manoeuvring about two issues which it was believed would greatly affect the balance of political power and the outcome of the general elections. These were the mode of election to the Chamber of Deputies and the choice of the seventy-five Life Senators.

The mode of election was an old issue in French politics. That practised under the Second Empire and most of the preceding regimes since 1789

1. At the beginning of July the Left had urged that the Organic Laws, the remainder of the budget, the electoral law and certain other Bills as well as the revision of the mayors' law and a new Press Bill could all be dealt with by 14 August.

2. *Nos amitiés*, p. 265; *Lettres*, no. 246.

3. *The Times*, 3 Aug.; cf. C. de B., letter of 3 Aug. (Rothschild pp.).

4. *The Times*, 25 Sept.

5. Thiers made an important speech at Arcachon on 17 Oct. urging all Republicans to maintain unity.

6. For this crisis and Gambetta's views on foreign affairs, see Chapter 21 below.

was *scrutin d'arrondissement* whereby each department was divided according to its population into a certain number of constituencies,[1] each of which was entitled to one deputy—hence the alternative designation *scrutin uninominal*—and the elector simply voted for one of the candidates soliciting his favour. But in 1848 Republican euphoria and in 1871 reaction against a *petit scrutin* identified with Bonapartist official candidatures had led to the adoption of the rival system of *scrutin de liste*. By this the elector was entitled to cast as many votes as there were deputies for the department.

Gambetta had been asked his views on this issue as early as July 1871 by a Republican newspaper published in Nantes, the *Phare de la Loire*. In the general elections of 1869 and 1871 the Republicans of the Loire department had gained a considerable majority in Nantes, but their votes had been submerged by those of the rural population and in consequence the deputies elected had all been royalist. The young Republicans felt bitterly about this and would have preferred *scrutin d'arrondissement* which would have given the town its own representation. But Gambetta, while sympathising with them, defended *scrutin de liste*. He pointed out that the circumstances of the elections of February 1871 had been exceptional all over France. Before continuing to campaign against *scrutin de liste* the Republicans of Nantes should consider what had happened in Bordeaux. There, too, in February 1871 the votes of the Bordelais had been submerged by those of the surrounding countrymen. But what had happened in the by-elections on 2 July? 'Thanks to the happy union of various sections of Republican opinion, to the ... attitude ... of the members of the committees astutely set up in the cantons; thanks to an intelligent, active and loyal propaganda; thanks finally to the activity of the Press', these same country dwellers changed their minds, made common cause with Bordeaux and accepted its candidates who gained a crushing majority. The system of *scrutin de liste*, Gambetta pointed out, had always been upheld by the democratic party and it was not one of those reforms which should be abandoned because it did not at first blush yield all the advantages it seemed to promise. It was the system 'most favourable to the creation of parties, to the expression of their ideas and the advent of men capable of serving them well'. Perhaps it could be improved: 'Might we not examine whether the representation of towns could not be secured by giving them ... deputies *intra muros* as in the days of the limited franchise or by choosing the *arrondissement* instead of the department as the unit for the electoral college, while still preserving *scrutin de liste*?' These were indeed important questions about which they ought to think

1. In 1871 one deputy was allotted to every 50,000 inhabitants.

in view of the electoral law which the National Assembly was doubtless preparing.[1]

In February 1871 *scrutin de liste* had favoured the Monarchists still more than the Republicans and so in May 1873 Thiers and his ministers had proposed a return to *scrutin d'arrondissement*, but this had come to nothing because of Thiers's overthrow. But by 1874, when the Commission of Thirty at last set to work to draft an electoral law, it was the Monarchists,[1] who, having lost by-election after by-election, had rediscovered a preference for *scrutin d'arrondissement*. The consequence was that most of the Republicans were now solidly in favour of *scrutin de liste*. But a complicating factor was that the Bonapartists as well as the Republicans appeared to be profiting from this system. Accordingly, some of the Left Centre were by no means convinced of the advantages of *scrutin de liste*: for them, as the *Journal des Débats* said, there was but one step from *scrutin de liste* to plebiscite.[2] Yet the spectre of Bonapartism did not cause Gambetta to change his views. Article after article in the *République Française* extolled the merits of *scrutin de liste* and condemned *scrutin d'arrondissement* for its parochialism and possibilities of corruption,[3] and when in July 1875 it was suggested to Gambetta that he might do a deal with the Conservatives and secure their consent to a speedy dissolution in return for abandonment of *scrutin de liste* he rejected the idea with scorn.[4] Fortified by the support of Thiers, who had in September publicly declared himself in favour of *scrutin de liste*, because 'the times were still exceptional' and because he believed that it would ensure the election of a relatively homogeneous and moderate Chamber, Gambetta also made *scrutin de liste* a main topic in what was his chief vacation substitute for a great public speech, namely a letter to the electors of Lyon at the end of October.

Since his return to political life at the end of June 1871 Gambetta had visited many parts of the country, but he had not been to this turbulent anticlerical 'second capital' of France since December 1870 when the red flag was flying on its Hôtel de Ville. Now he had been sent an invitation to a 'fraternal banquet' by a group of spokesmen for 'the democracy of the Rhône' who somewhat pointedly told him that at it he would 'learn to know the Lyonnais who complain that they are a little too much neglected by you'. A 'fraternal' visit to Lyon might well have been another propitiatory gesture to his 'tail', but it was one he could not risk

1. For the text, see P. Sorlin, 'Gambetta et les républicains nantais en 1871', *Revue d'Histoire Moderne et Contemporaine*, vol. x, avril–juin 1963, pp. 123–5.
2. D. Halévy, *La République des ducs*, p. 184.
3. e.g. 14 April; 4 May 1874; 23, 27, 29 April; 7, 30, 31 Oct. 1875.
4. *The Times*, 13 July. Cf. *R.F.*, 7 July.

at a moment when the dominant preoccupation was not to provoke the Marshal[1] or alienate the moderates of the Centre. Fortunately the imminence of the new session of the Assembly which was due to meet again on 4 November enabled him to excuse himself and at the same time to seize the opportunity to make his reply a masterly statement of policy before the new session and the forthcoming general election.[2] As for *scrutin de liste*, he reiterated his previous arguments and added a new one. All defenders of the new constitution should support it because it alone would allow conciliation and electoral alliances between 'all factions of the sincerely constitutional party'. The precious alliance concluded in the Assembly under the auspices of men such as Thiers, Casimir-Périer and Léonce de Lavergne should be shown to be a lasting cooperation. It was 'important for the success and durability of a policy of appeasement and moderation' that *scrutin de liste* should continue: 'It is difficult to understand why the authors or partisans of the Constitution of 25 February can hesitate on such a question. My information, indeed, allows me to declare that it is they alone who have everything to lose from *scrutin d'arrondissement*.'

Gambetta's letter was given great publicity—*The Times*, for example, printed a full translation and devoted a long leader to it[3]—but it did not suffice to allay hesitations in the Centre, despite the fact that the reconstituted Commission of Thirty had come down in favour of *scrutin de liste*. These hesitations were no doubt confirmed when Buffet let it be known that the government would resign if *scrutin d'arrondissement* were not carried. Prophets, like the Gallup pollsters of the twentieth century, were already prognosticating the majority by which *scrutin de liste* would be rejected. Meanwhile, with the advent of November and the imminence of what everyone knew must be positively the last session of the National Assembly, deputies were converging on Paris from all directions; 'extra-Parliamentary gatherings of all the groups are announced; Cabinet Councils follow one another; ... prayers are ordered in all the churches to invoke the Divine blessing on the Chamber and its decisions'. All that remained for it to do, wrote *The Times* correspondent, was for it to perform its last act—namely passing the electoral law; all the other measures, the Press Bill, 'the complement of the military organisation, the Budget ... even the laws of the magistracy' were subordinate matters.[4]

1. In an interview given to *Die Presse* in Vienna in September he had gone out of his way to speak well of MacMahon.
2. For the text, see *R.F.*, 29 October. The letter was also printed separately and sold for five centimes under the title 'Réflexions/de/M. Gambetta/sur la situation politique/lettre adressée aux Lyonnais/Le 25 Octobre 1875'.
3. 29 and 30 Oct., pp. 3 and 9 respectively.
4. *The Times*, 1 Nov., p. 5.

The Assembly in fact recognised the importance of the electoral law by giving it priority and the debates began at once. The climax came on 11 November when Ricard, one of the Commission of Thirty's two rapporteurs, spoke for two hours in defence of the Committee's support of *scrutin de liste* and Dufaure for the government argued the case for *scrutin d'arrondissement*, urging that it simplified the task of the less educated electors and safeguarded the interests of minorities. Then at 6.10 p.m. Gambetta ascended the tribune 'amid a general sensation'. *The Times* reporter (presumably Henri de Blowitz, who had been formally appointed to succeed Frederick Hardman on 1 February) was carried away by the momentous scene:

> Imagine [he wrote] a hall already excited by M. Ricard's speech and M. Dufaure's reply; the eager public unmindful of time, heat, and fatigue; the area whence interruptions, protests, and cheers scarcely restrained are ready to break forth from 700 or 800 Deputies; the Tribune occupied by that potent individuality [Gambetta] who seems hemmed in by the limited space in which he moves, his voice swelling to bursts of thunderclaps, his impressive, excited, menacing gestures obliging the ushers to take the precaution of removing one of the two lamps on the desk before him. Imagine this strange hall, half theatre, half forum, amid the noise of this special and impassioned audience, that massive and energetic head, that athletic frame agitated under the action of an over-flowing eloquence and pouring out above the repressed anger, enthusiastic accents, and cries of passion, irony, direct attack, and covert insinuation. All this must be imagined, together with the fact that the subject of discussion was the fall or maintenance of a Cabinet whose disappearance . . . may exert a decisive influence on the resolutions of the Chief of State.[1]

But Gambetta, though he delighted his hearers on the Left, was more eloquent than persuasive. He made a gratuitous attack on the Orleanists and his proposal at the very end of his speech that the vote should be taken by secret ballot appeared to some a confession of weakness, to others an all too transparent stratagem to win at least some of the waverers.[2] The Assembly voted as the prophets had foretold and *scrutin*

1. How different was the impression of one of Gambetta's warmest French admirers! Edmond Adam wrote and told his wife that in his speech Gambetta was 'calme, aisé, maître de lui, de sa parole, de sa voix . . . que de bon sens, de raison, de patriotisme, de force, que d'esprit surtout !' (Mme Adam, *Nos amitiés*, p. 287).

2. For the text of his speech, see *Discours*, vol. iv, pp. 398–424 and *Ass. Nat. A.*, vol. xlii, pp. 134–42. According to Edmond Adam the Bonapartists and Legitimists had promised 'un certain nombre de voix si nous obtenons que le vote ait lieu au scrutin secret' (*Nos amitiés*, p. 286). This was in order to cover up the divisions in their own ranks (cf. J. Rothney, *Bonapartism after Sedan*, 1969, p. 146). For an adverse comment on the secret ballot proposal, see C. de B. (Rothschild pp.) letter of 12 Nov.:

de liste was rejected by 357 votes to 326. This defeat, to which he himself contributed by his intemperate tone, was a severe blow to Gambetta. His anger was reflected in the *République Française*, which denounced the Orleanists anew and declared that they wished to introduce 'an oligarchic system of government installed within the Republic to fight and destroy universal suffrage'.[1] As Daniel Halévy remarked, Gambetta and his friends did not foresee that those who would enjoy the role of 'oligarchs' chosen by *scrutin d'arrondissement* would before long be the men of his own party.[2] Nor does he seem to have realised that *scrutin d'arrondissement* would weaken the Bonapartists much more than his own party. Meanwhile, however, in a letter to Juliette Adam, he tried to make light of the setback and attribute it to those now constant scapegoats the Vatican and the Church.[3] To be sure, the Republicans would have to modify their plan of campaign for the general election and this would cost more money and make their task more arduous, but the nation would support them in the *arrondissement* just as it would have done in the department.

There was, moreover, still a last chance to induce the Assembly to change its mind. On the 26th when the Bill came up for a third reading, another Gambetta, quiet in voice and restrained in manner, appeared to make a last effort to reverse 'a dangerous vote from the point of view of the government of this country'. He had never, he said, believed that *scrutin de liste* was a panacea and if it had been a question simply of a piece of electoral legislation without serious political implications he would not have been afraid to vote for *scrutin d'arrondissement* along with the majority; but the question was to adopt the method which would ensure a liberal government that was both moderate and strong and stood for a policy of conciliation. Without the majority to produce such a government 'the nightmare which has been weighing on the national conscience for five years' would continue. This was the point he came back to in his

1. 13 Nov.
2. *La République des ducs*, p. 185.
3. 'J'avais dès l'origine de la campagne redouté l'intervention à la dernière heure des ordres du Vatican; j'espérais enlever le succès, grâce au scrutin secret, qui favori-sait toutes les lâchetés, des amis au second degré du ministère. Mais le jésuite a parlé, Rome a parlé, et j'ai perdu la partie contre toute raison et toute sagesse' (*Lettres*, no. 255, 13 Nov.). In a letter to Ranc of the following day he also asserted that he had never regarded *scrutin de liste* as of capital importance (*ibid.*, no. 256).

'Voilà toutes les savantes manoeuvres de MM. Thiers et Gambetta encore déjouées! Les scrutins secrets, à l'honneur de cette Chambre, ne réussissent pas à ceux qui spéculent sur les capitulations de conscience et sur des honteux marchés.' see also E. Pillias, 'Gambetta et la loi électorale', *Revue d'histoire politique et constitutionnelle*, Oct.–Dec. 1938, pp. 554–5.

peroration after another prolonged tilting at the official candidatures which he believed *scrutin d'arrondissement* tended to favour:

> When a country possesses material strength and the ring of its frontiers is intact it can at leisure discuss questions of political metaphysics; but in a country which has not got all its frontiers, this is sacrilege, it is criminal. And since you are looking for the justification for the work of 25 February and of this policy of concord and pacification, I will give it you: 'Look towards the gap in the Vosges!'[1]

In its own way the speech was a notable performance which elicited from a lady in the gallery the comment: 'If he is not a great character, he is at all events a great actor.'[2] The brief patriotic cry at the end was moving and the whole speech won repeated applause from the Left, but it was uttered in vain. *Scrutin d'arrondissement* won the day once more (by 388 to 302) and Gambetta and his friends would have to modify their electoral plans.

In listing the labours still confronting the Assembly *The Times* correspondent had forgotten to mention one which to many was scarcely less important than the electoral law. As early as 8 April C. de B. had remarked that the deputies who had no hope of being reelected were seeking to obtain a retreat in the future Senate and on 27 May he observed that the majority of the Left who had triumphed in the votes for the new Commission of Thirty were preparing for a similar success in the election of the seventy-five life Senators: 'Their success is probable and it will exercise a great influence upon the choice made by the delegates of the communes.'[3] This, then, was the most vital battle of the last weeks of the Assembly's life. The idea that the seventy-five Senators might be men of distinction in all walks of French life, regardless of their political affiliations or their already sitting as deputies, had quickly been submerged by the passions of party strife. The seat of a life senator was now a political prize like any other and, as such, a legitimate object of any kind of bargain. If the Right were to present a solid front the seventy-five would be inexorably Conservative and their colouring might influence the countrywide elections of the other 225 in 1876. This was not a prospect that Gambetta could contemplate with equanimity—the man who had swallowed the second chamber so unpalatable to many of his Republican colleagues was bound to justify himself in their eyes by doing his utmost to win seats for Republicans. No doubt, too, after his discomfiture over *scrutin de liste* he was all the more delighted to dish the Orleanists with whom some Radical sharpshooters still alleged that he was in league. He had once as a

---

1. For the text, see *Discours*, vol. iv, pp. 425–47 and *Ass. Nat. A.*, vol. xlii, pp. 370–6.
2. *The Times*, 27 Nov.
3. Rothschild pp.

young man visited the Orleanist princes in their English exile at Twickenham and this was something that his Left-wing critics did not forget. Whenever he appeared to them too moderate, as he had of late, they repeated the old allegation that he was an Orleanist in fact or at heart.[1] 'The people who say this', he had told a police agent in June, 'are imbeciles. What interest should I have in supporting the d'Orléans who have no credit in the country when so many men who are rightly esteemed and influential have thrown in their lot with me?'[2] But the legend died hard and this was no doubt one of the reasons for his recent attack on the party:[3] he was looking over his left shoulder, but perhaps, too, he had come genuinely to detest the men who could still appear the most serious obstacle to the definitive establishment and continuance of the kind of Republic he wanted, the men who had remained deaf to his overtures and who still had in reserve such a commanding figure as the Duc d'Aumâle. Now he saw his chance: 'We will manoeuvre', he is alleged to have declared, and, fortunately for his manoeuvring, the Right was still as divided as ever. Gambetta was well aware of the continuing hostility between Orleanists and Legitimists and of the Bonapartists' readiness to adopt an independent line.[4] He took his chance and unscrupulously allied with both the latter. The Orleanists were routed more completely than he can have ever dared to hope. Thiers himself, who was at last beginning to warm towards him, admitted that he was 'a fine gambler'.[5]

Negotiations between different groups had started as soon as the parliamentary session had begun, if not before. They are a tangled tale which it would be tedious to try to unravel in detail. At first, however, Gambetta, perhaps despite objections from Thiers, was said to have made overtures to the Right Centre, offering the support of the Left for fifty men of their choice, provided that they had voted for the Republican constitution and could be regarded as *bona fide* constitutionalists. In return he proposed that the Right Centre should back twenty-five candidates nominated by the Left. Thus a Left–Right Centre combination would carry the day, ensuring that all the Senators were supporters of the constitution and that the Left would have a reasonable representation. But

---

1. C. de B., 17 March (Rothschild pp.).
2. Report dated 'June' (A.P.P., BA/918). Cf. report of 22 June, *ibid.*
3. Cf. Mme Adam, *Nos amitiés*, p. 287: 'Je pense qu'à présent personne ne soupçonnera Gambetta d'être orléaniste' (letter of 12 Nov. from her husband).
4. For the Bonapartists' attitude see Richard, *Le Bonapartisme sous la république*, pp. 150–1, and Rothney, *op. cit.*, pp. 147–8; for another account giving many details, see E. Daudet, *Souvenirs de la présidence du Maréchal de MacMahon* (1880), pp. 70–88.
5. 'Oui, vous êtes un joueur … un beau joueur, vous avez raison, pendant que vous êtes en passe, il faut faire *suer aux cartes* leur argent' (D. Halévy, *Le Courrier de M. Thiers*, p. 501); cf. *Nos amitiés*, p. 295.

the Orleanists of the Right Centre, without having secured a united front of the Right as a whole, overreached themselves: they tried to cut the Left's allotment to a mere thirteen and to eliminate the Radicals. Negotiations then not unnaturally broke down. Accounts of what happened subsequently vary. Much later, when Ranc wrote in an article in *Le Matin* that the Republican lists of Senators were drawn up by a committee of six, namely by Gambetta, Lepère, Jules Simon, Jules Ferry, Bordeaux and Ricard, Galliffet told him that he was wrong and that 'the senatorial elections were made by a triumvirate composed of MM. Duclerc, de La Rochette, Gambetta and—no others'. Moreover, the initiative, he said, came not from the Left but from the Legitimist leader La Rochette, a friend of one of those silent men *persona grata* with everyone, namely Duclerc. It was La Rochette, 'putting into practice the slogan *potius mori quam foedari* [sooner death than fusion]' who suggested to Duclerc an alliance between the Legitimists and the Left. Duclerc told Gambetta, who seized the unlooked-for opportunity with both hands and proceeded to mount the operation.[1] Quite different was the version given by Gambetta's friend Scheurer-Kestner, himself one of the last life senators to be elected. For him the initiative was Gambetta's. He had the brilliant idea of exploiting the natural enmities of the Right; he created the committee of six referred to by Ranc and it was this committee who, through Duclerc, approached La Rochette.[2] Both omitted to refer to the part played by the Bonapartists, most of whom were equally ready to dish the Orleanists. According to their most recent historian, Gambetta met one of their leaders, Raoul-Duval, every morning to agree upon the candidates whom Gambetta wished to support and Raoul-Duval to proscribe. It was perhaps from these encounters that Gambetta derived the respect for Raoul-Duval which soon made him wish that he were a Republican.[3]

Whoever took the initiative in these manoeuvres there is no doubt about the intensity of the eleven days' struggle or the importance of its ultimate outcome. For Gambetta it was a struggle which, added to his other political cares, was intensely wearing. At one of his Sunday lunches he was reported to have lost his temper with a friend who questioned the wisdom of his policy: 'My dear friend, put by your speech and produce it another time; for a week I have been going to bed at 4 in the morning and getting up at 7. I have to travel 15 leagues daily and I risk being hissed and shot at perhaps by the Irreconcilables. . . . I have had

1. Ranc, *Souvenirs-Correspondance*, pp. 428–31.
2. Scheurer-Kestner, *Souvenirs de jeunesse*.
3. Rothney, *op. cit.*, p. 148. Prof. Rothney has had the advantage of seeing the Raoul-Duval papers.

enough and should like to lunch in peace if possible.'[1] But such outbursts were rare. His absorption in the senatorial battle was mirrored both in his letters to Léonie Léon and in the *République Française*. They reflected his preliminary contentment with the behaviour of the Bonapartists and with the 'magnificent' conduct of the 'pure royalists' (he was now said to have been seen arm in arm with the Marquis de Franclieu, one of those diehard Legitimists who had shaken his fist at him in earlier days);[2] they showed him complimenting the sick and ailing members of the Left who had heroically turned out to vote; they revealed his dismay at the understandably flagging interest and failing discipline of his 'troops' as the proceedings became more and more protracted, his love of manoeuvring and yet his disgust with the more unsavoury side of such transactions and his exasperation at the recriminations levelled against him by some of the dissatisfied.[3] Wanting to follow Thiers's advice and 'sweat the last sovereign from the cards', he was dismayed when such a doughty clerical antagonist as Mgr Dupanloup was elected, but when all was over he was rightly triumphant. The unnatural alliance of the Left and Legitimists had secured fifty-seven seats for the Left and the Lavergne group, fifteen for the Legitimists and left only three for the Orleanists![4] Men as prominent in public life as Broglie and the Foreign Minister Decazes had been rejected and the Adams could soon rejoice that nearly all their friends had become senators. When the extent of the Republican victory began to be realised La Rochette (whom the *République Française* smothered in flowers)[5] was bitterly reproached. He had to resign the leadership of his group and died soon after. Irreparable damage had been done to the Monarchists' cause and men like Dupanloup were in despair. Once again they had been their own worst enemies; they had been unable to combine even to prevent a plan which each of them should have alike detected and detested. The *République Française* wrote with glee that the Republicans were taking possession of seats made ready in advance for the promoters of reaction and occupying as masters a fortress built against them: 'The Republic is no longer threatened; it is victorious.'[6]

1. Police report of 14 Dec. (A.P.P. BA/918).
2. Mme Adam, *Nos amitiés*, p. 297.
3. Letters of 11, 12, 14 and 16 Dec. (L.G.) and *R.F.*, leaders of 11–22 Dec.
4. The *R.F.* claimed that sixty-seven of the successful names had figured solely on the lists of the Left, five solely on those of the Right, and three on both lists.
5. Leader of 14 Dec.
6. Leader of 24 Dec. Cf. Dupanloup's lament in which he also spoke of the Senate as a fortress: 'Ce Sénat aurait pu être une barrière, mais c'est fini . . . . C'était une forteresse; M. Gambetta se vante d'y avoir mis garnison, et ce sont les nôtres qui lui ont ouvert les portes' (*cit.* D. Halévy, *La République des ducs*, p. 209). The Orleanists' defeat was all the more piquant since, as E. Beau de Loménie has pointed out, 'd'une

As for Gambetta, a friend of Juliette Adam, Jules de Lasteyrie, wrote to her that he was the father of the Senate just as Wallon was the father of the constitution.[1] It remained to be seen how happy he would continue to be with such an offspring.

façon générale, pour plus de moitié, la liste des sénateurs inamovibles républicains était compose de ralliés tout récents, presque tous rattachés par le passé de leur famille à la plus directe et la plus notoire des dynasties orléanistes' (*Les Responsabilités des dynasties bourgeoises*, vol. i, Paris 1948, p. 276).

18

The 1876 elections
December 1875–March 1876

'I have just got back from Versailles. At last the final step has been taken. Dissolution has been pronounced, France has been set free, she is going to be able to act and dispose of herself freely. . . . An enormous weight has been lifted from my chest.'[1] Thus curtly did Gambetta in a letter of 31 December 1875, dismiss the National Assembly which had been so long in dying and which indeed officially continued to exist until the formal transference of powers to the new parliament in March 1876. The *République Française* then printed a longer obituary. The intentions of the Assembly had not been good enough for it to do much good and it had lacked the self-confidence to do much harm. In grave circumstances it had shown energy and inspiration only when it was a matter of voting itself holidays. For long it might have been thought that it was 'threatened with history's indignation; it gained the right to her pity'. The enduring part of its work would be what it had done involuntarily.[2] Meanwhile a foreign paper, *The Times*, had been kinder. It had declared that the Assembly might occupy a place in French history greater 'than any Parliament since the Revolution'. But it added that it had 'brought to light very little capacity of a commanding order'. Thiers, of course, was incomparable, but he belonged to another generation. 'Alone among the younger men does M. Gambetta give promise of first-rate Parliamentary power.'[3]

Gambetta might well be relieved that the end had come, but to the end the political struggle had been intense. The last six months, he told his father, had been terrible.[4] He badly needed rest and fortunately dissolution gave him the chance of a holiday. He left at once for that

1. To Léonie Léon (L.G.).
2. 10 March 1876.
3. Leader, 3 Jan. 1876, p. 9.
4. *Lettres*, no. 261.

'Villa du Bon Repos', as Challemel-Lacour called it, Les Bruyères, where the Adams were as usual delighted to give him asylum. To put inquisitive admirers off the scent he travelled by way of Turin and Savona and, worn out on his arrival, slept until 1 p.m. the next day. Happily the weather was brilliant when he recovered from his fatigue. Soon he was out among the pine trees, climbing again to see the marvellous view and revelling in fresh oranges picked from the trees. Joined not long after by Spuller and Challemel-Lacour, the party made an expedition to the Ile Ste Marguerite, whence Marshal Bazaine had escaped sixteen months earlier, and visited Cap d'Antibes where Gambetta clambered over the rocks 'like a child'. His hostess as usual subjected him to one of her own literary products, making him listen to the first draft of her new novel *Jean et Pascal*, which she read to him even before it had been heard by Edmond Adam, her husband. In the evenings Gambetta played dominoes with Edmond and one day his own family came over from Nice to celebrate the betrothal of his sister Benedetta to Alexandre Léris. He in turn went to Nice on 9 January.[1]

The holiday came to an end on 17 January when Gambetta began his homeward journey and plunged once more into the waters of politics which were now swirling towards the electoral millrace. The first step in the choice of the remaining 225 Senators had been taken on the 16th, when the municipalities were called on to select their delegates, and on 30 January the delegates were to proceed to the chief towns in their departments to elect by *scrutin de liste* the Senators themselves. The first ballot for the new Chamber of Deputies was to take place on 20 February, to be followed by the second on 5 March. By the middle of March the two houses of parliament provided for by the Constitution of 1875 would have begun their labours at Versailles. But well before then Gambetta was again writing that he was exhausted, done up and 'deadbeat'.[2] There was no central committee set up to direct the Republicans' election campaign, but Gambetta was one of the foremost organisers of the campaign and the offices of the *République Française* were one of its main headquarters. Gambetta himself stood in no less than five different constituencies and during the six weeks from the middle of January to the end of February he was constantly on the move and continually under strain. 'I would not at this moment be in Gambetta's shoes for a million', Brisson told a police agent on 12 February: 'he no longer has a life of his own (*il ne vit plus*), his responsibility is terrifying. Think of it, if the elections are not completely Republican the whole democracy will fall upon

---

1. For a romantic account of Gambetta's holiday, see Mme Adam, *Nos amitiés*, pp. 303–16.
2. e.g. *Lettres*, nos. 268 and 269; letter of 14 Feb. to Léonie Léon (L.G.).

him, crush him and grind him to powder. He is irrevocably lost if he does not succeed beyond the bounds of probability.'[1]

Gambetta's electoral burdens (apart from the choice of the life senators) had begun to pile up even before the end of the year. As early as 3 December he had complained that all over the country there was a rash of candidates which threatened 'to exceed the locusts of Africa'; 'one must find one's way through this fine lot, set some aside, encourage others and often choose blindly, it's enough to make one lose one's temper'. He was already snowed under. What, he asked, would it be like during the electoral period?[2]

The business of the senatorial elections was less physically wearing than that of the elections to the Chamber since he was not a candidate. But he did not spare himself. As usual he had a practical eye to the mechanics of electioneering and the political education of the electors; and so a leader in the *République Française* on 29 December 1875, was the first in a series of articles directed to this end. The municipal council, it explained, elected the delegate who chose the Senator, but it nominated him 'without debate'. It was essential, therefore, to form committees of influential people whose task it would be to secure that the choice made was the one most in harmony with Republican institutions. Such preparatory deliberations were most important. There could not be too many discussions, conversations, and exchanges of view between electors. Republicans could not think of sending to the electoral assemblies any but Republicans and so it would be wise to exact serious guarantees of a candidate's sincerity. But while the elections would contribute to the political education of the whole country, the *République Française* was not trying to urge that there should be public meetings everywhere: 'We are talking only of discussions between friends and neighbours, of conversations . . . by the fireside. What is essential is to rouse everyone to political awareness. There is a well-known *mot* of a famous philosopher who said to a poet: "You are not concerned with politics, Sir? No. Well, take care; politics will be concerned with you." ' Two days later Gambetta wrote a letter to a municipal councillor of his native town of Cahors in the Lot, 'one of those departments in which political awareness [*l'esprit politique*] is still too drowsy [*assoupie*] and in which, for lack of cohesion, the servants of Republican democracy are ignorant of their strength and their numbers'. They ought, he said, to form a central committee of authorised representatives from all the *arrondissements* and develop a common programme, namely energetic defence of the Republican constitution of 25 February, resolute opposition to any attempt at monarchical or princely

1. A.P.P., BA/919.
2. L.G.

restoration and the postponement of constitutional revision until 1880. They should then meet the Senatorial electors and demonstrate to them the political condition of France by analysing the constitution and pointing to the exigencies of the international situation.[1]

Having thus given his directives on electoral tactics Gambetta left for his holiday in the Midi, but in the ensuing fortnight the *République Française*, no doubt following his instructions, reiterated various well-worn themes and multiplied advice to the electors of delegates: official candidatures were repeatedly denounced and the Republicans were again declared now to be the true Conservatives; the electors were urged not to choose a nominated mayor as delegate, for he was sure to be the prefect's candidate; they should remember also to choose a deputy delegate in case the delegate could not act and, having chosen a good Republican as delegate, they should not compromise by selecting a man of opposite views as his deputy.[2] Finally they were recommended to look at a 'Projet de cahier du délégué de commune aux élections sénatoriales' drafted by a M. Chassin, author of *Le Génie de la Révolution*, and published by the *Bulletin des Conseils municipaux*.[3] This included a 'simple programme' to be imposed on candidates, namely formal recognition of the Republic as the definitive form of government, a ban on foreign wars except those of legitimate defence, military service for all, the search for a more equitable allocation of taxes, free compulsory secular education, the exclusion of everything tending to a return of the *ancien régime*, and the elections of mayors and their assistants by municipal councils.[4]

Naturally the exhortations of the *République Française* were not ubiquitously followed. As might have been expected, respect for the men in office led to the choice of many mayors as delegates in rural districts. On 18 January C. de B. noted with satisfaction that he had been looking through several provincial newspapers and observed that the elections had been very favourable for the Conservatives:

> Many mayors have been nominated, which is contrary to orders given by the Republican committees. In the Vienne nearly all the mayors are delegates. Two-thirds of those in the Allier are Conservatives. Everything suggests, therefore, that the vote of the delegates on 30 January will produce a strong Conservative majority in the Senate, and such a result might exercise a good influence on the election of deputies.[5]

1. *R.F.*, 6 Jan. The letter was first published in *Le Républicain du Lot*.
2. See e.g. *R.F.*, 7, 8, 9 and 10 Jan.
3. Ch.-L. Chassin was an assiduous compiler of elementary political brochures. In 1877 he founded the *Semaine Républicaine*, a weekly devoted to 'propagande populaire et éducation civique'. Jean Macé was one of its contributors.
4. 14 Jan.
5. *Letters from Paris*, p. 214. Cf. Daniel, *L'Année politique, 1876*, p. 9: 'Le désir du

The *République Française* was, of course, aware of this danger and again urged the importance of winning over the isolated independent delegates. Arrangements should be made for the electors to meet first in small groups, between which it would be easier subsequently to establish general communication, so that meetings could be held, preferably in the cantonal capital, two or three times before election day. Wherever there was a Republican General Councillor he would be the obvious organiser and where there was none available the task should fall upon the mayor or municipal councillor who had gained most Republican votes. He should summon the meeting and be in touch with the central committee which sat in the chief town of the department and coordinated the information received from various parts of the area.[1]

His vacation over, Gambetta took a more direct part in this second stage of the senatorial elections. First of all he sought to pour oil on the stormy waters of local politics in the Bouches-du-Rhône where his friends Challemel-Lacour and Eugène Pelletan were candidates. This meant both braving or circumventing official attempts to prevent him from speaking and also exercising all his authority and tact in trying to obtain some kind of unity in Republican ranks, which were divided both because they were rent by personal rivalries and ambitions and because extreme Radicals disliked his opportunist tactics. At Marseilles, his first port of call, he was to have spoken at a banquet prepared for 250 guests at the restaurant Rossi on the evening of 17 January. But Marseilles was one of the four towns still under martial law.[2] Shortly before the company were due to sit down the police intervened and forbade the banquet. The disappointed guests had to withdraw. Gambetta consoled them as best he could by receiving them in groups at the Hôtel d'Orléans, sitting up until 1 a.m. for the purpose. He was satisfied with these talks, but none the less admitted that the situation was still very complex. He would refrain, he wrote, from giving Juliette Adam details of the petty and rather absurd quarrels in progress, but, he humourously added: 'You can't conceive of the number of apothecaries bitten by the electoral tarantula. At every street corner there are one or two Purgons setting out

1. R.F., 21 Jan.
2. The new Press law of 27 Dec. did away with martial law except in Paris, Lyon, Marseilles and Versailles.

---

gouvernement fut exaucé. Dans la grande majorité des communes les maires furent élus. Mais, comme les conseils municipaux ... avaient surtout obéi à des considérations locales ... il était fort difficile ... de pronostiquer l'issue du vote. ... *L'Agence Havas* et le *Bulletin Français*, organes du gouvernement, annonçaient néanmoins ... le succès des "conservateurs" qu'ils opposaient toujours aux "républicains" selon la langue adoptée au ministère de l'Intérieur.'

at full speed on the electoral turf. Thanks to this eruption of pharmacy we shall elude them all; the electorate clearly refuses to be injected and I approve its refusal.'[1]

On the following two days Gambetta went on to Aix and Arles, where the Buffet government continued its harassing tactics. Meetings arranged at Aix on the 18th and Arles on the 19th were forbidden by the military authorities, but this time Gambetta's admirers circumvented them more successfully. The Republican committee at Aix hastily arranged for a banquet for four hundred to be held at the Hôtel du Palais where he met most of the newly elected delegates and local councillors. The police did not interfere and on the 21st the *République Française* claimed that, while attempts had been made to prevent Gambetta from speaking to the General Councillors and Committees of *arrondissement* representing the Bouches-du-Rhône, 'he has seen them all. People wanted to prevent him from speaking: he has spoken at Marseilles, Aix and Arles; at Aix he even delivered an important speech which can be read in full in the papers.' He did indeed make a speech at the banquet. As befitted his audience, he was concerned to advise them on their conduct in the second stage of the senatorial elections. He did not fear, he said, for the Republican delegates, but for those sent by the municipalities of the smallest communes. These were the people who might be the victims of corrupt influences. These were men whom the Republican delegates must meet and convince of their duties. At the same time he enlarged on some of his now well-known themes. Politics was being transferred to new hands—from a disdainful and more or less enlightened élite to the *petit bourgeois*, the worker, the small capitalist and the peasant. The true Conservatives now were those who wanted a society free from privilege, such as had been organised by the Civil Code, those who wanted the liberty of conscience derived from the Declaration of the Rights of Man, and those who wanted freedom of thought as well as freedom to pray. The Senate, which he might now even go so far as to call the French House of Commons, had been greeted with distrust, but 'in some years we shall all gladly defend it'. Any Legitimists elected should bury their regrets for the past; any imperialists not irremediably compromised should answer the call and return to the great democratic family. In short, the elections should bear the stamp of appeasement and national reconciliation.[2]

Well pleased with his work in Provence, Gambetta hastened back to Paris to throw his weight into the electoral struggle in the Seine of which

1. *Lettres,* no. 264 of 17 Jan., A. Dansette *Le Boulangisme 1886–1890* (1938), p. 143; R. de Bonnières, *Mémoires d'aujourd'hui* (1888), pp. 178–84.
2. For the text see *Discours,* vol. v, pp. 32–52; or *R.F.* 22 Jan. It was sold separately for ten centimes.

he, as a deputy for the department, was also an elector. He claimed that he had routed 'the dissidents' in the south; in the Seine also he had to combat the extreme Left as well as the Right. The Intransigent Radicals were strong in the General Council of the Seine and the Municipal Council of Paris. If they were to gain the upper hand the Republicans might lose many votes in the provinces. This was the main reason why Gambetta attached great importance to the contest for the five Parisian seats. Moreover, instead of backing some new Barodet, he above all wanted to secure the election of his own chosen candidate, his wartime collaborator Freycinet, who was unlikely to succeed in the hurlyburly of election to the lower house, but might well render useful service as a Republican Senator. He had, before he went on holiday, persuaded Freycinet to stand and advised him how to promote his candidature: 'I can see only one really effective way', he told him.

It is to see the electors individually; there are not many more than two hundred. You will explain your position to them. You will strike a patriotic note to which they are sure to respond. You will tell them, if need be, that I gave you this advice. . . . I shall be there on the great day. And if anyone attacks you in the full meeting I will tell them what you have done. . . . Meanwhile be sure and pay a visit to Victor Hugo, who will probably be the grand master of the Senatorial election.[1]

Freycinet did as he was told and paid his 'academic visits', as Gambetta humourously called them, including one to the great poet who, he recorded, welcomed him with 'Olympian serenity'. Gambetta for his part kept his word. He was present at the four preparatory meetings or 'réunions plénières' of the 217 electors and he leapt to Freycinet's support when his candidature was criticised by a member of the extreme Left. He also skilfully prevented the gathering from discussing a political programme put forward by the Radicals and kept it to its task of hearing the candidates.[2] After a vigorous intervention on 23 January he wrote to Léonie Léon that he thought he had got the list he wanted, 'in spite of the reactionaries of the Right and the fools of the Left. M. Thiers was at the meeting. He had never been in such a furnace. On the way out he congratulated me warmly on "my forceful speaking" [*ma rude poigne*

1. Freycinet, *Souvenirs*, vol. i, pp. 322–3.
2. See *R.F.*, 28 Jan., report of meeting of 26 Jan. In the words of *The Times* (28 Jan., p. 5) Gambetta 'postponed the decision until the Ballot, and will naturally profit by the delay to make ill-inspired electors understand all the dangers to which they would expose the Republican cause by opposing men like MM. de Freycinet, Tolain and Hérold and supporting violent Irreconcilables, whose advent is always the precursor to despotism'.

oratoire]. Evidently the cunning old man prefers force to finesse. I am of the contrary opinion, but one day follows another and the means vary.'[1] In fact it proved impossible for the electors to evolve an agreed list and in the final meeting Gambetta blocked an attempt to create one. The means did indeed vary, but they were at any rate highly effective so far as Freycinet's candidature was concerned. On election day, 30 January, he came out top of the poll followed by two other supporters of Gambetta, Tolain and Hérold. To Gambetta's surprise and that of everyone else, the great Victor Hugo was elected only on the second ballot, while the fifth seat went to Peyrat. As delegate of Paris, 'this Babylon with the heroism of Saragossa', Hugo had taken it upon himself to issue a manifesto to the delegates of the 36,000 communes of France ending with a peroration telling them that thinkers were more useful than soldiers: 'There is one greater than Themistocles, namely Socrates; there is one greater than Caesar, namely Virgil; there is one greater than Napoleon, namely Voltaire.'[2] As for Louis Blanc and the defender of Belfort, Denfert-Rochereau, whose claims had been urged on Gambetta by Léonie Léon, they obtained only four votes each on the third ballot. The Republicans' success was complete, since they won all five seats, but it was a success that revealed their internal divisions. Louis Blanc and his supporters associated with the *Rappel* were embittered by their defeat and the triumph of Gambetta's friends and for a while there was something like a breach between the *République Française* and the *Rappel*.[3]

If the outcome in Paris was embarrassingly satisfactory there was no walkover for the Left in the country as a whole and Léonie Léon complained that some departments had conducted themselves ill.[4] In fact, as has been pointed out, if Republican central committees were set up in many departments they more often than not exercised only a remote control over the local committees whose existence was sporadic and whose tendencies varied.[5] The Left won ninety-three seats compared with 132 which went to the various groups of the Right, including

---

1. Letter of 23 Jan. (L.G.). It was presumably of this intervention that Léonie herself wrote the next day 'Votre éloquence va crescendo, elle se plie à toutes les exigences, multiplie ses efforts, et sait revêtir toutes les formes!' (*Ass. Nat.*, p. 244). *The Times* had earlier (7 Jan., p. 5) asserted that there were three Republican lists, Irreconcilable, Radical—i.e. Gambetta's, and Moderate and it named Hugo, Tolain, Freycinet, Béclard and Hérold as being on Gambetta's list.

2. *R.F.*, 22 Jan.

3. *Lettres*, no. 267 of 8 Feb. to Ranc. According to Freycinet, Victor Hugo's failure to be elected on the first ballot was due to his pressing too hard for an amnesty (*op. cit.*, pp. 328–9).

4. Letter of 1 Feb. (L.G.).

5. J. Chastenet, *L'Enfance de la Troisième 1870–1879* (1952), p. 210.

thirty-nine Bonapartists. They thus just failed to obtain a majority since, counting the Life Senators, the Right could claim 151 supporters to the Left's 149. The Right had indeed done better than many people had expected. But groupings in the centre were fluid. Three successive leaders in the *République Française* expressed satisfaction.[1] That of 3 February asserted that the results would ensure a Republican majority in the Senate and thereby prepare the way for the crushing of official candidates in the elections to the Chamber: 'For the first time since the beginning of the century the country districts which have been called on not to follow the lead of the towns but to precede it have expressed their preference for the Republican form of government and their firm wish to consolidate it.' 'To be sure', a further leader admitted,

> the senatorial majority is not throughout filled with the lively sort of demo-cratic feeling which paves the way for great reforms. It has not the élan for rapid progress. . . . But that is not what we expected. . . . What above all it was necessary to obtain was a Senate which would not stand in the way of progress and which would strengthen the Republic by its support (*adhésion*). That we have. The rest will come.

In fact the elections were a triumph for the moderates of the Centre, whether of the Right or the Left:[2] these men and their successors would often be suspicious of a more radical Chamber; they would not indeed thirst for great reforms and in the long history of the Third Republic it would often be Gambetta's Grand Council of the Communes that was the great obstacle to change. For the time being, however, when the regime itself had still to be secured beyond doubt, what seemed all important, as the *République Française* suggested, was that the majority in the Second Chamber did at least nominally support the Republic and that it would increasingly do so if the Republic continued to steer a moderate course. 'The Senate is reassuring', Gambetta claimed a few days later, 'it will fulfil its true function as a restraining influence.' This was indeed, 'to make the best of the situation'.[3] Before long he would regard his creation with a more jaundiced eye.

No sooner was the senatorial battle over and Juliette Adam able to rejoice that nearly all her friends were Senators, than Gambetta had to

1. 1, 2, and 3 Feb.
2. Thus of the 149 Republican senators, eighty-four belonged to the Left Centre and fifty to the Left or Republican Left, as it was sometimes called, while the extreme Left numbered only fifteen, namely Adam, Gen. Billot, Cazot, Challemel-Lacour, Crémieux, Elzéar Pin, Esquiros, Ferrouillat, Victor Hugo, Laurent Pichat, Lelièvre, Peyrat, Scheurer-Kestner, Schoelcher and Testelin. Eight of these were Life Senators.
3. Hanotaux, *Histoire de la France contemporaine (1871–1900).* vol. iii, p. 519.

face the still more strenuous election campaign for the Chamber of Deputies. He had declined an invitation to stand in the *3rd arrondissement* in Paris because he preferred to remain faithful to Belleville, but he contrived that Spuller should take his place. One constituency in Paris was enough, but since multiple candidatures were still permissible, he stood in three other great cities, namely Lille, Bordeaux and Marseilles. He stood, too, in Avignon, where his candidature was a challenge to the system of official pressures to which the administration in the department of Vaucluse was alleged to be especially prone. Such a quintuple effort laid him open to charges of seeking plebiscitary power and a new dictatorship, although he was not the only man to stand in more than one constituency. Buffet was a candidate in four and Louis Blanc, in a successful effort to recover from his rejection as a Senator, stood and was elected in three different places.[1] Undoubtedly Gambetta's multiple candidature emphasised his bid for Republican leadership, but at the same time he devoted his rhetorical powers unstintingly to the service of his party. The campaign was his greatest oratorical effort since the autumn of 1872 and the celebrated series of speeches culminating in that at Grenoble. He had to reassure the electors, to outline a policy, to deal with foes on the Left as well as the Right. He had to be constantly on the move and, time permitting, to speak on behalf of his friends as well as himself. Thus he spoke for Spuller, who was faced by Intransigent Radical opposition in the *3rd arrondissement*, before hastening to Lille to make his first great election speech in the provinces. There the flags were out in his honour and his audience on 6 February numbered some 3000.[2] His speech was hailed as a governmental programme by Emile de Girardin and saluted by the *Temps* as evidence of the political sense of the former revolutionary party.[3] On the 9th he addressed another 3000 people at Avignon, and at Bordeaux on the 12th, such was the fame of his oratory that 10,000 tried to get into the Cirque Lamartine which was made to hold 3000; 5000 succeeded, with the result that Gambetta himself, the man they had come to hear, was unable to do so! The meeting had to be abandoned; Gambetta prolonged his visit and addressed a smaller audience of 2000 in the Théâtre Français the following evening. Afterwards a large crowd processed along the Cours du Chapeau Rouge and demonstrated enthusiastically in front of the Hôtel de la Paix where Gambetta was staying.

---

1. Gambetta (*Lettres*, no. 267 of 8 Feb.) wrote of the 'manifestation "plébiscitaire" ' being made in favour of Louis Blanc.

2. Gambetta, never prone to underestimate, put the number at 4000 (*Lettres*, no. 266 of 6 Feb. to Juliette Adam).

3. E. de Girardin, *La Question d'argent, questions de l'année 1876* (1877), p. 38; Joughin, *The Paris Commune in French Politics*, p. 123.

Even the prefect and his friends joined in from the balcony of the prefecture nearby.[1] Back in Paris, Gambetta spoke on one and the same evening both in the *8th arrondissement* in support of Victor Chauffour, a former proscript of 1851, one of whose adversaries was the Foreign Minister Decazes, and in Belleville.

The meeting at Belleville and the speech he delivered there were of particular importance. When he arrived the chairman read out a long manifesto which reminded him of his original mandate and its modification and that between him and the Bellevillois there was a bond which no one wished to break. When he himself spoke he undertook a cogent definition and defence of his opportunist 'policy of results' against the Intransigents who would have liked to create a new world all at once. 'What I want', he said, 'is that once the Republican party has embarked upon a reform it should not leave it unfinished . . . to hasten on to another, making a muddle of everything and ending up with the miserable spectacle of a party which has meddled with everything and constructed nothing.' Such a policy perhaps demanded more real passion than those which were more doctrinaire.

> As for me, my policy is in accord with my philosophy, I deny the absolute everywhere, and so you can well imagine that I am not going to recognise it in politics. I belong to a school which believes only in the relative, in analysis, in observation, in the study of facts . . . a school which takes account of environment, races, tendencies, prejudices and hostilities. . . . No, Gentlemen, one is a politician only if one gets to the bottom of a subject and does as you do in your work; whether you have to carry out a work of thought (*travail de pensée*) or of craftsmanship or industry, you must hold on to your material . . . mould and perfect it day by day and only then are you sure to become past masters in your chosen career or profession.
>
> Is this a new procedure? . . . When have men been able to say that every problem must be tackled at once?

Moreover, politics were always changing.

> Politics today in 1876 will not be the same as in 1877, 1878 or 1880. It will change with our needs and interests. . . . And so it is necessary to alter one's conduct of policy in accordance with those very changes which have taken place in the world. You see then that politics is a matter for tact, study, observation and precision.

His audience listened to this lesson obediently and when he had done, the cries of 'Vive la République! Vive Gambetta!' were loud and long.[2]

1. E. Ginestous, *Histoire politique de Bordeaux sous la IIIe République* (1946), p. 60.
2. For the manifesto and speech see *Discours*, vol. v, pp. 142–59.

His double effort in Paris that evening left him 'happy but dead'.[1] He had not, he said, slept in a bed for five nights.

This was only a part of his Herculean labours. Despite his earlier visits there were still fierce battles to be fought in the south against both the Right and the Intransigents' 'League of evil',[2] the triumvirate Naquet, Blanc and Madier de Montjau who, he said, had been working immensely hard. There was no need for him to return to Bordeaux or Lille, but at Avignon and Marseilles he was much less secure. So, accompanied at Juliette's insistence by Edmond Adam, he set out once again for the Midi, embarking on a journey which was the most momentous of his campaign and which would provide matter for one of the longest and most vivid of all his many letters to Juliette Adam.[3] They dined ill at the Gare de Lyon, but were consoled in the train by a box of cigars, 'le myrte', as Juliette was wont to call it, while they rattled through the night to Auxerre. Then, the weather being bitterly cold, Gambetta wrapped himself up for sleep in 'the rabbit-skin furs so often and so justly denounced to an indignant Europe'. This was his own wry description of the fur coat he had worn when he made his celebrated escape by balloon from Paris on 7 October 1870, wry since his enemies had seized on the garment as evidence of 'the dictator's' luxurious tastes. But sleep in it he did, and when the travellers disembarked at Orange the next morning it was under an azure southern sky and to face a splendid reception prepared by Alphonse Gent, one of Gambetta's former prefects. There was a long procession through the town, the customary banquet, and a speech to be made from an improvised platform in a huge coach-house to a crowd of more than 3000. And what an audience it was!—an audience of humble southern folk unspoiled by their contact with civilisation—with these people the southerner brought up in the country town of Cahors felt 'solidarity' and 'mutual affection': 'We constantly understood and penetrated and traversed one another, this audience and I.' It was a splendid start to a gruelling tour.

Meanwhile a delegation had come from Carpentras to beg Gambetta to vary his itinerary and pass through their town. He yielded and he and Adam climbed into a carriage which was to take them sixty kilometres through the wonderful Provençal landscape by way of Carpentras to Cavaillon. At Carpentras, 'a white crown on a green hill', an 'ancient Celtic retreat surrounded by plane trees, green ilexes and tall dark cypresses', they were met by the Republican candidate, Cyprien Poujade, and another crowd including little girls in gala costume clutching bunches

1. Letter of 14 Feb. to Léonie Léon (L.G.).
2. Letter of 11 Feb. to the same (*ibid.*).
3. *Lettres*, no. 269, 22 Feb.

of flowers. Hemmed in by the throng they made their slow ascent to the old town, 'an acropolis gilded by the southern sun'. There they came to a halt in 'a colossal gateway' opening on to 'an immense Forum surrounded by high walls'. The crowd was vast, the atmosphere still more intoxicating than at Orange. Gambetta was carried away: 'I let myself go with all my political passion . . . all this country seems to be just one great public platform and for the first time I felt that my voice was powerful enough to harangue its immensity.' Here, too, was another audience spellbound by the magic of that voice: 'They felt what I was feeling; they responded to the cries I uttered, they themselves filled in what I had but sketched. . . . Ah! what a life! if only it could be prolonged!'[1] Here was the exaltation of the artist as much as the statesman. At such moments, remarked Daniel Halévy, that subtle writer over whom Gambetta cast a posthumous spell, he was a 'sublime chanteur des rues' and beloved as such, for he radiated happiness among those around him.[2] Yet he knew how illusory such triumphs could be. In an illuminating comment on his Spanish friend Castelar in 1874 he had written: 'I did not need this example to know how small is the value of eloquence alone . . . character, energy, confidence in one's party and complete lack of conceit and envy are qualities far more precious than this genius for oratory which serves to mislead you yourself as much as your audiences.'[3]

The travellers reached Cavaillon at sunset. Once again there was a splendid reception awaiting them. The whole town was astir: hats were doffed and heads inclined as Gambetta's cortège traversed the boulevards and everyone applauded. A vast throng accompanied him to the hotel in which he was to hold a meeting. But Cavaillon was in the constituency of Avignon where he was himself standing 'in order to come to grips with the fraudulent conduct of the clericals'. Suddenly the temperature changed. No sooner had he and his friends gone to their rooms than they heard beneath their windows a great din and shouts of abuse. On asking what was up, Gambetta was told that several carriages and omnibuses had come from Avignon and 'unloaded . . . a gang of from 100 to 200 individuals collected from the most unsavoury places, panders, wrestlers

1. Cf. Gambetta's letter of 18 Feb. to Léonie Léon: 'Ce Pays-ci n'est qu'une immense place publique, on peut à chaque instant rassembler une audience et répandre ses pensées' (L.G.). In his *Mon Village* (Paris, 1944, p. 183, n. 1) M. R. Thabault wrote: 'Melchior de Voguë remarque dans "les mots qui parlent", que les paysans de Gascogne n'étaient sensibles qu'au ton des discours politiques, aux gestes, à tous les signes extérieurs de la foi de l'orateur — non à la signification de ce qu'il disait.' May this not well also have been true of many of the peasants in Gambetta's rural audiences?
2. *La République des ducs*, pp. 218–19.
3. *Lettres*, no. 219, 22 Oct. 1874.

from fairs, old lags, professional thieves and assassins whom the fine gentlemen of moral order had hired to kick up a shindy. Among them was to be seen the Mayor of Cavaillon himself.' But these adversaries had arrived too late to prevent Gambetta from reaching the hotel and after they had indulged in some further hissing they withdrew to refresh themselves. Meanwhile the Republican candidate and his friends sat down to their meal; but it was an anxious affair, for a report came that an ambush had been prepared for them and that they must take the utmost precautions. Alarmists recalled the fate of Marshal Brune who was assassinated in 1815 and many of the company were in panic until Adam calmed them down, distributed some weapons and organised them for resistance. 'The bloodstained shade of Brune' hovered over the banquet. But in fact, wrote Gambetta, 'once the bulldogs got drunk' their masters feared the consequences and came to beg their adversary himself to intervene to preserve an order which they could no longer guarantee: 'I hastened to do so, I completely succeeded. I made these wretches appreciate true moral power and I was able to disentangle a horrible situation without bloodshed.' Yet, when towards 11 p.m. he and Adam left in an open carriage for the country château of Saint-Estève where they were to spend the night, 'some brigands' still tried to attack them and at one moment Adam was on the point of drawing his revolver. Such were the hazards of electioneering in the Midi in the mid-'seventies.[1]

But scenes like this were happily rare and they would do their promoters no good. Meanwhile Gambetta was a man who slept well. After a good night he rose next morning 'as fresh and as red as a rose of Provins', ready for the real fight at Marseilles, the last round of the electoral struggle against the Intransigent Radicals headed by Alfred Naquet.

In Naquet, the strange Jewish hunchback with fine eyes, a beautiful voice, and 'the hair of Samson', he had an irreconcilable foe. Early in 1875, it was true, Naquet in a meeting of the Republican Union had spoken in favour of the constitution and spoken so well that Gambetta had congratulated him and told him that if he continued to speak thus he would be indispensable. But Naquet had hoped that the Republicans would make constitutional revision a chief plank in their programme and, disappointed in this hope, he had voted against the Organic Laws, turned against Gambetta and in August begun a campaign against him particularly in the south.[2] In a long and revealing letter of 5 November defending his position, Naquet had told Scheurer-Kestner that he hated Gambetta just as he used to hate the Emperor: he was ruining the Republican

1. For a detailed account of the Cavaillon incidents taken from the *Républicain* of Vaucluse see the *R.F.* on 21 Feb.
2. See E. Pillias, *Autobiographie d'Alfred Naquet* (1939), p. 7.

cause just as Napoleon had ruined France. He professed that this hatred had nothing personal in it but that he had always thought Gambetta's policies were reckless, at one time inclining too much to the Right, at another too much to the Left, but always in a direction contrary to the needs of the political situation. For him Gambetta was a man devoid of character who thought only of his personal interests; so he believed that he had in 1870 proclaimed war to the knife not out of patriotism but to gain a hero's reputation and that he had induced the deputies of Alsace and Lorraine to resign in March 1871 'because he sensed that the Commune was coming and he wanted to go and hide himself. At the time of the Commune I thought he should have supported the movement instead of hiding himself in San Sebastian.'[1]

Naquet's campaign, supported by Louis Blanc, Madier de Montjau and others, had indeed been causing Gambetta great anxiety,[2] and he had had a further blow from the opposition of Rochefort, the celebrated journalist, who had escaped from New Caledonia whither he had been deported after the Commune. Gambetta had been one of those who had played an active part in raising funds to enable Rochefort to return to Europe and now his reward was 'a horrible letter. . . . When you see it', he wrote bitterly to Juliette Adam, 'it will show you how advantageous it is in life to render service to Vaudevillistes who have strayed into Politics.'[3] About the same time Naquet's supporters had refused to attend the banquet which was to have been held at Marseilles in Gambetta's honour.[4] They demanded an end to a policy of 'conciliation with a view to concessions which are never made';[5] and on 10 February it was by a majority of only seven votes (52 to 45) that the local electoral committee had adopted him as candidate in preference to Naquet.[6] Now, in

1. Scheurer-Kestner pp., B.N., N.a.fr. 22409, no. 123.

2. According to a police report of 12 Feb. on the eve of his departure for the south Gambetta had said to an employé of Carjat the photographer: 'Dites à votre patron . . . que je ne serai moi qu'après les élections. Dites-lui que je suis accablé d'ennuis, que j'ai plus que des ennuis, des tourments!' (A.P.P., BA/919).

3. *Lettres*, no. 264. Rochefort was now living in Geneva.

4. *The Times*, 21 Jan.

5. Kayser, *Les Grandes batailles du radicalisme*, p. 93.

6. According to *The Times* (14 Feb.) Gambetta had been asked whether in August 1870 he had not refused to take part 'in an attempt by M. Naquet, at the head of 5000 or 6000 persons to proclaim the Republic by surrounding the Palais Bourbon. . . . He replied that he never saw M. Naquet until the 7th of September . . . when he gave him a post he had called to solicit, and that he saw nothing of 5000 or 6000 men in August. M. Naquet was then sent for and repeated the charge . . . but [Gambetta] disclaimed all knowledge of such an incident. At a second meeting in the evening both of them spoke. M. Gambetta urged a policy of concord and moderation and explained his reasons for being a candidate at Lille, Bordeaux, Marseilles and Paris.

mid-February, there was to have been a public debate between the two men but once again the authorities intervened and the meeting was forbidden. None the less Gambetta campaigned indefatigably: 'I collect my troops, I fire them with enthusiasm. My meetings are forbidden, I hold a hundred.' He wanted 'to feel the pulse of public opinion' and so he took a box at the Grand Théâtre Lyrique to see one act of Rossini's *Moïse*. The news spread, a dense crowd gathered and he and his companions were applauded as they mounted the steps of the theatre. As they entered, by a strange coincidence, Pharaoh was singing 'Voilà le soleil, il paraît et tout s'incline dans la nature'. The spectators rose to their feet amid cries of 'Vive Gambetta!' and 'Vive la République!' The performance came to a halt as the actors joined the audience in incessant applause. After such an ovation Gambetta might well feel confident of victory. He sat up until 1 a.m. at his hotel discussing politics with his friends and, after a final election address to the people of Marseilles had been posted on the walls, he went to bed well satisfied. On the 19th, he told Juliette Adam, there was 'yet another meeting and another speech. In the evening another meeting of all the committees. A splendid evening.' But he added that he was exhausted and determined to leave for Nice (where he was due to attend his sister's wedding) 'in order not to die of fatigue in the midst of triumph'. From Nice he was more than thankful to take refuge once more in the Adams' hospitable villa for five days' infinitely needed rest. In the garden the mimosas were already in flower.

Polling took place on 20 February while Gambetta was still resting and in its issue of that date the *République Française* was moved to print a poem by one Gustave Mathieu entitled 'Sauvons la République!' It had the following refrain:

> Aux armes, citoyens. Votons!
> Et de la rage monarchique
> A coups de bulletins sauvons
> Sauvons, sauvons la République.

Yet in spite of poetic appeals and of all Gambetta's exhortations there were many abstentions in some even of the areas he had visited.

M. Naquet on the other hand took for his model Ledru-Rollin's attitude under Louis-Philippe. M. Gambetta rejoined by declaring that the time for Irreconcilables was past, a Republic being already established. . . . Asked whether he would agree to abide by the decisions of the Central Committee, he said he was not the man of a coterie, that he belonged to all the electors, and had no pledges to give.' Naquet's programme included a single assembly, the nationalisation of the Bank of France, mines and railways, a progressive tax on income or capital, equal rights for women in various respects, and the suppression of standing armies (Hanotaux, *op. cit.*, vol. iii, pp. 528–9).

'In the Var and Alpes-Maritimes less than 60 per cent went to the poll; in . . . Marseille and Saint-Etienne, fewer than 70 per cent',[1] but in several departments, such as the Côte d'Or, voting was heavier than in previous elections since 1870 and the hesitant had now veered to the Left. The result was in fact a crushing victory for the Republicans.

Superior organisation and propaganda had once again borne fruit and the Republicans won no fewer than 300 of the 435 seats for which deputies were elected outright.[2] As for Gambetta, the prediction that he would win in all his constituencies except at Avignon came true and there, in the Vaucluse, he had at least greatly quickened the pulse of political life.[3] As was expected, he was returned by handsome majorities in Belleville, Lille and Bordeaux, while at Marseilles his hard work was rewarded by the success which was so essential: he polled 6,357 votes compared with 1,959 cast for Naquet and 1,483 for the Legitimist candidate. At Avignon he did indeed fail, but the election of his successful Legitimist opponent, the Comte de Dumaine, mayor of Avignon since 1874, was in due course invalidated, partly as a result of the Cavaillon episode.[4] Gambetta's success and that of the Republicans in general was all the more striking in that Buffet, already defeated in the senatorial elections, was four times vanquished in those to the Chamber. That great target of Gambetta's political arrows was now no more than a wreck and he resigned on the 23rd without waiting for the second ballot or confrontation with the Chamber. His defeat was more crushing and irreparable than that of Broglie. Thiers, too, was outshone by Gambetta: Ludovic

1. Guy Chapman, *The Third Republic of France: the first phase 1871–1894* (1962), p. 162.

2. M. Viple in his *Sociologie politique de l'Allier* (p. 103) records that by 1876 the Republicans in that department had evolved a regular system of electoral organisation. First of all 'une réunion préalable de leaders, maires de villes importantes, élus cantonaux, baptisée "Comité d'organisation" décidait qu'il y avait lieu de tenir un congrès et fixait le nombre de délégués selon une proportion donnée et par communes. Ces délégués étaient désignés au cours de réunions publiques ou privées, les républicains "avancés" préférant les premières et critiquant les secondes . . . les délégués se réunissaient ensuite à la date fixée. . . . La proportion des délégués par rapport à la base ainsi que la définition de cette base . . . changèrent assez souvent. Selon . . . Pierre-Fr. Anjame . . . le règlement électoral de l'Allier prévoyait en 1876 un délégué pour 250 électeurs inscrits ou fractions de 250.' In this department, where there were more Conservative than Republican newspapers with a larger total printing, the Republicans nevertheless did better at the polls. M. Viple accounts for this by saying that whereas the Conservative papers seldom left the family the Republican ones passed from hand to hand and were read in cafés, often aloud (p. 261).

3. *The Times*, 19 Feb.

4. For the report of the commission of enquiry into the election, see *Discours*, vol. v, pp. 325–414.

Halévy noted that he had been elected 'only one poor little once, in Paris, in our *arrondissement*, and not very brilliantly'.[1]

The Republican triumph was so widely regarded as one of Gambetta over Buffet that the victor felt it incumbent on him to deliver a final election speech giving some further indication of Republican policy. It was the speech of a victor who might soon assume the role of leader of the first Republican majority in parliament, and, more than ever, the speech of a potential 'homme de gouvernement'. The place he chose for it was significant. Hitherto, since the war, except for a brief halt in September 1872 on his way to Chambéry, he had carefully avoided setting foot in Lyon, France's second capital. Now, however, he felt strong enough to revisit the 'red' city, a 'town', he said, 'that people have for five years delighted in representing as a volcano constantly smoking and ready to erupt'.[2] The speech he delivered there on 28 February (and with which he was only half content) was intended to guide and reassure opinion both at home and abroad and also to be his final shot in the election campaign, his main effort to influence the second ballot of 5 March.[3] It was a speech in which he played to an anticlerical audience by an initial diatribe against clericalism and by making the claim that the elections had been distinctly anticlerical in character, in conformity with France's domestic preoccupation and with the expectations of Europe. He then turned first to explain the peaceful and orderly character of a Republic which had renounced 'proselytism and cosmopolitanism'[4] and subsequently to expound firmly and clearly the desiderata of the Republican majority. Public opinion, he had told Léonie Léon, was satisfied, but also somewhat embarrassed by the extent of the Republican success.[5] Accordingly he warned his hearers that good fortune was still more difficult to bear than evil; they must be moderate, remain united and refrain from trying to meddle with everything at the risk of causing confusion. Finally, in order to achieve 'the union of all Frenchmen around a single flag', he made a last appeal to the Conservatives who had been let down by Buffet, and a last appeal to the errant troops of the Bonapartist

1. 'Les carnets de Ludovic Halévy', 22 Feb. 1876 (*Revue des Deux Mondes*, 15 Feb. 1937).

2. For the text of Gambetta's speech at Lyon, see *Discours*, vol. v, pp. 171–99. He sent Juliette Adam an outline of it (see *Nos amitiés*, pp. 351–3) which is preserved in her papers in the B.N. (N.a.fr. 13815, pp. 160 and 160 *bis*).

3. Letter of 24 Feb. (Fichier Charavay) and *Lettres*, no. 271 of 26 Feb. to A. Péphau.

4. 'Proselytism' he equated later in the speech with 'cette politique du second empire... qui allait chercher tantôt une querelle sur le Bas-Danube, tantôt une guerre... au Mexique... cette politique fatale... qu'on décore du nom de politique des nationalités'.

5. Letter of 26 Feb. (L.G.).

general staff to take the chance offered by the second ballot and be reconciled to democracy. The Republican majority that would shortly go to Versailles would ensure four years of calm and tranquillity; and when they had done so, thus falsifying the sinister predictions of hired criers, the Republic would be founded indeed and have the sympathy of the whole world.

The speech was received with enthusiasm by Gambetta's audience. Next day there was a banquet and in reply to a toast he drank to 'the union of all groups of the Republican party'.[1] On the following morning a crowd of 2000 gathered outside his hotel to acclaim him as he left for the station, and he could hardly get into his carriage for the press of admirers eager to shake his hand.[2] On the eve of the second ballot for the 105 seats in the Chamber yet to be filled the *République Française* exhorted the voters not to abstain and exclaimed 'anything rather than Bonapartism!'[3] On the evening of election day itself Gambetta scribbled a hasty line to Léonie Léon written 'in the middle of the furnace with 400 people in front of me fighting for the telegrams'.[4] France, he wrote, was repeating the splendid demonstration of 20 February. He was worn out but satisfied, and he told Princess Troubetskoï (with whom he had exchanged views on a number of individual candidatures) that, apart from two or three disappointments, the result of the second ballot had been much as he had foreseen.[5] In fact the Republican victory was far less striking than in February, the Left obtaining fifty-six of the vacant seats and the Right, including the Bonapartists, forty-nine. But the result of the two ballots taken together was still 'arch-Republican'. On the final reckoning 340 of the 533 deputies were Republican and 155 Conservative, while in the centre was a small but indecisive 'Plain' of thirty-five.

On the Right the Bonapartists, it was true, had not been shattered; they held ninety-four of the 155 seats, but it was a much smaller number than they had hoped for. They had suffered from divided counsels, shortage of funds had prevented them from putting many candidates into the field, and *scrutin d'arrondissement* had told against them. Perhaps, too, the incessant attacks of Gambetta and his followers had really damaged them and contributed to their defeat. The Empire would no longer be a menace to the Republic, for, although the Bonapartists could still goad the Republicans in parliament, their defeat led to 'a

1. *Discours*, vol. v, p. 198.
2. *R.F.*, 4 March.
3. *Ibid.*, leader of 5 March.
4. L.G.
5. *Lettres*, no. 3. The Princess had reopened her *salon* in the autumn.

decline that was never really arrested'.[1] Gambetta could indeed be relieved.

The country districts in Auvergne, Languedoc and the Lyonnais had swung over almost completely to the Republicans who had also made important gains in such traditionalist areas as Brittany and Anjou. There was no danger that 'the whole democracy' would fall upon their leader and rend him in their disappointment. The Republic looked secure. In the hour of victory Gambetta's thoughts turned, as they constantly did, to the mistress of whom he had seen but little during the last hectic months.[2] It was to her, he told Léonie Léon, that he owed the best of his triumphs. 'At the bottom of my heart', he added, 'I feel that it is only under your wing that I can complete and follow them through.'[3] Juliette Adam and other great ladies might still be his Egerias in society, his generous hostesses and his eager correspondents on political developments, but his mainstay to the end would be his mistress in the shadows, the delicate, nigh hypochondriacal Creole who had him under her spell.

1. Rothney, *op. cit.*, p. 230, and Appendix (pp. 321–7) for a list of the Bonapartists elected.

2. 'En vérité je ne suis pas une femme importune, si nous comptons bien je crois que nous n'avons pas passé ensemble six heures en six mois!' Léonie Léon to Gambetta, 16 March (Ass. Nat., p. 154).

3. *Lettres*, no. 275.

19

The soured fruits of victory
March–May 1876

The year 1876 marked a new stage in the history of the Third Republic and a new phase in Gambetta's career and mode of life. The main parts of the constitutional structure had come into being. 'The period of gestation' of the Republic, as Gambetta himself had put it, was over: 'It is now a question of bringing up the child, of nourishing and strengthening him; this will not be the least tough and tiring task, for we must show ourselves prepared to meet both our old adversaries and inveterate foes and also those who are impatient, foolish, vain and mischievous.'[1] The Senate and Chamber had to adjust both their mutual relationships and their relationship with the executive power personified in the Marshal-President. In addition, now that the Republicans had the majority in the Chamber, it could be expected that any new government would reflect their dominance and fulfil their policies: but how far these policies could be carried out would depend upon the balance of forces within their ranks, the attitude of the Senate, and the extent to which the President would tolerate men and manners that might be unpalatable to him.

Now that Thiers was ageing, Gambetta had more than ever been the outstanding personality among the Republicans in the recent election campaigns. He had in a sense been the father of the Senate and he had been the chief architect of the Republican victory in the Chamber. His adoring Léonie saw him as 'master of the situation by the unanimous wish of France and with the approval of Europe'.[2] He had, as a party leader, in various speeches given some indication of the relatively moderate policies which he wished to see pursued and, although he belonged to the Radical Left, he might well aspire both to secure places in any new government for members of his group, if not for himself, and to consolidate and lead the new majority in the Chamber. But these aspirations

1. *Lettres*, no. 255, of 13 Nov. to Mme Adam.
2. Letter to Gambetta, 6 March (Ass. Nat., p. 152).

were frustrated, the one because of the conservatism of the Marshal and his intimates, the other because of jealousies within the Republican ranks which were given freer rein owing to the size of the Republican majority. Gambetta had foreseen some of the difficulties. He was quickly to learn that

> It is the bright day that brings forth the adder
> And that craves wary walking.

On 8 March 1876, large but orderly crowds again gathered at the Gare St Lazare. They had come to see the newly elected senators and deputies who were about to embark on the parliamentary trains in order to hold their first formal meeting at Versailles. Gambetta left by the 12.25, 'the crowd silently making room for his passage', while Thiers departed an hour later. As Thiers passed hats were raised, but there was no cheering.[1]

The 300 Senators were to occupy the theatre in which the National Assembly had held its memorable debates, while the 533 deputies[2] were housed in a new hall especially built for them and which later served for the elections of Presidents of the Republic. There were only a few hundred yards between the two buildings, but between their occupants, as Daniel Halévy remarked, there was 'a moral abyss'.[3] Unfortunately the deputies found their new building cramped and, to begin with, acoustically deplorable so that the journalists in the Press gallery were loud in their complaints. But these defects were gradually rectified. The first days were taken up with the usual preliminaries of French parliamentary organisation such as the constitution of bureaux[4] and the election of officers. The Duc d'Audiffret Pasquier had been the last president of the National Assembly; now that he was a senator it was natural for him to be elected President of the Senate. But it was a choice that Léonie Léon had urged Gambetta to oppose. No doubt she remembered Pasquier's bitter attack on Radicalism in December 1872 and sensed that Pasquier's

1. *The Times*, 9 March.

2. 526 for metropolitan France and seven for Algeria and the colonies.

3. *La République des ducs*, p. 241; cf. Hanotaux, *Histoire de la France contemporaine*, vol. iii, p. 557: 'Le Sénat, trop voisin, a l'oeil sur sa pupille, la Chambre des députés. Elle se sent surveillée, suspecte. ... Quelle pitié de lui avoir donné, pour camarade de lit, ce Sénat chenu, en cet endroit somptueux et maussade!'

4. 'The division of the whole Chamber into a number of sections, entitled *bureaux*, for the preliminary consideration of some matters, ... is one of the oldest pieces of French procedure.' Members were at this time chosen by lot and 'from 1814 till the end of the nineteenth century it was the rule that all bills were considered in the *bureaux*, that is, in all the *bureaux*, before the Committee stage' (D. W. S. Lidderdale, *The Parliament of France*, n.d., p. 172).

influence in the Senate would be hostile to him.[1] Jules Grévy had been the first president of the Assembly; although of senatorial gravity and timber, he had preferred to remain a deputy. His election to preside over the Chamber also seemed a natural choice. But he, too, was one of those jealous elders who disliked and distrusted Gambetta. There were four vice-presidents, one of them being Lepère, a member of the Republican Union in the National Assembly and, on Gambetta's proposal, the number of secretaries was increased from six to eight. These included two members of the extreme Left who were destined to become prime ministers and to have long and chequered political careers, namely Gambetta's Marseilles friend Maurice Rouvier, and a formidable newcomer, Georges Clemenceau.

The Chamber of Deputies was an assembly in which, characteristically, lawyers well outnumbered any other profession.[2] Since it contained nearly 200 fewer members than its predecessor it should have been easier to manage and perhaps it was so far as its President was concerned. But what struck Gambetta was the number of newcomers, men who had not sat in any previous parliaments. Fewer than 200 of the total of more than 500 had been members of the National Assembly. The newcomers included some of his closest associates, men such as Spuller, Allain-Targé, Antonin Proust and Marcellin Pellet, but they were a handful in the mass of tyros. So it was that in his letter to Léonie Léon on the evening of 5 March, when the final results were still coming through, Gambetta wrote that his joy was not unmixed: 'The assembly is going to be terribly new. We shall hardly be able to count as many as twenty-five former deputies who have already spoken in debate. I shall find myself in the position of our generals during the war who did not know what to do with our young conscripts. . . . It is going to be a hard task to order and discipline all these people.'[3] He would not succeed until a major political crisis once again compelled the Republican ranks to close.

'Had the Constitution of France been as well established as our own', said a leader in *The Times*, 'it would have been the duty of the Marshal

---

1. Letters of 8 March and 13 May (Ass. Nat., pp. 153, 170).

2. According to an analysis in the *Rappel* (reproduced by *The Times* of 1 March) the 398 deputies elected on the first ballot were professionally distributed as follows: 189 'propriétaires' (these included several former prefects and sub-prefects), 85 barristers, 25 physicians, 40 manufacturers and merchants, 21 agriculturalists, 11 public officials, 10 retired officers, and 17 men of letters and journalists. M. Dogan in Marvick (ed.) *Political Decision-makers*, p. 69, puts the total number of lawyers (after the second ballot) at 192 compared with 237 elected to the much bigger National Assembly in 1871 and 202 to the Chamber in 1877.

3. L.G.

to call upon M. Gambetta to form a Cabinet.'[1] But the constitution was brand new, 'a synthesis of conflicting party demands',[2] and the Marshal had no such view of his duty. In fact, the result of the 1876 elections was eventually to bring about a violent opposition between the three powers in the state, President, Senate, and Chamber, and to upset the balance between them. Some such conflict was already foreseen even before the National Assembly had come to an end. As early as March 1874 Rémusat had recorded that the most thoughtful supporters of the government had it in mind, if a hostile Chamber were elected, to make a fight of it and sustain the struggle vigorously by legal or other means while profiting from the probable blunders of the enemy. 'This plan', he commented, 'is neither absurd nor inexcusable, but it is hazardous.'[3] From the outset, then, the position was precarious. In the words of a French constitutional historian:

> The President remained a Monarchist by conviction and tradition. He was a man of military background who stood for order, authority and discipline, a man who was chosen by a conservative Assembly to defend social order and conservative interests and who regarded himself as bound by his mandate. The Constitution had given him important powers.
>
> The Senate had a conservative majority . . . its constitutional mission was to serve as a brake or mentor . . . and to support the President of the Republic in case of conflict between him and the Chamber.
>
> The Chamber of deputies was in the hands of a Republican majority which had no serious opposition and was excited by its tremendous success and carried away by its five years' struggle to conquer power.
>
> Was it possible to conceive a more radical opposition between the three chief organs of state?[4]

Such was the background to the new struggle for power which would develop and gather momentum during the next eighteen months. Meanwhile, in his speech at Lyon, Gambetta had held out an olive branch to the President of the Republic. He had declared that the majority would support the government and not indulge in systematic opposition, and he had told MacMahon he could rest assured that the Republicans would in no way attempt to question, by reducing or modifying them, the powers he derived from 'the fundamental pact itself'. But the overture was ignored. The voting on 20 February had been a great blow to the

1. 21 April.
2. D. Thomson, *Democracy in France*, p. 100.
3. Rémusat, *Mémoires de ma vie*, vol. v, p. 491, 30 March 1874.
4. M. Deslandres, *Histoire constitutionnelle de la France*, p. 471. For a fuller and excellent summary of MacMahon's position, see Capéran, *Histoire contemporaine de la laïcité française*, vol. i, pp. 68–9.

Marshal and his entourage, obsessed as they were by the spectre of Radicalism. The stable order of the Septennate seemed in peril. To some the elections had been a trick contrived by Republican wolves in the clothing of Conservative sheep: the Marshal, they urged, should dissolve parliament even before it met and the new elections should be held under firmer guidance. But this was wild advice, and MacMahon had prudently listened to Broglie who counselled him to wait: dissolution should be deferred until the Republican Chamber committed some folly.

Buffet's position was, however, untenable after his crushing personal defeat in the elections, and, as has been seen, he had resigned on the morrow of the first ballot.[1] But there was no need for his ministers to resign too, and MacMahon asked one of them to carry on for the time being while he sought a new cabinet. This was the septuagenarian Minister of Justice and former Orleanist, Dufaure, a rough and rugged old lawyer, whose nickname was 'the boar'. He had earlier been one of Thiers's leading ministers and was one of those indispensable central figures so prominent in the history of the Third Republic. But in his negotiations for a new cabinet MacMahon did not consult Gambetta. The aristocratic Catholic world of the Marshal and his advisers was poles apart from that of Gambetta. To the Marshal, Gambetta, for all his olive branches, was still suspect as a dangerous Radical at heart. As for Gambetta, only eighteen months before, he had privately described the Marshal as 'the most worthless, incapable and imbecile of Frenchmen . . . the most insignificant of Imperial Knights'.[2] If the Chamber was certain to have a massive Republican majority, the Senate was far more Conservative. The Marshal saw no need to move an inch further to the Left than he could help. This being so, in more normal circumstances the obvious man to head a new government would have been Thiers, the power behind the Left Centre. But Thiers could not abide the Marshal, who had taken his place as President of the Republic, and would never have consented to serve under him. In default of Thiers, MacMahon fell back upon one of Thiers's leading henchmen, none other than Dufaure. On 9 March, regardless of the resolution of a meeting of Republican senators and deputies and before the Chamber itself could attempt to impose on him any directives, he announced the appointment of Dufaure as President of a Council of nine ministers, five of whom had been in the outgoing cabinet. It was a perfect example of the adage 'Plus ça change, plus c'est la même chose!' Moreover, respected and honest though he was,

1. See above, p. 279.
2. To Juliette Adam, 7 Sept. 1874 (*Lettres*, no. 206).

Dufaure was in power not because he was the man most fitted to pursue a definite policy but because he would keep others out.[1]

Of the nine, one belonged to the Right Centre, two to the Constitutional groups, four, including Dufaure himself, to the Left Centre, and one only to the Republican Left. Five were deputies, and three were senators. The ninth, Ricard, the able new Minister of the Interior, was not even a member of parliament. Not only was Gambetta himself not included but not a single portfolio went to any of his colleagues of the Republican Union. The *République Française* indignantly dubbed the new government 'a cabinet of the Left Centre of the old Assembly. . . . It is not a ministry of a majority, it is the ministry of a coterie. The time for this sort of arrangement is past.'[2] But the arrangement had been made and, what was more, it was soon apparent that it would be swallowed by most of the majority. It represented a kind of compromise between the divergent colours of Senate and Chamber 'and it manifested a determination not to let the Chamber of deputies be the arbiter of the Government, not to abdicate before the majority in the Chamber, and to pursue towards this majority a policy of independence, if not of combat'.[3] The Left Centre was happy enough that four of its members should be in the ministry and there is every indication that the leaders of the Republican Left, if not wholly content, were happy enough that Gambetta should be excluded. He himself had understandably been furious. To make a cabinet with 'such pieces', he told Léonie Léon, was both 'stupid and malevolent'. He was very angry and needed to see her to recover his calm. A day or two later he spoke of being back in opposition: 'How long will it last?'[4]

The fruits of victory were indeed hard to gather. The ministry was not the only great disappointment. Gambetta was at the same time foiled in his attempt to realise an old dream and to weld the Republicans into

1. A. Soulier, *L'Instabilité ministérielle sous la troisième République, 1870–1938* (Paris, 1939), p. 46. Dufaure's predecessors since September 1871 had held the title of Vice-President of the Council, for Thiers had at first in effect been President of the Council as well as President of the Republic.

2. Leader of 11 March. But of course the ministry was equally ill regarded by conservatives. Thus the Comte de Cumont wrote to Caillaux, a member of the outgoing cabinet: 'Quel triste cabinet, bon Dieu . . . ces médiocrités envieuses et vantardes, aussi avides du pouvoir qu'incapables d'exercer celui que nos divisions et nos malheurs ont fait tomber dans leurs mains!' (J. Caillaux, *Mes Mémoires*, I, *Ma jeunesse orgueilleuse 1863–1909*, Paris, 1942, p. 55 n.).

3. Deslandres, *op. cit.*, pp. 473–4. Dufaure presented his cabinet to the Senate as 'chosen by the President of the Republic to exercise in his name the powers conferred on him by the constitution.'

4. Letters of 9 and 14 March (L.G.).

one great party.[1] This dream he had returned to in a notable letter to Brisson on 20 October when he had expressed his belief that the elections would produce a real *governmental* majority capable of putting an end to the internal struggle of parties in parliament—'The Parties themselves will be reordered and apart from the sworn enemies of our Institutions, the numbers of whom will be very small, we shall at last see the establishment of two great parties corresponding to the two forces which divide every civilised society between them, the forces of resistance and progress'.[2] This dream of two 'great parliamentary groups, conservative and progressive, whigs and tories' was also reinvoked by the *République Française* in a leader of 28 February.

The first moves, according to Joseph Reinach, took place on the morrow of the election triumph of 20 February.[3] The upshot was that on 3 March a leader in the *République Française* proposed a full preliminary meeting of the Republicans in both houses 'in order that they might meet, get to know one another and exchange their first impressions': furthermore this general meeting, which might, it suggested, take place on 7 March, would have the advantage of approximately estimating the strength of the various groups of the Republican party and preparing a new distribution of their strength 'if occasion arises'. These proposals seemed both sensible and innocuous, but other Republican journals at once smelt a rat: the *Temps*, for example, said that such a meeting would be useless, the *Siècle* could see in it only drawbacks. The *République Française* had hastily to explain that it was not a matter of a meeting at which any binding resolutions would be taken or a matter of suppressing the existing parliamentary groups 'to which some of the newly elected members of the two Assemblies already belong, thanks to the zeal shown by some of their most active members'. In short, there was no question of 'overriding the individual opinions of the members of the meeting and of extracting from each decisions for which the time had not yet come'. What harm could there be in a preliminary exchange of ideas?[4]

This opening gambit was partly successful. After the preliminary

1. See above, pp. 28 and 74.
2. *Lettres*, no. 252.
3. 'C'étaient M. Gambetta et ses amis politiques les plus directs, M. Challemel-Lacour, M. Spuller, M. Paul Bert, M. Henri Brisson, M. Lepère qui s'étaient faits, dès le 20 février, les promoteurs de la fusion des groupes républicains' (*Discours*, vol. v, p. 201).
4. *R.F.*, 5 March. The *Siècle* (9 March) pointed out that such a proposal had once been made by Ernest Picard, but that it had been rejected by Grévy, Simon and Gambetta. Whilst agreeing that it was important that groups should not proliferate, it concluded: 'Les trois groupes que nous appellerons primordiaux, parce qu'ils ont existé dans les assemblées ... peuvent donc se perpétuer, au moins dans la chambre des députés, sans danger pour le discipline du parti républicain.'

parliamentary business the Left Centre held a meeting at the Hôtel de France while Gambetta's supporters foregathered at the Hôtel des Réservoirs, where Gambetta suggested a joint meeting of all the groups. A deputation was despatched to convey the proposal to the deputies in the Hôtel de France. There it met with objections from various people, including Jules Grévy's brother Albert, Jules Ferry, and a veteran of 1848, Leblond. In the end, however, the Left and some members of the Left Centre went round to the Hôtel des Réservoirs where they drew up a resolution which was intended to influence MacMahon in his choice of a new cabinet. It declared that the support of the majority in the Chamber would be given only to a homogeneous cabinet which was resolved to administer the country in a firmly Republican sense.

But MacMahon, as has been seen, took no notice. The Dufaure government was not at all the kind of homogeneous government generally expected. Indeed Republican doubts about its significance and intentions were sufficiently widespread for Gambetta to be able to boast to Léonie Léon three days later of having struck a good blow at 'the ministry of deception'.[1] He had succeeded in obtaining agreement to another general meeting and at it he had demanded the heads of the reactionary officials whom he and the *République Française* had repeatedly denounced ever since the government of moral order came to power in 1873.[2] Such a development had been foreseen very soon after the elections of 20 February by that shrewd and witty spectator of the political scene, Ludovic Halévy. He had noted that after the news of the Republican victory there had been a fall on the stock exchange for three successive days. When he asked his friends in the office of the *Temps* the reason why, they replied: 'The prefects are going to be changed.' This, he commented, was the basis of their policy, and 'I think it is more or less that of all the parties. Gambetta dismissed the prefects of the Empire, M. Thiers, Gambetta's prefects, M. Buffet, M. Thiers' prefects and now the great business is to lay M. Buffet's prefects low. You will see that this will come and come very rapidly!' Now that Dufaure was President of the Council,

people will shout in his ear: Change the prefects! He will at once replace a dozen or fifteen. . . . That done M. Dufaure will say, 'Well! That's been done. Are you satisfied?—Satisfied? And what about the others?—I can't dismiss them all.—But yes, yes.—But no, but no.' M. Dufaure will release another ten prefects to the circus and he will have a little respite for six weeks; but then the cries will begin again. Prefects! Prefects! Still more prefects! And

1. Letter of 12 March to Léonie Léon (L.G.).
2. He had reiterated the demand in his speech at Lyon, but added 'Je ne demande pas d'hécatombes.'

M. Dufaure who is a man of honour and courage will get angry and say: 'No, that's an end of it—that's enough. Indeed that's enough! Ah! you don't want to give our political friends the right to dispose of all the tobacconists' shops and all the little jobs of less than 1200 fr! Just wait a little!' And M. Dufaure will be neatly overthrown. And we shall see M. Léon Renault or M. Jules Simon come to power. And people will say: 'Give us the prefects of M. Dufaure.' And the whole business will begin again.[1]

The prognostication was not a mere parody. At the second general meeting, held in the salons de Lemardeley on 12 March and attended by more than 300 Republican senators and deputies, Gambetta succeeded in obtaining a resolution expressing the expectation that the cabinet would ensure that 'decidedly Republican administrators should be substituted for the officials who have hitherto combated the regime now established by the national will'.[2] On 22 March a decree relieved fourteen prefects of their posts and transferred twelve others. Further removals and transfers of prefects, sub-prefects and the holders of subordinate administrative posts followed on 14 April and 24 May,[3] and when in June, to the Republicans' fury, Buffet returned to the scene, having been elected a Life Senator in place of the deceased Minister of the Interior, four more prefects were promptly discarded as a sop to the angry Republican wolves. Moreover, six months later when Dufaure fell, it was, as Halévy had predicted, Jules Simon who succeeded him. He too, was to make the ritual sacrifice in response to fresh pressure. Early in 1877 eight prefects and fifty-one sub-prefects were replaced.

But the general meeting of 12 March was to be the last of its kind for several months. According to one observer, Paul Cambon, Gambetta's antagonism to the Dufaure ministry had had the effect not only of rallying the two Centres and the Republican Left to its support but also of scaring away a number of members of the Republican Left who had been disposed to draw nearer to Gambetta's Republican Union. (This, of course, was still the group furthest to the Left.) Moreover, Cambon suggested, some of the new deputies and senators were irritated by Gambetta's

---

1. 'Les Carnets de Ludovic Halévy' 24 Feb. 1876 (*Revue des Deux Mondes*, 15 Feb. 1937). The *R.F.* of 23 Feb. noted that the Bourse, 'qui passe, à juste titre, pour avoir des aspirations peu républicaines, a supporté le coup des élections avec mauvaise humeur sans doute, mais cette mauvaise humeur ne s'est traduite jour par une baisse de peu d'importance'; cf. 27 Feb.

2. *R.F.* 14 March. For the original draft by Brisson, see Ass. Nat., MS. 1550.

3. The *R.F.* each time declared them to be inadequate. The removal of eleven prefects and two sub-prefects in April was 'tout à fait dérisoire'; the 'mouvement administratif' of May was largely a recourse to a 'changement d'air' which deceived no one (159 sub-prefects and other officials were affected) (*R.F.*, 15 April, 29 May).

promptness in trying to bind them to a single organisation. In consequence, they fell 'like frightened flies' into the web of the more moderate Republican Left, at the heart of which, silent and motionless and eager to gobble them up, sat Gambetta's old antagonist of Bordeaux, Jules Simon. Gambetta had walked straight into a trap laid by Simon and Thiers.[1] However that might be, it was true that, as the *République Française* itself had remarked, the Republican Left and Left Centre had already begun to recruit some of the newcomers. They saw no reason to disband and merge in a larger whole at Gambetta's bidding. They were afraid that in a single whole they would be more subject to Radical pressures, while the less numerous Senators feared that they would be swamped by the deputies and lose their autonomy.[2] So Gambetta's arguments that the Republican forces were now larger and different in composition from those in the old Assembly and that the country would not understand why, when unity of purpose had brought them victory, they should begin their parliamentary career by splitting into three, fell on deaf ears. The Left Centre and Republican Left went ahead and set up their bureaux and elected their presidents on 18 and 19 March respectively. It was reasoning such as that of Jules Ferry, the newly elected President of the Republican Left and henceforward a figure of increasing importance, which prevailed:

> The real way to remain united, really united, is to stay distinct. The discipline without which the parliamentary system is at the mercy of chance or anarchy is learnt . . . only in separate groups, limited in numbers and homogeneous in composition. Negotiations between the extremes can operate only through intermediaries. Mutual sacrifices are obtained more easily in the deliberations of delegates than in full meetings. We would not, I assure you, have achieved in the last Assembly by the other method the results just consecrated by the country.[3]

Gambetta and his friends, however, would not accept this setback without protest.[4] In the view of a not unfriendly French diplomat, he

1. Cambon, *Correspondance*, vol. i, pp. 71–2. Jules Ferry later, in a letter of 19 July 1876 (*Discours et opinions de Jules Ferry*, ed. P. Robiquet, vol. ii, Paris, 1894, pp. 279–80) maintained that Gambetta was eager for 'réunions plénières' because he wanted to delay or avert the break-away from the Republican Union of the extreme Left faction who followed Louis Blanc and Naquet.

2. Freycinet, *Souvenirs, 1848–1878*, pp. 330–1.

3. Cf. the *Siècle* on 9 March: 'Mieux vaut se diviser pour se rapprocher que se confondre pour se désunir.'

4. Gambetta's irritation was clearly reflected in leaders in the *R.F.* of 20 and 21 March, e.g. the following passages: (1) 'Nous demandons seulement que l'on nous laisse nous étonner que ces efforts qui ont été tentés pour cimenter . . . cette union

was himself, because of his dominating personality, the chief obstacle to the formation of two great parties.[1] But naturally he did not see this himself. With the full approval of Léonie Léon, who perhaps had urged him on to such a course,[2] he persuaded a meeting of some seventy deputies held on the 22nd to resolve that, since the unity and cohesion of the Republican majority was the great interest of the democracy, there was no ground for forming groups. As one justification for this attitude he alleged his fear that the Conservatives or 'party of resistance' would contrive to form a majority with what remained of the Right Centre and the Left wing groups which they might succeed in dividing: 'They want to organise in the Senate and Chamber a kind of alternating game between Right and Left Centres and thus separate the Republicans from those they call Radicals. If you form distinct groups, you yourselves are putting into operation . . . just the division desired by our adversaries.'[3] Thus Gambetta was harking back to his old dread of a conjunction of the Centres and the isolation of his own group on the extreme left. He believed, moreover, that his more Conservative rivals on the Left deliberately wished to weaken his position: 'By constituting a Left Centre and a Left people have no doubt wanted to force you to constitute an Extreme Left and thus cause you to lose a large part of your strength. After that they would like to divide this Extreme Left.'[4] His speech was revealing of the mutual fears and jealousies of the victorious Republicans, but now that the other two groups had organised themselves the refusal to organise

1. Comte J. B. A. D. du Chaudordy, *La France à la suite de la guerre de 1870–1871* (1887), p. 35.
2. Letter of 21 March (Ass. Nat. p. 155).
3. *R.F.*, 24 March.
4. As was suggested by a remark of a member of one or other of the two constituted groups: 'It may be all very well for the Left Centre to amalgamate with the Left, but the country will not believe in our moderation unless there is a distinct group representing *intransigence*. If the Irreconcilables did not exist, it would be necessary to invent them' (*The Times*, 17 March). Gambetta's own awareness of the jealousies and intrigues to which he was subjected was very clearly expressed in a letter of 25 April to Léonie Léon: 'Je sens autour de moi la mauvaise volonté qui s'organise, on est un peu fatigué de mes légitimes exigences sur le travail commun, et on voudrait me faire payer cher le surcroît de pouvoir et d'influence qu'on[t] apportés dans ma situation les derniers événements' (L.G.).

aient été si mal compris, si persévéremment entravés et traversés de tant d'obstacles.' (2) 'Il est . . . étonnant de voir une majorité républicaine, nouvelle comme majorité . . . se diviser de parti pris, sans qu'aucun incident l'y ait amenée, sans savoir pourquoi ni même s'il y aura un pourquoi, en une série de minorités. C'est une nouvelle théorie des trois tronçons . . . dont M. Rouher célébra autrefois la découverte imaginaire.'

the extreme Left was an empty blow in the air, a mere thrust of vexation which could only prove to have been the skilful stroke of a knight in shining armour if the others repented or disintegrated. Neither repentance nor disintegration followed, although mutual suspicion and equivocation continued. Already Gambetta's supporters in the Senate had decided to constitute a Republican Union group in the upper house and less than three weeks later Crémieux was elected its President and Scheurer-Kestner Secretary-Treasurer.[1]

Gambetta held out for some time, but the return to politics of the 'Black Viper',[2] Buffet, who was elected in mid-June to the senatorial vacancy due to the death of Ricard, led him to change his mind. Buffet's candidature so soon after his shattering defeat had caused the greatest excitement. It had been encouraged by the Marshal's entourage, but discouraged by the cabinet. He might well have lost had not the Republicans been stupid enough to oppose him with a candidate of over eighty![3] Their blunder and Buffet's success roused the Republican majority in the Chamber to fury and dismay which was all the greater not only because they detested Buffet, but because it meant a reinforcement of the slender Conservative majority in the Senate. 'After such a blow', Gambetta wrote to Léonie Léon, 'people will feel the need to close the ranks. . . . Discipline must be imposed again on all these new recruits and as from tomorrow I am going to reconstitute the . . . Republican Union.'[4] He did so. Eighty-three deputies were present at the meeting at which the decision was taken. At a further meeting on 28 June the Union boasted over 120 members.[5] Two days earlier he had in his now customary speech at the annual Hoche commemoration publicly alluded to the need for discipline. What he feared most, he said, was majorities whose strength was such that they ceased to be reasonable.[6]

Given the recurrent tendency of France's political parties and groups to fragmentation, it could fatalistically be held that Gambetta's dream of two great parties was wholly visionary and ignored the abiding currents of her parliamentary history. Yet the attempt to weld the Republicans into a single whole was surely worth making and this had been the

---

1. *R.F.*, 24 March and 10 April. At the later meeting the three Republican groups in the Senate appointed delegates 'chargés de se concerter au nom des trois réunions'. In particular, they were to consider 'les conditions d'un accord permanent entre les groupes républicains du Sénat et ceux de la Chambre législative'.

2. Letter of 16 June to Léonie Léon (L.G.).

3. Renouard, procurator-general in the Cour de Cassation and a connection of Léon Say.

4. Letter of 16 June (L.G.).

5. *R.F.*, 19 and 30 June.

6. *Discours*, vol. v, p. 255.

moment to make it anew since he had not succeeded in 1871. In October, after seven months' experience of a divided Left he told his constituents at Belleville that he was convinced that he had been right.[1] Had he succeeded in 1876, it is indeed arguable that the crisis of 16 May 1877, which was to have such profound effects, might never have occurred and the pattern of French parliamentary life might have been permanently altered. He himself said almost as much at Amiens in June 1877.[2] Henceforward, however, only crises would produce Republican unions or Left-wing blocs. Groups would be the order of the day, groups which seldom if ever corresponded to a well-knit party, but served mainly as bucklers for vested interests and as springboards for ambitious politicians.[3]

Two steps might perhaps have facilitated Gambetta's task, but both would have been gambles and required great political courage. He might earlier, in logical progression with his growing opportunism and political caution, have gone over to the Republican Left,[4] taking with him as many of the Republican Union as would follow and leaving the doctrinaire Irreconcilables to represent the Extreme Left; and, secondly, despite his ties with Belleville and the possible charges of desertion and treachery, he might have cut off his 'tail' by electing to sit for some other city such as Lille.[5] It was not usual for deputies to change constituencies but he had already done so and March 1876 would have been a good moment to do so again: he could well have argued that it was now time for him to serve one of the other cities which had given him such a handsome majority.[6] But on 20 March it was announced that he had decided to represent Belleville and there is no knowing whether he ever seriously considered a change. The decision, though it might testify to Gambetta's generous sense of loyalty, was to cost him dear. As Ludovic Halévy noted with characteristic aptness and charm: 'A little comedy actress said to me the other day: "One always remains the wife of one's first love".'

1. *Discours*, vol. vi, p. 161.
2. *Ibid.* vol. vii, p. 64. He recalled 'la tactique si sage qu'ont adoptée, il y a trois semaines les quatre groupes de la Gauche, et qui, si elle eût été mise en pratique à Versailles après les élections du 20 février 1876, eût évité au pays des méprises, des mécomptes, et des désagréments nombreux.' A fourth group was formed in June 1876, pp. 320–1.
3. See Chastenet, *Gambetta*, p. 254.
4. Always assuming that they would welcome and accept him.
5. Bordeaux, which had welcomed him so warmly on his return to politics in June 1871, and where enthusiastic crowds had recently thronged to hear him in Feb. 1876 might have seemed an obvious choice, but it was soon to swing further Leftward, electing an Intransigent Radical, Mie, in 1877.
6. 'Of 4,892 deputies in the Third Republic only 110 changed *départements* during their careers as deputies' (M. Dogan in *Political Decision-makers*, ed. Marvick, p. 60).

The vexing thing for Gambetta is that his first love is Belleville.'[1] His election victory had been, as Juliette Adam wrote, too great. It had been exploited against him. The moderate Republicans went about saying that he was bound to be carried away by his tail: 'A member of the government representing Belleville—that would really be too alarming. It's all right for an opposition leader. Gambetta must be kept in opposition where he is admirable.'[2] Not least dismaying was the fact that Thiers himself contributed to this whispering campaign: 'Yes, a hundred times yes, he is deliberate, he is prudent, he is wise', Thiers kept telling Adam, 'but his tail! Remember he is deputy for Belleville, that he must satisfy Belleville, that he always chooses to represent Belleville and that there is a Belleville programme to fulfil. . . . If Gambetta triumphs, that programme is no longer a weapon of opposition, it is a governmental programme.'[3] The campaign was insidious and galling. By the end of April Gambetta complained to Léonie Léon that '*They* are organising around me a malevolent strike. . . . I have to deal with satisfied vanity and the help on which I was going to count will disappear on one pretext or another.'[4] The effect was understandably depressing and when he visited the Salon a few days later France's artists seemed to him as mediocre as her politicians.[5] Despite the setbacks of 1871 and the frustrations of the era of Moral Order there was something in the comment of one of the biographers most sympathetic to him: 'At this moment Gambetta did not perhaps reckon sufficiently with the resistance of men and things. Political genius requires infinite patience and fortune had not taught him this. He had succeeded in everything, even defeat', and when he met with rebuffs he exposed himself too much: 'he is unaccustomed to contrary winds; here are the reefs and rocks; he allows his ill-temper to be seen and lets his rival get across his bows (*il donne barre sur lui*)'.[6]

What a difference in a few short weeks! On 6 March Léonie had hailed her lover as master of the situation; on the 16th she could see nothing to console her politically: indeed it was difficult to see at all in the midst of the darkness in which she was 'plunged by so many accumulated sorrows'.[7] There were indeed sorrows and vexations enough for them to share. At the end of February 'La Tata', who had been a second mother to Gambetta

1. Cit. D. Halévy, *La République des ducs*, p. 248.
2. *Nos amitiés*, p. 366.
3. *Ibid.*
4. Letter of 25 April (L.G.).
5. Letter of 30 April: 'Je me suis fatigué au delà de toute mesure à regarder la médiocrité de nos beaux arts. La peinture est tout à fait digne de l'époque, sans idée, sans relief, sans grandeur. . . . La sculpture est beaucoup meilleure' (*ibid.*).
6. Deschanel, *Gambetta*, p. 195.
7. To Gambetta (Ass. Nat. p. 154).

and had managed his household for him ever since he was a student, had had a stroke while she was still at Nice after Benedetta's wedding. He was devoted to her and now it was increasingly clear that she was unlikely ever to recover sufficiently to return to Paris and resume charge of the flat in the Rue Montaigne. At the same time Léonie's delicate health, to which she often referred, gave them both cause for concern, while her dragon of a mother was more than ever a 'scourge'.[1] Gambetta in the moment of victory had held out the hope of a holiday in Italy or Holland,[2] but the hope was soon submerged by the relentless tide of politics, the politics which had recently delivered such major blows as 'the ministry of deception' and the refusal of the Republicans to unite, and such minor ones as the prosecution and condemnation of the *République Française* for an article attacking Buffet.[3] Now, in the latter part of March, politics inflamed an old problem and caused it to worry Gambetta and give him more anxiety than he allowed to appear in the *République Française* or the Chamber: 'More than ever', he wrote to Léonie Léon, 'I need Minerva's light.'[4] This problem was the problem of an amnesty. According to the report of the Pardons Commission there were still 5,496 condemned Communards, 3,609 of them people who had been deported, 240 condemned to hard labour, and 1,647 to imprisonment and solitary confinement.[5]

Various proposals for an amnesty had been presented to the National Assembly since July 1871 and Gambetta had sponsored some of them,[6] but they had never had any chance of success. The Commune was too recent, too moving and horrific a memory, and the men associated with it had been regarded with too much fear and hatred by the Right-wing majority. But now that five years had elapsed since its outbreak, now that a new era was beginning, those who sympathised with the Communards or who believed that the time had come to bury the past could hope that a Republican majority in a new parliament under a Republican constitution would take a generous view. Men like Victor Hugo and Clemenceau had repeatedly advocated an amnesty in their election campaigns and the demand for a total amnesty had been prominent in the programmes of the Irreconcilable Radicals. After parliament met,

---

1. Letter of 16 April: 'Mon coeur physique me fait un mal incessant' (Ass. Nat., p. 163).

2. *Lettres*, no. 275.

3. The original condemnation of 18 Feb. was upheld by the Cour des Appels de police correctionnelle on 17 March. The paper's manager (gérant) was condemned to one month's imprisonment and a fine of 2,000 fr.

4. Letter of 27 March (L.G.).

5. G. Bourgin, *La Guerre de 1870–1871 et la Commune* (1939), p. 425.

6. See above, p. 84; cf. Barodet's electoral programme, above p. 143.

two of its leading supporters, Victor Hugo and the elder Raspail, had on 21 March introduced Bills for a total amnesty simultaneously in the Senate and the Chamber. But one of the best known Communards in exile, Jules Vallès, knew that any immediate hope of return was vain. 'No', he wrote to a friend on 27 February,

> we shall not have the amnesty. The bourgeoisie still believe that those who fought for the Commune were raging madmen, as they have already termed Gambetta. At any rate they think that there were leaders in the orchestra of crime, men who perverted and were leaders of assassination and incendiarism. I, who followed the vanquished rising through to the last cartridge, know how little the words of those best known weighed in those days of dark despair. . . . I know that in such last hours it is the wind of the crowds which fans the flames and intoxicates (*emporte les têtes*). But the bourgeoisie does not know this.[1]

Gambetta was more understanding than Vallès's bourgeoisie. In a letter to Castelar in 1873 he had referred to 'the causes which explain but do not justify the Paris Commune'; they were 'the suspicion of a conspiratorial and royalist assembly', the morbid explosion of a patriotism which had been over-excited for too long and was finally deceived, 'the feverish agitation, which, as the result of the most terrifying disasters that could befall a great people, could possess the most balanced of men', and, finally, hunger and wretchedness, 'the ordinary counsellors of sedition'.[2] He might understand, but he was still in a dilemma. In June 1875 a police report had related that at one of his lunches, when there had been talk of amnesty, Gambetta had said that, in spite of his regrets, he could not propose such a big step to the Left Centre whose alliance was absolutely necessary. But in the first real sitting of the new Chamber he would himself raise the matter, which was his constant preoccupation. In the meantime a dossier concerning the horrors of the exiled Communards' captivity in New Caledonia would be assembled.[3] But, if this report of his intentions was true, he thought better of them when the time came. He well knew the attitude of 'the bourgeoisie' and hence of the majority in Senate and Chamber. He himself had never declared sympathy with the Commune. Least of all could he afford to appear to do so now, when he aspired to be an 'homme de gouvernement' and

1. To Hector Malot, *cit. Le Monde* 31 Aug. 1968, p. 1 of literary section. The fact that they were still inexorable was illustrated by the condemnation in October 1876 of F.-X. Raspail to eight months' imprisonment for the publication of a pamphlet entitled *Nécessité de l'amnistie* (Jonghin, *The Paris Commune*, pp. 120–1.).

2. *Lettres*, no. 161 bis.

3. A.P.P. BA/918.

when some Communard sympathisers were for the first time claiming that an amnesty was an inalienable right.[1] In his own election speeches he had studiously avoided the subject (as had the new government in their policy declaration of 14 March). Yet Spuller was one of the signatories of Raspail's motion of 21 March,[2] and others of Gambetta's friends and followers had supported alternative Bills proposed at the same time. Moreover, those who, like himself, appeared to be sitting on the fence were the targets of Rochefort, who had resumed his vitriolic journalistic role in a newly launched paper, *Les Droits de l'Homme*. It was indeed the amnesty question in the electoral period which made Rochefort bitingly coin the party label 'Opportunist' that was to become so celebrated:

> Apart from the Republicans, France thought she had only three parties: the Legitimists, the Orleanists and the Bonapartists. She was wrong. The public meetings have revealed a fourth, the party of the Opportunists. The Opportunist is the sensitive candidate who, deeply affected by the evils of civil war and full of solicitude for the families it deprived of their mainstays, declares that he is in favour of the amnesty, but that he will wait to vote for it at the 'opportune time'.... Electors take heed: *at the opportune time* is a term of parliamentary slang meaning: Never![3]

In the debate on 21 March the government had declared itself categorically opposed to an amnesty whilst ready to recommend the President of the Republic to make a generous use of his right to pardon. Urgency was voted (the government was naturally anxious to bury the matter as

1. e.g. Gabriel Deville in *Les Droits de l'Homme*, 7 March; see Joughin, *The Paris Commune in French Politics 1871–1880*, n. 101.

2. Cf. Spuller's explanation at an election meeting on 2 Feb. in Gambetta's presence: 'L'amnistie ce n'est pas une grâce que l'on accorde, un décret que l'on signe, c'est un pacte qui intervient entre le gouvernement et ceux qui profitent de l'amnistie.... De part et d'autre il faut qu'il y ait oubli, réconciliation...' (*Discours*, v, p. 57); also his letter of 18 Feb. printed in *Le Rappel* of 20 Feb., explaining his position and his support for 'l'amnistie pleine et entière, immédiate et sans restrictions'.

3. Article of 11 Feb., *cit.* A. Zévaès, *Henri Rochefort le pamphlétaire* (1946), p. 149. In Paul Verlaine's *Invectives* (Paris, 1896) there is a savage verse entitled 'Opportunistes (1874)' (no. xxxiii) which begins:

> Assez des Gambettards! Otez-moi cet objet,
> Dit le Père Duchêne, un jour qu'il enrageait.
> Tout plutôt qu'eux! Ce sont les bougres de naissance.
> Bourgeois vessards!...

It was originally part of a ten verse poem called 'Vieux Coppées' sent by Verlaine to his friend Le Pelletier in Aug. 1874: but it was not printed until the posthumous publication of the *Invectives*. It is probably the first literary reference to Gambetta's opportunism.

soon as possible) and the usual committee was set up to report on the four different motions. Gambetta could no longer keep silent. Yet if he vigorously attacked the government he would risk still further alienating the more conservative Republicans or even precipitating a ministerial crisis which no one wanted at this early stage in the life of the new parliament. In either case he might lay himself open to the charges of irresponsibility and of still being a 'Red' at heart. The articles in the *République Française* of 23 and 28 March betrayed his embarrassment. The first said that no one could contest 'that the moment has come to take a great resolution and bring about . . . a final pacification'. It could not be supposed that the question would not receive the scrupulous attention it deserved:

> The Chambers . . . know the various interests . . . that must be reconciled. The interest of society will not be sacrificed to that of humanity any more than the interest of justice to that of clemency. . . . An amnesty will be voted after ripe consideration, after a thorough study, an amnesty accepted through a deliberate agreement of the public authorities which will be a relief to all consciences and obtain the approval of France.

The second made a distinction between Paris, where an amnesty seemed a necessary act of humanity, and the provinces which were ready only for acts of pardon. So the question was very difficult. A great act of humanity was needed but there must be no rehabilitation of acts universally disapproved:

> This can be done. But how? It must be remembered that above all an amnesty is a political measure. . . . Politics has its difficulties, its duties, its obscurities, its attractions and its dangers. We are confronted by a measure that must be envisaged coolly. . . . With free enlightened and upright minds, inspired by sober and generous consciences, the solution may be found; but it is necessary to reflect and not to be in a hurry.

It was an embarrassed and laboured article indeed, as 'Minerva' frankly told her 'Monseigneur'. All the parties, she said,

> might well think it a bad or at least strange thing that you have no decided opinion on this serious subject. I think it would have been better if you had kept your irresolution to yourself and boldly told the public to have complete confidence in the decisions of the two Chambers both of which wished to combine the widest possible clemency with respect for the laws and the maintenance of order.[1]

---

1. Letter of 27 March (Ass. Nat., p. 156). A leader of 13 April in the *R.F.* took a line closer to that advocated by Léonie Léon.

Inevitably Gambetta's attitude to the amnesty was opportunist, but this did not mean that he would *never* be in favour of it. The debate on the parliamentary Commission's report on the Raspail Bill did not take place until May, since the new parliament, liking its ease no less than the old Assembly, voted itself a month's holiday from 10 April. Meanwhile the agitation for a full amnesty had increased and various Irreconcilable newspapers had been busy organising petitions. *The Times* on 6 May pointed to Gambetta's continuing dilemma. The only result of the petitioners' activities was to spread alarm, but

> The Party which promotes the Amnesty takes no thought of this result. It confounds agitation with progress. Some of its leaders, with Gambetta at their head, see very well that the Republic is endangered by these sterile agitations; but it is impossible for them to act on the ignorant and excited masses, and they are forced, in appearance at least, to make common cause with the agitators in order not to lose the direction of a whole Party. Thus ... M. Gambetta ... now ... wants an alteration, if not in the sense, at least in the consequences of the term 'Amnesty'. . . . M. Gambetta wants the men of the Commune to be divided into classes; the first ... those really recommending themselves to clemency, and so on, in order that the Assembly may proceed by partial Amnesties.[1]

This the correspondent thought a sophism, since the Marshal was ready to pardon the first category but 'this procedure is repelled, first, because the pardon is the result of a favour and not of a legal claim', and secondly because Gambetta, he believed, wanted to tell the masses that the Chambers 'have voted an amnesty, great or small, but, at any rate, an Amnesty'. In fact he was watching the extent to which the idea of a partial amnesty was gaining ground.

The debate began on 16 May; it aroused intense interest and all the galleries were full to overflowing. Ladies were predominant and the white flowers in their bonnets made one observer compare the effect to a light fall of snow.[2] Yet the speech which created the biggest stir was not pronounced by Gambetta but by Clemenceau. He claimed that rejection of an amnesty meant the exclusion not only of those who had played an active part in the Commune but of some 100,000 innocent people who had fled in fear of the savage repression, and he spurned pardon as a

1. In taking this line Gambetta was supporting a proposal put (no doubt with his connivance) by the meeting of the parliamentary committee on 7 April (see *R.F.*, 9 April). Cf. leader in *R.F.* of 12 May. It was perhaps some time in this year that Gambetta told Lord Lyons's private secretary, George Sheffield, that he was not inclined to grant a general amnesty and that he would not agree to the reestablishment of the National Guard (Newton, *Lord Lyons*, p. 351).
2. *The Times*, 17 May.

farce, because many of those recommended for pardon were not freed but merely had their sentences reduced. His arguments were interpreted by the Conservatives as evidence that an amnesty would be hailed as a justification of the Commune, and they were, as Vallès had foreseen, uttered in vain. In the words of one historian: 'Nothing said in the Chamber that day really meant anything. It was political show; there was little or no discussion of the merits of an amnesty. Everyone's mind was made up, and the measure was fought "by vote and not by speeches".'[1] Gambetta, on the watch, told Léonie Léon on the 18th that if the idea of a partial amnesty made sufficient progress he might 'plant his flag'. There would be every advantage in being able at one and the same time to give satisfaction by reassuring the timid and appeasing the legitimate aspirations of the people. He saw a gleam of hope and would tell her the next day if he decided to 'strike a blow'.[2] But the gleam was too slight. In the end he neither spoke nor voted.[3] Spuller was another of the fifty-eight deputies who abstained. The Raspail Bill was defeated by 392 to 50 and the proposals for a restricted amnesty were also decisively rejected. It was noteworthy that all the fifty who had voted for the total amnesty belonged to the Extreme Left; fifteen of the twenty-five deputies of the Seine had supported it and nearly all the others came from those southern strongholds of Radicalism, the Bouches-du-Rhône, the Rhône and the Var. Two days later the corresponding debate took place in the Senate. In fact it was no debate, but only an eloquent monologue from its sponsor, Victor Hugo. When he had finished there was silence and a voice cried: 'No one answers, because there is nothing to answer.' The vote was taken and those who supported Hugo were a mere handful. Thus the new parliament had rejected the amnesty as decisively as the old and Gambetta had sat on the fence. But it was not the end of the matter.

1. Joughin, *op cit.*, p. 113.
2. L.G. For Léonie Léon's reply see her letter of 19 May (Ass Nat., p. 172).
3. The *R.F.* came out with a leader in favour of partial amnesty on 20 May, but it was unavailing—Gambetta did vote for consideration of a Bill presented by Margue.

20

Two papers, a budget, and other problems April–November 1876

As has been said, 1876 marked a new phase in Gambetta's career. Despite the setbacks described in the previous chapter, he realised other ambitions. But these, too, brought their cares and vexations, although in the long run they enhanced his material wellbeing and his political influence. He founded a new paper and he became President of the most important committee in the Chamber, the Committee for the Budget.

One of the early acts of the Republican majority in the new Chamber was to vote for a month's holiday at Easter. In view of the scorn heaped by the Republicans on the former conservative majority for taking such long vacations, this was a measure which met with some understandable ridicule. In earlier days it would have given Gambetta much needed relief, and Léonie Léon wrote that no doubt he was dreaming of an escape from politics. But, she reminded him:

> 'You have two papers to inspire
> electors to enlighten
> diplomats to watch
> and a woman to console

statesman, remember this.'[1]

The statesman was only too well aware of the multiplicity of his tasks. Nearly a fortnight later he told his father that he had not a moment's freedom: 'The two papers, visitors, the budget, foreign policy, the elections[2] and the Devil's in them. I'm giving way beneath their weight.'[3]

Two papers and the budget. These were great new commitments and,

1. Letter of 12 April (Ass. Nat., p. 161).
2. By-elections were held in seven constituencies on 16 and 30 April. They marked a continuing swing to the Left.
3. *Lettres*, no. 276.

added to them, he had the temporary upheaval of moving house. Unfortunately the Devil seemed to have entered both the papers and the new abode; indeed Léonie later wrote that this was bewitched: 'All our misfortunes date from its purchase.'[1]

One of Gambetta's closest associates on the *République Française* was his childhood friend from Cahors, Alphonse Péphau. Péphau had become the business manager and in January 1874 he had taken over Gambetta's own rights in the title and ownership of the paper so as to leave Gambetta free to retire if and when he wished.[2] Unfortunately Péphau's ambitions for the success of his patron and his paper outran his business capacity. As the *République Française* prospered—its daily circulation had increased from 15,000 in 1872 to 18,469 in 1873[3]—and as the prospects of the definitive establishment of the Republic and of Gambetta's participation in government improved, so Péphau was eager that the paper should cut a more grandiose figure in the journalistic world. He it was who encouraged, if he did not originate, the idea that the *République Française* should sire an offspring in the shape of a *Petite République Française* to be sold for a *sou*. By June 1875 Gambetta was enthusiastic, seeing in it not only an additional means to extend his influence and to propagate Republican ideas, but also a useful weapon with which to parry the attacks of the Irreconcilables. Such a paper, he optimistically told a police agent, would bring to reason 'those members of our party who want to compromise everything by their precipitancy and their violence'.[4] The plan went ahead. According to Juliette Adam, it was one of the main topics of conversation during Gambetta's winter holiday at Les Bruyères, and it was warmly approved by Edmond Adam. Always the most upright and generous of friends to Gambetta, he saw in it a means not only of propaganda but of providing him with an income which would free him from financial worry. If the

1. Letter of 30 Sept. (Ass. Nat., p. 226): 'Imbue des légendes allemandes je crois votre . . . ensorcelé — tous nos maux datent de son acquisition.' The key word is unfortunately omitted in the typescript and as the original no longer exists it cannot be checked. It was probably 'hôtel' or a word with equivalent meaning.

2. A police report of 11 Jan. 1875 described Péphau 'le secrétaire' as 'un brave garçon, d'une intelligence médiocre et bavard à un point que l'on ne peut s'imaginer. Ce n'est pas lui qui gardera les secrets de la maison' (A.P.P. BA/918). The original statutes of the Société de la République Française had committed Gambetta to be a director for the duration of the society's existence, namely twenty years. This could prove an inconvenient tie for him and in January 1874 he had transferred his rights in the title and ownership of the paper to Péphau. He remained the paper's political and literary director, but was free to withdraw whenever he wished. 'La République Française journal de Gambetta. Extraits du Journal inédit de Scheurer-Kestner', *Etudes de Presse*, vol. xii, nos. 22–23, p. 15.

3. *Ibid.*

4. Report of June, date omitted (A.P.P., BA/918).

paper went well it could be sold at the height of its prosperity and Gambetta reap the financial reward. This plan to provide Gambetta with a larger income was alleged by Juliette to have met with Spuller's approval: 'You are right, Adam, for our friend will never make a rich marriage. . . . His love life is fixed, if not his fidelity.'[1]

The new paper was only one part of Péphau's plan. The other was a move from the comparatively modest premises which the *République Française* shared with other papers in the rue du Croissant to a larger and grander building in the rue Chaussée d'Antin. There, no. 53, the former Hôtel Benoist Chamfy, latterly occupied by Clément Duvernois, an able journalist and minister in the Palikao government at the end of the Second Empire, fell vacant in the autumn of 1875. Its purchase for the *République Française* was said to have been negotiated by Gambetta's old friend Clément Laurier for a price variously stated as 360,000, 544,000 and 550,000 francs, payable in five annual sums. The larger premises had several advantages. They bore a prestige value and demonstrated that the paper had 'arrived'.[2] There was room to receive large numbers of people, there was room for the production of the *Petite République* as well as the original paper, and there was room, too, for a small flat at the back for Gambetta, who by the middle of May had decided to leave the rue Montaigne now that 'la Tata' could no longer look after him. The offices of the *République Française* were transferred to the new premises on 9 April and Péphau celebrated the move by a slight change in the layout of the paper which appeared in its new guise on 12 April.

A little over a year later Gambetta in his new abode was the subject of an article in a series entitled 'Celebrities at Home' run by an English paper called *The World*. 'He lives very simply still', wrote the reporter,

> . . . although he has his own rooms, he may more accurately be said to share those appropriated to his infant charge. He is with his paper all the earlier part of the day, and he returns to it again after he has taken his walks abroad. The great *salle de rédaction* is virtually his drawing-room, a use for which it seems to have been originally designed. Here, at one vast table, sit the writers . . . associated with him. . . . The ex-Dictator's room . . . seems to be little better than a former passage. . . . It is almost as sparsely furnished as the cell of one of the monkish transcribers of the Middle Ages—a writing-table, a case of books, a chair for himself, a chair for a visitor, and that is all. . . . He has no litter of pamphlets, books, manuscripts about him, although he receives some dozens of them by every post. You see the sheet of paper on which he is now writing, his pen and the inkstand; but all that he has written or read . . . is

1. *Nos amitiés*, p. 310. This is one of Mme Adam's many more or less veiled and often barbed references to Léonie Léon.
2. P. Albert, *Colloque Gambetta*, 13 May 1972.

neatly stowed away, either here or in an adjoining room, with as much precision as if it belonged to the *dossiers* of the department of police.[1]

In the meantime, however, the move to these new premises had caused Gambetta much vexation. Péphau's grandiose plans had led to discontent, disruption and financial crisis. Having underestimated the costs of the new installation he found it necessary to economise and to reduce salaries. Gambetta, immersed in the elections and their aftermath, left everything to him, but Gambetta's old friends, Spuller, Challemel-Lacour and Allain-Targé increasingly resented Péphau's control. They mistrusted his financial capacity; they had doubts about the wisdom of founding the *Petite République* and, when Gambetta consulted them less and less and ignored their representations, they resigned.[2] For some time the paper was run by Gustave Isambert, who had taken over from Spuller as chief editor when the latter was electioneering.[3]

This breach with three of his most trusted lieutenants was surely one of the reasons why Gambetta smoked too much and was unusually irritable during the spring and summer of 1876.[4] But it was not the only reason. No doubt he missed 'La Tata' and the savoury ragouts and cassoulets of beans and smoked goose which she could cook so well. But still more important perhaps was the fact that Léonie Léon, too, disapproved of the move to the Chaussée d'Antin and took him to task: 'May not this socialite's mansion (hôtel de petit-maître) lessen the effects of that dignified simplicity which so well suited the great politician, the statesman wholly devoted to the triumph of a great cause? Luxury for the encouragement of arts and industry is a duty only for him who is actually in power.'

1. *The World*, 4 July 1877.
2. For Spuller's unhappiness about the situation, see his letters of 17 March to Ranc (Ranc, *Souvenirs-Correspondance*, pp. 307–11). Police reports make it clear that the breach between him and Gambetta occurred at the end of March or beginning of April. It is not clear whether the resignations all took place at the same time. Another police report of 11 Oct. alleged that the new premises had cost 800,000 fr, 'sur lesquels le Crédit Foncier avait avancé 500,000 f.; pour parfaire aux 300,000 f. restant à payer, M. Gambetta a emprunté cette somme à M. Soubeyran'. I am indebted to Mr John Parsons for this reference (BA/1272) but I have not found corroboration elsewhere. On the face of it, it would seem very improbable that Gambetta borrowed from a man such as Soubeyran who was a well-known Bonapartist.
3. There must have been some further rearrangement of duties. Auguste Laugel on 12 May noted that Antonin Proust was now writing the articles on foreign affairs ('Le Maréchal de MacMahon et le 16 mai', *Revue de Paris*, 1 Aug. 1926, p. 521).
4. Millaud, *Le Journal d'un parlementaire*, vol. ii, p. 13; a police report as late as 11 Oct. 1876 spoke of Gambetta's 'état d'irritation nerveuse' (A.P.P., BA/919). An additional vexation in June was the accusation brought against his friend and colleague Maurice Rouvier, the future prime minister, of having been guilty of 'obscénités devant des petites filles'.

Having written thus, she spent an uneasy day fearing the thunderbolts of Gambetta's reaction. But her 'sublime master' apparently reassured her, and she explained that she was not against the installation itself, whose motives she understood and approved, but against its rather garish luxury, 'which makes you prosaically enter the common rut of all successful people. Thus you provide evidence—quite contrary to the truth as I know well—that your relative simplicity of life was not the simplicity of principle, example or taste, but derived merely from the impossibility of living otherwise.'[1] Yet fundamentally she disapproved. Six weeks later she told Gambetta that the new acquisition had brought nothing but vexations and that it tied him down and made him melancholy. Still later she called it a vampire of a building.[2]

She was right. One day Péphau had come to Gambetta, who suspected nothing, and told him that he had run into financial difficulties. Gambetta, angry and anxious, asked his friend Scheurer-Kestner to investigate. He did so and found 'complete disorder': a sum of 75,000 francs was due in three days and a similar sum at the end of the month.[3] If they were not paid, the *République Française* would go bankrupt. Meanwhile the *Petite République*, announced as 'a political and literary morning paper' to be sold for five centimes, had been launched on 13 April, the day on which martial law had finally ended.[4] One of its initial attractions advertised was a serial by Erckmann-Chatrian on the Suez Canal. The paper was well laid out and varied in content, but its launching was a gamble and an additional liability for it was published at a loss during the first two years.[5] Scheurer-Kestner's immediate reaction was to advise Gambetta to obtain a loan from his wealthy and faithful Swiss friend and admirer, the gas king, Dubochet. But Gambetta would have none of it: 'Never', he cried, 'I don't want to be the prisoner of any financier, not even Dubochet! I should prefer ruin provided my honour was safe.' In this dilemma Scheurer-Kestner went to see Edmond Adam who, as former secretary-general of the Comptoir d'Escompte, had many financial connections.

---

1. Letters of 30 April and 2 May (Ass. Nat., pp. 166 and 167).
2. Letters of 30 June and 18 Oct. (Ass. Nat., pp. 188–9 and 234).
3. He does not make clear which month. It was either July or August. Cf. letter of 29 July to Léonie Léon (L.G.).
4. Unfortunately the copies preserved in the Bibliothèque Nationale begin only in January 1878. The *Illustrated London News* (8 April 1876) forecast that one immediate consequence of the ending of martial law would be 'the appearance of numerous cheap Republican journals in Paris'.
5. Scheurer-Kestner (*Etudes de Presse, art. cit.*, p. 15) wrote: '*La Petite République Française* avait mangé plus de 60,000 francs la première année, davantage la seconde.' But further on (p. 22) he said that the paper 'ne tarda pas à entrer dans une ère de prospérité extraordinaire'. The chief editor was Dionys Ordinaire.

His reaction was the same: 'ask Dubochet'; and, when Scheurer-Kestner told him of Gambetta's response, he decided to ignore it and ask him himself. Dubochet at once agreed to provide the loan, but, hurt that Gambetta had not himself approached him, stipulated that it should be repaid in weekly instalments. When Gambetta refused to allow any further appeals to Dubochet, Adam and Scheurer-Kestner had to take other urgent measures to restore solvency.

They decided to separate the affairs of the two papers. Adam agreed to raise the 300,000 francs estimated as necessary to provide additional capital for the little one. Scheurer-Kestner, for his part, made himself responsible for mobilising a similar sum to bolster up the big one. Had Gambetta been willing to appeal to the financial world, he would, wrote Scheurer-Kestner in his reminiscences, 'have got a million the next day and he well knew it'; but he did not share 'the modern journalists' indifference to the purity of the source to which the organs which offer them hospitality owe their existence. Gambetta had retained the principles and rigidities of the "vieux" so much rejected by the new Radicals of today.'[1] The money was, however, eventually raised. Among those who came to the aid of the *Petite République* were Léon de Roussey, Paul Bert, Paul Sandrique, Paul Ruiz, Dubochet's niece Mme Arnaud de l'Ariège, her brother Jules Guichard, Maurice Bixio, President of the Compagnie générale des voitures, and a young man called Eugène Etienne who was to make a great name in colonial affairs towards the end of the century. Among those who came to the aid of the *République Française* itself there were once again a number of Alsatians, among whom Scheurer-Kestner in his memoirs singled out Charles Blech and Hickel, a former Mulhouse lawyer, who also gave legal advice. By the end of August all was ready for the foundation of a joint stock company or Société anonyme with a capital of 300,000 francs to take over the *Petite République*. Henri Villain, a rich sugar manufacturer and deputy for the Aisne since 1871,[2] who was to be registered as the founder, wrote on 30 August to Gambetta that he and some friends, namely Camille Depret,[3] E. Adam, Cernuschi, Ruiz, Blech, Scheurer-Kestner, Fieuzal, de Roussey, A. Péphau, Girard, Steinbach and Engel had come together with the requisite money to purchase the title to the paper and all its equipment as well as to pay its debts and cover its anticipated expenses. They invited him to become the political director and agreed that he alone should choose the editorial staff. At the same time Villain informed him that they had decided to create a number of additional shares (*actions d'apport*) equal to the capital

1. Scheurer-Kestner (*Etudes de Presse, art. cit.*, p. 17).
2. In Feb. 1876 he had been elected unopposed at Saint-Quentin.
3. See *Lettres*, no. 284.

shares (*actions de capital*) and carrying the same rights. 'These "actions d'apport" will be allotted to you, both to give you a preponderant influence in the association and so to strengthen the paper's unity of political outlook, and also as a proper return for the strength you will give us by your aid.'[1] Thus did his friends generously provide for Gambetta's material wellbeing. Such fortune as he had in his latter years derived from the *Petite République*. By October it was selling 60,000 copies and Gambetta with characteristic optimism looked forward to a circulation of 100,000.[2] This optimism was to be justified during the great crisis of the Seize Mai in the following year when this figure was almost certainly attained and exceeded.[3]

At the same time Scheurer-Kestner insisted, in spite of Gambetta's reluctance, that the original company of the *République Française* should be converted into a limited liability company (*Société anonyme*), since it was the only way in which his responsibility could be safeguarded.[4] This transformation was effected in June 1877. Of the 850 shares of 1000 francs each, 300 were held by Gambetta in addition to those he held originally. All these transactions had two or three other consequences of some significance. One that was important for personal relations was the removal of Péphau and the return to the fold of Spuller, Challemel-Lacour and Allain-Targé. Another that was vexatious and protracted was a lawsuit brought against the *République Française* by one of its shareholders, Puthod, former prefect of the Ain, who had originally in 1871 been asked to raise money for it in Alsace.[5] He claimed that the directors had no right to sell the paper to a new society and in November he won his case before the Commercial Tribunal of the Seine.[6] He had to be bought out. Meanwhile the affair was vexatiously reported in the *Figaro* and elsewhere in

1. For the text of Villain's and Gambetta's letters, see Scheurer-Kestner (*Etudes de Presse, art. cit.*, pp. 23–4). They were also printed in *Le Figaro* 18 Oct. 1876. The nominal capital was 600,000 fr, of which 300,000 was paid up. The shares were of 5000 francs each.

2. *Lettres*, no. 289. A minor return was the use of a brougham, 'hired from the Paris General Cab Company at a cost of £26 a month' (Vizetelly, *Republican France*, p. 212).

3. I am indebted to M. Pierre Albert for this information. At the beginning of 1878 the paper itself advertised its circulation for Nov. and Dec. 1877 as having been 125,000 and 140,000 respectively.

4. *Ibid.*, *Etudes de Presse, art. cit.*, p. 20. A *société anonyme* required government authorisation, whereas for a *société en commandite par actions* this was unnecessary.

5. See above p. 56. Scheurer-Kestner described him as an 'avocat sans causes, journaliste sans talent' (*Etudes de Presse, art. cit.*, p. 19).

6. Gambetta's dismay was reflected in a letter of 29 Nov. to Léonie Léon (L.G.): 'Là aussi je dois avoir une belle collection d'amis qui ont trouvé piquant de fausser toutes les lois pour m'atteindre. Il ne me reste plus qu'à porter mon recours contre les juges d'appel, ce qui me prépare une belle déconvenue.'

such a way as to implicate Gambetta as well as Péphau.[1] At the end of the year Léonie feared that the unhappy business had caused Gambetta some loss of prestige,[2] but it is doubtful whether the charges and the publicity did him any permanent harm. By then a new parliamentary session had begun and within a short time the seasonal clouds of ministerial crisis began to loom on the horizon. These were darkened among other things by certain issues relating to the budget.

'You have a budget to calculate', Léonie Léon had written in April. Gambetta was neither President of the Council nor President of the Chamber—'He is no doubt young and can wait', remarked *The Times*[3]— but he could scarcely be denied a key position in the Chamber. On 4 April, though only by a narrow margin of sixteen votes to thirteen, he had been elected President of the Chamber's Budget Committee. It was his first responsible office since February 1871. At first sight the choice was a surprising one. As Hanotaux wrote, 'people were not yet accustomed to see the practical man and calculator . . . in the tribune. M. Gambetta was evidently anxious to destroy the legend in which he had been imprisoned by persistent hostile propaganda.'[4] To *The Times* the choice seemed to be 'an assurance that, if he continues to justify the hopes his career has raised, his time will not be long deferred'.[5] The post was indeed important and arduous. The Committee of thirty-three members, three from each of the Chamber's eleven bureaux and nearly all from the Left, divided its labours into two parts. It had the routine task of examining the cautious and temporising finance Bill for 1877 already presented to the Chamber by the Finance Minister, Léon Say.[6] For this purpose it was split up into five sub-committees which examined and reported on the various departmental estimates which were divided into five groups.[7] This was labour

1. *Le Figaro* 18 Nov., p. 3: 'Plusieurs commanditaires . . . à la tête . . . M. Puthod . . . protestent contre l'acquisition de l'hôtel. . . . Ils ajoutent que l'hôtel doit être payé, non par la caisse de la Société, mais par MM. Péphau et Gambetta qui l'habitent, et qui ont usé, disent-ils, du crédit et des fonds de la Société pour leur faire avantage personnel'; cf. *l'Univers* 19 Oct., *Le Pays* 20 Oct., *Lettres*, no. 289.

2. Letter of 20 Dec. (Ass. Nat., p. 252).

3. Leader of 21 April.

4. *Histoire de la France contemporaine*, vol. iii, p. 577.

5. *The Times*, 21 April.

6. 'Aucun impôt n'est aggravé, mais aucune réforme n'est proposée', said the preamble to the Bill (Hanotaux, *op. cit.*, vol. iii, p. 577). For this reason the budget had been severely criticised by the R.F. (24 March, p. 3): 'Non seulement l'étude du budget . . . montre qu'il n'y a . . . aucune initiative féconde, mais elle prouve aussi qu'il ne se préoccupe nullement du grand but que les nouvelles Chambres doivent avoir en vue, c'est à dire le dégrèvement des impôts, l'atténuation de la cherté.'

7. Finance; the Interior, Algeria and Foreign Affairs; War and Navy; Justice, Public Worship and Fine Arts; Public Works, Agriculture and Commerce.

enough, but in addition, it set up a special committee to report on the whole subject of tax reform. Gambetta, who drafted the report, was to claim that no such comprehensive survey had been made since 1791. Such a survey was indeed overdue. As government expenditure had increased earlier in the century the tendency had been to meet it by additional indirect taxation because this was more elastic than the old system of direct taxes and because, before 1848, those who paid direct taxes and qualified for the vote had no wish to have their own contributions increased or to see the electorate enlarged. The result was that by the 1870s the indirect taxes had become more onerous than the direct which had not been adjusted to social changes and so left certain categories of the community untouched. To obtain a radical reform from a French parliament would require decades, not one or two sessions. But it was Gambetta's great merit, one seldom mentioned, to have been the first President of the Budget Committee to point to the need and at the same time to make specific proposals for meeting it.

The Budget Commission was thus considerably more influential than a Select Committee of the House of Commons. To it the budgets of the spending departments were referred and its recommendations concerning expenditure and the means of raising revenue could have a considerable influence upon both government and Chamber. Furthermore the President of the Committee must sooner or later come into direct relationship both with ministers and with the President of the Republic. Moreover, later on, to critics looking back like Jules Richard, the Bonapartist journalist, or to the Catholic Minister of the Interior, Marcère, who was before long to clash with him, Gambetta in his new role was more than just the holder of the purse strings, the President of a key committee in parliament. He appeared, in Richard's words, to be 'the master of a government beside the government'. He made his position

a kind of fortress from which he dominates and snipes at the executive power. He peoples the higher administrative posts with his creatures; no transaction is definitive unless it has his agreement; he regulates the departments of war, the navy and public works. All the administrators come to him in the morning clicking their heels, like sergeant-majors reporting to the Colonel.[1]

Gambetta's covert reign, his notorious exercise of what after 1877 came to be known as 'occult power' (*le pouvoir occulte*) seemed to them to have already begun.

Gambetta set about learning his fresh duties with characteristic energy

---

1. Richard, *Le Bonapartisme sous la république*, p. 293, cf. Marcère *Histoire de la République de 1876 à 1879*, vol. i, pp. 89–90.

and enthusiasm.[1] Finance was no new subject to him. In an essay on Gambetta's reading Joseph Reinach printed a whole series of notes on the subject taken 'during his years of political apprenticeship'.[2] In addition to jottings on the mechanics of credit and the stock exchange, they included a methodical analysis of the principles of public finance and varieties of taxation and they showed that Gambetta had early come to the view that indirect taxes bore more hardly on the poor than on the rich and that a gently progressive income tax was preferable to a tax on capital. But since the war his main preoccupations had been elsewhere. He still had much to learn and in addressing himself to his new task he once again showed the remarkable powers of rapid assimilation which are such an asset to the politician who possesses them. In particular, if Juliette Adam is to be believed, he sought advice and clarification from his old friend Edmond Adam, who had throughout been a member of the Budget Committee of the National Assembly. He visited him nearly every day before going to the offices of the *République Française*: he harried him with questions: 'Mon petit, what do you think of this, what do you think of that?' and together they went through the fifty volumes of the last fifty budgets one by one.[3] But these new duties were exacting as well as absorbing, for he was President of the sub-committee on the army and navy as well as the leading member of the special committee on tax reform. By June he was overworked and depressed, had pains in the neck and was being urged by Léonie to see the doctor and take eau de Carmes.[4] A month later she was telling him that his preoccupation with the Budget was one of the reasons for the lack of cohesion of the Left-wing groups on whom he had been unable to keep sufficient watch.[5] She was nearer the mark than the exiled Empress Eugénie who had taken Gambetta's election as President of the Budget Committee as proof that he was in complete control of the majority in the Chamber.[6]

In his important letter of October 1875 to Henri Brisson, Gambetta had briefly outlined the policies to be pursued by the Republican majority whose return he had envisaged at the general election. At this time he had

---

1. 'Combien votre enthousiasme budgétaire me ravit!', wrote Léonie Léon on 5 May. 'Aimez-les, ces chiffres, scrutez les jusqu'aux profondeurs de leurs sources; ils sont au total . . . la base de la réhabilitation de la France qui est votre but, votre devoir, votre mission' (Ass. Nat., p. 168).

2. Reinach, *La Vie politique de Gambetta*, pp. 173–91. The notes are not dated, but were presumably written in the 1860s. Ass. Nat., MS 1673 is an analysis in Gambetta's hand of P. J. Proudhon's *La théorie de l'impôt*.

3. *Nos amitiés*, p. 361.

4. Letters of 7, 10 and 15 June (Ass. Nat., pp. 180–1).

5. Letter of 8 July (*ibid.*, p. 193).

6. Empress Eugénie, *Lettres familières* (1935), vol. ii, p. 58.

mentioned three great objectives, the modification of the finance laws in a liberal democratic sense, the completion of France's military structure, and the inauguration at last of a system of national education. In subsequent speeches during the election campaign he had sometimes enlarged upon or added to this programme. He had in addition demanded the liberties of the Press, meeting and association, and the restoration to municipalities of the right to elect their mayors, and he had renewed the demand for separation of Church and State as well as of Church and school. But he had also referred again to 'the better distribution of the financial and economic strength of the country',[1] and at Bordeaux he had very incidentally mentioned an income tax.[2] These references, however, had been cursory and uninformative. It was not until April that two successive numbers of the *République Française* published a memorandum which gave some indication of the content of the financial and economic, even social, reforms Gambetta and his friends had in mind.[3] It was the work of the man who, since its foundation, had been the paper's correspondent on all questions concerning social economy, the budget, taxation, public works and other kindred subjects. It had been read to a recent gathering of representatives of industry called to discuss measures which might be submitted to the Chamber.[4] After beginning with a defence of the *République Française* for having hitherto treated political questions before all others, it went on to say that now it would be possible to demand the immediate introduction of a number of easily applicable social reforms. These fell into three categories: those relating to the preservation of the worker from destitution; those concerned with the relations of capital and labour; and those relating to a reduction in the cost of living. So far as the first category was concerned, children needed the protection of a vast network of primary schools, adolescents of a network of vocational schools, adults the help of mutual aid societies, savings banks and other forms of banking (*banques de prêt sur nantissement*), and an accident insurance fund.

1. Speech at Lille, *Discours*, vol. i, p. 72.
2. *Ibid.*, p. 122.
3. 7 and 8 April.
4. Its author, either Gustave Hubbard or Allain-Targé (accounts differ as to who was the *R.F*'s principal contributor on these problems), said that he had beside him M. Paul Lanjalley who had been in direct touch with members of the audience. According to the *R.F.* of 28 Sept., when this programme was put forward, 'deux de nos amis ont-ils convoqué des représentants des chambres syndicales ouvrières, des membres des associations de production et de consommation, des ouvriers membres du conseil des prud'hommes, afin de leur soumettre leurs propres idées'. Perhaps this was the gathering referred to. A number of the questions included in the programme were discussed later in the Workers' Congress of October 1876, see below p. 323.

Many of these institutions existed already but they needed to be improved. The statutes of mutual aid societies needed to be scrutinised by an actuary and unemployment funds should be created. The savings bank system should be reformed on English lines with a central treasury able to make use of every post office. Pawnshops should be amalgamated in such a way as to provide the basis of a 'great popular bank which would be for the poor what the Bank of France is for the rich'. Accident and superannuation funds were new and their advantages needed to be publicised. Finally, the legislation governing conciliation boards in industry needed reform: the numbers and powers of the boards should be increased: the railway companies should come within their purview: their members should be paid and the conditions of election should be broadened.[1] The writer's proposals for his second category were much briefer, although they were important. They referred simply to the rights of meeting and association and the need to abolish articles 1 and 2 of the Le Chapelier law of 1791 and articles 291–294 of the Penal Code.[2]

It was the last section of the memorandum which dealt specifically with financial questions. The National Assembly had raised the additional revenue required to meet the increased debt charge, while other expenses resulting from the war had been raised almost entirely by indirect taxation. The author urged the reduction of indirect taxation and of the cost of living by the introduction of an income tax and economies in the organisation of the public services. In his view the advent of railways and the telegraph had rendered many of these superfluous: 'France voluntarily remains in the condition of an ill-equipped manufacturer who uses old machines and can only produce at a very high cost.' He advocated the revision of the law of 1853 on officials' pensions. Finally, he made an onslaught on the excessive power of the railway companies.[3] The methods of granting credits for public works, in particular railways, should be revised. As things were, the railway companies had effected no reduction

1. The Chamber passed a Bill to allow conciliation boards to choose their Presidents and Vice-Presidents, but to the indignation of the R.F., it was rejected by the Senate in Feb. 1877.

2. Article 1 of the Le Chapelier law abolished corporations of 'citoyens du même état et profession' and forbad their reestablishment, Article 2 forbade such citizens, 'les entrepreneurs, . . . ouvriers et compagnons d'un art quelconque' to meet and elect officers, keep registers or 'prendre des arrêtés ou délibérations, former des règlements sur leurs prétendus intérêts communs'. Articles 291–4 of the Penal Code dealt with unlawful associations or assemblies. In particular, Article 291 laid down that no association of more than twenty persons might be formed without the government's consent.

3. The R.F. printed many articles on this subject, see e.g. its attack on 15 March 1877 on the 'incroyables prétentions des Grandes Compagnies' which it denounced as constituting a 'féodalité financière'.

in freight costs, while the canals had been forced into a position in which they were unable to provide healthy competition. Nearly all the points in small print in this memorandum were a sort of curtain raiser to a series of leaders on the problems of the 1877 budget which singled out three measures for increasing revenue, namely the revision of the land tax, an income tax (of which Gambetta had long been a protagonist)[1] and the removal of a number of small indirect taxes. They echoed the memorandum in suggesting a reform of administrative boundaries and services and they urged the implementation in large part of a report on financial administration originally tabled by the Comte de la Monneraye in 1872. They referred also to the English system of income tax and demonstrated how its five schedules might be adjusted to French practice and they pertinently analysed the defects of the French system of direct taxes: this did not keep pace with the increases in movable wealth: it ignored the principle of proportionality; it was concerned only with gross and not net production; it was cumbrous and therefore costly in so far as concerned the allocation and collection of taxes; and it left untouched 'a considerable number of taxpayers such as State rentiers and pensioners, public servants, speculators, artists and those pursuing liberal professions. All these people have appreciable incomes without corresponding obligations.'[2]

Many of these points, in particular those relating to income tax, were to be taken up by Gambetta when he presented his sub-committee's proposals for financial reform to the whole Budget Committee in October. He had abandoned his earlier idea of a progressive tax, and it has been said by a French financial historian that what he and his colleagues now envisaged would better be described as a tax on income than an income tax, since it was neither global nor progressive.[3] What they proposed was to replace the four traditional direct taxes by a tax with five schedules on English lines; the revenue from this, they calculated, would be sufficient to permit the abolition of a number of indirect taxes. But many financial and business interests were strongly conservative and Léon Say, the Minister of Finance, acted as their champion in strenuously opposing the idea of any radical reform of the tax structure. Thus,

---

1. See above, p. 85.
2. Leaders of 18 and 29 April, article of 30 May (cf. also *The Times*, leader of 21 April). An article of 24 April on the forthcoming session of the General Councils urged that they should consider problems relating to taxation, such as the revision of the land register (*cadastre*) and an income tax as well as such practical matters as the building of new schools or enlargement of existing ones and the provision of public libraries; cf. also leader of 22 Aug.
3. M. Marion, *Histoire financière de la France depuis 1715*, vol. vi (1931), p. 5.

though Gambetta's was a notable document and though to Léonie Léon he seemed 'a great Colbert' whose work showed 'a clarity and elegance of style rare in this kind of thing',[1] it had little practical effect. No doubt, realising the opposition his proposals might encounter, he had himself said that for the moment he and his colleagues wished only to put forward general views and to point the way for their successors.[2] In consequence, although the report was adopted by the Budget Committee as a whole, despite Say's hostility, the Committee did not present it to the Chamber. There attention would be focused on the reductions made by the Committee in certain specific credits and on the conflict with the Senate to which these speedily gave rise.[3] But caution over general fiscal reform and constitutional conflict over particular financial credits did not prevent some of the measures advocated by the *République Française* from being adopted at least in part. Thus the Budget Committee increased the credits for education by seven million francs, nearly four of them for the much needed improvement of primary education,[4] and in March the Chamber voted in favour of the purchase by the State of the lines run by two lesser railway companies which were barely solvent.

Long before then, however, a number of other thorny problems had begun to rear themselves during the summer session. The constitutional tensions grew more acute and the existence of the cabinet looked more precarious. At the same time Gambetta himself came under fresh fire from the Irreconcilable Left.

Even before the rejection of the amnesty Bills in May the further question had been raised whether the time had not come to stop the continuing arrest and prosecution of persons still suspected of having been implicated in the Commune. At the end of the month a deputy named Gatineau had introduced a Bill to stay all further prosecutions. Once again Spuller was a sponsor, and once again—this was the time of the rift between them—Gambetta did not commit himself. The Bill was referred to the committee on legislation and the debate on the Committee's report, which was not tabled until the end of July, was postponed until the winter session. But the Government had meanwhile expressed its own desire to

---

1. Letter of 15 Oct. (Ass. Nat., p. 233). For the text of the report see *R.F.*, 16 Oct. and *Discours*, vol. vi, pp. 365–401.

2. A particular reason for Gambetta's restraint may well have been his reluctance at such a juncture to have an open brush with Thiers. When Etienne of the *Neue Freie Presse* asked him if he thought he could get his proposals through he had replied 'Nous verrons' and said that he had a powerful opponent who must be reckoned with. He had recently had a letter from Thiers at Cannes saying: 'My dear Gambetta, I shall come home in time to oppose your dreadful tax bill' (*Neue Freie Presse*, 19 Nov.).

3. See below, pp. 385–7.

4. The total sum was more than double that voted in 1869 (*R.F.* leader, 4 Aug.).

prevent people from continuing to live in fear of arrest and spoken of putting forward its own measure. Unable, however, to agree upon a draft, it adopted a different procedure and induced the President of the Republic to write to the Minister of War on 27 June enjoining upon him extreme caution in making further arrests and the maximum indulgence consistent with the maintenance of principles. The sentiments were unexceptionable, but the procedure came in for Radical criticism as an encroachment by the executive on the preserves of the legislature[1] and Benjamin Raspail promptly gave notice of an interpellation. This was to have been debated on 3 July and it was highly embarrassing to Gambetta. The last thing he wanted was the overthrow of the Dufaure cabinet and the crisis which might ensue and for which the Right was believed to be waiting. The Dufaure cabinet would, as someone said, be 'an embarrassing corpse'.[2] 'We must find a diversion', Gambetta told Léonie Léon on the 2nd; 'I believe I have one, the affair of the Rue des Postes; I am collecting the evidence and I shall raise the question tomorrow.'[3]

Once more he proved himself a masterly player of the parliamentary game. He raised the question and the Left were diverted and in full cry on an anticlerical witch-hunt. The 'affaire de la rue des Postes' was slight enough. In a geometry examination at the Ecole Polytechnique it had been discovered that a number of pupils knew the question in advance. It was alleged that it had been revealed by a teacher at the Polytechnic who was also attached to the Jesuit school in the rue des Postes. Gambetta deployed all his eloquence in depicting the horror of the situation, the emotion it had caused, the effect on candidates and their families, the reflection on the honour of State education, and the fresh anxiety which public opinion must feel concerning 'the favours accorded to certain institutions'. He demanded a full enquiry.[4] Turmoil ensued, especially when, in a skirmish with the Bonapartists, Gambetta referred to 'the rottenness of the Empire' (*la pourriture impériale*); the scene then, according to *The Times* correspondent, exceeded 'all that have gone before it'.[5] To Ludovic Halévy it seemed that 'the old Gambetta' had reappeared: 'For some time Gambetta has been watching himself and has shown a real "correctness" in conduct and language. Yesterday he had an attack of

1. See e.g. *R.F.* leader of 30 June.
2. *The Times*, 24 June.
3. *Lettres*, no. 279. The *R.F.* had already drawn attention to the affair on 1 and 2 July.
4. For the text see *Discours*, vol. v, pp. 261–89, and *Annales, Chambre*, vol. iii, pp. 209–17. The result of the enquiry was that the charge against pupils of the Jesuit school was dismissed, the finding being that an indiscretion had been committed by some person unknown.
5. 4 July.

violence.'[1] To the new Bayard of the Catholics, Comte Albert de Mun, it appeared that the question was but an incident in the open struggle of the majority in the Chamber against his coreligionists. In that struggle Gambetta was an acknowledged leader and de Mun's own election was shortly to be invalidated.[2]

The diversion worked like a miracle. After the turmoil the deputies were too weary to engage in a full-scale amnesty debate and they agreed to defer the discussion of the Raspail interpellation until the debate on the Gatineau Bill. Gambetta had triumphed, but the Radicals continued their amnesty campaign outside parliament.

A second question which came to the fore once more was the old one of the mayors. The government had promised a new Bill, but, like most governments in office, it was loth to relinquish power. While conceding the general principle that mayors and their assistants (*adjoints*) should be elected, it proceeded to restrict its application by reserving the right to nominate not only in the chief towns of each *arrondissement* and department but also in those of cantons. The Left were up in arms. They could stomach the departmental and, at a pinch, the *arrondissement* capitals, but not the 3000 cantonal ones.[3] A number of alternative Bills were also proposed. In its perplexity the committee (presided over by Jules Ferry), which had been appointed to consider the matter, favoured a compromise whereby the government proposal should be accepted provisionally until an all-embracing law on municipalities was passed. This did not satisfy Gambetta who had wanted a law dealing with the whole problem of municipalities to be approved before the Chambers broke up for the vacation.[4] But Marcère, the Minister of the Interior, stood his ground and insisted that until the complete law was ready the committee's compromise should be accepted. An amendment already put forward and supported by Gambetta demanding that the Bill should be referred back to the Committee pending the tabling of an all-embracing or organic law was rejected by 389 to 76. It was a conspicuous setback. Gambetta was much

1. *Revue des Deux Mondes*, 15 Feb. 1937, 'Les carnets de L. Halévy', note of 4 July. When Gambetta was involved in another scene with the Bonapartists on 22 July Léonie Léon wisely cautioned him: 'Je suis contrariée de voir votre éloquence céder trop aux caprices des bonapartistes, qui en persistant à vous provoquer espèrent toujours faire naître une violence pour la tourner ensuite contre vous . . . je trouve que vous avez suffisamment répondu aux attaques personnelles des bonapartistes et je ne veux pas qu'il soit en leur pouvoir de vous faire parler quand cela leur plaît' (letter of 24 July, Ass. Nat., p. 201).

2. He was, however, reelected later in the year with a much reduced majority.

3. See *R.F.*, leaders of 1, 3, 4, 30, 31 May and article on 20 May.

4. See *R.F.*, 8 July, for a resolution of the Republican Union on this subject and 9 July for a leader supporting it.

irritated with Marcère for having forced the issue and said to him afterwards 'You have won, but it is a Pyrrhic victory and you will remember
it!'[1] In the *République Française* he vented his displeasure with a government which so far had been content with 'half-measures, even equivocal
and contradictory measures'. It was time that it showed clarity in its
ideas and decisiveness in its actions: in fact that it was worth maintaining.[2]

But in this affair Gambetta had not been at issue with the government
alone. The debate had in part been a duel between Gambetta and Jules
Ferry, the *rapporteur* of the Bill, a duel between 'two companions of arms'
and 'two masters of the future'. It seemed to a discerning French historian
who was to work with both as interesting for the destinies of the Republic
as it was indicative of the nature of the two men: 'Jules Ferry, on the
defensive, irritates and wearies his brilliant adversary: his sometimes
sarcastic tone provokes and punctures the warm and passionate élan of
the tribune.'[3] It was with such sarcasm that Ferry referred to 'eminent
politicians of the Left' who were of a different school from his own and
dreamt that a thoroughgoing measure could be put through in no time
and that the Chamber could act, as though it were a single Chamber,
without any concern for the Senate: 'It is a policy, I admit, but it is not an
effective one', and he claimed that if it had been followed during the past
five years 'France would not today be in possession of the Republic'.
His Committee's policy was, he said, quoting Gambetta's phrase 'a policy
of results', that supported by Gambetta 'a bad and illusory policy'.[4] In all
the circumstances Léonie Léon's attempt to console her lover with the
thought that it was a great source of security and strength for a government to have all the mayors at its disposal can have been of little comfort.[5]

1. For Gambetta's intervention, see *Annales, Chambre*, vol. iii, pp. 313–17, and for
the text of the Bill, *ibid.*, *Annexes*, p. 312; see also Marcère, *op. cit.*, p. 100. According
to E. de Girardin (*Questions d'argent*, p. 146) when the Dufaure ministry was formed
MacMahon had agreed to the choice of mayors of the chief towns of departments,
etc., from among the municipal councillors on condition that they were nominated
by the government: 'Cet engagement pris par M. Richard lierait son successeur,
M. de Marcère, à tel point qu'il n'hésiterait point à se retirer plutôt que d'y manquer.'
Marcère (*op. cit.*, p. 96) just says 'M. le Maréchal pensait que, dans cette affaire, son
autorité personnelle était en jeu.'
2. Leader of 14 July.
3. Hanotaux, *op. cit.*, vol. iii, p. 605. On 12 July the *R.F.* taunted Ferry with forgetting the views on municipal freedom which he had expressed in his contribution
to a well-known pamphlet, *Un Projet de décentralisation*, published under the Second
Empire.
4. For Ferry's speech, see *Annales, Chambre*, vol. iii, pp. 310–13. The law was
eventually passed after modification by the Senate and it was published in the *Journal
Officiel* on 13 Aug.
5. Letter of 12 July (Ass. Nat., p. 195).

Meanwhile the Senate was preparing to oppose another Republican measure. At the end of March the new Minister for Public Instruction, Waddington (the only French Minister ever to have won a Cambridge rowing blue) had introduced in the Chamber a Bill to repeal the 1875 law allowing Catholic universities to confer degrees.[1] Spuller had acted as *rapporteur* of the Committee appointed to report on it, and on 7 June, after a passionate six days' debate, in which Gambetta took no part, the Bill had passed by a large majority. Nevertheless, the Senate had appointed a predominantly Right-wing Committee to examine the Bill. On 20 July, after a remarkable debate and a masterly speech by Broglie, the Senators rejected it, but only by five votes. For the *République Française*, which had long confidently supported the measure, its rejection was the exasperating victory of an old ducal enemy: 'We will repeat to the man of 24 May what we said to him on the morrow of his first and most dangerous victory: "Gentlemen, it is war; you must not complain if you are subjected to the laws of war." '[2] No wonder that at the end of the session Léonie Léon wrote bitterly of 'these elderly children in the Senate' and said that 'this constant and obstinate struggle between the two Chambers' boded ill. She thought it would become more bitter and, with the Intransigents helping to sow discord, lead to a catastrophe that must be avoided.[3] No wonder, too, that when the first ordinary session of the legislature of 1876 was ended by presidential decree on 12 August and the *République Française* asked itself whether the Republican representatives had been able to keep all the promises on their programme it had to reply that the answer was 'far from satisfactory'. It had to admit that the fulfilment of the programme had not even been begun. It had to confess that the situation was still fraught with 'extreme difficulties'. Gambetta for his part had plaintively told Léonie Léon that nothing was going to his liking. Politics were like Penelope's web: 'No sooner have I repaired it on the Right than it is torn on the Left and in the middle: I am up against miserable and constant difficulties.'[4]

'Torn on the Left': a fresh tear had come about there just a month earlier. It had been caused by the thorny question of the amnesty and by Intransigent dissatisfaction both with MacMahon's letter enjoining clemency and with the equivocal attitude of Gambetta and some of his friends. On 30 June sixteen deputies met in Louis Blanc's home and decided to break away from the Republican Union. They declared their

---

1. See above, pp. 249–50. The law had not yet been implemented. Waddington was No. 6 in the winning Cambridge crew of March 1849.
2. Leader of 23 July.
3. Letter of 12 Aug. (Ass. Nat., p. 213).
4. 29 July (L.G.).

opposition to temporary policies. The need to alert and enlighten public opinion must come before 'the expediency of certain parliamentary manoeuvres'. Some weeks later twenty-five deputies of the extreme Left published a lengthy manifesto denouncing clericalism and emphasising the need not to fear a conflict with the Senate if it was unavoidable.[1] Once again they proclaimed the primacy of principle and declared that temporising should not become a system. Their following gradually increased. In the view of the chief historian of the Radicalism of the time, those who by the end of the year could really be classified as belonging to the Extreme Left were as many as fifty-seven, four members of the Republican Left and thirty-seven of the Republican Union in addition to Louis Blanc and his fifteen henchmen: 'In consequence there was misunderstanding within the Republican Union and discontent and suspicion beset the majority.'[2] Furthermore, an incidental result of the split was the appearance at the end of October of yet another Intransigent paper, Louis Blanc's *L'Homme Libre*. But this, happily for Gambetta, was to demonstrate the truth of his earlier remark that it was one thing to found a paper, another to keep it going.[3] Louis Blanc's production would not last long.

Rents on the Left kept appearing, too, in the coarser part of the fabric, the electorate itself. Radical zealots demanded that deputies should render account of their conduct. Worse still, only a short time after the Chambers had been prorogued in the middle of a heatwave, *The Times* was reporting that Irreconcilables in Belleville had censured Gambetta for voting for the retention of the Embassy to the Pope and against the reduction of military service to three years with the abolition of the twelve months' *volontariat*, as also for his neutrality in the division on the Amnesty.

1. For the text, see *R.F.*, 14 Aug. The signatories were Barodet, Louis Blanc, Bouquet, Cantagrel, Clémenceau, Crozet-Fourneyron, Daumas, de Douville-Maillefeu, Armand Duportal, Durand, Charles Floquet, Girault, Lockroy, Madier de Montjau, Marcou, Nadaud, Naquet, Ordinaire, Georges Perin [*sic*], F.-V. Raspail père, Benjamin Raspail, Rollet, Talandier, Turigny and Vernhes. The *R.F.* of 15 Aug. immediately printed an approving and conciliatory leader on the manifesto.

2. Kayser, *Les Grandes batailles du radicalisme*, pp. 95–6. Cf. Jules Ferry's interesting comments on the secession of 'la nouvelle Montagne' and the state of the Republican Union in mid-July in a letter of 19 July (*Discours et Opinions de Jules Ferry*, ed. P. Robiquet, vol. ii, pp. 278–82; cf. also p. 288).

3. See above, p. 195. A historian of radicalism in the Nord has noted the appearance there 'Dès 1876' of the *Petit Radical* which he describes as 'le journal des travailleurs Dunkerquois' and which spoke of 'la confiscation de la République et denonçait en Gambetta et ses amis, des traîtres' (R. Vandenbussche, 'Aspects de l'histoire politique du radicalisme dans le département du Nord (1870–1905)', *Revue du Nord*, vol. xlvii, p. 227).

One of the speakers mentioned that in the lobbies of the Chamber M. Gambetta had been seen joking and laughing with M. Laurier.'[1] The man whom the Bonapartist paper *L'Ordre* had recently dubbed 'Opportunist the First' must be brought to book.[2] In October, moreover, a disappointed former associate printed a violent attack on him in an open *Lettre de Pierre Baragnon a Léon Gambetta*. It repeated what were to be familiar charges, whether they were levelled by foes on the Right or the Left. Gambetta had become 'the Grand Elector of the democracy'. He had missed the opportunity to proclaim the Republic on 12 August 1870. He had shown rank ingratitude to former helpers. He had been badly brought up and was irremediably Bohemian. France could not be ruled by such a man.

So once again Gambetta was embarrassed by 'his tail'. The Rothschilds' informant, C. de B., even alleged that he had received anonymous letters threatening him with death if he did not resign and that he had asked for police protection.[3] But he chose his own time and did not hurry to arrange a confrontation with his constituents at Belleville.[4] Preoccupied more than ever with foreign affairs now that an Eastern crisis had developed and Russia and Turkey were on the verge of war, he spent some time travelling in September.

He made an amorous and fascinating journey across Germany.[5] He also revisited Les Crêtes with its splendid view over the whole eastern end of the Lake of Geneva and walked and played quoits with Guichard, his aged host Dubochet's nephew. And while he was there he had the heartening experience of receiving a deputation of French and Swiss citizens of Lausanne who presented him with a splendid silver cup in recognition of his devotion to the Republican cause from 4 September 1870 to 20 February 1876. He returned to put the finishing touches to the big report he had to have ready for the Budget Committee by the middle of October. Thus it was not until the end of that month that he faced what in a letter to Léonie Léon he called 'this other monster more thick-

---

1. For the volunteer system and Gambetta's views on army reform, see below Ch. 22. The police archives contain many reports and newspaper cuttings in August and September to the effect that the electorate of Belleville were getting restive and demanding that Gambetta should give account of his conduct (A.P.P., BA/919). The Viennese *Neue Freie Presse* (25 Sept.) reported a Radical meeting at Marseilles on 22 Sept. in which there were loud cries of 'Down with Gambetta' and 'Out with him'.

2. 24 July, cutting in police file, A.P.P., BA/419.

3. *Letters from Paris*, p. 220, 23 Aug.

4. See his actual speech: 'J'ai tenu à venir ici, au milieu de vous à mon heure — car j'ai tenu à choisir mon heure' (*Discours*, vol. vi, p. 159).

5. See below, p. 339.

skinned and difficult than the one of Varzin' [Bismarck].[1] On the eve of the confrontation he was no less nervous than in April 1875 when he had sold the Senate to the Belleville workers. He had sketched for Léonie the draft of a speech, but on looking at it again he found it 'a painful harangue. I am accursedly embarrassed; ideas flow; their development piles up in my head; but order and clarity are lacking; it is as though I can't produce anything far from the heat of the audience. I seem to find nothing but vague banalities.' So, he said, he had decided to give up the task and to trust to the good luck of the moment. He added a profoundly disillusioned reflection: 'What a profession mine is! Before I can act I have to gain the right to bring about the triumph of reason and justice in the livery of violence. I must allay the suspicions of some, check the calumnies or fears of others, and deceive them all in order to serve them better.'[2]

The atmosphere was tense when at 8.30 p.m. in the Salle Graffard at Ménilmontant on the evening of 27 October Gambetta faced an audience of some four thousand; but 'the good luck of the moment', his capacity to judge the mood of his hearers and tune his speech accordingly, once again came to his rescue. Léonie Léon had wisely warned him against being long-winded: 'decisive victories are quickly won or lost'; and his speech was much briefer than his earlier Belleville orations. 'It's a question', she had told him, 'of charming rather than teaching, of carrying them with you rather than convincing them.'[3]

After the President had solemnly reminded the audience of the terms of the manifesto under which Gambetta's mandate had been renewed on 14 February 1876, their deputy rose, as he himself said, to render his account. At the outset he disarmed most of his audience by being absolutely frank; he said at once that he knew what passions were stirring them and that when he had opted for Belleville he was aware what difficulties he would encounter. But he asked them to be orderly because their meetings were watched by all the embittered and defeated reactionaries. They should take as their example the recent Workingmen's Congress which discussed the most burning questions without once giving a handle to their enemies.[4] This was a deft touch which met with prolonged

1. *Lettres*, no. 290. He wrote on 10 Oct. to the President of the Republican electoral committee of the 20th *arrondissement* stating his readiness to give a review of the political situation before the return of parliament (*Discours*, vol. vi, pp. 156–71).

2. *Lettres*, no. 290.

3. Letter of 26 Oct. (Ass. Nat., p. 236).

4. This Congress held early in October was the first of its kind to take place in Paris since the Commune. The *R.F.* gave it its blessing on 28 Sept. and devoted an approving leader to its orderliness on 9 Oct. Its correspondant was, however, critical of many of the sessions.

applause. Then followed his defence. There were only two ways of conducting politics: to negotiate or fight. France had had all too much violence. He was for negotiation. People said that the policy which had been followed was one of transaction. Yes, because men could only govern themselves by transactions. They said it was a policy of results and they ridiculed those results. Yet they were there for all to see. 'Less than a year ago we had martial law and the ministers you remember . . . you know in what hands the *mairies* had been placed. Parliament had sat for four months and there were people who said 'How is it that in these four months you haven't changed the face of the earth?' That could not be done in four years, let alone four months, but 'we have ploughed and traced the furrow and sown good seed and, if you persevere, others will raise it and the harvest will be yours'.

Much of all this was punctuated by loud applause. The bulk of the audience was with him. It was time to tackle the burning issue of which the Irreconcilables had made so much: 'I know that there is one question which divides us and excites you and I am too accustomed to democratic politics not to see your lips uttering this word "amnesty" (*pour ne pas distinguer sur vos lèvres ce mot d'amnistie*).' The audience was more tense than ever. Exclamations of 'Ah! Ah!' by some were drowned by cries of 'Silence! Listen!' from others. Now at last he was about to grasp the nettle. A generous policy earlier, he said, would have prevented the question from being raised in the way in which it had been raised. But some failed to understand the opportuneness of such a measure and others exaggerated it. He did not favour an amnesty such as had been 'demanded in certain formulas', principally because by putting the proposal forward 'in absolute and violent terms' opposition would be provoked to such a degree that nothing would be gained. He reminded his hearers that there were people who had skilfully represented the Commune 'as a sort of explosion and manifestation of a political sect or school when they knew perfectly well that this insurrection of 18 March was . . . a sort of convulsion of famine, misery and despair'. But, he continued, to claim in this way that 'the criminal insurrection of 18 March' represented the real expression of the Republican party and to attempt to confound the Republicans with the most depraved and tainted of the men mixed up with the Commune was a manoeuvre that could threaten the structure of the Republic itself. He had parried it by demanding as generous a partial amnesty as possible. 'I did not think and I still do not think that it was possible to go further': but everything ought to be done to procure a partial amnesty. Those who demanded a total one were of two kinds: those who were moved by generosity, 'as are some of my friends here—but let them allow me to tell them that they are the dupes of their feelings and unwittingly and unwillingly they are betraying the very interests they believe they are serving—and those who make the question a means for disorder and constant agitation (Murmurs and protests on some benches. Hear, Hear! and signs of approval on a large number of benches. Various interruptions).' Gambetta flung the nettle away with a promise and a firm reaffirmation of his attitude: he would give his unreserved support to the proposal to stop further prosecutions which would come before parliament when it resumed its sittings: 'But, you must understand that as long as I am convinced that I am right I am determined never to go beyond the limits prescribed by my conscience and my reason.'

He then reminded his hearers that, since he was convinced that the majority of the French people wanted all communes to have the right to elect their mayors, he had supported this principle in its entirety—this was, of course, an allusion to his attitude in July. This served as an effective springboard to a further defence of opportunism which is worth quoting at some length.

> So it is, whenever we are convinced that we have the country with us; this is the key to this policy which has been labelled with a . . . word which comes from Italy just as the word intransigent comes from Spain. . . . The key to this policy, rather ridiculously and scornfully dubbed opportunist, consists in only committing oneself completely to a question when one is convinced of having the country incontestably with one. But when there are hesitations, when the country has not clearly manifested its will, when it is divided . . . when the adoption of this measure would throw universal suffrage into disarray and be a cause of weakness and ruin for the government, however strong the pressures, I resist and shall always resist.

He clinched the argument by a reference to the history of Rome which provoked prolonged applause. (What working-class audience in England would so have responded?)

> Oh! it would be too easy to drape oneself in the toga of the ancient Romans and to die like Cato at Utica. What profit did the Roman Republic derive from Cato's death at Utica? (Laughter). I am for fighting to the end when Caesar is alive or to prevent Caesar's return (Prolonged applause).

He concluded with a warning. In the dark days he had spoken as he had because it was essential to inspire confidence; 'but today, no, I am not optimistic'. Republican union had never been more necessary.

> We are witnessing an unheard of recrudescence of reactionary passion . . . we have before us the strange spectacle of no longer having a political party in the

true sense to combat. . . . It is no longer a question of restoring royal or imperial houses; it is a question of saving the faith and religion, as though religion were not something different from fanaticism and theocracy: there is but one enemy . . . it appears everywhere . . . and this is the moment you choose to create dissidence and provoke divisions.

He did not utter the celebrated words, 'Clericalism, there is the enemy!', but this was the gist of the long denunciatory passage which followed. It was a ploy that never failed and Gambetta sat down to a 'double salvo of applause'.

But one man named Buffenoir, who claimed that he belonged to 'the advanced Radical party', was not satisfied and asked leave to speak. Gambetta insisted that he be heard. Buffenoir declared that while he did not doubt Gambetta's sincerity, the policy he advocated would not lead to democracy's goal, 'namely the direct government of the people by the people'. It was a policy 'which still upholds the old tradition of giving the nation a master; no matter whether or not he is called President of the Republic: he puts the nation in chains and chains are always chains, whoever inflicts them.' Amid increasing hubbub he queried Gambetta's interpretation of the amnesty. This was the really delicate point and could have seriously embarrassed Belleville's deputy. But, fortunately for him, Gambetta knew Buffenoir and gave him short shrift.

> Do you know where this gentleman . . . was at the time of the Commune? Well, he was in the hands of the clerical party. He came to me for help to escape—he brought me a piece of verse that he dedicated to me. . . . His sole preoccupation was not, as he said, with Communard radicalism, but to write no matter what . . . in a paper I had just founded; there were no platitudes and flatteries he did not address to your servant in order to gain admission. But there was nothing doing. I took the measure of this man and there he is.

That was the end of Buffenoir. Amid general laughter and applause the unhappy man left the rostrum. The meeting ended with a further salvo of applause for the deputy of the 20th *arrondissement*. Gambetta had won the day.[1] Léonie hailed her 'splendid victor'.[2] 'His success', noted Juliette Adam, 'was shattering and his reputation is perhaps still greater in Paris than at Belleville. Gambetta is well satisfied, but the Intransigents are not.

---

1. For the text of Gambetta's speech, see *Discours*, vol. vi, pp. 158–78. He professed to have let Buffenoir off lightly, for his friend Michel Etienne reported him as saying that, had he disclosed what he knew to be true, that Buffenoir was still a hireling of the priests and living in the Curé of Saint-Sulpice's house, the poor man might well have been beaten up (*Neue Freie Presse*, 19 Nov. 1876).

2. Letter of 29 Oct. (Ass. Nat., p. 237).

They all appeared much irritated yesterday at Versailles.'[1] If Gambetta was satisfied, he had also learnt a lesson. Henceforward he would keep in closer contact with his constituents.[2] There was no doubt, however, that he had regained a stature which had seemed to be diminished in the spring and summer. *The Times*, for instance, devoted a leader to the speech and praised the courage with which he had talked good sense. Besides, it concluded, 'Belleville does not rule France. The rulers of France are the middle class and the peasantry, and if no disaster should befall the Republic, M. Gambetta promises to become the accepted chief of both.'[3] In the next twelve months France was more than ever to need a man of Gambetta's stature to save the Republic from what looked like disorder. More than ever beset by internal problems, he would have little leisure for foreign affairs which increasingly fascinated him and at which it is time to glance.

1. Louis Blanc's *Homme libre* naturally took him to task.
2. Thus he visited Ménilmontant on 9 Jan. 1877 and saw Gérard, 'son ami, son agent très actif dans ce quartier' (Police report of 10 Jan., A.P.P., BA/919). He went there again on 10 Feb. and 9 May (Letters to Léonie Léon, L.G.).
3. 30 Oct., p. 9.

21

Foreign affairs
1871–1877

France's foreign policy after 1870 was circumscribed by the consequences of invasion and defeat. Her horizon was dominated by the blue line of the Vosges. The hegemony of Europe had passed to the new German Empire under the formidable guidance of Bismarck, and French statesmen were all too conscious of their country's weakness and isolation. They required time in which France could recover from the ravages of war and establish a stable regime. The German annexation of Alsace and Lorraine had created what looked like an irreparable breach between France and Germany and for most Frenchmen in the years immediately after the war the ultimate object of foreign policy must be the recovery of those lost provinces.[1] This was no imperialist aim. It was a profound and legitimate desire to right a great wrong and to recover territories and people regarded as an integral part of France. Their recovery would enhance French security instead of endangering it. It was an aim which was by no means inconsistent with the basically pacific and conservative character of French society. But it was an ultimate not an immediate aim. 'The true *revanche* of which we are thinking', Thiers had written to the French Minister in Rome on 6 April 1872, 'is the reconstitution of France. That is possible, indeed certain.'[2]

But it was an aim that could not be pursued in tranquillity. The vicissitudes of French politics, the reserve and suspicion with which monarchical Europe regarded a Republican regime, the fear that a restored Bourbon Monarchy would go crusading to restore the temporal power of the Papacy, and uncertainty and dread of Bismarck's ultimate intentions, all clouded the air. In the autumn of 1876 Lord Lyons, reviewing the different phases through which French public opinion had passed since the Treaty

1. A notable exception was Jules Grévy (see Scheurer-Kestner, *Souvenirs de jeunesse*, p. 262).
2. *D.D.F.*, vol. i, p. 139.

of Frankfurt, wrote as follows: 'At first rage and mortification engendered a wild and unreasoning longing for revenge. This was soon followed by a depression almost amounting to despair. Germany was looked at with absolute terror; and even so late as the spring of last year a rumour that an immediate attack from that quarter was to be apprehended produced something very like a panic.' (This was an allusion to the celebrated war scare of 1875). The resurrection of the French army, he said, had indeed been astonishing, but Frenchmen were still aware that single-handed they could be no match for Germany: 'The dread that an attack from Germany may come before France is ready to meet it, still weighs upon men's minds.'[1]

Such was the background, the climate in which Gambetta's views on foreign affairs were to evolve. He held, of course, no official position between his resignation as Minister for War and the Interior in the Government of National Defence in February 1871 and his election as President of the Budget Committee in 1876 and even then he had no formal concern with foreign policy, apart from budgetary control of the foreign policy vote. Yet his role early in 1871 and the conspicuous part he had played in French politics since his return from exile in June of that year meant that he could not be ignored. He had after all at one time been expected to succeed Thiers, he had been a principal leader of the opposition in the National Assembly, and after the elections of 1876 he was widely regarded as a potential prime minister or even head of state. Yet just as French foreign policy as a whole was circumscribed and conditioned by the events of 1870–71 and subsequent uncertainty about the regime, so was Gambetta's position and freedom of manoeuvre restricted by his own role at that time and by the fact that he stood on the Left of the Republican party. It was he who had demanded the continuation of war to the knife even after the fall of Paris, and in the heat of debate in February 1872 he could still defend his policy by accusing the Right of preferring peace to honour.[2] He had, too, been one of the deputies for Alsace and Lorraine. He had written their first protest, signed their second and resigned along with them in a dramatic gesture against annexation. At the funeral of one of them a few days later he had declared that France could have no other policy than the liberation 'of our brethren in these unhappy lands'.[3] On the morrow of the war,

1. Lyons to Derby, 31 Oct. 1876, F.O. 146, 1898. Cf. Connolly (the Britith Military Attaché) to Lyons, 28 July 1871, reporting on a journey back from Versailles in the same carriage with Gambetta and a number of Left-wing Deputies: 'The paramount feeling among the whole company was a thirst for revenge' (F.O. 146, 1539).

2. *Ass. Nat. A.*, vol. viii, p. 31.

3. See *Discours*, vol. ii, p. 14.

therefore, for most Frenchmen, he was the incarnation of the desire for *revanche*. He was a nationalist, eager to identify nationalism with Republicanism and proud of the title, given him by the well-known writer Jules Claretie (among others) of 'patriot before all else'.[1] But he was also a Radical and therefore to many conservatives at home and abroad a 'Red'; and this and his nationalism combined made it easy for his enemies at home and abroad to represent him as a bellicose Jacobin revolutionary.[2] Just as men like Thiers believed that he would at bottom always be a Radical demagogue giving way to his 'tail', so his foes abroad would, when it suited them, affect to believe that once in power again he would be a danger to European peace. Thus the first postwar German Ambassador in Paris, Count Arnim, recorded that in October 1871 Bismarck had told him to make it clear that Germany would view Gambetta's accession to power as an occasion for war (*Kriegsfall*).[3] Thus, too, in 1873 Bismarck tried to delay the evacuation of French territory on the grounds that the departure of the German troops would be the signal for fresh revolutionary activity and the possible reemergence of Gambetta at the helm. He affected, indeed, to dismiss Gambetta as a mediocrity, but admitted that he was energetic and said that 'in the government of peoples this is what is most dangerous.'[4] But while Bismarck was prepared to use any means to keep France cowed and isolated, before long he came to the conclusion that a French Monarchy would be more bellicose and more likely to attract allies than a Republic. In consequence, by 1874 he had also shifted his attitude so far as Gambetta was concerned. He

1. *Lettres*, no. 224.

2. Friends, too, watched him with anxiety. Thus in July 1872 Jules Ferry, then French Minister in Athens, wrote approvingly of Gambetta's 'sagesse' which 'le sert infiniment dans l'opinion européenne', but disapprovingly of his 'intempérances de Grenoble, qui nous ont mis en si grand péril' (*Lettres de Jules Ferry*, pp. 152, 174).

3. Galli, *Gambetta et l'Alsace-Lorraine*, p. 52, quoting *Pro nihilo, Vorgeschichte des Arnim'schen Processes* (Zurich, 1876), p. 8. Such an instruction was indeed understandable if Bismarck saw a despatch of 14 July 1871 from Waldersee, the German Ambassador in Paris. This reported that Gambetta had told an elderly German that France must and would by means of the Republic win the strength to wage a victorious war of revenge; and that he had added that she was already capable of waging a revolutionary war against Germany, the more so since there were revolutionary elements in Germany who could cripple Germany's war effort (W. Frank, *Nationalismus and Demokratie in Frankreich der dritten Republik (1871 bis 1918)*, Hamburg, 1933, p. 21). But as early as 13 Jan. 1872, speaking to the Italian Minister in Berlin, Bismarck took a different line: 'Quant à la République de M. Thiers, peu nous importe, qu'elle se consolide ou qu'elle soit remplacée par celle de M. Gambetta. Cette dernière aurait peut-être pour résultat une guerre civile, nouvelle cause d'affaiblissement pour cette nation' (De Launay to Visconti Venosta, 14 Jan. *D.D.I.*, Seconda Serie, 1870–96, vol. iii, Rome, 1969, no. 299).

4. *D.D.F.*, Série I, p. 215, Gontaut-Biron to Thiers, 9 March 1873.

was convinced, he said, that his advent to power would have the same effect on other European peoples as that of the Commune which had led to a widespread swing to the Right. For the time being then he regarded 'a Gambettist France as quite without danger for the peace of Europe'.[1] Two months later when he gave Arnim's successor, Hohenlohe, his instructions on his appointment to the Paris Embassy he told him that 'a republic and internal dissensions' were the best guarantees of peace.[2] He still adhered to this view nearly two years later. On 19 December 1875, Hohenlohe recorded having dined with Bismarck on a visit to Berlin:

> After dinner . . . I turned the conversation to Gambetta and the possibility that he might secure the reins of power. The Chancellor immediately interrupted me and said: 'He is not dangerous to us, however strongly he organises France. We shall always be superior even to a strong France. The danger lies solely in a coalition, and the French Republic will not be able to secure this against us.'[3]

For the Republican patriot who was the object of these speculations, Alsace-Lorraine and Franco-German relations were inevitably the central points in any thinking on foreign affairs. Inevitably he felt that he had special obligations to the people of the lost provinces. Inevitably he was obsessed by the problem of their recovery and by the policies of the man and the Empire that stood in its way.

Once the annexation of Alsace and Lorraine was complete some of their inhabitants were ready to accept the *fait accompli*. But such acceptance was intolerable to those most loyal to France. They instituted a secret Ligue d'Alsace to resist this acceptance and the league, it has been said, was inspired by Gambetta.[4] When he founded the *République Française* he wrote to an Alsatian friend and former deputy, Albert Boell, telling him that its dominant idea was 'patriotism which is in itself a whole policy. . . . As long as we have not restored France's integrity, we shall not have the right to consider ourselves satisfied.' He proposed, he said, to devote a special section of the paper to the affairs of Alsace and Lorraine, while his political efforts at home would always have as their 'secret or avowed motive the recovery of our heroic and honest people of the East.'[5]

---

1. *G.P.*, vol. i (Berlin, 1927), no. 151, 28 Feb. 1874, Bismarck to Prince Henry VII Reuss.

2. *Memoirs of Prince Chlodwig of Hohenlohe-Schillingsfuerst*, (London, 1906), vol. ii, p. 106.

3. *Ibid.*, p. 161.

4. H. Galli, *op. cit.*, p. 43.

5. *Ibid.*, pp. 45–8. This letter, however, is omitted from Halévy and Pillias's *Lettres*. They must have known of it since Pillias frequently referred to Galli's book in his own study of *Léonie Léon amie de Gambetta*. Did they doubt its authenticity?

But Gambetta was a cautious realist as well as a patriot. The *République Française* did not give any special prominence or frequency to news from the lost provinces, although from time to time it printed such news in a section headed 'Alsace-Lorraine' just as it printed news from Algeria or 'Letters' from Italy, Germany or Spain; nor was there any special reference to the lost provinces in its early leaders.[1] Its director knew that it was dangerous to excite hopes which it might take long years to fulfil. So at Saint-Quentin in November 1871 he had sounded his celebrated note of caution. He had reminded his hearers of the need for dignified reserve incumbent upon the vanquished: 'Let us preserve that dignity and never speak of the foreigner, but let it be understood that we are constantly thinking of him. . . . Then you will be on the real path to *revanche* because you will have learnt to govern and control yourselves.'[2] Six months later a deputation came to him bearing with them a bronze group symbolising the sufferings and hopes of Alsace. It was the work of the Colmar artist, Bartholdi, and thousands of loyal Alsatians had subscribed to this gift to Gambetta the great patriot. He was deeply moved, but once again the words he had to speak were words of restraint. It was hard to ask these 'abandoned brethren' to show a spirit of sacrifice and resignation, yet he appealed to them not to disturb the country in her task of reconstruction: 'You must give France the example of a people which can control its feelings and avoid provoking intervention. . . . Let us not speak of *revanche*, let us not utter rash words, let us keep silence (*recueillons-nous*). When we have completed this essential regeneration time enough will have passed for there to have been changes in the world around us.'[3]

So he preached restraint and prudence in the matter of *revanche* just as he urged them on his party in home affairs generally. But, though time passed, he would not forget. He kept in touch with Alsatians and Lor-rainers both at home and across the frontier and generally attended their children's Christmas tree party in Paris. When elections were held for the Reichstag in 1874 he did his best to secure the return of men still loyal to France. Not only that, but he, the anticlerical, urged the candi-dature of Roman Catholic priests, because, accustomed to preach in German, they would be the better equipped to take part in debates in the German parliament.[4] It is said, too, that it was he who inspired the

1. From the first number of 7 Nov. 1871 to the end of that year there were only four issues in which news from the lost provinces was published under the caption 'Alsace-Lorraine'. Articles on events there were more frequent later on, e.g. in 1877.
2. See above, p. 68.
3. *Discours*, vol. ii, p. 272.
4. Auguste Lalance, *Mes Souvenirs 1830–1914* (1914), p. 51.

celebrated demand of one of the Alsatian deputies, Teutsch of Saverne, that the German government should hold a plebiscite in Alsace-Lorraine to give their annexation a semblance of legality.[1] In the following year, in one of his moments of profounder gloom soon after the war scare of 1875, he wrote to Léonie Léon that he would be inclined to throw up politics and return to the bar, but for his duties to his country, 'whose frontiers must be redrawn on pain of dishonour'.[2] Of these duties the Bartholdi bronze in his study and Jean Jacques Henner's celebrated picture 'L'Alsacienne' were constant reminders. And he had reminded others of them too. In their bedroom in a black frame the Scheurer-Kestners had an engraving of 'L'Alsacienne'. It bore the inscription: 'There will be no peace in Europe, no order or rebirth in France until the day when we shall have freed the captive; let us prepare without fuss (*sans phrases*) and let us have no other thought than the recapture of our property. To Madame Scheurer-Kestner. Léon Gambetta.'[3]

He did not forget the lost provinces. But his concern was, for the time being, profoundly pessimistic. He shared that terror of Germany that Lord Lyons had discerned in French public opinion as a whole, terror of Germany and above all of Bismarck. In his correspondence Bismarck is 'the Monster', by whom he is fascinated and obsessed. Visitors to his flat noticed with surprise that he had a volume of Bismarck's speeches or a photograph of Bismarck on his desk.[4] But it was thus that Gambetta sought to know his adversary, this man of colossal power 'such a one as is born only every two centuries': just as in the Second World War intelligence officers would, as part of their training, wear the enemy's uniform. One day, however, he would hope to meet and wrestle with him in the flesh. Meanwhile he was full of the direst forebodings, for everywhere he saw the Monster's claw. 'Everywhere', he wrote to Juliette Adam in September 1874, 'he has sought and found support, allies and accomplices, at Vienna, at Rome, at St Petersburg, at Washington, at Madrid he is tightening round us the circle of his diplomatic siege works (*investissement*)'.[5] 'He waits and watches for us on the Pyrenees, he deceives us in Italy, he humiliates us in Switzerland and he relegates us to an inferior position in Egypt.'[6] Everywhere he detected 'the Monster's'

---

1. Galli, *op cit.*, pp. 89, 95–9.
2. Letter of 29 June 1875 (L.G.).
3. Scheurer-Kestner, *Journal inédit*, B.N., N.a.fr. 12, 706, p. 338.
4. Article by Léo Lespès in *L'Evénement*, 24 Aug. 1872; Nordheim pp.
5. *Lettres*, no. 205.
6. *Ibid.*, no. 213, 1 Oct. 1874; cf. interview recorded in the Viennese *Neue Freie Presse* (19 Nov. 1876) where he saw Bismarck's hand in the military preparations of Greece and Roumania.

Machiavellian influence, even in separatism in Nice. Thus when Juliette reported on this phenomenon without so much as mentioning Bismarck, he asked how she thought he could remain inactive in Nice any more than he himself, when there were elections in Alsace and Lorraine, could refrain from intervening there 'in order to help maintain national feeling and prepare in advance further claims against German domination.'[1] Nor did he think that Bismarck meant merely to isolate and humiliate France. He believed that peace was precarious, that Germany was irremediably aggressive and greedy, that Holland, for instance, was doomed to be her victim, and that she was preparing to attack France and seize more French territory.[2]

These forebodings were shared by many Frenchmen and there was justification enough for them. Many highly placed Germans spoke of waging a preventive war if France recovered strength too quickly. Bismarck himself told Hohenlohe in 1874 that Germany wanted to keep the peace, 'but if France goes on arming so that she is to be ready in five years, and bent on war at the end of that time, then we will declare war in three years'.[3] A year later, at the time of the war scare which Bismarck raised in 1875, it looked as though the declaration would come still earlier. But the scare passed, the time for the dissolution of the National Assembly drew near and with it the prospect of a Republican victory, and, for Gambetta, some sort of return to power. Preoccupied though he was with domestic problems, his correspondence makes it clear that he was increasingly fascinated by foreign affairs. Already in December 1874 he had urged Ranc to write on foreign policy, 'the only policy which can and should interest a great and noble nation that has been defeated and discouraged'.[4] At the same time he was concerned for the republicanisation of the foreign service no less than of other branches of the administration. He would have liked to place his own men in the embassies as well as the prefectures.[5] Subsequently, the possibility that he might himself play a part on the stage of European diplomacy made it all the more urgent that he should disarm those who still thought he would be a disturber of the peace. Thus, while during the election campaign in 1876 he expressed the hope that justice would triumph and France recover her 'separated brethren', in his final utterances at

1. *Lettres*, nos. 219 and 221, 22 Oct. and 15 Nov. 1874. For fresh Alsatian protests in the Reichstag, see Galli, *op. cit.*, pp. 95–9.
2. *Ibid.*, nos. 213, 219, and also no. 244 of 5 June 1875. It is noteworthy that in May 1875 at the time of the war scare Decazes suspected Bismarck of wishing to annex Holland (Adams to Derby, 6 May, F.O. 146, 1810).
3. Hohenlohe, *op. cit.*, vol. ii, p. 97.
4. *Lettres*, no. 228.
5. See, e.g., *R.F.*, 15 Nov. 1871, 8 Sept. 1872, 27 April, 20, 24 June, 27 Oct. 1876

Lyon, when the Republican victory was clear, he was at particular pains to try to reassure European opinion that the Republic was eminently pacific and had no intention of going crusading or causing fear or harm to her neighbours.[1]

Gambetta's views are mainly reflected in his correspondence and above all in his correspondence with two women, Juliette Adam and Léonie Léon. His realism led him fully to understand the limitations of France's position and the obstacles in the way of *revanche*. Fundamentally his position during most of the period before the great internal crisis of 1877 was identical with that of Thiers who, in the autumn of 1872, had told Le Flô that for the time being it was in France's best interest to be the friend of all the world.[2] In a letter of 5 June 1876 Gambetta wrote to Léonie: 'Our role is to be like Molière's Sosie, everybody's friend, free in our movements, and above all to postpone the ultimate collision as long as possible.'[3] Nine months earlier he had told Juliette: 'The supreme art will lie in keeping France free in her movements, reserved in the midst of the general agitation, able to defend her own territory without giving herself up to suspect alliances or to unfounded illusions.'[4] An eminent French historian has, however, remarked that Gambetta's letters showed that his views on foreign policy were 'neither precise nor the result of deep reflection, nor were they founded upon a serious observation of the facts. They contained a considerable dose of imagination.'[5] Yet an admittedly interested German contemporary of Gambetta's was to describe him to Bismarck as 'the only Frenchman who is reliably and precisely informed about what is going on in Germany'.[6] In view of these partially contradictory verdicts it is worth while enquiring what were the sources of information on which he relied, what other main views he expressed, particularly on the vexed subject of alliances, and how far they merit the historian's criticism.

In the first place it must be remarked that if Gambetta was a nationalist he was no parochial one, ignorant, like so many of his compatriots, of foreign lands and tongues. He knew Italian, of course, he set to work to

1. Speech at Lille 6 Feb. 1876 (*Discours*, vol. v, p. 81) and at Lyon 28 Feb. 1876 (*ibid.*, p. 181).
2. D. Halévy, *Le Courrier de M. Thiers*, p. 482.
3. *Lettres*, no. 244.
4. *Ibid.*, no. 255, 13 Sept. 1875; cf. no. 251, 5 Oct. 1875; also *Neue Freie Presse*, 19 Nov. 1876.
5. P. Renouvin, *La Politique extérieure de la IIIe République de 1871 à 1904* (Cours de Sorbonne), p. 90.
6. Count Henckel v. Donnersmarck to Bismarck 17 Oct. 1877, in E. Pillias, *Léonie Léon*, pp. 101–2. Henckel wished to bring about a meeting between Gambetta and Bismarck; hence my words 'admittedly interested'.

learn German and he could read English and probably 'even express himself in it if necessary'.[1] His sources of information were various. In France, for instance, he would seem to have been posted by Duclerc, a close friend both of the Adams and of Decazes, the Foreign Minister from 1873 to 1877.[2] Sometimes he must have had access to original documents, for in 1874 he was emphatic about having seen a demand from Bismarck that if need be the French government should allow a German observation corps of 50,000 men to pass through France to Spain.[3] He met diplomats.[4] He kept in touch either directly or through Laurier with the Comte de Chaudordy, a career diplomat who had done good service for the Government of National Defence and was ambassador in Madrid from 1874 to 1881.[5] He received reports from the foreign correspondents of the *République Française* and exiled informants such as Ranc in Belgium.[6] He had foreign friends who came to see him or wrote to him, mostly liberals or Radicals, such as the Spanish Republican leader Emilio Castelar, the English Radical politician Sir Charles Dilke, who became deeply attached to him,[7] and the Austrian Constitutionalist deputy Ignatius Kuranda.[8] He had contacts, too, with men who played a more shadowy role in 'the corridors of diplomacy' such as Jules Hansen, a Danish agent who entered French service in 1869 and was much used by Thiers and Decazes,[9] and, from 1873 with Louis Nordheim, a Hamburg industrialist, who until Gambetta's death wrote regular letters to Dumangin, one of Gambetta's secretaries, with the intention that they should be passed on to Gambetta.[10] There was also, from August 1875, another much wealthier

1. *New York Herald*, 27 Jan. 1873, p. 3, but J. Hanlon denied his ability to speak or even understand English (*Gambetta: orator, dictator, journalist, statesman*, 1881, p. 144).

2. *Nos amitiés*, pp. 207 and 240. Cf. letter of 19 Aug. 1875 to Léonie Léon (L.G.): 'Le Duc Decazes s'est enfin décidé à rentrer à Paris et j'espère pouvoir d'ici quelques jours me rendre compte de l'état de son esprit. On parle également d'une entrevue considérable entre M. Thiers et le Czarewitch, je saurai aussi ce qui se sera passé.'

3. See *Lettres*, no. 206, 7 Sept. 1874 and editors' footnote.

4. See, e.g., letter of 2 April 1875 to Léonie Léon (L.G.).

5. For a tribute to Chaudordy, see *R.F.*, 27 Nov. 1873.

6. See, e.g., police report of 4 June 1875: 'Ranc vient de recevoir de Gambetta l'ordre de se tenir au courant de la situation des républicains en Allemagne et de le renseigner très exactement sur la politique de ce pays' (A.P.P., BA/1,233).

7. 'It was Gambetta, I think, that saved me', wrote Dilke after the death of his first wife in 1874: see Gwynn and Tuckwell, *Life of Sir Charles Dilke*, vol. i, p. 183.

8. *Lettres*, no. 206.

9. According to his own account in his book *Les Coulisses de la diplomatie* (pp. 266–7) he fell out with Gambetta at the time of the Barodet election, but saw much of him from 1871–73.

10. Nordheim pp., Cahier I, '*Erinnerungen an Léon Gambetta*'. The letters transmitted German criticisms of France and also Nordheim's own views on Franco–German relations.

German industrialist, Count Henckel von Donnersmarck, who lived partly in France and whose wife, the former courtesan known as 'La Païva', held court in her mansion on the Champs Elysées.[1] These last were men from the enemy camp—Henckel indeed was in touch with Bismarck. Very different were two other informants on German affairs, Henri Cheberry, a wine merchant who numbered Bismarck among his customers, and (if he existed) a mysterious and patriotic Lorrainer in whom Juliette Adam alleged that she and her husband placed great confidence. She said that they called the latter 'the Talisman' and regularly passed on his views to Gambetta and Thiers. The suggestion that he was a man named Foucault de Mondion, who later went on secret missions to Germany on behalf of the Ministry of War,[2] has, however, been scouted by Juliette's most recent biographer who believes him to have been her invention.[3] The mystery remains.

But Gambetta was not content to receive information at home in France. He believed in seeking it abroad and even in making reconnaissances into enemy country. In January 1874 he paid a brief visit to Italy where he saw 'a great many people, from the most headstrong to the most cautious', and later, in 1876, when it was rumoured that Pope Pius IX had died, he was eager to go to 'the banks of the Tiber' if the news were confirmed.[4] Meanwhile in October 1874 he had told Juliette Adam that because he was sufficiently informed about the European situation he intended to travel as far as threatened Holland to seek for news: 'It is a corridor into which all the sounds of Europe find their way'.[5] The journey, as has been seen, was a holiday with Spuller and Ranc.[6] The

1. For a discussion of Gambetta's first contacts with Henckel, see Pillias, *Léonie Léon*, pp. 97–9.

2. See Pillias, *op cit.*, p. 90, for Cheberry; p. 113, n. 2 for 'the Talisman'; cf. *Nos amitiés*, pp. 14–15, 141, 143.

3. See Marcos, *Juliette Adam*, pp. 84 and 371, n. 103: 'Il ne pouvait s'agir de Foucauld de Mondion que Madame Adam connut beaucoup plus tard, mais tout simplement d'une ombre mystérieuse, ne cachant rien derrière elle, et qui intervenait dans le récit des *Mémoires* chaque fois que l'auteur tenait à se dérober pour n'avoir pas à prendre la responsabilité totale de ce qui allait être dit.'

4. Letters of 7 Jan. 1874 and 16 June 1876 (L.G.).

5. *Lettres*, no. 213. In an undated letter to Léonie Léon, which must from its content have been written before the fall of Thiers, he had expressed the intention of escaping for a month to study the foreign situation which was daily growing darker, but this intention cannot have been carried out (L.G., where the letter is erroneously placed with those of 1874).

6. See above, p. 214. It was probably on this holiday that he was recognised in a 'café-concert' at Amsterdam and that the 'Marseillaise' and a patriotic French song 'Le Maître d'Ecole Alsacien' were at once played and sung in his honour (Gheusi, *Gambetta par Gambetta*, pp. 338–9).

three friends were tourists exploring the country and its marvellous art galleries. But Gambetta also claimed to have seen men and things, for instance Dutch arsenals, that gave him pleasure without reassuring him about the fate of Holland or the continuance of peace. Who the men were, however, he did not disclose.[1] A year later he embarked upon a much longer journey which likewise combined holiday with the quest for information. He went with the Adams to Venice hoping perhaps that on the way Princess Troubetzkoï would arrange for him a secret interview with the septuagenarian Russian Chancellor, Prince Gortschakoff, who was staying at Vevey.[2] Then he continued alone to Vienna and Berlin and revisited Switzerland before returning to France. He came back much more optimistic about the way in which France was regarded abroad. 'Men of the greatest importance, devoted to Monarchy in their own countries', had been opposed to the idea of a Bourbon restoration, regarded the idea of a return of the Empire with disgust, and begged him 'jealously to defend and preserve our young Republic'. His conversations in Switzerland had been particularly reassuring.[3] But once again he did not reveal the identity of these important people or of the participants in his Swiss conversations.[4] 'Secrecy', he said, would long 'weigh upon these discreet conversations.' It still does.

By now the quest for foreign intelligence had become an annual habit. In the summer of 1876 as President of the Budget Committee he thought of going to England to see Dilke and to study the British income tax system on the spot.[5] But he changed his mind. He had wanted to take Léonie Léon with him,[6] but this could have created difficulties, as she well realised, divining in him a struggle between the statesman and the lover; 'the one fearing to compromise his dignity and his prestige; the other eager to add some gracious pages to a romance so full of poetry'.[7] Discretion was the better part of valour for the statesman. It was romance that won and the fresh pages would be added not in England but in Germany. He was discreet indeed. He abandoned the idea of going to

1. *Lettres*, no. 219, 22 Oct. 1874.

2, See below, pp. 345–6,

3. For his account of his impressiont see *ibid.*, no. 351 of 5 Oct. 1875 to Juliette Adam.

4. Mme Adam said that he was going to Vienna to make things up with his former friend the director of the *Neue Freie Presse* (*Nos amitiés*, p. 275). According to a police report of 16 April 1874 he made use of Gregory Ganesco 'pour faire dire ce qu'il veut à la "Nouvelle presse libre" de Vienne' (A.P.P., BA/918).

5. *Lettres*, no. 286 of 16 Aug. to Dilke.

6. Letter of Léonie Léon 18 Aug. (Ass. Nat., p. 215): 'Notre excursion d'outre-Manche me trotte toujours dans l'esprit.'

7. Letter of 25 Aug. (Ass. Nat., p. 219).

England at all and on 4 September left Paris ostensibly to stay with his friend Dubochet and once more enjoy the beauties of the Vaud. But, he told Juliette Adam, once he was by the Lake of Geneva he threw all his plans overboard, changed trains, took a ticket for Berne, shaved off his beard, 'becoming uglier than usual', and set off with 'a fixed idea'. This fixed idea he attributed to one of his talks with Juliette herself: 'We both said: how useful, how fruitful it would be *to go to Germany* and to take advantage of the season of manoeuvres to see for oneself on the spot the results of this military organisation of which we have been the victims and of which we still are the destined target.'[1] What he did not say was that the discarding of his plans was premeditated, that he was joined for a while by Léonie Léon and that it was the two of them together travelling either as M. and Mme Péphau or as M. and Mme Massabie (the maiden name of Gambetta's mother) that made a grand tour of the new empire.[2] He returned, however, 'laden with notes, impressions and information', and more than ever impressed by Bismarck's prodigious work and the might of Germany's 'formidable military organisation'. He had been, he said, to Mainz and Frankfurt and then across to Saxony, where the manoeuvres were being held. He saw military reviews at Leipzig and Merseburg where the Emperor had his headquarters and he returned by way of Berlin, Hanover, Magdeburg, Karlsruhe and Baden. It was an adventurous as well as an amorous foray and it showed Gambetta's remarkable determination to see things for himself. There is little doubt that he was well informed about Germany. But his notes have not survived and his informants are unknown.

In September 1875 Gambetta had referred to 'suspect alliances'. When France was isolated and clearly had no hope of military *revanche* without an ally the phrase may seem surprising. But what allies were possible in the German-dominated Europe of the 'seventies? Although at particular

1. *Lettres*, no. 287, 20 Sept.
2. Gambetta, in his letter to Juliette Adam (no. 287), said that he left Lausanne on 5 Sept. and did a grand tour of Germany 'en 15 jours'. Léonie Léon was back with her family on the 16th (letter to Gambetta of that date, Ass. Nat., p. 225), so Gambetta's visit was either shorter than he made out or she left him before it ended. He did not return direct to Paris but went to stay with his rich friend M. Dubochet at the Château des Crêtes. While he was there he visited the Simplon tunnel (the building of which he had supported in 1873—*Ass. Nat. A.*, vol. 17 an., p. 375) with Dubochet and a former President of the Swiss Confederation, Paul Cérésole. Presumably by this time he had grown his beard again! Pillias in his *Léonie Léon* (p. 84) asked whether it was in 1875 or 1876 that Gambetta was accompanied on his German visit by Léonie Léon and her son. Her son is unlikely to have gone with them in 1876, for in the Ass. Nat. letter just quoted she says that she was alone in her compartment from Strasbourg to Paris. There is no evidence that she and her son accompanied Gambetta in 1875, but very few letters have survived for that year.

moments Gambetta reviewed the European situation or elements in it and expatiated upon his hopes and fears, he nowhere committed himself to a systematic review of France's possible partners. It is, however, evident that he was well aware how limited was the choice. Austria was clearly ruled out after the Saxon Beust had been succeeded as Minister for Foreign Affairs by the Hungarian Andrassy. Indeed Gambetta affected to believe that it was already due to Andrassy that Austria had been prevented from intervening on France's side in the war of 1870; that she was a potential prey to nationalist disruption; that Germany and Hungary had entered into partnership, and that as a result Bismarck would one day take Vienna, thus realising what the twentieth century would call the Anschluss.[1] England, too, he appears to have discounted. The *République Française* reflected the traditional French anglophobia.[2] After Disraeli's Manchester speech on 3 April 1872, in which he had reminded his audience of England's imperial commitments and declared that her policy towards Europe would be one of proud reserve, it asked what help could seriously be expected from a nation which so easily deserted the field of its traditional policy.[3] A little later it was still more categorical. It agreed with Duvergier de Hauranne, the author of a recent article in the *Revue des Deux Mondes*, that an alliance with England would be insane: 'How can one conceive of an alliance between two nations whose feelings are in perpetual contradiction? Great Britain requires a Europe that is tributary. ... England seeks clients, she scorns making friends.'[4] On occasion Gambetta himself might speak differently. For instance, in January 1873 he told a *New York Herald* correspondent that he wanted to be on cordial terms with England which, with Switzerland, was the only country that would really be friendly to a republic in France.[5] On occasion, too, the tone of his paper might become less acid, but, despite her restraint of Germany in 1875, Gambetta for the time being seems to have had little real faith in the 'egotistical England'—a very few people, he wrote scornfully in the autumn of 1876, 'propose an alliance with Austria and

1. *Lettres*, no. 289, 17 Oct. 1876; cf. *R.F.*, 10 Nov. 1871: 'Faute d'avoir cherché dans l'égalité des droits la base de l'union des peuples qui la composent, l'empire d'Autriche est condamnée à une prochaine et inévitable dissolution.' The unpublished, undated letter quoted by Deschanel (*Gambetta*, p. 197) advocating a Franco-Austrian alliance is not included in Halévy and Pillias's *Lettres*. They presumably thought it suspect. Charles Maurras later (*Action Française*, 1 Jan. 1933) attributed what he called the failure of the Third Republic to effect 'une manoeuvre politique essentielle dont l'axe devait passer par Londres, Paris, Vienne' to Gambetta's anticlerical policy.

2. See, e.g., 5 Jan. 1872, 'Lettres d'Angleterre'.

3. 6 April 1872.

4. Leader of 7 June 1872.

5. *New York Herald*, 27 Jan. 1873.

England as though the three of us could fight the two northern courts' (Russia and Prussia).[1] England had ships but she did not have armed men.

Once Austria and England were eliminated, only two great European powers, Italy and Russia, remained. But in a letter of September 1874 he had written of strangling the Germanic monster between the Latins in the west and the Slavs in the east.[2] 'The Latins in the West'—did this loose phrase mean just the French or was he thinking not only of Italy but also of Spain? Italy, like England and Austria, had failed to come to France's aid in 1870 and since her occupation of Rome in 1870 she had lost the sympathy of French Catholics who periodically agitated for the restoration of the temporal power. Gambetta, with his Italian ancestry, naturally favoured friendship with Italy, but for the time being he had to recognise that the Roman question appeared to be almost as much an obstacle to this as Alsace-Lorraine in a bigger way was a barrier to good Franco-German relations.[3] But Spain was a different matter. Here in the early 1870s was a specific foreign problem on which Gambetta was bound to take a categorical line.

As a staunch Republican and one who had played so notable a part in the war originating from the Hohenzollern candidature for the Spanish crown, he was inevitably preoccupied by events across the Pyrenees. In the monarchical Europe of the early 'seventies the only other republic that might have counted in European politics and been both a friend and a possible basis for a future alliance of Latin peoples was the Republic of Spain. Gambetta knew a number of the Republican leaders and in February 1873 the British Ambassador in Madrid reported having heard 'from the best sources' that they had been in intimate communication with him and rarely acted without his advice.[4] This is very doubtful, yet for a brief time the Republic was under the guidance of his friend and counterpart, the great democratic orator Emilio Castelar, who, like Gambetta, was fundamentally a moderate.[5] But Republican Spain was in turmoil and at the end of August 1873, when Castelar was in a dominant position,

1. *Lettres*, nos. 289, 17 Oct. 1876, and 300, 27 Jan. 1877.
2. *Lettres*, no. 206.
3. For a curious report of Gambetta's expressing scorn for Italy, see, however, *D.D.I.*, Seconda Serie, vol. iii, no. 297, the Consul-General at Niceto Visconti-Venosta, 13 Jan. 1872. The Italian government's disquiet at French Catholic activities had been expressed to the French Minister in Rome in April 1872. It increased when MacMahon was elected President and the reign of 'Moral Order' was inaugurated (Renouvin, *op. cit.*, p. 86).
4. Layard to Granville, 26 Feb. 1873, F.O. 146, 1665. The *R.F.* printed a great deal of Spanish news in 1872–73.
5. For articles in the *R.F.* in praise of Castelar see 16/17 July and 17 Sept. 1873.

his government was hard pressed. It was faced by insurrection both from the Carlist Right and from the Internationalist Left who were supported by many French Communard refugees. This Left-wing revolt shocked and dismayed Gambetta who had hoped that extremists outside as well as within France would have learnt a lesson from the horrors of the Commune and from its repression. It was in his eyes a wholly unjustifiable and criminal insurrection. The very existence of the Spanish Republic rightly seemed to him to be at stake and at this crucial juncture he took it upon himself to write to Castelar, the one man, he said, in whom he had confidence, a long letter of affectionate encouragement and advice.[1] The French Republican party, he told him, utterly condemned 'the rebellion of your dissidents'. The supreme struggle must come before the end of the year. Castelar had only three months in which to save the situation, the three months during which the Cortes was prorogued.[2] 'Take advantage', Gambetta urged him, 'of this period of legal dictatorship to finish off the Red flag and the Carlist standard; be precise and implacable. Let everyone . . . who is in any sort an accomplice of the rebels be court-martialled and dealt with in the name of the Patrie en danger.' In this way he would rally the great majority who were thirsting for stability. He should, like the Northerners after the American Civil War, deprive all those involved in insurrection of their civil rights for ten years and he should dismiss and replace all officials who did not at once carry out his orders. Just as Gambetta himself had in February 1871 decreed the ineligibility of all former Bonapartist deputies and others, so he now urged a similar course upon Castelar, invoking, however, not his own abortive example but that of the U.S.A. He added that he did not understand how it was that from the outset the Republicans had not seized all the coastal landing places so as to stop Carlist supplies. If Castelar did not hesitate to take these energetic measures the Spanish Republicans could found the Republic in Spain (as Thiers had done in France, though he did not mention the precedent), through 'the ruthless repression of disorder'. Above all, Castelar must have the will to act, even if this meant 'veiling the statue of the law'. 'Act, act, my dear friend, the Republicans are with you.' Thus spoke the former 'dictator' of France to the man about to become virtual dictator of Spain.

But his advice and appeal and all Castelar's efforts were in vain. Castelar's difficulties were enormous; he was determined to crush the Internationalists, but did not succeed in recapturing the strategic port of

1. *Lettres*, no. 161 *bis*, 29 Aug. 1873.
2. Castelar was elected President of the Executive Power on 6 Sept. 1873 and the Cortes were in fact prorogued for four months, until 2 Jan. 1874. During this period Castelar governed by decree.

Cartagena; he was dependent on an army whose political sympathies were by no means wholly Republican; the Republicans were divided by personal feuds, and when the Cortes reassembled in January 1874 he was defeated and resigned. The way was open for the reestablishment of the Monarchy. Gambetta was bitterly disappointed and disillusioned with his friend. Castelar came to Paris in the autumn of 1874 and Gambetta entertained him to 'a Pantagruelic lunch', but his doubts of Castelar's political effectiveness were confirmed. When he was questioned about his period of rule and his country's foreign policy Gambetta found him evasive, obscuring the issues with a flood of words: 'While I listened to him I invariably thought of Lamartine and Ollivier and I found myself inwardly hating him.' When the two men parted Gambetta felt that a wall of bronze had come between them—'more than ever we are separated by the Pyrenees.'[1] They met again in November 1875 at dinner with another man of many words, Victor Hugo, and were superficially reconciled.[2] In January 1876 the *République Française* cordially hailed Castelar's election to the Spanish Cortes as a Republican deputy for Barcelona.[3] But fundamentally the rift remained and in the last year of his own life Gambetta would wonder how he had ever taken 'this troubadour' for a politician.[4]

Henceforward, after the restoration of Monarchy in 1874, Spain counted for little in Gambetta's calculations. The alliance of the Latin peoples, if he had ever seriously entertained it, was a chimera. When England and Austria were suspect as partners and Italy was kept apart by the Papal barrier, only Russia remained.

A writer with a taste for melodrama might, after reading Gambetta's letters, argue that his ideas on foreign policy were shaped by two women who were pulling him in different directions, Juliette Adam who ardently desired an alliance with Russia, and Léonie Léon who wanted an accommodation with Germany. To make his argument more titillating he might add that between these was a third who was a Russian agent, the Princess Troubetzkoï herself: and for good measure he might echo an unscrupulous romancer of the Action Française, Léon Daudet, and proclaim that Léonie Léon was a German spy. But he would simplify the facts, strain the evidence and be undeserving of the name of historian. Léonie Léon and Juliette Adam were indeed two of the women Gambetta saw and wrote to most frequently and his longest letters on foreign affairs were those addressed to Juliette. But this does not mean that they

1. *Lettres*, no. 219, 22 Oct. 1874 (cf. letter of 3 Oct. to Léonie Léon, L.G.).
2. *Lettres*, no. 257, 28 Nov. 1875.
3. 27 Jan.
4. *Lettres*, no. 556, 12 Aug. 1882.

dictated his views or that he had no independence of judgement. Princess Troubetzkoï was indeed a friend of Gortschakoff and may even have aspired to play in French politics of the 1870s a role not dissimilar to that of Princess Lieven in the 1840s, but whether that made her an 'agent' with the special connotations of that word is open to question.[1] As for the charge that Léonie Léon was a spy, there is no shred of evidence to sustain it.[2] But she and Juliette certainly pulled in different directions, and this the correspondence between Léonie and Gambetta which has recently come to light makes more than ever clear.

In an undated letter, probably of 1873, Léonie had told Gambetta of a *mot* which was going the round of the salons: 'You are marrying a Russian endowed with several millions and your reply to congratulations is: "My intention has always been to make an alliance with Russia".'[3] But while it is known that Thiers hoped for an eventual Russian alliance it is by no means evident that Gambetta did so. It is true that in 1874, after a visit from the Serbian minister Ristich, he wrote enthusiastically to Juliette Adam that in him he divined 'a proud and secret ally for the day when we must seize and strangle the Germanic monster between the Latins of the west and the Slavs in the east. . . . It is on the borders of Europe and Asia that we must find our comrades in war and deliverance.' The Serbs were destined to be 'The Piedmont of the East. . . . When they have created Southern Slavia, these Macedonians of the North will have had their day as dictators of Europe.'[4] This was indeed one of those many letters which contained 'a considerable dose of imagination'. As Juliette Adam was to remark, he much exaggerated the potential power of the Balkan peoples,[5] while for all his talk of 'the east' there was no specific word of Russia. He might often see Princess Troubetzkoï, he might assure her that the old French Republican who was enthusiastic in championing the Poles was now an extinct species and that 'we must be glad of it',[6] but, despite his friendship with her and despite the ardent Russophilia of his much closer 'Cossack' friend Juliette Adam, he seems to have been generally reserved so far as Russia was concerned. It was a reserve which was maintained even though he believed that Bismarck was basically

1. Many contemporaries simply refer to her as the hostess presiding over a brilliant salon. 'Diplomats', wrote C. de B. (*Letters from Paris*, p. 211, 21 Oct. 1875), 'call this princess the "Great Question Mark". She is always asking the most awkward questions with the most unruffled air.'
2. See Pillias, *op. cit.*, pp. 133–6.
3. Ass. Nat., p. 46.
4. *Lettres*, no. 206.
5. *Nos amitiés*, p. 166. There seems to be no justification for J. Chastenet's assertion (*Gambetta*, p. 230), 'il est russophile décidé.'
6. *Lettres*, no. 198, attributed to July 1874.

hostile to Russia.[1] His letters to the Princess reflect her interest in France's internal affairs, not his in Russia. Was his reserve because he, the staunch Republican, detested Russian autocracy? Possibly, yet his letters do not reveal such a motive and his realism might have been expected to rise superior to such dislikes.[2] Was it because he knew that Gortschakoff, the Russian Chancellor, was also reserved[3] or because he regarded the Tsar as irremediably hostile to Republicanism?

There is no clear evidence. But if he was cautious and 'more than ever suspicious of Russia's formidable appetite' in the Balkans as the Eastern question loomed up anew,[4] he was perhaps ready to try the Russian ground, particularly in the summer of 1875 after the war scare in which both Russia and Great Britain had intervened to keep the peace.[5] If Juliette Adam could be believed, the great diplomatic moment of 1875 for him would have been the interview with Gortschakoff which, to her bitter disappointment, failed to materialise. Unfortunately, her dramatic account of Gambetta's journey to Lausanne where she alleged that he had expected to meet the Chancellor is the only one and therefore inevitably suspect.[6] Once they had reached Lausanne Gambetta left the Adams at the station while he hurried off to keep his assignation. But he found only the Princess and no Gortschakoff. She told him that the Chancellor would be ready to meet him once he had received the Tsar's authorisation for which he had telegraphed on the previous day. He asked Gambetta meanwhile to go to Vevey or wait at Lausanne. But the last thing Gambetta desired was an *official* interview 'in which every word will be important'. What he had wanted, he said, was a secret and apparently fortuitous

1. See especially the interview reported in the *Neue Freie Presse* of Vienna, 19 Nov. 1876; also *R.F.*, 4 Sept. 1872, article expressing the view that the two countries' interests were irreparably opposed.

2. An article in the first number of the *R.F.* (7 Nov. 1871, p. 2) did, however, remark that the idea of 'une immense démocratie autoritaire' was profoundly repugnant to French democracy.

3. In a letter of 12 Oct. 1874, the Foreign Minister Decazes told his friend Chaudordy that the French Minister in Berne, Bernard d'Harcourt, had recently had two interviews with Gortschakoff at Vevey and that the Prince had been severely critical of France's internal divisions (Chaudordy papers, vol. i); cf. a severe leader in *Moscow Gazette* (Dec. 1876) referred to in *The Times*, 23 Dec. 1876, p. 10.

4. Letter of 19 Aug. 1875 (L.G.).

5. Deschanel (*Gambetta*, p. 198) and others at one time made much of certain letters alleged to have been written by Gambetta to Ranc in 1875 and 1876 in which he categorically favoured a Russian alliance. But for reasons which they preferred not to make public the careful editors of Gambetta's *Lettres* doubted their authenticity and did not include them in their collection of his letters.

6. *Nos amitiés*, pp. 271–6. As early as 4 Dec. 1874 Decazes, in a postscript to a letter to Chaudordy had written: 'Savez vous quelle est la personne qui soit d'intermédiaire entre Gortschakoff et Gambetta?' (Chaudordy Papers, vol. i).

meeting in which he and his interlocutor could talk with complete freedom and without commitment on either side. He evidently felt that he had been trapped and insisted on taking the first train on to Venice, even after the Princess had reappeared with the news that imperial authorisation had just arrived. The two women were almost in tears, but Gambetta was adamant and the train left. Later a letter came from the Princess saying that nothing was irremediably lost. It was in consequence of this, according to Juliette Adam, that Gambetta promised to pass through Switzerland again on his way back to France. But there is no evidence that the 'discreet' and secret conversations he had there on his return journey included any with Gortschakoff.[1]

The two women, the Russian aristocrat and the Russophile Frenchwoman, may have been discomfited on 3 September 1875. But Gambetta did not break with either; to break with the Princess would have been impolitic, while Juliette Adam was still one of his closest friends with whom he delighted to correspond and to stay. Indeed in the following year the tone of his letters to Juliette was warmer than ever before.[2] Yet the tenor of his correspondence with Léonie Léon in this same year following the Gortschakoff episode suggests that he thought that the Princess had deceived him or that she promised more than she could perform.[3] In 1876 with the exacerbation of the Eastern question his distrust of Russia had evidently increased. In the letter of October 1876 to Juliette already quoted he reviewed the situation at length: there were two parties who took diametrically opposed views of the origins and consequences of the Eastern crisis. One considered it to be the outcome of the Russo-German collaboration of 1860–71 and believed that while Russia was busy in the Balkans Bismarck would seize the opportunity for a fresh attack on France. They concluded that war was inevitable. 'Where is the remedy? Most of them do not speak of one, the boldest urge a Russian alliance for France, a very few propose an alliance with Austria and England, as though the three of us could fight the two northern courts.' Happily he was of the other party: he believed with them that Bismarck had stirred up the Eastern crisis, that he had deliberately encour-

---

1. Marcos, *op. cit.*, p. 392, n. 106, says that nothing is less certain than that Princess Troubetzkoï tried to arrange a meeting between Gambetta and Gortschakoff.

2. What would Léonie have thought if she had read the ending of Gambetta's letter of 20 Sept. 1876 to Juliette (*Lettres*, no. 287)? 'Je suis si doucement habitué à vivre dans votre rayonnement, que le reste de la terre sans vous me paraît toujours froid, vide et sans lumière. Je cheminerai dans les ténèbres jusqu'à ce que je vous aurai retrouvée.'

3. On 1 Jan. 1876 he sent the Princess his 'voeux les plus sincères pour le succès de vos patriotiques desseins', but we are left guessing what these were (*Lettres*, no. 260).

aged both tension between Austria and Russia and Hungarian preponderance in the Dual Monarchy in order eventually to lay his hands on Vienna. He believed that Germany and Hungary would be the godparents of a new Greco-Slav confederation which would serve as a barrier to Russian encroachment while making ready to eject the Turks. Bismarck was waiting for the moment to push Austria, Britain or Russia into conflict. But Gambetta's remedy was not a Russian alliance. Indeed he referred roundly to Russia's 'responsibility for a policy of usurpation and conquest' in the Balkans.[1] Far from allying with her, if a new conflict arose, France must wait uncommitted.[2]

> Europe has allowed her to be crushed. Europe has thought she can do without her, let Europe settle her affairs without us if she can. When much time and gold and many men have been lost ... people will come back to her and then she can say ... to those who invite her to join in concerted action, what will you give me? And who knows, it is perhaps from the side from which one least expects them that the most splendid proposals will come.

In his reserve or even hostility towards Russia he was certainly encouraged by Léonie Léon. Already in an undated letter attributed to the year 1873 she had expressed anxiety because she thought that Russia was exercising too great an influence.[3] Was it feminine jealousy of the Princess, and even perhaps of Juliette Adam to whom she never directly referred, that led her to write as she did in 1876? In March she told Gambetta roundly that, so far as concerned foreign affairs, she thought the help 'of *La P* quite and even more than useless; Europe has understood you; France approves you, the monster is being tamed'.[4] In May she reproved her 'dear great man' for being splendidly naïve, 'you who are ... the object of all feminine desires' (*toutes les convoitises féminines*); and she ended by saying that 'the marmoset' (the nickname she and Gambetta henceforward mysteriously gave to the Princess) had had the skill doubly to make his chords vibrate; by hoisting his colours and 'by lifting a corner of the veil which floats on the diplomatic horizon!'[5]

1. *Lettres*, no. 289. Already in Sept. 1875 he had referred to the increasing 'appétits des puissances du nord' (*ibid.*, no. 255).

2. The *R.F.* constantly urged that France must maintain an absolute reserve in the Eastern crisis, see e.g. leaders of 8 and 10 Oct. 1876.

3. Ass. Nat., p. 127.

4. *Ibid.*, p. 153, 8 March, J. Chastenet (*Gambetta*, p. 278) interprets '*La P*' as referring to La Païva.

5. Ass. Nat., p. 171, 18 May. In the meantime Gambetta had told her that he was engaged in a very big diplomatic affair (*rien d'ailleurs du Ouistiti*) in which he was quite pleased with 'the old soldier [MacMahon] and his ministers', but he could not say much about it on paper (letter of 30 March, L.G.; cf. letter of 19 April). Once more we are left mystified. I assume that the 'Ouistiti' was not Mme Adam.

How distasteful to her this evidently was! While Gambetta appears to have been hesitating in his attitude, Léonie Léon made no secret of hers: 'I persist in putting Russia aside, as having no community of interest with us from any point of view.'[1] 'M. Thiers's man will cause you to fall right back into the arms of the marmoset and we shall have a fresh struggle to extricate ourselves from Russia.'[2] Cialdini, the new Italian ambassador in Paris, 'can be a powerful support to you in your foreign negotiations, that is better than the marmoset'.[3] 'The tenderness the marmoset bestows on you from the top of her palm-tree keeps running in my head; at bottom, this is significant enough and very consoling, if she is really well informed of the way of thinking of foreign courts.'[4] But was she? This slight softening was only momentary—a month later Léonie was writing that 'this accursed marmoset, who is always a factor in our quarrels, is decidedly difficult to deal with: one must observe "prudence and silence" towards her as in the comic operas'.[5] In between, a letter of 22 July contained a paragraph of a single mysterious sentence in Léonie's sometimes precious style: 'And is the note the colour of hope on the way to the banks of the Neva?'[6] Another cryptic sentence in a letter of 4 August suggests that Gambetta was perhaps hoping that the Princess would make another attempt to arrange a meeting with Gortschakoff. But there is no certainty. This and the other secrets of the 'marmoset's' intrigues are arcana unlikely to be revealed except in some hitherto unexplored Troubetzkoï or Gortschakoff archives.[7]

If Léonie detested the Princess, distrusted the Princess's country, and hoped for peace and 'the withdrawal of the Cossacks in the Balkans' she shared Gambetta's fear and admiration of Germany and 'the Monster'.[8] She encouraged him in the idea that one day he might be Bismarck's

1. Ass. Nat., p. 178, 5 June.
2. *Ibid.*, p. 182, 12 June. The reference to 'M. Thiers's man' is obscure. Perhaps Léonie Léon was referring to Gen. Le Flô whom Thiers had appointed ambassador at St Petersburg in 1871 and who held the post until 1879.
3. *Ibid.*, p. 190, 2 July. She does not mention Cialdini by name, but wrote 'La nomination du général . . .', but it is clear from other evidence that it was to him that she referred.
4. *Ibid.*, p. 197, 15 July.
5. *Ibid.*, p. 211, 10 Aug.
6. *Ibid.*, p. 200, 22 July. Cf. another cryptic reference 28 July, p. 206: 'Cela chauffe du côté du ouistiti, elle embrasse la Russie quel volcan!!' It probably relates to the Eastern Question.
7. The Princess left Paris in the summer of 1877. 'De graves intérêts', wrote Juliette Adam, 'peut-être un ordre, la font rentrer en Russie' (J. Adam, *Après l'abandon de la revanche*, 1910, p. 9).
8. e.g. 'Le monstre est sublime, et ses retraites sont des abîmes insondables d'habileté diplomatique!' (Ass. Nat., p. 182, 12 June).

match, confront him, charm him and do a splendid deal. How marvellous, she might well think, that she, the obscure Creole in the shadows, should inspire such a move and that her 'divine beloved', the grocer's son from Cahors, should do business with the great Prussian Junker, the most formidable man in Europe! In her letters to Gambetta some such plan, clouded by obscure allusions, can be seen developing. In March 1876 she tells him with excessive adulation that his genius would dominate Bismarck's 'with all the superiority of your eloquence, the magnetism your talent exercises upon the masses, the subtlety of your mind which is far more perspicacious than his, the moderation you have learnt in the course of political life and finally the whole power of your will which has given birth to circumstances, whereas his only merit is to know how to profit by them'.[1] In April she suggests that 'the Monster's' intentions are perhaps not as hateful as Gambetta supposes.[2] In June she refers to 'the success of our plan, since you call it so. For the monster it will have the attraction of a new combination and one on diplomatic ground which he has not been able to consider seriously because he did not know if it was possible to encounter us except armed to the teeth.'[3] Eleven days later she exclaims: 'How dramatic it would be if on one of his morning outings he found himself face to face with the only intelligence which can be a match for his own!'[4] and at the end of July 'Ah! I know very well where I should like to go if I were free to travel! For the moment the important thing is to attain the conjunction of the two stars you know of as soon as the hour of vacation has struck.'[5]

It seems then as though the notion of a meeting with Bismarck was first toyed with by Gambetta and Léonie as early as 1876.[6] But, despite the reference to the 'new combination . . . on diplomatic ground', it is probable that for the time being they got no further with any serious attempts to arrange one and that at this stage it was little more than a wild idea which it amused them to talk about. If in their 'amorous tour' of Germany in September they had unexpectedly encountered Bismarck they could hardly have expected to force a serious interview. But how

---

1. Ass. Nat., p. 153, 8 March. Cf. *ibid.*, 16 Sept., p. 225: 'Votre génie vaut celui du monstre, vous êtes jeune, la France est riche . . .'
2. *Ibid.*, p. 163, 16 April.
3. *Ibid.*, p. 178, 5 June.
4. *Ibid.*, p. 184, 16 June.
5. *Ibid.*, p. 208, 31 July. I have interpreted the two stars as being Gambetta and Bismarck. But Léonie may have been simply alluding to herself and Gambetta and their being able to have a holiday together: or she may have been referring to Gambetta and MacMahon (see below, pp. 378).
6. Pillias and other authors ascribed the first moves to 1877; but Chastenet (*op. cit.*, p. 278) thinks that the idea first came to Henckel von Donnersmarck 'dès 1876'.

amusing if as a simple, unrecognised and, without his beard, unrecognisable tourist, Gambetta could contrive to have a preview of 'the Monster' with whom he hoped one day to do business! Perhaps this was what they did contrive, for sometime later he told Juliette Adam that while he was watching a review in Germany he had been brushed against by Bismarck who was on horseback.[1]

The German tour of September 1876 certainly did not weaken their desire to pursue their plan and in October a reference in one of Léonie's letters reveals that she was reading a description of 'the Monster's' house, probably Varzin in East Prussia.[2] But by then a new parliamentary session was imminent and, although Gambetta seldom lost sight of European developments, crises at home would speedily demand priority.

It must not be thought that the idea of improving Franco-German relations was something new and peculiar to Gambetta. At the time of the war scare of 1875 Bismarck had suggested that such fears of war would be reduced if some common ground of agreement between the two countries could be discovered and, although Decazes tactfully avoided any commitment, Bismarck realised that a change of attitude was desirable and allowed the tension to relax. The change, it has been said, was hastened by three factors in particular, the influence of Thiers, 'the dislike of both governments for the policy of Russia in the Near East; and last, the common anticlericalism of Bismarck and the Republican party in France'.[3] It was the last of the three which seems to have been uppermost in Gambetta's mind when he was himself searching for some diplomatic ground or pretext for entering into conversation with his foe.[4] On 12 October 1876 he had a long talk with Sir M. E. Grant Duff, the English Liberal M.P. and former Under-Secretary of State for India, to whom he had been introduced by John Morley, the editor of the *Fortnightly Review*. In the course of it Grant Duff asked him 'what he thought of the chances of a *guerre de revanche*'. He answered:

> I more and more doubt whether there will be any *guerre de revanche* at all. The fact is that nowadays, when peace is once made between two conterminous nations, so many joint interests grow up and become rapidly strong that, with every month that passes, the chances of war are lessened. There is another thing ... which has great influence upon myself and my friends—I mean

1. Pillias, *op. cit.*, p. 93.
2. Letter of 8 Oct. 1876 (Ass. Nat., p. 230).
3. P. B. Mitchell, *The Bismarckian policy of conciliation with France 1875–1885*. (1935), p. 50.
4. Whether this was 'the new combination' to which Léonie Léon had referred in her letter of 5 June, there is no means of knowing.

Prince Bismarck's ecclesiastical policy. His opposition to ultramontanism is so agreeable to us, that . . . it produces a very great effect upon our minds.[1]

Again in a letter to Juliette Adam on 27 January 1877, Gambetta wrote that the danger of renewed German aggression could be parried in only two ways. The first of these was by entering into relations with Bismarck through secret agents and persuading him to a community of views 'both from the point of view of his struggle against Ultramontanism and . . . of the big industrial and commercial interests'.[2] Ultramontanism, which Gambetta so constantly denounced as a factor which could lead to war,[3] was thus the common element in both the conversation and the letter.

Gambetta's alternative means of parrying the risk of renewed German aggression was still more dramatic. If Germany could not be won over the Concert of Europe must be revived against her. All the European nations now felt threatened by 'Prussia's preponderance'; even Russia felt resentment. And then he let his imagination run riot again, this time in a way reminiscent of his old enemy, Napoleon III, who had so dearly loved to redraw the map of Europe. It would not, he wrote, be difficult to incite Poland to widespread revolt and to persuade Austria to cede Galicia and accept Roumania and the mouths of the Danube by way of compensation. Moreover, if need be, Italy must be given back a stretch of territory in the bay of Genoa 'in order that she should not desert us until we have retaken Strasbourg and Metz'. Then Germany could be hemmed in by a circle of 'iron and fire' (*de fer et du feu*) and, 'however great her military vitality, she could not resist such a gigantic effort undertaken in the name of common security and the reestablishment of the European balance of power'. He asked Juliette for her views, but significantly added that he was going to consult Thiers.[4]

The conversation with Grant Duff and the letter to Juliette Adam thus make it evident that a *rapprochement* with Germany, in other words contact with Bismarck, was the course Gambetta himself favoured. As has been suggested, if Léonie Léon pushed Gambetta towards Bismarck she 'only pushed him to the side on which he wished to fall'.[5] It is equally clear that Gambetta no longer desired a war of *revanche* if France could gain her ends by peaceful means.[6] Here, it must be remembered, he was

1. M. E. Grant Duff, *Notes from a Diary 1873–1881*, vol. i (1898), p. 221.
2. *Lettres*, no. 300.
3. e.g. Speech at Lyon, 28 Feb. 1876 (*Discours*, vol. v, pp. 178–9).
4. *Lettres*, no. 300.
5. Pillias, *op. cit.*, p. 105.
6. An Alsatian deputy later alleged that at a meeting in Gambetta's flat as early as the end of 1871 Gambetta had said: 'Vous nous reviendrez par la paix' (A. Lalance,

no doubt in line with French public opinion, to which he was so sensitive. Already in May 1875 the British Chargé d'Affaires in Paris, Francis Adams, had reported Decazes as saying that

> no one in France is desirous of regaining Alsace and Lorraine by war; there is certainly in the minds of many Frenchmen ... a lively desire to get back the lost Provinces; there are hopes that some diplomatic means may be found whereby Lorraine at least may be restored to France ... this may, they hope, be effected by some compromise or other, one suggests the surrender of the French province in Cochin China, another, less scrupulous, would give compensation at the expense of other nations.[1]

'Was it not', as Pillias has written, 'a fine dream to gain *revanche* without a war, without any dead, without devastation?'[2] As early as 1874, the well-known journalist Emile de Girardin, for whom Gambetta then had no particular respect, had, in the course of a premature campaign for a Franco–German *rapprochement*, written: 'Could we hesitate for a moment between *revanche* without war and war without *revanche*?'[3] Gambetta, too, was to think in terms of colonial compensation. In September 1877 he told an Alsatian deputy in the Reichstag, Auguste Lalance, that a peaceful agreement between the two countries would be infinitely preferable to a war of revenge; by such an agreement Germany might restore her conquest in return for colonial, commercial, or tariff compensations.[4]

Meanwhile he had intended to consult Thiers. At some date unknown the two men, uneasy partners in opposition, had at last begun to resume personal contact. Already in March 1876 Hohenlohe had reported that they were said to be 'cherishing vain hopes of securing the neutralisation

---

1. Adams to Derby, 6 May 1875, F.O. 146, 1810. Cf. Connolly to Lyons 13 Feb. 1876: 'The most hot-headed of Gambetta's Generals and optimist of Thierist ones are now painfully aware that *Revanche* is out of the question for some time to come'; cf. Saint-Valry (*Les Souvenirs et réflexions politiques*, vol. i, p. 107), 22 April 1875: 'On ne trouverait pas un Français sur mille assez aveugle pour croire que la *revanche* ... soit une oeuvre de très longtemps réalisable.'

2. *Op. cit.*, p. 96.

3. *Ibid.*

4. Lalance, *op. cit.*, p. 70. A letter of 15 Oct. from Gambetta to Princess Troubetzkoï (*Lettres*, no. 342) referred to a 'singular project' which she had mentioned. He said he could not discuss it in a letter: 'Je suis d'ailleurs opposé à toute combinaison qui ne serait pas le retour au droit des gens et au droit historique.' No doubt it referred to Alsace-Lorraine.

---

op. cit., pp. 61 and 69). In another conversation, on 24 March 1877, Grant Duff noted that Gambetta's 'tone about Germany was now, as last autumn, very moderate and reasonable' (Grant Duff, *op. cit.*, vol. i, p. 241).

of France for four years'.[1] What Thiers's advice to Gambetta was at the
end of January 1877 is, alas! unknown, but all the indications are that it
favoured the first course outlined in Gambetta's letter of the 27th to
Juliette Adam, namely entering into relations with Bismarck through
secret agents and working for a *rapprochement*. Just as Gambetta went to
Henckel von Donnersmarck's salon in order to reconnoitre 'enemy'
territory, so Thiers talked freely to Hohenlohe and had even attended an
official reception at the German Embassy.[2] He had suggested to a correspondent of the *Kölnische Zeitung* that Alsace and Lorraine might be
bought back.[3] He constantly reiterated France's peaceful intentions and
denied the existence of a war party in Paris and he, too, took the line that
a community of interest in the overthrow of Ultramontanism was a
guarantee for the continuance of good relations between France and
Germany.[4] The crisis of the Seize Mai 1877 would, as will be seen,
strengthen the two Republican leaders' wish for a better understanding
with Germany. But Gambetta's reconciliation with Thiers probably
increased his hostility to the Foreign Minister Decazes. Thiers's was not a
forgiving nature. Decazes was one of the men of 24 May and Thiers
resented his still being in office. In 1877 even before the Seize Mai Gambetta wrote to Léonie Léon hoping that it would be possible to give the
Foreign Minister 'a final blow',[5] but that hope was not to be fulfilled for
another six months.

Meanwhile a *rapprochement* with Italy began to look possible. In an
article of 13 April 1873, the *République Française* had written that the
course of Italian foreign policy would depend on France's internal
evolution: 'The Italian government will be more or less inclined to move
closer to Germany according to the extent to which France inclines to
the Right or to the Left.'[6] Now, in 1876, France had moved to the
Left, while in March a change of ministry had brought the Left into
power in Italy. One consequence was the replacement of the Italian
ambassador in Paris, Nigra, by a man who, Léonie Léon believed, might

1. Hohenlohe, *op. cit.*, p. 52. The story emanated from E. Simon, editor of the
Mémorial diplomatique.
2. Mitchell, *op. cit.*, p. 52. For Thiers's numerous conversations with Hohenlohe
(deliberately encouraged by Bismarck), see Hohenlohe, *passim*, Frank, *op. cit.*,
pp. 63–6, and G.P., vol. i, *passim*.
3. Bülow to Hohenlohe, 28 Dec. 1875 (G.P., vol. i, no. 195).
4. See, e.g., Hohenlohe to Bismarck, 27 Jan. and 3 March (*ibid.*, nos. 201 and 203);
Hohenlohe, *op. cit.*, p. 168, 16 April 1876.
5. Letter of 13 May (L.G.). See also Daudet, *Souvenirs de la présidence du Maréchal
de MacMahon*, pp. 143, 156.
6. For a brief survey of Gambetta's attitude to Italy before the fall of Thiers see
my 'Gambetta, la *République Française* e l'Italia', in *Il Risorgimento e l'Europa*, ed.
V. Frosini (1969), pp. 59–68.

powerfully support Gambetta in his 'negotiations'.[1] On 20 July Gambetta had a long interview with this man, General Cialdini, with which he was very satisfied,[2] and later he consented to see Crispi, the President of the Italian Chamber of Deputies (who was paying a brief visit to Paris) although he had once referred to Crispi's 'faction' as being in Bismarck's pay[3] and although Crispi had the reputation of being fanatically anti-French as well as anticlerical. They had a long and cordial conversation which touched upon disarmament as well as French affairs when Crispi dined with him on 3 September. Gambetta wrote to him in October, hoping to keep in touch.[4] But there was a large dose of opportunism in Gambetta's anticlericalism when it came to international relations. Here at least he was no fanatic. Thus on 11 November 1876 when, in the debate on the budget of the Ministry of Foreign Affairs, de Montjau had proposed to abolish the credits for maintaining the French Embassy to the Vatican, Gambetta had replied with a statesmanlike speech which anticipated his later assertion that anticlericalism was not for export. After pointing out that it was not for a finance committee to resolve the complex question of relations between the French Church and the Holy See, he said that French interests must be considered. However much of a freethinker one might be, it was impossible not to realise that only a detestable

---

1. See above, p. 348. For a leader on the new Italian government's programme see *R.F.*, 2 April.

2. *Lettres*, no. 282. The *R.F.* had hailed Cialdini's appointment on 3 July and urged that the French Legation in Rome should be raised to the status of Embassy; cf. 9 and 25 July. When in the Chamber on 11 Nov. Keller made a derogatory reference to Cialdini Gambetta defended the latter with what must have been embarrassing warmth: 'Messieurs, il n'y a pas dans toute l'Italie une âme plus française et plus devouée à la grandeur de la France !' (*Annales Chambre 1876*, Session Extra-ordinaire, vol. i, p. 157).

3. *Lettres*, no. 221, 15 Nov. 1874.

4. The *R.F.*, 4 Sept., printed a letter from its correspondent in Rome, dated 30 Aug. which described Crispi as 'un des personnages les plus marquants du groupe parlementaire qui, à la Gauche, professe une haine profonde pour la France et une admiration servile pour l'Allemagne'. On the 7th, however, announcing Crispi's presence in Paris, it added: 'C'est à tort qu'on a souvent représenté l'homme d'Etat italien comme un adversaire de la France; M. Crispi qui a tant contribué au delà des Alpes au triomphe des idées modernes, n'a jamais été l'adversaire de notre pays; il n'est l'ennemi que de la théocratie et du césarisme, qui sous le gouvernement de Napoléon III, le firent expulser de France, où il était exilé. . . . Aujourd'hui . . . Crispi ne peut être chez nous qu'un hôte sympathique.' For Crispi's brief account of his interview with Gambetta, published nearly twenty-two years later, see his article 'La conferenza pel disarmo' in *Nuova Antologia*, May 1899, p. 364; also *The Memoirs of Francesco Crispi*, ed. T. Palamenghi-Crispi, vol. ii (1912), pp. 16–18 and 36–7. This gives the text of Gambetta's letter to Crispi of 21 Oct. which was to be taken to him by Armand Ruiz.

foreign policy would fail to take account of the country's diplomatic traditions and of her 'Catholic clientèle in the world'. Yet at the same time he understandably seized the opportunity to express the desirability of ever closer relations between France and Italy.[1] It was significant that when in December 1877 Dufaure at last formed the ministry which ended the protracted crisis of the Seize Mai, the man nominated to the Ministry of Foreign Affairs so long directed by Decazes was the Protestant Waddington, whom some people regarded as a nominee of Gambetta. *The Times* correspondent hailed Waddington's appointment as 'a pledge for England, Germany and Italy'. He would hasten, it said, to resume negotiations concerning the Commercial Treaty with England and he would guarantee Italy and Germany 'against imprudent complaisance' towards clericalism.[2] But the crucial question would still be whether relations with Italy could be so improved as to prevent her from moving still closer to Germany at the expense of France.

Thus the international situation had undergone various changes since 1871 and Gambetta's views had fluctuated in a fluctuating situation. Being mercurial in temperament and writing especially to women, he had sometimes let his imagination run riot according to his mood. Being a nationalist obsessed by Franco-German relations he had no doubt made himself better informed about Germany than about some other European countries. Being for much of the time without formal responsibilities and writing privately he was under no compulsion to formulate a clear-cut policy and stick to it. In 1876 and at the beginning of 1877, as in 1871 he was as mindful as ever of the lost provinces and as fearful as ever of the dangers of France's isolation and the impasse in which it confined her.[3] But he was also no less aware of the perils of any move away from France's basic position of reserve. He saw two ways of escape from her present danger but both were full of risk. The outcome of the battle with clericalism might determine which he would choose, while victory in the battle would certainly open up for him still greater vistas of power and diplomatic influence. Meanwhile, it must be remembered that, ever since 1871, he had been concerned also for the repair of that crucial instrument of power, without which an effective French role in foreign affairs would be unthinkable; he had the army to watch as well as the diplomats.

1. *Discours*, vol. vi, pp. 54–6, and *Annales Chambre, Session Extraordinaire de 1876*, vol. i, pp. 154–8. For comment in the *R.F.*, see leaders of 13 and 16 Nov.
2. *The Times*, 14 Dec., pp. 5–6.
3. Cf. speech at Lille, 6 Feb. 1876, referred to above, p. 272. On the same day he wrote to Juliette Adam: 'Tout va bien. La République est fondée, il reste à la faire grande, forte et de la mener aux Frontières naturelles' (*Lettres*, no. 266).

22

The army
1870–1877

In many of his speeches in 1871 and 1872 Gambetta had spoken of the regeneration of France and the buoyant future which lay ahead under the aegis of the Republic. One of the vital instruments of this regeneration was the army. But the shadows of war and defeat, the dramatic collapse of the Empire, the bloody civil war of the Commune, the fall of one regime and the halting progress of another still darkened the past and clouded men's view of the present. Inevitably the army itself was profoundly shaken by the succession of upheavals in twenty months. Everyone agreed that it must be reformed and made ready for the day of *revanche*, but behind the façade of agreement there were deep cleavages, differences about the kind of army which was required and differences about the kind of society it should serve. With all these issues Gambetta, the man who, against all odds, had desperately attempted to snatch victory from defeat, was profoundly concerned.

Once peace was concluded generals and politicians took up their pens and wrote their apologias. Gambetta himself was not given to this sort of task, but he had immediately seen the importance of publishing an authoritative justification of the conduct of the 'national defence'. He had insisted that Freycinet, who had been his delegate at the Ministry of War, should undertake the work. He had made him go to San Sebastian and read his manuscript to him; he had corrected it himself and urged that it should be published 'as soon as the events of the Commune had ceased to engross attention'.[1] The result was *La Guerre en province pendant le siège de Paris* which appeared later in 1871. The most weighty Republican defence of the war in the provinces, it went through ten editions in less than a year.

At the same time the Assembly had instituted a series of official enquiries

1. Freycinet, *Souvenirs 1848–1878*, pp. 272–3.

into governmental and administrative activities during the war. The battles over the past were thus fought also in parliamentary commissions and courts martial. There was a commission of fifteen to review wartime ranks, a commission of thirty to enquire into the acts of the Government of National Defence and one of sixty to examine war contracts entered into since 18 July 1870. Finally, there was a commission to investigate the circumstances of various capitulations, notably those of Sedan and Metz. The reports of these bodies were gradually completed and presented to parliament in and after 1872. Then the encounters between the men of 4 September and the predominantly Monarchist commissioners became public and added fresh fuel to the flames of parliamentary passion.

In particular they provided material for the continuing fight against the Bonapartists. Just as Thiers had once condemned Gambetta for continuing the war beyond all reason so Gambetta and his friends lost no chance to condemn the Empire for starting and mismanaging it. But the Republicans' failure to win it gave the Bonapartists the chance to try and shift responsibilities. They argued that the final disasters were due to the incompetence of the men of 4 September and not least of Gambetta and his followers. So the fight was all the more bitter and the echoes of the past reverberated anew in the tempestuous incidents of present debate. One celebrated occasion was in May 1872 when Rouher spoke for two hours in a debate on war contracts. It was the former 'Vice-emperor's' first speech since his election to the Assembly, and the Left strikingly demonstrated their growing discipline by hearing him in virtual silence.[1] But when, in a second intervention, 'this lawyer of the Empire at bay', as Gambetta called him, sought to divert the wrath of some of his critics by a violent attack on the men of 4 September, Gambetta bounded to their defence:

> If you had arms, why . . . did you conclude forty-eight contracts on iniquitous terms? And if you had no arms . . . you were traitors and thieves. . . . Oh! you will not escape your responsibilities. . . . Mexico has already made short work . . . of . . . this detestable crew . . . justice has begun, it has seized Morny and Jecker in turn, and Maximilian and Napoleon III! It holds Bazaine! It awaits you![2]

It did indeed hold Bazaine, the Marshal who had capitulated at Metz in October 1870, the man whom Gambetta had in a fiery proclamation

1. *The Times* (18 May, p. 7) reported that Rouher spoke 'with only two interventions and the culprits were instantly silenced by the captains and leaders of parties . . . General Chanzy, M. Gambetta, M. Carayon-Latour and one or two others seemed to act like Generals of Division of their respective Parties'.

2. For the text of Gambetta's indictment, see *Ass. Nat. A.*, vol. xi, pp. 489–93, and *Discours*, vol. ii, pp. 292–3.

immediately branded as a traitor. Bazaine had been grossly incompetent, but he was not a traitor;[1] yet, because of that proclamation and because he was a Bonapartist, his trial and condemnation seemed all the more necessary to many of the opponents of the Empire, above all those on the Left. When he was brought before a court martial Gambetta and his friends continued to assume his guilt. They and the *République Française* exulted over Bazaine's condemnation to death in December 1873 and did their utmost to exploit the whole affair in order to discredit the political party they still feared most.[2] Thus, in this and other ways the war was still a living and momentous issue. But how effective Gambetta's exploitation of it for anti-Bonapartist purposes was, it is impossible to judge. It may sometimes have prevented Bonapartism from making converts; but, on the whole, it is likely that most men's attitudes to the events of 1870–71 were firmly fixed and that all the propaganda and all the fiery speeches of deputies and censures by commissions of enquiry did little to change them.

The results of the investigations of the Commission appointed to enquire into the acts of the Government of National Defence were published in eighteen volumes which appeared at intervals between 1872 and 1875. Gambetta had, of course, been one of the numerous witnesses and he had been hard pressed by some members of the Commission. But he had been treated courteously by the president, the Orleanist Saint-Marc Girardin,[3] and had been allowed to begin his evidence with a long personal statement which was scarcely interrupted. In his testimony, as also subsequently in public debate, he accepted responsibility for actions taken in accordance with his general instructions and he had been prompt to defend former subordinates such as Freycinet, Le Cesne and Naquet who were particularly under attack.[4] The enquiries did not impair his

1. See, e.g., Michael Howard, *The Franco-Prussian War* (1961), p. 283.

2. See, e.g., *Lettres*, nos. 165, 166 and 168 to Ranc. Gambetta gave evidence before the court martial on 21 Nov. 1873 (see *Discours*, vol. iv, pp. 91–108). The death sentence was immediately commuted to one of twenty years' imprisonment.

3. Saint-Marc Girardin, unwell, had been replaced for a while by the Vice-President of the Commission, the Bonapartist Daru. Gambetta declined to be interrogated when Daru was in the chair and Saint-Marc Girardin consented to return to duty when Gambetta gave evidence. For his evidence, see *Ass. Nat. A.*, vol. xxiii, pp. 480–506. The publisher E. Leroux, who printed most of Gambetta's speeches in pamphlet form, thought it worth doing the same for his 'déposition', which was put on sale for fifteen centimes.

4. See, e.g., *Ass. Nat. A.*, vol. xiii, pp. 458ff, *Discours*, vol. i, p. 441. After the end of the war contracts debate in which Rouher had spoken, Léonie Léon was horrified to learn that Gambetta had accepted a motion by Broglie on 22 May expressing confidence in the Assembly's war contracts commission. She said he had been caught in a web like an innocent fly and that Le Cesne was 'un infâme gredin' who had

reputation except among those for whom it was already tarnished. They helped to keep controversy alive and they might be used as electoral propaganda, as in 1876 when the Buffet government had the Boreau–Lajanadie report upon the acts of the Delegation of Tours and Bordeaux published in the *Journal Officiel*. In the end, however, their main function, like that of many similar investigations, was to provide material for historians.

But it was with the future of the army that Gambetta and Freycinet were above all concerned. When they looked back at the war it was not only to justify themselves but to learn and teach its lessons. They had ended *La Guerre en province* with a warning: 'We must not be taken unawares! Let history not be able to say of us that we wasted time in debate while the enemy was still encamped on our soil.' France, Freycinet had said in his book, had been defeated because of her inferiority in numbers, armament and organisation. It was clearly with Gambetta's approval that he had emphasised the importance of training and discipline, urged the need for a general staff comparable with that of Prussia, and stressed the desirability of standardising small arms and improving the organisation of the supply services. Before long the seriousness with which Gambetta and his friends took the problems of army reform would be demonstrated by their new paper, the *République Française*. In it Freycinet was to write a whole series of articles elaborating on the ideas already put forward in *La Guerre en province*, and for a while the paper devoted an almost daily section to 'Military Affairs'.

The war had indeed been Gambetta's road to Damascus. Before 1870 he had shared the prevailing Republican distrust of the long-term professional army as a tool in the hands of a detested regime. In 1869 he had accepted the celebrated Belleville programme which had included a demand for the suppression of standing armies; his preference apparently was for the kind of citizen army enshrined in revolutionary legend. But the conduct of war opened his eyes to military realities. It gave him first-hand knowledge. It led him, no doubt, to mistrust the value of the National Guards and he made no attempt to speak against their dissolution in August 1871.[1] It impressed on him the value as well as the defects of the professional soldier and it gave him an abiding interest in military questions as such, so that, like Thiers, he was ready to discuss them with the experts irrespective of their political views. It taught him, as nothing else could, the need for effective training and organisation. No one was more

1. He abstained in the vote of 24 Aug.

joined 'dans une commune haine et jalousie de vous avec cette horreur de Naquet' (letter of 'Mardi 7 heures', Ass. Nat., p. 31, wrongly attributed to Dec. 1872).

surprised to discover this than the British Military Attaché, Colonel Connolly, who met him on the way back from Versailles one day towards the end of July 1871. The two men were introduced to one another by Chaudordy, and Connolly reported that he had never 'heard sounder ideas upon the necessity of instruction, discipline and drill to an Army' than those expressed by Gambetta.[1] Gambetta, indeed, was now under no illusions on the point of discipline. In a very interesting letter written two months later to Denfert-Rochereau, the defender of Belfort, thanking him for dedicating to him a book on the defence of that fortress, he discussed the question and told him that he did not think that the existing armies, 'composed of men of little education often ignorant of the simplest notions about science [*les sciences*] and their duties to their country', were ready for the lofty sort of purely moral discipline advocated by Denfert. He added: 'What we must hope for is that we shall succeed in remaking the army by remaking the whole nation through universal compulsory education.'[2]

In coupling army reform with the reform of education Gambetta was touching upon a favourite theme. Nearly everyone now, whether of the Right or the Left, was convinced of the military importance of numbers and the desirability of securing them by that compulsory service which the *République Française* had demanded in its very first issue. The great novelty politically was the conversion of the Right to the principle of compulsion. But the Left also had strong political reasons for supporting it. For them it was a facet of the basic principle of equality which should apply alike to civil and military training. 'It is in educating the citizens', wrote Freycinet in *La Guerre en province*, 'that one creates good soldiers; and it is in making good soldiers that one also educates them as citizens.'[3] At Bordeaux in his first speech on his return from exile Gambetta had declared: 'Everywhere alongside the schoolmaster we must put the gymnast and the soldier . . . so that our children . . . may all be fit to hold a sword, handle a rifle, go for long marches, sleep in the open and bravely undergo every kind of ordeal for the sake of the *patrie* . . . let it be understood that every boy is born a soldier as well as a citizen.'[4] Just as civil and military education had been provided for in a single law of 1794 when France was at bay, so for Gambetta and his colleagues compulsory education and military service were twin requisites of France's regeneration in the 1870s. They never tired of saying so.[5]

1. Connolly to Lyons, 28 July 1871, F.O. 146, 1539.
2. *Lettres*, no. 126, 20 Sept. 1871.
3. p. 357.
4. *Discours*, vol. ii, pp. 23 and 25. See above, p. 26.
5. See, e.g., *ibid.*, p. 274, vol. iii, p. 355.

Yet there was no possibility of compulsory education until the Republicans were firmly and fully in power. Army reform was urgent and could not wait upon the outcome of the struggle between Catholics and anti-clericals on the educational battlefield. All parties recognised this[1] and the great task was promptly tackled and eventually completed by the National Assembly. The legislation in which it was embodied comprised three principal laws, that of 1872 concerning recruitment, that of 1873 dealing with organisation, and that of 1875 determining the cadres and effectives. Together they formed one of the Assembly's most notable legislative achievements. As has been said, they 'provided the essential framework within which French military institutions were to function and to evolve for the next forty years. The conscription laws would be changed three times, while the laws on the organisation of the army and on the cadres would be frequently modified and even disregarded, but the general shape of the army would remain the same until 1914.'[2]

The conscription or recruitment Bill of eighty articles drafted by a commission of forty-five members took fourteen months to prepare. But although everyone accepted the notion that party prejudices should be laid aside and gave lip service to the principle of compulsory service, one man, the President of the Republic himself, clung to the view that the best army was the long-term professional army and held that the defects of 1870 were due not to inferior numbers but to government blunders and strategic errors. Thiers was as keen an armchair soldier as Machiavelli; he took immense pride in his military knowledge and believed passionately that he was right. When he expounded his views at length in his presidential message to the Assembly of 8 December 1871 and advocated a limited annual peacetime contingent liable to eight years' service, five on active service and three 'on renewable leave', it was clear that length of service would be the great bone of contention. Very different were the views of Gambetta and his friends and indeed of many members of the Commission of Forty-Five. They believed that the Prussian victory was due to the superiority of the Prussian system, under which every ablebodied man did three years' active service and then successively spent four in the reserve and five in the Landwehr or militia.

1. In April 1872 Gambetta was one of those who urged that discussion of the army Bill should take precedence over Bills relating to taxation and the Conseil d'Etat. These views were reflected in Republican pamphlets, e.g. No. 4 issued by La Société d'Instruction Républicaine (*La Question militaire et la République*, 1872). On p. 22 the author wrote: 'Tout le monde sait que, si nous voulons être inattaquable ... il nous faut une armée réunissant ces deux qualités: 1° le *nombre*; 2° l'*instruction* et la *discipline*.'

2. David B. Ralston, *The Army of the Republic, the Place of the Military in the Political Evolution of France 1871–1914* (1967), pp. 62–3.

Gambetta and his associates favoured the relatively short term of three years' active service for three reasons: because the Prussian system with its large number of trained men and ample reserves had proved so successful, because a long-term service for all would be too costly, and because it was undesirable that recruits should be too long divorced from their normal civic functions. The *République Française* at once sharply criticised Thiers's views: his prejudices were what they had always been, he had not changed, it said: indeed he still clung to the principles of the army law of 1832 sponsored by Marshal Soult.[1] When it heard that the Commission itself had recommended the maintenance of five years' service,[2] without prejudice to service in the reserve, and that all but one of the nine generals on it held that it was impossible to give the rural populations an adequate military training in a shorter time, it declared that, if this were so, France must be despaired of. The Commission seemed to confuse what was good for the officers and what was good for the men. The officers could never be too well-trained or seasoned. But the events of 1870 had shown the fallacy of the idea that the military art was 'an impenetrable mystery only to be acquired after a long novitiate'. 'They have taught us that after a certain time the soldier is deformed . . . by barrack life and that he loses in intelligence, morality and faith more than he gains in precision of movement, discipline and solidity.' If all that was going to happen was to maintain the old system with a greater number of men under arms how could the budget be adapted to the reform? 'We are told that there will be a large number of exemptions. . . . And all this is called equality! . . . a democratic law!'[3]

Yet, despite the sustained campaign against it by Freycinet in the *République Française* and by others elsewhere, this was the kind of law that emerged. When the great debates took place in the Assembly in the summer of 1872 General Trochu, former President of the Government of National Defence, and others, not by any means all on the Left, argued eloquently in favour of a three years' term of service, but their amendment was rejected by 455 to 227. Then a further amendment was proposed by a member of the Commission, General Chareton, who suggested a variable term of not more than four years and not less than one. This was an ingenious compromise which might have won the day had it not been for the renewed intervention of Thiers. In a speech of two hours, which was an astonishing feat for a man of seventy-six, he declared that he would not accept responsibility for enforcing a law in which he

1. Leader of 8 Dec. It subjected Thiers's proposals to detailed criticism on 14 Dec. (p. 3).
2. The five years' term was already operating under a law of 1868.
3. 1 Jan. 1872. The author was no doubt Freycinet.

did not believe. If the Assembly did not vote for the five years' term he would resign. Once again, as six months earlier, the old man used the threat of resignation to get his way.[1] Yet on this occasion it is probable that his action was not due solely to the wish to impose his own will. He was seriously alarmed by the menacing grumbles from Germany about the dangerous speed and character of France's army reform and, like other Frenchmen, he feared the danger of a fresh German attack to check France's recovery.[2] The German system of compulsory service might be a model, but it was not one that Bismarck wished to see too successfully imitated in France. So Thiers was all the more anxious to prevent any shorter term than five years. By pressing for five years he could assure Berlin that France was grasping only the shadow and not the substance of compulsory service: her army could not possibly be a serious menace to her powerful neighbour.

Thiers's action transformed the situation. What was hitherto primarily a military issue abruptly became a political one of the first order. The Left would gladly have voted for Chareton's amendment on military grounds, but so now, it appeared, would many of the Right in order to be rid of Thiers. Chareton withdrew his amendment but it was at once reintroduced by General Martin des Pallières. The problem of France's military regeneration had suddenly placed Gambetta and his colleagues in an acute dilemma.

The military issue itself was a major one and in the long debates about it Gambetta might have been expected to play a leading part. But he did not, and the *République Française*, his mouthpiece, appeared sometimes to express views more radical than his own.[3] Apart from one stormy incident, he spoke on only three clauses of the Bill. He supported the veto on voting by soldiers, although it had earlier been objected to by the *République Française*, but he opposed certain proposals relating to deferment of

1. See above, pp. 87–8.
2. See Chapman, *The Third Republic of France*, pp. 30–2.
3. Edward L. Katzenbach Jr., 'Charles-Louis de Saulces de Freycinet and the Army of metropolitan France—1870–1918', (unpublished thesis, Princeton, 1952), p. 179. Freycinet, the R.F.'s writer, wrote in his *Souvenirs* (p. 333) that the Bill he prepared on army administration in the latter part of 1876 was the first question on which he was not 'en complet accord avec M. Gambetta'. He wished, in particular, to subordinate the commissariat directly to the C. in C. of Army corps instead of allowing them, as hitherto, to correspond directly with the Minister of War, but 'L'intendant Richard, qui était entré dans les bureaux de la *République Française* et qui voyait M. Gambetta journellement, avait suscité des doutes dans son esprit. Toutefois, avec sa largeur de vues habituelle, il ne chercha pas à peser sur moi, et même son journal, auquel je ne pouvais plus collaborer régulièrement, me consacra des articles très sympathiques.' For a leader expressing disquiet about the changes after they had been approved by the Senate, see *R.F.*, 11 Nov. 1876.

call-up and to the exemption of members of teaching orders. But his opposition was moderate in tone and in the second instance he successfully secured an amendment to the original clause (no. 23).[1] The reasons for his reticence can only be surmised. It is probable that he was still ill at ease in a hostile Assembly and also that, because of his own contentious role in the war, he preferred to let others, especially soldiers like Trochu, bear the brunt of arguing the Republican case. It is no less probable that he still wished to avoid a personal collision with Thiers. It is also possible that, as Joseph Reinach suggested, Thiers had indirectly let him know that, in his view, Germany's threatening attitude was an additional reason for maintaining the five years' term: it would enable two or three classes to be mobilised at once if there were a sudden attack.[2] So Gambetta voted in favour of the three years' amendment but he did not speak and it was rejected. When on the following day Thiers threatened to resign if there were not an immediate vote in favour of five years and when a member of the Right urged that the vote should be adjourned to the following day, 'in order that time should bring counsel', in other words time to concert the President's downfall, there was the kind of turmoil which Gambetta loved to try to dominate. He leapt to the tribune and, making his voice heard above the hubbub, demanded that the Assembly should vote at once. He added that 'the only patriotic course' for him and his friends was abstention.[3] Abstain they did. The Right's game was checkmated and des Pallières's amendment was rejected by 477 to 56. There were nearly 200 abstentions. With the aid of Gambetta Thiers had triumphed and by the end of July the whole law had been passed.

The law of 1872 made it possible for France in time of war to put into the field an army of 740,000 men, which was about the same number as that provided for by Germany's legislation. This approximate parity was maintained for some twenty years.[4] The law thus achieved its authors' main object so far as numbers were concerned. But it was not a democratic law and its inequalities were criticised by men as different as Trochu

1. *Ass. Nat. A.*, vol. xii, pp. 104–8, 114–16, 123–4, 292–4.
2. Reinach, *La Vie politique de Léon Gambetta*, pp. 280–1. Léonie Léon in her 'Charlotte Corday' anger over the War Contracts Commission had vented her indignation against Thiers as well for allowing 'un pareil scandale'. She had urged Gambetta to see Thiers 'lui exposer la faiblesse et l'indignité de son attitude après ce que vous avez fait pour lui et le menacer s'il ne vous fait pas rendre par ses ministres une justice complète ... de lui faire une opposition systématique, acharnée à outrance' Ass. Nat., p. 31, letter wrongly dated '(déc. 1872)'.
3. *Ass. Nat. A.*, vol. xii, p. 247.
4. P. Renouvin, 'Les relations franco-allemandes de 1871 à 1914', in A. O. Sarkissian, ed., *Studies in Diplomatic History* (1961), p. 309.

and the Right-wing Keller.[1] The cost of maintaining every conscript under arms for five years would have been ruinous. So the annual contingent was to be divided by lot into two parts. The conscript who drew 'a good number' would have to serve for only six or twelve months, whereas the drawer of a 'bad' one would do the full term. Thus the principle of five years' service was maintained, but it was unequally applied. At the same time the law incorporated two other provisions which transgressed the Republican principle of equality. The first, a device borrowed directly from Prussia, provided that young men who had passed certain examinations and paid the State approximately 1,500 francs for uniform and maintenance might be permitted to volunteer for one year's service in the active army before passing to the reserve. The second allowed for exemption for various categories, including those training to be teachers or priests as well as young men with widowed mothers and those whose labour was indispensable for the running of a family farm or business.[2] As a result some 60,000 men were excused service.

These provisions, it has been said, would have provided material for acrimonious and protracted debate 'if the deputies had not really been intent on the great work of restoring the military strength of France as rapidly as possible'.[3] Nevertheless on the very day on which the law finally passed the *République Française* roundly declared that it would have to be immediately revised and Gambetta himself at Belleville in April 1873 would call it 'a misshapen, ill-made and contradictory law worth less than what went before'.[4] An income tax, he added, would have provided the money for both a proper military law and a proper system of compulsory education. The army provided by the law fell short of the 'truly national army' which he had pictured as the Republican ideal in a speech at Annecy a few months earlier.[5] Yet revision of the law was unlikely when so many people had been at such pains for so long to arrive at the compromise which it represented. Gambetta might proclaim in April 1873 that the Republic would eventually establish a military system in which neither wealth nor privilege would receive special benefits,[6] and a truly effective system of compulsory service for all

1. J. Monteilhet, *Les Institutions militaires de la France (1814–1932)*, 2nd edn, (1932) p. 125.
2. The effect of these provisions was that 30 per cent of the annual contingent were wholly exempt from service and 20 per cent served for a maximum of only one year.
3. Ralston, *op. cit.*, p. 41.
4. *Discours*, vol. iii, p. 356.
5. *Ibid.*, p. 167.
6. F. Bédarida, 'L'Armée et la République: Les opinions politiques des officiers français en 1876–1878', *Revue Historique*, July–Sept. 1964, p. 131.

might figure in many Radical election programmes in 1876: yet when in that same year 1876 Laisant and some 130 mainly Left-wing deputies introduced a new Bill to reduce the service in the active army to three years and abolish the one year volunteers Gambetta opposed it.[1] He argued that the moment was not yet opportune (he, the 'opportunist', did in fact use the word *opportun*). The Bill, he said, confused two different issues which ought to be kept apart. The primary need was for 'a good law' governing the recruitment and organisation of non-commissioned officers. In emphasising this need he was now echoing the argument of the professional soldiers who 'believed that until the French army had a solid core of N.C.O.s, to introduce the three years' service would be not only unwise but dangerous.[2] So although he admitted the defects of the volunteer system, defects denounced more than once by the *République Française*,[3] he maintained his opposition to the Bill which included a proposal to abolish it, but in November he himself introduced a Bill to improve the conditions of the N.C.O.s in order to attract a larger recruitment.[4] Perhaps, too, there was another reason for his regarding Laisant's Bill as inopportune, a reason which he preferred not to mention. Might it not antagonise Bismarck and cause a deterioration in Franco-German relations just when he was seeking to improve them? However that might be, Gambetta and the policy of caution carried the day, though only by a comparatively small majority (230 to 195); but, as has been seen, in speaking as he did, he provided fresh ammunition with which the Intransigent Radicals could shoot at his opportunism.[5]

In spite of such temporising, the ultimate aim of the Left, Gambetta included, was indeed the 'republicanisation' of the army. 'In such an army', it has been said, 'the citizen in uniform would be more important than the professional soldier, the term of service would be so short that the conscript would not be militarised, and every man would serve the same length of time.'[6] But it would be many years before such a goal was in sight.

1. For the text of his speech, see *Discours*, vol. v, pp. 237–44, and *Annales, Chambre* 1876, vol. iii, pp. 23–4.
2. Ralston, *op. cit.*, p. 98.
3. e.g. 12 Sept. 1875. The defects were widely criticised. One writer in 1874 had dubbed the system 'a means to avoid five years . . . service placed at the disposal of those who have 1,500 francs to spend' (Ralston, *op. cit.*, p. 101).
4. For the text, see *Annales Chambre, Session Extraordinaire 1876*, vol. i, Annexes no. 542, pp. 91–5. The proposals included 'une installation spéciale pour les sous-officiers mariés. Un mess de sous-officiers par régiment ou détachement' and 'Un cercle-bibliothèque de sous-officiers par quartier', as well as better pay.
5. See above, p. 321.
6. R. D. Challener, *The French Theory of the Nation in Arms 1866–1939* (1955), p. 45.

Meanwhile the National Assembly had completed the work of army reform and Gambetta had successfully upheld its sharply contested claim to legislate on cadres against those who maintained that it was exceeding its constitutional limits and that such decisions should remain the prerogative of the Minister of War.[1] On the same day the Assembly had voted that battalions should consist of four strong companies instead of six weak ones. Gambetta was triumphant and, in one of his most adoring letters to Léonie, wrote that the French army was saved and the future assured.[2]

In addition, much had been accomplished independently of the Assembly. A new Ecole de Guerre or Staff College had been founded and its first head, Colonel Lewal, was a man of whom the *République Française* thought highly.[3] A General Staff had been instituted in 1874. A number of new weapons had been introduced and measures were being taken to improve the fortifications on the eastern frontier. The *République Française*, like Gambetta himself and men such as the pamphleteer Charles L. Chassin, had urged the importance of gymnastics, and in 1876 it advocated training children in 'the handling of the rifle adopted by the French army'.[4] A new spirit was indeed abroad: among Frenchmen generally there was a widespread patriotic ardour and pride in the army. Already by the beginning of 1875 Spuller, Gambetta's 'other self', could rejoice that the spirit of innovation and reform had triumphed.[5] A year later, after that army had held autumn manoeuvres in the presence of MacMahon, Lord Lyons reported that 'all the officers of Foreign Armies and the English officers especially who have been out with the French troops . . . , seem to agree in regarding the improvement as being . . . very considerable. In short, it may not unreasonably be expected that in about three years . . . France will count for as much, or nearly as much, in the balance of power in Europe, as she did before 1870.'[6]

While these developments marked the progress of military regeneration under the aegis of the Republic, but without any very specific 'republicanisation', there was also another sense in which the battle for republicanisation was fought. The army might be traditionally a neutral body devoted only to the service of the state, but in the course of the war of National Defence and the fight against the Commune it had become 'a politicised corps in the service of an ideology: in the first case of Jacobin

1. *Ass. Nat. A.*, 12 Jan., vol. xxxvi, pp. 42–4.

2. *Lettres*, no. 233, For the military arguments for and against smaller or larger companies, see Ralston, *op. cit.*, pp. 59–62.

3. e.g. 16 Nov. 1871, 6 March 1872.

4. 5 Dec. 1875, 17 April 1876; cf. Chassin's *Cahier général des électeurs républicains de 1876*, p. 20.

5. Mme Adam, *Nos amitiés*, pp, 220–1.

6. Lyons to Derby, 26 Sept. 1876 (Newton, *Lord Lyons*, p. 352).

patriotism and in the second of social order'.[1] Men had been torn by conflicts of conscience and been obliged to make decisions with political implications. Alongside the moral conflicts to which they had been subjected came an intellectual shakeup. Gone were the prewar days when MacMahon had said that he would remove from the promotion list any officer whose name he saw on the cover of a book. Defeat had aroused a new will to work and criticise and rise superior to the dullard routine of garrison life. But all this had occurred and was occurring while the future of the regime was still in doubt. If ever there was a political crisis in which the Republic itself was in jeopardy the role of the army could be crucial. No true Republican could forget the part it had played in strangling the Second Republic in 1851. Gambetta might tell the *New York Herald's* correspondent that he had no fear of any military *pronunciamiento*[2]—the army was indeed unlikely of its own initiative to make and unmake governments—but in such a crisis the political sympathies of the officers might be all-important. It was all the more necessary therefore both to keep a watchful eye upon the officers and, if possible, to win their support for the Republican cause.

The task was not an easy one, but it was one to which Gambetta paid constant attention. He sought as always to outbid the Bonapartists and, by propaganda, to stress the Republicans' solicitude for the army and its officers; he remained in close touch with those on whom he knew he could count, and he gathered information about and kept watch on the rest.

The *République Française* from the outset devoted much space not only to army reform but also to the army's wellbeing. It invited officers to write to it and air their views or grievances and later it censured the Minister of War, General du Barail, for prohibiting them from writing for publication. It showed its concern for the low rates of army pay and urged equal pay for all branches.[3] It evinced, too, a continuous concern for the improvement of intellectual standards in the army. It praised the educational work of bodies such as the Ligue privée de l'enseignement which by February 1875 had established more than 150 regimental libraries.[4] It encouraged the discussion of technical problems and reviewed the latest books and periodicals on military subjects. If the striking intellectual ferment of the 1870s, unimaginable a decade earlier, was mainly generated by the professional soldiers themselves, Gambetta's

---

1. Bédarida, *art. cit.*, p. 131.
2. *New York Herald*, 27 Jan. 1873; cf. his speech at the Hoche banquet in the same year (*Discours*, vol. iv, p. 26).
3. Katzenbach, *op. cit.*, pp. 185–6.
4. 19 Feb. 1875.

paper none the less did its best to stimulate it. In its director the more intelligent officers and military writers could, if they were so minded, recognise a man eager for reform and the exchange of information and new ideas.[1] In him, too, some of those who were aggrieved might hope to find a champion.

In 1870–71 as in every war, there had been an inflation of the officer ranks. But the situation had been bedevilled by the two stages of the war, Imperialist and Republican. There was a cleavage between two categories of officer, those of the Empire who had been at Sedan and Metz and spent the rest of the war in captivity and those who had served the Government of National Defence and gained promotion under the Republic.[2] When the war was over those who returned from Germany 'felt that their vital interests had been endangered by the wholesale promotions of the Government of National Defence'.[3] The Commission for the revision of ranks, although they claimed to be guided by 'equity and good faith', tended to share this view. They censured the men who had broken parole and escaped in order to fight for the National Defence. Patriotism in their eyes was no excuse for the violation of a man's word of honour, particularly, no doubt, if it meant serving Gambetta. However conscientiously they performed their task, the net result was, in the words of an American historian, that 'the men in command of the French army over the next two or three decades would all have begun their careers under Napoleon III or even before'.[4] The great review at Longchamps at the end of June 1871 was indeed a stirring event which moved Thiers and Gambetta as much as any non-Republican; but there was much truth in the remark of one spectator, the French novelist 'Gyp', when she wrote: 'It was still the magnificent army of the Empire!'[5]

The work of the Commission for the revision of ranks was naturally

1. Some of the *R.F.*'s military contributors saw large. Thus the author of a review of 'Le bilan militaire de l'année 1875' wrote that now that England was installed in the Suez isthmus Calais had become the bridgehead of a vast network of commercial interests. In consequence France should transform it into 'une ville de guerre du premier ordre', press on with the Channel Tunnel plans and improve the railway to Marseilles and Brindisi.

2. The Government of National Defence had on 13 Oct. 1870 suspended the normal rules for military promotion and made subsequent regulations to permit rapid advancement in special circumstances. This measure was annulled when the Commission for the revision of ranks was set up. Gambetta in Aug. 1871 had vainly endeavoured to secure for 'généraux en chef' and others who had held command in face of the enemy the right to be heard by the commission (*Ass. Nat. A.*, vol. iv, pp. 529–32).

3. Ralston, *op. cit.*, p. 31.

4. *Ibid.*, p. 33.

5. L. Thomas, *Le Général de Galliffet (1830–1909)* (1910), p. 104.

bitterly criticised by the men of 4 September and it perpetuated the cleavage.[1] Fourteen generals appointed while Gambetta was Minister of War were reduced to their previous ranks and four were placed on the retired list. Such men in turn had a sense of grievance and tended to look to Gambetta as their protector.[2] He had to admit that for the time being he had no influence, but he did what he could, in particular supporting the petition to the Assembly in March 1873 of General Carrey de Bellemare against the Commission's decision depriving him of the rank of General of Division.[3] Men like Carrey de Bellemare were to become staunch Republicans, if they were not so already, and thus form a nucleus of Republican supporters in the predominantly conservative officer corps. They were the 'Gambetta's Generals' referred to by the British Military Attaché,[4] men who were alleged often to visit Gambetta, who wanted to make of them 'the general staff of a revolution',[5] the generals whose visits were noted by police agents, generals such as Gougeard, Faidherbe and Cremer or Farre.[6] The last named wrote from Algeria to show his zeal for the Republican cause and in 1876 Gambetta toyed with the idea of having him put forward as a candidate for the senatorial elections in the Nord.[7]

Yet if the army were to be strong and effective for its purpose it was desirable that it should be as little concerned with politics as possible. Fortunately none were more eager for political neutrality than the professional soldiers themselves. This was the reason for disfranchising the soldier on active service. He should in the words of General de Cissey, the Minister of War in 1872, 'remain a stranger to all factions and to all political struggles'[8] and Gambetta, as has been seen, supported this view. This was why in 1875 soldiers were denied the right to sit in the Chamber although they still remained eligible for the Senate. These measures were legislative acts intended to have a unifying effect and to keep the soldier aloof from the 'contagious defects of civil society'. But a different event,

1. See e.g. the criticisms of the *R.F.* 12 Dec. 1871, 2/3 Jan., 16 Jan., 18 April 1872.

2. Gambetta's papers in the Quai d'Orsay (vol. lv) contain the copy of a furious letter of resignation from General Cremer who had just been told that he had been downgraded to 'chef d'escadron', He signed it

> 'Cremer Lorrain annexé
> Ex Général Gambettiste'.

3. See Ass. Nat., vol. xvii, pp. 32–5, and *Discours*, vol. iii, pp. 315–26.

4. e.g. 13 Feb. 1876, Connolly to Lyons, F.O. 146, 1889.

5. C. de B., 15 March 1872 (Rothschild pp.).

6. A.P.P., BA/918, 26 July 1873.

7. Gen. Farre to Gambetta, 14 Feb., 19 Aug. 1872 (Reinach pp., B.N., N.a.fr. 24900), *Lettres*, no. 265, 20 Jan. 1876.

8. Ralston, *op. cit.*, p. 65.

the death of Napoleon III in 1873, was also widely regarded as having a similar result. It was good for the army, wrote the *République Française* on 10 January: there would now be no more divisions, 'for there was a schism and anyone would be blind who did not recognise this'.[1] Certainly this was the effect in some instances: for example the well-known General de Galliffet was supposed to have publicly stated: 'It is true that the Emperor was very kind to me, but he is dead and I owe nothing to his son. I would only act on his behalf in so far as my chiefs gave me the order, for discipline alone is my watchword.'[2] Even before then Connolly had quoted the opinion of a 'good' French authority that the army 'without being frankly Republican' was neither Orleanist nor Legitimist and neither Imperialist nor Red. It contained, he said, only fractions of parties. The leaders were very divided in opinion: 'In short those who are ready to sacrifice their personal feelings to the cause of order and stability are in the great majority.'[3] If he were to be believed the move to neutrality was already well under way.

Nevertheless, given the continued political uncertainties, it was wise for Gambetta and his Republican associates to be watchful and wary. To keep watch effectively they needed to have detailed and accurate information concerning the state and temper of the army and this was what they obtained.

In June 1875 Gambetta confidently told a police agent that the army would not lend itself to a *coup de main*: 'He knows very well what is going on there.'[4] And so no doubt he did, for by the end of February 1876, that is to say significantly on the morrow of the general elections, there had been completed for his information two remarkable memoranda, which seem to have been closely connected but only one of which has survived. The one still extant described army corps by army corps, and in each division, brigade and regiment, the attitude and opinions of the principal officers, especially those opposed to the Republic. The authorship is unknown, but it is clear that the freemasons had a hand in compiling a similar memorandum for Gambetta's information in 1878. Whether or not their services had already been enlisted in 1875–76, a French historian could justly remark that 'here, long before the celebrated scandal provoked by General André in 1904, there are veritable files, comments in which the professional worth and political sympathies of officers are recorded

1. See also C. de B., 13 Jan. 1873 (Rothschild pp.).
2. Ralston, *op. cit.*, p. 79.
3. Connolly to Lyons, 10 July 1872, F.O. 146, 1602.
4. Report of June 1875, no date of the month (A.P.P., BA/918). Cf. Scheurer-Kestner to Ranc, 22 March 1876: 'Déjà dans chaque régiment les amis des Thiers, des Gambetta, MM. Billot, Chadois et Denfert ont des protégés qui redoublent de propagande' (Ranc, *Souvenirs-Correspondance*, p. 312). He was quoting Broglie.

under their names'.[1] Not surprisingly, the anonymous author regarded the Bonapartist officers as more dangerous than the Royalist. Not surprisingly he gave good marks to those who were 'favourable to the ideas of M. Gambetta' or who had acquitted themselves well in the National Defence. But the memorandum was no merely partisan document. Its author made a serious attempt at an objective appraisal of the competence of the officers on whom it reported and he did not hesitate to describe Republicans as 'mediocre' if he thought they deserved it. Thus Gambetta was provided with a very valuable dossier which shows, as did his earlier chart of the municipalities of France, the thoroughness with which he and his henchmen were prepared to work in the cause of republicanisation.

Yet if Gambetta was bound to show an optimistic face in front of a police agent, the documentary basis for such optimism might seem slender indeed. M. Bédarida's analysis of the memorandum shows that three-quarters of the generals whose opinions were recorded were hostile to the Republic, approximately half being Bonapartist and half Royalist, while only one in ten supported it, the others being neutral. Indeed of all the eighteen metroplitan army commanders only one, Clinchant, was reckoned to be a Republican. Much the same was true of the colonels, although here the great majority of those opposed to the Republic were Bonapartist and not Royalist. It was no wonder, then, that in private Gambetta was dissatisfied and that he told Léonie Léon, for instance, on 10 February 1877, that he intended to press the government to make changes in the army command as well as to reorganise the diplomatic service. Commands, he wrote, were still held by 'the vanquished and incompetent men of the last war: our poor rulers still do not seem to understand that the largest armies and the best equipped arsenals are but costly follies without an efficient (*forte*) organisation of the high command. . . . Ah! when shall I be able to talk freely with the old soldier?'[2]

When indeed? The political crisis later in the year, the crisis known as the Seize Mai, made the chance of such a talk between Gambetta and MacMahon ever more remote. Meanwhile in a remarkably frank conversation with a police agent on 1 May 1877, a fortnight before the crisis began, Gambetta had disclosed how closely he continued to watch the army personnel.[3] Berthaut, the Minister of War, was, he said, better than his predecessor General de Cissey, but none the less a man of fourth-rate ability without any real authority over the corps commanders. The man who really controlled 'the vast machine', he asserted, was General Ducrot.[4]

1. Bédarida, *art. cit.*, p. 119.
2. L.G.
3. Report of 2 May, A.P.P., BA/919.
4. Commander of the 8th army corps, whose headquarters were at Bourges.

He was imperious and detested, but no one dared resist him; he got rid of those who stood in his way and he was working for the Empire. His ultimate intentions alarmed him. It was imperative that his movements should be kept under continual watch. It was also inadmissible that Montaudon, Lebrun, Douai, Picard, Bourbaki and others, 'the grotesque Espivent', for instance, 'on whom I have up there some very interesting documents which would soon reduce him to silence', should continue to hold posts of authority which at any moment they might be tempted to abuse.[1] Nevertheless, as has been seen, the Republicans had some supporters and in this conversation Gambetta declared that he was 'more and more satisfied with Galliffet ... everything leads me to think that he is now definitely one of ours.[2] We hope that before the end of the year de Bellemare and Saussier will be promoted generals of divisions, especially the latter who is highly to be recommended.'[3] There were others, too, who were making approaches to Gambetta such as General Pajol and a staff commandant named Darras who would be a very valuable recruit. 'We are not on the eve of a *coup d'état*', Gambetta assured his hearer, 'and we are working to make it impossible.'[4] The Seize Mai would put the matter to the test and would show how far his prognostication was right and how far his efforts were successful. Meanwhile the Budget Committee, no doubt with his encouragement, would have made its own contribution towards republicanisation. It refused to vote the money necessary for the maintenance of army chaplains, being convinced, as *The Times* put it, 'that they put reactionary political ideas into soldiers' heads'.[5] This, too, would furnish matter for conflict.

1. Commanders of the 2nd (H.Q. Amiens), 3rd (H.Q. Rouen), 6th (H.Q. Châlons-sur-Marne), 13th (H.Q. Clermont-Ferrand), 14th (H.Q. Lyon) and 11th (H.Q. Nantes) army corps respectively. Bédarida, *art. cit.*, p. 141, n. 3, lists Montaudon and d'Espivent as Royalists and Lebrun, Douai and Bourbaki as Bonapartists.

2. The Marquis de Galliffet was in command of the 15th division stationed at Dijon. He had been a hero at Sedan and one of the suppressors of the Commune. Able and ambitious, he was probably in direct or indirect touch with Gambetta as early as 1874 (Bédarida, *art. cit.*, p. 127).

3. Bellemare and Saussier were still listed as brigadiers in the *Almanach National* for 1878, but had become divisional commanders by 1879.

4. Gambetta added, according to the police agent: 'J'ai beaucoup insisté pour le départ des régiments dont les casernes étaient construites, et avant peu les autres auront évacué la capitale et les environs, emmenant avec eux les généraux les plus hostiles à la République' (A.P.P., BA/919).

5. Leader of 1 Jan. 1877: cf. *R.F.*, 2 April 1876, article denouncing the activity of a chaplain at Lorient who had distributed a pamphlet called *Soldat sans religion*.

23

The fight for leadership and the Simon ministry October 1876–May 1877

The Chambers returned to work on 30 October after the summer vacation of 1876. *The Times*, preoccupied by the Eastern Question, had no space to describe the scenes at the Gare Saint Lazare as the deputies and Senators made their way to the parliamentary trains, but it deemed it a good sign that the new session was beginning quietly without the stir of a presidential message.[1] A week later, on 6 November, when a compromise had been reached in the Chamber of Deputies over the Gatineau Bill to stop further prosecutions of people implicated in the Commune, excepting those 'inculpated as principal actors or instigators in cases of assassination, incendiarism or robbery', it hailed the result as 'an encouraging illustration of the growth of Parliamentary Government in France'.[2] Indeed its leader declared: 'Our impression is that if Versailles sees nothing more alarming in the course of the coming Parliamentary year than M. Gatineau's proposals, even as they were first submitted by him . . ., the French people will have some cause to complain of the dullness of the Session.' But it wisely added: 'It will not be so; something unexpected will happen.'

Much indeed was to happen, expected and unexpected. In fact, from the outset many people anticipated that the days of the Dufaure cabinet might soon be numbered and that before long the antagonisms between Chamber and Senate and Chamber and President would come to a head. Fresh collisions were in any case likely and two events in the timetable of the next two years made it probable that a final trial of strength between Conservatives and Republicans would come sooner rather than later. One was the holding of a great Universal Exhibition in Paris in 1878. The other was the renewal of a third of the Senate which was due at the

1. Leader of 31 Oct., p. 7.
2. Dufaure, who had refused to support the Bill, because of its implied criticism of MacMahon, also opposed the compromise. This was for him the first of a series of defeats.

end of January 1879. It would be unfortunate for a major political crisis to coincide with an exhibition held to demonstrate the recovery of France. But could the Conservatives afford to wait until 1879 and then probably see their last precarious stronghold taken from them? Already the Senate, instead of being a great Conservative fortress, was but a frail stockade. In two years' time it was only too probable that it would be broken down. In March 1876 the Senate had, as *The Times* put it, been divided into Red, Blue and Yellow Senators. A 'pretty little map of France' had been prepared with the departments painted in three colours in alphabetical order.[1] A draw had then taken place to determine which third should retire first, and the Reds, namely the Senators 'from Garonne to Oise', drew the 'bad' number. As chance would have it, the Red departments were those held predominantly by Conservative Senators. It was they who would have to offer themselves for reelection first and their prospects would be slender unless the Republican tide were stemmed. In the meantime half the General Councils were due for reelection in August 1877 and all the municipal councils in November. 'In fact', wrote the *République Française* on 6 January 1877, 'the battle to be fought in 1879 ... will be decided this very year by the outcome of these elections.' So, on the Left, men like the journalist Girardin had urged that there was no need for the Republicans to precipitate a crisis. All that they needed to do was play a waiting game and control of both houses would be theirs.[2]

But two years is a long time for the day-to-day politician. If the Conservatives were nervous and knew that the sands were running out, the Republican majority in the Chamber was impatient and eager to assert its power. Quite apart from the timetable, impatience on one side and nervousness or deliberate policy on the other might force a crisis well before 1879. Already on 17 October in a letter to Juliette Adam, Gambetta had written: 'The worries of home politics have begun again and all along the line one feels that the reaction is making a supreme effort against the cabinet and the very existence of the Chamber ...; it will need a strong hand to keep the present ministry steady, but ... I am without anxiety about the final issue.'[3]

But it was not going to be easy to bolster a ministry which still wished to 'pursue a policy of independence if not of combat' and which was no more disposed than before to toe Gambetta's line.[4] In accordance with his promise to his electors at Belleville, Gambetta had vigorously supported the Gatineau Bill on the amnesty, but it had, of course, been opposed by

1. 30 March.
2. e.g. Girardin, *La Question d'argent:* p. 150.
3. *Lettres*, no. 289.
4. See above, p. 288.

Dufaure.[1] This was one cause of dissension with the ministers. The Budget Committee's proposals and financial questions provided several more. Gambetta might, as has been seen, support Decazes in the debate on the Ministry of Foreign Affairs vote and oppose a Left-wing amendment to do away with the credits for the French Embassy to the Vatican,[2] and he could hardly endorse a motion to abolish the estimates for the Ministry of Public Worship (the motion was indeed overwhelmingly rejected by 430 votes to 62). But to the anger of the Catholic Conservatives, his Committee did make many cuts in those estimates and all Dufaure's efforts to oppose them were vain. Furthermore Gambetta crossed swords with the Minister of Finance, Léon Say, more than once in the budget debates as he had already in the hearings of the Committee; and when a controversy began over the Senate's power to amend finance Bills it looked as though Say and his cabinet colleagues would again take a different line from that of the President of the Budget Committee. No less delicate and still more inflammable was another question which brought the Left into conflict with the Minister of the Interior, Marcère, and precipitated the first crisis of the session. This was the vexed question of military honours at funerals of members of the Legion of Honour.

Provision for such honours had been made by a decree of messidor in the Year XII (1804), but, since the fall of Thiers, successive Ministers of War had interpreted the decree in such a way as to make it inapplicable to civil burials. Here was a nice subject of controversy, and tension flared up when at the beginning of September the commander of the Lyon garrison, supported by a new Minister of War, General Berthaut, refused to provide an escort for the remains of the well-known composer Félicien David. The Republicans protested that according to the decree the army should accompany the corpse to both church and cemetery. But no, said the Conservatives, the church is mentioned first, so if there is no church to go to when a man has civil burial, there can be no escort to the cemetery. The dispute, as Halévy said, became 'endless and Talmudic';[3] but it also became more serious when the anticlericals of the Left denounced the refusal of an escort as an infringement of liberty of conscience.[4] Marcère hoped to reduce the risks of repeated tension by limiting the provision of an escort to military members of the Legion of Honour on

---

1. See above, p. 316. The *R.F.* also stressed the Bill's importance, see e.g. leader of 24 Oct. For the text of Gambetta's intervention on 3 Nov., see *Discours*, vol. vi, pp. 187–200 and *Annales, Chambre*, Session Extraord. 1876, vol. i, pp. 15–18, 27–8.
2. See above p. 354.
3. D. Halévy, *La République des ducs*, p. 244. For a vivid and indignant account of the funeral, see *R.F.*, 3 Sept., p. 3; cf. leader of the 4th.
4. e.g. *R.F.*, 6 Sept., 25 Nov.

the active list at the time of their decease. But this proposal, too, in Gambetta's colourful words, 'vomited flames'.[1] He himself refrained from speaking when it was debated on 23 November because, he said, he wished 'to avoid parliamentary war'; he would bridle his 'intemperate tongue' by thinking on his 'wise Minerva'.[2] Nevertheless Marcère's Bill caused an outcry on the Left and in Gambetta's eyes the Minister and his colleagues had cut a sorry figure. The impassioned debate of 23 November ended with the reference of the Bill to a hostile committee and Marcère eventually withdrew it. The 'strong hand' had 'steadied' the ministry only by checking it publicly and too many public rebuffs must make its position untenable. Already by the 25th Gambetta was writing that it was a terrible week: 'we are in the midst of a crisis', but his paper none the less continued to criticise the ministry.[3] The final rebuff came from the Senate on the ever-recurring amnesty question. Although Dufaure had accepted an amendment to it, the Senate on 1 December rejected the compromise on the Gatineau Bill recently voted by the Chamber. This was the last straw. Dufaure had already remarked: 'There is an age at which a too heavy burden should no longer be undertaken.'[4] He was seventy-nine and on the following day he thankfully resigned: but he had been adroit enough to fall when he was defeated by the Senate and not by the Chamber. The rest of the cabinet quickly followed suit.

Nine months earlier the *République Française* had written that it wanted 'durable and solid ministries, long ministries which would have time to do many good things, to bring about reforms and to serve the democracy.'[5] The sentiments were excellent, but, as Emile de Girardin remarked: 'He who wills the end must will the means.'[6] The Dufaure cabinet had not been the means the *République Française* had sought, and once it had fallen it would be no easier to find a better. It had taken some days for the Marshal to decide on the Dufaure cabinet in March. The ten days' crisis leading to its fall was now followed by another of ten days before

1. *Lettres*, no. 293 of 22 Nov. to Léonie Léon. For Marcère's defence of his policy, see his *Histoire de la République de 1876 à 1879*, vol. i, pp. 144–59. It is interesting to note that Thiers had little patience with rabid anticlericalism and mistrusted Gambetta on this account. *The Times* later recalled that on the day when Marcère's Bill was introduced Thiers had told its correspondent that although, as former President of the Republic he was entitled to a large escort, he would gladly go without a single red trouser at his funeral if this would put an end 'to this stupid discussion' *The Times*, 7 Sept., 1877). For a vivid account of a civil funeral earlier in the year, that of Gen. Cremer, see *The Times*, 5 April 1876.
2. Letter of 23 Nov. to Léonie Léon (L.G.).
3. L.G. Cf. *R.F.* leaders of 27 and 29 Nov.
4. *The Times*, 2 Dec.
5. 20 March 1876.
6. *La Question d'argent*, p. 121.

a successor emerged: yet once again—'Plus ça change plus c'est la même chose'—with the exception of its head, the new cabinet appeared remarkably like the old. And all this, wrote a hostile writer a little later, 'for a question of funeral ceremonies'.[1] To one of the outgoing ministers, Marcère, looking back in disillusioned old age, it seemed that these crises, and particularly 'the little scenario' of the funeral ceremonies, provided a brief illustration of the whole pattern of politics from 1876 to 1879:

> There were the same questions at issue, the same intrigues and the same personalities. The Left Centre played the leading parts; the intrigues were concerted and passionately pursued by the Right in the two Chambers; whilst the many-faced personage who performed the role analogous to that of the traitor in the plays, lorded it in the same Press offices or in the Budget Committee's room in the Chamber of Deputies.[2]

One continuing difficulty in 1876 was that of personalities. The worlds of MacMahon and of Marcère's 'many-faced personage', Gambetta, were very different, but Gambetta's influential position as President of the Budget Committee and virtual leader of the Republican majority in the Chamber should have brought him into touch with the President of the Republic; it should have given Gambetta an opportunity to exercise his immense charm and dispel some of the old soldier's prejudices. Yet, just as it had been difficult for him to bridge the gulf and renew personal contact with the septuagenarian Thiers, so it was still more difficult for him to bridge the gulf and make contact at all with the sexagenarian MacMahon. According to MacMahon's biographer, Gambetta had made several attempts to do so but in vain.[3] These attempts to effect a meeting were little known. What was publicly evident was the lack of contact. Thus, when on 9 November the Marshal held an official reception at the Elysée, *The Times* correspondent reported that it had been announced that Gambetta was to be there but that there had been no sign of him.

1. J. J. Weiss, 'La chambre de 1876' in *Combat Constitutionnel (1868–1886)* (1893), p. 60. Simon replaced Marcère at the Ministry of the Interior and Martel replaced Dufaure at the Ministry of Justice. Otherwise there were no changes, apart from the head of the government.

2. Marcère, *op. cit.*, pp. 159–60.

3. Silvestre de Sacy, *Le Maréchal de MacMahon*, p. 328. 'Que n'êtes-vous en relation avec ce vieux militaire?' Léonie Léon asked Gambetta on 13 May 1876 after Ricard's death, and in July she wrote, 'Je rêve à des moyens violents de vous mettre face à face avec le vieux militaire.' 'Comment guérir de ses préventions cet irascible militaire?' (Ass. Nat., pp. 170, 201 and 204). Joughin, *The Paris Commune in French Politics* (p. 125) erroneously says that Gambetta went privately to see MacMahon after the President of the Republic had written to the Minister of War on 27 June 1876 urging him to show restraint in making further arrests in connection with the Commune. She does not quote her source.

'The friends of M. Gambetta', he said, 'must regret that he . . . abstained . . . the distance at which he keeps himself from the Head of the Government cannot pass unobserved.'[1] Because it was not unobserved all the more interest was aroused when it was known that the two men were to meet on the 17th at Sèvres where the Marshal was to open a new porcelain factory. It was a brilliant morning and Léonie Léon hastened to write to her 'illustrious love': 'What a marvellous sun is lighting up the ceremony over which you are presiding and at which the old soldier [*le vieux militaire* was the expression she and Gambetta habitually used when referring to MacMahon] will be present as a supernumerary (*en comparse*). I think the ice will be broken, how was it that you never told me of such an important event?'[2]

The important event was described in a letter from Edmond Adam to Juliette three days later. He had, he said, had the details from Gambetta himself:

> The Marshal wanted to say a few words but found it impossible. He spoke, but nobody heard what he said. He was much moved and showed only his usual diffidence. It was then that Gambetta replied with the sentence you have read in the *République Française*.[3] They visited some of the halls and workshops together, but without conversing. . . . On the way out they came face to face again at the foot of some staircase. The Marshal certainly half stretched out his arm, but not enough for Gambetta to go the rest of the way without showing too much eagerness. He bowed and each of them departed in his own direction (*de son côté*) as in the Marlborough song. In short [Adam concluded] the ice has been broken but it cannot be said that it has melted.[4]

1. 11 Nov.
2. Letter of 17 Nov. (Ass. Nat., p. 244). In fact it was Waddington who as Minister of Public Instruction and Fine Arts presided over the ceremony.
3. 'M. Gambetta s'est déclaré personnellement heureux que la Commission du budget l'ait chargé de la représenter dans cette cérémonie, et d'avoir à porter de sa part au maréchal-président l'expression de l'esprit de concours qui l'anime pour le développement et l'amélioration de tous les services publics du gouvernement de la République' (*R.F.*, 19 Nov., p. 3).
4. *Nos amitiés*, p. 243. The allusion is presumably to the 18th verse of 'Marlbrough s'en va-t-en guerre', i.e.

> La cérémonie faite
> Mironton, tonton, mirontaine;
> La cérémonie faite,
> Chacun s'en fût coucher'

MacMahon's account of the meeting revealed his determination not to melt: 'Je le saluai sans lui adresser la parole. Choqué de cette froideur, M. Gambetta chercha à se rendre compte si elle était l'effet d'une surprise ou d'une résolution bien arrêtée. Il se dirigea donc de manière à se trouver en face de moi: mais l'ayant aperçu, je fis semblant de ne pas le reconnaître' (S. de Sacy, *op. cit.*, p. 346).

It did not melt, and at the end of January 1877 Girardin found it necessary to write: 'There is another lack of correct usage which the President should cause to disappear: that which consists in not giving to M. Gambetta the consideration due to the man who has twice been elected President of the Budget Committee.'[1] The consequences had been seen in December. Already in July the Marshal had told Marcère in a cabinet meeting that he, Marcère, was his 'extreme limit . . . it is a mistake . . . if it is thought that I will look . . . further to the Left . . . or change the Ministers of War and Foreign Affairs.' If people wanted a dissolution they could have it, for he had confidence in the country.[2] An oblique admonition to him from Gambetta in the Assembly a little later not to desert his constitutional role cannot have endeared Gambetta to the Marshal.[3] When it was again suggested that he should see Gambetta he was alleged to have replied: 'One of the most painful sacrifices I have made was in refusing to see M. le Comte de Chambord; I will not make that of seeing M. Gambetta.'[4] In fact his remarks in July had thrown a lightning gleam on the conflict ahead. The Ministry of War would be a key position and the big question was how far either side really wanted to force a dissolution. It appears that both the Marshal and Gambetta would have been glad to do so, but that they were restrained by their followers. The Marshal would have liked to have procured a wholly Right-wing ministry although he knew it must be unacceptable to the Chamber;[5] Gambetta wanted a Left-wing one, truly representative of the majority in the Chamber, and he was ready to withold the vote on the budget in order to force the 'old soldier' to capitulate. If he did not, he would welcome a dissolution 'while we still enjoy the plenitude of popular favour.'[6] But Broglie and Fourtou advised the Marshal that a Right-wing cabinet was unobtainable—they no doubt wanted to give the Republicans more rope with which to hang themselves—while Decazes probably counselled him against dissolution at a moment when the deterioration

1. Hanotaux, *op. cit.*, vol. iii, p. 651. According to *The Times* (8 Feb.) Gambetta attended an Elysée reception for the first time on 6 Feb. and exchanged a few courteous words with the Marshal.

2. *The Times*, 5 July 1876. It added: 'the words of the Marshal are, if not verbatim, at least authentic, and . . . the Marshal himself will not contest the exact sense'.

3. *Annales, Chambre*, vol. iv, p. 115. Gambetta denounced his opponents' tactics of always dragging in the Marshal and said: 'Il faut donc qu'un ordre du jour catégorique instruisant celui à qui vous prétendez adresser vos avertissements, lui apprenne que cette Chambre, tout en respectant la Constitution sait y rappeler tous ceux qui s'en écartent.'

4. P. Dalloz, 4 Dec. 1876, quoted by C. Barjac 'Autour du 16 mai' (*Le Temps*, 12 March, 1937).

5. MacMahon's *Souvenirs inédits, cit.* F. Pisani-Ferry, *Le Coup d'état manqué*, p. 132.
6. Letter of 23 Nov. to Léonie Léon (L.G.).

of the Eastern Question made the foreign situation more menacing. The Marshal therefore sought a cabinet as closely as possible resembling the one with which he had just parted. He succeeded mainly because Gambetta's weapons misfired.

To begin with all had gone well. The emergency was such that Gambetta was able to obtain a joint meeting of the delegates of all three Left-wing groups. On 4 December they unanimously passed a resolution similar to that of 7 March:[1] they would give their support to a truly parliamentary cabinet resolved on putting an end to the contradictions still existing between the outlook of the majority elected on 20 February and the attitude of too many officials. The *République Française* declared that the solution was perfectly simple. It lay in the choice of a ministry from among the Left-wing groups of the Senate and Chamber: only thus could there come into being the durable cabinet which the Chamber had always wanted.[2] But on 7 December Gambetta met with 'two grave disappointments'. He had not succeeded in getting an adjournment of the vote on the budget: 'At the decisive moment, under double pressure from the President of the Chamber and those who want to be ministers, part of my troops lost heart and we have met with a setback which is all the more serious in the present circumstances because it shows a vexatious tendency of the majority to take fright at the moment of attack.'[3] The second disappointment was still more disquieting. Delegates of the three Left-wing groups had met but been unable to agree and, after a protracted and confused discussion, they had sent a deputation to ask the advice of the President of the Chamber, Jules Grévy.[4] Grévy, influenced according to Gambetta by 'the reaction at bay', had simply advised the return of the Dufaure ministry:

> This singular resurrection was suggested, advocated and defended by the President of the Chamber in an extra-parliamentary meeting as the last word in political wisdom. His language seems to have made a great impression upon my conscripts and here we are back again confronted by our dead ministers galvanised until there is some new development. I still count a little on a return of good sense and dignity . . . I would not dare to affirm that in

1. See above, pp. 284–90. For a draft declaration of the Republican Union, in Spuller's hand, expressing the wish for a common deliberation of the groups which would 'porter sur l'obligation pour le nouveau ministère, quel qu'il soit, de gouverner suivant les règles du régime', see Ass. Nat., MS 550.

2. *R.F.*, 6, 7 Dec.

3. Letter of 7 Dec. (L.G.).

4. According to the *R.F.* (10 Dec.) the delegates had been invited by Grévy to meet him so that he could tell them the upshot of his discussions with the Marshal. They all accordingly went to see Grévy, except 'M. Gambetta, qui s'est abstenu'.

the struggle we shall not lose a number of soldiers who have little desire to see their electors again so soon.[1]

In fact the majority of the Left were not after all convinced by Jules Grévy. They deputed Demaine and Jules Grévy's own brother Albert to see the leading members of the Dufaure cabinet and tell them that they would not have their support unless they gave preliminary undertakings satisfactory to the majority. In particular, they wanted a Republican Minister of War. But even this they would not obtain.

During this time the Marshal, wearied and put out, was continuing his search for a cabinet sufficiently conservative to be tolerable to him. After D'Audiffret-Pasquier and Léon Say had both declined his invitation, he, too, had looked once more to Dufaure; but Dufaure made his acceptance conditional on the Ministry of the Interior being given to another prominent member of the Left Centre, Jules Simon, who, like Dufaure himself, was close to Thiers. Simon, however, had been a member of the Government of National Defence and a prewar Radical. He could be regarded as a shade further to the Left than Dufaure or Marcère. Meanwhile Gambetta, through Freycinet and Freycinet's friend General Borel, had conveyed to MacMahon the suggestion that the man who might be acceptable to both sides was Duclerc. Not only was Duclerc a friend of Gambetta but he was a Senator and known to enjoy the Marshal's esteem.[2] As MacMahon's biographer has remarked: 'Perhaps a subtle politician would have profited from this opportunity to disarm the leader of the Left. . . . But the Marshal had to reckon with his supporters and for him radicalism was still the enemy with whom no arrangement was possible.'[3] The Marshal was indeed no subtle politician, but a blunt soldier who believed in laying his cards on the table. On the evening of the 9th he called his ministers together (Dufaure and his colleagues were still carrying on pending the nomination of a new cabinet) and told them precisely what his position was. He could not accept the claims of the Left to demand undertakings concerning the composition of the cabinet. In order to meet Dufaure he was ready to accept the inclusion of Jules

1. The *R.F.* wrote bitterly (9 Dec.): 'On dirait . . . que ce n'est plus le cabinet qui est responsable devant les Chambres, mais les Chambres qui sont responsables devant le cabinet.'

2. Freycinet, *Souvenirs*, pp. 339–42. According to *The Times* of 14 Dec., p. 5, Gambetta proposed the following ministers: Duclerc, Interior; Le Royer, Justice; Gen. Borel, War; Freycinet, Public Works. Paul Cambon wrote that a Duclerc ministry was Gambetta's dream: '1° Parce que Jules Simon n'en serait pas. 2° Parce que Duclerc est muet et que Gambetta continuerait à faire joujou avec le Ministère' (*Correspondance*, vol. i, p. 75, 12 Dec.).

3. Silvestre de Sacy, *op. cit.* p. 328.

Simon, but on certain conditions: 'He must reject M. Gambetta's doctrines concerning the omnipotence of the Chamber and recognise the independence of the President of the Republic within the limits traced by the constitution. He must also promise . . . only to strike at those officials who have failed in their professional duties or in the respect they owe to the constitution.' People had said he could find other ministers such as Duclerc who had also recently come to him with a suggestion from Gambetta that he should meet the Marshal in the Bois de Boulogne: 'Very well! Are you going to advise me to take a ministry from the hands of M. Gambetta, a ministry of which he would be the patron and hidden president (*le président occulte*). For my part, I cannot do it.' A Dufaure–Simon ministry was as far as he could go, and if the majority of the Chamber opposed it, all he could do would be to appeal to public opinion and let the country decide between him and parliament.[1]

Public opinion did not have to decide. MacMahon's advisers were against a dissolution and Gambetta was unable to force one. At the very moment that he had belatedly won a victory in the Chamber adjourning the vote on the budget the cabinet was at last formed. Its head was not Dufaure, who had retired from the fray, but Jules Simon himself, and the majority of the Chamber would be prepared to give it a trial. But, in the view of one of Gambetta's friends, Charles Floquet, this sort of ministry would never have emerged had the Left maintained its unity and continued to hold full meetings of all its groups as Gambetta had wished: 'As a consequence of the abandonment of such meetings personal power has been allowed to gain upon the nation's representatives. Result: a cabinet emerging from the will of the executive which itself declares that it is not free.'[2]

Gambetta was disgusted. Once again he had been foiled; his friends were again excluded from the cabinet; his 'troops' had failed to support him at the critical moment, and, although the man now in power was a genuine Republican and not a converted Orleanist like Dufaure, he had been Gambetta's antagonist at Bordeaux in February 1871 and was one of those who earlier in 1876 had frustrated his plan for a united Republican party. Moreover, he had, in Gambetta's view, been too eager for power. He had indeed himself kept the Ministry of the Interior, always a key post, but he had also, Gambetta believed, sold the pass by making virtually no conditions: above all he had failed to insist on replacing Berthaut by a Republican Minister of War. Nowhere did Gambetta's

1. After the cabinet meeting the Marshal dictated a note of what he had said. The text, from which I have quoted extracts, is printed in Hanotaux, *op. cit.*, vol. iii, pp. 643–7.
2. *Cit.* Capéran, *Histoire contemporaine de la laïcité française*, vol. i, p. 70.

preoccupation with the army come out more clearly than in the letter of 12 December to Léonie Léon in which he expressed his dismay. Behind MacMahon he saw the shadow of his old enemy Broglie. This cabinet, he told her, would allow the Broglie faction to pursue its aims, and the last resource of the faction

> lies wholly in the role of the army . . . it is upon it, upon its bad disposition, carefully maintained and stimulated, towards the Republicans, that the reactionaries of all kinds are speculating. If the minister of war was republican, there would be an end of these criminal aims; in the ranks [*sic*], the numerous Republican officers would lift their heads instead of undergoing daily humiliations.

He added an interesting point:

> Still better, if the minister of war were republican, the majority in the Senate would change character, it would become docile . . . for it contains nearly forty officers who always wait to know their chief's opinion before they vote. . . . So I understand only too well the desperate energy with which Broglie must have insisted on saving the ministry of war from the hands of the republicans.[1]

Léonie shared her lover's dismay. The ministry, she said, made her despair:

> Simon is as much our enemy as de Broglie, an intriguer of the worst kind and all the more dangerous because it is difficult for you to fight him. The attitude to adopt towards such a cabinet will be a delicate matter: you will have the intransigents and the reactions alternately against you, whilst dissolution, which at this moment would be favourable for you and which you will have to renounce as the time of the exhibition draws near, will be adjourned.[2]

The situation was indeed delicate and Gambetta's personal power and ascendancy over the majority were for a month more than ever in the balance. The constitutional question of the Senate's power to amend finance Bills came to a head and the Budget Committee itself, the main seat of his power, was due to be reelected in the New Year.

On 16 December Gambetta won a victory over the Minister of Finance who had opposed an article in the Budget of Receipts abolishing a

---

1. Letter of 12 Dec. (L.G.). Cf. letter of 13 Dec. The *Almanach National: Annuaire Officiel de la République Française* for 1877 listed thirty-four senators as officers in the army or navy.

2. Letter of 13 Dec. (Ass. Nat., p. 250). The *R.F.*'s attitude to the new cabinet was understandably guarded at first (see leader of 15 Dec.), but much warmer after Simon had made his initial declaration in the Chamber (leader of 16 Dec.). After that it relapsed into an admonitory attitude, e.g. 18 Dec.: 'La majorité . . . a le droit de se croire arrivée à la saison des fruits. Elle attend que ce ministère d'automne [*sic*] mette quelquechose dans son pressoir.'

surtax on salt. The Chamber voted for the article by a large majority and the budget was passed. Gambetta was cock-a-hoop. It had been the most splendid success of the session; his majority had increased; nothing less had been at stake than 'the next Budget Committee, the Presidency, the direction of the government, the authority of the assembly over the senate, the popularity of the Left'. The ministry had been laid low: 'I gently picked it up and strangled it with bonds of silk and honey.'[1] Léonie was delighted, but wisely reminded him of the mobility of politics: 'I found you too ready to take alarm just as today I find you too ready to rejoice'—no certainty could be based on a single vote, 'the bizarre result of oscillations which are almost always inexplicable, and above all unforeseen'.[2] She was right: the vote of the 16th was only an incident in a struggle in which the New Year vacation would provide a brief respite. Gambetta might win a victory over Léon Say. It was not so easy to defeat the Senate.

'France which promised to give the world a political millennium ninety years ago', wrote *The Times* with lofty disdain on the first day of 1877, 'is still uncertain which of its two Chambers shall possess the supreme power of the purse.'[3] Article 8 of the constitutional law of 1875 relating to the Senate had declared that it, concurrently with the Chamber, had the initiative in legislation: 'Nevertheless the finance laws ought in the first place to be presented in the Chamber of deputies and voted by it.' But the Senate, greatly influenced by Mgr Dupanloup's eloquence, now proceeded to restore or modify a number of anticlerical cuts made by the Budget Committee in the Minister of Finance's estimates and voted by the Chamber; they included those relating to army chaplains, the Catholic Faculties of Aix and Rouen, and Catholic priests and Protestant pastors. Was its action constitutional? Gambetta and his friends naturally claimed that it was not. As Léon Blum was to write much later, Gambetta had raised a question which was still a live one in the late 1930s, the question who was to have the last word.[4] Gambetta held that the Senate had power only to reduce but not to increase estimates voted by the Chamber and that, if the interpretation of an article of the constitution was in doubt,

1. To Léonie Léon 16 Dec. (L.G.). For Gambetta's part in the debate, see *Annales, Chambre* Session Extraordinaire 1876, vol. ii, pp. 282–5, 289–96.
2. Letter of 17 Dec. (Ass. Nat., p. 251). She was clearly concerned at this time lest Gambetta's mercurial temperament and readiness to talk should make him vulnerable. Thus on 20 Dec. she wrote: 'Je regrette toujours votre trop grande franchise avec certains ministres; les persécutions suivent invariablement l'expansion' (*ibid.*, p. 252).
3. Leader, p. 9.
4. *L'Oeuvre de Léon Blum, 1937–1940* (1965), pp. 60 and 132, Blum's speech in the Senate, 9 April 1938.

the doubt must be resolved jointly by both houses. But Simon and his colleagues supported the Senate. The issue, as *The Times* noted and as Gambetta knew only too well, was not simply an academic one of constitutional law, it was at bottom 'a struggle against the personal influence of M. Gambetta'.[1] Gambetta himself wrote with an excess of indignant exaggeration on 21 December: 'The battle is engaged. The Senate has resolutely opened hostilities, the usurpation is flagrant, it tends to do nothing less than transform the Chamber of Deputies ... into a modest General Council which would have nothing to do but voice futile wishes and which would be deprived of its financial power.' Once again he complained bitterly of lack of support—not one of the Senators of the Left had defended the constitution and their treachery would make it 'all the more difficult to maintain unity among the Republicans in the Chamber. .... These are the first fruits of the Simon arrangement (*combinaison*). .... They want to put me in a minority and deprive me of the leadership in the Chamber.' What would the Chamber do? That was the great question: 'If I can gather all the deputies together before the discussion I think I can convince them of the justice of our claim and the legitimacy of our resistance.'[2]

The battle was indeed hotly engaged. When the Budget Committee met on 27 December Gambetta's proposal that it should declare that the Senate had the right only to call for the revision of the budget by the Chamber or to suppress estimates, but in no case to reinsert them was rejected by twelve votes to eleven. Already *The Times* had been certain that 'this first difference would be resolved in the sense of an implicit recognition of the right of the Senate'.[3] And this was what happened. On Tuesday the 28th the question came up for general discussion in the Chamber and Gambetta made a great oratorical effort in defence of his view of the Chamber's rights, an effort all the greater in that Léonie Léon, at his request, was present to give him courage.[4] The effort was in vain. Jules Simon, unlike the Marshal, was a subtle politician and he too had a store of 'bonds of silk and honey'. He offered the Chamber a choice of two policies, either to appeal to the country or to do what the Senate had done and take the ten articles over which there was disagreement and vote on them afresh: 'The first', he said, 'raises a conflict, the

1. *The Times*, 23 Dec., p. 5.

2. L.G.

3. 23 Dec.

4. 'Je veux t'avoir ce jour-là à Versailles et lutter sous tes yeux. J'en serai plus confiant et plus fort' (letter of 21 Dec., L.G.). For the text of his speech, see *Annales, Chambre*, S.E. 1876, vol. ii, pp. 370–9, 385–9, and *Discours*, vol. vi, pp. 207–33 and 252–69, and for supporting articles R.F. leaders of 22–26 Dec.

second causes it to disappear'. The Chamber preferred the second, despite
a further speech by Gambetta, and voted for it with no uncertain voice
by 358 votes to 136. Conflict was averted: the budget was passed and
published in the *Journal Officiel* on 30 December. Gambetta had suffered a
resounding defeat—Louis Blanc in an article in *L'Homme Libre* called it
his Waterloo[1]—and the Right was gloating over the divisions of the
Left. But Léonie Léon, after a sleepless night 'endlessly reliving' and
meditating on the excitements of the debate, very wisely consoled her
'light' and her 'life': 'It is really preferable that the trouble of ministerial
crisis or a dissolution should not arise out of a wholly personal struggle,
above all when it is regarded as such by public opinion. What an electoral
argument your enemies would have!'[2] As she had already told him, she
did not think that outside the political world public opinion was much
concerned with the Senate's usurpation of power. It would simply
see the issue as one between Gambetta and the government and side
accordingly.

Léonie was certainly right. Gambetta would indeed have placed himself
in a false position if he had appeared to force another cabinet crisis so
soon or a dissolution because of his personal animosity against the new
government. But he was only partly consoled. Two or three days later
he left to pay his usual New Year visit to the Adams at Les Bruyères.
This time, however, it was a sad holiday, although the sea was 'delicious'
and the fields, full of roses and oranges in flower, made him think of the
gardens of Armide. He arrived 'dead beat, harassed and much depressed'
by the newspapers he had read on the journey, for they vied with one
another in recording his defeat.[3] His hostess had just lost her father and
La Tata was slowly dying at Nice. He had to spend all too much time
wading through the details of new commercial treaties,[4] his future was
at stake and the political horizon generally was overcast. He felt lonely
without Léonie to console him, remind him that his genius could overcome all obstacles and tell him that the worms could not devour his
marble base.[5] No wonder that his walks with the Adams along the sun-
drenched roads were melancholy and that they constantly asked one
another 'What will this new year bring?'[6] It would bring little that was
good: it would bring political crisis and fresh bereavements.

Nevertheless the rest benefited Gambetta and he went back to Paris

1. Wormser, *Gambetta dans les tempêtes*, p. 205.
2. Letter of 29 Dec. (Ass. Nat., p. 256). For a good discussion of the issue, see
P. Mathieu-Bodet, *Les Finances françaises de 1870 à 1878* (1881), pp. 338–45.
3. Letter of 2 Jan. 1877 (L.G.).
4. The Anglo-French commercial treaty was about to be revised.
5. Letter of 21 Dec. (Ass. Nat., p. 253).
6. *Nos amitiés*, p. 434.

in good trim for the next round, the fight for the Budget Committee. The man who had dished the Orleanists in the elections for Life Senators might dish his new antagonists with similar means. His next letter to Juliette Adam was written not from Paris but from 'the golden town' of Naples where 'we are in a climate as radiant as the sky of Baia and Pozzuoli'.[1] 'We' no doubt meant he and Léonie, which was all the more reason for the letter to breathe complete confidence. Luck had been with him in the composition of the Chamber's bureaux and he was busy unravelling all the threads with which his foes sought to tie him down and prevent his reelection as President of the Budget Committee. Courtesy and diplomacy were doing the rest and for these he thanked another Minerva, his 'Minerva of Les Bruyères'. Stage by stage he succeeded. His rival for the presidency of the Budget Committee, Henri Germain of the Crédit Lyonnais Bank, was induced to stand down. Then the three Left-wing groups were prevailed on to agree each to nominate eleven members to the Committee and to accept Gambetta as President provided that the Left and Left Centre each had a Vice-President. This was not enough for Gambetta, who wanted once more 'to sweat the last sovereign from the cards'. When it came to the point the Republican Union refused to abide by the agreement that the groups should choose eleven members each. They claimed and successfully asserted the right to vote freely. When the vote was taken no fewer than nineteen of their members were elected compared with eight of the Left and four only of Jules Simon's Left Centre.[2] What had happened? In the words of Jules Ferry: 'When faced by a misdeed, the old judges used to say, "Where is the woman?" In parliament we have only to say, where is the Right?'[3] The Bonapartists and Right had once again pursued 'la politique du pire' and voted for those furthest to the Left. No doubt they hoped thereby to widen the rift in the Republican ranks between the followers of Gambetta and the followers of Simon, but Gambetta, knowing their frame of mind, had not scrupled to exploit it to strengthen his own position. It now looked impregnable. What matter if, according to the *Figaro*, the new Committee contained twenty-eight lawyers or journalists and only three financiers?[4] He had won the second round and the intoxication of victory inspired

---

1. *Lettres*, no. 298, 17 Jan.

2. *The Times*, 25 and 26 Jan. Daniel, *L'Année politique 1877*, p. 5, gives the figures as 16, 10 and 6, plus 'un du groupe constitutionnel'. For the Republican Union's resolution of 24 Jan. see *R.F.*, 26 Jan. For a pencil draft of the resolution, see Ass. Nat., MS 1550. For an interesting letter of Jules Ferry on the Republican Union's attitude, see *Discours et Opinions de Jules Ferry*, vol. ii, pp. 312–5.

3. *Discours et Opinions de Jules Ferry*, vol. ii, p. 313.

4. *The Times*, 27 Jan.; cf. its leader of 29 Jan. on Gambetta's election. It deplored this apparent lack of financial expertise.

him to write one of the most ardent of his many love-letters to the woman who was his 'protection and guide', his 'recompense and good fortune'.[1] Soon after this victory one observer wrote that Jules Simon's honeymoon was over and that he was kept up only at the end of a string held by Gambetta.[2] Had he not already been warned by the *République Française* not to let himself be suspected of having two sorts of friends, 'those whom one acknowledges but for whom one does nothing, and those whom one conceals but for whom one does everything'?

For *The Times* the duel that was being fought was one between 'M. Jules Simon . . . the partisan and defender of the Conservative Republic, and M. Gambetta . . . defender and representative of a progressive Republic, contrary to the Republican ideal of M. Thiers, M. Jules Simon, M. Dufaure, M. Grévy and others'.[3] It believed that Simon would try to constitute a majority on the basis of driving Gambetta into a corner and preventing

> every measure which might furnish a pretext for the triumph of the reaction. If he does not succeed . . . he will dissolve with the aid of the Senate. . . . Hitherto the danger was that—the dissolution . . . could be only effected with the cooperation of MM. de Fourtou, Buffet, de Broglie and their partisans, to the advantage of the reaction. With M. Jules Simon . . . it will be for the advantage of the Conservative Republic and everything leads to the belief that with such a programme, directed by so able and profoundly Republican a politician, France . . . would answer by elections which would be a triumph for the reassuring Republic.[4]

In other words, there was now under way 'the decisive and famous campaign' for the conjunction of the centres, or what the *République Française* scornfully called 'the chimerical plan pursued by the alchemists of the National Assembly'.[5]

This was at the end of December. It had then seemed that Gambetta had indeed been driven into a corner. But a month later, with the elections to the Budget Committee, he had retrieved his position. A lull then ensued. The Simon cabinet, like its predecessor, wished to pursue a policy of independence if not of combat, and it looked for a while as though it might be successful, for Simon was younger and more supple than Dufaure. As someone said when he had just formed his cabinet and made his first speech as its head: 'It will now be worth coming to Versailles.

---

1. *Lettres*, no. 299, 27 Jan.; for the R.F.'s satisfaction, see leaders of 28 and 29 Jan.
2. A. Laugel, 19 Feb. 1877, in *Revue de Paris*, 1 Aug. 1926.
3. 23 Dec. 1876.
4. 30 Dec. 1876.
5. Hanotaux, *op. cit.*, vol. iii, p. 652; R.F., leader of 1 Jan. 1877; Marcère, *op. cit.*, pp. 190–6.

It is just as if an impresario in a difficulty had engaged the tenor Niccolini in the room of a provincial singer. The words are the same perhaps, but they are better sung.'[1] Yet Simon, too, like Dufaure, was walking a tightrope, as Léonie Léon saw.[2] The majority in the Chamber was eager to embark on its programme of reforms; many deputies, particularly among the Intransigents, were busy introducing Bills, and the *République Française* demanded that the government should stir itself and take the initiative.[3] A well-known Intransigent, Bonnet-Duverdier, was elected President of the Paris Municipal Council in February and to Gambetta's discomfiture Left-wing Republicans were victorious in by-elections at Bordeaux and Avignon.[4] Such developments convinced the Conservatives and the Marshal's entourage at the Elysée that Radicalism was once more on the march. Simon in the middle was at the mercy of one side or the other, both hoping to capture him for their own purposes or to trip him up. There would be no question of his choosing his own time to secure a dissolution and a new, conservative but Republican Chamber and government of which he could be master.

For a month or so, however, there was comparative calm. Gambetta made no notable speeches in the Chamber and outside it spoke only at three ceremonies, two in aid of public libraries and the other of a secular school. During this time he had a recurrence of bronchitis which confined him for some time to his room.[5] He was troubled, too, by continued complications resulting from the financial and administrative troubles of the big and little *République Française*.[6] But there were perhaps other preoccupations or distractions.[7] After all the many letters from Léonie

1. *The Times*, 15 Dec.
2. 'Simon . . . campe sur un terrain qu'il lui faudra diviser en premier choc soit à droite soit à gauche, et alors finira la dernière incarnation de Simon' (Letter of 29 Dec., Ass. Nat., p. 256).
3. See, e.g., leaders of 21 Jan., 20 Feb., 25 April.
4. In both these constituencies the Intransigents put up their own candidates against more moderate Republicans. No doubt, however, Gambetta was pleased that at Avignon his old enemy the Legitimist Comte du Demaine had been defeated. The R.F. (28 March and 11 April) did its best to explain that Louis Mie, the successful candidate at Bordeaux, was not so red as he was painted and that there was really little to choose between the various Republican candidates' programmes.
5. *Lettres*, nos. 301, 302 of 26 Feb. and 3 March.
6. These apparently continued for some time, see, e.g., letter from Challemel-Lacour, 18 July 1877, to Scheurer-Kestner: 'Les relations avec la *Petite République* sont plus tendues que jamais' (Scheurer-Kestner pp., B.N., N.a.fr. 2409, p. 197) and to Ranc, 21 Oct. 1877 (Ranc, *Souvenirs-Correspondance*, pp. 313–15).
7. Sometime he had found leisure to sit for a portrait by the American painter Healy. It was commissioned by the American Minister, Washburne and exhibited in the 1877 Salon. The R.F. (25 April) described it as a painting 'd'une énergie et d'une ressemblance remarquable'.

Léon in 1876 there are only one or perhaps two, for the second is undated, which survive for the first five months of 1877. The one dated 24 March began significantly with a couplet:

> Ami puis-je penser que d'un zèle frivole
> Tu te laisses aveugler pour une vieille idole?

and went on to speak of 'the wounds which pierce my heart and sap my strength'. Had Marie Meersmans or some other mistress of the past reappeared and was another charmer also luring him away from his idol? Gambetta adored flowers and was used to receiving them—Juliette Adam had sent him a 'trophy', flowers that were 'like a crown prepared' for his victory of 27 January[1]—but now in April he had from a new admirer not only a 'magnificent bouquet', but a seal bearing the likeness of 'the most incomparable madwoman of the eighteenth century' and having on its base a maxim which the donor had had especially engraved.[2] It was an odd gift, but the donor, the daughter of a Radical Senator of the Seine, Alphonse Peyrat, and now the Marquise Arconati-Visconti, was intelligent, generous, Republican and very rich. Moreover, she had recently lost her husband and she was two years younger than Gambetta. Before long he would be writing to her as 'cara mia', 'mignonne', 'ma mie' and 'Bimbella carina' and thanking her for her tenderness as well as her liberality.[3]

Before long—yet the storms with Léonie were brief and quickly over. Gambetta's reply to her letter of 24 March, if he made a written one, has not survived, but soon he was writing to his 'Moumour' more passionately than ever. Now that the Easter vacation had begun they would go and hunt for lilies of the valley together, revisit their fine rocks in the forest of Fontainebleau and look once more for the fairies' lake and the 'little circle of Druidic oaks'.[4] In May he was writing that their love was cloudless.[5] More than ever he needed to have Léonie at hand to tell her of his projects and hear her reactions:[6] more than ever he wanted her

1. *Lettres*, no. 300.
2. *Ibid.*, no. 305, 12 April, to the Marquise Arconati-Visconti. An editorial note says: 'Nous n'avons pu identifier ni folle ni maxime.'
3. *Lettres*, nos. 336–9, 341: also the section of 'Lettres non datées'.
4. Letters of 11 and 14 April 1877 (L.G.).
5. Letter of 10 May (*ibid.*).
6. See, e.g., letter of 29 May: 'Je . . . te narrerai les divers incidents' (i.e. of his day's political activities); letter of 6 May: 'on dit qu'il y a des tiraillements graves dans le cabinet. Je m'informerai . . . et mardi nous en raisonnerons à fond'; 11 May, letter saying that he is dining with Cialdini on Monday evening—he would at least have the consolation of telling her 'ce qui sera passé; 14 May: 'à la soirée nous avons fait un assez grand pas vers la réalisation de la Politique que tu préconises' (*ibid.*).

to be in the Chamber if he had a great speech to make. She was, he said, his visible and always active providence. But, much as he valued her comments and advice, he kept his independence of judgement. She might be his counsellor, she might restrain his impulsiveness, but he was no woman's marionette.

It was in the summer of 1877, however, that there took place an event which revolutionised his way of life and brought him still closer to Léonie. Astonishingly, the change was due to Bismarck. An old friend, Henri Cheberry, was a wine merchant who went each year to Germany and counted Bismarck among his customers. Bismarck knew of the friendship and often asked Cheberry about Gambetta. Bismarck told him that in his opinion Gambetta drove himself too hard. He was burning the candle at both ends and should follow his example and have a house in the country to which he could retire and relax. Cheberry reported to Gambetta what Bismarck had said, and 'the Monster's' opinion made a great impression upon him, the more so, no doubt, as he was lonely in his 'accursed hotel' and a country dwelling would give him a greater chance to be with Léonie. He decided to follow the great adversary's advice and rented a cottage in the Chemin des Ronces at Ville d'Avray, a little place conveniently situated near the railway between Paris and Versailles. According to Léonie Léon's biographer she spent four months there.[1] It was the first time that they had been so long together and their doing so accounts for the relative dearth of letters. They liked this country retreat so well that Gambetta eventually decided to buy one near by. Ville d'Avray was to give him a modest country home to the end of his days.

But work did not cease, and already, he told Léonie Léon in February, he had reverted to one of his moods of pessimism. The cabinet was living from day to day: 'You see it's the rock of Sisyphus that I am rolling, each time I have got it to the top of the mountain the weight of the boulder pushes me back and it begins to roll towards the abyss.'[2] The events that were to give Gambetta his chance to go over to the offensive and bind Jules Simon to his chariot were beginning to gather momentum. The government was at the mercy of an incident and the first of these took place far away in Rome. In January the Italian Chamber had passed a Clerical Abuses Bill, naturally approved of by the *République Française*,[3] which empowered the state to prosecute agitator-priests. It gave the aged

---

1. Pillias, *Léonie Léon*, pp. 90–1. It is remarkable that none of the surviving letters between Gambetta and Léonie make any clear references to the rented cottage or their staying there.
2. 10 Feb. (L.G.).
3. 1 Feb.

Pius IX an opportunity for yet another protest against the loss of his temporal power and the humiliations to which he was subjected by the temporal state. In an allocution on 12 March he called upon the clergy to make known these iniquities to their flocks and exhort them to appeal to their governments on his behalf. Once again the Roman Question, which for more than quarter of a century had caused intermittent trouble in France, had come to life. French militant Catholics were roused and Catholic Action committees organised a petition to the President of the Republic asking him to use all means in his power to secure respect for the Holy Father's independence. Jules Simon at once acted, dissolved the Catholic Committees and instructed the prefects to stop petitions which were 'offensive to the authorities of a neighbouring and friendly country': but he could not silence the bishops and, whilst most of them were moderate in the way in which they obeyed the Papal behest, one in particular, the Bishop of Nevers, Mgr de Ladoue, not only wrote a public and belligerent letter to MacMahon on 7 April but circulated copies of it to all the mayors and justices of the peace in his diocese.[1]

The fat was in the fire. The government reprimanded the turbulent prelate and did its best to bury the affair, but the Radicals would not let it rest.[2] It was a heavensent opportunity for them to strike at the political pretensions of the clergy; a heavensent opportunity for Gambetta to attack Ultramontanism and move a step further towards the possible meeting ground with Bismarck, a heavensent opportunity to bring the Simon ministry to heel. Early in April Gambetta had given a dinner attended by all the Republican deputies and Senators of Paris to discuss the elections for General Councils later in the year.[3] A week later he was reported to have been urging his colleagues to press ahead with various proposals for reform, even though they were likely to be turned down by the Senate, in order to demonstrate that the majority in the Chamber was faithful to its electoral programme.[4] But these constructive plans were now overshadowed by the clerical issue. Parliament was due to reassemble on 1 May after five weeks' vacation. On 30 April the three Left-wing groups met and decided at the house of one of them, Leblond, that he should interpellate the government on the measures it proposed to take to check the clerical intrigues (*menées*), whose recrudescence was causing anxiety. The debate was to take place on 3 May. On the evening of the 1st, at no. 53 rue Chaussée d'Antin, Gambetta had a remarkably frank conversation with a police agent in his confidence, but it was mostly

1. It was published in the *Univers* on 13 April.
2. See, e.g., the *R.F.*'s outraged leaders of 21 April and following days.
3. Police report, 4 April (A.P.P., BA/919).
4. *Ibid.*, report of 11 April.

about MacMahon and the army, who appeared to give him much more concern than the immediate political situation. This, he said, was a little easier. The return of parliament had damped the ardour of 'the clericals'; their claims, which had not much chance of being supported by the Senate, would be condemned by a solemn vote of the Chamber at the end of a debate in which he would take part. He feared that Jules Simon was not quite up to his task: 'I see him from time to time and try to show him things as they are.' But it would not be a light undertaking to overthrow him, for, if he fell, the difficulty would be to find a successor who was both 'devoted to our interests and agreeable to the Marshal'.[1]

The debate on 3 May attracted an immense crowd. Leblond, an able lawyer of the Left group, so thin that he looked on the point of expiring, opened the attack and Jules Simon replied with a long, closely documented, and moderate speech which was intended to lower the temperature. He undertook to call the episcopate to order, if need be with all the means that the Concordat placed at his disposal, but argued that the need had not yet arisen because the majority of the bishops had acted temperately—the incidents referred to had been isolated happenings. 'We may be sure', commented Halévy, 'that had Gambetta been in Jules Simon's place he would have spoken as he did; only the accent would have been different.'[2] But Gambetta was not in Simon's place, the *République Française* called the speech 'a long and deplorable error',[3] and the Left insisted that the debate should be continued. When it resumed on the 4th Gambetta was the main speaker. Jules Ferry was down to speak, but he gave way. What was the reason? A French historian has asked: 'Was it not above all because the two Republican statesmen had agreed upon taking a fundamentally new position? The moment was favourable to a change of programme.'[4] Men like Littré and Renouvier had pointed out the danger of any hasty separation of Church and State, and Renouvier, in particular, had emphasised the judicial importance for the state of not renouncing its right to impose conditions upon all associations within its territory.[5] In the words of Georges Weill, 'the language of the philosophers was heard by the politicians',[6] but it was Gambetta rather than Ferry who took the manoeuvre in hand because he above all 'excelled in

1. *Ibid.*, report of 2 May.
2. *La République des ducs*, p. 261.
3. Leader, 5 May. The leader of the 4th had been a vigorous attack on the tergiversations and inertia of the Cabinet in face of the clerical danger.
4. Capéran, *op. cit.*, p. 58.
5. G. Weill, *Histoire de l'idée laïque en France au XIXe siècle* (1929), pp. 256-8.
6. *Ibid.*, p. 258.

concealing a moderate policy under verbal vehemences offered up to party passions'.[1]

The Catholics had organised a movement for the defence of religion and society and, since the fall of Thiers, this movement under the guidance of congregations like the Assumptionists and bishops like Dupanloup had gained great momentum. Now the Republican riposte was a neo-Gallicanism, the defence of the rights of the secular state, the riposte of many earlier governments since the Revolution. It was a countermovement which was to attain its climax in 1880–83.[2] The invocation of the rights of the state was the essence of Leblond's interpellation and of Gambetta's carefully prepared but much more powerful intervention of 4 May, an intervention which raised all the greater expectations because he had made no notable speech in the Chamber for more than four months. How was it, he asked, that such a letter as that addressed by the Pope to the University of Lille had been allowed to cross the frontier without any protests from the magistrates? How was it that the frightening multiplicity of congregations had a freedom of association not admitted by the law? The triumph of Ultramontanism in the Vatican Council of 1870 had shaken the Concordat and brought it into question. It was time for the Concordat and the Organic Articles to be rigorously applied 'for the defence of our liberties and the protection of our ecclesiastical freedom'. He was, he said, a supporter of the system which bound the Church to the State.

This was 'the new position' which was indeed a notable shift of ground for an erstwhile Radical Republican. The Radical Gambetta (like many other Radicals) had demanded the separation of Church from State in 1869, and although, grown more moderate, he had soft-pedalled it in his speech at Saint-Quentin in 1871, it was not until now that he openly advocated the maintenance of the Concordat. But this new 'moderate policy' was concealed by verbal vehemence. Five and a half years earlier, at Saint-Quentin, he had made a vigorous attack on the clergy and the Papacy. Now his onslaught was still more damning. Now, 'since the evil caused by the Ultramontane agitation' had reached the point of alarming France and disturbing Europe, he would go to the root of the question. He would denounce 'the political activity of a political faction' and point to the striking similarity between 'the ruling personnel of the clerical agitation and the ruling personnel of reaction', between the men of 'the government of combat' and those who had been signing petitions.

---

1. Capéran, *op. cit.*, p. 58.
2. See J. Gadille, 'La politique de défense républicaine à l'égard de l'église de France (1876–1883)', *Bulletin de la Société d'Histoire Moderne*, 14e série, no. 1, 1967.

When the Pope spoke, everyone among the clergy obeyed: 'We are in the presence of an army which has a general and which manoeuvres as disciplined armies do.' 'The clerical evil' had infiltrated deeply among the ruling classes, in the schools, in public administration and in the spheres of government. So much so that 'we have come to the point of asking ourselves whether the State is not within the Church instead of the true principle which wills that the Church should be within the State'. The government must declare that it intends to liberate France from the clutches of Ultramontane policy. There was one thing this country and its peasants detested as much as the ancien régime and that was clericalism. 'I am doing no more than translating the innermost feelings of the people of France when I say of clericalism what was once said by my friend Peyrat: "Clericalism? There is the enemy!"'[1] It was a tremendous indictment, following what has been called 'the first of the great interpellations of the regime'.[2] But it was not only the indictment that mattered, it was also the wording of the order of the day that followed. After Gambetta's onslaught Jules Simon had to accept the most virulent of the three wordings proffered—a formula in which, it was alleged by Broglie, Gambetta had refused to insert any mention of confidence in the government.[3] This was no 'bond of silk and honey'. 'The Chamber', it ran, 'considering that the Ultramontane manifestations, whose recrudescence could compromise the internal and external security of the country, constitute a flagrant violation of the laws of the State, invites the government to make use of the legal means at its disposal to repress this antipatriotic agitation.' It was voted by 346 to 114.

Simon, in Paul de Cassagnac's metaphor, had swallowed, not just accepted, the order of the day, but Gambetta, having administered the dose, had no wish that the unwilling patient should die as a result. Yet less than a fortnight later Simon was no longer in power. The routed Catholics and Right were indignant and dismayed by the debate. The Marshal was a Catholic and his heart was on the Right. He was infuriated. Moreover, he had no love for his First Minister. Not only was Simon the man who in a speech against the Septennate had expressed astonishment that the Right should have made a hero of a man who lacked the lineage of Chambord, the intelligence of the Comte de Paris and the military

---

1. For the text, see *Discours*, vol. vi, pp. 330–54, and *Annales, Chambre 1877*, vol. iii, pp. 31–8. For Gambetta's reference to Peyrat, see above, p. 70.

2. D. Halévy, *La République des ducs*, p. 260.

3. See Broglie's speech of 21 June in Senate: *Annales Sénat, 1877*, vol. iii, pp. 127–8. Marcère, however (*op. cit.*, pp. 211–12), no lover of Gambetta and, as President of the Left Centre, much concerned with the group manoeuvrings, makes no mention of Gambetta's refusal.

genius of Napoleon,[1] but he was a man whose silky and fawning manner was repugnant to him. He had respected Dufaure. He did not respect Simon, and although in the debate both Simon and Gambetta had made complimentary references to him, he was angered by Simon's capitulation and wounded by an unjust phrase that Gambetta had let fall in the heat of the moment—namely that it was rare to find in a Catholic the spirit of a patriot. While his wife, in dejection, wept 'like a weeping willow', MacMahon made up his mind to be rid of Simon at the first opportunity.[2]

The opportunity was not long in presenting itself. The greatest and most prolonged crisis of all was at hand. Ironically enough, four days before it began, the act which had set this momentous train of events in motion was nullified. On 12 May the Italian Senate rejected the Clerical Abuses measure which had led the Pope to rouse the Catholic world. In Italy, too, the Senate could act as a brake upon anticlerical enthusiasm.

1. It is, however, only fair to note that in his statement on 9 Dec. 1876 the Marshal explicitly said that he bore Simon no ill-will on this account.
2. Capéran, *op. cit.*, p. 68; Pisani-Ferry, *op. cit.*, pp. 142–3.

24

The Seize Mai and dissolution
15 May–July 1877

On 15 May 1877 the Chamber began to discuss a Bill about Press offences. According to a law of 29 December 1875, some of these were reserved for summary jurisdiction. The Republicans wished to restore trial by jury for all kinds of offence, but Jules Simon had promised the Marshal to uphold the 1875 law. Hard pressed, he made an embarrassed speech in which he declared that he could not make public his motives for opposing the abrogation of the existing provisions, but that his general opinion on the liberty of the Press had not changed and when the day came to make a law on it he would be its foremost defender. Gambetta realised the difficulties of Simon's position and recommended that an additional article proposed in the course of debate on the Bill be referred back to the appropriate commission. But the majority had the bit between its teeth and voted for the abrogation of the law by 377 to 55. The Marshal, angered anew, believed that his minister had broken faith. His opportunity to be rid of him had come.[1] Next morning Simon found on his desk a letter asking for an explanation which Simon, glad to escape from an increasingly difficult position, took to be a virtual dismissal. In it the Marshal declared that if he was not, like Simon, responsible to parliament he had a responsibility towards France. Without consulting his colleagues Simon resigned at once. He was the third head of a ministry to fall in fifteen months. The Third Republic was already stamped with the mark of governmental instability for which it was to be so notorious.

It was not the fall of another cabinet which made such a stir when the news was generally known in Paris, it was the manner of its going.

1. Lord Lyons in a letter of 16 May to Lord Derby averred that one of MacMahon's reasons for dismissing Simon was that 'he would not, or could not, get from the Chamber powers to restrain the Press from attacking Germany in the dangerous manner in which it has written against that country lately' (Newton, *Lord Lyons*, p. 360).

MacMahon's action appears to have been the exasperated impulse of an old soldier and not the deliberate and judiciously timed application of a carefully devised plan.[1] His letter was not countersigned by any minister and it was widely regarded as contrary to the spirit of the constitution. As Gambetta himself later recognised, it was not a *coup d'état* but an impulsive act, a *coup de tête*.[2] Yet to many it seemed almost tantamount to a *coup d'état* if not a *coup de force* and many talked of it as such.[3] It was, as Gambetta at once perceived, a declaration of war against the Left and what the Marshal conceived to be Radicalism:[4] and MacMahon had made no attempt to disguise the fact when Simon went to the Elysée to tender his resignation. 'I accept your resignation,' he said, 'I am a man of the Right. We can no longer work together. I prefer to be overthrown than to remain at the orders of M. Gambetta.'

Gambetta had indeed reestablished his position since his reelection as President of the Budget Committee. He had exploited the clerical issue to bring the cabinet to heel and, whether they liked it or not, both Left and Right had to admit the fact of his political ascendancy. But it had been a partly occult power, wielded, as Marcère would later write, 'from the room of the President of the Budget Committee or the offices of the *République Française*'.[5] In turn he and his friends had denounced 'the camarilla' surrounding the Marshal and exercising their sinister influence upon the head of state. Now both sides were to be forced into the open and Gambetta's ascendancy would be all the greater once the battle was overtly joined. On the morrow of the crisis of 24 May 1873, he had taken the lead in preaching calm, confidence and unity in the discomfited Republican ranks. Now more than ever he was the man of the hour. This was apparent on the very first day of the drama that had just begun.

On 16 May most of the ministers and a large number of Republican deputies and senators attended at the church of Saint-Germain-l'Auxerrois the funeral of Ernest Picard, the first of Gambetta's former colleagues in the Government of National Defence to die.[6] Just as the funeral procession

---

1. For a discussion of the controversy over the origins and timing of the Marshal's letter, see Pisani-Ferry, *Le Coup d'état manqué*, pp. 148–9. The *Journal des Débats* pointed out that MacMahon's action had a parallel in Louis-Napoleon's dismissal of the Odilon Barrot cabinet in 1849 (*The Times*, 26 May).

2. L. Halévy, *Trois dîners avec Gambetta* (1929), p. 45.

3. e.g. Jules Bravard in his Journal covering 1 Jan.–31 July 1877 (Ass. Nat., MS 1587).

4. *Lettres*, no. 309.

5. *Histoire de la République de 1876 à 1879*, vol. i, pp. 89–90; cf. pp. 120, 178.

6. Gambetta, who did not like Picard, commented: 'La perte est minime, mais le moment est assez mal choisi; c'est un vide au Sénat toujours difficile à combler' (letter of 13 May, L.G.). Curiously enough, Picard had made gloomy prophecies at

was about to move off the ministers present received brief notes, signed by the Marshal, informing them that Simon had resigned and that his resignation had been accepted. They were soon to follow suit. The news spread and caused stupefaction among the mourners, many of whom at first refused to believe it. When it was clear that it was true, the deputies of the Left group were summoned to meet in the conference hall of the Boulevard des Capucines in Paris. Many members from other groups joined them and Gambetta broke off a meeting of the Budget Committee in order to attend. As in 1873, he appealed for calm and determination; at the same time he urged that a full meeting of all four Republican groups[1] should be held that very evening to approve a collective declaration; this would immediately make clear to the country the Republican majority's attitude and unanimity. Despite the opposition of Ferry, Marcère, Bernard Lavergne and others, who thought it sufficient to obtain a common front by agreement between the bureaux of the different groups, most of those present were this time swayed by Gambetta. A meeting was arranged for 10 p.m. in the Grand Hotel in Paris. Immediately after the gathering at the conference hall had dispersed the Republican Union in turn held a meeting which endorsed the proposal; moreover, in view of the exceptional circumstances, the Union added Gambetta, Spuller and Lepère to its bureau. Once again, as in March and December 1876, it was a question of making clear, clearer than ever, the kind of cabinet tolerable to the majority of the Chamber in a parliamentary system.

When some 300 deputies met at the Grand Hotel that evening, the chairman Devoucoux at once invited Gambetta to speak.[2] What he said was brief and to the point. This was not the moment, he declared, for passionate and empty discussions: 'When people want to take a grave step, marked with the stamp of strength and authority, they must be

1. There were now four, since Louis Blanc had broken away from the Republican Union and formed his own group (see above, pp. 320–1).
2. According to the *R.F.*'s report (18 May) Devoucoux said: '... M. Gambetta qui a assisté aujourd'hui aux réunions des différents groupes républicains et à la réunion des quatre bureaux de gauche, va vous faire connaître l'ordre du jour qui est sorti de leurs délibérations'.

the opera on 4 April, as his companion, Mme C. noted in her diary: 'Tout l'intérêt à écouter M. Picard à propos de la politique de M. Jules Simon qui réussit à mécontenter aussi bien la Droite que la Gauche. Il nous a fait un véritable discours au noir: le pays ne se doute pas d'un grand danger prochain: entourage de la maréchale exaspérée ... maréchal se laissera faire un coup d'état par les ducs ... la dissolution en juin, nouvelles élections peut-être ... — Où serez-vous emprisonné, M. Picard? demandais-je. — Qui sait? En tout cas je saurai maigrir en prison' (M. Reclus, *Ernest Picard 1821–1877*, 1912, p. 350, n. 1).

dignified and their language must be correct, constitutional and legal.' The President's letter asserted a special responsibility, the claim to a personal power.

> You are replying by asserting the authority of the country whose representatives you are. Your delegates have thought that they should assert three main ideas: the reestablishment of the principles of parliamentary government, on the basis of ministerial responsibility which must be scrupulously respected; a reminder that Republican policy is the guarantee of order and prosperity at home; resistance to any risky policy which . . . might involve France, this country of peace, order and thrift, in warlike and dynastic adventures.

These three ideas were contained in the motion or order of the day which he then proceeded to read:

> The Chamber,
> Considering that, in order that it should fulfil the mandate it has received from the country, it is in the present crisis its duty to recall that the preponderance of the power of parliament exercised by a responsible ministry is the first condition of that government of the country by the country which it was the aim of the constitutional laws to establish;
> Declares
> That the confidence of the majority can be given only to a cabinet which is free to act and which is resolved to govern in accordance with those Republican principles which can alone guarantee order and prosperity at home and peace abroad
> And passes to the order of the day.[1]

This motion, Gambetta went on, was not an attack upon the head of State, but a reply to the activities of the camarilla which possessed him and from whose intrigues he should be extricated. He besought his hearers to vote for it at once, without debate and unanimously. They did as he bade them, spurred on no doubt by the thought, voiced by one of them and echoed by Gambetta, that they were emulating the 221 deputies who had opposed Polignac and Charles X in 1830.[2] Gambetta's staff work had been admirable and he was well pleased. When he got home he wrote to Léonie Léon that his positions were impregnable; 'we are in occupation of the heights of the law from which we can fire at our ease upon the miserable troops of the reaction who are floundering in the plain'. What had, moreover, pleased him particularly was the acclaim of the Parisians who had gathered outside the Grand Hotel:

> I was almost suffocated by the enthusiasm of the crowd; the cries of Vive la République, vive Gambetta, filled the air. As usual I preached calm and

1. For Spuller's MSS drafts of this declaration, see Ass. Nat., MS 1550.
2. For the full text of his speech, see *Discours*, vol. vii, pp. 7–10.

moderation and it was with great difficulty that I succeeded in getting them to disperse quietly, once I had given them the assurance that the cause of right was in good hands and that the final victory would fulfil all their wishes.[1]

He was serene and confident. This was one of his great qualities at such a time. But some who remembered the last days of the Second Republic feared preventive arrests. Louis Blanc is said to have asked him on the way out of the hotel: 'Where are you going to sleep tonight?' 'Why, in my bed,' replied Gambetta laughing.[2]

The first step was thus concerted outside parliament. It remained to implement it in the Chamber. 'I shall go tomorrow to Versailles,' he had told Léonie, 'where perhaps a reactionary ministry will await us and our sittings will be suspended.'[3] As was to be expected, great crowds gathered at the Gare Saint Lazare on the 17th to see the parliamentarians entrain for what promised to be a historic session, and there were loud cheers for many of the Left. At Versailles the galleries of the Chamber were packed. The business was the Left's interpellation of the government upon the ministerial crisis. There was no debate, since there was only one of the resigning ministers present and he declined to answer on behalf of colleagues whom he had not been able to consult. Gambetta had the floor to himself. He ascended the tribune amid profound silence. 'Never', wrote *The Times* correspondent, 'did the Chief of the Radical Party display greater, more bitter, more overpowering eloquence.... Only from having heard this speech and being present at the scene could anyone understand how much the earnestness of the situation added to the orator's habitual eloquence.'[4] He again disclaimed any intention of uttering anything which could be regarded as an act of hostility towards the President of the Republic, but the first reaction of public opinion was, he said, to think that very probably the President had about him advisers, 'a kind of government already made', who had denatured his actions and had not hesitated to precipitate him into an adventurous policy.[5] It was the

1. *Lettres*, no. 309. For an account of this incident by an Englishman who was 'in the thickest part of the crowd', see J. Hanlon, *Gambetta, orator*... (2nd edn, London, 1881), pp. 131–2.

2. Marcellin Pellet, 'Souvenirs sur Gambetta', *Revue de France*, 15 Nov. 1927, p. 285.

3. *Lettres*, no. 309.

4. *The Times*, 18 May, p. 5.

5. D. Halévy in *La République des ducs* misleadingly tends to put in quotation marks his own summaries of speeches. Here (p. 282) he makes play with the fact that the reporter of the *Journal des Débats* (18 May) made Gambetta say 'Quels conseils dépravent son action' (actually the reporter wrote: 'Quels conseillers, quels inspirateurs secrets "dépravent ainsi l'action" du chef de l'état'). He comments: 'Sur ce mot, sensation profonde: c'est Mgr. Dupanloup que Gambetta visait ainsi.' The text in

Chamber's duty to tell the President that he had been deceived and to appeal to him to return to the true path of the constitution:

> In effect what is it that we have come to ask? That the Constitution should be a reality . . . and we say to M. the President of the Republic that the phrase . . . in which you claim a responsibility beyond your legal responsibility . . . does not correspond to the true position. . . . We appeal to his reason . . . to his patriotism . . . and say: Monsieur the President of the Republic, remain within the Constitution, always within the Constitution. . . . Gentlemen, we must put an end to this situation. . . . With the Constitution in your hands and the country behind you, ask whether it is the intention to govern with the Republican party in all its shades or if, on the contrary, by recalling to power men who have been three or four times rejected by popular suffrage, it is intended to impose on this country a dissolution which would mean consulting France anew. . . . If the decision is for dissolution we shall go back with confidence to the country . . . which knows that it is not we who are troubling peace at home and disturbing it abroad.

Disturbing it abroad! He ended with what Halévy called a treacherous sally: 'If dissolution comes . . . beware lest it should be found to conceal another manoeuvre and the country say: Dissolution is the prelude to war! Those who had such an object in mind would be criminals!'[1] This, as the Conservatives at once appreciated, was dangerous propaganda. After 1870–71 there was nothing that Frenchmen feared so much as war.

The order of the day, prepared by the deputies at the Grand Hotel the previous evening, was voted by a large majority—349 to 147, since the Left Centre, which had hesitated the day before, had now fallen into line. Gambetta, well satisfied, but aware of the strategic importance of this group, was willing to give it a sort of precedence;[2] yet in effect he was more than ever the leader of the Republican resistance. To Léonie that night he wrote that he had given battle and believed that he had won. The question had been clearly posed: either a Republican government or dissolution. He added that Broglie was taking over the control of affairs: 'We are going to have three difficult laborious months and at the end revenge and the punishment of intriguers and the perverse. I answer for it.'[3] 'We are back on the morrow of 24 May', exclaimed the *République*

1. For the full text, see *Discours*, vol. vii, pp. 13–23, and *Annales, Chambre 1877*, vol. iii, pp. 234–7.
2. See Marcère, *op. cit.*, pp. 239–42.
3. *Lettres*, no. 310.

Discours (vol. vii, p. 17) and the *R.F.* (19 May) as well as *Annales Chambre*, vol. iii, p. 236 runs: 'Il se trouvait . . . des conseillers, une sorte de gouvernement tout formé, qui dénaturait l'action du chef de l'Etat.'

Française, '. . . but how much stronger and more numerous than we were then. . . . The country . . . is ready to resist.' Broglie's return to power was, of course, taken to mean the dissolution already talked of six months earlier.[1] The order of the day had left open for the Marshal a way of escape, but by recalling Broglie he had promptly closed it. 'The supreme effort against . . . the very existence of the Chamber' was about to be made.[2] It began in detestable weather, probably, wrote Gambetta, because the sun itself was indignant at the return of 'these birds of the night'.[3]

The day before, Gambetta had remarked to Freycinet that the Republican protest would make the Marshal realise the full extent of the blunder he had committed.[4] Although MacMahon was said to have had second thoughts about his famous letter to Simon and tried to retrieve it before it was too late, once he had committed himself to dismissing Simon it would indeed be difficult to find a successor who was both agreeable to him and also devoted to Republican interests. He had not listened to the Left's representations in March or December 1876: still less would he listen to their still clearer representations in May 1877. His advisers had persuaded him that conservative interests and the defence of all that he believed he stood for demanded an end sooner or later to the experiment of governing with a Republican majority in the Chamber. No doubt, too, they had emphasised the importance of having a resolutely conservative cabinet in power to conduct the various crucial elections of the coming year. He had seized his opportunity and the time had come for the experiment to end. For a moment perhaps, he thought of falling back once more on Dufaure, but Broglie had all along been regarded as the man for the supreme emergency and this time there would be no prolonged ministerial crisis and protracted cabinet-making. Broglie's men were ready to answer his call and the composition of the new government was announced in the *Journal Officiel* of the 18th. Broglie himself and Decazes (who remained at the Ministry of Foreign Affairs after some hesitation and in response to a special appeal from the Marshal) along with Eugène Caillaux and Auguste-Joseph Paris represented the Orleanists or Right Centre, Brunet the Bonapartists, and the Vicomte de Meaux the Legitimists. The key post of the Ministry of the Interior was entrusted to Fourtou, a relatively young and energetic man who had held a number of ministerial offices in the past five years. Wrongly labelled a Bonapartist by his enemies, he was in reality one of those wholehearted Conservatives

1. See above, p. 380.
2. Leader of 20 May.
3. Letter of 21 May (L.G.).
4. Freycinet, *Souvenirs 1848–1878*, p. 356.

who were little troubled by constitutional scruples.[1] Since the support of the Senate was all important, four of the nine ministers were Senators. Berthaut was retained at the Ministry of War, although (or because) he was regarded as a non-political general who had resisted some of the political demands of the Left. It was a new ministry of combat and moral order, but not a dictatorship. As Broglie left the Elysée with de Meaux and looked at the fashionable crowd near the Arc de Triomphe, he remarked with disdain that these people were more fitted to submit to a *coup d'état* than to make the effort he was going to demand of them.[2]

Broglie might speedily form a cabinet, but the Marshal had blundered by precipitating him into doing so in May. It was not the moment of Broglie's choosing and he is said to have exclaimed: 'Who would have thought that of the Marshal? But what is the good of groaning? We have been clumsily thrown into the water. We must swim.'[3] But the waters would be strong and treacherous, and if they reached land at all the troops might only too easily flounder in the plain. Gambetta himself later allowed that 'the Duc de Broglie, Fourtou and the others did not want to desert MacMahon and they bravely followed him although they knew that the fight had begun badly and was lost in advance. They had indeed loaded the gun, but it went off all on its own without being "au point." '[4] The Marshal would have done better to wait a month or more, by which time Simon might have succumbed, as had Dufaure in effect, to fresh attacks from the Left, or even better, as Naquet and Freycinet thought, until the budget had been voted and other parliamentary combinations had been used up: 'Then he might have dissolved two or three times if need be and he would probably have succeeded in obtaining a Chamber to his liking.'[5] As it was, the Conservative ranks were taken by surprise. Some provincials in the Sarthe believed that the 16 Mai was a Bonapartist coup. A disillusioned intellectual, Taine, wrote that the more he thought of the Marshal's last step, the more imprudent it seemed:

It is like the charge at Reichshoffen after the fight was lost, and only adds to the disaster of defeat. In my opinion the social and political battle we are fighting has already long been lost. . . . The task still left was to show the

1. M. Reclus, *Le Seize Mai* (1931), pp. 41–5.
2. de Meaux, *Souvenirs politiques*, p. 315.
3. Pisani-Ferry, *Le Coup d'état manqué*, p. 160.
4. L. Halévy, *Trois dîners*, p. 45.
5. Silvestre de Sacy, *Le Maréchal de MacMahon*, p. 355, n. 30; Pillias, *Autobiographie d'Alfred Naquet*, p. 9; Freycinet, *op. cit.*, p. 363. But cf. Joseph Caillaux's scornful reference to Broglie's envisaging a 'dissolution à l'anglaise' (*Mes mémoires*, vol. i, 1942), pp. 61–2. Joseph Caillaux was son of the Finance Minister in the Broglie cabinet.

Republicans by contact with actualities the distance that lies between theories and practice.... As we are in the power of the brutes, we must learn to tame them.... The Marshal's attempt will only exasperate them and hasten their day of power.[1]

This was just what Gambetta was optimistically reckoning. He believed that the Marshal would be forced to resign. In consequence the Septennate would end three years earlier and 'Republican democracy' would be the gainer by ten years![2]

When the deputies returned to Versailles on the 18th the reactionary ministry expected by Gambetta awaited them. But there was no immediate dissolution. Instead Fourtou read a presidential message adjourning parliament for a month, the maximum period allowed by the constitution, 'in order that the emotion caused by the recent incidents may be allowed to calm down'. But the message made clearer than ever MacMahon's opposition to 'the fraction of the Republican party which believes that the Republic cannot be consolidated without the *radical* modification of all our institutions', men who differed from one another 'only upon the means and the *opportune* moment'[3] to apply their programme. The allusion to Gambetta and his followers was patent, as also in the appeal to patriotism 'which, thank God, in France is not lacking in any class of citizens'. The message no less clearly indicated that dissolution was in the offing: 'If the country were consulted anew and in such a way as to avert all misunderstanding it would reject this confusion.'

Gambetta's attempts to speak after the adjournment decree had been read were ruled out of order. Parliament stood prorogued and a debate on the message had to be deferred until it reassembled. Thereupon the deputies of the Left, like their predecessors who went to the Tennis Court in 1789, repaired to the Hôtel des Réservoirs. Although Marcère presided, it was once again Gambetta who took the lead. The prorogation, he declared, could be a prelude only to dissolution. They must draw up an appeal to the country and protest against an act which was contrary to the spirit, if not to the letter, of the constitution. A manifesto was drafted then and there by Spuller (who had no doubt concerted the gist if not the precise wording beforehand with Gambetta).[4] It recalled the 24th of May and appealed for the same patience, coolness and determination that had

---

1. *Life and Letters of H. Taine*, part iii, pp. 174–5, 21 May.

2. *Lettres*, no. 313, 30 May. Cf. *R.F.*, leader of same day: 'M. le président de la République paiera bientôt de sa démission l'erreur de ses amis et de ses courtisans'; also leader of 3 June.

3. My italics.

4. For the original draft and the signatures of the 363 deputies who subscribed to it, see Ass. Nat., MS 1550.

been shown then. It declared that France would not be intimidated, despite the economic uncertainties and international anxieties resulting from the fresh crisis. It invited Frenchmen to choose between the policy of reaction and adventure, which was suddenly imperilling all the gains of the last six years, and the 'wise, firm, peaceful and progressive policies' which they had already approved by their votes. At Gambetta's particular request it included both an appeal to Republican officials to remain at their posts until they were replaced and an assurance to the nation that this new trial would not last for more than five months. Then the Republic would emerge stronger than ever, the parties of the past would be finally vanquished and France could look to the future with confidence and serenity. It was a stirring document and it was signed by 363 deputies. With the prorogation and the publication of this manifesto of the 363 the first round of the struggle was done. The speed and unanimity of action obtained by Gambetta were indeed impressive. Since 16 May, claimed the *République Française* on the 24th, there were no longer four separate Left-wing groups, there was 'only the Republican party closely united with a single mind and hope'.

If the 'dismissal' of the Simon ministry had been a Conservative blunder so, too, almost certainly, was the prorogation of the Chamber instead of its immediate dissolution. Had there been an immediate dissolution, wrote Freycinet, the Republicans would not have had time to organise for fresh elections, and 'the government, by a rapid offensive, would have won over the timid and the hesitant'.[1] But the cabinet had been divided and eventually it was the policy of Fourtou, who wanted a longer period in which to mount a great system of official candidatures, supported by loyal agents, that prevailed. Thus the month's delay gave the Republicans more time for propaganda, a month, moreover, in which they could still benefit from parliamentary immunity. It gave them time, too, to prepare more fully for the deferred and tremendous debate on the composition of the new government.

The second round began at once. Republican deputies and senators wrote to their constituents denouncing personal power, and patriotic citizens voted addresses to senators and deputies.[2] The government of combat lost no time in laying about it with its administrative weapons. Sixty-two prefectoral changes were made within twenty-four hours and during the whole month's prorogation 484 prefects and subprefects, 184 magistrates, 83 mayors and 381 justices of the peace were replaced. The Second Empire itself had not been more thorough or speedy. Broglie reminded the procurators-general that the laws were intended to protect

1. *Op. cit.*, p. 365; cf. Pisani-Ferry, *op. cit.*, p. 168.
2. See H. Gautier, *Carnet d'un journaliste pendant le seize-mai* (1881), pp. 76–8.

morality, religion and property and that 'any lies' publicly uttered might be punished. Fourtou ordered a watch on cafés and cabarets where meetings were held and instructed the prefects to be severe in their licensing and control of newsvendors. But the Republicans refused to be rattled or indulge in provocative acts which would play into their enemies' hands. Gambetta as ever insisted on calm and good order. For some salon wits the 'fou furieux' had now become a 'faux furieux', in other words 'one who keeps a cool head for the guidance of a warm heart'.[1] To foreign visitors and others who interviewed him he expressed complete confidence. There would not be a vestige of disturbance and, he assured Grant Duff, 'he and his friends would play out the political game against the Marshal, as quietly as if it were a *parti de whist*'. Fourtou's attempts to muzzle opinion were laughable, he told the American Minister. 'To want to stop Frenchmen from talking is like wanting to stop Americans from taking action (*d'agir*).'[2] He declined a suggestion that he should speak to his constituents at Belleville because of the risk of provoking excitement when the greatest calm was essential.[3] A speech at Belleville of all places at such a time would indeed have been injudicious, but he did speak elsewhere and sharpened his attack. On 31 May he told a deputation of Paris students that he and his friends were not merely fighting for the constitution. The struggle was 'between all that remains of the old world, the old castes, the privileged of the old regimes, between the agents of Roman theocracy and the sons of 1789'.[4] In June he paid a brief visit to the Somme to consolidate unity in the ranks of the Republicans there. On the 9th at Amiens, in reply to a toast given by his colleague Goblet, mayor of the city, he derided the 'handful of dukes, infatuated by their prestige' who claimed to take over the nation, and at Abbeville, two days later, in a speech of reply to the Marshal's message of 18 May, he denounced 'the so-called ruling classes' and 'the handful of incorrigible political coxcombs', who had emerged from their concealment and hoped to put an end to the Republic.[5] Both these latter speeches won the admiration of

---

1. *The World*, 4 July 1877.
2. Grant Duff, *Notes from a Diary 1873–1881*, vol. i, p. 262, 19 May; E. B. Washburne, *Recollections of a Minister to France 1869–1877* (London, 1887), vol. ii, p. 346, 6 June. Cf. Gambetta's words at the Hoche banquet on 24 June: 'on croit pouvoir empêcher ce peuple de plaisanter, de railler, de rire, et de se moquer de ce qu'il trouve ridicule et même grotesque. Non! Non! on pourra vexer les Gaulois, mais on ne supprimera jamais la Gaule.'
3. Police report of 24 May (A.P.P., BA/919).
4. *Discours*, vol. vii, p. 54.
5. *Ibid.*, pp. 60 and 72. Goblet was at once attacked by the Right for his part in welcoming Gambetta and on 28 June the Government dismissed him and his 'adjoints'.

The Times. That at Abbeville it thought 'even more finely conceived' than the one at Amiens. It was 'at once sober and firm and strong'.[1] In it, of course, Gambetta also returned to the clerical charge. The government might try to restrain the Ultramontanes, but France had been warned: 'We know what clericalism is and where it is leading us and you will not get it out of the heads of our French peasants that the hand of the Jesuit is in all this affair.' It was good propaganda and the tone of many of his letters suggests that Gambetta sincerely believed in it. But it was unfortunate that constitutional issues in the battle ahead should be too often submerged by denunciation of such vague and imprecise horrors as 'clericalism' and 'radicalism'.[2]

Meanwhile during the prorogation there were rumours that the cabinet was divided and hesitating about dissolution. But Gambetta was now eager for victory. His immediate reaction was to press on: 'We must push for dissolution and force everyone to accept the nation's verdict as final. This is the only way to clear things up and give France a white shirt. Ever since 4 September she has been left with old linen spotted with the stains of all the parties.' All that he feared, he said, was an enemy retreat and another refurbishing (*replatrage*) of the cabinet 'which would take us back into the marshes into which the Ricards and the Simons led us'.[3] At one moment that interesting observer, Saint-Valry, even wondered whether the Marshal's intention was after all to call upon Gambetta to take office: 'It could be quite a deep though risky political game, but it is doubtful whether it is being seriously entertained.'[4] It was not. As soon as parliament reassembled on 16 June Broglie asked the Senate to agree to dissolution. On the same day the Chamber embarked upon the discussion of the Republicans' interpellation on the composition of the new government which they had been debarred from debating in May.

The bureaux of the Left-wing groups had issued a statement declaring that in order that the debate should be fruitful the utmost calm should reign in the Chamber. In addition, citizens were urged to refrain from going to the Paris stations to await the arrival and return of the deputies. But, whether or not good citizens kept away from the stations, the scene in the Chamber was said to have been more tumultuous than any for years even in a French parliament, and that was saying a good deal. Feelings

1. Leader of 13 June. Gambetta certainly was pleased. He told Léonie Léon that his welcome had been splendid and that the crowd had included not only peasants but 'l'élite de la bourgeoisie' (L.G., 11 June).

2. For an able article arguing that clericalism had hitherto been 'un mot vide de sens', see J. J. Weiss 'La chambre de 1876', *Combat constitutionnel*, p. 61.

3. *Lettres*, no. 313. As late as 10 June in his speech at Abbeville he expressed doubt about the government's intentions.

4. Saint-Valry, *Souvenirs et réflexions politiques*, p. 186.

were in any case strong, but they were deliberately goaded by some of the Bonapartists, only too ready to seize any chance to discredit parliamentary institutions. The sitting lasted four and three-quarter hours. 'During that long time', wrote *The Times* correspondent, 'amid an immense crowd, heaped up, as it were, in every gallery, filling the passages, staircases and waiting-rooms, there was one prolonged roar of vociferation rebounding from one side of the Chamber to the other.'[1] The Swiss and American ministers, present in the diplomatic gallery, had never seen anything like it and believed that it must portend civil war.[2] Bethmont, who opened for the Left, was followed by Fourtou who proved himself no mean adversary and made a powerful attack upon the majority, its leader Gambetta and the Belleville radicalism still hidden behind his opportunist policies.[3] The atmosphere was still more tense when Gambetta rose to reply. He spoke for between two and three hours amid an intermittent hail of interruptions (the vituperative and irrepressible Bonapartist Paul de Cassagnac interrupted more than ninety times). His irony and sarcasm were superb, his quickness of repartee was admirable, his denunciations became more violent with the violence of the interrupters. He came back to 4 May and in different language unscrupulously enlarged upon the same anticlerical theme: it was 'from the depths of the Vatican' that there came the blow that felled the Simon ministry.[4] No one was deceived 'and you will soon hear a cry ... which will spell liberation and punishment: the cry "It is the government of the priests (Bravos on the Left— denials on the Right). It is the ministry of the curés," the peasants are saying! (Repeated Bravos on the Left).' A little later, amid redoubled interruptions, he poured scorn on the government's claim to have reassured Europe. Their policy had been condemned by the Press of Europe and America. He referred to a debate in the Italian parliament, but could not finish the phrase. But eventually, in a moment's lull, he was allowed to utter three consecutive sentences and in the last of them

1. *The Times*, 18 June, p. 7. *The Times* correspondent thought it lasted 5½ hours. Feelings were already aroused by exchanges arising from the tabling of a bill concerning the accounts of the Government of National Defence. In the course of these Gambetta was referred to as 'dictateur de l'incapacité' and invited to go back to Belleville (*Annales Chambre 1877*, vol. iii, pp. 256–7).

2. Washburne, *op. cit.*, p. 347.

3. Extracts from Fourtou's speech were liberally quoted in pro-government propaganda, e.g. *Le Programme de M. Gambetta* (Tours, n.d.). In particular, Fourtou reminded his hearers of Gambetta's Belleville programme of 1869 and his declaration on 24 May 1875 that 'le contrat tient toujours'. For the text of Fourtou's speech see *Annales, Chambre 1877*, vol. iii, pp. 264–70.

4. There is no evidence that this was so, see the discussion in Capéran, *op. cit.*, pp. 76–7.

declared: 'We have the right and duty to make it known beyond the Alps that, if by a wholly passing accident, the government of France can fall into suspect hands (M. de Baudry d'Asson—"Into yours, for example!") the nation disowns them!' This was too much. Paris, the Minister of Public Works, sought to intervene, deputies of both sides rushed down from their benches, and Washburne thought there was going to be a free fight and that Gambetta would be forcibly dragged from the tribune.[1] It did not happen, but it was no wonder that a little later, after he had finally stepped down amid the vociferous applause of his supporters, he fainted. The speech had been a colossal effort.[2] It made a tremendous impression. Admirers flocked later to the *République Française* to congratulate him. It was read throughout the country the next day and caused the same passionate reactions. The rows in the Chamber were echoed *in petto* in family circles, and at lunch in Dinan the liberal Cosme de Satgé had a furious altercation with his conservative uncle, Baron de Thoren.[3]

The debate continued for another two days, but all the din and insults could not affect the result. When it came to the vote on 19 June the Left-wing motion of no confidence was carried by 363 to 158. It was 'perhaps the most sweeping vote of censure ever passed on any Ministry'.[4] The announcement of the figures, recorded one of the 363, was greeted with

applause ten times repeated. A thrill stirred the whole hall and the tribunes, people laughed, sang, shook one another by the hand and embraced. There was no longer a Left Centre, a Left or Republican Union; we were united in a single party . . . against the enemies of the Republic. 'That's it! It's splendid! Long live the Republic! Down with the priests! Let them come on now!' Such were the cries which mingled with one another.[5]

1. Washburne, *op. cit.*, pp. 345–8.
2. According to Marcellin Pellet's *Notes et Souvenirs 1876–1882* (Ass. Nat., MS 1474 bis) the temperature was 'sénégalienne' and Gambetta 'ruisselait comme s'il sortait de l'eau'. He therefore went and changed his underclothes. Pellet does not mention the fainting. For the text of the speech see *Discours*, vol. vii, pp. 115–57, and *Annales Chambre 1877*, vol. iii, pp. 271–83. The R.F., exceptionally, published a second edition of its issue of 18 June. This contained the 'texte sténographié in extenso' of Gambetta's speech. Perhaps Gambetta was inspired, as on a previous occasion, by the presence of Léonie Léon. On the 18th she wrote that she understood his exhaustion and added: 'J'ai savouré le discours que j'avais beaucoup mieux entendu que je ne le pensais; chacune de vos paroles se trouve en mon coeur et vibre encore à mes oreilles avec l'intonation que vous lui aviez donnée' (L.G.).
3. 17 June (extract kindly communicated to me by Canon J. C. de Satgé from his grandfather's diary).
4. Stannard, *Gambetta*, p. 188, for the text, see *R.F.*, 21 June.
5. Millaud, *Journal d'un parlementaire*, vol. ii, p. 24.

More than ever the figure '363' had a symbolic character like '221' in 1830. It represented both opposition to personal power and defence of the constitution, and it became an electoral talisman.

In the Senate, too, there had been notable speeches, not least one by Broglie himself—a speech in which he rebutted the accusations of unconstitutionality, clericalism and warmongering and, above all, disclosed his grand strategy of making the struggle a combat between that 'Bayard of modern times', MacMahon, and Gambetta. Jules Simon, he said, might have been content to be a puppet in Gambetta's hands, not so the President of the Republic.

> When one bears the name of Marshal MacMahon; when one represents law [*la règle*] order and discipline . . . when one has passed a blameless life fulfilling all one's duties . . . one does not suddenly think of becoming the ally and soldier of the contrary . . . one is not the ally and accomplice of the honourable M. Gambetta. . . . Universal suffrage will have to choose between Marshal MacMahon and the dictator of Bordeaux or the orator of Belleville, who can barely restrain the quivering masses of Radicalism and the uprising of the new social strata.

But, as Hanotaux was to write: 'The subtle Duke was deceiving himself; things were not so simple and, if there was to be a choice between the two men, the parallel itself would be a dangerous one to draw.'[1] Broglie in the course of his speech had, for instance, admitted that Gambetta was the 'true incarnation, the natural chief' of the parliamentary majority in the Chamber and that had the President of the Republic wished to choose a prime minister from the parliamentary majority he would have had to summon Gambetta.[2]

Three days later, on 22 June, the Senate assented by 150 votes to 130 to the President's request for a dissolution. On the preceding day the Chamber had made its last act of defiance when on the advice of the Budget Committee it refused the Finance Minister Caillaux's request that it should detach the four direct taxes from the rest of the budget and vote them as a matter of urgency so that the General Councils could allocate them during their summer sessions which were due to begin on 14 August. To do this would, as Cochery for the Budget Committee pointed out, be to give the ministry the means of delaying the elections and this would increase the country's anxieties and the undoubted sufferings of France's trade and industry.[3] Thus the Republican majority

1. *Histoire de la France contemporaine*, vol. iv, p. 43.
2. For the text of Broglie's speech, see *Annales Sénat 1877*, vol. iii, pp. 123–32.
3. *Annales Chambre, 1877*, vol. iii, p. 352. Gambetta vigorously supported Cochery in this debate.

reminded the government that in the last resort it had the power of the purse. The government soon retorted by adjourning the partial elections for the renewal of the General Councils for as long as it dared, namely until 4 November. Meanwhile, on the 25th, the Chamber elected early in 1876 had met for the last time and dispersed amid cries of 'Vive la République! Vive la paix!' from the Left and Centre and of 'Vive la France!' and 'Vive le Maréchal!' from the Right. It was the only legislature of the Third Republic which lasted for less than two years. Now 'the galleries were empty . . . the ushers, so busy for ten days were motionless on their benches and the half-open doors of the boxes testified to the impending abandonment of the building'. By 4 p.m. it was virtually deserted. 'At the Paris terminus there were no spectators. The ex-Deputies . . . greeted each other a last time and then dispersed . . . surprised at finding themselves back in Paris at so unusual an hour, and forced to reflect that they no longer had to take the train for Versailles.'[1] But the *République Française*, writing their obituary, declared that the members of the defunct Chamber resembled those young men dead in the flower of their youth of whom the ancients said that they were beloved by the gods. Had not its president, Grévy, affirmed that it had succumbed like a soldier on the field of honour and that its greatest praise was that it had deserved well of the country?[2] Thus ended the second round of the great fight. The third would be much more protracted and end only with the climax of the elections themselves.

Although the Chamber had been dissolved, no mention had been made of the election dates. Gambetta had challenged the government to summon the voters before the end of July and the Republican lawyers contended that this should be done within three months of the dissolution. But Fourtou wanted to play for time and to keep the enemy in suspense. Although by the latter part of August it was anticipated that the first ballot would be held on 14 October,[3] it was not until 22 September that the *Journal Officiel* published decrees fixing the dates. They were to be 14 and 28 October, and the new Chamber was to meet on 7 November. In effect, however, campaigning had begun from the moment of dissolution, if not well before, and Gambetta and his colleagues had long been mustering and organising their forces. A number of directing committees

1. *The Times*, 26 June, p. 5.
2. Leader of 27 June. The reference to succumbing like a soldier was not in Grévy's brief closing speech as recorded in *Annales, Chambre, 1877*, Session Ordinaire, vol. iii, p. 423.
3. *R.F.*, 21 Aug., p. 1.

were now formed, a committee of Senators, to help to collect and distribute funds, a committee to give legal advice, a committee of Parisian newspaper editors to direct Press strategy, and a committee, largely of dismissed officials and young lawyers, to disseminate propaganda.[1] The expenditure on both sides was enormous; the electoral expenses of the government were later estimated at eight million francs, but, fortunately for them, the Republicans were not poor. Their needs, as Gambetta said, were 'pressing and extensive', but they were backed by many wealthy business interests, and men like Gambetta's friend Dubochet, the gas king, Emile Menier the industrialist and chocolate manufacturer (himself one of the 363), Boucicaut of the big Parisian store the Bon Marché, Cernuschi the bimetallist, and the Alsatians Koechlin and Scheurer-Kestner, subscribed liberally or helped to raise money.[2] Once again in a great speech at Lille in August Gambetta could hail the alliance of the bourgeoisie and proletariat.[3]

For Gambetta himself one of the most important committees was no doubt that concerned with the Press. To his great grief, his old friend Edmond Adam had died of anthrax on 14 June after a comparatively short illness.[4] He was only sixty. One of the last services he had rendered Gambetta was to help disentangle the affairs of Gambetta's two newspapers in the preceding year. It was thanks to him, Gambetta tactfully told his widow, that he now had 'the sinews of war'. But Juliette, despite her bereavement, could still play a part. She soon reopened her salon, which become one of the social and political centres of Republican resistance and she claimed that it was with her help that Gambetta enlisted the aid of two of the ablest journalists of the day, the veteran Emile de Girardin, now owner of *La France*, and Edmond About of the *XIXe Siècle*.[5] With them he formed a kind of triple alliance which was

1. Freycinet, *op. cit.*, p. 371; *R.F.*, 27 June, 17 July, p. 2; 5 Nov., p. 1. The Senatorial Committee had notepaper headed 'Comité Général Electoral des Gauches du Sénat, 9 Rue Louis-le-Grand' (Ass. Nat., MS 1669). The last of the committees listed above was presumably the Comité de Propagande referred to in Ass. Nat., MS 1669.

2. *Lettres*, no. 321, 13 July; E. Spuller, *Figures disparues* (1891), vol. ii, pp. 251–2; G. Leti, *Henri Cernuschi* (1936), p. 240. The *R.F.* (6 Aug.) reported that Dubochet had sent to the Republican propaganda committee 200,000 fr., 'le produit de diverses souscriptions', and Menier a subscription of 100,000 fr.

3. *Discours*, vol. vii, p. 225.

4. For an obituary, see *R.F.*, 16 June.

5. Mme Adam, *Apres l'abandon de la revanche* (1910), pp. 4 and 13. Her account of Adam's financial assistance is, however, largely inaccurate (see Marcos, *Juliette Adam*, pp. 78 and 396, n. 153). According to F. Giles, *A Prince of Journalists: ... Henri Stefan Opper de Blowitz* (1962), p. 123, n. 1, Girardin was often called 'le roi des journalistes', Blowitz, 'le prince des journalistes'.

strengthened by the support of such other notable journalists as Hébrard of the *Temps*, Bapst of the *Journal des Débats* and Vacquerie of the *Rappel*. But Gambetta was the leader and the offices of the *République Française* became the main headquarters of the Republican Press campaign. 'You are the captain of the ship,' said Girardin, 'command and we will obey.'[1] Such was the enthusiasm of the captain and his original crew that for the first time since its foundation the *République Française* kept its printing presses (*ateliers*) going on 14 July, the great national holiday. But in doing so it promised that after the Republican victory in the battle now being waged there would be a double celebration in 1878![2]

Thus organised at the centre, the Republicans mobilised a veritable army of agents to work in the provinces where the real battlefield lay.[3] There was a spate of polemical literature and an intense propaganda drive which naturally met with increasing obstacles owing to government obstruction. The *République Française*, for example, announced towards the end of June that, because of the difficulties it was encountering it would have to pay its agents more and raise its price to twenty centimes as from 1 July. At the same time, for propaganda purposes, it started fortnightly and monthly subscriptions; previously the shortest subscription period had been three months. A month later it printed a further announcement: 'The ban on the sale of Republican papers is becoming general. Street selling is forbidden and newly established bookshops are threatened and prosecuted. Republicans must combine and redouble their zeal to defeat these manoeuvres. Men with initiative should form groups in every commune to take the banned papers and then, after reading them, pass them round.'[4] New propaganda subscription rates were also announced and readers were reminded of the official form of declaration necessary for opening a bookshop. Driven from the bookstalls, tobacconists and kiosks, Republican papers took refuge in bookshops and there the *République Française* could still be easily obtained.[5] As government repression intensified many Republican papers were prosecuted. The *République Française* itself was twice a victim, first being charged with the

---

1. Freycinet, *op. cit.*, p. 371. According to an English journalist, the captain was usually to be found at the offices of the *République Française* about midnight, directing operations 'in a worn-out brown worsted jacket with long sleeves and smoking a cigar' (Hanlon, *op. cit.*, p. 107).

2. *R.F.*, 15 July.

3. 'Le gouvernement n'avait pas la prétention d'intimider une ville comme Paris. ... A quoi bon d'ailleurs disputer à la *démagogie* "l'inconvenable capitale"? Elle n'entrait que pour 20 voix dans les comptes électoraux' (H. Gautier, *op. cit.*, p.v).

4. 23 July ff.

5. See *The Times*, 25 Aug., p. 8 (article by 'an Englishman in the French provinces', said by the *World* to be Frederick Harrison).

alleged publication of false news[1] and on the second occasion with publishing Gambetta's speech at Lille on 15 August which was alleged to defame the Marshal. There were in all 421 prosecutions for Press offences, 849 of newsvendors, 216 of bookshops and 170 for seditious cries.[2] Nevertheless the sales of the *Petite République* soared to 120,000 copies.[3] Republican pamphleteers were undeterred and although the official pressure was far heavier in the provinces than in Paris, where the Press remained relatively free, the Republican propaganda organisation was both thorough and effective. In August Jules Ferry, for example, wrote with satisfaction that in his constituency in the Vosges there were some 2,000 agents who received the *Mémorial*, the *Gazette*, the *XIXe Siècle* or the *Temps*. They had been carefully chosen in each village and constituted excellent cadres.[4] Ever since 21 June, moreover, the Propaganda Committee had been busy sending out copies of the *Petite République* and the *Bien Public*, to which it soon added the *République Française* and Girardin's *France*. In September it widened its scope still further and added the *Rappel*, the satirical paper the *Lanterne de Boquillon*, and the *Journal des Débats* to its list.[5] As *The Times* later reported: 'Political pamphlets, catechisms, almanacks, and songs have been left at the homes of the peasants by an army of enthusiastic volunteers. Pedlars have distributed them by stealth, and the humblest railway servants have helped to give them a safe and often a free passage. Commercial travellers have been enthusiastic preachers of Republican doctrines.' Never had 'volunteer agencies been so skilfully organised or worked with so passionate a zeal'.[6]

Meanwhile a meeting of Republican deputies on 3 July had decided to create a single electoral committee. It met weekly at no. 9 rue Louis-le-Grand and its secretary was their Benjamin, Marcellin Pellet. The 363 were urged to form committees in each cantonal capital and there was to be no inter-Republican rivalry, for from the very day of the dissolution of parliament it had been decided that the 363 were to be regarded as a bloc.[7] Thus even Napoleon III's turbulent cousin, Prince Napoleon,

1. See *R.F.*, 29 June.
2. Pisani-Ferry, *op. cit.*, p. 232. The commission of enquiry into the Seize Mai later estimated the total number of Press prosecutions between 16 May and 13 Dec. at 2,500 (I. Collins, *The Government and the Newspaper Press in France 1814–1881* (1959), p. 178.
3. A. Tournier, *Gambetta, Souvenirs Anecdotiques*, p. 235.
4. *Lettres de Jules Ferry 1846–1893* (1914), 28 Aug., p. 246. He made no mention of the *République Française*.
5. Ass. Nat., MS 1669.
6. Leader of 15 Oct. One of those seized by the authorities was 'La République c'est la paix, la Monarchie c'est la guerre' by 'un Alsacien' (*R.F.*, 25 Sept.).
7. Marcère, *op. cit.*, vol. ii, pp. 18–27.

would be unopposed by the Left in spite of the doubts many people felt about his republicanism. The simple and telling slogan was 'Send back the 363'—the 363 whose manifesto was printed in many forms and on many materials including silk handkerchiefs. But nervous officialdom was such that it intervened to prevent the *République Française* from sending to its subscribers even a single sheet bearing the portraits of all the 363.[1] The government had good reason to be nervous, as events would show.

1. A copy of this sheet and an example of one of the silk handkerchiefs are preserved in Ass. Nat., MS 1550.

25

The death of Thiers and Republican victory at the polls May–October 1877

In the summer of 1877 Gambetta and his colleagues were not planning merely for an election victory. From the outset they had begun to think about its consequences. In letters as early as 21 and 30 May Gambetta was envisaging the Marshal's resignation and the holding of a Congress of the two Chambers, in accordance with the constitutional law of 16 July 1875, in order to elect a successor.[1] On the same day Taine was gloomily prophesying that in four months' time Gambetta would be President: 'Instead of a gradual descent into democracy we shall probably rush into it with a crash.'[2] But, whatever his private and ultimate ambitions, it is probable that Gambetta had no great desire to be elevated— or relegated—to the Elysée at the early age of thirty-nine. For the moment all his energies were concentrated on the new struggle to preserve the Republic itself. He knew that his adversaries believed their master-stroke was to represent the struggle as one between him and the Marshal and, in one of these letters of May, he wrote that he was determined at the right moment to upset their calculations by putting forward Grévy as candidate for the Presidency.[3] Ten days later, however, he had different views. He told the Paris student deputation that the Republican party had no lack of eminent men who would make perfectly constitutional Presidents of the Republic: 'There is one above all who has already been tested, who has already occupied the presidency and who left it with simplicity, disinterestedness and dignity.'[4] Thiers was, of course, the man. Thiers had recently celebrated his eightieth birthday, but age has seldom been an obstacle to power in France and Thiers's prestige was great. Moreover, he was still full of vigour and excited by the prospect of revenge

1. *Lettres*, nos. 312 and 313.
2. *Life and Letters*, part iii, p. 176.
3. *Lettres*, no. 312.
4. Speech of 31 May, *Discours*, vol. vii, p. 54.

on the men who had overthrown him. In Reinach's words, he thought himself

> back in 1830, in the days of the great struggle of the 221 against Polignac. The offices of the *République Française*, like those of the *National* earlier, became the headquarters of the Republican and liberal army. The oldest combatants came down into the arena with a new ardour. M. Crémieux and M. Senard ... M. Henri Martin ... M. de Montalivet ... M. de Girardin ... M. Thiers was the most ardent and impatient of them all. We have heard him accuse Gambetta of being too *moderate*.[1]

Thiers thus became the ace in the Republican pack and the value of that ace was dramatically enhanced by an unforeseen incident which occurred in the tumultous debate on 16 June. When Fourtou was making his speech he at one point referred to the National Assembly as having liberated the territory. Immediately someone interrupted and, pointing to Thiers, cried 'There is the liberator of the territory!' Thereupon the whole Left and Centre had risen to their feet and applauded the little old man for several minutes. Thiers sat motionless with bowed head, but he was greatly moved. It was a stirring moment which unforgettably brought Thiers back into the limelight. But popular imagery soon represented Gambetta as the leader in the scene and thus another legend was born. Henceforward the names of Thiers and Gambetta were constantly coupled, and in Republican propaganda their portraits appeared together, on the silk handkerchiefs and elsewhere, along with the manifesto of the 363. At long last, the greatest of the Conservative Republicans and the greatest of the Radicals, now himself much more Conservative, had joined hands. Gambetta, so much the younger man, still inevitably played the leading part in the campaign, but he could defer to Thiers with perfect good grace and be all the more reassuring because of the alliance.[2] The combination seemed unbeatable.

1. *Ibid.*, p. 51.
2. Already on 10 June the moderate Republican Clamageran (*Correspondance, 1849–1902*, p. 407) had noted as one of several encouraging symptoms 'l'effacement de Gambetta devant le vieux Thiers'. Later, in a conversation after Thiers's funeral Gambetta recalled 'un joli mot' of Thiers when he and Gambetta were reconciled: 'Nous ne sommes pas toujours aussi bien entendus que maintenant; je vous ai même appelé fou furieux. Il faut m'excuser, car alors vous étiez si jeune et j'étais si vieux !' (Lalance, *Mes Souvenirs*, p. 69). Gambetta's effigy also, however, appeared alone. The police reported that the sale of matchboxes with Gambetta's likeness had been announced at the end of June and that small photographs of him were on sale for thirty centimes all over Lyons at the beginning of October (reports of 25 June and 6 Oct., A.P.P., BA/919 and A/921). According to *The Times* (2 Oct.), a Lyons house was fined 100 fr for issuing handkerchiefs bearing the portraits of Thiers and Gambetta.

Pitted against it was an uneasy coalition. A member of the Right was said to have boasted to Girardin that they would march against the Republic 'some with the cock, some with the eagle and the third with the lilies'. 'You will have cock against cock,' replied Girardin, 'both will peck the lilies and the eagle can only hover over the charnel house of Sedan.'[1] They had no adequate cause except the saving of society (most of which saw no need to be saved), no popular leaders comparable to those of the Republicans, and they were beset by mutual jealousies and quarrels over tactics which discredited them when they became public.[2] They were defending Catholicism, but dared not mobilise the clergy because of the unpopularity of clericalism. Having no prince on whom they could agree they had to fall back upon the Marshal. So when official candidatures were restored the government's men were put forward as 'candidates of the government of the Marshal'. The Marshal was their ace, the ace they sought to play not against Thiers but Gambetta, and they played him for all they were worth. The *Moniteur*, for example, printed 20,000 copies of his portrait and 300,000 copies of pamphlets lauding his policies as well as tens of thousands of copies of a poster which displayed a terrible looking Gambetta and a reassuring Marshal.[3] An official organ of the Ministry of the Interior, the *Bulletin des Communes* (soon known to Republicans as *Le Menteur des Communes*) had even declared that the country had to choose between the Marshal 'shedding his blood for France and the incompetent dictator who had enriched himself and whose name is bound up with our misfortunes'.[4] The Marshal was defending the country against Gambetta and all the dangerous Radicalism his name inspired, and in July the defender, having declared his intention of fulfilling his mission to the end, was induced to tour the south-west and centre as part of the great preelection campaign. Although the tour was

1. Mme Adam, *Après l'abandon* . . ., p. 8.
2. For vivid illustrations of some of their internecine rivalries, see A. Daniel, *L'Année politique 1877*, pp. 261ff. Their difficulties were well described by one of Fourtou's harassed prefects, the Vicomte de la Morandière on 8 Sept. He wrote of the situation in his department of Ille-et-Vilaine as follows: 'Division, fractionnement infini des groupes conservateurs, aveuglement absolu de l'extrême droite, absence de notabilités et d'influences locales . . . hostilité d'un grand nombre de municipalités; trahison ou défaillances de presque tous les employés de l'administration et des finances — voilà avec quelles armes faussées avec quelles poudres mouillées il nous faut combattre' (M. A. E., Fond Chaudordy, vol. iv, Lettres Particulières); cf. de Meaux, *Souvenirs politiques*, pp. 328–34, for a good account of the Conservatives' difficulties by a member of the government.
3. Reclus, *Le Seize Mai*, p. 76.
4. The *R.F.*, 10 July, had been particularly incensed by this 'libellous' article. Jules Ferry complained that he was similarly accused by the *Vosgien* of having enriched himself (*Lettres de Jules Ferry*, p. 236).

far from being the success the government hoped for—the Marshal was no orator and lacked the common touch, except among his troops—it was time for someone to reply. 'The battle was in danger of being lost sight of [*se perdre*] in the skirmishes of sharpshooters. It was the dog-days. The suspense was enervating. The overladen atmosphere could only be relieved by a storm.'[1] The storm came with Gambetta's speech at Lille on 15 August.

Gambetta's journey to Lille was improvised at short notice and kept dark until the last moment to prevent the risk of official interference. On 11 August he wrote to his friend Dr Testelin, now a Senator, expressing his wish to 'expound the country's electoral situation' on the 15th. If he thought he could assemble an audience of sixty to eighty people Testelin was to telegraph as follows: 'Send me the collection of Senate speeches on army administration.'[2] All went well. If the 'cabinet noir' intercepted the telegram it suspected nothing. Gambetta arrived at Lille late on the 14th and on the following evening, at a private banquet for 163 people at the Hôtel de l'Europe, he delivered his assault.

This celebrated speech breathed complete confidence in Republican unity and ultimate victory. It was a powerful résumé of most of the Republican arguments. As in 1873 and two months earlier at the Hoche banquet, he asserted that it was the Republicans who were the true Conservatives and the Right the party of disorder. And to the government's spectre of Radicalism he opposed the much more horrifying spectres of clericalism, Bonapartism and war. It was the Bonapartists who had the whip hand in the cabinet of 16 May and who paid the papers which pressed for the use of force, and Bonapartism was 'the party which succumbed at Sedan . . . the party whose name is Brumaire and December . . . the party the foreigner would like to see back because . . . it is the party of invasion!' But it was the final sentence and its consequences which made the great sensation: 'When France has spoken with her sovereign voice, believe me, Gentlemen, it will be necessary to submit or resign.'[3] Gambetta had said not a word of the Marshal in any part of the speech, but everyone knew to whom he was referring.[4]

1. Hanotaux, *Histoire de la France contemporaine*, vol. iv, p. 146.
2. *Lettres*, no. 325 *bis*.
3. For the text, see *Discours*, vol. vii, pp. 209–30. Freycinet (*Souvenirs 1848–1878*, p. 372, n. 1) claimed the parentage of the famous phrase. He wrote that, at a dinner sometime earlier, he had said that if the Republicans won the elections 'il faudra bien que le Maréchal se soumette ou se démette' — 'Je retiens le mot, dit en riant M. Gambetta, je lui ferai un sort'. Joseph Reinach, for his part, thought he might have inspired it, for a similar phrase occurred in his brochure *La République ou le Gâchis* (1877). It is interesting, however, to note that the R.F. as early as 22 Jan. 1875 had written that the Marshal must either place himself at the disposition of a Republican

The battle was indeed no longer confined to the skirmishers. The leaders reemerged in the forefront and both sides were roused to still more frantic exertions. Thiers wrote to congratulate Gambetta on a speech which he said was 'both eloquent, extremely patriotic, and firm as circumstances demanded'.[1] Tension mounted anew and people on opposing sides were no longer on speaking terms.[2] Incensed and embarrassed by the speech at Lille, the government decided to prosecute both the speaker and the *République Française*, which had printed the speech, for insulting the President of the Republic. The decision created a sensation both at home and abroad. To Flaubert it was the madness (*le délire*) of stupidity.[3] To *The Times* it seemed that Gambetta's words 'se soumettre ou se démettre' had almost 'passed into a proverb'.[4] It was astonished by the proposed prosecution: 'Fancy Mr Bright—the Mr Bright of a dozen or score of years ago—summoned before a Magistrate at Bow St. on a charge of having assisted in the publication . . . of a report of a speech . . . calculated to excite mutual hatred among Englishmen!' The idea was ludicrous and the prosecution 'a self-inflicted sentence of disqualification on the score of political incapacity'.[5]

Quos Deus vult perdere prius dementat. Perhaps the government's main object was again to focus on Gambetta as the dire alternative to the Marshal and to prevent him from being given office even if the cabinet were defeated.[6] But, whatever their motives, Broglie and his colleagues could hardly have devised a better way of winning sympathy for their great adversary. It was rumoured that they intended to arrest him or at

1. This letter is reproduced in facsimile, facing p. 10 of Ernest Hecht's *Thiers et Gambetta* (1905), extrait des *Publications de la Société Gambetta*.

2. Ferry, *op. cit.*, p. 245. Letter of 21 Aug. to Mme Jules Ferry: 'Ici [i.e. in Epinal] les divisions s'accentuent; on ne se parle plus, à peine si on se salue.'

3. *Correspondance*, vol. viii, p. 76.

4. 27 Aug.

5. 31 and 27 Aug. Later, after the elections, it declared that 'Of all the evil incidents of the late campaign' Gambetta's prosecution 'was the worst' (leader, 30 Oct.).

6. *The Times*, 29 Aug., reported an admirer of Broglie as saying: 'The Marshal . . . cannot offer a portfolio to a person judicially convicted of insulting him.' Cf. G. W. Smalley, *London Letters and some others* (1890), vol. i, p. 39.

---

majority or resign. In a letter of 30 May 1877 (*Lettres*, no. 313) Gambetta had used the words 'céder ou partir': and the *Moniteur du Puy-de-Dôme*, had, as Gautier pointed out (*op. cit.*, p. 106, n. 1) posed the dilemma several times since 19 May 1877 'sans donner lieu à des poursuites. . . . C'est que M. Gambetta consacrait, il faut bien le dire, par l'immense autorité de sa parole, cette formule *se soumettre ou se démettre*. En prenant plus d'éclat, elle devenait subitement une offense.'

4. Daniel Halévy, so often inaccurate in his quotations, wrote 'Gambetta, le 15 [édat] août, s'écria: "Il faudra que *le Président* se soumette ou se démette" ' (*La République des ducs*, p. 297), my italics.

least to secure a conviction which would disqualify him from sitting in the next parliament. But his immediate arrest would have made him a martyr and been an act too arbitrary even for Fourtou and most of his colleagues.[1] Gambetta had not been a lawyer for nothing and he was determined to make the most of the opportunities for delay afforded by the complicated procedure of the Correctional courts. 'I am in no danger,' he reassured the Marquise. 'In my life I have been too much involved with legal procedure not to get the better of all these conscripts.'[2] Indeed, he was soon enjoying his new position. He appeared before the examining magistrate on 31 August and took full responsibility for his speech and its publication, but denied the charge that he had committed a misdemeanour and insulted the head of state. Nevertheless, he and Murat, the manager (*gérant*) of the *République Française*, were summoned before the 10th Correctional Tribunal of the Seine at the Palais de Justice, on 11 September. They asked for an adjournment, since their counsel had been away and had insufficient time to prepare the case. It was refused and they were each condemned to three months' imprisonment and the payment of a 2,000 francs fine, the equivalent of £80 in contemporary English money. The condemnation was, declared Gambetta, 'the last act of a government at bay'.[3] He and Murat immediately objected to the sentence on a point of law and, when it was confirmed on 22 September, appealed.[4] 'Dame Justice' had been capricious, but Gambetta would, he said, outwit her servants 'and cock a snook at the Janissaries of Monsieur le Duc'. 'However keen my judges are to see me locked up,' he told Princess Troubetzkoï, 'I shall snap my fingers at them for a long time still, and it may be that *those* who have so clumsily prosecuted me are destined to go and occupy the comfortable lodgings they have doubtless prepared for me in Sainte-Pélagie.'[5] And snap his fingers he did. The appeal had yet to be heard when the elections took place and in December a new cabinet dropped the case. Gambetta and his lawyers had successfully played for time and later, in his election address, he did not scruple to repeat his challenge—'submit

---

1. De Meaux (*op. cit.*, p. 360) would have liked to arrest Gambetta forthwith, but, he admitted: 'La détention préalable n'était pas usitée en matière de presse.'

2. *Lettres*, no. 336, 13 Sept.

3. *The Times*, 3 Sept., p. 9.

4. At this second hearing Gambetta spoke briefly with a 'grace, simplicity and subtle irony' which *The Times* correspondent found it difficult to describe (*The Times*, 24 Sept.).

5. Letter of 10 Sept. to Léonie Léon (L.G.) and *Lettres*, no. 340, 28 Sept. For accounts of the proceedings against Gambetta, see *Discours*, vol. vii, pp. 233–54, *R.F.* 13 Sept. ff. and *The Times*, 13 Sept. ff. Sainte-Pélagie was a famous Paris prison. On 12 Sept. Gambetta humourously wrote to Victor Hugo: 'prévenu, condamné, et même détenu, je viendrai toujours à vos invitations' (*Lettres*, no. 335).

or resign!'—and incur a second condemnation. Many Frenchmen enjoyed the game and a bad verse was composed:

> Par un arrêt comminatoire
> Gambetta fut exécuté
> On se souviendra de l'histoire
> Elle est bien bonne en vérité.[1]

Meanwhile his first condemnation had so moved some Midland English Liberals that they sent him through the editor of the *Birmingham Daily Post*, a cheque for 2,000 francs to pay his fine.[2]

Soon after his collapse at the end of his great speech on 16 June Gambetta had thought it wise to see a doctor. He had been told that there was nothing much wrong with him; the treatment prescribed was 'a purgative—milk and water—chloroform on the chest, a light diet and, once well again, a trip to Holland'.[3] But despite the doctor's advice and despite a persistent cold at the end of July, there was to be no foreign holiday in this hard and litigious campaigning summer. He had all too little time even for his poor mother. She had decided to make a round of visits. Deprived of the news she used to have of him from La Tata and feeling neglected, at the end of July she suddenly took it into her head to come and see him in Paris. The moment was ill chosen. When he heard of her impending visit he wrote at once to say that, had she given him any warning, he would have told her he could not receive her, first of all because at this moment he was 'too, much too, occupied by electoral operations' and secondly because he had no bed to give her. 'In the whole building I have only *one bedroom* and a study apart from François's room in the attic.'[4] But it was too late; the old lady arrived two days later and Gambetta wrote in haste to appeal to Juliette Adam to tell her gently not to stay too long.[5] She remained for the best part of three weeks and, when she left, Gambetta wrote cheerfully to his father that he believed she had passed them 'in the most agreeable way in the world. Unfortunately I could not give her much time because of the frightful task [*besogne*] which overwhelms me more and more.'[6] But there were younger women for

---

1. Halévy, *La République des ducs*, p. 298. In October there was a rumour that Gambetta had been arrested (Millaud, *Journal d'un parlementaire*, vol. ii, p. 42).

2. Ass. Nat., MS 1669.

3. Letter of 28 June (L.G.).

4. *Lettres*, no. 324, 27 July. François Roblin was Gambetta's manservant.

5. *Ibid.*, no. 325.

6. *Ibid.*, no. 326. Yet perhaps he introduced her successfully to Léonie Léon, for on 19 Aug. he wrote to Léonie: 'Tu as dû sentir comme moi que depuis qu'une troisième tête adorée s'est glissée entre nous il y a plus de certitude... dans nos communions' (L.G.).

whom he found time in this tense summer. He slipped away to Léonie and escaped with her to the country, to the cottage at Ville d'Array where she comforted him and embroidered slippers for him.[1] He had time, too, to talk politics with Juliette Adam and Princess Troubetzkoï and time to visit his Marquise and his latest conquest, the beautiful Comtesse de Beaumont, who was a sister-in-law of the Marshal himself. But women, whom he adored, could be devils as well as angels, and ghosts from the past could return to haunt and threaten. Marie Meersmans had in fact reappeared. She had various compromising papers dating from her association with Gambetta and, worst of all, so Juliette Adam claimed, a photograph on which, in a mad amorous moment, he had written 'A ma petite Reine que j'aime plus que la France!' She was threatening to sell them to Rouher! Many of Gambetta's friends and associates had vainly tried to induce her to give them up. In despair Girardin appealed to Juliette. The two women had an interview, dramatically described in Juliette's *Après l'abandon de la revanche*,[2] and Juliette succeeded in buying them back for 6,000 francs. The Bonapartists lost their chance of making a sensational coup on the eve of the elections and Gambetta's reputation was saved.

Meanwhile, before the elections took place a real and greater blow had befallen him. On 7 July Gambetta had received a gold watch from a deputation of Alsatian admirers from Bienne in Switzerland. In his speech of thanks he had told them that Thiers's health had never been better. So it seemed to the general public. Indeed on 1 September a satirical paper published a cartoon showing the old man 'giving a helping hand to

1. *Lettres*, no. 333. Gambetta was delighted when the slippers were admired by Thiers on 19 Aug.: 'Mignonne, sois fière, tes pantoufles ont brillé du plus vif éclat aujourd'hui. J'ai reçu la visite du vieux de la montagne St Georges . . . et il n'a pas pu résister au plaisir de . . . dire en riant "on vous aime de la tête aux pieds" ' (letter of 19 Aug., L.G.).

2. pp. 55–65. As so often, Mme Adam omits the date and once again we are left guessing how much of her story is true. Marcos, very sceptical of his 'heroine's' veracity, writes of 'le récit probablement imaginaire, de cette photographie dédicacée par le tribun à une ancienne maîtresse' (*Juliette Adam*, p. 83); but later (*ibid.*, p. 400, n. 196) he comments: 'Nous ne pouvons démentir Juliette Adam à ce sujet, faute de documents. Mais n'est-il pas piquant de constater que les lettres rachetées à Marie Meersmans et brulées totalement par Gambetta aient pu reparaître et être publiées par Halévy et Pillias?' Two police reports, however, one of 28 Dec. 1877 and the other of 16 Jan. 1878, refer to the purchase of compromising letters from a former mistress whom the second report names as 'La dame de Moölle'. Both mention Mme Adam as the purchaser or as contributing to the purchase, the purchase money being stated to be 50,000 fr. Moreover, the second report added that as the vendor had kept 'une centaine des plus drôles, elle n'a pas déprecié sa propriété' (A.P.P., BA/921). An earlier report of 15 Dec. 1875 had referred to the breach between Gambetta and Marie Drouel [*sic*] (A.P.P., BA/918).

poor old Father Time, who was portrayed in the last stages of decrepitude, no longer able even to carry his scythe . . . of which his companion had kindly relieved him'.[1] Two days later Thiers was taken ill at Saint-Germain-en-Laye and died within a few hours. Gambetta was to have seen him by appointment in Paris that very afternoon. With his death an era of French history had come abruptly to an end.

The government at once offered the state funeral which in normal times would have been a matter of course, but Madame Thiers made conditions that were unacceptable to the authorities. Yet there was a great funeral all the same, in spite of wind and rain, and the Republican leaders did all they could to make it a tremendous Republican manifestation. Gambetta, who walked bareheaded in the front row of the 363 former Republican deputies,[2] was deeply moved and wrote lyrically to Léonie Léon that it had been the most magnificent ceremony of the century. 'Caesar returning from Gaul met with nothing like it in Rome and Bonaparte had no such civic splendours after Austerlitz.' But it was the political aspect which had impressed him still more, for, after all, 'What could be more surprising and at the same time more reassuring politically than this passionate crowd of the people of Paris who six years ago were bombarded, shot down and bled white by M. Thiers and now . . . have the courage to pardon the victor and number him among the gods?' It was this that had made the ceremony a dazzling success: he had witnessed

> a million men inspired by the same passion for justice and the Republic . . . all united round the same flag and . . . by their discipline and good conduct presenting the spectacle of a people that scorns brutal provocations and . . . is ready for the most sublime sacrifices in defence of its ideas and its representatives . . . above the thousands of bared heads . . . one could not but see hovering the august image of Republican France.

Paris, he wrote,

> has just ensured the justice of our cause, completed our election task, and shown those who dream of a *coup d'état* their impotence and their imminent

---

1. Vizetelly, *Republican France*, p. 215.
2. Halévy, *op. cit.*, p. 314. Hanotaux (*op. cit.*, vol. iv, p. 172) wrote that no special place was reserved for Gambetta at the funeral and the heading in the margin of his History at this point read 'M. Gambetta est oublié'. But there does not appear to be any evidence for this and it was natural that the speeches at the funeral should be made by older men who had had a longer association with Thiers. On the other hand Galli (*Gambetta et l'Alsace-Lorraine*, p. 123), equally without quoting evidence in support of his assertion, described Gambetta as 'le véritable metteur en scène, l'ordonnateur autorisé' of the funeral ceremony.

dismissal. Nothing can express the emotion I felt during this long journey across Paris.[1]

Yet, as Hanotaux pointed out, the first of these letters, ardent, enthusiastic, ended on a different note: after the cry of triumph 'a faint note of complaint, a *nescio quid amare*': 'I am loaded with fortune's favours: yesterday the joy of the heart, today the reward of the people. But *what shelters me from disappointment* is to tell myself that our love is imperishable and inviolable, *whatever the vicissitudes of popular* favour.' 'Why', asked the historian who had been one of Gambetta's disciples, 'why this introspection on this day of triumph, these thoughts of refuge and withdrawal, in the midst of victory? What arrow (*pointe*) has grazed the victor and what drop of blood trickles from the first wound?'[2]

Thiers's funeral might seem to an optimist like Gambetta to be a glowing presage of Republican victory in the elections. But not everyone was so sanguine. To one contemporary Frenchman, as he recounted the events of the year 1877, the death of Thiers was

an incalculable loss for the French liberal party.... In spite of his great age, he was still capable of playing a part in public affairs and his eventual candidature for the Presidency of the Republic, should the office fall vacant, was in the minds of all. His sudden disappearance on the eve of the electoral battle was an event whose impact it was impossible to foresee. All parties realised this and the tributes paid in the Republican Press were coloured with a personal sadness and discouragement.[3]

On the other hand, many of the Right rejoiced in the disappearance of one whom they called the 'sinister old man'. But, if the loss to the 'liberals' was incalculable, there was but one man in France, according to another Republican observer, to whom it might prove 'a real disaster' and this the man whom it thrust 'into a position of extraordinary difficulty'.[4] That man was Gambetta and this perhaps accounted for the phrase in that letter to Léonie Léon of which Hanotaux made so much. The difficulty was not that the incorrigible Paul de Cassagnac had warned

1. *Lettres*, nos. 333 and 334. For other vivid accounts of the funeral, see *R.F.* and *The Times*, both of 10 Sept. and J. Ferry's letter to his wife of 8 Sept. (Ferry, *op. cit.*, pp. 247–9); also the tribute of the Italian statesman Crispi: 'the calmness of the people was really admirable. There were a few shouts of Vive la République! Honneur à Thiers! and Vive Gambetta! but that was all, and the programme was carried out in perfect order' (*The Memoirs of Francesco Crispi*, vol. ii, p. 21).

2. Hanotaux, *op. cit.*, vol. iv, p. 173.

3. Daniel, *L'Année politique 1877*, p. 290.

4. *The Times*, 12 Sept., p. 6.

him that his turn would come: 'Apoplexy is waiting for him on the threshold of the restaurant.'[1] It was that the aged partner who gave him respectability and might have given him office was gone. Thiers, as Saint-Valry remarked, had provided Gambetta with 'a screen, a shelter beneath which he could complete the process of making for himself a relatively conservative wrapping',[2] With the disappearance of the screen Gambetta was exposed, while his prospects of ministerial office became more remote.

Once back at the Elysée, Thiers, according to Juliette Adam, had intended to call upon Gambetta to form a cabinet and take charge of foreign affairs.[3] He would, he had said, 'present him to Europe', and it was no doubt with this in mind that he had invited the German Ambassador, whom he saw frequently, to meet Gambetta early in July.[4] The governmental programme would have included *scrutin de liste*, a full amnesty, freedom of the Press and free compulsory education.[5] This would have been a logical outcome of the Thiers–Gambetta partnership, but it was not the sort of programme formerly associated with the Conservative Republic of M. Thiers, and, to judge by a letter of 20 August to Ranc, Gambetta himself did not expect it to be carried out—at least not all at once. He wrote of organising a strong ministry, including members of all four groups, and of a ruthless and immediate purge of the administrative personnel. But then, he added, it would be necessary to wait and be patient concerning laws and reforms, 'for M. Thiers is always M. Thiers'. However, 'one would grant a slight amnesty whilst preparing the way

1. In *Le Pays*, quoted by H. Gautier, *op. cit.*, p. 199.

2. *Les Souvenirs et réflexions politiques*, p. 239. Thiers's old friend Mignet told Ludovic Halévy in 1883 that he believed that Thiers 's'il avait vécu, aurait contenu, modéré Gambetta, l'aurait eu docile, souple, obéissant, comme ministre ou comme chef de sa majorité', But Halévy thought Mignet wrong and commented: 'Gambetta bien vite se serait cabré, révolté. Il n'aurait jamais su se résigner à être second' (*Trois dîners avec Gambetta*, p. 99).

3. Mme Adam, *Après l'abandon*, pp. 39–40: she said that the composition of the cabinet had already been settled: 'Campenon à la guerre, Ferry à l'intérieur, Léon Say aux finances, Giraud, de l'Institut, à la justice, Pothuau à la marine, Krantz aux travaux publics etc.'. Cf. Reinach, *Récits et portraits contemporains*, p. 30.

4. Reinach, *La Vie politique de Gambetta*, p. 64. *Memoirs of Prince Hohenlohe-Schillingsfuerst*, vol. ii, p. 195. Hohenlohe said that, after talk on current affairs, 'Thiers told his old stories about Metternich, Talleyrand and Louis Philippe. Gambetta and I listened respectfully. I have never seen the present and the past so incarnated as in these men.' He concluded by noting: 'Gambetta makes a good impression. He is courteous and friendly, and, at the same time, you can see in him the confident, vigorous statesman.' Gambetta himself had written to Léonie Léon on 30 June: 'Tout va bien, surtout quand je pense que je te verrai mardi avant cette importante entrevue' (L.G.).

5. *Après l'abandon*, pp. 39–40.

for the big one' and Ranc would be included in it.[1] It would have remained to be seen how far the Republican majority would have tried to force the pace. Perhaps de Meaux was right in commenting that by a timely death the historian of Napoleon was saved from his own 'Hundred Days'.[2]

But Thiers, had he lived, could not have returned to the Elysée until the Marshal had resigned. Now that he had died, like Moses in sight of the Promised Land, it was necessary for the Republicans to give him a successor, one who could both take up his mantle as the party's elder statesman and, perhaps quite soon, step into the Marshal's shoes. Earlier, when Thiers was President of the Republic, Gambetta had been spoken of as 'the Dauphin' and he himself had jokingly referred to the old man as an uncle he might succeed.[3] In January 1877 the old man himself had told Hohenlohe that Gambetta was preparing to be President[4] and at the time of his death many still thought of him as 'the heir'; the improbable rumour even went round that he was about to marry a kinswoman of Thiers, Mlle Dosne.[5] But for Gambetta to be the acknowledged heir at this moment would have been to play directly into the hands of the government which so strenuously sought to represent the great electoral battle as a fight between him and MacMahon. Moreover, however great Gambetta's standing in the country, it was less assured among the parliamentarians. Despite his moderation, the moderates of the Left feared his ambition and still suspected that he was a Radical at heart. On 5 September, even before Thiers was in his grave, the Senators of the Left had in a manifesto to the country intimated their wish for a man who would continue the tradition of Thiers, and, like him, devote himself to the founding of a Liberal and Conservative Republic. Before long they and their friends had secured the designation of Jules Grévy to take Thiers's place as a candidate for election in the 9th *arrondissement*. With such backing Grévy gradually emerged as the man most likely to be their choice to succeed MacMahon.

How did Gambetta react? Ludovic Halévy noted at the time that he was furious. But Ludovic's son, Daniel, commented that if this were so it did not last, for Gambetta 'was good-hearted and quick to calm down'.[6] In fact Grévy's candidature was no new idea. As long before as December 1871 the *République Française* had written that, were there to be a question

1. *Lettres*, no. 327. Optimistically he said he hoped to see Ranc back in Paris before Christmas.
2. *Op. cit.*, p. 390.
3. See above, p. 37.
4. Hohenlohe to Bismarck, 27 Jan. (*G.P.*, vol. i, no. 201).
5. D. Halévy, *La République des ducs*, p. 315.
6. *Ibid.*

of replacing Thiers, acclimatising France to a Republic which was at one and the same time peaceful, modest, and dignified, and having at its head a magistrate who was serious and calm with a simple and grave authority, then Grévy might well be President.[1] And, as has been seen, in a recent letter of 21 May 1877, Gambetta had talked of himself putting Grévy forward 'at the right moment'. This would give him the advantage both of appearing disinterested and 'steering opinion towards an impersonal solution' and also 'of ending military power and ensuring the triumph of the civilian outlook'.[2] But at the end of September, nearly a month after Thiers's death, he seems to have been less decided, for in a letter assuring Princess Troubetzkoï that the loss of Thiers would not affect the Republicans' victory at the polls, he said that there were others who might take his place: 'Turenne is no longer there, but we will coin his likeness if need be with Grévy and Pothuau.'[3] Pothuau was one of the few naval officers of high rank to be an avowed Republican and in November there was still talk of preferring him to Grévy as a candidate for the Presidency.[4] But it was Grévy who prevailed.

Jules Grévy had none of Thiers' international prestige or sparkling vivacity and his role in French history had been far less spectacular. But he was a solid, middle-class lawyer from the Franche-Comté, measured, cautious, shrewd and eminently respectable, a man who could never be accused of Radicalism, but whose Republicanism was beyond reproach. He had been Vice-President of the Constituent Assembly of the Second Republic in 1848, President of the National Assembly from 1871 to 1873 and, from March 1876 until the recent dissolution, President of the Chamber. Just seventy, he was a veteran in politics and a man who, possessing something of the *gravitas* of a Roman senator, seemed born to preside. Such a choice, it was reckoned, could not but be reassuring to moderate men, and in the interests of party unity Gambetta eventually gave him his wholehearted support. The *République Française* extolled Grévy's virtues, defending him from the attacks of the Right who derided him as an unknown nonentity, and it was Gambetta who was chairman of the Republican Committee which, when the electoral period formally began, proposed Grévy for adoption as parliamentary candidate in the 9th *arrondissement*.[5] Moreover, in his own election speech of 9 October

1. 17 Dec. 1871.
2. *Lettres*, no. 312 to Ruiz. See above, p. 418.
3. *Ibid.*, no. 340.
4. Clamageran, *Correspondance*, p. 415. Chapman (*Third Republic*, p. 179) says that on Thiers's death the group leaders invited Dufaure who refused. 'After that they could think of no one better than Jules Grévy.'
5. Grévy, like Barodet in 1873, but with more justification, had no great yearning to meet his Parisian constituents. He was already a candidate for reelection in the

in Belleville he went out of his way to disclaim presidential ambitions himself and to hail Grévy as the new Republican leader: he himself had never, he said, sought to be anything but 'the representative of opinion'.[1] Although Gambetta had no reason to love Grévy, he can hardly have realised that in him he was supporting a man who would become one of his most jealous and dangerous foes. Meanwhile, there were widespread tributes to the good grace with which he had given way to the older man.

As polling day, namely 14 October, drew near, the election campaign gathered still greater momentum. Propaganda redoubled, as is shown by returns of newspapers distributed between 21 June and 26 September by the Republican Propaganda Committee. Whereas in August the average number of weekly despatches was 21,257, in September it went up to 44,192.[2] The sums disbursed for electoral purposes likewise soared: in the six weeks from 17 August to 30 September Joseph Richard, the treasurer of the Republicans' central election fund, had distributed 229,550 francs; but in the mere twelve days from 3 to 15 October he paid out 232,000.[3] Meanwhile the leading Republican papers had been busy raising contributions to the election fund. They themselves each contributed 2,000 francs and they printed long lists of subscribers. By 2 October the receipts amounted to 376,428 francs; by the 6th they had risen to 484,669 francs 35 centimes. The lists contained many picturesque or touching entries; thus in contrast to such handsome donations as those of Thiers and Victor Hugo (5,000 francs and 1,000 francs respectively) there were the 10 francs of 'an admirer of Gambetta', the 2 francs each of 'a Darwinist' and 'a Rabelaisian', the 50 centimes of 'a little Swiss' and the 1 franc 25 centimes of '25 poor folk from the Eure'.[4]

1. *Discours*, vol. vii, p. 290.
2. Ass. Nat., MS 1669. The figures for the period 26 Sept. to 14 Oct. do not appear to have been preserved.
3. *Ibid.*
4. The first list was printed in the *R.F.* on 27 Aug.; see also lists on 2, 9 and 23 Sept., 6 and 23 Oct. Some lists in the form of printed sheets headed 'Souscription Républicaine pour les prochaines élections' with the names of the contributors and

Jura and in a letter of 5 October to Gambetta sending him his election address, he said that it was quite impossible for him to go to Paris: 'Je suis obligé de visiter tout mon arrondissement qui est très étendu: mes adversaires m'en ont fait une nécessité par les calomnies qu'ils y répandent.' Moreover, he did not see much point in a meeting in Paris: 'On sait bien qui je suis. . . . Que pourrai-je y dire autre chose que je n'ai écrit dans la lettre aux électeurs que je vous envoie. Je ne pourrai que la paraphraser.' But he thanked Gambetta for his 'concours si obligeant', and ended, with unusual warmth: 'Je vous prie de croire aux sentiments affectueux et dévoués de votre ancien Collègue et de votre Confrère Jules Grévy' (Ass. Nat., MS 1684).

At the same time Senators and would-be deputies issued fresh appeals to the electorate, each incidentally exploiting the death of Thiers as it suited them. More than ever the Right made desperate efforts to scare the voters with the spectre of Gambetta and a red terror. The *République Française* itself quoted some choice examples, such as the following from the *Moniteur du Cantal*:

> M. Thiers is dead! M. Gambetta is condemned! The Radicals no longer have a leader. Who would dare speak of M. Gambetta today? The actual chief of the Radicals has been condemned by a police court . . . and is morally dead. . . . If you want the Commune with Gambetta and his fellows, that is to say the amnesty of the criminals, the incendiaries and 'fusillards', the closure of the churches, the removal of all officials . . . the terror with drownings like those of Carrier and the guillotine . . . vote for the 363![1]

To the dismay of those who hoped that he would not further compromise himself but leave to his government the responsibility for conducting the battle the Marshal himself reentered the fray and issued a manifesto on 19 September. Its language was naturally less exaggerated, but he too, referred to the great Revolution, when he accused the accepted chiefs of Radicalism of aiming to substitute 'the despotism of a new Convention' for the necessary equilibrium of powers.[2] Moreover, he reiterated his intention to remain at his post to the end: 'As for me . . . I could not obey the behests of the demagogues. I could not become the tool of radicalism or abandon the post in which I have been placed by the Constitution.' This authoritarian note was cold comfort for the constitutionalists, whether on the Right or the Left. John Lemoinne in the formerly Orleanist *Journal des Débats* asked: 'In what year are we living? Is the French Revolution an invention of historians and novelists? Are we living under Louis XIV who said "L'Etat c'est moi!" or under Louis XV who said "Après moi le déluge!"?'[3] As for the *République Française*, it suggested

---

1. *R.F.*, 23 Sept. Carrier was a celebrated Jacobin member of the Convention who sent many people to death by drowning. This language was highly exaggerated, but events such as the circulation of an anti-Royalist manifesto by the French Federation of the International no doubt gave some grist to the Monarchist propaganda mill (D. Stafford, *From Anarchism to Reformism*, 1971, pp. 109–10).

2. An address circulated by Right-wing Senators also referred to 'the dictatorship of the Convention'.

3. 20 Sept.

---

the amounts of their contributions entered in ink are preserved in Ass. Nat., MS 1669. At the bottom of each sheet a printed note indicated that 'le montant des Souscriptions reçues par chaque Journal est versé chaque semaine, tous les samedis, au Comptoir d'Escompte, au Compte no. 2 de M. Vincent du Bochet'.

that the country was back in 1830; it reprinted Charles X's declaration of 13 June that year for comparison with the Marshal's manifesto.[1] Three days later there was a further riposte to the propaganda of the Right, 'a Parthian arrow', as *The Times* put it, from the grave. On the 24th (25th for the *République Française*) the leading Republican papers printed a characteristically vigorous and lengthy election address which Thiers had drafted before his death.

Meanwhile Gambetta had to think of his own constituency. Since all the 363 were standing again there could now be no question of multiple candidatures. But Belleville needed watching, for there, despite the general agreement among Republicans not to oppose the 363, a small number of Intransigent Radicals had tried to substitute Bonnet-Duverdier, the ebullient and extreme President of the Paris Municipal Council, for Gambetta as the Republican candidate. Their attempt failed miserably and Bonnet-Duverdier (like Ranc earlier) was adopted instead by Lyon. Gambetta's candidature was carried with acclamation and in his election address of 6 October, as has been seen, he still more categorically repeated his challenge to MacMahon to submit or resign.[2] Three days later he delivered a final election speech in the hall of the Cirque Américain in the Place du Château d'Eau. The vast room was packed and many were unable to gain admission. The 6,000 or 7,000 who did heard Gambetta declare that what was at stake was 'both the existence of universal suffrage and the very future of the French Revolution and the principles it had promulgated for the world'. If official pressure and corruption triumphed, the enemies of the Republic would say: 'Back with you, you people, return to slavery, since you are keen to give yourself masters after having had the omnipotence which will now be taken from you for ever.' But his peroration, as might be expected, was reserved for the Church: 'On the morrow of the poll the vanquished must be not merely such and such a party hostile to the Republic, but the party which . . . leads all the others, the great enemy. We have said: clericalism, there is the enemy; it is for universal suffrage to declare . . . Clericalism, there is the vanquished!' The words were greeted with an explosion of applause and the cries of 'Vive la République! Vive Gambetta!' were loud and long.[3] With this and similar stirring doctrines proclaimed from a myriad of Republican

1. 21 Sept., cf. 23 Sept.

2. p. 421 above. The relevant sentence ran as follows: 'Elle [i.e. France] condamnera la politique dictatoriale; elle ne laissera au chef ou pouvoir exécutif, transformé en candidat plébiscitaire, d'autre alternative que de se soumettre ou se démettre.' For the full text of the address, see *Discours*, vol. vii, pp. 271–3.

3. For the text, see *Discours*, vol. vii, pp. 277–303. The speech cost 400 fr. to stenograph (Ass. Nat., MS 1669).

platforms it was not surprising that the anxious Fourtou had just issued a further circular reminding inn-keepers that on pain of losing their licences they must not allow their premises to be used for the reading aloud of newspapers and election addresses.[1]

On the same day Broglie had made one of his rare utterances, a speech to the Conservative election committees in Paris. It was an apologia for the Seize Mai and once again a pitting of MacMahon against 'the heir', the dangerous Radical Gambetta. Grévy was subtly swept aside in a passage no doubt designed to force open any rift in the Republican ranks: 'We think M. Grévy himself only half lends himself to playing a role which fundamentally consists of making his face a mask concealing that of Gambetta.' Gambetta's words 'submit or resign', said the Duke, meant only one thing: 'You must submit to me, or resign in my favour.'[2]

Broglie ended his speech by declaring that France was on the eve of a great battle. 'At the moment when the armies are taking up their positions, a morning fog, the dust which rises from the tread of men and horses, often forms a thick cloud, which prevents them from making out their positions and respective forces.' But then, he said, the sun rises and all becomes clear. 'Let us hope that the sun will not set without shining on the triumph of justice and right.'

The sun did indeed shine: 14 October was, reported *The Times*, 'the most beautiful day for months'[3] and the poll was proportionately high, attaining 80 per cent or more in as many as twenty-two departments. But the sun did not shine for Broglie's view of justice and right. Although Thiers's death and government pressure had pulled some waverers back to the Right, Fourtou's efforts had been largely unavailing. He had hoped that the government parties would win a hundred seats but they gained no more than forty. Although Gambetta was, as so often, over-optimistic when he had predicted that the Republican 363 would increase to 400 or even 408,[4] the outcome of the elections was still a notable Republican victory. Moreover, it was gained on the first ballot, for after the polling on 14 October only fifteen out of the total of 533 contested

---

1. A number of cafés were in fact closed. Thus the historian of the Allier records that 'Au 16 mai, la résistance se fit par de petites réunions tenues dans des cafés et le pouvoir prononça de nombreuses fermetures. Cette politique de "bistrot" amenait les candidats et les élus de la gauche, au sens large, à protester contre les droits sur les alcools et la surveillance des agents des "indirectes". Non sans raison les gens de droite, au sens large, les accusaient de favoriser, ce faisant, l'alcoolisme' (Viple, *Sociologie politique de l'Allier*, p. 84).

2. *The Times*, 10 Oct.

3. 15 Oct.

4. *Lettres*, nos. 340 and 342.

seats required a second ballot. The *République Française* could aptly quote an ancient saw: 'Il n'faut qu'un coup/Pour assommer un loup',[1] and on the night of 14–15 October there were understandable cries of triumph in its offices where Juliette Adam heard Gambetta call out the results as they came in.[2] The poll had been the heaviest since 1848. Some 4,200,000 votes had been cast for the Republicans compared with 3,600,000 for the government parties. In Belleville Gambetta had increased his vote by 2,400 and similar increases were achieved by Spuller, Louis Blanc and Barodet. Although the 363 on the final count after the second ballot on 28 October were in fact reduced to 326, the Republicans still had a majority of 119 over their opponents who had won 207 seats in all. Gambetta could write with pride that, in spite of the fact that the government had committed more hateful acts in three months than the Empire in twenty years, its efforts had been in vain: 'In what other country or parliament does the opposition have a majority of 120?'[3] When the overall picture was complete it mattered little that Gambetta, unsparing as ever in his efforts to make victory as complete as possible, had travelled in vain to the Nièvre where he addressed a largely rural audience at Château-Chinon on 24 October.[4] In that *arrondissement* Monarchist and Bonapartist traditions were still strong and the Republican candidate, Gudin, was defeated by a little over a thousand votes. The *République Française* consoled itself by noting that the Republican vote had increased by 183.

Gambetta, despite this check, and the attempt of hostile critics to belittle his role, had been the major architect of the Republican victory.[5] No doubt Fourtou and his colleagues had often overreached themselves with their harsh administrative measures. No doubt, as 'an Englishman in the Provinces' more than once reiterated in an interesting series of reports to *The Times*, the frequent changes of administrative personnel had interfered with local development programmes and unsettled and disconcerted rural populations by creating a climate of uncertainty and

1. 23 Oct.
2. *Après l'abandon*, p. 67.
3. *Lettres*, nos. 324 and 342. Cf. *The Times*, 17 Oct.: 'There is not a Chamber in all Europe containing such a majority.'
4. His expenses for two for four days' travelling etc. amounted to 283 francs 65 centimes. The cost of stenography for his speech and those of three other speakers was 150 fr (Ass. Nat., MS 1669).
5. Marcère, who did not like Gambetta, later wrote that Gambetta's role was exaggerated subsequently by 'ses admirateurs et thuriféraires' and that at the time of the elections his influence was nil 'sauf peut-être en quelques endroits clairsemés' (*Histoire de la République 1876–1879*, vol. i, pp. 113–14). But there is plenty of contemporary evidence that Gambetta was regarded as the chief director of the Republican campaign, see e.g. *Memoirs of Prince Hohenlohe*, vol. ii, p. 196.

insecurity.[1] No doubt the Right had suffered from its own internal divisions and the mutual suspicions and conflicting tactics of its component parties. But if the Left had once again benefited from superior unity, discipline and organisation, this was in no small measure due to Gambetta's directing energy, persuasiveness and self-abnegation. He had from the outset preached the need for unity; he had the combination of charm and drive to secure it; and he had the sagacity to preserve it by giving way to the elder statesmen, Thiers and then Grévy, who could retain the confidence of the more conservative and timorous Republicans of the Left Centre. He had rallied the ablest journalists of the day to support the 363.[2] He himself was the most powerful of many able Republican speakers in the Chamber; outside it he was incomparable in his popular appeal, and, although he made but one speech in the provinces between dissolution and polling day, that speech at Lille with its challenging 'submit or resign' made a tremendous impression which was enhanced by the government's action in prosecuting him. Moreover, Gambetta from the first had divined the three main charges which would be most damaging to the enemy and which they would find hardest to rebut. They were none of them new, but in the Republican propaganda campaign he gave the cue for them to be employed more ruthlessly than ever: they were the charges that Broglie and his followers were the men of the past, the clerical party, and the party that wanted war. Afraid of giving substance to the clerical charge the government had refrained from trying to mobilise the clergy. The freemasons, on the other hand, had worked actively on behalf of the Left, doubtless with the connivance and encouragement of Gambetta and the other influential Republicans who two years earlier had attended the ceremonial admission of Ferry and Littré into the masonic ranks.[3]

1. *The Times*, 31 Aug., 14 Sept., etc. The Second Empire, he pointed out, had got things done, but not so the present government: 'The accounts cannot be balanced; the budget is adjourned; the new Prefect is struggling with recalcitrant Mayors or battling with a petty journal in the law courts; the new Mayor is devoted ... but hardly ready for business. ... The farmer who hoped to have that new road settled has to wait; the projected waterworks are still in the air.'

2. He was later reported to have said 'les trois hommes qui ont tué le Seize Mai, ce sont Girardin Blowitz et moi' (Giles, *A Prince of Journalists*, p. 13). Blowitz's articles in *The Times* had been very critical of the Broglie government.

3. The extent of the freemasons' political influence at this time is, of course, a vexed and no doubt insoluble question. But the claim of one of them, Anatole de la Forge, in 1887 that 'pendant la réaction cléricale du Seize Mai ... d'un même coeur tous les républicains ... se portèrent spontanément vers le Grand-Orient. Ils comprirent tous, Gambetta en tête, qu'il y avait dans cette vaste association de braves gens, une force considérable à utiliser au profit des libertés nationales' (*Bulletin du Grand Orient*, 25 April 1887, p. 173) is obviously exaggerated.

Afraid of the charge of belligerent intentions, the government had from the first sought to parry it abroad, but their efforts had been only partially successful, particularly with the power that mattered most to France, her eastern neighbour, Germany. While the old Emperor, William I, naturally sympathised with MacMahon and the Conservatives and would have rejoiced in a restoration of Monarchy in France, Bismarck, as we have seen, took a very different line.[1] He distrusted MacMahon and disliked the prospect of a 'clerical' victory in France while he was still at war with the Roman Catholic Church and Ultramontanism in Germany. Moreover, he believed that a Republican victory would keep France disunited and incapable of alliances. Therefore, he had on 18 June instructed Bülow to mobilise the German governmental Press in such a way as to convince the French electorate that it would be choosing war if it voted for Broglie and his colleagues. And later, on 6 September he had told his ambassador in Paris, Hohenlohe, that it would be necessary 'to assume a somewhat menacing attitude' while the French elections were in progress: 'But that need not be done in Paris, it would be stage-managed from Berlin.'[2] And so indeed it had been. Thus, to give but one example, on 11 October, three days before the poll, Bismarck's own paper, the *Norddeutsche Allgemeine Zeitung*, had printed a threatening article in which it declared that Italo-German negotiations then in progress were tending towards a mutual agreement in case the two countries found themselves faced by a clerical and therefore aggressive France after the general elections. This article was naturally reproduced in the French Republican papers and, although the Broglie government at once published a denial of aggressive intentions, there is little doubt that the threat assisted the Republicans. Some Frenchmen spoke of Bismarck's having become France's Grand Elector, and Broglie in his last fighting speech in the Chamber on 15 November accused the Republicans of being in league with the German Press. It was the first time, he claimed, that Frenchmen had used such a weapon, for when in 1818 an extreme party had attempted a similar move it had at once been disowned by Louis XVIII and his party. If such dealings continued it would be a sign of irremediable decadence: 'Read the sad lessons of history! Was it not in the Agora of dying Athens that the ghost of Philip of Macedon had been conjured up? Was it not in the Polish Diets that men waited to vote until they knew what Catharine's ambassadors thought and wanted?'[3]

1. Above, pp. 300–1.
2. Hohenlohe, *op. cit.*, vol. ii, p. 198 (6 Sept.); cf. Bismarck to Hohenlohe 29 June (*G.P.*, vol. i, no. 212). For a good brief summary of the 'war scare' propaganda indulged in in Germany and also Italy, see Pisani-Ferry, *op. cit.*, pp. 242–6.
3. *Annales Chambre, 1877*, Session Ordinaire, vol. i, p. 169.

Was there anything in the charge? It was significant that Gambetta ignored it and attacked his enemy on the home front. In fact he had guessed Bismarck's reactions to the Seize Mai, but it was not for want of patriotism that he had lost little time in trying to exploit them in his own and the Republican interests. On 24 May Hohenlohe had reported what the Republicans were saying,

> and Herr Hartmann was asked by Gambetta to inform me, that they have given up every thought of revenge. If they did think of recovering the lost provinces or part of them, they merely had in view friendly discussions in the event of territorial changes in Europe.... On the other hand the Monarchist parties could not dispense with war, because of their need to strengthen their prestige at home.

But if this was one reason for Germany to prefer a Republican form of government in France there was also another, namely the fact that, once in power, the Republicans intended to embark on a thorough-going campaign against Ultramontanism: 'Therein lay the means of forging good relations with Germany.'[1]

Bismarck wrote 'Correct' in the margin against the sentence relating to the Monarchists' need of war to maintain prestige, and 'No' in answer to a question put by Gambetta asking whether he had really opened negotiations with the German episcopate: 'Such a development', he commented, 'will not encourage the Republican party.'[2] These and other observations were no doubt relayed to Gambetta through Hartmann, but what other exchanges there were through this intermediary before the elections of 1877 we do not know. In any case Bismarck had acted and Gambetta, who had impressed Hohenlohe as a 'confident, vigorous statesman', had helped to gain a powerful but uncomfortable ally for the Republican cause. By October he had penetrated all the weak points in the Conservatives' armour.

---

1. Frank, *op. cit.*, p. 62. It appears from the original despatch (No. 92, Akten I.A.B. c. (Frankreich) 79, Bd. 15), a copy of which has been kindly sent me by Dr Weinardy of the Auswärtiges Amt, that Hartmann was Frédéric Hartmann of Münster in Alsace, an industrialist and one of the deputies of the Bas-Rhin who resigned in 1871 in protest against the Treaty of Frankfurt.

2. *Ibid.*, p. 63.

26

The end of the crisis
September–December 1877

At the end of September Gambetta had written to Princess Troubetzkoï:
'On the morrow of the poll we must not lose a day or a vote, but fall upon
the routed enemy and take all this lot prisoner as at Sedan.'[1] More than
ever the Marshal was the key figure. If he would not resign, he must
submit and take a ministry from the Republican majority. Gambetta
lost not a day, indeed scarcely a moment, hoping, it would seem, that the
Marshal, downcast and abashed by his defeat, would be willing at last to
meet him, hear him and surrender to his charm. On the evening of
14 October, even before the election results were fully known, MacMahon
received a visit from Gambetta's friend Duclerc who told him that
Gambetta would be delighted to see him secretly. He proposed—in
MacMahon's own words—'to come and see him in the Elysée on the
following night at midnight. He would enter the President's domain by
the little garden gate opening on to the Champs Elysées. He already
knew that the elections would give his party a large majority and he said
that he wished to come to an understanding with the Marshal about the
way in which it would be best to proceed in the general interest.'[2]

But the Marshal refused. His was not a conspiratorial nature and he disliked clandestine interviews. Besides nothing had occurred to diminish
his dislike of the Republican leader who only a few weeks earlier had been
judicially convicted of insulting him. On the contrary, for it was apparently
about this time that Gambetta was enjoying an intimacy with no less a
person than the Marshal's own sister-in-law, the beautiful Comtesse de
Beaumont. 'It can easily be imagined', writes MacMahon's latest biographer, 'that this liaison offended the religious feelings of the Marshal
and his wife, quite apart from wounding the *amour propre* of the Duchesse

1. *Lettres*, no. 340.
2. Memo by Marshal MacMahon, quoted in Silvestre de Sacy, *Le Maréchal de
MacMahon*, p. 345.

de Magenta whose aristocratic prejudices are well known.'[1] Moreover, this biographer suggests, the Marshal may have suspected that Gambetta wished to do a deal; believing that once in office he might have difficulty in establishing good relations with foreign powers, he wanted MacMahon to remain President on condition that he himself should virtually control home affairs. For the Marshal this was inadmissible.

So Gambetta failed to take the Marshal prisoner as at Sedan. Perhaps he hardly expected to, in spite of his assertion that he was convinced that he could have come to a good arrangement with 'the obstinate old man' had he had but ten minutes' talk with him.[2] But the failure must none the less have been a bitter disappointment. Such an arrangement would have been a splendid coup had he won from the Marshal the promise of office already offered by Thiers, and the history of France in the later 'seventies might indeed have been different.

But the Marshal was in any case too stiff and unbending to be capable of such an imaginative and conciliatory *volte-face*. For the next few days he withdrew into discomfited seclusion surrounded by his 'camarilla', who gave him conflicting advice and who appeared to *The Times* correspondent to be keeping him as invisible 'as the Emperor of China in the most secluded of his palaces'.[3] He showed no sign of submitting and the schemes of Republicans like Jules Ferry and Paul Cambon to set a soldier to catch a soldier and to utilise General Chanzy, now Governor-General of Algeria, to persuade him to yield came to nought.[4] Nor would he resign as Gambetta's paper now urged him to, on the grounds that 'care for his reputation, self-respect and patriotism' all made this his duty.[5] He on the contrary believed that it was his duty to remain in office particularly when de Vogüé, the French Ambassador in Vienna, told him that he inspired confidence abroad, whereas Gambetta would have no prestige, and that his departure might precipitate a foreign war.[6] Yet most Republicans were confident of the eventual outcome. 'The President', said one of those whom MacMahon had most injured, to wit Jules Simon, 'was a harpooned whale—he would give a good deal of trouble but

---

1. *Ibid.*, pp. 345–6. Pillias (*Léonie Léon*, pp. 291–2) gives a different account, saying that in December the Marshal 'rencontra dans une allée solitaire du Bois sa belle-soeur et Gambetta se promenant en grande intimité, et rompit net le projet', i.e. the plan of a *rapprochement* with Gambetta. The Duchesse de Magenta was MacMahon's wife.

2. In a letter of 20 Aug. to Ranc he had said that it was unlikely that the Marshal would capitulate 'et subir toutes les conditions de la nouvelle majorité' (*Lettres*, no. 329).

3. 23 Oct.

4. Cambon, *Correspondance*, vol. i, p. 86, letter of 9 Sept. to Jules Cambon.

5. *R.F.*, leader of 3 Nov.; cf. e.g. 9 and 12 Nov.

6. Silvestre de Sacy, *op. cit.*, p. 348.

must give in at last.'[1] The trouble he could give might consist in refusing to part with his ministers or to appoint men acceptable to the majority in the new Chamber, in attempting to dissolve the Chamber a second time, or even in being persuaded to essay a *coup d'état*.

'M. de Broglie had long been tottering under the weight of universal unpopularity.' These words had been written by Louis Blanc not in the 1870s but early in the 1840s with reference to Broglie's father.[2] Now in 1877 he might have applied them to the son. But even if he were tottering, Broglie, too, was in no hurry to fall. In February 1876, after his resounding personal defeat in the general election, Buffet had resigned without awaiting the result of the second ballot. Not so Broglie after 14 October 1877. He was ready to remain as long as the Marshal wished and the Marshal was only too glad to accept his offer. So Broglie not only remained but claimed a partial victory—the Conservatives had in fact won more than forty seats—and, to the scandalised dismay of the *République Française*, announced that the ministry had no intention of resigning.[3] He was determined to see the elections through, and this meant not only the second ballot of the general elections on 28 October but also the elections on 4 November for the partial renewal of the General Councils. But the latter gave him no comfort. The Republicans gained 113 seats and, worst of all, Broglie himself was defeated in his home fief in the Eure. After this fresh blow he and his colleagues at last handed in their resignations, but, in a quandary over who should take their place, since the Right were still in disarray, the Marshal begged them to stay on and stay they did.[4] Once again they would meet a hostile Chamber, for the new session was due to begin on 7 November.

The advent of winter was often a bad time for Gambetta's health. After his journey to Château-Chinon he had had to hurry back to Paris to attend yet another funeral, that of his old friend and benefactor Vincent Dubochet, who had died at the age of seventy-eight. Exhausted by the immense strain of the election campaign and saddened by this second loss of an older man who had been of such help to him, he was more than ever vulnerable to cold and bronchitis or chest complaints. According to police reports, he retired to bed soon after Dubochet's funeral, was in

1. Grant Duff, *Notes from a Diary 1873–1881*, vol. i, p. 312.
2. *History of Ten Years* (1845), vol. ii, p. 380.
3. *R.F.*, 22 Oct.
4. For the Marshal's difficulties, see Silvestre de Sacy, *op. cit.*, p. 347: 'Le Maréchal ne demandait pas mieux que de former un nouveau ministère conservateur, mais les députés de la droite restaient divisés, même dans la défaite, et n'arrivaient pas à se mettre d'accord sur la composition de ce ministère.' D'Audiffret-Pasquier refused the invitation to form a government. Dufaure made unacceptable conditions and Pouyer-Quertier failed.

bed again early in November and still very unwell ten days later.[1] But the political situation was such that nothing barring serious illness could have kept him long from the scene of action, and he was soon writing that his day began at 8 a.m. and finished at 1 a.m.—he hardly had time to sit down or eat.[2] As the Marshal and his cabinet, a cabinet now dubbed Trompe-la-Mort, still remained in power, political tension continued. Fourtou had issued a circular declaring that the Marshal could not abandon his post, and more officials had been replaced. Old friends and acquaintances still cut one another. A man like Thiers's former henchman Barthélemy St Hilaire could write on 22 October of his hope that punishment was at hand 'for all these bandits; this is no longer politics, but brigandage', and three weeks later the prefect of the Nord, Paul Cambon, immobilised by a riding accident, consoled himself by dreaming that Broglie and Fourtou had been transported to New Caledonia and were being eaten by savages.[3]

As was to be expected, the Gare Saint Lazare was again crowded when the deputies and senators set out for Versailles on 7 November, but the crowd was reported to have been 'silent and downcast' while the deputies selected their compartments in the train with exceptional care 'for fear of falling into some Conservative or Republican den'.[4] The first two days of the session were, however, occupied by the usual but necessary formalities of a new parliament. The Chamber was busied in verifying its powers, invalidating those of its members (mostly of the Right!) whose elections were fraught with dubious procedures—a process which continued for several days and always earned it a sermon from *The Times*[5]—and electing its officers. To emphasise its continuity with its predecessor, it chose the same Bureau, elected Jules Grévy once more as its President

---

1. A.P.P., BA/921, 27 Oct., 6 Nov., 16 Nov.; cf. letters from Gambetta to Léonie Léon of 30 Oct., 3 Nov. and 11 Nov. referring to his cold and fatigue (L.G.). The *R.F.* of 18 Nov. thought it necessary to rebut 'les mystifications imbéciles des feuilles réactionnaires à propos de la santé de M. Gambetta'.

2. Letter of 9 Nov. to Léonie Léon (L.G.).

3. Letter from Barthélemy St Hilaire to an unknown correspondent (in the author's possession); letter of 15 Nov. (Cambon, *Correspondance*, vol. i, p. 87). Cf. *The Times*, 30 Oct., p. 8, for a vivid allusion to the continued tensions in personal relationships.

4. *The Times*, 8 Nov.

5. e.g. leader of 30 Oct. which said that the French procedure was 'much the same as ... in our own House of Commons until the Grenville Act corrected the scandal of these multitudinous decisions. It would be a ... triumph for the liberal majority ... if, in this hour of their victory, they could be persuaded to delegate to small Committees ... the power of finally deciding. ... It ought not to be impossible for a French Chamber to do to-day what an English House of Commons was able to do more than a hundred years since.'

and, a fortnight later, designated most of the same men (twenty-four out of thirty-three) to serve on the Budget Committee, of which Gambetta again became President.

Meanwhile the Republican majority had begun to make plans to frustrate and embarrass the government and to meet any emergency. According to *The Times*, the deputies of the Left had held a meeting to this end on the evening of 5 November which seemed 'to have been at times rather stormy'.[1] Three days later, after parliament had reassembled, they met again in the big salon of the Hôtel des Réservoirs at Versailles and elected a directing Committee of Eighteen, chosen from all four groups, in order to coordinate policy during the critical days ahead. It was given full powers to act and its deliberations were to be kept secret.[2] It met several times a week, if not daily.[3] Its members, in alphabetical order, were Bethmont, Louis Blanc, Brisson, Horace de Choiseul, Clemenceau, Jules Ferry, Floquet, Gambetta, Germain, Goblet, Albert Grévy, Lepère, Lockroy, Madier de Montjau, de Marcère, Antonin Proust, Léon Renault and Tirard. Despite his indisposition, his friends claimed that Gambetta was its directing spirit,[4] and it was probably largely to the initiative of the man who had hitherto led the struggle against

1. 6 Nov. The *R.F.* (7 Nov.) reported a meeting of members 'des bureaux de Gauches de l'ancienne Chambre . . . rue Malesherbes, 8, chez M. Camille Sée', which adopted the following resolution: 'Pendant toute la durée de la crise actuellement pendante, aucune communication ne sera faite aux journaux sur les motions, propositions, et délibérations des réunions des Gauches . . .'.

2. *R.F.*, 10 Nov.

3. According to Mme Adam it met daily in an apartment on the Boulevard Malesherbes (*Après l'abandon*, p. 83); according to René Goblet ('Souvenirs de ma vie politique', *Revue politique et parlementaire*, 10 Sept. 1928, p. 378) it met several times a week in Léon Renault's flat in the Bd Haussmann (Marcère, *Histoire de la République*, vol. ii, p. 135, says Bd. Malesherbes).

4. e.g. Goblet, *art. cit.*, p. 377. According to a police agent (No. 8), who on 17 Dec. claimed to have had several meetings with Ranc, Ranc said that Gambetta had shown particular skill in handling 'en même temps Madier de Montjau, l'exalté radical et les membres modérés du comité de dix-huit', and the agent commented, apparently echoing Ranc: 'Le comité de 18 est son oeuvre personnelle. C'est ce comité qui a tout dirigé et c'est Gambetta seul qui le dirigeait lui-même' (A.P.P. Dossier Ranc Ba/1, 233). Cf. Reinach, *La Vie politique de Léon Gambetta*, p. 65: 'Gambetta fut l'âme de ce comité.' An undated letter in L.G. perhaps bears out his part in the formation of the Committee: 'très belle journée, je rentre à une heure du matin; j'aurai demain une assez rude tâche, mais tout marche bien. Réunion plénière très réussie, commission fermée [? formée] par moi, élue par acclamation.' On the other hand, the sentence in this letter, 'Les ministres sont de nouveau démissionnaires, c'est du moins la nouvelle de ce soir', suggests that the reference may be to the resignation of the Broglie cabinet on the 19th and to the choice of the Budget Commission, formally elected on the 20th.

the men of 16 May that its formation was due. Grévy, it will be noted, was not a member, but in view of his position as Thiers's successor, all the decisions taken by the Committee were to be communicated to him.[1]

On the eve of the assembling of parliament Gambetta had written to Léonie Léon that 'the sick man' was 'in the pangs of death': he reckoned that 'in two or three weeks we shall be able to publish the news of decease (*les lettres de décès*)'; two days later he told his father that the situation was serious, but that all would end well, 'thanks to the determination of the country and its representatives. We have three weeks of crisis still before us and then all will be settled.'[2] For once his prophecies were not far wrong; his later estimate fell short by a mere fortnight.

While urging the Marshal that it was his duty to resign, the *République Française* drew attention to the danger of a second dissolution. As early as July the *Bulletin des Communes* had threatened such a dissolution, should the Chamber emerging from the elections 'declare war on the Marshal'.[3] Now, since it was clear that the Republican majority, whose predecessor had 'declared war' on the Broglie government in May and June, was more than ever bound to open hostilities in November, it was evident that the role of the Senate would once again be crucial. Of this the *République Française* was well aware. Already on 21 October it had printed a violent article criticising the Senate and declaring that it must more than ever be watched. Now in November it reported that the Right-wing Press was suggesting that government would be carried on with the support of the Senate; 'The budget would be voted by the Senate; the Senate would be the answer to everything.' The ministers were beseeching the Senate to save the Marshal and to save them along with him,[4] but a second dissolution would be an unconstitutional act,

> a *coup d'état*, and an unacceptable violation of the pact of 1875. . . . The 1877 Chamber would have no more right than that of 1830 to renounce its mandate and . . . submit to arbitrary decrees or ordinances. If it were permissible to have recourse to a second dissolution then there could be a third and a fourth. . . . The Senate would be transformed into a single assembly . . . the country's regular government and parliamentary regime would no longer exist. This was not what was intended by the Constitution of 1875. Therefore it would be the deputies' duty to resist a second attempt at dissolution.

This leader of 13 November waxed still more eloquent before it drew to a conclusion:

1. Mme Adam, *Après l'abandon*, p. 83.
2. 6 Nov. (L.G.); *Lettres*, no. 345.
3. *R.F.*, 25 July.
4. Leaders of 10 and 11 Nov.

Never since 1789 has the French *patrie* been threatened by a greater internal danger. If the vote of 14 October is scorned . . . if the men elected on 14 October refuse to submit to such an outrage, France will have to be tamed by force. . . . What should we become? Another Spain, minus the Pyrenees. . . . Is it worth it?

Once the preliminary formalities in the Chamber were over the Republican majority lost no time in opening hostilities. The Committee of Eighteen had decided on its tactics and Jules Grévy's younger brother Albert tabled a resolution for the establishment of a Commission of Enquiry into the actions which since 16 May had been designed to exert illegal pressure upon the elections.[1] Thus, no doubt, Gambetta hoped to procure his 'revenge and the punishment of the intriguers and the perverse'.[2] The great clash, the last great fight between Broglie and his enemies was at hand and spectators flocked to Versailles to see and hear the battle. According to a correspondent of the *New York Tribune*, writing later, half Paris 'streamed out to the portals of the palace. . . . The streets of Versailles were filled with troops. The doors of the palace were guarded. . . . In the tribunes not a seat was vacant. . . . Outsiders were offering £20 for a place to hear.'[3] These spectators had come, wrote the *République Française*, to see 'the unheard-of sight of condemned ministers . . . who persist in remaining on their benches like the servants of some Asiatic tyrant'.[4] The excitement was, if possible, even greater than in any previous debate since the war: women, recorded another reporter, could be heard 'stamping with rage or delight' and on all sides people were exclaiming 'ce misérable de Fourtou', 'cet infâme Gambetta', or 'hideux de Broglie'.[5] Their expectations of a tremendous encounter were amply fulfilled, for both sides rose to the momentous occasion. The debate lasted three days and during those days Broglie and his colleagues fought with determination and skill against the Republican resolution, arguing that such an enquiry was itself illegal and that it was not they but the Republicans who had won the elections by deceit, invoking foreign support to spread the calumny that it was the Right which wanted war.[6]

It was not until the third day, the 15th, that Gambetta entered the fray to utter the final and devastating kind of denunciation of which he was a master and which inevitably precipitated frequent uproar. On 16 May, he

1. See *Annales Chambre*, 2nd session 1877, vol. i, p. 89.
2. See above, p. 403.
3. Smalley, *London letters*, vol. i, pp. 40–1.
4. 15 Nov.
5. *The Times*, 15 Nov.
6. For Broglie's references to this, see also above, p. 437.

declared, a minority had taken power and made the Head of State 'not only a candidate, but the country's grand elector': it had thrown him into the electoral arena, it had thrust the clergy to the voting urns and in the end by fraud and theft it had succeeded in winning forty seats. It had demeaned itself by making its officials, the government press and national printing office instruments of slander and public calumny. It had endeavoured to make the election into a kind of plebiscite between him and the Marshal but, he went on—and the whole Left rose to its feet and applauded as he did so—'A Republican before all else, I serve my party not to enslave or compromise it, but, so far as my strength, my hard work, and intelligence permit, to bring about the victory of its ideas, its aspirations and its rights!' When universal suffrage had spoken it was absurd to talk of two powers against one. The two Chambers (which he had helped to set up) and the executive were all organs of universal suffrage and made to serve it. If the Senate were to arrogate to itself the right to revise the elections it would no longer be an upper Chamber but a Convention which would be none the less formidable or criminal for being a white Convention. But he knew that the Senate, like the constitution itself, was the product of a gleam of patriotism. He adjured its members to have a care for their own cause and for that of liberty— 'The truth is [addressing the government] that you are clinging to power; that you do not hesitate to ruin the very man whose honour you are exploiting against his constitutional duty—all for a few hours' more of this domination for which you are not merely ambitious but a glutton!'[1]

It was a tremendous riposte, the reply of a man who claimed to be of his own time[2] to the aristocratic figure from the past, one whom he had so often denounced, but whom, he had the generosity to concede, it was a pleasure to fight, since the Duke had plenty of pluck (*un rude estomac*).[3] It was a tremendous riposte despite the fact that Léonie Léon (who had a new purple veil) had not, to his sorrow, been there to hear him. Yet it was to her, he told her, that he had spoken his reply to the born adversary of his policies, and he thought she would be pleased: 'It is our battle of Arques,' he added, 'but the absence of the lovely Gabrielle weighed upon my heart.'[4] His elation was justified. A noble spectator, a young diplomat,

1. For the text, see *Discours*, vol. vii, pp. 343–63, and *Annales, Chambre* 2nd Legisl. 1877, vol. i, pp. 160–6.
2. As, ironically, did Gambetta's old enemy Napoleon III! Gambetta's words here no doubt wounded his adversary: 'vous êtes resté un ennemi de la démocratie, un aristocrate! . . . je suis un homme de mon temps et vous n'êtes plus un homme de votre temps.'
3. D. Halévy, *La République des ducs*, p. 318.
4. 15 Nov. (L.G.). Henry IV of France had defeated the Duc de Mayenne at Arques in 1589. Gabrielle d'Estrées was one of the King's most celebrated mistresses.

the Vicomte de Vogüé, thought his performance 'superb' and G. W. Smalley, the journalist, later wrote that it was 'the greatest single effort of oratory' he had ever heard. He asked Gambetta's friends 'who had heard him often if he had ever made a greater speech. "Never", was the uniform answer.'[1] The Republican majority applauded Gambetta enthusiastically as he left the tribune and the resolution for appointing a Commission of Enquiry of thirty-three members was voted by 312 to 205. So there ended a day which seemed to the *République Française* to have witnessed 'the most moving and solemn of all the parliamentary sittings for seven years'. Victory, it was true, was not complete, but the campaign had opened under the most favourable auspices.[2]

Defeated in the Chamber, Broglie still hoped to exploit what the *République Française* called 'the ridiculous theory of two against one' and to play the Senate against the lower house. If the Senate rejected the Commission of Enquiry, then there would be a conflict between the two houses and a second dissolution could yet follow. So, reported *The Times*, the Cabinet was 'going before the Senate, according to some, to ask of it the right to live, according to others, to ask permission to die'. It proved to be the latter. Whether or not he was moved by reading Gambetta's eloquent appeal in the Chamber, the President of the Senate, D'Audiffret-Pasquier, would do no more than permit a debate on 'the measures the government proposes to take with regard to the enquiry ordered by the Chamber'. Moreover, the Right Centre Senators would vote only for a motion 'taking note' instead of 'approving' the government's declarations and this on condition that Broglie and his colleagues then resigned.[3] Broglie had won but a Pyrrhic victory and on the 19th he and his cabinet resigned for the second time since the general elections. This time their resignations were accepted. The Duke's second and last 'government of combat' had lasted just six months, six of the most

1. Vicomte E.-M. de Vogüé, *Journal Paris, Saint-Petersbourg 1877–1883*, ed. F. de Vogüé (1932), p. 67; Smalley, *op. cit.*, vol. i, p. 44.

2. 17 Nov., p. 2; leader of 18 Nov. The Commission of Enquiry did not report until March 1879, by which time in Marcère's words (*op. cit.*, p. 141) 'il ne correspondait plus à l'esprit public'. It recommended the impeachment before the Senate of the members of the ministries of 17 May and 23 Nov. 1877, but the government of the day arranged 'pour que cette mise en accusation ne fût jamais suivie d'effet, on n'en entendit parler' (*ibid*).

3. The text of this 'ordre du jour motivé' was as follows: 'Le Sénat, prenant acte des déclarations du Gouvernement, est résolu, conformément aux principes conservateurs qu'il a toujours soutenus, à ne laisser porter aucune atteinte aux prérogatives qui appartiennent à chacun des pouvoirs publics, passe à l'ordre du jour (*Annales, Sénat 1877 (suite)*, vol. i, p. 78). The R.F. (leader, 20 Nov.) naturally regarded it as an unfortunate motion in which the spirit of the Church was at work: 'Abîmons tout plutôt; c'est l'esprit de l'Eglise.'

momentous and in some ways futilely frenzied months in the early history of the Third Republic.

But the departure of this 'mischievous personage and his acolytes' from the scene was not the end of the battle and it did not satisfy the *République Française*.[1] It saw in the motion voted by the Senate (by a majority of 151 to 129 and not, as originally announced, 142 to 138) a declaration of war on universal suffrage and its chosen representatives. With the hateful tenacity characteristic of the clerical spirit the Duc de Broglie, it declared, had wished to make inevitable the conflict he himself was no longer able to sustain. It was not a change of person but a change of policy that France was demanding. Broglie and his fellows could be replaced by 'les premiers venus' without the country's feeling that it had been freed. The Marshal had previously been unable to find presentable ministers to take up Broglie's heritage. The prospect of carrying out the terms of Broglie's will would now be still less attractive to serious politicians.[2] In the war that had been declared by incorrigible factions the President of the Republic, their docile instrument, was seeking the support of an assembly which affected to believe itself superior to the decisions of universal suffrage. But let the Senate beware! 'It is a great misfortune for a political body to run counter to the country's wishes.' One way out of the conflict, the paper suggested, would be for the President to use his constitutional power and call a Congress or National Assembly, in other words a joint meeting of Chamber and Senate.

> What can he fear? It is said that it is a point of honour with him not to yield to the Chamber of Deputies. He will yield to this general assembly of the mandatories of the nation, similar in majesty and equal in authority to that Assembly of 1871 which placed him in the post where he is. . . . The patriotism of M. the President of the Republic, his modesty, his self-sacrifice, his disinterestedness, have often been lauded. What better opportunity of demonstrating them than by summoning this national Congress which can resolve all the difficulties peacefully in the space of an hour?[3]

Needless to say, the Marshal did not respond to this invitation although this was not the last that was to be heard of it. It was to crop up again soon in a curious way.[4] He and his advisers were still fighting a rearguard action and preoccupied with the succession to Broglie. In a letter of 21 November to Léonie Léon, Gambetta wrote that there was as yet no cabinet: 'We

1. 19 Nov.
2. Leaders of 19 and 21 Nov.
3. Leader of 23 Nov. The idea was taken up by Floquet in the Chamber on the 24th, cf. *R.F.*, 27 Nov.
4. See below, pp. 453–4.

do not know who are the commissioners charged with bearing the old soldier's words to the Chamber. I do not care. Everything, absolutely everything, is ready to give them a hot reception.'[1] Fortified by this knowledge, he went to the theatre that evening to see a revival of Victor Hugo's *Hernani* and he and the author were warmly applauded by waiting crowds when they left. But he confided to Léonie that he had rarely seen 'a more puerile play' and that nothing was 'more sepulchral and fossilised than the Romanticism of 1830'.[2]

The great weapon with which to beat 'the Commissioners', whoever they might be, had already been forged by the Chamber when on the 19th it had elected the Budget Committee of which Gambetta again became President. On the 22nd the *République Française*, announcing the news of the election, issued a solemn warning. With a few exceptions, it pointed out, the Committee was the same as that which in June had categorically refused to grant M. Caillaux the four direct taxes which he had demanded in advance.[3] The new Committee had not forgotten that its chief task was

> to secure respect for the decision made by universal suffrage in the vote of 14 October. There is not a single one of the deputies who does not know that control of the budget is the only sanction at the disposition of legislative Assemblies in a parliamentary regime. How then can it for an instant be doubted that they will know how to make the use of this power which should be made . . . ? It is for the Chamber to save the country. . . . No budget, so long as there is no ministry in which the Chamber can have confidence; no budget, so long as the President of the Republic fails to obey the decision made by universal suffrage in the vote of 14 October.

On the following day the paper's leading article started with the words 'War is declared'. The situation was indeed alarming; in the Senate between the 16th and 24th six men of the Right had been elected to fill vacancies resulting from deaths among the Life Senators and this and the size of the majority who had voted for the compromise motion on the 19th led to fresh talk of dissolution. This, as *The Times* explained, would render the Chamber's refusal of a budget 'of irremediable gravity'. It would be

> impossible for a fresh Chamber to be in a condition to vote before 12th or 15 January. Hence the Budget would not have been voted at the beginning of

1. L.G.
2. *Ibid.*
3. See above, p. 412. As early as 18 Oct. *The Times* had written that it was known what the Left would do if they encountered a hostile government: they would immediately pass a vote of 'want of confidence' and refuse to vote funds.

the financial year of 1878; the Councils General could not fix the fiscal assessments; fiscal anarchy would prevail.... Moreover ... the country has just voted, and there would be no advantage from voting immediately again. The question, then, is just this—either a compromise, the chances of which have disappeared since yesterday; or resignation if the future Cabinet is overthrown and its fall is accepted; or the *coup d'état* with the arbitrary collection of taxes, state of siege, and all the calamities which follow it.[1]

The names of the new ministers were announced on the 23rd. 'I thought', the Marshal wrote to D'Audiffret-Pasquier, 'that the best way to let tempers cool was to take men from outside parliament and not involved in my latest political struggle.'[2] It was a transitional cabinet composed mainly of officials and headed by a relatively obscure general, the Comte de Grimaudet de Rochebouët, who also took charge of the Ministry of War, thus displacing the well-liked Berthaut. There was to be no other such cabinet headed by a non-parliamentarian until Doumergue's ministry of February 1934, also formed at a time of crisis. The new ministers were little known and the Left greeted the appointments with 'gales of laughter'.[3] Gambetta dubbed them 'the ministry of the last prayers'[4] and the *République Française* wrote sarcastically:

> We suppose that these little-known statesmen will arrive with their papers in good order so as to establish their identity.... The *Dictionnaire des Contemporains* unfortunately refuses to relieve our readers' embarrassment. It only mentions two of the new ministers.... On M. Faye it recommends his works on Saturn's ring and on the parallax of a nameless star in the Great Bear. As for M. Collignon ... the most outstanding detail ... is that he was born on a 16 May. No doubt M. de MacMahon saw in this a predestination.[5]

In the circumstances, no government not representative of the parliamentary majority could hope to win the confidence of the Chamber, whatever its claims to be no more than a business government to bring about appeasement. But this particular government was feared as well as derided by the Left, for in their eyes its contained disquieting elements. The most forceful member, Welche, the Minister of the Interior, had been one of Fourtou's prefects, and there were soon people who remembered that Rochebouët himself, a Bonapartist turned Legitimist, had been one of the officers who executed Louis Napoleon's *coup d'état* of

1. 21 Nov., p. 5.
2. Chastenet, *L'Enfance de la Troisième République*, pp. 239–40.
3. *R.F.*, leader of 24 Nov.
4. *The Times*, 24 Nov. In a letter of the 23rd to Princess Troubetzkoï he called it 'un ministère de dépit, pour finir, sans avenir' (*Lettres*, no. 346).
5. 24 Nov. Faye was Minister of Public Instruction, Collignon of Public Works.

2 December 1851.[1] It was no wonder then that the ministry met with 'a hot reception' and that it was defeated on 24 November, the very first day on which it confronted the Chamber. The Committee of Eighteen sponsored a vote of no confidence which was carried by 315 to 207. Gambetta believed that the end, the final decision by the Marshal to submit or resign was at hand.[2] But his paper was less optimistic. It wrote that the ministry was 'merely a screen behind which the occult government which has ruled for five years is preparing for action, to show that it is armed and ready to fight, perhaps for a *coup d'état* and civil war when the favourable moment comes'. It bade the ministers be gone as quickly as possible and, when they did not immediately resign, it again raised the spectre of armed intervention and 'the violent dispersal' of the deputies.[3]

For a while the pessimism of the *République Française* looked like being justified. Neither Marshal nor ministry resigned and the crisis lasted another three weeks. They were three weeks during which Gambetta wrote that he was living in a state of feverish activity and during which he was worried by Léonie's having an attack of nerves; yet he hoped that they might soon go and laugh together at the Palais Royal, for he was 'in great need of distraction, tenderness and gaiety' to enable him to continue putting up with 'the heartrending tedium of politics'.[4]

Of the details of his hectic activity during this critical period we know all too little, but clearly he was much taken up by his duties in the Budget Committee, by the frequent meetings of the Committee of Eighteen and by planning to forestall any desperate moves by the men in power, quite apart from his normal preoccupations with the *République Française*.[5] Certainly, he played a key part as President of the Budget Committee.

1. There was a devastating entry on him in the second memorandum on army officers specially compiled for Gambetta (see Ch. 22 above) in the autumn of 1878, but this was no doubt partly coloured by his role in 1877 (Bédarida, 'L'Armée et la République', *Revue historique*, July–Sept. 1964, p. 158).

2. Letter of 25 Nov. to Léonie Léon (L.G.).

3. Leaders of 25 and 27 Nov. There were rumours that the government would, like Louis Napoleon in 1851, disperse the Chamber and arrest leading Republican deputies.

4. Letters of 25, 28, 29, 30 Nov. and 1 Dec.

5. He also presided during this period over a series of electoral meetings in the 9th *arrondissement* where a candidate was to be selected to replace Grévy, who had chosen to sit for his old constituency, the Jura. The choice fell on Emile de Girardin who was unanimously adopted on 5 Dec. at a meeting in the Paz Gymnasium. Polling day was to be 16 Dec., but the political situation was such that Gambetta in his concluding speech had to say he did not know whether it would take place, 'car nous vivons à une époque singulière, où, même lorsqu'il s'agit des prescriptions de la loi l'on ne sait pas si l'on peut compter sur huit jours de sécurité ou seulement de probabilité' (*R.F.*, 7 Dec.).

Despite its defeat, the Rochebouët cabinet remained in power, 'prolonging a miserable resistance whilst the real battle continued behind the scenes'.[1] It remained in office, like its predecessor, until the Marshal could find successors and make up his mind what to do in the further corner into which he had now been driven. And the real battle was not wholly behind the scenes. There was an open and vital engagement in the Chamber early in December. The Rochebouët ministry might continue in office, but no government could do so indefinitely without funds; the calendar year was drawing to an end, and the budget had still to be passed. So the ministers tried to persuade the deputies to vote the budget or at least, like Caillaux in June, to coax them to sanction the four direct taxes. But they tried in vain. In the debate on 4 December Jules Ferry, speaking on behalf of the Budget Committee, took the line already foreshadowed by the *République Française*: the Committee, he declared, was willing to grant these taxes only to a truly parliamentary ministry. Gambetta eloquently reinforced him. The Committee had been working hard, he said; its reports would all be ready soon and it could then claim to have done its duty: 'But we shall only surrender our gold, our responsibilities, our sacrifices, the fruits of our devoted labour, when the will expressed on 14 October has been satisfied, when we know whether it is the nation which governs in France or a man who commands.'[2] (Prolonged applause on the Left and in the Centre.) For the first time the Marshal's personal responsibility was formally challenged.

MacMahon had indeed brought the challenge upon himself by his indecision. The Republicans had made clear that they were ready to withhold money; they also now applied wider economic pressure. A general economic depression was developing in Europe, but, apart from the metallurgical, silk, sugar-beet and wine industries, the French economy in 1877 was still in a relatively healthy state. Yet there is no doubt that the political crisis had heightened a growing business recession. In 1873 the Republicans had alleged that uncertainty about a possible restoration of Monarchy was damaging the economy and very early in the Seize Mai crisis they had sounded a similar

1. Pisani-Ferry, *op. cit.*, p. 290. To a man of the Right, like Decazes, who had just ceased to be Foreign Minister, the new ministers 'font bonne contenance', but, he added 'le Budget! le Budget!!!' (letter of 26 Nov. to Chaudordy, M.A.E., Fond Chaudordy, vol. i, ff. 130–1).

2. *Annales, Chambre*, 1877, vol. v, p. 43; *Discours*, vol. vii, pp. 382–4. In the course of his intervention Gambetta rebutted Rouher's suggestion that the Committee of Eighteen was a kind of 'comité supérieur qui asservirait à ses volontés et à son caprice l'indépendance des votes de la Chambre' (Gambetta's words). The same charge was made earlier on the same day by Paul de Cassagnac (*Annales, ibid.*, p. 56). For a retrospective defence of the Committee see Marcère, *op. cit.*, pp. 169–70.

note.[1] Now that note rose to a crescendo.[2] Traders and businessmen from many parts of the country sent petitions and deputations to the Marshal beseeching him to relieve the economic situation by ending the political uncertainty, and from 24 November onwards, the *République Française* was full of their complaints. Although MacMahon refused to receive these deputations, he must have been aware of the growing discontent and his position was increasingly uncomfortable. He was urged by some to resign (which he would have been only too glad to do), by the Orleanists to submit, and by others, especially the Bonapartists, to resist and impose martial law or once more dissolve parliament, and he veered now one way and now another. It was an extraordinary situation and a Republican journalist in the provinces, Hippolyte Gautier, might well ask whether 'this perpetual alternation of incomprehensible advances and retreats could be called government?'[3]

One curious incident in the tortuous manoeuvring of these last weeks of crisis was the reemergence of the idea of a Congress. On 4 December a report by the semi-official Havas news agency was posted 'in the corridors of the Chamber'. It asserted that the Left-wing groups had tried to press the Marshal to summon a Congress to discuss the article in the constitutional laws which gave him power to dissolve the Chamber with the agreement of the Senate. The report was at once formally repudiated in the Chamber by Léon Renault speaking on behalf of the Left.[4] At the same time Gambetta's friend Duclerc sent a denial to the Press, as did the Committee of Eighteen. Yet, if MacMahon's unpublished memoirs are to be believed, Gambetta, ever fertile in expedients, had again taken up the idea of a Congress as a means of reaching a settlement. He had had dinner with de Lesseps of Suez Canal fame and asked him to convey a message to the Marshal to the effect that, if he were willing to summon a Congress to abrogate the dissolution article, he, Gambetta, would exert all his influence to get the budget through parliament, no matter what the ministry in power.[5]

1. See, e.g., Gambetta's brief references in his speech at Abbeville to 'les intérêts troublés' (*Discours*, vol. vii, pp. 73 and 85).

2. See *R.F.*, 24 Nov.: 'une crise industrielle, commerciale et financière, laquelle touche à son paroxysme.' According to a police report of 6 Dec. these petitions were organised by 'l'hôtel de la Chaussée d'Antin' (A.P.P., BA/921).

3. *Cit.* Pisani-Ferry, *op. cit.*, p. 293.

4. *Annales, Chambre 1877*, vol. v, p. 54.

5. Duclerc in his note to the Press, dated 5 Dec., said that he had given in writing his view that a Congress would be 'le meilleur moyen de procurer à la Chambre une garantie efficace contre l'abus possible du droit de dissolution et de sauver en même temps la dignité de M. le président de la République' (*R.F.*, 7 Dec.). He may well have reflected Gambetta's view, but more cautiously. Marcère (*op. cit.*, pp. 187–9)

It is a strange story illustrative of Gambetta's love of a 'combinazione'. Did he really think that the Marshal would consent to such a proposal and was he really prepared to back it in order to weaken the executive, 'no matter what the ministry', or did he simply believe that it might at least lead to negotiations which would give him at last the interview with MacMahon which he had so much desired? There is no means of knowing. But MacMahon recorded his reply in his unpublished memoirs: 'I considered this proposal as inadmissible, and that I could not divest myself of a right which in a difficult situation might be the only means of rescuing the country from a great danger.'[1] Little did he realise that by his conduct during the last months he had already virtually divested himself and his successors of that right.

Meanwhile he had at last seen the Presidents of the two Chambers to allay their fears that he intended to disperse parliament by force. D'Audiffret had told him he could not count on the Senate and both he and Grévy urged him to take a ministry from the Left Centre. Swayed by their arguments, he turned once more to that elderly stalwart Dufaure. It looked as though he was about to submit, and once again men believed and hoped that at long last the crisis was ended. But the *République Française* was emphatic that 'the solution must be serious and not resemble the dangerous combinations which the preceding Chamber had made the mistake of accepting and the object of which had been to make way for the return of the Duc de Broglie and for adventures'.[2] When Freycinet consulted Gambetta about accepting a place in the proposed new cabinet Gambetta made his position plain:

> You should accept without hesitation. ... I do not mind whom M. Dufaure takes provided that he takes genuine Republicans. But he must not give way on principles! The Marshal claims to keep his ministers of Foreign Affairs, War and Marine in order, so he says, to keep them aloof from the vicissitudes of politics. That is an exercise of personal power to which we cannot subscribe. The ministry must be jointly responsible (*solidaire*); all its members must be in it on the same footing. Tell M. Dufaure that in the Chamber we can support only a Republican and clearly parliamentary cabinet.[3]

1. Quoted in Pisani-Ferry, *op. cit.*, p. 299.
2. Leader of 8 Dec., cf. also 9 Dec.
3. Freycinet, *Souvenirs 1848–1878*, pp. 384–5.

---

refers to de Lessep's presence at a dinner given by Girardin. He says that those present thought that de Lesseps was the only man who could induce MacMahon to submit and that in consequence 'il s'engagea à se faire auprès du Maréchal et du monde de l'Elysée ... l'organe de l'opinion qu'il recueillait partout'. He does not refer to a possible Congress in this connection or mention Gambetta as one of the guests at the dinner. But de Vogüé (*op. cit.*, p. 71) noted on 1 Dec.: 'Gambetta a fait tenir par Lesseps un ultimatum demandant le congrès et la révision.'

But the Marshal still wished, as before, and 'as a matter of principle' to reserve the right to select the holders of the three ministries in which he was specially interested. Neither side would give way and the negotiations broke down. Announcing the breakdown, owing to the conditions imposed by the Left,[1] the Havas agency reported that the Marshal had asked M. Batbie to form a cabinet.

The news caused fresh dismay and alarm in the Republican ranks. Batbie had been the original advocate in 1872 of a 'government of combat' and he was now ready to fight again and, if he could muster support, to take extreme measures—to promulgate the budget by decree, proclaim martial law and arrest the leading Republicans, beginning with Gambetta. The breakdown of the negotiations with Dufaure led the *République Française* to renew more insistently than ever its demand for MacMahon's resignation. This should have taken place at the outset; he had no choice now but resignation or 'crime', in other words a second dissolution which would be tantamount to a *coup d'état*.[2] Would he dare resort to 'crime'? The air was full of the most fantastic and contradictory rumours. MacMahon was reported to have told Pasquier that he had said his last word. *The Times* believed that all hope of making him 'see the perils of his conduct must be dismissed'.[3] The Committee of Eighteen was supposed to be in more or less permanent session. The Republican Union reiterated its resolve 'not to vote the Budget under any form or in any proportion whatever until complete satisfaction has been given to the national will'.[4] Guy de Maupassant wrote to Flaubert a tirade against 'this general [MacMahon] who ... has ruined the poor, exasperated the peaceful and pricked them on to civil war like the wretched bulls enraged in the Spanish arenas', and on the 12th Anatole de la Forge also told the exiled Ranc of imminent civil war: 'We are waiting for the solution of the crisis like people resolved to do their duty by descending armed into the streets to resist a military *coup d'état*.'[5]

In 1873, when the Republic appeared to be in danger of being ousted by a restoration of Monarchy, an old politician had rightly remarked: 'It all depends upon the army.'[6] Now more than ever this appeared to

1. The Committee of Eighteen denied having had 'aucun entretien ni aucune relation directe ou indirecte avec l'honorable M. Dufaure à l'occasion de la mission qui lui etait confiée' (*R.F.*, 10 Dec.).
2. Leaders of 9, 10, 12 and 13 Dec.
3. 14 Dec.
4. *R.F.*, 14 Dec. The Union met on the 12th, having already passed a similar resolution on 30 Nov. (*ibid.*, 1 Dec.).
5. G. de Maupassant, *Chroniques, études, Correspondance*, ed. R. Dumesnil and J. Loize (1938); Ranc, *Souvenirs — Correspondance*, p. 316.
6. See above, p. 172.

be true. The idea of a *coup d'état* had often been ventilated during the preceding six years and Gambetta had issued a warning to MacMahon on 24 June 1873—'the world would pass the severest judgement on the man who deserted legality to enter upon crime'.[1] But from then on until the Seize Mai he had always pooh-poohed the idea in public and generally also in private.[2] At Abbeville, however, on 10 June 1877 he had thought it right to issue a warning: 'We are at such a pass that we hear the cut-throats of December, who still exist, say that we shall only get out of it by going on to the end and that the end would be a violent coup, that is to say a crime. . . . I do not believe that anyone in this country can think of a *coup de force* and I say that in all circumstances such a *coup de force* would be condemned to a terrible expiation.' It was scandalous that the name of the national army should be mixed up with such infamous intrigue.[3] Meanwhile, as has been seen, he had already taken precautions to be as well informed as possible about the political sympathies of the officers.[4] Now, after the Seize Mai, there is little doubt that he and his friends began to take further soundings, to multiply their contacts with the army and to make contingency plans for possible resistance.[5] Was it of some resistance organisation that he was already thinking when in July, despite Léonie Léon's objections, he told her that everything, all the excesses of the reaction, all the rumours he heard, convinced him that his plan was right? 'Today it may seem premature, in some weeks' time it will be demanded, imposed, barely adequate.'[6] The letter is too allusive for a clear answer to be given, but a month later Gambetta was assuring Ranc that 'precautions still better than in 1873' had been taken against any attempts at a *coup d'état,* and a month later still a police agent reported that he (Gambetta) had had two lively discussions with Ferdinand Hérold about forming a secret resistance committee, the membership of which would be kept dark.[7]

It is clear that whereas in 1873 Gambetta was opposed to the idea of armed resistance he was ready to countenance it in 1877. Plans seem to have been made for the execution of the Loi Tréveneuc of 15 February 1872, should the parliament be illegally dissolved or prevented from

1. See above, p. 162.
2. But see above, p. 223, for an exception in Jan. 1875.
3. *Discours*, vol. vii, pp. 81–2.
4. See above, pp. 371–2.
5. See e.g. police report of 28 June: 'Gambetta s'occupe bien des élections, mais ce qu'il "travaille" surtout en ce moment c'est l'armée. Il a des relations très suivies avec des officiers supérieurs, voire même des généraux qui l'ont connu en 1870' (A.P.P., BA/919).
6. 25 July, L.G.
7. *Lettres*, No. 327, 20 Aug.; A.P.P., BA/921, 4 Oct.

meeting. This meant that the General Councils should meet at once to choose delegates to form a new Chamber. These delegates and/or Republican members of the existing Parliament still free to move were then to proceed in small groups to eastern France, almost certainly to Lille, the headquarters of General Clinchant, the one army corps commander who was a staunch Republican.[1] The young Joseph Reinach later claimed that he was one of those who helped to prepare the resistance, and the young Gabriel Hanotaux later recorded that Henri Martin had let him into the secret: 'The fight would be concentrated in the departments of the east and north.'[2] But from remarks Gambetta made to the American Minister in June it appears that he expected all the big towns to rise in support.[3] In the east he was alleged to have sounded Galliffet at Dijon who was regarded by the Republicans as absolutely reliable— he had told Gambetta that if the Republican majority in parliament went to Dijon he would defend the majority.[4] It also appears that the Duc D'Aumâle, who commanded at Besançon, had seen Gambetta and was likely to support the Republicans because of his fear that a coup could only too easily play into the hands of the Bonapartists.[5] Meanwhile Generals Farre, Saussier and Campenon had also promised Gambetta their support and it was asserted that he had seen General de Wimpffen in Paris and persuaded him, in the event of trouble, to accept the Ministry of War—Wimpffen had sent him a plan of the military measures which it would be necessary to take to ensure the success of 'the legal resistance'.[6] In Paris, Hanotaux, then still a student, recalled: 'We collected recruits. The Latin Quarter was determined to march. One name rallied us... that of Gambetta.'[7] An article in the *République Française* of 22 November

1. L. Delabrousse, *Joseph Magnin et son temps 1824–1910* (Paris, 1916), vol. ii, p. 269 n. Cf. R. Goblet, *art. cit.*, p. 379; Col. Connolly to Lord Lyons, 29 Nov. (F.O. 146, 1980). One of the reasons Connolly mentioned for the choice of Lille was 'its proximity to the frontier... thereby offering a safe line of retreat'.

2. Reinach, *op. cit.*, p. 68. Hanotaux, *Mon Temps*, vol. ii (Paris, 1938), p. 21.

3. Washburne, despatch of 8 June, in Katzenbach, 'Freycinet and the Army of Metropolitan France' (thesis, 1952), p. 231.

4. Mme Adam, *Après l'abandon*, p. 5; cf. Delabrousse, *op. cit.*, vol. ii, p. 269 n., and police report 22 May 1877, A.P.P., BA/919.

5. Scheurer-Kestner, *Journal inédit* (quoted in S. de Sacy, *op. cit.*, p. 350). M. Pellet 'Souvenirs sur Gambetta', *Revue de France*, 15 Nov. 1927, p. 287. Pellet's information came from 'Mme Léon'.

6. Delabrousse, *op. cit.*, vol. ii, p. 269 n. According to Mme Pisani-Ferry (*op. cit.*, p. 302), this plan involved 'sabotage des fils télégraphiques entre Versailles et la province, remise en place des maires, préfets et sous-préfets destitués par Fourtou, remplacement de la plupart des généraux, installation à Paris, au palais du Luxembourg, des députés républicains qui se constitueraient en Assemblée nationale, proclamation de la déchéance du maréchal de MacMahon et de ses ministres'.

7. *Mon Temps*, p. 21.

entitled 'The *Coup d'Etat* and the Army' seemed almost to welcome the idea of a clash, 'for this convulsion ... would be the last' and if (as was rumoured) Ducrot were to be appointed Minister of War to carry through a coup, 'he might keep the word he had failed to keep before, but it would not be by returning victorious'.[1]

But Gambetta was reckoning without Grévy. When informed of the plans afoot he minimised the danger of a coup and replied that, so long as there were regular authorities in existence, resistance should be by regular means. Any proposal which meant that deputies were contributing to civil war filled him with horror and he would never be a party to it.[2] His reply, said Goblet, one of the Committee of Eighteen, made a painful impression,[3] but what is not clear is whether Gambetta and his friends went ahead with their plans despite Grévy's attitude.[4]

Grévy was, however, right in playing down the risk of a *coup d'état*. Each side by crying wolf had exaggerated the other's nefarious intentions. No doubt there were civilians like Batbie and generals like Ducrot or Rochebouët himself who, given the necessary support and freedom of action, would have been prepared to carry out a coup. No doubt, when all was uncertain, the Rochebouët government had understandably instructed army commanders to provide emergency rations in case the Marshal finally decided to pursue a hard-line policy which met with resistance.[5] But Gambetta had been right when in August he had told Ranc that he thought a coup impossible because the army *leaders* were divided—'impossible to risk such an adventure without being obeyed and by *all*'.[6] *The Times* had been right, too, when, as early as 3 November,

---

1. During the siege of Paris Ducrot had rashly sworn to return from an attempted sortie 'victorious or dead'. The author of this interesting article said he had served under both MacMahon and Berthaut and thought them 'les derniers que je croirais capables de trahir le mandat qu'ils ont reçu'.

2. Marcère, *op. cit.*, vol. ii, p. 155.

3. Goblet, *art. cit.*, p. 382.

4. Pisani-Ferry, *op. cit.*, pp. 302–3, implies that they did not. The date of the interview with Grévy is uncertain.

5. Pisani-Ferry, *op. cit.*, p. 301.

6. *Lettres*, no. 327. The very interesting article 'Le coup d'état et l'Armée', R.F., 22 Nov., by a man who had served under both MacMahon and Berthaut and claimed to be 'en mesure de bien connaître les sentiments de l'armée' gave an analysis of army opinion which closely corresponded with that in the secret memorandum compiled earlier for Gambetta's use (see above, pp. 371–2). This strongly suggests either that he was the author of the memorandum or that he had had access to it. The following parts of the analysis are worth quoting: 'Les généraux de division sont, quelques-uns légitimistes, quelques-uns orléanistes, le plus grand nombre, et de beaucoup, bona-partistes. Si l'opinion républicaine commence à compter des adeptes parmi les généraux de brigade, c'est encore en petit nombre: leur classement, comme opinion politique, est à peu près le même que celui des généraux de division (*contd.*)

it had pointed out that the circumstances were not the same as in 1851: even if Marshal MacMahon were inclined to emulate the deeds of Prince Louis Napoleon he could not, it said, 'command the requisite weapons', Berthaud [*sic*] (then still Minister of War) was no Saint-Arnaud, Voisin, the Prefect of Police, no Maupas, and Ladmirault, the Military Governor of Paris, no Magnan. 'But, of course,' it had continued, 'he is too honourable to use them even if they lay ready to his hands.' And here, too, it was right—at least in the end. MacMahon had no personal ambition and he had a horror of doing anything illegal. Had he been assured that a majority of the Senate would have been ready to grant him a second dissolution, he would no doubt have dissolved parliament because, although the Left would have denounced dissolution as a *coup d'état*, he would have regarded it as entirely legal and within his constitutional rights. Thus the *République Française* was right in hammering away at the Orleanist Senators and reminding them of their terrible responsibility were they to favour dissolution. They were the weak point in the Conservative armour. They refused to support Batbie and when the Marshal boggled at the illegality of proclaiming the martial law Batbie deemed essential, and when he was also ultimately convinced that he would be acting illegally if he attempted to collect taxes without a vote from the Chamber, the end had come. There was no need for the Republicans to invoke the Loi Tréveneuc, which was not conjured up again until 1943.[1] The Marshal realised at last that he must resign or submit and he told his ministers that he intended to resign. But they implored him to stay: he consented against his better judgement, and had to submit.

1. Thomson, *Democracy in France*, p. 98.

'Parmi les colonels, lieutenant-colonels et chefs de bataillon, il y a encore quelques légitimistes, quelques orléanistes, quelques bonapartistes: tout le reste est républicain, et dans une proportion d'autant plus grande que le grade est moins élevé.

'Parmi les capitaines, lieutenants et sous-lieutenants, il n'y a plus d'autres bonapartistes que les Corses, d'autres légitimistes que les élèves de la rue des Postes et ils ne le sont pas tous; le reste dans la proportion de 99 sur 100, est républicain.'

The Times special correspondent in the provinces (*The Times*, 5 Nov.) had gone further in his reports of the army's loyalty to the Republic; 'Wherever I have been I have constantly heard this language: "We are in daily communication with the officers of the garrison, and we are perfectly certain that the mass of them will be no parties to a crime against the nation. A very large proportion of the younger officers are known to be Republicans, and in every command there are Colonels and general officers who are known to be with us." ' Cf. earlier (14 Oct.) the Vicomte de Vogüé's note in his diary at La Fère where he was doing a course as a reserve artillery officer: 'Je suis frappé de l'attitude des officiers . . . de leurs voeux républicains' (F. de Vogüé, *op. cit.*, p. 60); cf. also Clamageran's observation (7 Sept.) that most of the sapper officers were Republican (Clamageran, *Correspondance, 1849–1902*, p. 409).

Submission meant following the advice of the Orleanist Senators and having recourse once more to that 'glorious veteran', as Freycinet called him,[1] the indispensable Dufaure. This time the surrender was complete and unconditional. Dufaure chose all his ministers and the Marshal reluctantly had to sign a message which had been drafted for him by three members of the cabinet and formally approved by Gambetta before being submitted for signature. It was an adroit statement of the Republicans' interpretation of the constitution:

> The elections of 14 October have once again demonstrated the country's confidence in Republican institutions.
>
> In conformity with parliamentary rules, I have formed a Cabinet chosen from the two Chambers and composed of men who are resolved to defend and maintain these institutions by sincere application of the constitutional laws. . . . The exercise of the right of dissolution . . . cannot be erected into a system of government. I thought it my duty to make use of this right and I accept the country's response.
>
> The constitution of 1875 established a parliamentary Republic in which it provided that I should be irresponsible while instituting the collective and individual responsibility of the ministers.
>
> Thus our respective duties and rights are defined . . .
>
> The end of this crisis will be the beginning of a new era of prosperity. All the public powers will contribute to its development. The agreement brought about between the Senate and the Chamber of Deputies which is now certain of regularly attaining the end of its term, will enable the completion of the great legislative labours demanded by the public interest. The Universal Exhibition will soon open . . . and we shall give the world fresh proof of the vitality of our country.

Gambetta had won, but what did he think of the victory? He was the parliamentary leader of the majority, but once again he was not in the government, and he had told Freycinet a few days earlier that Dufaure's policy was not his: 'But after the upheavals France has experienced we must put up with it.'[2] As on the morrow of the passing of the Wallon statement which 'made' the Republic in 1875, the *République Française* was once again cumbrously but distinctly cautious: 'Without abandoning ourselves to unmixed satisfaction, for all danger has not yet been averted, it would not seem to us right not to state that the cabinet formed by M. Dufaure appears (*se présente*) in circumstances well adapted to secure the favour of public opinion'; but, it added, 'this is enough for us to hope for a prompt and decisive victory'.[3] No doubt for Gambetta the

1. *Op. cit.*, p. 381.
2. Freycinet, *op. cit.*, pp. 384–5.
3. Leader of 16 Dec. Cf. (17 Dec.) report in *The Times* of a remark by a member of

test would come in the garnering of the spoils, in what way he could govern France and what use could be made of the fruits of victory. But that is a subject for another volume. Meanwhile he replied to someone who asked if he was satisfied with MacMahon's message: 'How should I be dissatisfied when I see so grievous a crisis so happily ended? It is the first victory gained by the legislative power over the proceedings of personal power, and that without any revolution, riot, or disturbance. That is a new event in our history and all due to Democratic institutions. If you are not satisfied, you are very hard to please.'[1]

1. *The Times*, 17 Dec.

'the Extreme Left' after the close of the sitting at which the Marshal's message was read: 'We are like men who have taken possession of a hostile town, but are afraid of the explosion of a mine on entering it. When we know there is really no mine there, we shall be more enthusiastic.'

Appendix

Extract from an interview with Gambetta which appeared in the *New York Herald*, 9 January 1873.

Gambetta's Ideas of a French Constitution

This criticism upon the English constitution encouraged your correspondent to ask M. Gambetta whether he himself had elaborated any scheme of constitutional government for France as the idea of the Left when it came to power.

'Yes,' said M. Gambetta; 'I have my ideas, and if you have time I will give them to you.'

Your correspondent added that he knew of nothing concerning France that would be more interesting to the American people.

'Well,' he answered, 'briefly these. Of course we must have a President. I will never consent to the government of France by a triple consulate or a directory or a general commission or anything of that kind. There should be an executive head to France—a President, who should be elected for a term of four or five years. He should not be elected by direct universal suffrage, as hitherto. I think there is a better plan than that for France. We have seen national misfortune come from the election of a President by the direct universal suffrages of the people. I mean after 1848. In America, where you practically elect a President by the direct national vote, it was not so intended by the founders of the American constitution. They never foresaw, nor do I think they ever intended, that the electoral colleges should have what we call in France a *mandat impératif* forced upon them in the matter of choosing a President.' The response was made to this criticism that in the United States political affairs were so much in the hands of parties—skilfully organised and obedient in every way—that virtually the electoral colleges had their decrees indicated when they were nominated in the conventions; that no man of honour after accepting such a nomination, and receiving an election, would violate the pledge, and that

462

they were voted for by the people upon the express idea that they would respect their pledges!

'But,' said M. Gambetta, 'they are puppets. The election is the direct act of the nation. There is the difference that in France the nation votes as one State, while the States so vote in America that a President might be elected by a majority of electoral votes and a minority of popular voice. I think Lincoln was a minority President. Now I should avoid what seems to be a difficulty in the United States, and what was certainly a difficulty in France, in our "universal suffrage", as we called it, by having the National Assembly elect the President. I would have also a Grand Council of State, somewhat like the American Senate, and with similar functions. It would resemble the Grand *Conseil d'Etat* in Switzerland, except that it should not be chosen as there, by universal suffrage. One half of the members should be named by the Assembly and one half by the President. I would make this council about as large as your Senate—eighty members in all—forty named by the Assembly, forty by the Executive. I would direct that no nominations be made from the Assembly. I think this council would act as a great conservative, strengthening force, a balance wheel as it were, acting as a check upon an Executive with despotic aspirations and a sedative upon an angry and unreasonable Assembly. This council should be the chief seat of power in France and its term of office should be longer than that of the Assembly. As for the Assembly I would favour a general election every two years. I would not favour a partial election or any scheme of renewal. I would have the Ministers among the council. They should not be allowed to take part in the debates of the Lower House. They should have an existence and a responsibility apart. Whenever the House desired to interpellate the government or whenever the government wished to communicate with the Assembly delegates could be chosen by the Council of State to communicate with the Assembly. But I would not allow Ministers to act as delegates. Furthermore, carrying out the idea the Americans preserve in confirming appointments to the service, I would give this general council an authoritative voice in all great state appointments—ambassadors, for instance, the designation of generals to important commands and so on. So it would come to have an influence in the direction of foreign affairs and in the appointment of the judiciary.'

'You do not favour, then' said the correspondent 'an elective judiciary?'

'No,' said M. Gambetta, with a quiet meaning smile, 'nor am I encouraged to favour it by the results of an elective judiciary in America.'

Your correspondent explained that even in America, in the Supreme Court of the United States, for instance, and all national Courts, there was no election of judges, and that with us it was an experiment, as many things were experimented in France and elsewhere. Passing from this the question was asked as to how M. Gambetta would arrange the National Assembly?

A Smaller Assembly Needed

'The first thing to do with the Assembly,' said M. Gambetta, 'is to greatly decrease its members. I presume it is really the largest Assembly in the world, and I am afraid enjoys the distinction of being the most turbulent. We do not require 750 members. The presence of so many gives opportunity to discord, intrigue and needless party divisions. We have too many parties and shades of parties. So in planning a new and permanent republican constitution I would provide for an Assembly of about four hundred members. This would be sufficient to represent the country, and would give us peace and quiet in many cases where peace seems to be impossible now.'

Your correspondent referred to the mode of voting, mentioning Paris as an instance, where the electors voted all in a heap for forty-three members on one ticket, electing all or defeating all, having so many candidates that few electors could know their real merit, and asked whether this would be changed in the proposed plan.

'Certainly,' said M. Gambetta. 'In Paris there should be voting by *arrondissement*. I would provide that each *arrondissement* should be represented in proportion to its population, and not arbitrarily, as under the Empire. These arbitrary imperial divisions were not honest. They were meant to influence votes. I would make representation fair, each member representing so many people, and have the term like that in America, for two years. This would bring the Assembly close to France, and give France the chance of expressing her will. The misfortune of France has been and is now that the nation is antagonised by the legislative power, and there is no way out of the problem but by revolution. This danger would be increased by the scheme of partial elections and renewal, and that is why I am so bitterly opposed to it. Such a scheme seems to absorb all the defects. An Assembly must represent the country fairly or it is not a National Assembly. Now, if an Assembly really represents the average prevalent public opinion of France, then no election is necessary. But if an Assembly like the one now in session, as I regard it, does not represent the country, then of what use is partial election? The country could not speak by a partial election, and the result would be to swell the minority and bring out in more glowing colours the discrepancy between the Assembly as it now exists and general public opinion. I cannot think of an invention more absurd than this of partial election. It springs from an apprehension that is as baseless as a dream—that general elections would disturb the public peace in France.'

No Ministerial Responsibility

Your correspondent said that the impression made upon him by M. Gambetta was that he did not approve of the doctrine of Ministerial responsibility. 'I do not,' M. Gambetta said, 'so far as France is concerned. We are a peculiar people, and our faults of character—for each nation has its virtues and faults—make any Ministerial responsibility impossible. It would lead to personal intrigues and strifes of the most deplorable character. Its forty years of existence in France shows that. It is not suited to our habits or our temperament. I am not discussing Ministerial responsibility as an abstract political principle; I only think it is not suited to France. What we want here is a strong executive. There can be no true government here with that condition wanting—no government that can inspire respect abroad and preserve peace at home. I am convinced that a constitution without this feature would be like a temple of sand. Now, a strong executive means, for France, stability, power, peace. This we want. France suffers more than any but a Frenchman would believe from these periodical strifes at Versailles. No nation, especially one so uneasy and sensitive as France, can exist in peace under the strain produced by a condition of affairs in which we may have a new President and a new policy in twenty-four hours.'

Map 1   The Departments

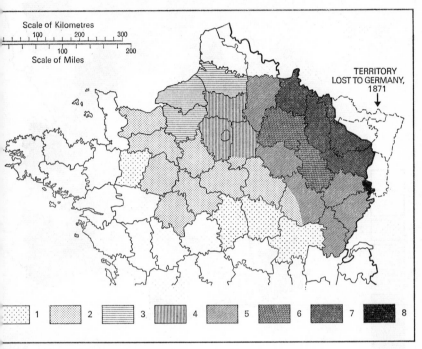

Map 2   The German occupation 1871–73

Departments evacuated: 1 Immediately after the armistice
                         2 In March–April 1871
                         3 In July 1871
                         4 In September 1871
                         5 In October 1871
                         6 In November 1872
                         7 In July 1873
                         8 On 2 August 1873

(Map devised by G. Dupeux)

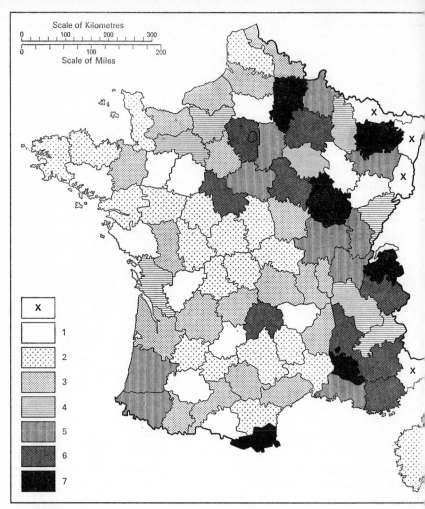

Map 3 The General Election of 8 February 1871. Republicans elected in the different departments.

1 None
2 Only one
3 A minority
4 Half
5 A majority
6 All but one
7 All

This map does not take account of the multiple elections, resignations and unseatings which mutilated the representation of some departments. In the departments marked with a cross the cleavage between Republicans and Conservatives had no significance in 1871 because of local issues, namely loyalty to France in Alsace-Lorraine and separatism at Nice in the Alpes-Maritimes.

(From J. Gouault, *Comment la France est devenue républicaine. Les éléctions générales et partielles à l'Assemblée Nationale 1870–1875*, F.N.S.P., Colin, 1954)

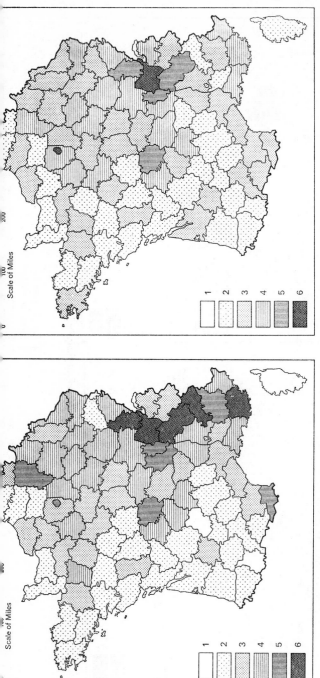

Map 4 *Left*: Republican votes in the elections of 20 February 1876
       Right: Republican votes in the elections of 14 October 1877

Percentage of the votes cast:

1 Less than 40%   4 From 60 to 70%
2 From 40 to 50%   5 From 70 to 80%
3 From 50 to 60%   6 Over 80%

(Maps by A. Lancelot based on H. Avenel *Comment vote la France, Dix-huit ans de suffrage universel, 1876–1893*, Quantin, 1894.)

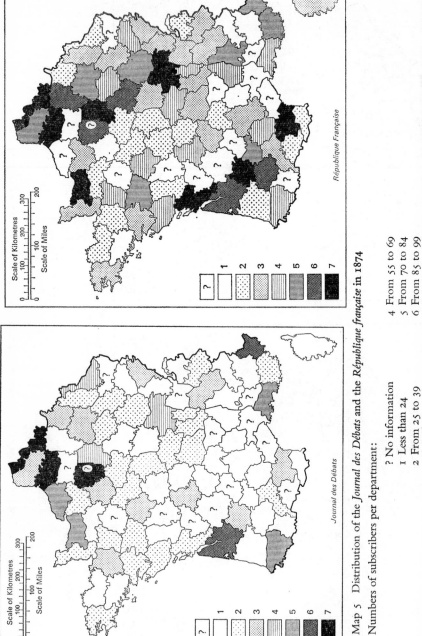

Map 5 Distribution of the *Journal des Débats* and the *République française* in 1874
Numbers of subscribers per department:

? No information		4 From 55 to 69
1 Less than 24		5 From 70 to 84
2 From 25 to 39		6 From 85 to 99

Journal des Débats

République Française

Map 6   Places associated with Gambetta 1838–77.
Before his return to France June 1871, thus: Tours
Speeches—June 1871 to December 1875, thus: *Auxerre*
Speeches—1876 to 1877, thus: ORANGE
During all three periods, thus: **Marseilles**

Bibliography

Manuscript Collections

I. *Gambetta papers*

1. Gambetta's letters to Léonie Léon (transcripts in the possession of M. Jacques Desmarest)
2. Léonie Léon's letters to Gambetta (transcripts in the Library of the Assemblée Nationale)

The correspondence between Gambetta and Léonie Léon has undergone strange vicissitudes. According to Léonie, Gambetta wrote some 3,000 letters to her. Halévy and Pillias, who in 1938 published 593 of his letters to various correspondents (including 113 to Léonie) during the period from 26 December 1868 to 20 November 1882, believed that most of the 3,000 were destroyed by Léonie Léon herself. The exception was a quantity of between 500 and 600: these she bequeathed to Georges Pallain who burnt them in 1922. The only ones of which the text was thought to have survived were 112 which Léonie had copied in quintuplicate, 'in order to demonstrate the importance of the role she herself had played', together with seven others. Copies of the 112 were transmitted by 'friendly hands' to the *Revue de Paris* which published them in 1906–07 with the consent of Mme Léris-Gambetta (Gambetta's surviving sister, Benedetta). In fact, however, more than 600 letters escaped what M. Jacques Chastenet has called 'this double auto-da-fé' and they are, in his words, 'preserved in a safe place'. They were apparently given by Léonie Léon to her confessor, the Dominican R. P. Janvier. At least one typescript copy of them was made, the one used by M. Chastenet in his book on Gambetta published in 1968, and this I have also been able to use, since it was very kindly lent to me by its owner, M. Jacques Desmarest.

It was also for a long time thought that virtually all Léonie's letters to Gambetta had been burnt. But this, too, was an erroneous belief, for in 1938 the Library of what was then the Chamber of Deputies and is now the National Assembly acquired 496 of these letters. Once again, however, fate intervened to destroy or render the originals inaccessible. In 1940 the Germans made off with them and they have not been found again. Fortunately, however, typescript copies ('parfaitement authentiques' in the words of one of the librarians) had been made. These letters were the subject of a lively account by Gambetta's kinsman, P.-B. Gheusi, in the second volume of his *Cinquante ans de Paris* (1938) and some of them were subsequently printed *in extenso* by M. André Beauguitte in his book *Le Tiroir secret* (1968).

3. *Gambetta pp.* (Ministère des Affaires Etrangères)

II. *Other private papers*

4. Juliette Adam pp. (Bibliothèque Nationale)
5. Jules Bravard, diary (Assemblée Nationale)
6. Chaudordy pp. (Ministère des Affaires Etrangères)
7. Louis Nordheim pp. (in the possession of M. Rupert Nordheim)
8. Marcellin Pellet pp. (Assemblée Nationale)
9. Ernest Picard pp. (Bibliothèque Nationale)
10. Joseph Reinach pp. (Bibliothèque Nationale)
11. Rothschild pp. (Newsletters from 'C. de B.' in the possession of the Rothschild family, St Swithin's Lane, London)
12. Scheurer-Kestner pp. (Bibliothèque Nationale)

III. *Official Collections*

13. Archives de la Préfecture de Police (Dossiers Gambetta *et al.*)
14. Foreign Office papers (Public Record Office)

Printed Sources

1. *Official publications and reference works*

Almanach National
Annales de l'Assemblée Nationale 1871–75
Annales de la Chambre et du Sénat 1876–77
L'Année politique, ed. A. Daniel

Annuaire de l'Armée française
Annuaire diplomatique et consulaire de la République Française
Biographie des sénateurs et des députés, ed. F. Ribeyre, Paris, 1877
Collection complète des lois . . ., ed. J. B. Duvergier
Dictionnaire universel des contemporains, 5th edn, ed. L. G. Vapereau, Paris, 1880
Documents diplomatiques français, Série I, vols i and ii, Paris, 1929, 1930
I Documenti diplomatici Italiani, Seconda Serie, vol. iii, Rome, 1969
Die Grosse Politik der europäischen Kabinette, vol. i, ed. J. Lepsius, A. M. Bartholdy and F. Thimme, Berlin 1927

Memoirs, speeches, correspondence and other contemporary works

ADAM, JULIETTE. *Après l'abandon de la revanche*, Paris, 1910
ADAM, JULIETTE. *Mes Angoisses et nos luttes (1871–1873)*, Paris, 1907
ADAM, JULIETTE. *Nos amitiés politiques avant l'abandon de la revanche*, Paris, 1908
AUDIFFRET-PASQUIER, DUC D'. *La Maison de France et l'Assemblée Nationale: Souvenirs, 1871–1873*, Paris, 1938
AVENEL, GEORGES. *Lundis révolutionnaires, 1871–1874*, Paris, 1875
B., C. DE. *Letters from Paris, 1870–1875, written by C. de B., a political informant, to the head of the London House of Rothschild*, ed. R. Henrey, London, 1942
BAC, F. *Intimités de la IIIe République. De Monsieur Thiers au Président Carnot*, Paris, 1935
BALLEYGUIER, E., *see* FIDUS
BARAGNON, PIERRE. *Lettre de Pierre Baragnon à Léon Gambetta*, Paris, 1876
BARAIL, GEN. F. C. DU. *Mes Souvenirs*, vol. iii, *1864–1879*, Paris, 1896
BARODET, D. *L'Election Parisienne du 27 avril 1873*, Lyons, 1903
BEAUGUITTE, A. *Le Tiroir secret. Récit historique avec lettres de Léonie Léon*, Bar-le-Duc, 1968
BIENVENU, LÉON, *see* MARTIAL, G.
BIGOT, C. *La Fin de l'anarchie*, Paris 1878
BLANC, L. *Histoire de la constitution du 25 février, 1875*, Paris, 1882
BLANC, L. *Questions d'aujourd'hui et de demain*, 2e série, Paris, 1874
BOSQ, PAUL. *Souvenirs de l'Assemblée Nationale, 1871–75*, Paris, 1908
BROGLIE, DUC DE. *Mémoires du Duc de Broglie*, vol. ii, *1871–1875*, Paris, 1941
CAILLAUX, J. *Mes Mémoires*, vol. i, *Ma jeunesse orgueilleuse, 1863–1909*, Paris, 1942
CAMBON, PAUL. *Correspondance*, vol. i, Paris, 1940

MARQUIS DE CASTELLANE, ANTOINE. *Men and Things of My Time*, London, 1911

CAVALIER, GEORGES. *Gambetta*, Brussels, 1875

CHESNELONG, C. *L'Avènement de la République 1873–1875. Mémoires publiés par son petit-fils*, Paris, 1934

CHESNELONG, C. *Les Derniers jours de l'empire et le gouvernement de M. Thiers*, Paris, 1932

CLAMAGERAN, J. J. *Correspondance, 1849–1902*, Paris, 1906

CLARETIE, JULES. *Histoire de la révolution de 1870–1*, Paris, 1872

CLARETIE, JULES. *Portraits contemporains*, Paris, 1873–75

CLAVEAU, A. *Souvenirs politiques et parlementaires d'un témoin*, Paris, 1913

CRISPI, F. *The Memoirs of Francesco Crispi*, ed. T. Palamenghi-Crispi, vol. ii, London, 1912. 'La conferenza pel disarmo' (*Nuova Antologia*, May 1899)

DAUDET, E. *Souvenirs de la présidence du Maréchal de MacMahon*, Paris, 1880

DELAFOSSE, J. *Figures contemporaines*, Paris, 1899

DELPIT, M., *see* VALADES, P. B. DES

DEPASSE, H. *Célébrités contemporaines*, Paris, 1883–88

DUFF, M. E. GRANT. *Notes from a Diary, 1873–1881*, vol. i, London, 1898

DUMAS, ALEXANDRE, fils. *Nouvelles lettres sur les choses du jour*, Paris, 1872

DUPANLOUP, MGR. *Lettre de M. l'évêque d'Orléans à M. Gambetta*, Orléans, n.d.

EUGÉNIE, EMPRESS. *Lettres familières de l'impératrice Eugénie*, vol. ii, ed. the Duke of Alba, Paris, 1935

FERRY, J. *Discours et opinions de Jules Ferry*, ed. P. Robiquet, vol. ii, Paris, 1894

FERRY, J. *Lettres 1846–1893*, Paris, 1914

FIDUS (BALLEYGUIER, E.). *Journal de Fidus*, vol. iii, *L'Essai loyal*, Paris, 1890

FLAUBERT, GUSTAVE. *Correspondance*, vol. vi, Paris, 1930

FREYCINET, C. DE. *Souvenirs de 1843–1878*, 6th edn, Paris, 1914

GAMBETTA, L. *Discours et plaidoyers politiques de M. Gambetta*, ed. J. Reinach, 7 vols, Paris, 1881–2

GAMBETTA, L. *Lettres de Gambetta, 1868–1882*, ed. D. Halévy and E. Pillias, Paris, 1938

GAUTIER, H. *Carnet d'un journaliste pendant le seize-mai*, Paris, 1881

GÉRARD, A. *La Vie d'un diplomate sous la troisième République. Mémoires d'Auguste Gérard*, Paris, 1928

GHEUSI, P. B. *Gambetta par Gambetta*, Paris, 1909

GILL, A. *Le Bulletin de Vote*, Paris, 1877

GIRARDIN, E. DE. *La Question d'argent, questions de l'année 1876*, Paris, 1877

GIRAUDEAU, F. *Bleus, Blancs, Rouges: Lettres réactionnaires adressées aux Directeurs du Paris-Journal par un Provincial*, Paris, 1873

GOBLET, R. 'Souvenirs de ma vie politique', *Revue politique et parlementaire*, 10 Sept., 1928

GOLTZ, C. VON DER. *Léon Gambetta und seine Armeen*, Berlin, 1877

GONTAUT-BIRON, A. A. E. VICOMTE DE. *Mon Ambassade en Allemagne, 1872–1873*, ed. A. Dreux, Paris, 1906. *Dernières années de l'ambassade en Allemagne de M. de Gontaut-Biron*, ed. A. Dreux, Paris, 1907

HALÉVY, D. *Le Courrier de M. Thiers d'après les documents conservés au département des manuscrits de la Bibliothèque Nationale*, Paris, 1921

HALÉVY, L. *Notes et souvenirs 1871–1872*, Paris, 1899

HALÉVY, L. 'Les Carnets de Ludovic Halévy', II, *Revue des Deux Mondes*, 1 Feb. 1937.

HALÉVY, L. *Trois dîners avec Gambetta*, Paris, 1929

HANOTAUX, G. *Mon Temps*, vol. i, *De l'Empire à la République;* vol. ii, *La Troisième République, Gambetta et Jules Ferry*, Paris, 1933, 1938

HANSEN, J. *Les Coulisses de la diplomatie. Quinze ans à l'étranger (1864–1879)*, Paris, 1880

HOHENLOHE–SCHILLINGSFUERST, PRINCE CHLODWIG OF. *Memoirs of Prince Chlodwig of Hohenlohe–Schillingsfuerst*, ed. F. Curtius, vol. ii, London, 1906

HUGO, VICTOR. *L'Année terrible*, Paris, 1872

JOLLIVET, G. *Souvenirs d'un Parisien*, Paris, 1928

LACOMBE, CHARLES DE. *Journal politique de Charles de Lacombe, député à l'Assemblée Nationale*, ed. A. Hélot, vol. i, Paris, 1907

LAFFITTE, JULES. *Gambetta intime, sa vie et sa fortune*, 2nd edn, Paris, 1879

LALANCE, A. *Mes Souvenirs, 1830–1914*, Paris, 1914

LANFREY, P. *Correspondance*, vol. ii, Paris, 1885

LAUGEL, A. 'Le Maréchal de MacMahon et le 16 mai', *Revue de Paris*, 1 Aug. 1926

LAUR, F. *Le Coeur de Gambetta*, Paris, 1907

LAVERTUJON, A. *Gambetta inconnu*, Bordeaux, 1905

LITTRÉ, F. *De l'Etablissement de la troisième République*, Paris, 1880

MACKIE, A. *Italy and France. An editor's holiday*, London, 1874

MARCÈRE, E. L. G. H. DE. *Histoire de la République de 1876 à 1879*, vol. i, Paris, 1908

MARCÈRE, E. L. G. H. DE. *L'Assemblée Nationale de 1871*, Paris, 1904

'MARTIAL, G.' (*pseudonym for* LÉON BIENVENU). *50 Lettres Républicaines de Gervais Martial ouvrier recueillies par Touchatout*, Paris, 1875

MAUPASSANT, G. DE. *Chroniques, études, correspondance*, ed. R. Dumesnil and J. Loize, Paris, 1938

MEAUX, VICOMTE DE. *Souvenirs politiques, 1871–1877*, Paris, 1905

MILLAUD, EDOUARD. *Le Journal d'un parlementaire (de l'Empire à la République, mai 1864–février 1875)*, Paris, 1914

NAQUET, A. *La République radicale*, Paris, 1873

NEWTON, LORD. *Lord Lyons, a record of British diplomacy*, London, n.d., Nelson Library of Notable Books

OLLIVIER, EMILE. *Lettres de l'exil 1871–1874*, Paris, 1921

ORDINAIRE, D. *La République, c'est l'ordre*, Paris, 1872

PELLET, M. 'Souvenirs sur Gambetta', *Revue de France*, 15 Nov. 1927

PELLETAN, C. *Le Théâtre de Versailles. L'Assemblée au jour le jour du 24 mai au 25 février*, Paris, 1875

PESSARD, H. *Mes Petits papiers*, 2e série, *1871–1873*, Paris, 1888

RANC, A. *Souvenirs-Correspondance, 1831–1908*, Paris, 1913

RANC, O. *De Bordeaux à Versailles*, Paris, 1877

REINACH, J. 'Gambetta (souvenirs personnels)', *Mercure de France*, 1 Jan. 1918

REINACH, J. *La République ou le Gâchis*, Paris, 1877

REINACH, J. *Gambetta Orateur*, Paris, 1884

REINACH, J. *La Vie politique de Léon Gambetta*, Paris, 1918

REINACH, J. *Léon Gambetta*, Paris, 1884

REINACH, J. *Récits et portraits contemporains*, Paris, 1915

RÉMUSAT, C. DE. *Mémoires de ma vie*, vol. v, Paris, n.d.

RENAN, E. *La Réforme intellectuelle et morale de la France*, ed. P. E. Charvet, Cambridge, 1950

ROCHEFORT, H. *Les Aventures de ma vie*, 5 vols, Paris, 1896–98

ROUQUETTE, J. *Célébrités contemporaines*, Paris, 1872–73

SAINT-VALRY, G. DE. *Souvenirs et réflexions politiques. Documents pour servir à l'histoire contemporaine*, 2 vols, Paris, 1886

SARDOU, VICTORIEN. *Rabagas, Comédie en cinq actes, en prose*, Paris, 1872

SCHEURER-KESTNER, A. *Souvenirs de Jeunesse*, ed. M. Pellet, Paris, 1905

SCHEURER-KESTNER, A. '*La République Française*, journal de Gambetta (Extraits du journal de Scheurer-Kestner)', *Etudes de Presse*, vol. xii, nos 22–23, 1960

SIMON, JULES. *Le Gouvernement de M. Thiers, 8 février 1871–24 mai 1873*, 2 vols, Paris, 1878

SIMON, JULES. *La Politique Radicale*, 2nd edn, Paris, 1968

SIMON, JULES. *Le Soir de ma journée*, ed. G. Simon, Paris, 1902

SMALLEY, G. W. *London Letters and some others*, vol. i, London, 1890

SOCIÉTÉ D'INSTRUCTION RÉPUBLICAINE, LA. *La Question militaire et la République*, 1872

SPULLER, E. *Figures Disparues. Portraits contemporains politiques et littéraires*, 3 vols, Paris, 1891–94

TAINE, H. *Life and Letters of H. Taine, 1870–1892*, London, 1908
TOURNIER, A. *Gambetta, souvenirs anecdotiques*, Paris, 1893
VALADES, P.-B. DES. *Martial Delpit, député à l'Assemblée Nationale. Journal et correspondance*, Paris, 1897
VERLAINE, PAUL. *Invectives*, Paris, 1896
VINOLS DE MONTFLEURY, BARON J. G. DE. *Mémoires politiques d'un Membre de l'Assemblée Nationale Constituante de 1871*, Le Puy, 1882
VOGÜÉ, VICOMTE E. M. DE. *Journal Paris, Saint-Petersbourg 1877–1883*, ed. F. de Vogüé, Paris, 1932
WASHBURNE, E. B. *Recollections of a Minister to France 1869–1877*, London, 1887
WEISS, J. J. *Combat Constitutionnel, 1868–1886*, Paris, 1893

Secondary Works

(a) Books

ANDREW, C. *Théophile Delcassé and the Making of the Entente Cordiale*, London, 1968
ALLAIN-TARGÉ, H. *La République sous l'Empire*, Paris, 1939
AVENEL, HENRI. *Histoire de la presse française, 1789 jusqu'à nos jours*, Paris, 1900
BARRAL, P. *Le Département de l'Isère sous la Troisième République*, Paris, 1962
BARRAL, P. *Les Fondateurs de la Troisième République*, Paris, 1968
BARRAL, P. *Les Périer dans l'Isère au XIXe siècle*, Paris, 1964
BARTHÉLEMY, A. *Gambetta à San Sebastian*, Niort, 1930
BEAU DE LOMÉNIE, E. *Les Responsabilités des dynasties bourgeoises*, vol. i, Paris, 1948
BELLESSORT, A. *Les Intellectuels et l'avènement de la Troisième République (1871–1875)*, Paris, 1931
BLOCH, C. *Les Relations entre la France et la Grande-Bretagne (1871–1878)*, Paris, 1955
BLUM, L. *L'Oeuvre de Léon Blum, 1937–1940*, Paris, 1965
BÖHMER, B. *Frankreich zwischen Republik und Monarchie in der Bismarckzeit*, Munich, 1966
BONNER, H. B. *Charles Bradlaugh. A record of his life and work*, vol. i, 2nd edn, London, 1895
BOUNIOLS, G. *Thiers au pouvoir*, Paris, 1921
BOURGIN, G. *Gambetta*, vol. vii in *Les Grands Orateurs Républicains*, Monaco, 1949–50

BOUVIER, J. *Le Crédit Lyonnais de 1868 à 1882*, vol. i, Paris, 1967

BOUVIER, J. *Les Rothschild*, Paris, 1967

BRABANT, F. H. *The Beginning of the Third Republic in France*, London, 1940

BRULAT, P. *Histoire populaire de Léon Gambetta*, Paris, 1909

BURY, J. P. T. *Gambetta and the National Defence*, London, 1936

CAPÉRAN, L. *Histoire contemporaine de la laïcité française*, vol. i, Paris, 1957

CARROLL, E. M. *French Public Opinion and Foreign Affairs, 1870–1914*, New York, 1931

CARTIER, R. *Léon Gambetta*, Lyon, 1946

CHALLENER, R. D. *The French Theory of the Nation in Arms, 1866–1939*, New York, 1955

CHANLAINE, P. *Gambetta, père de la République*, Paris, 1932

CHAPMAN, GUY. *The Third Republic of France, The First Phase, 1872–1894*, London, 1962

CHARNAY, J. P. *Société militaire et suffrage politique en France depuis 1789*, Paris, 1964

CHASTENET, J. *Gambetta*, Paris, 1968

CHASTENET, J. *L'Enfance de la Troisième 1870–1879*, Paris, 1952

CHAUDORDY, COMTE J. B. A. D. DE. *La France à la suite de la guerre de 1870–1871*, Paris, 1887

CHEVALIER, L. *La Formation de la population parisienne au XIXe siècle*, Paris, 1950

CHEVALLIER, J. J. *Histoire des institutions politiques de la France de 1789 jusqu'à nos jours*, Paris, 1952

COLLINS, I. *The Government and the Newspaper Press in France, 1814–1881*, Oxford, 1959

CARRIÈRE, F. AND PINCHEMEL, P. *Le Fait urbain en France*, Paris, 1963

COMPAYRÉ, G. *Jean Macé et l'instruction obligatoire en France*, 2nd edn, Paris, 1902

CONTAMINE, H. *La Revanche 1871–1914*, Paris, 1957

DANSETTE, A. *Le Boulangisme 1886–1890*, Paris, 1938

DANSETTE, A. *Histoire religieuse de la France contemporaine: sous la IIIème République*, Paris, 1951

DAUDET, E. *Souvenirs et révélations. Histoire diplomatique de l'alliance franco–russe, 1873–93*, Paris, 1894

DAVID, R. *La Troisième République. Soixante ans de politique et d'histoire, de 1871 à nos jours*, Paris, 1934

DELABROUSSE, L. *Joseph Magnin et son temps, 1824–1910*, vol. ii, Paris, 1916

DELABROUSSE, L. *Jules Grévy*, Paris, 1882

DESCHANEL, P. *Gambetta*, Paris, 1919

DESLANDRES, M. *Histoire constitutionnelle de la France: l'avènement de la troisième République*, Paris, 1937

DIGEON, C. *La Crise allemande et la pensée française (1870–1914)*, Paris, 1959

DREYFUS, R. *De Monsieur Thiers à Marcel Proust*, Paris, 1939

DREYFUS, R. *La République de Monsieur Thiers (1871–1873)*, Paris, 1930

DREYFUS, R. M. *Thiers contre l'Empire, la guerre, la Commune, 1869–1871*, Paris, 1928

DUBOIS, J. *Le Vocabulaire politique et social en France de 1869 à 1872 à travers les oeuvres des écrivains, les revues et les journaux*, Paris, 1963

DUBREUIL, L. *Paul Bert*, Paris, 1935

DUPEUX, G. *Aspects de l'histoire sociale et politique du Loir-et-Cher, 1848–1914*, Paris, 1962

FARMER, PAUL. *France Reviews its Revolutionary Origins, social politics and historical opinion in the Third Republic*, New York, 1944

FRANK, W. *Nationalismus und Demokratie in Frankreich der dritten Republik (1871 bis 1918)*, Hamburg, 1933

GADILLE, J. *La pensée et l'action politique des évêques français au début de la IIIe République, 1870/1883*, 2 vols, Paris, 1967

GALLI, H. *Gambetta et l'Alsace-Lorraine*, Paris, 1911

GILES, F. *A Prince of Journalists: the Life and Times of Henri Stefan Opper de Blowitz*, London, 1962

GHEUSI, P.-B. *La Vie et la Mort singulières de Gambetta*, Paris, 1932

GIMPL, M. C. A. *The Correspondant and the Founding of the French Third Republic*, Washington, 1959

GINESTOUS, E. *Histoire politique de Bordeaux sous la IIIe République*, Bordeaux, 1946

GIRARD, LOUIS, ed. *Les Elections de 1869*, Paris, 1960

GIRARD, LOUIS, PROST, A. AND GOSSEZ, R. *Les Conseilleurs généraux en 1870*, Paris, 1967

GOOCH, R. K. *The French Parliamentary Committee System*, New York and London, 1935

GOUAULT, J. *Comment la France est devenue Républicaine: les élections générales et partielles à l'Assemblée Nationale 1870–1875*, Paris, 1954

GWYNN, S. AND TUCKWELL, G. M. *The Life of the Rt. Hon. Sir Charles Dilke*, vol. i, London, 1917

HALÉVY, D. *La Fin des Notables*, Paris, 1930

HALÉVY, D. *La République des ducs*, Paris, 1937

HANLON, J. *Gambetta: orator, dictator, journalist, statesman*, 2nd edn, London, 1881

HANOTAUX, G. *Histoire de la fondation de la Troisième République:* vols i and ii, *Le Gouvernement de M. Thiers, 1870–1873*, Paris, 1925; vols iii and iv, *L'échec de la Monarchie et la fondation de la République* (*mai 1873–mai 1876*), Paris, 1926

HANOTAUX, G. *Histoire de la France contemporaine*, vol. iii, Paris, n.d.

HEADINGS, M. J. *French Freemasonry under the Third Republic*, Baltimore, 1949

HECHT, E. *Thiers et Gambetta*, Paris, 1905 (extrait des *Publications de la Société Gambetta*)

HOWARD, MICHAEL. *The Franco-Prussian War*, London, 1961

JOUGHIN, JEAN T. *The Paris Commune in French Politics, 1871–1880*, Baltimore, 1955

KATZENBACH, E. L., JR. 'Charles-Louis de Saulces de Freycinet and the Army of Metropolitan France, unpublished thesis, Princeton, 1952

KAYSER, J. *Les Grandes batailles du Radicalisme des origines aux portes du pouvoir, 1820–1901*, Paris, 1952

KAYSER, J., ed. *La Presse de province sous la Troisième République*, Paris, 1958

KRAKOWSKI, E. *La Naissance de la IIIe République, Challemel-Lacour le philosophe et l'homme d'état*, Paris, 1932

LABARTHE, E. *Gambetta et ses amis*, Paris, 1938

LECANUET, E. *L'Eglise de France sous la Troisième République*, Paris, 1907

LEFÈVRE, A. *Histoire de la ligue d'union républicaine des droits de Paris*, Paris, 1881

LETI, G. *Henri Cernuschi*, Paris, 1936

LÉVY, R. *Trois hommes d'Etat Républicains*, Le Havre, 1908

LIDDERDALE, D. W. S. *The Parliament of France*, London, n.d.

LOLIÉE, F. '*La Païva*', Paris, 1920

LOVIE, J. *La Savoie dans la vie française de 1860–1875*, Paris, 1963

MARCOS, S. *Juliette Adam*, Cairo, 1961

MARICHY, J. P. *La Deuxième chambre dans la vie politique française depuis 1875*, Paris, 1969

MARION, M. *Histoire financière de la France depuis 1715*, vol. vii, Paris, 1931

MARVICK, D., ed. *Political Decision-Makers*, New York, 1961

MATHIEU-BODET, P. *Les Finances françaises de 1870 à 1878*, Paris, 1881

MILHAUD, A. *Histoire du Radicalisme*, Paris, 1951

MITCHELL, P. B. *The Bismarckian policy of conciliation with France 1875–1885*, Philadelphia, 1935

MONTEILHET, J. *Les Institutions militaires de la France (1814–1932)*, 2nd edn Paris, 1932

MOREAU-NELATON, E. *Manet raconté par lui-même*, Paris, 1926

NAQUET, A. *Autobiographie*, see Pillias, E. ed.

NEUCASTEL, E. *Gambetta, sa vie, ses idées politiques*, Paris, 1885

OSGOOD, S. M. *French Royalism under the Third and Fourth Republics*, The Hague, 1960

PHILLIPS, C. S. *The Church in France, 1848–1907*, London, 1936

PILLIAS, E. *Léonie Léon, amie de Gambetta*, Paris, 1935

PILLIAS, E., ed. *Autobiographie d'Alfred Naquet*, Paris, 1939

PISANI-FERRY, F. *Le Coup d'état manqué du 16 mai 1877*, Paris, 1965

RALSTON, DAVID E. *The Army of the Republic. The place of the military in the political evolution of France, 1871–1914*, Massachusetts Inst. Tech., 1967

RECLUS, M. *Emile Girardin, le créateur de la presse moderne*, Paris, 1934

RECLUS, M. *L'Avènement de la 3ème République, 1871–75*, Paris, 1930

RECLUS, M. *Le Seize mai*, Paris, 1931

REGAMEY, F. *Gambetta 1838–82*, Paris, 1884

RÉMOND, R. *La Droite en France de 1815 à nos jours*, Paris, 1954

RÉMOND, R. *La Vie politique en France depuis 1789*, vol. ii, *1848–1879*, Paris, 1969

RENARD, E. *La Vie et l'oeuvre de Louis Blanc*, Toulouse, 1922

RENOUVIN, P. *La Politique Extérieure de la IIIe République de 1871 à 1904*, Les Cours de Sorbonne, n.d.; *Les relations franco–allemandes de 1871 à 1900*, 1952

RIHS, CHARLES. *La Commune de Paris: sa structure et ses doctrines (1871)*, Geneva, 1955

RICHARD, J. *Le Bonapartisme sous la République*, 2nd edn, Paris, 1883

ROTHNEY, J. *Bonapartism after Sedan*, Cornell, 1969

ROUGERIE, J. *Paris libre 1871*, Paris, 1971

ROUX, MARQUIS M. DE. *Origines et fondations de la troisième République*, Paris, 1933

SCHUMAN, F. L. *War and Diplomacy in the Third Republic*, New York and London, 1931

SEIGNOBOS, C. *Le Déclin de l'Empire et l'établissement de la 3e République*, vol. vii, in E. Lavisse, *Histoire de France Contemporaine*, Paris, 1921

SILVESTRE DE SACY, J. *Le Maréchal de MacMahon, Duc de Magenta (1808–1893)*, Paris, 1960

SOULIER, A. *L'Instabilité ministérielle sous la Troisième République, 1870–1938*, Paris, 1939

STANNARD, H. *Gambetta*, London, 1921

THE TIMES. *History of The Times*, vol. ii, *The Tradition Established, 1841–1884*, London, 1939

THOMAS, L. *Le Général de Galliffet (1830–1909)*, Paris, 1910

THOMSON, D. *Democracy in France*, London, 3rd edn, 1958

THOUMAS, C. *Les Transformations de l'armée française*, 2 vols, Paris, 1887

THURAT, H. *Gambetta, sa vie, son oeuvre*, Paris, 1883

VIER, J. *La Comtesse d'Agoult et son temps*, vol. vi, Paris, 1963

VIPLE, J. F. *Sociologie politique de l'Allier. La vie politique et les élections sous la Troisième République*, Paris, 1967

VIZETELLY, E. A. *Republican France 1870–1912*, London, 1912

WEILL, G. *Histoire de l'idée laïque en France au XIXe siècle*, Paris, 1929

WORMSER, G. *Gambetta dans les tempêtes, 1870–1877*, Paris, 1964

WYROUBOFF, G. N. *Louis Blanc et Gambetta*, Paris, 1883

ZÉVAÈS, A. *Au temps du Seize Mai*, 1932; *Henri Rochefort le pamphlétaire*, Paris, 1946

(b) *Articles*

BARRAL, P. 'Gambetta et l'armée', *Revue de défense nationale*, Oct. 1970

BÉDARIDA, F. 'L'Armée et la République: les opinions politiques des officiers français en 1876–1878', *Revue historique*, July–Sept. 1964.

BOUVIER, J. 'Les banquiers devant l'actualité politique en 1870–1871', *Revue d'Histoire Moderne et Contemporaine, April–June 1958.* 'Aux origines de la Troisième République. Les Réflexes sociaux des milieux d'affaires', *Revue Historique*, vol. ccx, Oct.–Dec. 1953

BURY, J. P. T. 'The Seine and the Rhône. Two French bye-elections in 1873', *The Historical Journal*, vol. x, no. 4, 1967. 'Gambetta, la République Française e l'Italia', *Il Risorgimento e l'Europa*, ed. V. Frosini, Catania, 1967

DELUNS-MONTAUD. 'La philosophie de Gambetta', *Revue politique et parlementaire*, 10 Feb. 1897.

DREYFUS, R. 'Gambetta et la Naissance de l'Opportunisme', *Revue de France*, 1 and 15 Dec. 1934. 'Les Premières Armes de Gambetta (1869–1873)', *Revue de France*, 15 Dec. 1932, and 1 Jan. 1933. 'La déception monarchique de 1873', *Revue de France*, 15 June 1933. 'Saint-Valry, ou le Conservateur hérétique', *Revue de France*, 15 Nov. 1937

ELWITT, SANFORD H. 'Politics and social classes in the Loire: triumph of Republican order, 1869–1873', *French Historical Studies*, vol. vi, no. 1, 1969

GADILLE, J. 'La politique de défense républicaine à l'égard de l'église de France (1876–1883)', *Bulletin de la Société d'Histoire Moderne*, 14e série, no. 1, 1967

GAILLARD, JEANNE. 'La Presse de province et la question du régime au début de la IIIe République', *Revue d'histoire moderne et contemporaine*, Oct.–Dec. 1959

HALÉVY, D. 'Gambetta connu par ses lettres', *Revue des Deux Mondes*, 1 March 1938

LENORMAND, G. 'Le mouvement républicain dans la Somme au début de la IIIe République (1870–1877)', *Revue historique*, vol. cxcvi, Jan.–March 1946

PILLIAS, E. 'Gambetta et la loi électorale', *Revue d'histoire politique et constitutionnelle*, Oct.–Dec. 1938

RENOUVIN, P. 'Les relations franco–allemandes de 1871 à 1914', in A. O. Sarkissian, ed., *Studies in Diplomatic History . . . in honour of G. P. Gooch*, London, 1961

ROBINET, DR. 'Gambetta positiviste', *Revue occidentale philosophique, sociale et politique*, vol. x, 1883

SCHEURER-KESTNER, A. 'Les Républicains de l'Alsace et de la Lorraine à l'Assemblée Nationale de Bordeaux', *Revue Alsacienne*, May and June 1887

SORLIN, P. 'Gambetta et les Républicains Nantais en 1871', *Revue d'histoire moderne et contemporaine*, April–June 1963

VANDENBUSSCHE, R. 'Aspects de l'histoire politique du radicalisme dans le département du Nord (1870–1905)', *Revue du Nord*, vol. xlvii

SPULLER, E. 'Lettres à Gambetta', *Revue de Paris*, 1 June 1900.

Newspapers and Periodicals *not mentioned under Articles*

L'Acacia, nos 46–7, 1928
Le Bien Public
Le Bulletin du Grand Orient, 1887
La Constitution
L'Eclipse
L'Evénement
Le Figaro
L'Homme Libre
The Illustrated London News
Le Journal des Débats
Le Monde Maçonnique, 5 Jan. 1883
Die Neue Freie Presse, 19 Nov. 1876
The New York Herald, Jan. 1873
La Petite République Française
Le Progrès du Nord
Le Rappel
La République Française
La Revue des deux Mondes

Le Siècle
Le Soir
The Times★
The World, 4 July 1877

★ *The Times* gave a remarkable coverage to French affairs during this period and I have used it frequently. This coverage was reduced to some extent in 1876–77 when the Eastern Question and the Russo–Turkish war stole the limelight.

Index